AIR FORCE COMBAT UNITS
OF WORLD WAR II

Edited by

Maurer Maurer

Office of Air Force History
Washington, D.C.
1983

Library of Congress Cataloging in Publication Data
Main entry under title:

Air Force combat units of World War II.

Reprint. Originally published: Washington, D.C. : U.S. Govt. Print. Off., 1961.
Includes index.
Supt. of Docs. No.: D 301.2:C73/3/983
1. United States. Army Air Forces—History.
2. World War, 1939–1945—Aerial operations, American.
I. Maurer, Maurer.
D790.A533 1983   940.54'4973   83–600169
ISBN 0–912799–02–1

For sale by the Superintendent of Documents, U.S. Government Printing Office
Washington, D.C.

Foreword

Like all chronologies, bibliographies, and encyclopedias, *Air Force Combat Units of World War II* serves a very special historical function. It traces the lineage of each Army Air Corps and U.S. Air Force combat group or higher organization active in World War II, from its origins to 1956.

It is a concise official record of those units: their assignments, subordinate organizations, stations, commanders, campaigns, aircraft, and decorations. But it is more than that.

As an important source of ready information, this volume not only serves as a reference tool for historians and researchers; but it also provides commanders with a corporate memory of vital statistics. With these facts, a unit documents its heritage, the basis for unit *esprit de corps.*

Originally this volume had been printed in 1961. Its worth has been proven, and the demand for it has been great. With this reprint, it will continue to serve the United States Air Force in all quarters in years to come.

Richard H. Kohn
Chief, Office of Air Force History

United States Air Force
Historical Advisory Committee

(As of September 1, 1983)

Lt. Gen. Charles G. Cleveland,
USAF
Commander, Air University,

Mr. DeWitt S. Copp
The National Volunteer Agency

Dr. Philip A. Crowl
Annapolis, Maryland

Dr. Warren W. Hassler, Jr.
Pennsylvania State University

Brig. Gen. Harris B. Hull, USAF,
Retired
National Aeronautics and Space
Administration

Dr. Alfred F. Hurley
Brig. Gen., USAF, Retired
North Texas State University

Mr. David E. Place
The General Counsel, USAF

Gen. Bryce Poe II, USAF, Retired
Alexandria, Virginia

Lt. Gen. Winfield W. Scott, Jr.
Superintendent, USAF Academy

Dr. David A. Shannon (Chairman)
University of Virginia

iv

Preface

Purpose. Over a period of several years the USAF Historical Division has received hundreds of requests for brief histories of Air Force organizations. Air Force units ask for historical data they can use for the orientation of new personnel and for building morale and *esprit de corps*. USAF Headquarters and the commands need historical data for organizational planning. Information officers throughout the Air Force want historical materials for public relations purposes. Members and former members of the Air Force are interested in the units with which they have served. Government agencies and private individuals, for various reasons, seek information about Air Force units and their histories. As a result of the great demand for and the interest in such histories, it appeared that a book containing brief sketches of Air Force combat organizations would be of value as a reference work. The task of preparing such a volume was undertaken by the USAF Historical Division as a phase of its work on World War II.

Scope. This book is concerned primarily with the combat (or tactical) groups that were active during the Second World War. Although such groups had numerous designations, nearly all fell within four major categories: bombardment, fighter, reconnaissance, and troop carrier. The book covers both the combat groups that served overseas and those that remained in the United States. It also covers combat organizations above the group level. It does not deal with provisional organizations or with air base, maintenance, supply, medical, transport, and other service or support organizations.

Although this book is devoted exclusively to organizations that were active during World War II, its coverage of those organizations is not confined to the World War II period. Instead, each organization is traced back to its origin and forward to 1 January 1956, with later activations being mentioned if they took place prior to the time the draft of the book was prepared in 1957-1958.

The organizations are presented under the designations they carried on 2 September 1945. For each organization there is information concerning insigne, lineage, operations, assignments, aircraft (for groups only), components, stations, commanders, campaigns, and decorations. A guide to the way these materials are treated is provided in the *Explanatory Notes* that follow this *Preface*.

Revision. It is impossible to handle the vast amount of detailed data used in the preparation of a work of this kind without some errors appearing in the published volume. A considerable portion of the material in this book represents judgments that historians made in their efforts to determine facts from conflicting data found in various sources. Because of the nature of the volume, there was little opportunity to employ the qualifying words and phrases that historians normally use to indicate weaknesses in their sources or suggest the possibility of other interpretations of available data. Like any historical work, this book is subject to revision in the light of evidence that may be discovered or may become available in the future.

Sources. Most of the sources used in the preparation of this volume are found in the archives of the USAF Historical Division. The most important of these are histories that Air Force organizations at all echelons have forwarded periodically to the archives in accordance with directives pertaining to the Air Force historical program. These histories consist of narratives, plus supporting documents, such as plans, orders, directives, operational reports, organizational charts, statistical summaries, and correspondence. The narratives and documents for many organizations are excellent. Unfortunately, the coverage for some organizations is inadequate and in some cases is lacking for considerable periods of time. Coverage is especially thin, or absent, for the years before 1943, the date the historical program became operative, and for the period immediately following World War II, when the program was disrupted by demobilization and by numerous changes in Air Force organization. Lower echelons of some commands, as well as reserve and national guard organizations not in active service, have not forwarded narratives and documents to the archives.

Other important sources were papers of the Air Service, the Air Corps, and the Air Staff of Army Air Forces; numbered letters of the War Department and the Department of the Air Force; general and special orders; reports and staff studies; statistical digests; organizational directories; personnel rosters; and station lists.

Monographs prepared by the USAF Historical Division and by the historical offices of the various commands were very useful. Another secondary source of great value was the USAF Historical Division's seven-volume history, *The Army Air Forces in World War II,* edited by W. F. Craven and J. L. Cate, and published by the University of Chicago Press.

Acknowledgments. This volume is, in a large measure, the work of Miss Mary Frances Morgan (M.A., University of Georgia), Miss Merlin Elaine Owen (M.A., Tulane University), Mr. Sam H. Frank (M.A., Florida State University), Mr. Herman A. Higgins (M.A., Peabody College), Mr. Richard C. Lukas (B.A., Florida State University), and Mr. Wesley P. Newton, Jr. (M.A., University of Alabama). These young graduate students, who joined the USAF Historical Division in the summer of 1957, were well qualified for the task of conducting the research and preparing the draft of the book. Each had excellent training in history and historical methodology. Each proved to be a first-class researcher. But these historians brought more than technical competence to their job. They had enthusiasm for their work, a vast store of good humor, and the personal qualities that enable people to work together in the finest spirit of cooperation. When this team broke up in the summer of 1958, Miss Morgan and Mr. Newton stayed on for another year to finish the draft and assist with the editing.

Many other persons contributed to the production of this volume. Miss Marguerite Kennedy and her staff in the archives of the USAF Historical Division provided numerous services that expedited the research. Mr. David Schoem of the Air University Historical Liaison Office in Washington assisted with many administrative matters. Mr. Gordon W. Benson and members of his staff furnished copies of the unit history cards maintained by the Organization Branch, Directorate of Statistical Services, Headquarters USAF. Miss Eleanor Cox, Chief of the Heraldic Section, Directorate of Military Personnel, Headquarters USAF, assisted by Miss Anna D. Osso of the Heraldic Section, supplied the insignia and their descriptions. Dr. Chauncey E. Sanders, Mr. Robert T. Finney, Dr. Wilson Howell, Dr. Edith C. Rodgers, Major Ruth P. Boehner, Lieutenant James D. Secor, Lieutenant Eugene Pascuzzi, and other members or former members of the USAF Historical Division who at various times were associated with the Division's unit history program, prepared many unit histories that supplied valuable data for this volume. Mrs. Lois L. Lynn maintained the voluminous files required for the project and typed the various drafts of the book. Although this brief note can not name all the persons who assisted in one way or another, it should mention two men whose interest and support were vital to the project: Col. G. C. Cobb, Director of Research Studies Institute during the time the book was being written; and Dr. Albert F. Simpson, Chief, USAF Historical Division.

15 September 1959

Explanatory Notes

These notes, which are designed as an aid to the use of this volume, are keyed to the various kinds of information presented in the historical sketches of the combat organizations.

Heading. The heading gives the numerical and general functional designation of the organization at the end of World War II.

Insigne. The insigne is the last one approved prior to the end of World War II if such an insigne was available. If the organization had no insigne at that time but had one approved after the war, the latter is shown. A regulation issued in 1953 required each combat group to use the insigne of the combat wing of the same number; consequently, in this book wing insignia are given for some groups.

Lineage. The lineage, which was traced through official documents, is presented in a narrative that also covers the major activities of the organization. Organizational actions (e.g., activation, redesignation, etc.) relating to lineage are highlighted by means of italics. Minor redesignations (e.g., a change from Bombardment Group, H to Bombardment Group, Heavy), as well as organizational changes that had no effect on lineage, were omitted. The terms used to describe actions that establish the lineage of Air Force organizations are defined in Appendix I: Organizational Terms.

Operations. The narrative for each group gives a brief summary of the organization's major activities, especially its combat operations. A general statement concerning major functions or area of operations is provided for organizations above the group level.

Assignments. The narrative includes information concerning the organization's assignments, or its attachments for operational control. For World War II, this information is generally restricted to the numbered air forces with which the organization operated;

for the post-World War II period, it is usually confined to the major command. Because of peculiarities and changes in the Air Force structure between 1946 and 1950, assignments to Air Defense, Tactical Air, and Continental Air Command during that time are, as a general rule, not shown. In references to Air National Guard (ANG) organizations, names of states, shown as abbreviations in parentheses, indicate allotments of headquarters.

Aircraft. The narrative for each group supplies information concerning the aircraft used by the organization.

Organizational Components. The major combat elements are listed immediately following the narrative. The list shows only the components at the first subordinate echelon in any particular period. Components were omitted in some cases in which the structure of the subject organization changed frequently and the assignments of components usually were of brief duration. Attached components, as well as service and support elements, were omitted. Components of national guard organizations are given only for those periods in which the guard organizations were on extended active service.

Only numerical designations are shown if the functional designations (e.g., fighter, bomber) of the components and subject organization were similar. For components assigned during World War II, the numerical designation shown is the one in use at the end of the war. If the numerical designation of a component changed during the period of assignment to the subject organization, the former or later designation is supplied in parentheses.

A semicolon separating dates indicates that the subject organization was inactivated. A comma indicates that the component was relieved of assignment and later reassigned during a period in which the subject organization remained active.

Stations. The list of stations shows the locations and movements of the organization. Temporary stations are not listed. The name given for each base is the one in use at the time the organization arrived. *Webster's Geographical Dictionary* was used as the primary authority for the spelling of place names. For places not listed there, the *NIS Gazetteers* were used. For places not given in either of those sources, it was necessary to rely on station lists and other Air Force documents. Geographical place names, rather than base names, are generally shown for stations overseas. If the organization moved frequently, as some organizations did in the Mediterranean and Pacific areas during World War II, countries, rather than specific places, are shown. Stations for national guard organizations are given only for those periods in which the guard organizations were on extended active service.

A single date indicates the arrival of the organization's headquarters or, if that could not be determined, the arrival of the first major element of the organization. Where double dates are given, the second date, if followed by a semicolon, shows when the organization (or the first major element) began an extended movement either overseas or within a theater; if followed by a period, the second date indicates that the organization was inactivated.

Commanders. The list of commanders gives the names of the organization's commanding officers, the highest rank held by each during the period of command, and the date each assumed command. As a general rule, temporary or acting commanders are not shown. Because of difficulties encountered in obtaining data concerning commanders of reserve and national guard organizations, commanders of such organizations are shown only for those periods the organizations were on extended active service.

Where double dates are shown, the second date, if followed by a period, indicates that the organization was inactivated; if followed by a semicolon, the second date indicates that there is, or may be, a gap in the list of commanders.

Campaigns. The campaigns listed are those in which the organization participated, the determination in each instance being based upon a careful analysis of the organization's operations. If the listing shows Asiatic-Pacific Theater or European-African-Middle Eastern Theater, the organization served, but was not engaged in combat, in the theater. If the listing includes American Theater, the organization either served in the theater area outside the United States, or was stationed in the United States for a total time of one year or more. The theater is not shown if any campaign in the theater is listed. When some components of the organization were engaged in activities that could not be attributed to the entire organization, those activities are not covered by the list of the organization's campaigns. For example, if a squadron on detached service from a group in the European-African-Middle Eastern Theater served in combat in the Asiatic-Pacific Theater, the campaigns listed for the group do not include the Asiatic-Pacific campaigns in which the squadron participated. A list of all the campaigns in which Air Force organizations have participated is provided in Appendix II: Theaters and Campaigns.

It should be emphasized that the listings in this book are for groups, wings, divisions, commands, and air forces rather than for the headquarters of these organizations or for the squadrons. Consequently, *units are cautioned not to use the listings in this volume as the basis or authority for claiming or displaying service streamers.* The Awards Branch, Personnel Services Division, Directorate of Military Personnel, Headquarters USAF is responsible for determining what service streamers each unit is entitled to display.

Decorations. Under decorations are listed the citations and other awards made to the organization. In cases where citations were found to be suitable for such treatment, they are mentioned in the narrative in connection with operations (as well as listed under "Decorations") in order to provide additional data about the activities covered by the citations. In many instances dates for citations have been omitted or have been revised and set in brackets because the dates given in orders pertaining to the citations are obviously incorrect. For example, the dates given in an order may extend over a period before or after the organization was engaged in the activity for which it was cited. Information concerning the various citations and other awards that have been bestowed on organizational elements of the Air Force is provided in Appendix III: Decorations.

As in the case of the campaigns, *the listings in this volume are not to be used by units as the basis or authority for claiming or displaying streamers and other devices that represent awards.* The Awards Branch determines the awards to which each unit is entitled.

Contents

INTRODUCTION

AIR FORCE COMBAT ORGANIZATION

At the peak of its strength in World War II, the United States Army Air Forces (AAF) had more than 2,400,000 men and women in uniform. There were pilots, navigators, bombardiers, gunners, and radio operators, clerks and typists, artists and flautists, teachers, mechanics, statisticians, and engineers—for it took many talents and skills to conduct and support the war in the air. All these persons, from privates to generals, had to be welded into an organization capable of giving direction and coordination to their diverse activities. For combat the men were formed into squadrons, and squadrons into groups. Above the groups were wings, and wings were organized into commands, and commands into the 16 air forces of the AAF. The upper part of the structure had to be built while the war was on, but the foundation was old. Some of the squadrons, two of the groups, and one wing had combat records from the First World War. One squadron, the oldest in the Air Force, could trace its history back to 1913.

1913–1917

The Army had established an Aeronautical Division in the Signal Corps on 1 August 1907 and had acquired its first plane in 1909. Army men had learned to fly, but for some time the aviators were not organized into units for operations. Consequently in 1913, when relations between the United States and Mexico were strained as a result of a revolution in Mexico, there was no aviation unit for service along the Mexican border. The Army, however, sent some of its flyers and planes to Texas, and on 5 March 1913 these were formed into the 1st Aero Squadron, a provisional organization made up of two companies. Later that year, in December, after the provisional unit had moved to San Diego for training, it was organized officially as an Army squadron. Following Pancho Villa's raid on Columbus, New Mexico, in March 1916, the squadron joined the force that Brig. Gen. John J. Pershing organized to try to capture the Mexican bandit. Thus the 1st Aero Squadron, which provided communication and reconnaissance services during the Mexican expedition, was the first American aviation unit to take the field for a military campaign.

Meanwhile, although war had broken out in Europe, little progress had been made toward expanding the Army's air arm. Congress created an Aviation Section in the Signal Corps by an act approved on 18 July 1914, but the legislators provided little money for the new service. Moreover, the Signal Corps naturally used the meager resources to develop aviation as a means of communication, observation, and reconnaissance, rather than as an instrument for combat. One company of the 2d Aero Squadron was organized in 1915 and sent to the Philippines. The following year plans were made for five more squadrons. One, the 7th, was formed in February 1917 for duty in the Panama Canal Zone. Another, the 6th, was organized in Hawaii in March 1917. Three others, the 3d, 4th, and 5th, were being formed in the United States at the time the nation entered World War I in April 1917.

World War I

Pershing, who became commander of the American Expeditionary Forces (AEF) soon developed a plan for the deployment of 260 combat squadrons to France. Later the plan was revised with the number of squadrons reduced to 202, all of which were to be at the front by 30 June 1919. In Pershing's view, the main functions of the AEF's Air Service were to drive off hostile aircraft and to obtain information about enemy movements. Half of the 202 squadrons, therefore, were to be observation units assigned to 3 armies and 16 corps. Of the remainder, 60 were to be pursuit squadrons. But the plan also provided for 27 night-bombardment and 14 day-bombardment squadrons.

The first American aviation unit to reach France was the 1st Aero Squadron, an observation organization, which sailed from New

York in August 1917 and arrived at Le Havre on 3 September. As other squadrons were organized at home, they too were sent overseas, where they continued their training. It was February 1918 before any American aviation squadron entered combat, but by Armistice Day, 11 November 1918, 45 combat squadrons (20 pursuit, 18 observation, and 7 bombardment) had been assigned to the front. During the war the aero squadrons played important roles in such famous battles as the Aisne-Marne, St. Mihiel, and the Meuse-Argonne. Some, like the 94th Squadron that had Captain Eddie Rickenbacker for its commander, or the 27th that had "balloon buster" Frank Luke as one of its aviators, made distinguished records in combat.

Observation planes frequently operated individually, and pursuit pilots often went out alone to attack a balloon or to meet the enemy in a dogfight. But the tendency was toward formation flying for pursuit as well as for bombardment operations. The dispersal of squadrons among the various army organizations made it difficult, however, to obtain coordination of aerial activities. Some higher organization was required. Squadrons with similar functions were formed into groups, the first of these being the 1st Corps Observation Group, organized in April 1918. The following month the 1st Pursuit Group was formed, and by 11 November 1918 the AEF had 14 groups (7 observation, 5 pursuit, and 2 bombardment). In July 1918 the AEF organized its first wing, made up of the 2d and 3d Pursuit Groups and, later, the 1st Day Bombardment Group.

Some airmen, including William Mitchell, were advocating the formation of an air force that would concentrate control over military aviation for heavy blows against the enemy. In September 1918, for the Allied assault against the German salient at St. Mihiel, Mitchell brought together almost 1,500 American and French planes for coordinated operations in which observation and pursuit supported ground forces, while the other two-thirds of the air force bombed and strafed behind the lines. Later, during the Meuse-Argonne offensive, Mitchell attained a somewhat smaller concentration of air power for use in keeping the enemy on the defensive.

In France the Air Service was part of Pershing's expeditionary force. In the United States the Chief Signal Officer was responsible for organizing, training, and equipping aviation units until 21 May

1918. At that time the President created a Bureau of Aircraft Production and made it responsible for aeronautical equipment; training of personnel and units was the responsibility of the Division of Military Aeronautics, which had been created by the War Department on 27 April 1918. Although the bureau and division were recognized by the War Department on 24 May 1918 as forming the Army's Air Service, no Director of Air Service was appointed until 27 August 1918.

1919–1939

After the war the Army quickly demobilized most of its air arm, including the wing, all of the groups, and most of the squadrons. Almost immediately, however, it began to create new organizations for peacetime service. In many instances these new organizations had no connection with those that had been active during the war. For example, at Selfridge Field in August 1919 the Army organized a 1st Pursuit Group that was in no way related to the AEF's 1st Pursuit Group, which had been demobilized in France in December 1918. A little later, however, the Army began a series of organizational actions that eventually enabled many active organizations to trace their histories back to World War I. In the case of the 1st Pursuit Group, for instance, the Army reconstituted the World War I group of that name and consolidated it with the active group. This process of reconstituting old units and consolidating them with active units has continued up to the present time.

In 1920 an act of Congress (approved on 4 June) created the Air Service as a combatant arm of the United States Army. But the Air Service and the Air Corps that replaced it in 1926 (act of 2 July) did not control the combat units, for their training and operations came under the jurisdiction of ground forces. With this arrangement the Air Service and Air Corps were responsible for matters relating to personnel and materiel logistics, particularly training individual pilots and other specialists, and developing, procuring, storing, and distributing aeronautical equipment.

The composition, organization, and command of the combat elements of the air arm during the 1920's and early 1930's were based on principles laid down by the War Department General Staff in 1920. These principles, as they related to military aviation, were reflected in a war plan that called for the following aviation organizations as part of an expeditionary force: one observation squadron for each of 54 divisions and one for each of 18 corps; one observation group (four squadrons), plus one attack wing (one attack and two pursuit groups), for each of 6 armies; one attack wing, one observation group, and one bombardment group for General Headquarters (GHQ). Thus the war plan placed the greatest emphasis on observation aviation. It gave lesser roles to pursuit aviation, which was to destroy enemy planes and assist in attacking enemy troops and other objectives, and to attack aviation, which was to harass the enemy's ground forces. It assigned a minor place to bombardment aviation, with the mission of destroying military objectives in the combat theater and in the enemy's zone of interior. Furthermore, it placed aviation under the command of ground officers at division, corps, army, and GHQ levels. As a result, the structure was condemned by Billy Mitchell and other Air Service officers who discounted the importance of observation aviation, sought recognition for bombardment as a major instrument of warfare, desired a greater proportion of pursuit units for counter-air operations, and wanted aviation units organized as an air force under the command of airmen. One of the important facets of the history of the Army's air arm during the 1920's and 1930's was the conflict between air and ground officers over the composition, organization, and command of military aviation. While this is not the place for a detailed review of that subject, the progress that the airmen made toward gaining acceptance for their point of view is reflected in organizational changes mentioned in subsequent paragraphs.

The principles behind the war plan were applied to the smaller peacetime organization that was to be capable of rapid expansion in an emergency. For several years the striking force based in the United States consisted of three groups, the 1st Pursuit, the 2d Bombardment, and the 3d Attack. There also was one observation group (the 9th), and there was one observation squadron for each of the Army corps. During the same period there were three composite groups on foreign service, the 4th being in the Philippines, the 5th in Hawaii, and the 6th in Panama.

In 1926 the Army began to expand its air arm, and in the years that followed new groups were activated: the 18th Pursuit (in Hawaii) in 1927; the 7th Bombardment in 1928; the 12th Observation and 20th Pursuit in 1930; the 8th and 17th Pursuit in 1931; and the 16th Pursuit (in the Canal Zone) and the 19th Bombardment in 1932. Consequently by the end of 1932 there were 15 groups (45 squadrons). The distribution of the squadrons by function is significant. The number of attack squadrons (4) was the same as it had been a decade earlier, while the strength in observation aviation had decreased from 14 to 13 squadrons. The growth had, therefore, been in other types of aviation, the number of bombardment squadrons having increased from 7 to 12, and pursuit squadrons from 7 to 16. Five more pursuit squadrons were activated in 1933, bringing the total strength to 50 squadrons.

The most important change in the combat organization of the air arm in the two decades between World Wars I and II came on 1 March 1935. At that time the War Department established General Headquarters Air Force (GHQAF) and placed it under the command of an air officer to serve as an air defense and striking force. Some observation units remained assigned to corps areas, but all the pursuit, bombardment, and attack units in the United States became part of the new combat organization. The combat elements of GHQAF were organized into three wings: the 1st Wing (with headquarters at March Field) had two bombardment groups, one attack group, and three observation squadrons; the 2d Wing (Langley Field) had two bombardment and two pursuit groups, plus three observation squadrons; the 3d Wing (Barksdale Field) had an attack and a pursuit group, plus one bombardment, one attack, and two pursuit squadrons. The commanding general of GHQAF, who reported to the Army's Chief of Staff and was to report to the commander of the field force in time of war, was responsible for the organization, training, and operations of this air force. The Chief of the Air Corps still retained the responsibilities associated with personnel and materiel logistics.

The change of the 9th Group from observation to bombardment in 1935 should be noted because that redesignation was an indication of the decline of observation and the growth of bombardment aviation. Two years later the 12th Observation Group was inactivated. And the same year (1937) the 10th Transport Group, the first group of its kind, was activated. But there were no other significant changes, the number of groups remaining at 15 (10 in the United States and 5 on foreign service), until 1939.

World War II

In January 1939 President Franklin D. Roosevelt asked Congress to strengthen America's air power, which, the President said, was "utterly inadequate." On 1 September 1939 Hitler attacked Poland, and the Second World War began. In the months that followed, as Axis forces won one victory after another, the Army's air arm expanded rapidly. By the end of 1940 there were 30 groups. Within another year, that is, by the time the Japanese attacked Pearl Harbor and the United States entered the war, the number of active groups had increased to 67, but many of them were still in the process of being organized and few had aircraft suitable for combat.

The air arm grew even more rapidly in the months following Pearl Harbor, and by the end of 1943 there were 269 groups. At that time 133 of the groups were in the United States: 77 were being manned or trained; 56, which provided the strategic reserve, served as part of the defense force, as operational training units (OTU's) that prepared new units for combat, or as replacement training units (RTU's) that trained replacements for organizations overseas. Early in 1944 most of the OTU's and RTU's were inactivated or disbanded, the training activities being given to base units. As a result the number of combat groups fell to 218, but the formation of new groups brought the figure up to another peak of 243 in February 1945. When Allied forces landed on the beaches of Normandy on 6 June 1944, the United States had 148 combat groups in the European-African-Middle Eastern Theater for the war against Germany. By August 1945, when combat operations in the Asiatic-Pacific Theater came to an end, the United States had 86 groups in the war against Japan.

In addition to the expansion, other important changes had taken place in the air arm. By 7 December 1941 more emphasis was being placed on bombardment. Of the 67 groups active at that time, 26 were bombardment organizations; half of the 26 were heavy and the other half were medium and light bombardment groups, the light groups having replaced the attack organizations of an earlier time. There also were 26 pursuit, 9 observation, and 6 transport groups. During the war, pursuit units were redesignated fighter, observation became reconnaissance, and transport became troop carrier. With the development of B–29 aircraft, very heavy bombardment organizations were added to the combat force. In the spring of 1945, when America's air strength in the overseas theaters of operations reached its peak, the 243 combat groups of the AAF were divided as follows: 25 very heavy, 72 heavy, 20 medium, and 8 light bombardment groups; 71 fighter groups; 29 troop carrier groups; 13 reconnaissance groups; and 5 composite groups. At the same time there were 65 separate squadrons, mostly reconnaissance and night fighter, which were not assigned to groups but to higher echelons of organization.

As the number of groups increased, the number of wings multiplied. Earlier, during World War I and in GHQAF, wings had been composite organizations, that is, had been made up of groups with different kinds of missions. Most of the wings of World War II, however, were composed of groups with similar functions.

The growth of the air arm resulted in important organizational changes and developments above the group and wing levels. The separation of the combat organization (GHQAF) from the logistic organization (Air Corps) created serious problems of coordination. To correct this condition, GHQAF was placed under the Chief of the Air Corps, Maj. Gen. Henry H. Arnold, in March 1939. The two organizations were separated again in November 1940, but about the same time Arnold joined the War Department General Staff as Deputy Chief of Staff for Air, a position that enabled him to coordinate the two sections of the air arm. On 20 June 1941 the War Department created the Army Air Forces with the Air Corps and GHQAF, the latter redesignated Air Force Combat Command, as its major components and with Arnold as chief. In an Army reorganization on 9 March 1942 the Air Corps and Air Force Combat Command were discontinued and Arnold was made Commanding General of Army Air Forces.

During the war most of the AAF's combat groups and wings were assigned to numbered air forces. The first four of these air forces had their origins late in 1940 when GHQAF was becoming so large that its headquarters could not exercise adequate control over the training and operations of the various GHQAF organizations. General Headquarters Air Force was subdivided, therefore, into four air districts (Northeast, Northwest, Southeast, and Southwest), which were redesignated First, Second, Third, and Fourth Air Forces early in 1941. These four air forces remained in the United States throughout the war, but others were established for service overseas: the Fifth, Seventh, Tenth, Thirteenth, Fourteenth, and Twentieth served in the Asiatic-Pacific Theater; the Eighth, Ninth, Twelfth, and Fifteenth operated in the European-African-Middle Eastern Theater, the Eighth being redeployed to the Pacific after the war ended in Europe; the Sixth was in the Panama Canal Zone and the Eleventh in Alaska.

Some air forces, particularly the larger ones, had subordinate commands (or sometimes divisions) that provided an additional echelon of organization, by bringing together wings (or groups) with similar functions. An air force, such as the Ninth, could have a bomber, a fighter, a troop carrier, and a tactical air command, the number and kind depending upon the size, functions, and peculiar needs of the air force. There also were some separate commands, such as the Antisubmarine Command, which were not assigned to numbered air forces.

The arrangement of the various layers of organization is best seen by looking at the organizational position of some particular squadron, such as the 93d Bombardment Squadron, which took part in the B–29 offensive against Japan in 1945. That squadron was assigned to the 19th Bombardment Group, of the 314th Bombardment Wing, of the XXI Bomber Command, of the Twentieth Air Force. But the organization was much more complex than is indicated by such a chain, for operational and administrative requirements resulted in the establishment of organizations above the numbered air forces. There was, for example, the U.S. Strategic Air

Forces in Europe, which had some administrative control over both the Eighth and Ninth Air Forces (the one engaged primarily in strategic and the other in tactical operations), and which exercised some operational control over the two strategic air forces in Europe (the Eighth in England and the Fifteenth in Italy). Furthermore, American organizations sometimes became part of combined (i.e., Allied) commands. In April 1942, for instance, an organization called Allied Air Forces was created in Australia to control operations of Australian, Dutch, and American air forces; and in February 1943 American, British, and French elements in North Africa were combined to form the Northwest African Air Forces. The complexity of these organizational arrangements was compounded by the assignment of AAF units overseas to United States Army organizations, and by the relationships of those Army organizations to joint (i.e., Army-Navy) and combined commands.

This volume is not concerned with all of this vast organization but with the AAF structure from groups to numbered air forces. Within those limits, the major attention is focused on the groups, the basic operational organizations in the aerial war that America fought in the years between the attack on Pearl Harbor on 7 December 1941 and the Japanese surrender on 2 September 1945.

1946–1956

Once the victory had been gained, the United States plunged into demobilization, just as it had done at the end of the First World War. Officers and men were sent home. Bases were closed. Airplanes were stored or sold. And by July 1946 the Air Force had only 2 groups that were ready for combat, although 52 were carried on the list of active organizations. A new Air Force had to be built on the ruins of demobilization, the goal being 70 groups, the strength that was authorized for peacetime. In addition, reserve and national guard forces would be available for active duty in an emergency. There was much opposition, however, to a large military establishment in peacetime, and to the financial burden such an establishment placed on the nation. Consequently, the Air Force had to cut to 48 groups.

Then came the Korean War, precipitated by the Communist attack on the Republic of Korea on 25 June 1950. The United States rushed combat forces across the Pacific to strengthen those already present in the Far East. Others were sent to Europe to meet the increasing threat of Communist aggression in that part of the world. At home the air defense force was expanded. Under these conditions the number of groups jumped from 48 to 87 within a year. In June 1952, when the strength was stated in terms of wings rather than groups, the Air Force had 95. By the end of the Korean War on 27 July 1953 the number of wings had increased to 106. The expansion had been accomplished in part by ordering reserve and national guard organizations to active duty. Those organizations were called for 21 months, but some were relieved before the end of that period. In fact, some reserve organizations were in active service for only a few days, just long enough to assign their personnel to other organizations. Most of the reserve and guard elements that served the full term of 21 months were replaced by newly-activated organizations of the regular Air Force.

The program for expansion had first provided for 95 wings, but that goal was revised in November 1951 when the Joint Chiefs of Staff authorized a force of 143 wings to be attained by mid-1955. In 1953 the goal was reduced temporarily to 120 wings by June 1956, but later the same year it was changed to provide for 137 wings by June 1957. Under these changing programs the strength of the Air Force, in terms of the number of active wings, increased steadily. By the beginning of 1956 there were 127 wings, made up of 392 combat squadrons.

There had been many organizational changes in the period from 1946 to 1956, but the most important one in the view of the professional airmen was that which gave the Air Force its independence. Congress provided the necessary legislation in 1947 when it created a Department of the Air Force and established the United States Air Force as a separate service equal to the Army and the Navy in the nation's military establishment. On 18 September 1947, W. Stuart Symington became the first Secretary of the Air Force. And a week later, on 26 September, Gen. Carl Spaatz, who had succeeded Arnold

as Commanding General of the Army Air Forces, became the first
Chief of Staff, United States Air Force.

Earlier, on 21 March 1946, Spaatz had undertaken a major reorganization that had included the establishment of three new combat commands in the United States: Strategic Air Command (soon
known everywhere as SAC), to provide a long-range striking force
capable of bombardment operations in any part of the world; Air
Defense Command (ADC), to defend the United States against
attack from the air; and Tactical Air Command (TAC), to support
the operations of ground forces. TAC and ADC were reduced from
major commands to operating commands when they were assigned
to the Continental Air Command (ConAC) at the time the latter
was established on 1 December 1948. ADC was discontinued on 1
July 1950 but re-established as a major command on 1 January 1951.
A month earlier, on 1 December 1950, TAC had been removed from
the control of ConAC and again made a major command. As a
result of these changes ConAC became responsible mainly for super-
vising reserve and national guard affairs. In addition to its commands
in the United States, the Air Force had combat forces stationed overseas, with Far East Air Forces, United States Air Forces in Europe,
Caribbean Air Command, and Alaskan Air Command as the major
commands for the various areas of operations.

The World War II commands, which had been subordinate to
the numbered air forces, were eliminated in the reorganization of
1946, and the numbered air forces were made components of the
major commands at home and overseas. The new organizational
hierarchy thus contained the following levels: squadron, group,
wing, air force, command. In 1948, and afterward, wings were redesignated divisions, and placed immediately below the numbered
air forces in the organizational pyramid, new wings being constituted
and activated to take the place of the ones that had been elevated to
the division level. In addition to support and service elements, each
of these new wings, as a general rule, had one combat group, which
carried the same numerical designation as the wing itself. In 1952,
however, the Air Force began to inactivate the combat groups and
assign their combat squadrons directly to the wings. Consequently
no organizations in the Air Force perpetuated the histories of the

World War II combat groups that had been inactivated. The Air Force decided, therefore, to bestow the histories of combat groups on like-numbered wings. For example, the 9th Bombardment Wing, created after World War II, received the history of the 9th Bombardment Group, together with the campaign credits and decorations that had been earned by the group during the war.

Despite all the changes that had taken place since V–J Day, the Air Force in 1956 was to a large extent made up of elements that carried on the traditions of organizations that had been active during World War II. The history of each of those organizations had been shaped by many forces. Domestic politics, the national economy, and international affairs were important factors in fixing the size, and hence the number of active groups or wings, of the Air Force. Science and technology determined the kind of equipment available at any particular time. Fortune, too, had a part in forming the histories of the various organizations. It is evident, for example, that chance, rather than design, sometimes decided which organizations would be kept active and which would be retired. The results are reflected in the historical sketches presented in this book. Some groups, for instance, have lengthy records of service; others were created at a relatively late date or have been inactive for long periods. Some were sent overseas for combat; others were kept at home. Some received the newest planes from the production lines; others were forced to use old, worn-out craft.

But no organization had its life shaped entirely by forces beyond its control, for its own people, the men and women who gave the organization a living existence, made history in many ways. A fighter pilot flew out to battle and came back an ace. A gunner returned from a bombing mission to be decorated for bravery above and beyond the call of duty. But one did not have to be a hero to have a place in history. The mechanic armed with his wrench, the clerk with his typewriter—each had his own important part to play. And at their head to lead them was a commander who, by virtue of his authority and responsibility, had a special role in the historical process.

Thus, through the workings of numerous and diverse forces, each organization acquired a historic character and personality of its own.

At the same time, each contributed to the development of a larger history that goes back to a day in 1907 when the Army named a captain to take "charge of all matters pertaining to military ballooning, air machines, and all kindred subjects."

COMMANDERS

I.   *Aeronautical Division, Signal Corps*

Officer in Charge: Capt Charles DeF Chandler, 1 Aug 1907; Capt A S Cowan, 1 July 1910; Capt Charles DeF Chandler, 20 Jun 1911; Lt Henry H Arnold, 18 Nov 1912; Maj Edgar Russell, 15 Dec 1912; Lt Col Samuel Reber, 10 Sep 1913–18 Jul 1914.

II.   *Aviation Section, Signal Corps*

Officer in Charge: Lt Col Samuel Reber, 18 Jul 1914; Lt Col George O Squier, 20 May 1916; Lt Col J B Bennett, 19 Feb 1917; Maj Benjamin D Foulois, 30 Jul 1917; Brig Gen A L Dade, 12 Nov 1917; Col Laurence Brown, 28 Feb 1918–21 May 1918.

III a. *Division of Military Aeronautics*

Director: Maj Gen William L Kenly, 27 Apr 1918– (under Director, Air Service after 27 Aug 1918).

III b. *Bureau of Aircraft Production*

Director: Mr John D Ryan, 21 May 1918–(under Director, Air Service after 27 Aug 1918).

IV.   *Air Service*

Director: Mr John D Ryan, 27 Aug 1918; Maj Gen Charles T Menoher, 23 Dec 1918–4 Jun 1920.

Chief: Maj Gen Charles T Menoher, 4 Jun 1920; Maj Gen Mason M Patrick, 5 Oct 1921–2 Jul 1926.

V a. *Air Corps*

Chief: Maj Gen Mason M Patrick, 2 Jul 1926; Maj Gen J E Fechet, 14 Dec 1927; Maj Gen Benjamin D Foulois, 19 Dec 1931; Maj Gen Oscar Westover, 22 Dec 1935; Maj Gen Henry H Arnold, 22 Sep 1938; Maj Gen George H Brett, 30 May 1941–(under Chief, AAF after 20 Jun 1941).

V b. *General Headquarters Air Force,* redesignated *Air Force Combat Command*

Commanding General: Maj Gen Frank M Andrews, 1 Mar 1935; Lt Gen Delos C Emmons, 1 Mar 1939–(under Chief, AAF after 20 Jun 1941).

VI. *Army Air Forces*

Chief: Lt Gen Henry H Arnold, 20 Jun 1941–9 Mar 1942.

Commanding General: General of the Army Henry H Arnold, 9 Mar 1942; Gen Carl Spaatz, 15 Feb 1946–26 Sep 1947.

VII. *United States Air Force*

Chief of Staff: Gen Carl Spaatz, 26 Sep 1947; Gen Hoyt S Vandenberg, 30 Apr 1948; Gen Nathan F Twining, 30 Jun 1953; Gen Thomas D White, 1 Jul 1957–.

AIR FORCE
COMBAT UNITS

GROUPS

1st AIR COMMANDO GROUP

Constituted as 1st Air Commando Group on 25 Mar 1944 and *activated* in India on 29 Mar. The group, which began operations immediately, was organized to provide fighter cover, bombardment striking power, and air transportation services for Wingate's Raiders, who were operating behind enemy lines in Burma. The organization consisted of a headquarters plus the following sections: bomber (equipped with B-25's); fighter (P-51's); light-plane (L-1's, L-5's, and helicopters); transport (C-47's); glider (CG-4A's and TG-5's); and light-cargo (UC-64's). The group supported operations in Burma by landing and dropping troops, food, and equipment; evacuating casualties; and attacking airfields and transportation facilities. Received a DUC for operations against the enemy, Mar-May 1944. Withdrew from the front late in May 1944 and, with the bomber section eliminated and the P-51's replaced by P-47's, began a training program. Reorganized later, with the sections being eliminated and with fighter, liaison, and troop carrier squadrons being assigned. Transported Chinese troops and supplies from Burma to China in Dec 1944, and carried out supply, evacuation, and liaison operations for Allied troops in Burma until the end of the war. Attacked bridges, railroads, barges, troop positions, oil wells, and airfields in Burma and escorted bombers to Rangoon and other targets during the early months of 1945. Changed from P-47's to P-51's in May 1945, the fighter squadrons being engaged in training from then until the end of the war. Moved to the US in Oct 1945. *Inactivated* on 3 Nov 1945. *Disbanded* on 8 Oct 1948.

SQUADRONS. 5*th* Fighter: 1944–1945. 6*th* Fighter: 1944–1945. *164th* Liaison: 1944–1945. *165th* Liaison: 1944–1945. *166th* Liaison: 1944–1945. *319th* Troop Carrier: 1944–1945.

STATIONS. Hailakandi, India, 29 Mar 1944; Asansol, India, 20 May 1944–6 Oct 1945; Camp Kilmer, NJ, 1–3 Nov 1945.

COMMANDERS. Col Philip G Cochran, 29 Mar 1944; Col Clinton B Gaty, 20 May 1944; Col Robert W Hall, c. 7 Apr 1945–unkn.

CAMPAIGNS: India - Burma; Central Burma.

DECORATIONS. Distinguished Unit Citation: Burma and India, [Mar 1944]–20 May 1944.

INSIGNE. None.

1st COMBAT CARGO GROUP

Constituted as 1st Combat Cargo Group on 11 Apr 1944 and *activated* on 15 Apr. Equipped with C–47's. Moved to the CBI theater in Aug 1944. Began operations in Sep 1944 by transporting supplies and reinforcements to and evacuating casualties from Imphal, Burma. Continued to support Allied operations in Burma, flying in men and supplies from India, moving equipment required to construct and operate airstrips, dropping dummy cargoes to lead the enemy away from Allied offensives, dropping paratroops for the assault on Rangoon (May 1945), and evacuating prisoners of war who were freed by Allied advances. Meanwhile, part of the group had been sent to China, and for a short time (Dec 1944–Jan 1945) the group's headquarters was located

there. Operations in China included helping to evacuate the air base at Kweilin during a Japanese drive in Sep 1944, moving Chinese troops, and flying many supply missions, some of which involved ferrying gasoline and materiel over the Hump from India. The group, partially re-equipped with C–46's in Jun 1945, engaged primarily in transporting men, food, arms, and ammunition until the end of the war. *Redesignated* 512th Troop Carrier Group in Sep 1945. Returned to the US in Dec 1945. *Inactivated* on 24 Dec 1945.

Redesignated 512th Troop Carrier Group (Medium) and allotted to the reserve. *A c t i v a t e d* on 2 Sep 1949. Equipped with C–46's. Ordered to active service on 15 Mar 1951. *Inactivated* on 1 Apr 1951.

Allotted to the reserve. *Activated* on 14 Jun 1952. Equipped with C–46's.

SQUADRONS. *1st* (later 326th): 1944–1945; 1949–1951; 1952–. *2d* (later 327th): 1944–1945; 1949–1951; 1952–. *3d* (later 328th): 1944–1945; 1949–1951; 1952–. *4th* (later 329th): 1944–1945; 1949–1951.

STATIONS. Bowman Field, Ky, 15 Apr–5 Aug 1944; Sylhet, India, 21 Aug 1944; Tulihal, India, 30 Nov 1944; Tsuyung, China, 20 Dec 1944; Dohazari, India, 30 Jan 1945; Hathazari, India, 15 May 1945; Myitkyina, Burma, Jun 1945; Liuchow, China, 30 Aug 1945; Kiangwan, China, 9 Oct–3 Dec 1945; Camp Anza, Calif, 23–24 Dec 1945. Reading Mun Aprt, Pa, 2 Sept 1949; New Castle County Aprt, Del,

1 May 1950–1 Apr 1951. New Castle County Aprt, Del, 14 Jun 1952–.

COMMANDERS. Lt Col Robert J Rentz, 21 Apr 1944; Lt Col Walter P Briggs, 28 Apr 1945; Maj Samuel B Ward, 18 Aug 1945; Maj Maurice D Watson, 9 Sep 1945; Maj Wilbur B Sprague, 18 Sep 1945; Col J H Snyder, 24 Nov 1945; Capt Dixon M Jordan, 29 Nov–c. 24 Dec 1945.

CAMPAIGNS. India-Burma; China Defensive; Central Burma; China Offensive.

DECORATIONS. None.

INSIGNE. *Shield:* On a shield azure, over a sphere argent, with shading of the field, a stylized aircraft gules, with highlights of the second, its road-like jet stream encircling the sphere or, shaded gules, with center dash-like markings and all outlines of the first. (Approved 21 Jan 1958.)

1st FIGHTER GROUP

Organized as 1st Pursuit Group in France on 5 May 1918. Began operations immediately and served at the front until the end of the war, using Nieuport-28, Spad, and Sopwith Camel aircraft. Protected friendly observation balloons and planes, and made strafing attacks on enemy ground forces, but engaged primarily in counter-air patrols in which the group's pilots gained many victories over enemy aircraft and destroyed numerous observation balloons. Two of the group's pilots were awarded the Medal of Honor: 1st Lt (later Capt) Edward V Rickenbacker—America's World War I "Ace of Aces" who served as commander of the 94th (Hat-in-the-Ring) Squadron—received the medal for action near Billy, France, on 25 Sep 1918 when, disregarding the heavy odds, he attacked a flight of seven enemy planes and shot down two of them; 2d Lt Frank Luke Jr—the "balloon buster"—was awarded the medal for attacking and shooting down three German balloons on 29 Sep 1918 before his plane was hit and forced to land near Murvaux, France, where he died while defending himself against capture by enemy ground troops. *Demobilized* in France on 24 Dec 1918.

Reconstituted in 1924 and *consolidated* with 1st Pursuit Group that had been *organized* in the US on 22 Aug 1919. *Redesignated* 1st Pursuit Group (Interceptor) in Dec 1939, and 1st Pursuit Group (Fighter) in Mar 1941. Trained, participated in exercises and maneuvers, put on demonstrations, took part in National Air Races, tested equipment, and experimented with tactics, using Spad, Nieuport, DeHavilland, SE–5, MB–3, PW–8, P–1, P–6, PT–3, P–16, P–26, P–35, P–36, P–38, P–41, P–43, and other aircraft during the period 1919–1941. Was the only pursuit group in the Army's air arm for several years; later, furnished cadres for new units. Moved to the west coast immediately after the Japanese attack on Pearl Harbor and flew patrols for several weeks. *Redesignated* 1st Fighter Group in May 1942.

Moved to England, Jun–Jul 1942. Assigned to Eighth AF. Entered combat with P–38 aircraft on 28 Aug and flew a number of missions to France before being assigned to Twelfth AF for duty in the Mediterranean theater. Moved to North Africa, part of the ground echelon landing with the assault forces at Arzeu beach on 8 Nov 1942. The air echelon arrived a few days later and the group soon began operations, attacking enemy shipping, escorting bombers, flying strafing missions, and performing reconnaissance duties during the campaign for Tunisia. Participated in the reduction of Pantelleria. Escorted bombers to targets in Sicily and later aided ground forces during the conquest of that island by strafing and dive-bombing roads, motor transports, gun emplacements, troop concentrations, bridges, and railways. Flew missions against the enemy in Italy and received a DUC for its performance on 25 Aug 1943 when the group carried out a strafing attack on Italian airdromes, destroying great numbers of enemy aircraft that presented a serious threat to the Allies' plans for landing troops at Salerno. Also escorted bombers to Italy, receiving another DUC for a mission on 30 Aug 1943 when the group beat off enemy aircraft and thus enabled bombers to inflict serious damage on marshalling yards at Aversa. Supported the invasion at Salerno in Sep and continued operations with Twelfth AF until Nov 1943. Assigned to Fifteenth AF with the primary mission of escorting bombers that attacked targets in Italy, France, Germany, Czechoslovakia, Austria, Hungary, Bulgaria, Rumania, Yugoslavia, and Greece. Received third DUC for covering the withdrawal of B–17's after an attack on Ploesti on 18 May 1944. Also flew strafing and dive-bombing missions in an area from France to the Balkans. Supported the landings at Anzio in Jan 1944 and the invasion of Southern France in Aug 1944. Continued operations until May 1945. *Inactivated* in Italy on 16 Oct 1945.

Activated in the US on 3 Jul 1946. Equipped first with P–80's and later (1949) with F–86's. *Redesignated* 1st Fighter-Interceptor Group in Apr 1950. *Inactivated* on 6 Feb 1952.

Redesignated 1st Fighter Group (Air Defense). *Activated* on 18 Aug 1955. Assigned to Air Defense Command and equipped with F–86 aircraft.

SQUADRONS. *17th* (formerly *147th*): 1918; 1919–1940. *27th*: 1918; 1919–1945;

1946–1952. *71st:* 1941–1945; 1946–1952; 1955–. *94th:* 1918; 1919–1945; 1946–1952; 1955–. *95th:* 1918; 1919–1927. *185th:* 1918.

STATIONS. Toul, France, 5 May 1918; Touquin, France, 28 Jun 1918; Saints, France, 9 Jul 1918; Rembercourt, France, c. 1 Sep 1918; Colombey-les-Belles, France, c. 9–24 Dec 1918. Selfridge Field, Mich, 22 Aug 1919; Kelly Field, Tex, c. 31 Aug 1919; Ellington Field, Tex, 1 Jul 1921; Selfridge Field, Mich, 1 Jul 1922; San Diego NAS, Calif, 9 Dec 1941; Los Angeles, Calif, 1 Feb–May 1942; Goxhill, England, 10 Jun 1942; Ibsley, England, 24 Aug 1942; Tafaraoui, Algeria, 13 Nov 1942; Nouvion, Algeria, 20 Nov 1942; Biskra, Algeria, 14 Dec 1942; Chateaudun-du-Rhumel, Algeria, Feb 1943; Mateur, Tunisia, 29 Jun 1943; Sardinia, 31 Oct 1943; Gioia del Colle, Italy, c. 8 Dec 1943; Salsola Airfield, Italy, 8 Jan 1944; Vincenzo Airfield, Italy, 8 Jan 1945; Salsola Airfield, Italy, 21 Feb 1945; Lesina, Italy, Mar–16 Oct 1945. March Field, Calif, 3 Jul 1946; George AFB, Calif, 18 Jul 1950; Griffiss AFB, NY, 15 Aug 1950; George AFB, Calif, 4 Jun 1951; Norton AFB, Calif, 1 Dec 1951–6 Feb 1952. Selfridge AFB, Mich, 18 Aug 1955–.

COMMANDERS. Maj Bert M Atkinson, 5 May 1918; Maj Harold E Hartney, 21 Aug–24 Dec 1918. Lt Col Davenport Johnson, 22–29 Aug 1919; Capt Arthur R Brooks, unkn; Maj Carl Spaatz, c. Nov 1921–Sep 1924; Maj Thomas G Lanphier, unkn; Maj Ralph Royce, 1928; Lt Col Charles H Danforth, c. 1930; Maj George H Brett, unkn; Lt Col Frank M Andrews, c. Jul 1933; Lt Col Ralph Royce, 1934; Maj Edwin J House, 30 Apr 1937; Col Henry B Clagett, c. 1938; Col Lawrence P Hickey, c. 1939; Lt Col Robert S Israel, Jul 1941; Maj John O Zahn, 1 May 1942; Col John N Stone, 9 Jul 1942; Col Ralph S Garman, 7 Dec 1942; Maj Joseph S Peddie, 8 Sep 1943; Col Robert B Richard, 19 Sep 1943; Col Arthur C Agan Jr, 15 Nov 1944; Lt Col Milton H Ashkins, 31 Mar 1945; Lt Col Charles W Thaxton, 11 Apr 1945; Col Milton H Ashkins, 28 Apr 1945–unkn. Col Bruce K Holloway, 3 Jul 1946; Col Gilbert L Meyers, 20 Aug 1946; Col Frank S Perego, Jan 1948; Lt Col Jack T Bradley, Jul 1950; Col Dolf E Muehleisen, Jun 1951; Col Walker M Mahurin, 1951; Capt Robert B Bell, Jan–c. Feb 1952. Col Norman S Orwat, 1955–.

CAMPAIGNS. *World War I:* Lorraine; Champagne; Champagne-Marne; Aisne-Marne; Oise-Aisne; St Mihiel; Meuse-Argonne. *World War II:* Air Combat, EAME Theater; Air Offensive, Europe; Algeria-French Morocco; Tunisia; Sicily; Naples-Foggia; Anzio; Rome-Arno; Normandy; Northern France; Southern France; North Apennines; Rhineland; Central Europe; Po Valley.

DECORATIONS. Distinguished Unit Citations: Italy, 25 Aug 1943; Italy, 30 Aug 1943; Ploesti, Rumania, 18 May 1944.

INSIGNE. *Shield:* Vert five bendlets enhanced sable fimbriated or, as many crosses patee in bend debased three and two of the second fimbriated argent. *Crest:* Upon a wreath of the colors or and vert upon a hurte wavy an arrow palewise reversed between two wings displayed conjoined in lure or. *Motto:* AUT VINCERE AUT MORI—Conquer or Die. (Approved 10 Feb 1924.)

1st PHOTOGRAPHIC GROUP

FIDELITER ET DILIGENTER

Constituted as 1st Photographic Group on 15 May 1941. *Activated* on 10 Jun 1941. *Redesignated* 1st Mapping Group in Jan 1942, and 1st Photographic Charting Group in Aug 1943. Charted and mapped areas of the US and sent detachments to perform similar functions in Alaska, Canada, Africa, the Middle East, India, the Caribbean, Mexico, Central and South America, and the Kurils. Used a variety of aircraft, including F-2's, F-3's, F-7's, A-29's, B-17's, B-18's, B-24's, and B-25's. *Disbanded* on 5 Oct 1944.

SQUADRONS. *1st:* 1941–1943. *2d:* 1941–1944. *3d:* 1941–1943. *4th:* 1941–1944.

6th: 1943–1944. *19th:* 1943. *91st:* 1943–1944.

STATIONS. Bolling Field, DC, 10 Jun 1941; Peterson Field, Colo, Dec 1943; Buckley Field, Colo, Jul–5 Oct 1944.

COMMANDERS. Lt Col Minton W Kaye, 10 Jun 1941; Lt Col George G Northrup, c. 1 Feb 1942; Col Paul T Cullen, 8 Jul 1942; Col Minton W Kaye, c. 1 Jul 1943; Col George G Northrup, c. 18 Nov 1943; Lt Col Frank N Graves, c. 1 Dec 1943–unkn.

CAMPAIGNS. American Theater.

DECORATIONS. None.

INSIGNE. *Shield:* Per pale, vert and azure, a pile or debruised by a barrulet arched of the field upon and over the pile a camera lens proper rimmed sable. *Motto:* FIDELITER ET DILIGENTER —Faithfully and Diligently. (Approved 24 Oct 1942.)

1st SEARCH ATTACK GROUP

Constituted as 1st Sea-Search Attack Group (Medium) on 8 Jun 1942 and *activated* on 17 Jun. *Redesignated* 1st Sea-Search Attack Group (Heavy) in Jun 1943, 1st Sea-Search Attack Unit in Sep 1943, and 1st Search Attack Group in Nov 1943. Assigned directly to AAF in Jun 1942; assigned to First AF in Nov 1943. Tested equipment and developed techniques and tactics for use against submarines and surface craft; also flew patrol missions and searched for enemy submarines. Late in 1943 became concerned primarily with radar training for combat crews. Used B–17, B–18, and B–24 aircraft. *Disbanded* on 10 Apr 1944.

SQUADRONS. *2d:* 1942–1944. *3d:* 1942–1944. *4th* (formerly 18th Antisubmarine): 1943–1944.

STATIONS. Langley Field, Va, 17 Jun 1942–10 Apr 1944.

COMMANDERS. Col William C Dolan, 17 Jun 1942–10 Apr 1944.

CAMPAIGNS. Antisubmarine, American Theater.

DECORATIONS. None.

INSIGNE. None.

2d AIR COMMANDO GROUP

Constituted as 2d Air Commando Group on 11 Apr 1944 and *activated* on 22 Apr. Trained for operations with P–51, C–47, and L–5 aircraft. Moved to India, Sep-Nov 1944. Between Nov 1944 and May 1945 the group dropped supplies to Allied troops who were fighting the Japanese in the Chindwin Valley in Burma; moved Chinese troops from Burma to China; transported men, food, ammunition, and construction equipment to Burma; dropped Gurka paratroops during the assault on Rangoon; provided fighter support for Allied forces crossing the Irrawaddy River in Feb 1945; struck enemy airfields and transportation facilities; escorted bombers to targets in the vicinity of Rangoon; bombed targets in Thailand; and flew reconnaissance missions. After May 1945 the fighter squadrons were in training; in Jun the group's C–47's were sent to Ledo to move road-building equipment; during Jun–Jul most of its L–5's were turned over to Fourteenth AF. The group returned to the US during Oct–Nov 1945. *Inactivated* on 12 Nov 1945. *Disbanded* on 8 Oct 1948.

SQUADRONS. *1st* Fighter: 1944–1945. *2d* Fighter: 1944–1945. *127th* Liaison: 1944–1945. *155th* Liaison: 1944–1945. *156th* Liaison: 1944–1945. *317th* Troop Carrier: 1944–1945.

STATIONS. Drew Field, Fla, 22 Apr–28 Sep 1944; Kalaikunda, India, 12 Nov 1944–4 Oct 1945; Camp Kilmer, NJ, 11–12 Nov 1945.

COMMANDERS. Capt L H Couch, 22 Apr 1944; Col Arthur R DeBolt, 1 May 1944; Col Alfred J Ball Jr, 15 May 1945–unkn.

CAMPAIGNS. India-Burma; Central Burma.

DECORATIONS. None.

INSIGNE. None.

2d BOMBARDMENT GROUP

Organized as 1st Day Bombardment Group in France on 10 Sep 1918. Equipped with DH–4 and Breguet aircraft and entered combat on 12 Sep. Attacked troop concentrations and communications to interfere with the enemy's movement of reinforcements and supplies to the front during the Allied offensive at St Mihiel. Also took part in the Meuse-Argonne campaign, attacking the enemy behind the line, and conducting bombing operations that helped to protect Allied

ground forces by diverting German pursuit planes from the battle zone. Participated in one of the great bombing raids of the war on 9 Oct when 353 Allied planes (including 200 bombers) under the command of William Mitchell struck a concentration point where German troops were preparing for a counterattack against the Allied offensive in the Meuse-Argonne area. *Demobilized* in France in Nov 1918, soon after the armistice.

Reconstituted (in 1924) and *consolidated* with a group that was organized in the US as 1st Day Bombardment Group on 18 Sep 1919 and *redesignated* 2d Bombardment Group in 1921. Used LB-5A, B-10, B-17 (1937-), B-15 (1938-), and other aircraft during the 1920's and 1930's. Engaged in routine training; tested and experimented with equipment and tactics; participated in maneuvers; took part in Mitchell's demonstrations of the effectiveness of aerial bombardment on battleships; flew mercy missions to aid victims

of a flood in Pennsylvania in 1936 and victims of an earthquake in Chile in 1939; and made good-will flights to South America in the late 1930's. *Redesignated* 2d Bombardment Group (Heavy) in 1939. Trained with B-17's.

Served on antisubmarine duty for several months after the US entered World War II. Moved to North Africa, Mar-May 1943, and remained in the theater until after V-E Day, being assigned first to Twelfth and later (Dec 1943) to Fifteenth AF. Flew many support and interdictory missions, bombing such targets as marshalling yards, airdromes, troop concentrations, bridges, docks, and shipping. Participated in the defeat of Axis forces in Tunisia, Apr-May 1943; the reduction of Pantelleria and the preparations for the invasion of Sicily, May-Jul 1943; the invasion of Italy, Sep 1943; the drive toward Rome, Jan-Jun 1944; the invasion of Southern France, Aug 1944; and the campaigns against German forces in northern Italy, Jun 1944-May 1945. Engaged primarily in long-range bombardment of strategic targets after Oct 1943, attacking oil refineries, aircraft factories, steel plants, and other objectives in Germany, Poland, Czechoslovakia, Austria, Hungary, Yugoslavia, Rumania, and Greece. En route to bomb a vital aircraft factory at Steyr on 24 Feb 1944, the group was greatly outnumbered by enemy interceptors, but it maintained its formation and bombed the target, receiving a DUC for the performance. On the following day, while on a mission to attack aircraft factories at Regensburg, it met similar opposition equally well and was awarded a second DUC. Served as part of the occupation force in Italy after V–E Day. *Inactivated* in Italy on 28 Feb 1946.

Redesignated 2d Bombardment Group (Very Heavy). *Activated* in the US on 1 Jul 1947. Assigned to Strategic Air Command and equipped with B–29's. *Redesignated* 2d Bombardment Group (Medium) in May 1948. Converted to B–50's early in 1950. *Inactivated* on 16 Jun 1952.

SQUADRONS. *11th*: 1918; 1919–1927. *20th*: 1918; 1919–1946; 1947–1952. *49th* (formerly 166th): 1918; 1919–1946; 1947–1952. *96th*: 1918; 1919–1946; 1947–1952. *429th*: 1942–1946.

STATIONS. Amanty, France, 10 Sep 1918; Maulan, France, 23 Sep–Nov 1918. Ellington Field, Tex, 18 Sep 1919; Kelly Field, Tex, c. 25 Sep 1919; Langley Field, Va, 1 Jul 1922; Ephrata, Wash, 29 Oct 1942; Great Falls AAB, Mont, 27 Nov 1942–13 Mar 1943; Navarin, Algeria, Apr 1943; Chateaudun-du-Rhumel, Algeria, 27 Apr 1943; Ain M'lila, Algeria, 17 Jun 1943; Massicault, Tunisia, 31 Jul 1943; Bizerte, Tunisia, 2 Dec 1943; Amendola, Italy, c. 9 Dec 1943; Foggia, Italy, 19 Nov 1945–28 Feb 1946. Andrews Field, Md, 1 Jul 1947; Davis-Monthan Field, Ariz, 24 Sep 1947; Chatham AFB, Ga, c. 1 May 1949; Hunter AFB, Ga, 22 Sep 1950–16 Jun 1952.

COMMANDERS. Unkn, Sep–Nov 1918. Unkn, Sep 1919–May 1921; Maj Thomas J Hanley Jr, May–Sep 1921; Maj Lewis H Brereton, Jun 1925; Maj Hugh Knerr, Jul 1927–Sep 1930; Capt Eugene L Eubank, 26 Dec 1933; Maj Willis H Hale, 1 Jul 1934; Lt Col Charles B Oldfield, 1935; Lt Col Robert C Olds, c. 1937–unkn; Lt Col Harold L George, Feb 1940–unkn; Lt Col Darr H Alkire, 6 Jan 1942; Col Dale O Smith, c. Sep 1942; Col Ford J Lauer, 29 Oct 1942; Lt Col Joseph A Thomas, 20 Apr 1943; Col Herbert E Rice, 5 Sep 1943; Col John D Ryan, 8 Jul 1944; Col Paul T Cullen, 25 Sep 1944; Col Robert K Martin, 23 May 1945–20 Feb 1946. Unkn, Jul–Sep 1947; Col Dalene E Bailey, 24 Sep 1947; Col William E Eubank Jr, 3 Aug 1948; Col James B Knapp, Jan 1950; Col Earl R Tash, Jan 1951; Brig Gen Frederic E Glantzberg, 10 Feb 1951; Col John M Reynolds, c. 14 Feb–16 Jun 1952.

CAMPAIGNS. *World War I:* St Mihiel; Lorraine; Meuse-Argonne. *World War II:* Antisubmarine, American Theater; Air Combat, EAME Theater; Air Offensive, Europe; Tunisia; Sicily; Naples-Foggia; Anzio; Rome-Arno; Normandy; Northern France; Southern France; North Apennines; Rhineland; Central Europe; Po Valley.

DECORATIONS. Distinguished Unit Citations: Steyr, Austria, 24 Feb 1944; Germany, 25 Feb 1944.

INSIGNE. *Shield:* Or, in fess four aerial bombs dropping bend sinisterwise azure, on a chief engrailed paly of five vert and sable a fleur-de-lis argent. *Crest:* A cloud (gray) rifted disclosing the firmament (blue) crossed by a bolt of lightning (yellow) striking bend sinisterwise all proper. *Motto:* LIBERTATEM DEFENDI-

MUS—Liberty We Defend. (Approved 19 Jan 1924. The motto then approved was replaced on 15 Apr 1940 by the one shown above.)

2d COMBAT CARGO GROUP

Constituted as 2d Combat Cargo Group on 25 Apr 1944. *Activated* on 1 May 1944. Trained with C–46 and C–47 aircraft. Moved to the Southwest Pacific, Oct–Nov 1944, and assigned to Fifth AF. Operated from Biak to fly passengers and cargo to US bases in Australia, New Guinea, the Admiralties, and the Philippines. Also dropped supplies to US and guerrilla forces in the Philippines. Moved to Leyte in May 1945. Maintained flights to bases in Australia, New Guinea, and the Philippines; transported personnel and supplies to the Ryukyus, and evacuated casualties on return flights. Moved to Okinawa in Aug 1945. Transported personnel and equipment of the occupation forces to Japan and ferried liberated prisoners of war to the Philippines. Moved to Japan in Sep 1945. *Inactivated* on 15 Jan 1946. *Disbanded* on 8 Oct 1948.

SQUADRONS. *5th:* 1944–1946. *6th:* 1944–1946. *7th:* 1944–1946. *8th:* 1944–1946.

STATIONS. Syracuse AAB, NY, 1 May 1944; Baer Field, Ind, 9–27 Oct 1944; Biak, Nov 1944; Dulag, Leyte, May 1945; Okinawa, c. 20 Aug 1945; Yokota, Japan, c. 22 Sep 1945–15 Jan 1946.

COMMANDERS. Col William J Bell, May 1944; Maj Arthur D Thomas, 10 Dec 1945–unkn.

CAMPAIGNS. Air Offensive, Japan; New Guinea; Western Pacific; Leyte; Luzon; Southern Philippines; Ryukyus.

DECORATIONS. Philippine Presidential Unit Citation.

INSIGNE. None.

2d RECONNAISSANCE GROUP

IN ARDUA PETIT

Constituted as 2d Photographic Group on 1 May 1942 and *activated* on 7 May. *Redesignated* 2d Photographic Reconnaissance and Mapping Group in May 1943, and 2d Photographic Reconnaissance Group in Aug 1943. Assigned first to Second AF, later to Third AF. Trained crews and units for photographic reconnaissance and mapping; occasionally provided personnel to help man new groups and squadrons. Aircraft included B–17's, B–24's, B–25's, L–4's, L–5's, P–38's, and A–20's. *Disbanded* on 1 May 1944.

SQUADRONS. *6th:* 1942. *7th:* 1942–1944. *10th:* 1942–1944. *11th* (formerly *5th*): 1942–1944. *29th:* 1943–1944.

STATIONS. Bradley Field, Conn, 7 May 1942; Colorado Springs, Colo, c. 13 May 1942; Will Rogers Field, Okla, c. 7 Oct 1943–1 May 1944.

COMMANDERS. Capt Paul C Schauer, 9 May 1942; Lt Col Charles P Hollstein, c. 13 May 1942; Lt Col David W Hutchinson, c. 5 Jul 1942; Lt Col Charles P Hollstein, c. 13 Aug 1942; Lt Col Hillford R Wallace, c. 11 Sep 1942; Lt Col David W Hutchinson, c. 27 Feb 1943; Lt Col Karl L Polifka, c. 13 Mar 1943; Lt Col Hillford R Wallace, c. 29 Apr 1943; Lt Col Charles P Hollstein, 18 Sep 1943; Lt Col Frank L Dunn, 4 Dec 1943–unkn.

CAMPAIGNS. American Theater.

DECORATIONS. None.

INSIGNE. *Shield:* Per bend nebuly and azure, in sinister chief a stylized camera, lens to base sable. *Motto:* IN ARDUA PETIT—He Aims at Difficult Things. (Approved 12 Nov 1942.)

3d AIR COMMANDO GROUP

Constituted as 3d Air Commando Group on 25 Apr 1944. *Activated* on 1 May 1944. Moved to the Philippines late in 1944. Assigned to Fifth AF for operations with P–51, C–47, and L–5 aircraft. Attacked Japanese airfields and installations in the Philippines, supported ground forces on Luzon, provided escort for missions to Formosa and the China coast, made raids on airfields and railways on Formosa, and furnished cover for convoys. Also transported personnel, dropped supplies to ground troops and guerrilla forces, evacuated casualties from front-line strips, adjusted artillery fire, and flew courier and mail routes. Moved to the Ryukyus in Aug 1945. Flew some patrols over Japan, made local liaison flights, and hauled cargo from the Philippines to Okinawa. Moved to Japan in Oct 1945. *Inactivated* on 25 Mar 1946. *Disbanded* on 8 Oct 1948.

SQUADRONS. *3d* Fighter: 1944–1946. *4th* Fighter: 1944–1946. *157th* Liaison: 1944–1946. *159th* Liaison: 1944–1946. *160th* Liaison: 1944–1946. *318th* Troop Carrier: 1944–1946.

STATIONS. Drew Field, Fla, 1 May 1944; Lakeland AAFld, Fla, 5 May 1944; Alachua AAFld, Fla, c. 20 Aug 1944; Drew Field, Fla, 6–24 Oct 1944; Leyte, Dec 1944; Mangaldan, Luzon, c. 26 Jan 1945; Laoag, Luzon, Apr 1945; Ie Shima, Aug 1945; Chitose, Japan, c. 27 Oct 1945–25 Mar 1946.

COMMANDERS. Maj Klem F Kalberer, May 1944; Col Arvid E Olson Jr, Jun 1944; Lt Col Walker M Mahurin, Sep 1945; Lt Col Charles H Terhune, 20 Oct 1945–unkn.

CAMPAIGNS. Air Offensive, Japan; China Defensive; Western Pacific; Leyte; Luzon; China Offensive.

DECORATIONS. Philippine Presidential Unit Citation.

INSIGNE. None.

3d BOMBARDMENT GROUP

Organized as Army Surveillance Group on 1 Jul 1919. *Redesignated* 1st Surveil-

NON SOLUM ARMIS

lance Group in Aug 1919. Used DH–
4B's to patrol the border from Brownsville,
Tex, to Nogales, Ariz, until 1921. *Redesignated* 3d Attack Group in 1921, and 3d
Bombardment Group (Light) in 1939.
Equipped with O–1, O–2, A–5, A–12, A–17,
A–18, A–20, A–24, and other aircraft, 1921–
1941. Trained, participated in maneuvers,
tested new equipment, experimented with
tactics, flew in aerial reviews, patrolled the
Mexican border (1929), and carried air
mail (1934). Furnished personnel for and
helped to train new organizations, 1939–
1941.

Moved to Australia early in 1942 and
became part of Fifth AF. *Redesignated*
3d Bombardment Group (Dive) in Sep
1942, and 3d Bombardment Group
(Light) in May 1943. Served in combat
from 1 Apr 1942 until V–J Day. Used
A–20, A–24, and B–25 aircraft for operations.

The group had its headquarters in
Australia until Jan 1943, but its squadrons
operated from New Guinea, bombing and
strafing enemy airfields, supply lines, installations, and shipping as the Allies
halted the Japanese drive toward Port
Moresby and drove the enemy back from
Buna to Lae. At the end of that campaign
in Jan 1943, headquarters moved to New
Guinea. For the next year and a half the
group continued to serve in the Southwest
Pacific, where it played an important role
in the offensives in which the Allies pushed
along the northern coast of New Guinea,
taking Salamaua, Lae, Hollandia, Wakde,
Biak, and Noemfoor. In Mar 1943 it took
part in the Battle of the Bismarck Sea,
which ended Japanese attempts to send
convoys to Lae. In Aug 1943, when Fifth
AF struck airfields at Wewak to neutralize
Japanese airpower that threatened the advance of Allied forces in New Guinea, the
group made an attack in the face of
intense antiaircraft fire on 17 Aug, destroyed or damaged many enemy planes,
and won a DUC for the mission. In the
fall of 1943 the group struck Japanese naval
and air power at Rabaul to support the assaults on Bougainville and New Britain.
In an attack on shipping at Simpson Harbor, New Britain, on 2 Nov 1943, the 3d
group encountered heavy opposition from
enemy fighters and from antiaircraft batteries on the ships. In that attack Maj
Raymond H Wilkins, commander of the
8th squadron, sank two ships before he was
shot down as he deliberately drew the fire
of a destroyer so that other planes of his

squadron could withdraw safely—an action for which Maj Wilkins was posthumously awarded the Medal of Honor. The group moved to the Philippines late in 1944. Equipped with A-20's, it bombed and strafed airfields; supported ground forces on Mindoro, Luzon, and Mindanao; attacked industries and railways on Formosa; and struck shipping along the China coast. Moved to Okinawa early in Aug 1945 and flew some missions to Japan before the war ended. Moved to Japan in Sep 1945 and, as part of Far East Air Forces, became part of the army of occupation.

Served in combat in the Korean War from 27 Jun 1950 until the armistice on 27 Jul 1953. Operated first from Japan and later from Korea, using B-26 aircraft. Flew most of its missions at night to attack such targets as airfields, vehicles, and railways. Capt John S Walmsley Jr was posthumously awarded the Medal of Honor for his actions on 14 Sep 1944: flying a night mission in a B-26, Capt Walmsley discovered and attacked an enemy supply train, and after exhausting his ammunition he flew at low altitude to direct other aircraft to the same objective; the train was destroyed but Walmsley's plane crashed in the target area. The group returned to Japan in 1954. *Redesignated* 3d Bombardment Group (Tactical) in Oct 1955.

SQUADRONS. *8th:* 1919-. *12th:* 1919-1921. *13th* (formerly 104th): 1919-1924; 1929-. *26th:* 1921-1929. *51st:* 1935-1936. *89th* (formerly 10th): 1941-1946. *90th:* 1919-.

STATIONS. Kelly Field, Tex, 1 Jul 1919; Ft Bliss, Tex, 12 Nov 1919; Kelly Field, Tex, 2 Jul 1921; Ft Crockett, Tex, 1 Jul 1926; Barksdale Field, La, 28 Feb 1935; Savannah, Ga, 6 Oct 1940-19 Jan 1942; Brisbane, Australia, 25 Feb 1942; Charters Towers, Australia, 10 Mar 1942; Port Moresby, New Guinea, 28 Jan 1943; Dobodura, New Guinea, 20 May 1943; Nadzab, New Guinea, 3 Feb 1944; Hollandia, New Guinea, 12 May 1944; Dulag, Leyte, 16 Nov 1944; San Jose, Mindoro, c. 30 Dec 1944; Okinawa, 6 Aug 1945; Atsugi, Japan, c. 8 Sep 1945; Yokota, Japan, 1 Sep 1946; Johnson AB, Japan, c. 15 Mar 1950; Iwakuni, Japan, 1 Jul 1950; Kunsan, Korea, 22 Aug 1951; Johnson AB, Japan, c. 5 Oct 1954-.

COMMANDERS. Maj B B Butler, 1 Jul 1919; Maj William G Schauffler Jr, 1 Sep 1919; Lt Col Henry B Clagett, 27 Sep 1919; Maj Leo A Walton, 20 Nov 1919; Maj Leo G Heffernan, 10 Oct 1921; Lt Col Seth W Cook, 22 Aug 1922; Maj Lewis H Brereton, 5 Feb 1923; Maj Harvey B S Burwell, 25 Jun 1924; Capt Joseph H Davidson, Feb 1926; Maj Frank D Lackland, 26 Jun 1926; Maj John H Jouett, 15 Aug 1928; Maj Davenport Johnson, 27 Feb 1930; Lt Col Horace M. Hickam, 18 Jun 1932; Lt Col Earl L Naiden, 5 Nov 1934; Col J A Rader, Jul 1937; Maj O S Ferson, Aug 1938; Col John C McDonnell, Sep 1938; Lt Col R G Breen, Nov 1940; Lt Col Paul L Williams, Dec 1940; Lt Col Phillips Melville, 18 Aug

1941; 1st Lt Robert F Strickland, 19 Jan 1942; Col John H Davies, 2 Apr 1942; Lt Col Robert F Strickland, 26 Oct 1942; Maj Donald P Hall, 28 Apr 1943; Lt Col James A Downs, 20 Oct 1943; Col John P Henebry, 7 Nov 1943; Lt Col Richard H Ellis, 27 Jun 1944; Col John P Henebry, 30 Oct 1944; Col Richard H Ellis, 28 Dec 1944; Col Charles W Howe, 1 May 1945; Lt Col James E Sweeney, 7 Dec 1945; Maj L B Weigold, c. 7 Feb 1946; Col Edward H Underhill, 23 Apr 1946; Lt Col John P Crocker, 3 Jan 1947; Col Edward H Underhill, 28 Mar 1947; Col James R Gunn Jr, 2 Jun 1947; Lt Col Joseph E Payne, 27 Sep 1948; Col Donald L Clark, 3 Jan 1950; Lt Col Leland A Walker, Jr, 5 Aug 1950; Col Henry C Brady, 17 Oct 1950; Col Chester H Morgan, 4 Jan 1952; Col William G Moore, 17 Jan 1952; Col Sherman R Beaty, 1952; Col John G Napier, 1 Apr 1953; Col Straughan D Kelsey, 22 Jul 1953; Col William H Matthews, 18 Aug 1953; Col Sam L Barr, 2 Feb 1954; Col Rufus H Holloway, 21 Sep 1954; Lt Col William D Miner, 9 Jun 1955; Lt Col Charles E Mendel, 25 Jul 1955; Col Rufus H Holloway, 17 Aug 1955–.

CAMPAIGNS. *World War II:* East Indies; Air Offensive, Japan; China Defensive; Papua; New Guinea; Bismarck Archipelago; Western Pacific; Leyte; Luzon; China Offensive. *Korean War:* UN Defensive; UN Offensive; CCF Intervention; 1st UN Counteroffensive; CCF Spring Offensive; UN Summer-Fall Offensive; Second Korean Winter; Korea Summer-Fall, 1952; Third Korean Winter; Korea Summer-Fall, 1953.

DECORATIONS. Distinguished Unit Citations: Papua, 23 Jul 1942–23 Jan 1943; New Guinea, 17 Aug 1943; Korea, 27 Jun–31 Jul 1950; Korea, 22 Apr–8 Jul 1951; Korea, 1 May–27 Jul 1953. Philippine Presidential Unit Citation. Republic of Korea Presidential Unit Citation: 27 Jun–31 Jul 1950.

INSIGNE. *Shield:* Party per bend vert and sable in chief a cactus (prickly pear) or, a bend azure fimbriated of the third, all within a bordure argent charged with nineteen crosses patee of the second. *Crest:* On a wreath of the colors an arm couped near the shoulder paleways with hand clenched proper between two wings conjoined in lure argent. *Motto:* NON SOLUM ARMIS—Not by Arms Alone. (Approved 17 Jan 1922. This insigne was modified 22 Dec 1952.)

3d COMBAT CARGO GROUP

Constituted as 3d Combat Cargo Group on 1 Jun 1944 and *activated* in India on 5 Jun. Equipped with C-47's. Supported ground forces during the battle for northern Burma and the subsequent Allied drive southward. Flew Allied troops and materiel to the front, transporting gasoline, oil, vehicles, engineering and signal equipment, and other items that the group either landed or dropped in Burma. Also evacuated wounded personnel to India. Moved to Burma in Jun 1945. Hauled gasoline and other supplies to bases in

SUBSIDIA FERIMUS

western China. *Redesignated* 513th Troop Carrier Group in Sep 1945. Moved to China in Nov. *Inactivated* on 15 Apr 1946.

Redesignated 513th Troop Carrier Group (Special). *Activated* in Germany on 19 Nov 1948. Assigned to United States Air Forces in Europe. Using C-54's, transported food, coal, and other supplies during the Berlin airlift, 1948–1949. *Inactivated* in Germany on 16 Oct 1949.

Redesignated 513th Troop Carrier Group (Assault, Fixed Wing). *Activated* in the US on 8 Nov 1955. Assigned to Tactical Air Command and equipped with C-123 aircraft.

SQUADRONS. *9th* (later 330th): 1944–1946; 1948–1949; 1955–. *10th* (later 331st): 1944–1945; 1948–1949; 1955–. *11th* (later 332d): 1944–1946; 1948–1949; 1955–. *12th* (later 333d): 1944–1945; 1948–1949.

STATIONS. Sylhet, India, 5 Jun 1944; Dinjan, India, 2 Aug 1944; Myitkyina, Burma, 3 Jun 1945; Shanghai, China, 1 Nov 1945–

15 Apr 1946. Rhein-Main AB, Germany, 19 Nov 1948–16 Oct 1949. Sewart AFB, Tenn, 8 Nov 1955–.

COMMANDERS. Col Charles D Farr, 5 Jun 1944; Col Hiette S Williams Jr, 25 Oct 1944; Col G Robert Dodson, 21 Apr 1945; Col Hugh D Wallace, 17 Jun 1945; Lt Col George H Van Deusan, unkn–1946. Unkn, 1948–1949. Col John R Roche, 8 Nov 1955–.

CAMPAIGNS. India-Burma; Central Burma.

DECORATIONS. None.

INSIGNE. *Shield:* On a shield per fesse dancette azure and vert an American bald eagle volant, marked with three stars, red, blue, and green, wings spread upward, carrying with his talons an aircraft wing section loaded with a gun, supply box, and a combat soldier, all or; in chief a lightning bolt of the last. *Motto:* SUBSIDIA FERIMUS—We Fly Men and Materiel. (Approved 3 Apr 1957.)

3d RECONNAISSANCE GROUP

Constituted as 3d Photographic Group on 9 Jun 1942 and *activated* on 20 Jun. *Redesignated* 3d Photographic Reconnaissance and Mapping Group in May 1943, 3d Photographic Group (Reconnaissance) in Nov 1943, and 3d Reconnaissance Group in May 1945. Moved, via England, to the Mediterranean theater, Nov–Dec 1942, and assigned to Twelfth AF. Used F-4 and F-5 aircraft. Provided photographic intelligence that assisted the campaigns for Tunisia, Pantelleria, Sardinia,

ARCHEZ BIEN

and Sicily. Reconnoitered airdromes, roads, marshalling yards, and harbors both before and after the Allied landings at Salerno. Covered the Anzio area early in 1944 and continued to support Fifth Army in its drive through Italy by determining troop movements, gun positions, and terrain. Flew reconnaissance missions in connection with the invasion of Southern France in Aug 1944. Received a DUC for a mission on 28 Aug 1944 when the group provided photographic intelligence that assisted the rapid advance of Allied ground forces. Also mapped areas in France and the Balkans. *Inactivated* in Italy on 12 Sep 1945. *Disbanded* on 6 Mar 1947.

SQUADRONS. *5th:* 1942–1945. *12th:* 1942–1945. *13th:* 1942–1943. *14th:* 1942–1943. *15th:* 1942–1944. *23d:* 1944–1945.

STATIONS. Colorado Springs, Colo, 20 Jun–13 Aug 1942; Membury, England, 8 Sep 1942; Steeple Morden, England, 26 Oct–22 Nov 1942; La Senia, Algeria, 10 Dec 1942; Algiers, Algeria, 25 Dec 1942; La Marsa, Tunisia, 13 Jun 1943; San Sev-

ero, Italy, 8 Dec 1943; Pomigliano, Italy, 4 Jan 1944; Nettuno, Italy, 16 Jun 1944; Viterbo, Italy, 26 Jun 1944; Corsica, c. 14 Jul 1944; Rosia, Italy, c. Sep 1944; Florence, Italy, 17 Jan 1945; Pomigliano, Italy, 26 Aug–12 Sep 1945.

COMMANDERS. Capt George H McBride, 20 Jun 1942; Maj Harry T Eidson, 25 Jun 1942; Maj Elliott Roosevelt, 11 Jul 1942; Lt Col Furman H Limeburner, 13 Aug 1942; Col Elliott Roosevelt, 30 Sep 1942; Lt Col Frank L Dunn, c. Mar 1943; Lt Col James F Setchell, c. 4 Nov 1943; Maj Hal C Tunnell, 19 Jan 1944; Maj Thomas W Barfoot Jr, c. 29 May 1944; Col Duane L Kime, 17 Sep 1944; Lt Col Oscar M Blomquist, 29 May 1945; Lt Col James E Hill, 2 Aug–c. Sep 1945.

CAMPAIGNS. Air Combat, EAME Theater; Tunisia; Sicily; Naples-Foggia; Anzio; Rome-Arno; Southern France; North Apennines; Rhineland; Central Europe; Po Valley.

DECORATIONS. Distinguished Unit Citation: MTO, 28 Aug 1944.

INSIGNE. *Shield:* Per chevron or and azure, in center chief point a stylized camera, lens to base sable. *Motto:* ARCHEZ BIEN—Shoot Well. (Approved 29 Oct 1942.)

4th COMBAT CARGO GROUP

Constituted as 4th Combat Cargo Group on 9 Jun 1944 and *activated* on 13 Jun. Trained with C–46 and C–47 aircraft. Moved to India in Nov 1944. Began operations with C–46's in Dec 1944. Trans-

ported reinforcements and supplies for Allied forces in Burma until May 1945. Operations included moving equipment and materials for the Ledo Road in Dec 1944; transporting men, mules, and boats when the Allies crossed the Irrawaddy River in Feb 1945; and dropping Gurkha paratroops during the assault on Rangoon in May 1945. Moved to Burma in Jun 1945 and hauled ammunition, gasoline, mules, and men to China until the war ended. Returned to India in Nov 1945. *Inactivated* on 9 Feb 1946. *Disbanded* on 8 Oct 1948.

SQUADRONS. *13th:* 1944–1945. *14th:* 1944–1946. *15th:* 1944–1945. *16th:* 1944–1945.

STATIONS. Syracuse AAB, NY, 13 Jun 1944; Bowman Field, Ky, 17 Aug–6 Nov 1944; Sylhet, India, 28 Nov 1944; Agartala, India, Dec 1944; Chittagong, India, 5 Jan 1945; Namponmao, Burma, Jun 1945; Pandaveswar, India, Nov 1945; Panagarh, India, 15 Jan–9 Feb 1946.

COMMANDERS. Col Stuart D Baird, 13 Jun 1944–unkn.

CAMPAIGNS. India-Burma; Central Burma; China Offensive.

DECORATIONS. None.

INSIGNE. None.

4th FIGHTER GROUP

Constituted as 4th Fighter Group on 22 Aug 1942. *Activated* in England on 12 Sep 1942. Former members of RAF Eagle Squadrons formed the nucleus of the group, which served in combat from Oct 1942 to Apr 1945 and destroyed more enemy planes in the air and on the ground than any other fighter group of Eighth AF. Operated first with Spitfires but changed to P-47's in Mar 1943 and to P-51's in Apr 1944. On numerous occasions escorted bombers that attacked factories, submarine pens, V-weapon sites, and other targets in France, the Low Countries, or Germany. Went out sometimes with a small force of bombers to draw up the enemy's fighters so they could be destroyed in aerial combat. At other times attacked the enemy's air power by strafing and dive-bombing airfields. Also hit troops, supply depots, roads, bridges, rail lines, and trains. Participated in the intensive campaign against the German Air Force and aircraft industry during Big Week, 20–25 Feb 1944. Received a DUC for aggressiveness in seeking out and destroying enemy aircraft and in attacking enemy air bases, 5 Mar–24 Apr 1944. Flew interdictory and counter-air missions during the invasion of Normandy in Jun 1944. Supported the airborne invasion of Holland in Sep. Participated in the Battle of the Bulge, Dec 1944–Jan 1945. Covered the airborne assault across the Rhine in Mar 1945. Moved to the US in Nov. *Inactivated* on 10 Nov 1945.

Activated on 9 Sep 1946. Equipped with P–80's. Converted to F–86 aircraft in 1949. *Redesignated* 4th Fighter-Interceptor Group in Jan 1950. Moved to Japan, Nov–Dec 1950, for duty with Far East Air Forces in the Korean War. Began operations from Japan on 15 Dec 1950 and moved to Korea in Mar 1951. Escorted bombers, made fighter sweeps, engaged in interdiction of the enemy's lines of communications, flew armed reconnaissance sorties, conducted counter-air patrols, served as an air defense organization, and provided close support for ground forces. One member of the group, Maj George A Davis Jr, commander of the 334th squadron, was awarded the Medal of Honor for action on 10 Feb 1952 when, leading a flight of two F–86's, Davis spotted twelve enemy planes (MIG's), attacked, and destroyed three before his plane crashed in the mountains. The group returned to Japan in the fall of 1954. *Redesignated* 4th Fighter-Bomber Group in Mar 1955.

SQUADRONS. *334th:* 1942–1945; 1946–. *335th:* 1942–1945; 1946–. *336th:* 1942–1945; 1946–.

STATIONS. Bushey Hall, England, 12 Sep 1942; Debden, England, Sep 1942; Steeple Morden, England, Jul–Nov 1945; Camp Kilmer, NJ, c. 9–10 Nov 1945. Selfridge Field, Mich, 9 Sep 1946; Andrews Field, Md, Mar 1947; Langley AFB, Va, c. 30 Apr 1949; New Castle County Aprt, Del, Aug–Nov 1950; Johnson AB, Japan, Dec 1950; Suwon, Korea, Mar 1951; Kimpo, Korea, Aug 1951; Chitose, Japan, c. 1 Nov 1954–.

COMMANDERS. Col Edward W Anderson, Sep 1942; Col Chesley G Peterson, Aug 1943; Col Donald J M Blakeslee, 1 Jan 1944; Lt Col Claiborne H Kinnard Jr, Nov 1944; Lt Col Harry J Dayhuff, 7 Dec 1944; Col Everett W Stewart, 21 Feb 1945–unkn. Col Ernest H Beverly, Sep 1946; Lt Col Benjamin S Preston Jr, Aug 1948; Col Albert L Evans Jr, Jun 1949; Col John C Meyer, c. 1 Sep 1950; Lt Col Glenn T Eagleston, May 1951; Col Benjamin S Preston Jr, Jul 1951; Col Walker M Mahurin, 18 Mar 1952; Lt Col Ralph G Kuhn, 14 May 1952; Col Royal N Baker, 1 Jun 1952; Col Thomas D DeJarnette, 18 Mar 1953; Col Henry S Tyler Jr, c. 28 Dec 1953; Lt Col Dean W Dutrack, c. 19 Jul 1954; Col William D Gilchrist, c. 9 Aug 1954; Col George I Ruddell, c. 4 May 1955–.

CAMPAIGNS. *World War II*: Air Offensive, Europe; Normandy; Northern France; Rhineland; Ardennes-Alsace; Central Europe. *Korean War*: CCF Intervention; 1st UN Counteroffensive; CCF Spring Offensive; UN Summer-Fall Offensive; Second Korean Winter; Korea Summer-Fall, 1952; Third Korean Winter; Korea Summer-Fall, 1953.

DECORATIONS. Distinguished Unit Citations: France, 5 Mar–24 Apr 1944; Korea,

22 Apr–8 Jul 1951; Korea, 9 Jul–27 Nov 1951. Republic of Korea Presidential Unit Citations: 1 Nov 1951–30 Sep 1952; 1 Oct 1952–31 Mar 1953.

INSIGNE. *Shield*: Azure on a bend or, a spear garnished with three eagle feathers and shaft flammant to base all proper. *Crest*: On a wreath of the colors, or and azure, a lion's face or. *Motto*: FOURTH BUT FIRST. (Approved 26 Sep 1949.)

4th RECONNAISSANCE GROUP

Constituted as 4th Photographic Group on 14 Jul 1942 and *activated* on 23 Jul. Trained for overseas duty with F-4's. Moved to the South Pacific late in 1942. Assigned to Thirteenth AF in Jan 1943. *Redesignated* 4th Photographic Reconnaissance and Mapping Group in May 1943, 4th Photographic Group (Reconnaissance) in Nov 1943, and 4th Reconnaissance Group in May 1945. From Dec 1942 to May 1945 the group, based successively on New Caledonia, Espiritu Santo, Guadalcanal, and Morotai, flew reconnaissance missions over enemy territory to supply air force units with target and damage-assessment photographs and to provide army and navy units with intelligence on Japanese troop concentrations, installations, shore defenses, supply routes, and shipping. It also produced maps of Allied and enemy-held territory and prepared navigation charts for US units. During the last three months of the war the group photographed Japanese positions and installations on Mindanao and Borneo to aid US and Australian operations. Moved to Leyte in Sep 1945. *Inactivated* on 15 Jan 1946. *Disbanded* on 6 Mar 1947.

SQUADRONS. *17th*: 1942–1946. *18th*: 1942–1944. *19th*: 1942–1943. *20th*: 1942–1943. *38th*: 1945–1946.

STATIONS. Colorado Springs, Colo, 23 Jul–24 Oct 1942; New Caledonia, 22 Nov 1942; Espiritu Santo, 22 Jan 1943; Guadalcanal, 6 May 1944; Morotai, 12 Dec 1944; Leyte, Sep 1945–15 Jan 1946.

COMMANDERS. 2d Lt Everett E Shaw, 23 Jul 1942; Lt Col Francis L Rivard, 10 Aug 1942; Lt Col Charles P Hollstein, 3 Sep 1942; Col Paul C Schauer, 18 Jul 1943; Lt Col Hillford R Wallace, 7 Jun 1944; Maj Sidney L Hardin, 4 Aug 1944; Lt Col Hershell E Parsons, 20 Jan 1945–unkn.

CAMPAIGNS. Guadalcanal; New Guinea; Northern Solomons; Bismarck Archipelago; Western Pacific; Leyte; Southern Philippines.

DECORATIONS. Philippine Presidential Unit Citation.

INSIGNE. *Shield:* Azure, three piles and three like ordinaries transposed conjoined in honor point or. (Approved 28 Nov 1942.)

5th BOMBARDMENT GROUP

KIAI O KA LEWA

Authorized as 2d Group (Observation) on 15 Aug 1919 and *organized* in Hawaii. *Redesignated* 5th Group (Observation) in Mar 1921, 5th Group (Pursuit and Bombardment) in Jun 1922, and 5th Group (Composite) in Jul 1922. Used DH-4, MB-2, B-12, LB-5, LB-6, PW-9, P-12, O-19, and other aircraft. Activities included training, participating in Army-Navy maneuvers, staging aerial reviews, sowing seeds from the air for the Territorial Forestry Division, and bombing a stream of lava flowing from Mauna Loa to divert it from the city of Hilo. *Redesignated* 5th Bombardment Group in Mar 1938, 5th Bombardment Group (Medium) in Dec 1939, and 5th Bombardment Group (Heavy) in Nov 1940. Equipped with B-17's and B-18's by Dec 1941. Assigned to Seventh AF in Feb 1942. Engaged primarily in search and patrol missions off Hawaii from Dec 1941 to Nov 1942.

Left Hawaii in Nov 1942 and, operating from bases in the South and Southwest Pacific with B-17 and B-24 aircraft, served in combat with Thirteenth AF during the Allied drive from the Solomons to the Philippines. Flew long patrol and photographic missions over the Solomon Islands and the Coral Sea, attacked Japanese shipping off Guadalcanal, and raided airfields in the northern Solomons until Aug 1943. Then struck enemy bases and installations on Bougainville, New Britain, and New Ireland. Raided the heavily defended Japanese base on Woleai during Apr and May 1944 and received a DUC for the action. Helped to neutralize enemy bases on Yap and in the Truk and Palau Islands, Jun–Aug 1944, preparatory to the invasion of Peleliu and Leyte. Flew missions to the Netherlands Indies, receiving a DUC for an attack, conducted through heavy flak and fighter defenses, on oil installations at Balikpapan, Borneo, on 30 Sep 1944. Completed a variety of missions from Oct 1944 until the end of the war, these operations including raids on enemy bases and installations on Luzon, Ceram, Halmahera, and Formosa; support for ground forces in the Philippines and Borneo; and patrols off the China coast. Remained in the theater as part of Far East Air Forces after the war, but all personnel evidently had been withdrawn by early in 1946. *Redesignated* 5th Bombardment Group (Very Heavy) in Apr 1946, and 5th Reconnaissance Group in Feb 1947. Remanned in Mar 1947, equipped with FB–17's and F–2's, and engaged in mapping areas of the Philippines, Formosa, and the Pescadores.

Moved to the US in May 1949. Assigned to Strategic Air Command. *Redesignated* 5th Strategic Reconnaissance Group in Jul 1949. Equipped with RB–29's. *Redesignated* 5th Strategic Reconnaissance Group (Heavy) in Sep 1950. Began converting to B–36's. *Inactivated* on 16 Jun 1952.

SQUADRONS. *6th* Pursuit: 1919–1927. *19th* Pursuit: 1924–1927. *23d:* 1922–1930, 1938–1947, 1947–1952. *26th* Attack: 1930–1938. *31st:* 1938–1947, 1949–1952. *38th:* 1947–1949. *72d:* 1923–1930, 1938–1947, 1949–1952. *338th:* 1947–1949. *394th* (formerly 4th): 1920–1922, 1927–1938, 1939–1946. *431st* (formerly 50th, later 5th): 1930–1938, 1946, 1947.

STATIONS. Luke Field, TH, 15 Aug 1919; Hickam Field, TH, 1 Jan 1939; Espiritu Santo, 1 Dec 1942; Guadalcanal, 19 Aug 1943; Munda, New Georgia, 4 Feb 1944; Momote Airfield, Los Negros, 7 Apr 1944; Wakde, 17 Aug 1944; Noemfoor, 22 Sep 1944; Morotai, Oct 1944; Samar, 5 Mar 1945; Clark Field, Luzon, Dec 1945–6 May 1949; Mountain Home AFB, Idaho, 26 May 1949; Fairfield-Suisun AFB, Calif, 9 Nov 1949–16 Jun 1952.

COMMANDERS. Unkn, 1919–1938; Col Shepler W FitzGerald, c. Sep 1938–unkn; Lt Col Edwin B Bobzien, 1941; Col Arthur W Meehan, 1942; Col Brooke E Allen, 1 Nov 1942; Col Marion D Unruh, 10 Aug 1943; Lt Col Joseph E Reddoch Jr, 31 Dec 1943; Col Thomas C Musgrave Jr, 4 Apr 1944; Col Joseph E Reddoch Jr, 21 Apr 1944; Col Thomas C Musgrave Jr, 15 Aug 1944; Maj Albert W James, 28 Feb 1945; Col Isaac J Haviland, 15 Mar 1945; Lt Col Albert W James, 5 Jul 1945–unkn; Col Herbert K Baisley, 16 Jan 1947–unkn; Col William E Basye, 1949; Col Walter E Arnold, 27 Feb 1950–16 Jun 1952.

CAMPAIGNS. Central Pacific; Guadalcanal; New Guinea; Northern Solomons; Eastern Mandates; Bismarck Archipelago; Western Pacific; Leyte; Luzon; Southern Philippines.

DECORATIONS. Distinguished Unit Citations: Woleai Island, 18 Apr–15 May 1944; Borneo, 30 Sep 1944. Philippine Presidential Unit Citation.

INSIGNE. *Shield:* Party per pale nebuly vert and sable a death's head argent winged or. *Crest:* On a wreath of the colors (argent and vert), a bull's head caboshed azure and armed or. *Motto:* KIAI O KA LEWA—Guardians of the Upper Regions (Approved 21 Jun 1924.)

5th RECONNAISSANCE GROUP

Constituted as 5th Photographic Group on 14 Jul 1942 and *activated* on 23 Jul. *Redesignated* 5th Photographic Reconnaissance and Mapping Group in May 1943, and 5th Photographic Reconnaissance Group in Aug 1943. Trained and participated in maneuvers. Moved to the Mediterranean theater, Jul–Sep 1943. As-

BEWARE, WE SNAP

signed first to Twelfth AF and later (Oct 1944) to Fifteenth. Flew missions to Italy, France, Germany, Austria, Czechoslovakia, Poland, and the Balkans, using F–5 aircraft. Also flew some photographic missions at night with B–17's and B–25's. Photographed areas near Anzio prior to the Allied landings. Provided reconnaissance of road and rail targets to support US Fifth and British Eighth Army in southern Italy. Made bomb-damage assessments at Cassino. Operated over northwest France, photographing rail targets to be bombed in connection with the invasion of Normandy. Mapped coastal areas in preparation for the invasion of Southern France. Received a DUC for action on 6 Sep 1944 when the group secured photographic intelligence of German Air Force installations in the Balkans and thus enabled fighter organizations to destroy large numbers of enemy transport and fighter planes. Provided reconnaissance services for Fifteenth AF's campaign against the enemy's oil industry, aircraft production, and communications. Also assisted the advance of ground forces in

northern Italy by supplying intelligence on enemy installations in the area. *Redesignated* 5th Reconnaissance Group in May 1945. Returned to the US in Oct. *Inactivated* on 28 Oct 1945. *Disbanded* on 6 Mar 1947.

SQUADRONS. *15th:* 1944–1945. *21st:* 1942–1943. *22d:* 1942–1943. *23d:* 1942–1944. *24th:* 1942–1943. *32d:* 1944–1945. *37th:* 1944–1945.

STATIONS. Colorado Springs, Colo, 23 Jul 1942–8 Aug 1943; La Marsa, Tunisia, 8 Sep 1943; San Severo, Italy, 8 Dec 1943; Bari, Italy, 11 Oct 1944–Oct 1945; Camp Kilmer, NJ, 26–28 Oct 1945.

COMMANDERS. 2d Lt Frederick A Williams, 23 Jul 1942; Maj J D Russell, 1942; Maj James F Setchell, 12 Jan 1943; Lt Col Waymond A Davis, 27 Feb 1943; Maj Leon W Gray, 23 Oct 1943; Maj Lloyd R Nuttall, 4 Feb 1944; Col Wilbur H Stratton, 21 Sep 1944; Lt Col Bernard S Hendler, 9 Aug 1945–unkn.

CAMPAIGNS. American Theater; Air Combat, EAME Theater; Air Offensive, Europe; Naples-Foggia; Rome-Arno; Normandy; Northern France; Southern France; North Apennines; Rhineland; Central Europe; Po Valley.

DECORATIONS. Distinguished Unit Citation: MTO, 6 Sep 1944.

INSIGNE. *Shield:* Azure, on a chevron inverted or two wings conjoined in lure and elevated of the field, in chief a camera lens proper ringed of the second. *Motto:* BEWARE, WE SNAP! (Approved 25 Jan 1943.)

6th BOMBARDMENT GROUP

PARATI DEFENDERE

Organized as 3d Observation Group in the Panama Canal Zone on 30 Sep 1919. *Redesignated* 6th Group (Observation) in 1921, 6th Group (Composite) in 1922, 6th Bombardment Group in 1937, 6th Bombardment Group (Medium) in 1939, and 6th Bombardment Group (Heavy) in 1940. Operations, which were concerned chiefly with defense of the canal, included training, participating in maneuvers, flying patrol missions, photographing the canal area, staging aerial reviews, making good-will flights to Central and South American countries, and flying mercy missions in Jan 1939 to earthquake victims at Santiago, Chile. Equipped with R–4's and DH–4's in 1919; used SE–5A, MB–3A, and P–12B aircraft in the period 1922–1929; received B–10's in 1936 and B–18's in 1939; used B–17, B–18, B–24, LB–30, and L–4E aircraft after the US entered World War

II. *Disbanded* in the Canal Zone on 1 Nov 1943.

Reconstituted on 29 Jun 1944 and *consolidated* with 6th Bombardment Group (Very Heavy), which had been *constituted* on 28 Mar 1944 and *activated* in the US on 19 Apr 1944. Equipped first with B–17's; later trained for combat with B–29's. Moved to Tinian, Nov 1944–Feb 1945. Assigned to Twentieth AF. Commenced operations by attacking Iwo Jima and the Truk Islands in Feb 1945. Afterward, struck industrial targets in Japan, flying in daylight and at high altitude to carry out these missions. Began incendiary raids on area targets in Japan in Mar 1945 and was awarded a DUC for action on 25 May when the group flew at night and at low altitude through alerted enemy defenses to drop incendiaries on Tokyo. Participated in mining operations in the Shimonoseki Strait and received second DUC for contributing to the blockade of the Japanese Empire by mining harbors in Japan and Korea in Jul 1945. Assisted the invasion of Okinawa in Apr 1945 with strikes on Kyushu, hitting airfields that were used by kamikaze pilots. After the war, dropped food and supplies to Allied prisoners and took part in show-of-force flights over Japan. Moved to the Philippines in Jan 1946 and to the Ryukyus in Jun 1947. *Inactivated* on Okinawa on 18 Oct 1948.

Redesignated 6th Bombardment Group (Medium). *Activated* in the US on 2 Jan 1951. Assigned to Strategic Air Command and equipped with B–29's. *Inactivated* on 16 Jun 1952.

SQUADRONS. *3d:* 1940–1942. *24th:* 1922–1929; 1944–1948; 1951–1952. *25th:* 1922–1943. *29th:* 1943. *39th:* 1944–1948; 1951–1952. *40th:* 1944–1948; 1951–1952. *44th:* 1930–1937. *74th:* 1940–1942, 1943. *395th:* 1942–1943. *397th* (formerly 7th): 1919–1940, 1942–1943.

STATIONS. France Field, CZ, 30 Sep 1919; Rio Hato, Panama, 9 Dec 1941; Albrook Field, CZ, 14 Jan 1943; Howard Field, CZ, Oct–1 Nov 1943. Dalhart AAFld, Tex, 19 Apr 1944; Grand Island AAFld, Neb, 19 May–18 Nov 1944; North Field, Tinian, 28 Dec 1944; Clark Field, Luzon, 28 Jan 1946; Kadena, Okinawa, 1 Jun 1947–18 Oct 1948. Walker AFB, NM, 2 Jan 1951–16 Jun 1952.

COMMANDERS. Unkn, 1919–1923; Maj Follett Bradley, 1923–1926; Lt Col Lewis H Brereton, Aug 1931–c. Jun 1935; Lt Col William O Butler, c. Jan. 1937–Jul 1939; Lt Col Edwin J House, 1939–1940; Maj Samuel M Connell, c. Sep 1940–Feb 1941; Col Henry K Mooney, 15 Sep 1941–20 Jan 1943; unkn, 20 Jan–1 Nov 1943. Maj William E Taylor, 19 Apr 1944; Lt Col Howard D Kenzie, 28 Apr 1944; Col Kenneth H Gibson, 17 Jun 1944; Lt Col Theodore W Tucker, 31 Aug 1945; Col John P Kenny, 29 Aug 1946; Col Frank P Sturdivant, 4 Dec 1946–unkn. Col William K Martin, 15 Jan 1951–16 Jun 1952.

CAMPAIGNS. Antisubmarine, American Theater; Air Offensive, Japan; Eastern Mandates; Western Pacific.

DECORATIONS. Distinguished Unit Citations: Tokyo, Japan, 25 May 1945; Japanese Empire, 9–19 Jul 1945.

INSIGNE. *Shield:* Per fess debased or and azure issuant against the rays of the setting sun a full rigged ship (black hull and white sails), in the gaillard cut (light and dark green), in chief a biplane (black) diving bend sinisterwise all proper. *Crest:* On a wreath of the colors (or and azure) a pirate's head and shoulders tattooed on the chest with skull and bones proper, garbed and coifed or and sable. *Motto:* PARATI DEFENDERE—Ready to Defend. (Approved 22 Jan 1924.)

6th RECONNAISSANCE GROUP

Constituted as 6th Photographic Group on 5 Feb 1943 and *activated* on 9 Feb. *Redesignated* 6th Photographic Reconnaissance and Mapping Group in May 1943, 6th Photographic Reconnaissance Group in Aug 1943, and 6th Reconnaissance Group in May 1945. Moved to the Southwest Pacific, Sep–Oct 1943, and assigned to Fifth AF. Used F–5's and F–7's to photograph Japanese airfields, harbors, beach defenses, and personnel areas in New Guinea, the Bismarcks, Borneo, and the southern Philippines. Reconnoitered target areas and enemy troop positions to provide intelligence for air force and army units. Received a DUC for unescorted flights to Leyte during Sep 1944 when in a minimum period of time the group obtained information about Japanese defenses, such information being necessary for planning the amphibious assault on the Philippines. After moving to the Philippines in Nov 1944, flew missions to Formosa and China, engaged in mapping parts of Luzon and Mindanao, and provided intelligence for US ground forces concerning Japanese movements. Moved to Okinawa in Jul 1945 and flew some missions over Kyushu before the war ended. Moved to Japan in Sep 1945. *Inactivated* on 27 Apr 1946. *Disbanded* on 6 Mar 1947.

SQUADRONS. *8th:* 1943–1946. *20th:* 1943–1946. *25th:* 1943–1946. *26th:* 1943–1945. *27th:* 1943. *36th:* 1944–1945.

STATIONS. Colorado Springs, Colo, 9 Feb–7 Sep 1943; Sydney, Australia, 10 Oct 1943; Brisbane, Australia, 27 Nov 1943; Port Moresby, New Guinea, 10 Dec 1943; Nadzab, New Guinea, 17 Feb 1944; Biak, Aug 1944; Leyte, 3 Nov 1944; Clark Field, Luzon, 1 May 1945; Okinawa, 31 Jul 1945; Chofu, Japan, 27 Sep 1945; Irumagawa, Japan, Jan–27 Apr 1946.

COMMANDERS. Lt Col Waymond A Davis, 9 Feb 1943; Maj Cecil Darnell, 27 Feb 1943; Col David W Hutchison, 13 Mar 1943; Lt Col Cecil Darnell, 24 Mar 1943; Maj Arthur L Post, 24 Jul 1944; Lt Col Alexander Guerry, c. 1 Sep 1944; Lt Col Ben K Armstrong Jr, 5 Jan 1945; Lt Col Joseph Davis Jr, 31 May 1945–unkn.

CAMPAIGNS. Air Offensive, Japan; China Defensive; New Guinea; Bismarck Archipelago; Western Pacific; Leyte; Luzon; Ryukyus; Southern Philippines; China Offensive.

DECORATIONS. Distinguished Unit Citation: Philippine Islands, 18–25 Sep 1944. Philippine Presidential Unit Citation.

INSIGNE. None.

7th BOMBARDMENT GROUP

MORS AB ALTO

Organized as 1st Army Observation Group on 1 Oct 1919. *Redesignated* 7th Group (Observation) in Mar 1921. *Inactivated* on 30 Aug 1921.

Redesignated 7th Bombardment Group in 1923. *Activated* on 1 Jun 1928. *Redesignated* 7th Bombardment Group (Heavy) in 1939. Trained, participated in aerial reviews, dropped food and medical supplies to persons marooned or lost, and took part in maneuvers and experiments. Aircraft included B–12's, B–18's, and B–17's.

The group was on its way to the Philippines when the Japanese attacked Pearl Harbor on 7 Dec 1941. The ground echelon, on board ship, was diverted to Australia and later sent to Java. Six of the group's B-17's, which had left the US on 6 Dec, reached Hawaii during the enemy attack but were able to land safely. Later in Dec the remainder of the air echelon flew B-17's from the US to Java. From 14 Jan to 1 Mar 1942, during the Japanese drive through the Philippines and Netherlands East Indies, the group operated from Java, being awarded a DUC for its action against enemy aircraft, ground installations, warships, and transports.

Moved to India in Mar 1942 and assigned to Tenth AF. Resumed combat with B-17's and LB-30's; converted to B-24's late in 1942. Operations were directed primarily against the Japanese in Burma, with attacks on airfields, fuel and supply dumps, locomotive works, railways, bridges, docks, warehouses, shipping, and other targets. Also bombed oil refineries and railways in Thailand, hit power plants in China, attacked enemy shipping in the Andaman Sea, and ferried gasoline over the Hump to China. Received second DUC for damaging the enemy's line of supply in southeast Asia with an attack against rail lines and bridges in Thailand on 19 Mar 1945. Returned to the US in Dec 1945. *Inactivated* on 6 Jan 1946.

Redesignated 7th Bombardment Group (Very Heavy). *Activated* on 1 Oct 1946. Assigned to Strategic Air Command. Equipped first with B-29's, later with B-36's. *Redesignated* 7th Bombardment Group (Heavy) in Jul 1948. *Inactivated* on 16 Jun 1952.

SQUADRONS. *9th:* 1919-1921; 1928-1946; 1946-1952. *11th:* 1919-1921; unkn-1942. *22d:* 1939-1942. *30th:* 1928-1931. *31st:* 1919-1921; 1928-[1939?]. *436th* (formerly 88th): 1939-1946; 1946-1952. *492d:* 1942-1946; 1946-1952. *493d:* 1942-1946.

STATIONS. Park Field, Tenn, 1 Oct 1919; Langley Field, Va, 28 Oct 1919-30 Aug 1921. Rockwell Field, Calif, 1 Jun 1928; March Field, Calif, 30 Oct 1931; Hamilton Field, Calif, 5 Dec 1934; Merced Field, Calif, 5 Nov 1935; Hamilton Field, Calif, 22 May 1937; Ft Douglas, Utah, 7 Sep 1940-13 Nov 1941; Brisbane, Australia, 22 Dec 1941-Feb 1942; Karachi, India, 12 Mar 1942; Dum-Dum, India, 30 May 1942; Karachi, India, 9 Sep 1942; Pandaveswar, India, 12 Dec 1942; Kurmitola, India, 17 Jan 1944; Pandaveswar, India, 6 Oct 1944; Tezpur, India, 7 Jun 1945; Dudhkundi, India, 31 Oct-7 Dec 1945; Camp Kilmer, NJ, 5-6 Jan 1946. Ft Worth AAFld, Tex, 1 Oct 1946-16 Jun 1952.

COMMANDERS. Unkn, 1919-1921. Capt Frank H Pritchard, 1928-unkn; Maj Carl A Spaatz, c. May 1929-c. Oct 1931; Col Clarence I Tinker, c. Dec 1935-1938; Col Ralph Royce, 1938-unkn; Maj Stanley K Robinson, unkn-29 Jan 1942; Maj Austin A Straubel, c. 29 Jan-3 Feb 1942; Col Cecil E Combs, 22 Mar 1942; Col Conrad F Necrason, 1 Jul 1942; Col Aubrey K Dodson, 27 Mar 1944; Col Harvey T Alness, 6 Nov 1944; Col Howard F Bronson Jr, 24 Jun 1945-unkn. Col John G Eriksen, 1 Oct 1946; Col Hewitt T Wheeless, 16 Dec 1946-unkn; Col Alan D Clark, c. Nov 1947-unkn; Col Charles D Farr, 7 Feb

1949; Col John A Roberts, 17 Aug 1949; Col Richard T Black, c. 24 Oct 1950; Col John A Roberts, Feb 1951; Col George T Chadwell, c. May 1951; Col John A Roberts, Apr–Jun 1952.

CAMPAIGNS. Burma, 1942; East Indies; India-Burma; China Defensive; Central Burma; China Offensive.

DECORATIONS. Distinguished Unit Citations: Netherlands Indies, 14 Jan–1 Mar 1942; Thailand, 19 Mar 1945.

INSIGNE. *Shield:* Azure, on a bend or three crosses pattee sable. *Crest:* On a wreath of the colors (or and azure) a drop bomb palewise sable piercing a cloud proper. *Motto:* MORS AB ALTO— Death from Above. (Approved 30 Jan 1933. This insigne was modified 12 Sep 1952.)

7th RECONNAISSANCE GROUP

Constituted as 7th Photographic Group on 5 Feb 1943. *Activated* on 1 May 1943. *Redesignated* 7th Photographic Reconnaissance and Mapping Group in May 1943, 7th Photographic Group (Reconnaissance) in Nov 1943, and 7th Reconnaissance Group in Jun 1945. Transferred, without personnel and equipment, to England on 7 Jul 1943 and assigned to Eighth AF. Used Spitfires and L-5's to obtain information about bombardment targets and damage inflicted by bombardment operations; provide mapping service for air and ground units; observe and report on enemy transportation, installations, and positions; and obtain data on weather conditions. Prior to Jun 1944, photographed airfields, cities, industrial establishments, and ports in France, the Low Countries, and Germany. Received a DUC for operations during the period, 31 May–30 Jun 1944, when its coverage of bridges, marshalling yards, canals, highways, rivers, and other targets contributed much to the success of the Normandy campaign. Covered missile sites in France during Jul, and in Aug carried out photographic mapping missions for ground forces advancing across France. Provided reconnaissance support for the airborne attack on Holland in Sep and for the Battle of the Bulge, Dec 1944–Jan 1945. Used P-51's to escort its own reconnaissance planes during the last months of the war as the group supported the Allied drive across the Rhine and into Germany. Took part in the final bomb-damage assessment following V–E Day. *Inactivated* in England on 21 Nov 1945. *Disbanded* on 6 Mar 1947.

SQUADRONS. *13th:* 1943–1945. *14th:* 1943–1945. *22d:* 1943–1945. *27th:* 1943–1945. *28th:* 1943. *29th:* 1943. *30th:* 1943.

STATIONS. Peterson Field, Colo, 1 May–7 Jul 1943; Mount Farm, England, 7 Jul 1943; Chalgrove, England, Mar 1945; Hitcham, England, Oct–21 Nov 1945.

COMMANDERS. Col James G Hall, 7 Jul 1943; Col Homer L Saunders, Sep 1943; Col Paul T Cullen, 1 Jan 1944; Lt Col George A Lawson, 17 Feb 1944; Lt Col Norris E Hartwell, 7 May 1944; Lt Col Clarence A Shoop, 9 Aug 1944; Col George

W Humbrecht, Oct 1944; Maj Hubert M Childress, 18 Jun 1945–unkn.

CAMPAIGNS. Air Offensive, Europe; Normandy; Northern France; Rhineland; Ardennes-Alsace; Central Europe.

DECORATIONS. Distinguished Unit Citation: France, 31 May–30 Jun 1944. French Croix de Guerre With Palm: 1944.

INSIGNE. None.

8th FIGHTER GROUP

ATTAQUEZ ET CONQUEREZ

Authorized on the inactive list as 8th Pursuit Group on 24 Mar 1923. *Activated* on 1 Apr 1931. *Redesignated* 8th Pursuit Group (Fighter) in 1939, and 8th Pursuit Group (Interceptor) in 1941. Trained, took part in maneuvers and reviews, and tested planes and equipment, using PB–2, P–6, P–12, P–35, P–36, P–39, and P–40 aircraft prior to World War II. In Dec 1941, became part of the defense force for the New York metropolitan area. Moved to the Asiatic-Pacific Theater early in 1942.

Redesignated 8th Fighter Group in May 1942. Became part of Fifth AF. Equipped first with P–39's, added P–38's and P–40's in 1943, and used P–38's after May 1944.

Established headquarters in Australia in Mar 1942 but sent detachments to New Guinea for operations. Moved to New Guinea in Sep 1942 and served in combat until malaria forced the organization to withdraw to Australia in Feb 1943. Resumed operations in Apr 1943 and served in the theater through the rest of the war. Covered Allied landings, escorted bombers, and attacked enemy airfields in New Guinea; supported operations of the US Marines at Cape Gloucester, Feb–Mar 1944; flew long-range escort and attack missions to Borneo, Ceram, Halmahera, and the southern Philippines; provided cover for convoys, attacked enemy shipping, and won a DUC for strafing a strong Japanese naval force off Mindoro (26 Dec 1944); covered landings at Lingayen; supported ground forces on Luzon; escorted bombers to targets on the Asiatic mainland and on Formosa; and, in the last days of the war, attacked airfields and railways in Japan. Remained in the theater after V-J Day, being based in Japan for duty with Far East Air Forces. Converted to P–51's early in 1946 and to F–80's early in 1950. *Redesignated* 8th Fighter-Bomber Group in Jan 1950.

Began operations in the Korean War on 26 Jun 1950 by providing cover for the evacuation of US personnel from Seoul. Entered combat the following day.

Shifted to F–51 aircraft in Oct 1950 but converted back to F–80's in Dec 1950. Began operating from bases in Korea in Oct 1950, but resumed operations from Japan in Dec 1950 when Communist forces drove far south in Korea. Returned to Korea in Jun 1951. Served in combat until the end of the war, supporting UN ground forces and attacking such targets as airfields, supply lines, and troop concentrations. Maj Charles J Loring Jr was awarded the Medal of Honor for his action on 22 Nov 1952: after his plane had been hit and badly crippled as he was leading a flight of four F–80's against enemy artillery at Sniper Ridge, Maj Loring deliberately dived his plane into the gun emplacements. The group converted to F–86's in the spring of 1953 and returned to Japan the following year.

SQUADRONS. *33d:* 1932–1941. *35th:* 1932–. *36th:* 1931, 1932–. *55th:* 1931–1932. *68th:* 1945–1947. *80th:* 1942–1945, 1947–.

STATIONS. Langley Field, Va, 1 Apr 1931; Mitchel Field, NY, c. 5 Nov 1940–26 Jan 1942; Brisbane, Australia, 6 Mar 1942; Townsville, Australia, 29 Jul 1942; Milne Bay, New Guinea, 18 Sep 1942; Mareeba, Australia, Feb 1943; Port Moresby, New Guinea, 16 May 1943; Finschhafen, New Guinea, 23 Dec 1943; Cape Gloucester, New Britain, c. 20 Feb 1944; Nadzab, New Guinea, 14 Mar 1944; Owi, Schouten Islands, 17 Jun 1944; Morotai, 19 Sep 1944; San Jose, Mindoro, 20 Dec 1944; Ie Shima, 6 Aug 1945; Fukuoka, Japan, 22 Nov 1945; Ashiya,

Japan, 20 May 1946; Itazuke, Japan, Sep 1946; Ashiya, Japan, 13 Apr 1947; Itazuke, Japan, 25 Mar 1949; Tsuiki, Japan, 11 Aug 1950; Suwon, Korea, 7 Oct 1950; Kimpo, Korea, 28 Oct 1950; Pyongyang, Korea, 25 Nov 1950; Seoul, Korea, 3 Dec 1950; Itazuke, Japan, 10 Dec 1950; Kimpo, Korea, 25 Jun 1951; Suwon, Korea, 24 Aug 1951; Itazuke, Japan, 20 Oct 1954–.

COMMANDERS. Unkn, 1931–1932; Maj Byron Q Jones, 25 Jun 1932; Capt Albert M Guidera, 31 Mar 1934; Lt Col Adlai H Gilkeson, 1 Jul 1935; Lt Col William E Kepner, 7 Jul 1938; Lt Col Edward M Morris, 1 Feb 1940; Lt Col Frederic H Smith Jr, 17 Jan 1941; Lt Col William H Wise, 22 May 1942; Lt Col Leonard B Storm, 8 Mar 1943; Lt Col Philip H Greasley, 10 Apr 1943; Lt Col Emmett S Davis, 18 Jan 1944; Lt Col Philip H Greasley, 28 Jun 1944; Col Earl H Dunham, 8 Aug 1944; Lt Col Emmett S Davis, 16 Jun 1945; Lt Col Robert L Harriger, Dec 1945; Lt Col Fergus C Fay, 24 May 1946; Lt Col Luther H Richmond, Jul 1946; Col Stanley R Stewart, Feb 1947; Col Henry G Thorne Jr, 12 Apr 1947; Col Charles T Olmstead, c. 28 May 1948; Lt Col Richard C Banbury, 18 Aug 1948; Lt Col Woodrow W Ramsey, 18 Mar 1949; Lt Col Charles D Chitty Jr, 21 May 1949; Col William T Samways, 1 May 1950; Col Edward O McComas, 19 May 1951; Col Harvey L Case Jr, 31 Jul 1951; Col Levi R Chase, 22 Jan 1952; Col Walter G Benz Jr, 12 Sep 1952; Col John L Locke, 16 Sep 1953; Lt Col Walter A Rosenfield, 13 May 1954; Col Woodrow B Wilmot, 16 Jul 1954–.

CAMPAIGNS. *World War II:* East Indies; Air Offensive, Japan; China Defensive; Papua; New Guinea; Bismarck Archipelago; Western Pacific; Leyte; Luzon; Southern Philippines. *Korean War:* UN Defensive; UN Offensive; CCF Intervention; 1st UN Counteroffensive; CCF Spring Offensive; UN Summer-Fall Offensive; Second Korean Winter; Korea Summer-Fall, 1952; Third Korean Winter; Korea Summer-Fall, 1953.

DECORATIONS. Distinguished Unit Citations: Papua, [Sep] 1942–23 Jan 1943; Philippine Islands, 26 Dec 1944; Korea, 16 Sep–2 Nov 1950. Philippine Presidential Unit Citation. Republic of Korea Presidential Unit Citations: 27 Jun 1950–31 Jan 1951; 1 Feb 1951–31 Mar 1953.

INSIGNE. *Shield:* Azure, a chevron nebule or. *Crest:* On a wreath of the colors (or and azure) three fleur-de-lis or in front of a propeller fesswise azure. *Motto:* ATTAQUEZ ET CONQUEREZ—Attack and Conquer. (Approved 6 Sep 1934.)

8th RECONNAISSANCE GROUP

Constituted as 8th Photographic Reconnaissance Group on 15 Sep 1943. *Activated* on 1 Oct 1943. Trained to provide photographic intelligence for air and ground forces. Moved to India, Feb–Mar 1944. Equipped with F–5, F–6, F–7, and P–40 aircraft. Conducted photographic-reconnaissance, photographic - mapping, and visual-reconnaissance missions. Produced maps, mosaics, terrain models, and target charts of areas in Burma, China,

French Indochina, and Thailand. Also bombed and strafed enemy installations and provided escort for bombardment units. *Redesignated* 8th Reconnaissance Group in Jun 1945. Returned to the US, Oct–Nov 1945. *Inactivated* on 5 Nov 1945. *Disbanded* on 6 Mar 1947.

SQUADRONS. *9th:* 1944–1945. *20th:* 1944–1945. *24th:* 1944–1945. *40th:* 1944–1945.

STATIONS. Peterson Field, Colo, 1 Oct 1943; Gainesville AAFld, Tex, 26 Oct 1943—12 Feb 1944; Bally, India, 31 Mar 1944–7 Oct 1945; Camp Kilmer, NJ, 3–5 Nov 1945.

COMMANDERS. Lt Col Paul A Zartman, 1 Oct 1943; Col Charles P Hollstein, 12 Dec 1943; Col James W Anderson Jr, 24 Jan 1945; Lt Col John R Gee, Oct 1945–c. 5 Nov 1945.

CAMPAIGNS. India-Burma; China Defensive; Central Burma.

DECORATIONS. None.

INSIGNE. None.

9th BOMBARDMENT GROUP

Authorized as 9th Group (Observation) on 19 Jul 1922. *Organized* on 1 Aug 1922. *Redesignated* 9th Bombardment Group in 1935, 9th Bombardment Group (Medium) in 1939, and 9th Bombardment Group (Heavy) in 1940. Trained, took part in maneuvers, and participated in air shows, during the period 1922–1940. Equipped with B–10's and B–18's in the late 1930's and early 1940's. Moved to Panama late in 1940 to serve as part of the defense force

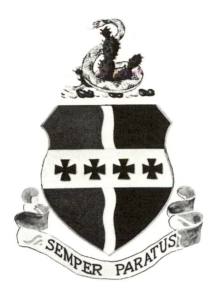

SEMPER PARATUS

for the canal. Used B–17's for antisubmarine operations in the Caribbean. Returned to the US in 1942. Equipped with B–17, B–24, and B–26 aircraft. Trained cadres for bombardment units and tested equipment.

Redesignated 9th Bombardment Group (Very Heavy) in Mar 1944. Prepared for combat with B–29's. Moved to the Pacific theater, Nov 1944–Feb 1945, and assigned to Twentieth AF. Commenced operations late in Jan 1945 with attacks against Japanese-held Maug. After that, struck industrial targets in Japan, conducting the missions in daylight and at high altitude. Received a DUC for bombing the industrial area of Kawasaki in Apr 1945. Beginning in Mar 1945 the group carried out incendiary raids at night on area targets in Japan. During Apr and May it assisted the Allied assault on Okinawa by hitting airfields that the Japanese were using to launch planes against the invasion force. Also conducted mining operations against Japanese shipping, receiving second DUC for such actions in the Inland Sea during May 1945. After the war, dropped food and supplies to Allied prisoners and took part in show-of-force missions over the Japanese home islands. Moved to the Philippines in Apr 1946 and to the Marianas in Jun 1947. *Inactivated* on Guam on 20 Oct 1948.

Redesignated 9th Strategic Reconnaissance Group. *Activated* in the US on 1 May 1949. Assigned to Strategic Air Command. Equipped primarily with B–29's although a few B–36's were assigned during 1949–1950. *Redesignated* 9th Bombardment Group (Heavy) in Apr 1950, and 9th Bombardment Group (Medium) in Oct 1950. *Inactivated* on 16 Jun 1952.

SQUADRONS. *1st:* 1922–1923; 1929–1948; 1949–1952. *5th:* 1922–1923; 1929–1948; 1949–1952. *99th:* 1929–1948; 1949–1952. *430th:* 1943–1944.

STATIONS. Mitchel Field, NY, 1 Aug 1922–6 Nov 1940; Rio Hato, Panama, 12 Nov 1940; Waller Field, Trinidad, 30 Oct 1941; Orlando AB, Fla, 31 Oct 1942; Dalhart AAFld, Tex, 9 Mar 1944; McCook AAFld, Neb, 19 May–18 Nov 1944; North Field, Tinian, 28 Dec 1944; Clark Field, Luzon, 15 Apr 1946; Harmon Field, Guam, 9 Jun 1947–20 Oct 1948. Fairfield-Suisun AFB, Calif, 1 May 1949–16 Jun 1952.

COMMANDERS. Unkn, 1922–1929; Maj William O Ryan, 1929–unkn; Col Follett Bradley, Jun 1933–May 1934; Col Walter

H Frank, Aug 1934–1936; Lt Col Carl W Connell, 1 Sep 1936–unkn; Col Ross F Cole, Apr 1940; Maj Charles F Born, Aug 1941–unkn; Lt Col Stuart P Wright, 1942; Lt Col Gerald E Williams, 1942; Col Harry G Montgomery, 10 Nov 1942; Col James T Connally, 15 Dec 1942; Col Donald W Eisenhart, 1 May 1944; Col Henry C Huglin, 6 Mar–Aug 1945; Col David Wade, Sep 1945–c. 25 Apr 1947; unkn, Apr 1947–20 Oct 1948. Lt Col Walter Y Lucas, 1 May 1949; Col Donald W Eisenhart, 24 Aug 1949; Col William P. Brett, 27 Mar 1950; Lt Col Walter Y Lucas, 24 Jun 1950; Col Clifford J Heflin, 6 Jul 1950–16 Jun 1952.

CAMPAIGNS. Antisubmarine, American Theater; Air Offensive, Japan; Western Pacific.

DECORATIONS. Distinguished Unit Citations: Kawasaki, Japan, 15/16 Apr 1945; Japan, 13–28 May 1945.

INSIGNE. *Shield:* Per pale vert and sable a pallet wavy argent; over all on a fess or four crosses patee of the second (sable). *Crest:* On a wreath of the colors (argent and vert) a rattlesnake entwined about a prickly pear cactus all proper. *Motto:* SEMPER PARATUS—Always Ready. (Approved 20 Mar 1924.)

9th RECONNAISSANCE GROUP

Constituted as 9th Photographic Reconnaissance Group on 15 Sep 1943. *Activated* on 1 Oct 1943. Assigned to Third AF. With·squadrons attached but none assigned, the group trained crews and units for photographic reconnaissance and combat mapping. Aircraft included B–17's, B–24's, F–4's, F–5's, F–7's, and A–20's. *Disbanded* on 6 May 1944.

SQUADRONS. (See narrative.)

STATIONS. Will Rogers Field, Okla, 1 Oct 1943–6 May 1944.

COMMANDERS. Lt Col Paul A Zartman, 11 Nov 1943; Lt Col Hiette S Williams Jr, c. 5 Dec 1943–unkn.

CAMPAIGNS. None.

DECORATION. None.

INSIGNE. None.

10th RECONNAISSANCE GROUP

ARGUS

Constituted as 73d Observation Group on 21 Aug 1941. *Activated* on 1 Sep 1941. Engaged in training activities, participating in the Tennessee Maneuvers in 1943. *Redesignated* 73d Reconnaissance Group in Apr 1943, 73d Tactical Reconnaissance Group in Aug 1943, and 10th Photographic Group (Reconnaissance) in Dec

1943. Moved to the European theater, Jan–Feb 1944, for duty with Ninth AF. Used F–3, F–5, F–6, L–1, L–4, and L–5 aircraft for operations, Feb 1944–May 1945. Photographed airfields, coastal defenses, and ports, and made bomb-damage assessment photographs of airfields, marshalling yards, bridges, and other targets, in preparation for the Normandy invasion; received a DUC for flying at low altitude to photograph the coast from Blankenberghe to Dunkirk and from Le Touquet to St-Vaast-la-Hougue, 6–20 May 1944. Supported the invasion in Jun by making visual and photographic reconnaissance of bridges, artillery, road and railroad junctions, traffic centers, airfields, and other targets. Assisted the Allied drive toward the German border during the summer and early fall of 1944 by flying daylight and night photographic missions; also performed tactical reconnaissance for ground and air units, directing artillery to enemy positions and fighter-bombers to opportune targets. Aided Third Army and other Allied organizations in the battle to breach the Siegfried Line, Sep–Dec 1944. Participated in the Battle of the Bulge, Dec 1944–Jan 1945, by flying reconnaissance missions in the combat zone. From Feb 1945 to V-E Day, assisted the advance of Third Army across the Rhine, to Czechoslovakia, and into Austria. Remained in Germany after the war as part of the army of occupation, being assigned to United States Air Forces in Europe. *Redesignated* 10th Reconnaissance Group in Jun 1945. Transferred, without personnel and equipment, to the US in Jun 1947. Remanned and equipped with RF–51's. *Redesignated* 10th Tactical Reconnaissance Group in Jun 1948. *Inactivated* on 1 Apr 1949.

Activated in Germany on 10 Jul 1952. Assigned to United States Air Forces in Europe. Equipped with RB–26, RB–57, RF–80, and RF–84 aircraft.

SQUADRONS. *1st:* 1945–1949; 1952–. *12th:* 1941–1942, 1944–1946. *14th:* 1943. *15th* (formerly Observation): 1942–1943, 1944–1945, 1947–1949. *15th* (formerly Photographic): 1947. *16th:* 1941–1942. *22d:* 1941–1942. *30th:* 1944. *31st:* 1944–1945. *32d:* 1952–. *33d:* 1944. *34th:* 1944, 1945. *36th* (formerly 28th): 1942–1943. *38th:* 1952–. *39th:* 1945. *42d:* 1952–. *91st:* 1941–1942, 1942–1943. *111th:* 1945. *152d:* 1943. *155th* (formerly 423d, later 45th): 1944–1945, 1945–1947. *160th:* 1945–1947. *162d:* 1945.

STATIONS. Harrisburg, Pa, 1 Sep 1941; Godman Field, Ky, c. 7 Nov 1941; Camp Campbell AAFld, Ky, c. 23 Jun 1943; Key Field, Miss, Nov 1943–Jan 1944; Chalgrove, England, Feb 1944; Rennes/St-Jacques, France, c. 11 Aug 1944; Chateaudun, France, c. 24 Aug 1944; St-Dizier/Robinson, France, Sep 1944; Conflans/Doncourt, France, Nov 1944; Trier/Evren, Germany, Mar 1945; Ober Olm, Germany, c. 5 Apr 1945; Furth, Germany, c. 28 Apr 1945; Furstenfeldbruck, Germany, Apr–Jun 1947; Langley Field, Va, 25 Jun 1947; Lawson Field, Ga, c. 8 Sep 1947; Pope Field, NC, c. 27 Sep 1947–1 Apr 1949. Furstenfeldbruck AB, Germany, 10 Jul

1952; Toul/Rosiere AB, France, Nov 1952; Spangdahlem AB, Germany, May 1953–.

COMMANDERS. Maj Edgar M Scattergood Jr, 1 Sep 1941; Lt Col John C Kennedy, c. 6 Nov 1941; Capt Phillip H Hatch, c. 24 Jan 1942; Lt Col Robert M Lee, c. 9 Feb 1942; Maj Burton L Austin, c. 26 Dec 1942; Lt Col Bernard C Rose, c. 19 Jan 1943; Lt Col Crawford H Hollidge, c. 28 Jan 1943; Maj William A Daniel, c. 4 Aug 1943; Col William B Reed, 9 Sep 1943; Col Russell A Berg, 20 Jun 1944–unkn; Lt Col W D Hayes Jr, 1945; Col Marvin S Zipp, 11 Jan 1946–19 Jun 1947; Lt Col James L Rose, 1 Oct 1947; Lt Col Harrison R Christy Jr, 16 Dec 1947; Lt Col Edward O McComas, 6 Jan 1948; Col William A Daniel, 26 Jan 1948–unkn. Lt Col Barnie B McEntire Jr, 10 Jul 1952; Col Willie O Jackson Jr, Dec 1952; Lt Col Steven R Wilkerson, c. 22 Sep 1953; Col Howard J Withycombe, 23 Feb 1954; Col Arthur E Smith, 13 Jul 1954; Col Fred W Dyer, c. 23 Jun 1955–.

CAMPAIGNS. American Theater; Air Offensive, Europe; Normandy; Northern France; Rhineland; Ardennes-Alsace; Central Europe.

DECORATIONS. Distinguished Unit Citation: France, 6–20 May 1944.

INSIGNE. *Shield:* Azure a sphere or, latitude and longitude lines sable, in chief the head and arms of the Greek mythical god Argus, head facing base, arms fesswise both hands toward dexter of the second, outlined of the field. *Motto:* ARGUS—

Ceaseless Watch. (Approved 29 Dec 1942.)

10th TROOP CARRIER GROUP

ALATUM SERVITIUM

Constituted on the inactive list as 1st Transport Group on 1 Oct. 1933. *Consolidated* with the 10th Observation Group (which had been constituted on the inactive list on 1 Oct 1933), *redesignated* 10th Transport Group, and *activated,* on 20 May 1937. Trained with C–27's and C–33's. As part of the logistic organization, assigned first to Office of Chief of the Air Corps and later (1941) to Air Service Command, the group transported supplies, materiel, and personnel within the US. Assigned to Air Transport Command (later I Troop Carrier Command) in Apr 1942. *Redesignated* 10th Troop Carrier Group in Jul 1942. Converted to C–47's. Trained cadres for troop carrier groups and in 1943 was given the additional duty of training replacement crews. *Disbanded* on 14 Apr 1944.

SQUADRONS. *1st:* 1937–1943. *2d:* 1937–1943. *3d:* 1937–1940. *4th:* 1937–1940. *5th:* 1937–1944. *27th:* 1942–1943, 1943–1944. *38th:* 1942–1944. *307th:* 1943–1944. *308th:* 1943–1944.

STATIONS. Patterson Field, Ohio, 20 May 1937; Wright Field, Ohio, 20 Jun 1938; Patterson Field, Ohio, 17 Jan 1941; General Billy Mitchell Field, Wis, 25 May 1942; Pope Field, NC, 4 Oct 1942; Dunnellon AAFld, Fla, 13 Feb 1943; Lawson Field, Ga, 30 Nov 1943; Grenada AAFld, Miss, 21 Jan 1944; Alliance AAFld, Neb, 8 Mar–14 Apr 1944.

COMMANDERS. Maj Hugh A Bevins, May 1937; Capt Lyman Whitten, Jun 1938; Maj Fred Borum, 1939; Capt Murray E Woodbury, Jan 1941; Capt Theodore Q Graff, 2 Sep 1941; Capt Maurice Beach, 1 Apr 1942; Maj Loren Cornell, 1 Aug 1942; Maj Douglas M Swisher, 30 Aug 1942; Lt Col Boyd R Ertwine, 25 Oct 1942; Lt Col Erickson S Nichols, 28 Jan 1943; Lt Col Henry P King, 12 May 1943–14 Apr 1944.

CAMPAIGNS. American Theater.

DECORATIONS. None.

INSIGNE. *Shield*: Azure, ten bendlets or surmounted by a torteau fimbriated of the second charged with a wheel winged bend sinisterwise of the like. *Motto*: ALATUM SERVITIUM—Winged Service. (Approved 9 Dec 1941.)

11th BOMBARDMENT GROUP

Constituted as 11th Observation Group in 1933. *Redesignated* 11th Bombardment Group (Medium) in 1938. *Activated* in

Hawaii on 1 Feb 1940. *Redesignated* 11th Bombardment Group (Heavy) in Nov 1940. Assigned to Seventh AF in Feb 1942. Trained with B–18's; received B–17's for operations. Flew patrol and search missions off Hawaii after the Japanese attacked Pearl Harbor. Moved to the New Hebrides in Jul 1942. Became part of Thirteenth AF. Struck airfields, supply dumps, ships, docks, troop positions, and other objectives in the South Pacific, Jul-Nov 1942, and received a DUC for those operations. Continued operations, attacking Japanese airfields, installations, and shipping in the Solomons, until late in Mar 1943. Returned to Hawaii, reassigned to Seventh AF, and trained with B–24's. Resumed combat in Nov 1943 and participated in the Allied offensive through the Gilberts, Marshalls, and Marianas, while operating from Funafuti, Tarawa, and Kwajalein. Moved to Guam in Oct 1944 and attacked shipping and airfields in the Volcano and Bonin Islands. Moved to Okinawa in Jul 1945 to take part in the final phases of the air offensive against Japan, bombing railways, airfields, and harbor facilities on Kyushu and striking airfields in China. After the war, flew reconnaissance and surveillance missions to China and ferried liberated prisoners of war from Okinawa to Luzon. Remained in the theater as part of Far East Air Forces but had no personnel assigned after mid-Dec 1945 when the group was transferred to the Philippines. *Redesignated* 11th Bombardment Group (Very Heavy) in Apr 1946. Transferred to Guam in May 1946, remanned, and equipped with B–29's. Terminated training and operations in Oct 1946. *Inactivated* on Guam on 20 Oct 1948.

Redesignated 11th Bombardment Group (Heavy). *Activated* in the US on 1 Dec 1948. Assigned to Strategic Air Command. Equipped with B–36 aircraft. *Inactivated* on 16 Jun 1952.

SQUADRONS. *14th:* 1940–1941. *26th:* 1940–1948; 1948–1952. *42d:* 1940–1948; 1948–1952. *98th:* 1941–1948; 1948–1952. *431st:* 1942–1946.

STATIONS. Hickam Field, TH, 1 Feb 1940; New Hebrides, Jul 1942; Hickam Field, TH, 8 Apr 1943; Funafuti, Nov 1943; Tarawa, 20 Jan 1944; Kwajalein, 5 Apr 1944; Guam, 25 Oct 1944; Okinawa, 2 Jul 1945; Manila, Dec 1945; Guam, May 1946–20 Oct 1948. Carswell AFB, Tex, 1 Dec 1948–16 Jun 1952.

COMMANDERS. Lt Col Walter F Kraus, Feb 1940; Lt Col St Clair Streett, 15 Jun 1940; Lt Col Albert F Hegenberger, 1 Apr 1941; Col LaVerne G Saunders, Mar 1942; Col Frank F Everest, Dec 1942; Col William J. Holzapfel Jr, 26 Apr 1943; Col Russell L. Waldron, 7 Jul 1944; Col John J Morrow, Mar 1945–c. Dec 1945; Col Vincent M Miles Jr, 20 May 1946; Capt Thomas B Ragland Jr, Nov 1946; Capt Thomas B Hoxie, 27 Dec 1947–20 Oct 1948. Maj Russell F Ireland, Dec 1948; Lt Col Harry E Goldsworthy, 11 Jan 1949; Col Richard H Carmichael, May 1949; Col Bertram C Harrison, 4 Mar 1950; Col Thomas P Gerrity, 3 Apr 1950–16 Jun 1952.

CAMPAIGNS. Central Pacific; Air Offensive, Japan; Guadalcanal; Northern Solomons; Eastern Mandates; Western Pacific; Ryukyus; China Offensive.

DECORATIONS. Distinguished Unit Citation: South Pacific, 31 Jul–30 Nov 1942.

INSIGNE. *Shield:* Azure (Air Force blue), on a bend or (Air Force yellow), three grey geese volant proper (in their natural colors). *Crest:* On a wreath or and azure a grey goose proper with wings displayed and inverted. *Motto:* PROGRESSIO SINE TIMORE AUT PRAEJUDICIO—Progress without Fear or Prejudice. (Approved 11 Jun 1941.)

11th PHOTOGRAPHIC GROUP

Constituted as 11th Photographic Group (Mapping) on 19 Nov 1943. *Activated* on 1 Dec 1943. Engaged in photographic mapping in the US and sent detachments to carry out similar operations in Africa, the CBI theater, the Near and Middle East, Mexico, Canada, Alaska, and the

Caribbean. Used B–17, B–24, B–25, B–29, F–2, F–9, F–10, and A–20 aircraft. *Disbanded* on 5 Oct 1944.

SQUADRONS. *1st:* 1943–1944. *3d:* 1943–1944. *19th:* 1943–1944.

STATIONS. Reading AAFld, Pa, 1 Dec 1943; MacDill Field, Fla, Jan–5 Oct 1944.

COMMANDERS. Lt Col Thomas D Brown, 8 Jan–5 Oct 1944.

CAMPAIGNS. None.

DECORATIONS. None.

INSIGNE. None.

12th BOMBARDMENT GROUP

SPIRITUS OMNIA VINCET

Constituted as 12th Bombardment Group (Light) on 20 Nov 1940. *Activated* on 15 Jan 1941. Trained with B–18, B–23, and PT–17 aircraft. Patrolled the west coast after the Japanese attack on Pearl Harbor. *Redesignated* 12th Bombardment Group (Medium) in Dec 1941. Using B–25's, began training early in 1942 for duty overseas. Moved to the Middle East, Jul–Aug 1942, and assigned to Ninth AF. Attacked storage areas, motor transports, troop concentrations, airdromes, bridges, shipping, marshalling yards, and other targets in Egypt, Libya, Tunisia, Pantelleria, Lampedusa, Crete, Sicily, and Italy, Aug 1942–Jan 1944. Supported the Allied drive from Egypt to Tunisia, Oct 1942–Apr 1943. Early in 1943 two squadrons operated with Twelfth AF, assisting Allied forces moving eastward across North Africa, while the other squadrons continued operations with Ninth AF, bombing enemy defenses along the Mareth Line. Received a DUC for action against the enemy in North Africa and Sicily from Oct 1942 to Aug 1943. While attached to Twelfth AF, Jun–Aug 1943, the group operated from bases in Tunisia and Sicily against targets in Pantelleria, Lampedusa, Sicily, and Italy. Assigned to Twelfth AF in Aug 1943 and operated primarily against targets in Italy until Jan 1944. Flew some missions to Albania and Yugoslavia.

Moved to India, Feb–Apr 1944, and assigned to Tenth AF. Engaged chiefly in missions against the enemy in Burma, Apr 1944–May 1945. Bombed communications, military installations, and other objectives. Delivered ammunition to Allied forces at Imphal. Also attacked some targets in China. Began training with A–26 aircraft in the summer of 1945. Returned to the US, Dec 1945–Jan 1946. *Inactivated* on 22 Jan 1946.

Redesignated 12th Bombardment Group (Light). *Activated* on 19 May 1947. Not manned during 1947–1948. *Inactivated* on 10 Sep 1948.

Redesignated 12th Fighter-Escort Group. *Activated* on 1 Nov 1950. Assigned to Strategic Air Command. Trained with F–84's. *Inactivated* on 16 Jun 1952.

SQUADRONS. *81st:* 1941–1946; 1947–1948. *82d:* 1941–1946; 1947–1948. *83d:* 1941–1946; 1947–1948. *434th* (formerly 94th): 1941–1942, 1942–1946. *559th:* 1950–1952. *560th:* 1950–1952. *561st:* 1950–1952.

STATIONS. McChord Field, Wash, 15 Jan 1941; Esler Field, La, c. 21 Feb–3 Jul 1942; Deversoir, Egypt, c. 31 Jul 1942; Egypt and Libya, Oct 1942; Medenine, Tunisia, 3 Apr 1943; Sfax, Tunisia, c. 15 Apr 1943; Hergla, Tunisia, 2 Jun 1943; Ponte Olivo, Sicily, c. 2 Aug 1943; Gerbini, Sicily, c. 22 Aug 1943; Foggia, Italy, c. 2 Nov 1943; Gaudo Airfield, Italy, 19 Jan–6 Feb 1944; Tezgaon, India, c. 21 Mar 1944; Pandaveswar, India, 13 Jun 1944; Fenny, India, 16 Jul 1944; Pandaveswar, India, 8 Jun 1945; Karachi, India, 15 Nov–24 Dec 1945; Ft Lawton, Wash, 21–22 Jan 1946. Langley Field, Va, 19 May 1947–10 Sep 1948. Turner AFB, Ga, 1 Nov 1950; Bergstrom AFB, Tex, Dec 1950–16 Jun 1952.

COMMANDERS. Unkn, Jan–May 1941; Col Charles G Goodrich, 6 May 1941; Col Edward N Backus, 16 Sep 1942; Lt Col William W Wilcox, 21 Sep 1943; Col Lloyd H Dalton Jr, c. 29 Sep 1944; Lt Col Samuel C Galbreath, 4 Sep 1945; Lt Col Lewis B Wilson, 23 Sep 1945–22 Jan 1946. Capt H Carney, Nov 1950; Col Charles

A Gayle, 20 Nov 1950; Col Cy Wilson, Feb 1951; Col Charles A Gayle, Apr–16 Jun 1952.

CAMPAIGNS. Air Combat, EAME Theater; Egypt-Libya; Tunisia; Sicily; Naples-Foggia; Rome-Arno; India-Burma; China Defensive; Central Burma.

DECORATIONS. Distinguished Unit Citation: North Africa and Sicily, Oct 1942–17 Aug 1943.

INSIGNE. *Shield:* Azure, a sword point to base or, hilt flamant proper; a bordure gyronny of twelve of the second and the first. *Motto:* SPIRITUS OMNIA VINCET—The Spirit Conquers All. (Approved 3 Feb 1942.)

13th BOMBARDMENT GROUP

Constituted as 13th Bombardment Group (Medium) on 20 Nov 1940. *Activated* on 15 Jan 1941. After the US entered the war the group searched for enemy U-boats and covered friendly convoys off the east coast of the US. Served with First AF and later with AAF Anti-

ALERT DAY OR NIGHT

submarine Command, using B-18, B-25, and A-29 aircraft for operations. *Inactivated* on 30 Nov 1942.

SQUADRONS. *3d* Antisubmarine (formerly 39th Bombardment): 1941-1942. *4th* Antisubmarine (formerly 40th Bombardment): 1941-1942. *5th* Antisubmarine (formerly 41st Bombardment): 1941-1942. *6th* Antisubmarine (formerly 393d Bombardment): 1942.

STATIONS. Langley Field, Va, 15 Jan 1941; Orlando, Fla, c. 6 Jun 1941; Westover Field, Mass, 20 Jan-30 Nov 1942.

COMMANDERS. Brig Gen Westside T Larson, 21 Jan 1941; Col Walter G Bryte Jr, c. 4 Mar 1942; Col John G Fowler, c. 2 May-c. Nov 1942.

CAMPAIGNS. Antisubmarine, American Theater.

DECORATIONS. None.

INSIGNE. *Shield*: Per bend azure and or, a sword point to base with wings displayed and inverted argent, that portion to base fimbriated of the first. *Motto*: ALERT DAY OR NIGHT. (Approved 2 Jan 1942.)

14th FIGHTER GROUP

Constituted as 14th Pursuit Group (Fighter) on 20 Nov 1940. *Activated* on 15 Jan 1941. Trained with P-40's and P-43's. Converted to P-38's, which were used in flying patrols on the west coast of the US after the Japanese attack on Pearl Harbor. *Redesignated* 14th Fighter Group in May 1942. Moved to England, Jul-Aug 1942. Began operations with

TO FIGHT TO DEATH

Eighth AF in Oct 1942, escorting bombers to targets in France. Arrived in North Africa shortly after the campaign for Algeria and French Morocco (8-11 Nov 1942) had ended, and remained in the Mediterranean theater until the end of the war, being assigned first to Twelfth AF and later (Nov 1943) to Fifteenth. Flew escort, strafing, and reconnaissance missions from the middle of Nov 1942 to late in Jan 1943 and then withdrew from combat, some of the men and planes being reassigned. Resumed operations in May. Flew dive-bombing missions during the Allied assault on Pantelleria. Helped prepare for and support the invasions of Sicily and Italy. Engaged primarily in escort work after Nov 1943, flying many missions to cover bombers engaged in long-range operations against strategic objectives in Italy, France, Germany, Czechoslovakia, Austria, Hungary, Yugoslavia, Rumania, and Bulgaria. Received a DUC for a mission on 2 Apr 1944 when the group, by beating off attacks by enemy fighters, enabled bombers to strike important ball-bearing works in Austria. Also provided escort for reconnaissance operations, supported the invasion of Southern France in Aug 1944, and on numerous occasions flew long-range missions to strafe and dive-bomb motor vehicles, trains, bridges, supply areas, airdromes, and troop concentrations in an area extending from France to the Balkans. *Inactivated* in Italy on 9 Sep 1945.

Activated in the US on 20 Nov 1946. Equipped first with P–47's and later with F–84's. *Inactivated* on 2 Oct 1949.

Redesignated 14th Fighter Group (Air Defense). *Activated* on 18 Aug 1955. Assigned to Air Defense Command and equipped with F–86 aircraft.

SQUADRONS. *37th:* 1943–1945; 1946–1949; 1955–. *48th:* 1941–1945; 1946–1949. *49th:* 1941–1945; 1946–1949. *50th:* 1941–1942.

STATIONS. Hamilton Field, Calif, 15 Jan 1941; March Field, Calif, c. 10 Jun 1941; Hamilton Field, Calif, 7 Feb–16 Jul 1942; Atcham, England, 18 Aug–Nov 1942; Tafaraoui, Algeria, 15 Nov 1942; Maison Blanche, Algeria, 18 Nov 1942; Youks-les-Bains, Algeria, 22 Nov 1942; Berteaux, Algeria, 9 Jan 1943; Mediouna, French Morocco, 5 Mar 1943; Telergma, Algeria, 5 May 1943; El Bathan, Tunisia, 3 Jun 1943; Ste-Marie-du-Zit, Tunisia, 25 Jul ·1943; Triolo Airfield, Italy, 12 Dec 1943; Lesina, Italy, Sep–9 Sep 1945. Dow Field, Maine, 20 Nov 1946–2 Oct 1949. Ethan Allen AFB, Vt, 18 Aug 1955–.

COMMANDERS. 1st Lt Troy Keith, 15 Jan 1941; Col Thayer S Olds, 18 Apr 1941; Lt Col Troy Keith, 28 Jan 1943; Col Oliver B Taylor, 26 Sep 1943; Col Daniel S Campbell, 18 Jul 1944; Col Thomas B Whitehouse, Mar 1945–unkn. Lt Col Lewis W Chick Jr, 24 Dec 1946; Col Loring F Stetson Jr, 7 Jan 1948; Col George A McHenry, Jul 1949; Lt Col Arvie E Olson Jr, Aug 1949–unkn. Col Harry L Downing, 1955–.

CAMPAIGNS. Air Combat, EAME Theater; Air Offensive, Europe; Tunisia; Sicily; Naples-Foggia; Rome-Arno; Normandy; Northern France; Southern France; North Apennines; Rhineland; Central Europe; Po Valley.

DECORATIONS. Distinguished Unit Citation: Austria, 2 Apr 1944.

INSIGNE. *Shield:* Per bend argent and sable. *Motto:* TO FIGHT TO DEATH. (Approved 17 Jun 1942.)

15th FIGHTER GROUP

Constituted as 15th Pursuit Group (Fighter) on 20 Nov 1940. *Activated* in Hawaii on 1 Dec 1940. *Redesignated* 15th

PROSEQUOR ALIS

Pursuit Group (Interceptor) in Feb 1942, and 15th Fighter Group in May 1942. Served as part of the defense force for the Hawaiian Islands, using A-12, OA-9, B-12, P-36, P-39, and P-40 aircraft. The Japanese attack on Hawaii on 7 Dec 1941 caused numerous casualties in the group and destroyed many of its aircraft; nevertheless, during the raid several of the group's pilots succeeded in taking off and in destroying some enemy planes, including four shot down by Lt George Welch and two credited to Lt Kenneth M Taylor. Afterward the group, which was re-manned, reorganized, and assigned to Seventh AF, remained part of the Hawaiian defense system. Sent squadrons (including some that had been attached) to the Central or South Pacific at various times for operations against the Japanese. Began training in Apr 1944 for very-long-range escort missions. Obtained P-51 aircraft late in 1944. Moved to Iwo Jima in Feb 1945. Supported the invasion force on Iwo early in Mar by bombing and strafing trenches, cave entrances, troop concentrations, and storage areas. Began strikes against enemy airfields, shipping, and military installations in the Bonin Islands by the middle of Mar. Flew its first mission to Japan on 7 Apr 1945, receiving a DUC for escorting B-29's that bombed the Nakajima aircraft plant near Tokyo. Struck Japanese airfields on Kyushu late in Apr and early in May 1945 to curtail the enemy's suicide attacks against the invasion force at Okinawa. Also hit enemy troop trains, small fac-

tories, gun positions, and hangars in the Bonins and Japan. Assigned to Twentieth AF during the summer of 1945. Continued its fighter sweeps against Japanese airfields and other targets, and flew long-range escort missions to Japanese cities until the end of the war. Transferred, without personnel and equipment, in Nov 1945 to Hawaii, where the group was re-manned and re-equipped. *Inactivated* on 15 Oct 1946.

Redesignated 15th Fighter Group (Air Defense). *Activated* in the US on 18 Aug 1955. Assigned to Air Defense Command.

SQUADRONS. *6th:* 1943–1944. *12th:* 1942. *18th:* 1943–1944. *45th:* 1940–1946. *46th:* 1940–1944. *47th:* 1940–1946; 1955–. *78th:* 1943–1946.

STATIONS. Wheeler Field, TH, 1 Dec 1940; Bellows Field, TH, 3 Jun 1944–5 Feb 1945; South Field, Iwo Jima, 6 Mar 1945; Bellows Field, TH, 25 Nov 1945; Wheeler Field, TH, 9 Feb–15 Oct 1946. Niagara Falls Mun Aprt, NY, 18 Aug 1955–.

COMMANDERS. Maj Clyde K Rich, 1 Dec 1940; Maj Lorry N Tindal, 6 Dec 1940; Lt Col Paul W Blanchard, 20 Sep 1941; Lt Col William S Steele, 12 Feb 1942; Lt Col Sherwood E Buckland, 5 Mar 1943; Col James O Beckwith Jr, 27 Sep 1943; Lt Col DeWitt S Spain, 16 Apr 1945; Lt Col Julian E Thomas, 17 May 1945; Col John W Mitchell, 21 Jul 1945; Col William Eades, c. Nov 1945; Col Oswald W Lunde, 25 Nov 1945–15 Oct 1946. Col Stanley E Matthews, 1955–.

CAMPAIGNS. Central Pacific; Air Offensive, Japan.

DECORATIONS. Distinguished Unit Citation: Japan, 7 Apr 1945.

INSIGNE. *Shield*: Or, on a bend azure, two (2) terrestrial lightning flashes issuant from base of the first, over all a gunsight counterchanged. *Motto*: PROSEQUOR ALIS—I Pursue with Wings. (Approved 5 Oct 1942.)

16th BOMBARDMENT GROUP

Constituted as 16th Bombardment Group (Very Heavy) on 28 Mar 1944. *Activated* on 1 Apr 1944. Trained for combat with B–29's. Moved to Guam, Mar–Apr 1945, and assigned to Twentieth AF. Entered combat on 16 Jun 1945 with a bombing raid against an airfield on Moen. Flew first mission against the Japanese home islands on 26 Jun 1945 and afterwards operated principally against the enemy's petroleum industry. Flying unescorted in the face of severe enemy attack, the 16th bombed the oil refinery at Shimotsu, the Mitsubishi refinery and oil installations at Kawasaki, and the coal liquefaction plants at Ube, Jul–Aug 1945, and was awarded a DUC for the missions. After the war the group dropped food and supplies to Allied prisoners of war in Japan, Manchuria, and Korea, and participated in several show-of-force missions over Japan. *Inactivated* on Guam on 15 Apr 1946.

SQUADRONS. *15th*: 1944–1946. *16th*: 1944–1946. *17th*: 1944–1946. *21st*: 1944.

STATIONS Dalhart AAFld, Tex, 1 Apr 1944; Fairmont AAFld, Neb, 15 Aug 1944–7 Mar 1945; Northwest Field, Guam, 14 Apr 1945–15 Apr 1946.

COMMANDERS. Unkn, Apr–Jun 1944; Capt William W Hosler Jr, 24 Jun 1944; Maj Richard W Lavin, 1 Jul 1944; Col Samuel C Gurney Jr, 11 Jul 1944; Lt Col Andre F Castellotti, 11 Jul 1945–1946.

CAMPAIGNS. Air Offensive, Japan; Eastern Mandates; Western Pacific.

DECORATIONS. Distinguished Unit Citation: Japan, 29 Jul–6 Aug 1945.

INSIGNE. None.

16th FIGHTER GROUP

Authorized on the inactive list as 16th Pursuit Group on 24 Mar 1923. *Activated* in the Panama Canal Zone on 1 Dec 1932. Served as a part of the defense force for the canal. Used various types of aircraft, including P–12's, P–26's, P–36's, and

P–39's, prior to World War II; equipped with P–40's in 1941. *Redesignated* 16th Pursuit Group (Interceptor) in 1939, and 16th Fighter Group in 1942. *Disbanded* in the Canal Zone on 1 Nov 1943.

SQUADRONS. *24th:* 1932–1943. *29th:* 1933–1943. *43d:* 1940–1943. *44th:* 1938–1939. *74th:* 1934–1938. *78th:* 1932–1937.

STATIONS. Albrook Field, CZ, 1 Dec 1932–1 Nov 1943.

COMMANDERS. Unkn, 1932–1933; Maj Robert L Walsh, c. 2 Sep 1933–c. 14 Aug 1935; Lt Col Willis H Hale, c. 11 Jul 1938–c. 8 Aug 1939; Maj Arthur L Bump, c. 1939–c. Feb 1941; Capt Roger J Browne, 24 Feb 1941; Lt Col Otto P Weyland, 20 May 1941; Lt Col Philip B Klein, 10 Apr 1942; Lt Col Hiette S Williams Jr, Sep 1942; Maj James K Johnson, 1943; Maj Erwin Bishop Jr, 25 Sep 1943–unkn.

CAMPAIGNS. American Theater.

DECORATIONS. None.

INSIGNE. *Shield:* Azure, four lightning flashes bendwise or. *Crest:* On a wreath of the colors (or and azure) a portcullis or. *Motto:* PURGAMUS COELUM— We Clear the Skies. (Approved 4 Dec 1934.)

17th BOMBARDMENT GROUP

Authorized as 17th Observation Group on 18 Oct 1927. *Redesignated* 17th Pursuit Group in 1929. *Activated* on 15 Jul 1931. *Redesignated* 17th Attack Group in 1935, and 17th Bombardment Group (Medium) in 1939. Trained and participated in maneuvers, using P–12 and

TOUJOURS AU DANGER

P–26 (1931–1932), A–17 (1933–1939), and B–18 (1940–1941) aircraft. Used B–25's for patrol duty on the west coast after the Japanese attack on Pearl Harbor, and later patrolled the Gulf of Mexico and the Atlantic coast. Converted to B–26's in the summer of 1942.

Moved to North Africa late in 1942 and began operations on 30 Dec. Served in combat in the Mediterranean theater until the end of the war, being assigned first to Twelfth AF, then to Fifteenth (Nov 1943), and again to Twelfth (Jan 1944). Flew interdictory and close-support missions, bombing bridges, rail lines, marshalling yards, harbors, shipping, gun emplacements, troop concentrations, and other targets. Helped to bring about the defeat of Axis forces in North Africa in May 1943; assisted in the reduction of Pantelleria and Lampedusa in Jun 1943; participated in the invasions of Sicily in Jul and of Italy in Sep 1943; and took part in the drive toward Rome, receiving a DUC for a bombing attack on airdromes at Rome on 13 Jan 1944. Also received the French Croix de Guerre with Palm for operations in Italy, Apr–Jun 1944. Took part in the invasion of Southern France in Aug 1944, and continued bombardment operations in northern Italy, France, and later in Germany. Received second DUC for bombing attacks on enemy defenses near Schweinfurt on 10 Apr 1945. Assisted in the disarmament of Germany after V–E Day. Returned to the US in Nov. *Inactivated* on 26 Nov 1945.

Redesignated 17th Bombardment Group (Light). *Activated* on 19 May 1947. Apparently did not become operative. *Inactivated* on 10 Sep 1948.

Activated in Korea on 10 May 1952. Assigned to Far East Air Forces and equipped with B–26's for service in the Korean War. Engaged in interdiction and provided close support for UN ground forces until the armistice in Jul 1953. Moved to Japan in Oct 1954; returned to the US, Mar–Apr 1955. Assigned to Tactical Air Command and equipped with B–57 aircraft. *Redesignated* 17th Bombardment Group (Tactical) in Oct 1955.

SQUADRONS. *34th:* 1931–1945; 1947–1948; 1952–. *37th:* 1931–1945; 1947–1948; 1952–. *73d:* 1947–1948; 1952–. *95th:* 1931–1945; 1947–1948; 1952–. *432d:* 1942–1945.

STATIONS. March Field, Calif, 15 Jul 1931; McChord Field, Wash, 24 Jun 1940; Pendleton, Ore, 29 Jun 1941; Lexington County Aprt, SC, 9 Feb 1942; Barksdale Field, La, 23 Jun–Nov 1942; Telergma, Algeria, Dec 1942; Sedrata, Algeria, c. 10 May 1943; Djedeida, Tunisia, 23 Jun 1943; Sardinia, Nov 1943; Corsica, c. 14 Sep 1944; Dijon, France, c. 20 Nov 1944; Horsching, Austria, Jun 1945; Clastres, France, c. 3 Oct–Nov 1945; Camp Myles Standish, Mass, Nov–26 Nov 1945. Langley Field, Va, 19 May 1947–10 Sep 1948. Pusan, Korea, 10 May 1952; Miho, Japan, 10 Oct 1954–16 Mar 1955; Eglin AF Aux Field No 9, Apr 1955–.

COMMANDERS. Capt Frank O'D Hunter, 1931–unkn; Lt Col Walter R Peck, Mar 1941; Lt Col William C Mills, Feb 1942; Lt Col Flint Garrison, 16 Jun 1942; Lt Col Curtis D Sluman, 26 Jun 1942; Lt Col Karl E Baumeister, 11 Mar 1943; Lt Col Charles R Greening, 25 May 1943; Lt Col Robert A Zaiser, 18 Jul 1943; Col Donald L Gilbert, 14 Oct 1943; Col R O Harrell, 21 Jul 1944; Col Wallace C Barrett, 20 Mar 1945; Lt Col Stanford W Gregory, 1 Jun 1945–unkn. Unkn, 1947–1948. Col James D Kemp, 10 May 1952; Col William C Lindley Jr, 11 Jul 1952; Col Robert E Keating, 14 Feb 1953; Col Gordon D Timmons, 8 Apr 1953; Col George D Hughes, 1954; Col Norton W Sanders, 1954–.

CAMPAIGNS. *World War II:* Antisubmarine, American Theater; Air Combat, EAME Theater; Tunisia; Sicily; Naples-Foggia; Anzio; Rome-Arno; Southern France; North Apennines; Rhineland; Central Europe. *Korean War:* Korea Summer-Fall, 1952; Third Korean Winter; Korea Summer-Fall, 1953.

DECORATIONS. Distinguished Unit Citations: Italy, 13 Jan 1944; Schweinfurt, Germany, 10 Apr 1945; Korea, 1 Dec 1952–30 Apr 1953. French Croix de Guerre with Palm: Apr, May, and Jun 1944. Republic of Korea Presidential Unit Citation: 24 May 1952–31 Mar 1953.

INSIGNE. *Shield:* Or, seven crosses pattee in pale sable. *Crest:* On a wreath of the colors (or and sable) a griffin rampant of the first, beaked, fore-legged and winged of the second, and langued gules. *Motto:* TOUJOURS AU DANGER—Ever Into Danger. (Approved 19 Jan 1934.)

18th FIGHTER GROUP

Organized as 18th Pursuit Group in Hawaii in Jan 1927. *Redesignated* 18th Pursuit Group (Interceptor) in 1939, and 18th Fighter Group in 1942. Before World War II the group engaged in routine flying and gunnery training and participated

in joint Army-Navy maneuvers, using DH-4, PW-9, P-12, P-26, P-36, and other aircraft. When the Japanese attacked Pearl Harbor on 7 Dec 1941, the group, which had recently converted to P-40's, sustained severe losses. The two planes that its pilots were able to get into the air during the attack were quickly shot down. The group, assigned to Seventh AF in Feb 1942, had to be re-equipped before it could resume training and begin patrol missions.

Moved to the South Pacific in Mar 1943. Assigned to Thirteenth AF. Began operations from Guadalcanal. Flew protective patrols over US bases in the Solomons; later, escorted bombers to the Bismarcks, supported ground forces on Bougainville, and attacked enemy airfields and installations in the northern Solomons and New Britain. Used P-38, P-39, P-61, and P-70 aircraft. Moved to New Guinea in Aug 1944. Equipped with P-38's. Escorted bombers to targets in the southern Philippines and Borneo, and attacked enemy airfields and installations in the Netherlands Indies. Received a DUC for actions at Ormoc Bay: on 10 Nov 1944 the group withstood intense flak and vigorous opposition from enemy interceptors to attack a Japanese convoy that was attempting to bring in additional troops for use against American forces that had landed on Leyte; on the following day a few of the group's planes returned to the same area, engaged a large force of enemy fighters, and destroyed a number of them. Moved to the Philippines in Jan 1945. Supported ground forces on Luzon and Borneo, attacked shipping in the central Philippines, covered landings on Palawan, attacked airfields and railways on Formosa, and escorted bombers to such widely-scattered targets as Borneo, French Indochina, and Formosa.

Remained in the Philippines as part of Far East Air Forces after the war. Flew patrols and trained with F-80's. Lost all personnel in Mar 1947 but was remanned in Sep 1947. Equipped first with F-47's, later with F-51's, and still later (1949) with F-80's. *Redesignated* 18th Fighter-Bomber Group in Jan 1950.

Moved to Korea in Jul 1950 and entered combat, using F-51's. Supported UN ground forces and attacked enemy installations and supply lines. Maj Louis J Sebille was posthumously awarded the Medal of Honor for his action on 5 Aug 1950: although his plane was badly damaged by flak while attacking a concentration of enemy trucks, Maj Sebille continued his strafing passes until he crashed into an armored vehicle. The group converted to F-86's early in 1953 and remained in Korea for some time after the war. Moved to Okinawa in Nov 1954.

SQUADRONS. *6th:* 1927-1943. *12th:* 1943-. *19th:* 1927-1943. *36th:* 1931-1932. *44th:* 1941-1942, 1943-. *55th:* 1931. *67th:* 1945-. *68th:* 1945-. *70th:* 1943-1945. *73d:* 1929-1931, 1941-1942. *74th:* 1929-1932. *78th:* 1940-1943. *333d:* 1942-1943. *419th:* 1943-1944.

STATIONS. Wheeler Field, TH, Jan 1927; Espiritu Santo, 11 Mar 1943; Guadalcanal, 17 Apr 1943; Sansapor, New Guinea, 23 Aug 1944; Lingayen, Luzon, c. 13 Jan 1945; San Jose, Mindoro, c. 1 Mar 1945; Zamboanga, Mindanao, 4 May 1945; Palawan, 10 Nov 1945; Floridablanca, Luzon, Mar 1946; Clark Field, Luzon, 16 Sep 1947; Taegu, Korea, 28 Jul 1950; Ashiya, Japan, 8 Aug 1950; Tongnae, Korea, 8 Sep 1950; Pyongyang, Korea, c. 21 Nov 1950; Suwon, Korea, 1 Dec 1950; Chinhae, Korea, 9 Dec 1950; Hoengsong, Korea, 26 Dec 1952; Osan-Ni, Korea, 11 Jan 1953; Kadena AB, Okinawa, 1 Nov 1954-.

COMMANDERS. Unkn, 1927-1940; Maj Kenneth M Walker, 22 Mar 1940; Maj William R Morgan, 1941; Lt Col Aaron W Tyer, Dec 1941; Lt Col W H Councill, 10 Dec 1943; Col Milton B Adams, 8 Jul 1944; Col Harry L Donicht, 24 May 1945; Lt Col Bill Harris, 1 Aug 1945; Lt Col Wilbur J Grumbles, 18 Oct 1945-unkn; Col Victor R Haugen, 1946; Col Homer A Boushey, 7 Aug 1946-Mar 1947; Maj Kenneth M Taylor, 16 Sep 1947; Lt Col Joseph J Kruzel, 1 Oct 1947; Col Marion Malcolm, 3 Sep 1948; Lt Col Henry H Norman Jr, 24 Jul 1949; Col Ira L Wintermute, 16 Jun 1950; Lt Col Homer M Cox, 20 Feb 1951; Col William P McBride, May 1951; Col Ralph H Saltsman Jr, 5 Jun 1951; Col Seymour M Levenson, 30 Nov 1951; Col Sheldon S Brinson, 17 May 1952; Lt Col Albert J Freund Jr, 25 Nov 1952; Col Maurice L Martin, 24 Jan 1953; Lt Col Edward L Rathbun, 17 Dec 1953; Col John H Buckner, 1 Feb 1954; Lt Col Edward L Rathbun, 24 May 1954; Lt Col Clifford P Patton, 17 Aug 1954; Col Nathan J Adams, 7 Sep 1954; Col John B Murphy, 1 Nov

1954; Lt Col Clifford P Patton, 10 Nov 1954; Col Paul E Hoeper, 1 Jan 1955; Lt Col Joseph E Andres, 22 Jul 1955; Col Leo C Moon, 21 Nov 1955–.

CAMPAIGNS. *World War II:* Central Pacific; China Defensive; New Guinea; Northern Solomons; Bismarck Archipelago; Western Pacific; Leyte; Luzon; Southern Philippines. *Korean War:* UN Defensive; UN Offensive; CCF Intervention; 1st UN Counteroffensive; CCF Spring Offensive; UN Summer-Fall Offensive; Second Korean Winter; Korea Summer-Fall, 1952; Third Korean Winter; Korea Summer-Fall, 1953.

DECORATIONS. Distinguished Unit Citations: Philippine Islands, 10–11 Nov 1944; Korea, 3 Nov 1950–24 Jan 1951; Korea, 22 Apr–8 Jul 1951. Philippine Presidential Unit Citation. Republic of Korea Presidential Unit Citations: 24 Jul 1950–31 Jan 1951; 1 Feb 1951–31 Mar 1953.

INSIGNE. *Shield:* Or, a fighting cock with wings displayed sable wattled and combed gules. *Crest:* On a wreath or and sable two wings conjoined and displayed tenne (orange). *Motto:* UNGUIBUS ET ROSTRO—With Talons and Beak. (Approved 21 Feb 1931.)

19th BOMBARDMENT GROUP

Authorized as 19th Observation Group on 18 Oct 1927. *Redesignated* 19th Bombardment Group in 1929. *Activated* on 24 Jun 1932. *Redesignated* 19th Bombardment Group (Heavy) in 1939. Equipped first with B–10's, later with

In Alis Vincimus

B–18's, and still later (in 1941) with B–17's. Moved to the Philippine Islands, Sep–Nov 1941.

On 7 Dec 1941 (8 Dec in the Philippines), when the Japanese first attacked Clark Field, the group suffered numerous casualties and lost many planes. The 93d squadron, however, was on maneuvers at Del Monte and therefore missed the attack. Supplies and headquarters were hastily moved from Clark Field to comparatively safe points nearby, and planes that had not been too heavily damaged were given emergency repairs and dispatched to Del Monte. There the 19th began reconnaissance and bombardment operations against Japanese shipping and landing parties. Sustaining heavy losses, the group ceased these actions after about two weeks, and the ground personnel joined infantry units in fighting the invaders. Some of the men were evacuated, some escaped, but most were either killed or captured.

Meanwhile, late in Dec 1941 the air echelon moved to Australia to transport medical and other supplies to the Philippine Islands and evacuate personnel from that area. The men in Australia moved to Java at the end of 1941 and, flying B–17, LB–30, and B–24 aircraft, earned a DUC for the group by attacking enemy aircraft, ground installations, warships, and transports during the Japanese drive through the Philippines and Netherlands Indies early in 1942. The men returned to Australia from Java early in Mar 1942, and later that month the group evacuated Gen Douglas MacArthur, his family, and key members of his staff from the Philippines to Australia. After a brief rest the group resumed combat operations, participating in the Battle of the Coral Sea and raiding Japanese transportation, communications, and ground forces during the enemy's invasion of Papua. From 7 to 12 Aug 1942 the 19th bombed airdromes, ground installations, and shipping near Rabaul, New Britain, being awarded another DUC for these missions. Capt Harl Pease Jr was posthumously awarded the Medal of Honor for his actions during 6–7 Aug 1942: when one engine of his bomber failed during a mission over New Britain, Capt Pease returned to Australia to obtain another plane; unable to find one fit for combat, he selected the most serviceable plane at the base and rejoined his squadron for an attack on a Japanese airdrome near Rabaul; by skillful flying

he maintained his position in the formation and withstood enemy attacks until his bombs had been released on the objective; in the air battle that continued after the bombers left the target, Capt Pease's aircraft fell behind the formation and was lost. The group returned to the US late in 1942 and served as a replacement training unit. *Inactivated* on 1 Apr 1944.

Redesignated 19th Bombardment Group (Very Heavy). *Activated* on 1 Apr 1944. Trained for combat with B–29's. Moved to Guam, Dec 1944–Feb 1945, for duty with Twentieth AF. Entered combat on 12 Feb 1945 with an attack against a Japanese airfield on Rota. Flew its first mission against the Japanese home islands by striking Tokyo on 25 Feb 1945. Conducted daylight raids against strategic objectives, bombing aircraft factories, chemical plants, oil refineries, and other targets in Japan. Participated in incendiary operations, receiving one DUC for its low-altitude attacks on the urban industrial areas of Tokyo, Nagoya, Kobe, and Osaka, in Mar 1945, and another DUC for striking the industrial section of Kobe on 5 Jun. Struck airfields from which the enemy was launching kamikaze planes against the invasion force at Okinawa, Apr–May 1945. Dropped supplies to Allied prisoners and took part in show-of-force missions over Japan after the war. Remained overseas as part of Far East Air Forces. Trained, participated in sea-search operations, and flew photographic-mapping missions. *Redesignated* 19th

Bombardment Group (Medium) in Aug 1948.

On 28 Jun 1950 the group flew its first mission against the North Korean forces that had invaded the Republic of Korea. It moved to Okinawa early in Jul 1950 and continued operations against the enemy until 1953. Targets included troops, supply dumps, airfields, steel mills, hydroelectric plants, and light metal industries. *Inactivated* on Okinawa on 1 Jun 1953.

SQUADRONS. *14th:* 1941–1942. *23d:* 1935–1938. *28th:* 1941–1944; 1944–1953. *30th:* 1932–1944; 1944–1953. *32d:* 1932–1941. *76th:* 1932–1936. *93d:* 1939–1944; 1944–1953. *435th:* (formerly 40th): 1941–1944.

STATIONS. Rockwell Field, Calif, 24 Jun 1932; March Field, Calif, 25 Oct 1935; Albuquerque, NM, 7 Jul–29 Sep 1941; Clark Field, Luzon, 23 Oct 1941; Batchelor, Australia, 24 Dec 1941; Singosari, Java, 30 Dec 1941; Melbourne, Australia, 2 Mar 1942; Garbutt Field, Australia, 18 Apr 1942; Longreach, Australia, 18 May 1942; Mareeba, Australia, 24 Jul–23 Oct 1942; Pocatello, Idaho, 9 Dec 1942; Pyote AAB, Tex, 1 Jan 1943–1 Apr 1944. Great Bend AAFld, Kan, 1 Apr–7 Dec 1944; North Field, Guam, 16 Jan 1945; Kadena, Okinawa, 5 Jul 1950–1 Jun 1953.

COMMANDERS. Lt Col Harold M McClelland, c. 24 Jun 1932–1934; Col Harvey S Burwell, 1939; Col Eugene L Eubank, 2 Apr 1940; Maj David R Gibbs, 10 Dec 1941; Maj Emmett O'Donnell Jr, 12 Dec 1941; Lt Col Cecil E Combs, Jan 1942; Lt Col Kenneth B Hobson, 14 Mar 1942; Lt Col James T Connally, 15 Apr 1942; Lt Col Richard N Carmichael, 10 Jul 1942; Lt Col Felix M Hardison, 1 Jan 1943; Lt Col Elbert Helton, 13 Feb 1943; Col Louie P Turner, 5 May 1943; Lt Col Frank P Sturdivant, 27 Jan 1944; Col Bernard T Castor, 11 Feb–1 Apr 1944. Maj Joseph H Selliken, 28 Apr 1944; Col John G Fowler, 20 May 1944; Lt Col John C Wilson, 29 May 1944; Lt Col Philip L Mathewson, 30 Jun 1944; Col John A Roberts Jr, 16 Jul 1944; Lt Col George T Chadwell, Sep 1945; Col Vincent M Miles Jr, 1 Mar 1946; Col Elbert D Reynolds, 13 Apr 1946; Col David Wade, 26 Apr 1947; Col Francis C Shoemaker, 8 Nov 1947; Col Robert V DeShazo, 2 Dec 1947; Lt Col Clarence G Poff, 1949; Col Theodore Q Graff, 17 Sep 1949; Col Payne Jennings, 26 Sep 1950; Col Donald O Tower, 29 Mar 1951; Col Adam K Breckenridge, 26 Jul 1951; Col Julian M Bleyer, 6 Feb 1952; Col Willard W Smith, 8 Jul 1952; Col Harvey C Dorney, 24 Dec 1952–1 Jun 1953.

CAMPAIGNS. *World War II:* American Theater; Philippine Islands; East Indies; Air Offensive, Japan; Papua; Guadalcanal; Western Pacific. *Korean War:* UN Defensive; UN Offensive; CCF Intervention; 1st UN Counteroffensive; CCF Spring Offensive; UN Summer–Fall Offensive; Second Korean Winter; Korea Summer–Fall, 1952; Third Korean Winter; Korea Summer–Fall, 1953.

DECORATIONS. Distinguished Unit Citations: Philippine Islands, 7 Dec 1941–10 May 1942; Philippine Islands, 8–22 Dec 1941; Philippine Islands and Netherlands

Indies, 1 Jan–1 Mar 1942; Philippine Islands, 6 Jan–8 Mar 1942; Papua, 23 Jul–[Oct 1942]; New Britain, 7–12 Aug 1942; Japan, 9–19 Mar 1945; Kobe, Japan, 5 Jun 1945; Korea, 28 Jun–15 Sep 1950. Philippine Presidential Unit Citation. Republic of Korea Presidential Unit Citation: 7 Jul 1950–[1953].

INSIGNE. *Shield:* Azure, within the square of the constellation of Pegasus, a winged sword, point to base, all or. *Crest:* On a wreath of the colors (or and azure) an osprey guardant, rising, wings elevated and addorsed proper. *Motto:* IN ALIS VINCIMUS—On Wings We Conquer. (Approved 19 Oct 1936.)

20th FIGHTER GROUP

Authorized on the inactive list as 20th Balloon Group on 18 Oct 1927. *Redesignated* 20th Pursuit Group in 1929. *Activated* on 15 Nov 1930. *Redesignated* 20th

Pursuit Group (Fighter) in 1939, 20th Pursuit Group (Interceptor) in 1941, and 20th Fighter Group in 1942. Equipped successively with P–12, P–26, and P–36 aircraft prior to World War II; used P–39's and P–40's during the early part of the war; converted to P–38's in Jan 1943. Trained, participated in maneuvers and tactical exercises, and took part in aerial reviews and demonstrations during the period 1930–1939. Provided personnel for and helped to train new units during 1940–1941. Served as an air defense organization after the Japanese attack on Pearl Harbor. Began intensive training late in 1942 for combat duty overseas.

Moved to England in Aug 1943 and became part of Eighth AF. Entered combat with P–38's late in Dec 1943 and for several months was engaged primarily in escorting heavy and medium bombers to targets on the Continent. Frequently strafed targets of opportunity while on escort missions. Retained escort as its primary function until the end of the war, but in Mar 1944 began to fly fighter-bomber missions, which became almost as frequent as escort operations. Strafed and dive-bombed airfields, trains, vehicles, barges, tugs, bridges, flak positions, gun emplacements, barracks, radio stations, and other targets in France, Belgium, and Germany. Became known as the "Loco Group" because of its numerous and successful attacks on locomotives. Received a DUC for performance on 8 Apr 1944 when the group struck airfields in central Germany and then, after breaking up an attack by enemy interceptors, proceeded to hit railroad equipment, oil facilities, power plants, factories, and other targets. Flew patrols over the Channel during the invasion of Normandy in Jun 1944. Supported the invasion force later that month by escorting bombers that struck interdictory targets in France, Belgium, and Holland, and by attacking troops, transportation targets, and airfields. Converted to P–51's in Jul 1944 and continued to fly escort and fighter-bomber missions as the enemy retreated across France to the Siegfried Line. Participated in the airborne attack on Holland in Sep 1944. Escorted bombers to Germany and struck rail lines, trains, vehicles, barges, power stations, and other targets in and beyond the Siegfried Line during the period Oct–Dec 1944. Took part in the Battle of the Bulge, Dec 1944–Jan 1945, by escorting bombers to the battle area. Flew patrols to support the airborne attack across the Rhine, Mar 1945. Carried out escort and fighter-bomber missions as enemy resistance collapsed in Apr 1945. Returned to the US in Oct. *Inactivated* on 18 Oct 1945.

Activated on 29 Jul 1946. Equipped first with P–51's and later with F–84's. *Redesignated* 20th Fighter-Bomber Group in Jan 1950. Moved to England in 1952 and became part of the United States Air Forces in Europe. *Inactivated* in England on 8 Feb 1955.

SQUADRONS. *24th:* 1930–1932. *55th:* 1930–1931, 1932–1945; 1946–1955. *74th:* 1932. *77th:* 1930–1932, 1932–1945; 1946–1955. *78th:* 1931–1932. *79th:* 1933–1945; 1946–1955. *87th:* 1935–1936.

STATIONS. Mather Field, Calif, 15 Nov 1930; Barksdale Field, La, Oct 1932; Moffett Field, Calif, Nov 1939; Hamilton Field, Calif, Sep 1940; Wilmington, NC, c. 2 Feb. 1942; Morris Field, NC, Apr 1942; Paine Field, Wash, Sep 1942; March Field, Calif, Jan–c. 11 Aug 1943; Kings Cliffe, England, c. 26 Aug 1943–c. 11 Oct 1945; Camp Kilmer, NJ, c. 16–18 Oct 1945. Biggs Field, Tex, 29 Jul 1946; Shaw Field, SC, Oct 1946; Langley AFB, Va, Nov 1951–May 1952; Wethersfield, England, c. 1 Jun 1952–8 Feb 1955.

COMMANDERS. Maj Clarence L Tinker, c. 15 Nov 1930; Capt Thomas Boland, c. 14 Oct 1932; Lt Col Millard F Harmon, c. 31 Oct 1932–unkn; Maj Armin F Herold, c. 7 Oct 1936–unkn; Lt Col Ross G Hoyt, 1937; Col Ira C Eaker, c. 16 Jan 1941; Maj Jesse Auton, c. 1 Sep 1941; Maj Homer A Boushey, Jan 1942; Lt Col Edward W Anderson, c. 9 Mar 1942; Lt Col Jesse Auton, Aug 1942–unkn; Col Barton M Russell, 1943; Lt Col Mark E Hubbard, 2 Mar 1944; Maj Herbert E Johnson Jr, 19 Mar 1944; Lt Col Harold J Rau, 20 Mar 1944; Lt Col Cy Wilson, Jun 1944; Col Harold J Rau, 27 Aug 1944; Col Robert P Montgomery, 18 Dec 1944; Maj Jack C Price, 3 Oct 1945–unkn. Col Joseph L Laughlin, 29 Jul 1946; Col Archie J Knight, c. 24 Feb 1947; Col William J Cummings, 31 Jul 1947; Col George R Bickell, Aug 1948–unkn; Col John A Dunning, 1949; Lt Col Jack R Brown, c.

22 Oct 1951; Col William D Ritchie, 29 Apr 1952–unkn.

CAMPAIGNS. American Theater; Air Offensive, Europe; Normandy; Northern France; Rhineland; Ardennes-Alsace; Central Europe.

DECORATIONS. Distinguished Unit Citation: Central Germany, 8 Apr 1944.

INSIGNE. *Shield:* Per fess azure and gules, a fess nebule or. *Crest:* On a wreath of the colors (or and azure) a sun in splendor proper radiating from the center thereof thirteen darts gules. *Motto:* VICTORY BY VALOR. (Approved 18 Dec 1934.)

21st BOMBARDMENT GROUP

Constituted as 21st Bombardment Group (Medium) on 13 Jan 1942. *Activated* on 1 Feb 1942. Began training with B–25's; later converted to B–26's. Served as an operational training unit in Third AF; also flew some antisubmarine patrols over the Gulf of Mexico. *Disbanded* on 10 Oct 1943.

SQUADRONS. *313th:* 1942–1943. *314th:* 1942–1943. *315th:* 1942–1943. *398th:* 1942–1943.

STATIONS. Bowman Field, Ky, 1 Feb 1942; Jackson AAB, Miss, 8 Feb 1942; Columbia AAB, SC, 21 Apr 1942; Key Field, Miss, 24 May 1942; MacDill Field, Fla, 27 Jun 1942–10 Oct 1943.

COMMANDERS. Col Robert D Knapp, 9 Feb 1942; Col William L Lee, 26 Apr 1942; Lt Col John F Batjer, 13 Aug 1942; Col Carl R Storrie, 5 Oct 1942; Col Guy L McNeil, 7 Nov 1942; Col Don Z Zimmerman, 19 Apr 1943; Lt Col L F Brownfield, 6 June 1943; Col Richard T Coiner Jr, 6 Jul–10 Oct 1943.

CAMPAIGNS. Antisubmarine, American Theater.

DECORATIONS. None.

INSIGNE. *Shield:* Per fess nebule azure and or, three drop bombs, two and one, counterchanged. *Motto:* ALIS ET ANIMO—With Wings and Courage. (Approved 26 Nov 1942.)

21st FIGHTER GROUP

Constituted as 21st Fighter Group on 31 Mar 1944. *Activated* in Hawaii on 21 Apr 1944. Assigned to Seventh AF and served as part of the defense force for the Hawaiian Islands. Equipped first with P–39, later with P–38, and still later (Jan 1945) with P–51 aircraft. Moved to Iwo Jima, Feb–Mar 1945. Sustained some casualties when Japanese troops attacked the group's camp on the night of 26/27 Mar 1945, but flew first combat mission the following day, bombing and strafing airfields on Haha Jima. Flew its first mission

to Japan on 7 Apr, being awarded a DUC for escorting B–29's that struck the heavily-defended Nakajima aircraft factory near Tokyo. Operations from Iwo Jima included attacking airfields that the enemy was using to launch suicide planes against the Allied forces on Okinawa; striking enemy barracks, airfields, and shipping in the Bonins and Japan; and escorting B–29's that bombed Japanese cities. Assigned to Twentieth AF during the summer of 1945. Trained, participated in aerial reviews, and served as a part of the defense force for Iwo Jima, Saipan, and Guam after the war. Re-equipped with P–47's during the summer of 1946. *Inactivated* on Guam on 10 Oct 1946.

Redesignated 21st Fighter-Bomber Group. *Activated* in the US on 1 Jan 1953. Assigned to Tactical Air Command. Equipped for a few months with F–51's, later with F–86's. Moved to France, Nov–Dec 1954, and assigned to United States Air Forces in Europe.

SQUADRONS. *46th:* 1944–1946. *72d:* 1944–1946; 1953–. *416th:* 1953–. *531st:* 1944–1946; 1953–.

STATIONS. Wheeler Field, TH, 21 Apr 1944; Mokuleia Field, TH, 13 Oct 1944–9 Feb 1945; Central Field, Iwo Jima, 26 Mar 1945; South Field, Iwo Jima, 16 Jul 1945; Isley Field, Saipan, Dec 1945; Northwest Field, Guam, 17 Apr–10 Oct 1946. George AFB, Calif, 1 Jan 1953–26 Nov 1954; Chambley AB, France, 13 Dec 1954–.

COMMANDERS. Col Kenneth R Powell, 21 Apr 1944; Col Charles E Taylor, 14 Jun 1945; Lt Col Charles E Parsons, 15 Oct 1945; Col William Eades, 25 Nov 1945; Col Lester S Harris, Feb–10 Oct 1946. Col Paul P Douglas Jr, 1 Jan 1953; Col Verl D Luehring, 26 Apr 1954; Col R C Franklin Jr, 27 Apr 1955; Lt Col Ira M Sussky, 6 May 1955; Col R C Franklin Jr, 1 Aug 1955–.

CAMPAIGNS. Air Offensive, Japan.

DECORATIONS. Distinguished Unit Citation: Japan, 7 Apr 1945.

INSIGNE. *Shield:* Azure, a broad sword argent, shaded silver, hilt and pommel or, shaded yellow, outlined of the field, between four red lightning streaks proper, two and two, bendwise. *Motto:* FORTITUDO ET PREPARATIO—Strength and Preparedness. (Approved 23 Jul 1957.)

22d BOMBARDMENT GROUP

Constituted as 22d Bombardment Group (Medium) on 22 Dec 1939. *Activated* on 1 Feb 1940. Trained with B–18

and B–26 aircraft, and used the latter to fly antisubmarine patrols off the west coast, Dec 1941–Jan 1942. Moved to the Southwest Pacific early in 1942, became part of Fifth AF, and served in combat in that area until V–J Day. Attacked enemy shipping, installations, and airfields in New Guinea and New Britain and supported ground forces in New Guinea, using B–26's until Oct 1943 when B–25's were added. Continued to support the Allied offensive in New Guinea, striking troop concentrations, installations, and shipping, being awarded a DUC for knocking out enemy entrenchments (5 Nov 1943) that were preventing the advance of Australian ground forces. *Redesignated* 22d Bombardment Group (Heavy) in Feb 1944. Equipped with B–24's, bombed Japanese airfields, shipping, and oil installations in Borneo, Ceram, and Halmahera. Began attacking the southern Philippines in Sep 1944 to neutralize Japanese bases in pre-

paration for the invasion of Leyte. From Dec 1944 to Aug 1945, struck airfields and installations on Luzon, supported Australian ground forces on Borneo, and bombed railways and industries in Formosa and China. Moved to Okinawa in Aug 1945 and flew some armed reconnaissance missions over southern Japan.

Remained in the theater after the war as part of Far East Air Forces. Transferred, without personnel and equipment, to the Philippines in Nov 1945. *Redesignated* 22d Bombardment Group (Very Heavy) in Apr 1946. Transferred to Okinawa in May 1946, remanned in Jun, and equipped with B–29's. Moved to the US in May 1948. Assigned to Strategic Air Command. *Redesignated* 22d Bombardment Group (Medium) in Jul 1948. Moved temporarily to Okinawa in Jul 1950 and attached to Far East Air Forces for duty in the Korean War. Began combat immediately, and until Oct 1950 attacked marshalling yards, bridges, highways, airfields, and industries and supported UN ground forces in Korea. Returned to the US, Oct–Nov 1950. *Inactivated* on 16 Jun 1952.

SQUADRONS. *2d:* 1940–1952. *19th:* 1940–1952. *33d:* 1940–1952. *408th:* 1942–1952.

STATIONS. Mitchel Field, NY, 1 Feb 1940; Langley Field, Va, 14 Nov 1940; Muroc, Calif, c. 9 Dec 1941–31 Jan 1942; Brisbane, Australia, 25 Feb 1942; Ipswich, Australia, 7 Mar 1942; Townsville, Australia, 7 Apr 1942; Woodstock, Australia, 5 Jul 1942; Iron Range, Australia, 29 Sep

1942; Woodstock, Australia, 4 Feb 1943; Dobodura, New Guinea, Oct 1943; Nadzab, New Guinea, Jan 1944; Owi, Schouten Islands, 17 Aug 1944; Leyte, 15 Nov 1944; Angaur, 26 Nov 1944; Samar, 21 Jan 1945; Clark Field, Luzon, Mar 1945; Okinawa, 15 Aug 1945; Luzon, Nov 1945; Okinawa, 15 May 1946–May 1948; Smoky Hill AFB, Kan, May 1948; March AFB, Calif, May 1949–16 Jun 1952.

COMMANDERS. Lt Col Ross F Cole, Feb 1940; Lt Col John L Moore, 1940; Maj Lewis M Merrick, 20 Feb 1941; Maj Mark L Lewis Jr, Oct 1941; Lt Col Millard L Haskin, 10 Dec 1941; Lt Col Dwight D Divine II, 19 May 1942; Lt Col George R Anderson, Mar 1943; Lt Col Roger E Phelan, Jun 1943; Col Richard W Robinson, c. Feb 1944; Col Leonard T Nicholson, 21 Jan 1945; Lt Col James E Sweeney, 24 Sep 1945; Lt Col Charles W Johnson, 7 Oct 1945; Maj John E Pryor, c. 17 Oct 1945–unkn; Col Joseph F Carroll, Jun 1946; Lt Col Alvin J H Mueller, Jan 1947; Col Francis L Rivard, Oct 1947; Col Walter E Arnold, 19 Dec 1947; Lt Col Paul L Barton, 7 Jun 1948; Capt William L Lemme, 29 Jun 1948; Maj John W Swanson, 3 Jul 1948; Lt Col Payne Jennings Jr, 7 Jul 1948; Col James V Edmundson, 19 Aug 1949; Col John B Henry Jr, Mar–16 Jun 1952.

CAMPAIGNS. *World War II:* Antisubmarine, American Theater; East Indies; Air Offensive, Japan; China Defensive; Papua; New Guinea; Bismarck Archipelago; Western Pacific; Leyte; Luzon; China Offensive. *Korean War:* UN Defensive; UN Offensive.

DECORATIONS. Distinguished Unit Citations: Papua, 23 Jul 1942–23 Jan 1943; New Guinea, 5 Nov 1943. Philippine Presidential Unit Citation.

INSIGNE. *Shield:* Azure, a cougar's left gamb erased palewise claws to base or armed gules. *Motto:* DUCEMUS—We Lead. (Approved 19 Jun 1941.)

23d FIGHTER GROUP

Constituted as 23d Pursuit Group (Interceptor) on 17 Dec 1941. *Redesignated* 23d Fighter Group in May 1942. *Activated* in China on 4 Jul 1942. Chennault's American Volunteer Group supplied experienced pilots and a name—"Flying Tigers." Using P–40's and later P–51's, the 23d group provided air defense for the Chinese terminus of the Hump route from India; conducted a counter-air campaign to whittle down Japanese air strength by destroying enemy planes in the air and on the ground; strafed and bombed Japanese forces, installations, and transportation; escorted bombers; and flew reconnaissance missions. It intercepted Japanese planes that attempted to bomb Allied airfields; attacked Japanese airdromes; strafed and bombed river craft, troop concentrations, supply depots, and railroads; and protected bombers that attacked Hong Kong, Canton, Shanghai, and other targets. Its area of operations extended beyond China to Burma, French Indochina, and Formosa. The "Flying Tigers" operated against the Japanese during the enemy's drive toward Changsha and Chungking in May 1943, supported Chinese forces during the Japanese offensive in the Tungting Hu region in Nov 1943, and took part in the effort to halt a Japanese force that pushed down the Hsiang Valley in Jun 1944. In the latter battle the group, despite bad weather and heavy flak, repeatedly struck boats, trucks, aircraft, troops, and other objectives, receiving a DUC for its operations. The 23d helped to turn the enemy's offensive in the spring of 1945 and then harassed the retreating Japanese by strafing and bombing their columns. Remained in China until Dec 1945. Moved to the US. *Inactivated* on 5 Jan 1946.

Activated on 10 Oct 1946 on Guam. Assigned to Far East Air Forces and equipped with P-47 aircraft. Moved to the Panama Canal Zone in Apr 1949. *Inactivated* on 24 Sep 1949.

Redesignated 23d Fighter-Interceptor Group. *Activated* in the US on 12 Jan 1951. Assigned to Air Defense Command and equipped with F-86's. *Inactivated* on 6 Feb 1952.

Redesignated 23d Fighter Group (Air Defense). *Activated* on 18 Aug 1955. Assigned to Air Defense Command. Equipped with F-89 aircraft.

SQUADRONS. *16th:* 1942-1943. *74th:* 1942-1946; 1946-1949; 1951-1952. *75th:* 1942-1946; 1946-1949; 1951-1952; 1955-. *76th:* 1942-1946; 1946-1949; 1955-. *132d:* 1951. *134th:* 1951.

STATIONS. Kunming, China, 4 Jul 1942; Kweilin, China, c. Sep 1943; Liuchow, China, 8 Sep 1944; Luliang, China, 14 Sep 1944; Liuchow, China, Aug 1945; Hangchow, China, c. 10 Oct-12 Dec 1945; Ft Lewis, Wash 3-5 Jan 1946. Guam, 10 Oct 1946; Howard AFB, CZ, 25 Apr-24 Sep 1949. Presque Isle AFB, Maine, 12 Jan 1951-6 Feb 1952. Presque Isle AFB, Maine, 18 Aug 1955-.

COMMANDERS. Col Robert L Scott Jr, 4 Jul 1942; Lt Col Bruce K Holloway, 9 Jan 1943; Lt Col Norval C Bonawitz, 16 Sep 1943; Col David L Hill, 4 Nov 1943; Lt Col Philip C Loofbourrow, 15 Oct 1944; Col Edward F Rector, 12 Dec 1944-c. Dec 1945. Col Lester S Harris, 10 Oct 1946; Maj Leonard S Dysinger, 1 Nov 1947; Lt Col Hadley V Saehlenou, Nov 1947-unkn; Col Louis R Hughes Jr, 1 Sep 1948-unkn. Unkn, Jan-Jul 1951; Col Norval K Heath, c. Jul 1951-6 Feb 1952. Col Frank Q O'Connor, 1955; Lt Col Frank J Keller, Dec 1955-.

CAMPAIGNS. India-Burma; China Defensive; Western Pacific; China Offensive.

DECORATIONS. Distinguished Unit Citation: Hunan Province, China, 17–25 Jun 1944.

INSIGNE. *Shield:* Azure, over a bolt of lightning, in pale, or, a Flying Tiger proper, tongue red, winged argent; all outlines black; a diminutive border silvergrey. (Approved 24 Jan 1957.)

24th PURSUIT GROUP

Constituted as 24th Pursuit Group (Interceptor) on 16 Aug 1941. *Activated* in the Philippine Islands on 1 Oct 1941. Augmented by two attached squadrons (21st and 34th) and equipped with P-35 and P-40 aircraft, this group comprised the entire pursuit force in the Philippines in Dec 1941. When enemy aircraft were reported to be approaching Luzon on the morning of 8 Dec (7 Dec in the US), the 24th group attempted to intercept but failed because radar and visual sighting facilities were inadequate. Later that day, after the group's planes either had landed for refueling or had run so low on fuel that they could not fight, the Japanese attacked and inflicted heavy losses on the organization. In the days that followed, the group's strength declined rapidly, but the 24th flew some patrol and reconnaissance missions, engaged the enemy in the air, and attacked enemy airfields and shipping. By late in Dec the ground personnel were absorbed by infantry units and some pilots were evacuated to Australia. One of these pilots

was Lt Boyd D "Buzz" Wagner, who already had become the first AAF ace of World War II. The remaining pilots continued operations in the Philippines with the few planes that were left. Eventually all of the men, except the few who had gone to Australia, were either killed or captured by the enemy. Although not remanned, the group was carried on the list of active organizations until after the war. *Inactivated* on 2 Apr 1946.

SQUADRONS. *3d:* 1941–1946. *17th:* 1941–1946. *20th:* 1941–1946.

STATIONS. Clark Field, Luzon, 1 Oct 1941; Mariveles, Luzon, c. 1 Jan–May 1942.

COMMANDERS. Col Orrin L Grover, 1 Oct 1941–Apr 1942.

CAMPAIGNS. Philippine Islands.

DECORATIONS. Distinguished Unit Citations: Philippines, 7 Dec 1941–10 May 1942; Philippines, 8–22 Dec 1941; Philippines, 6 Jan–8 Mar 1942. Philippine Presidential Unit Citation.

INSIGNE. None.

25th BOMBARDMENT GROUP

Constituted as 25th Bombardment Group (Heavy) on 22 Dec 1939. *Activated* on 1 Feb 1940. Trained with A-17's and B-18's. Moved to the Caribbean late in 1940. *Redesignated* 25th Bombardment Group (Medium) in May 1942. Flew antisubmarine patrols, escorted convoys, and served as part of the defense force of the area. Aircraft: B-18's (1940–1942), A-20's (1942–1943), and B-25's (1943–1944). Returned to the US early in 1944,

GUARD WITH POWER

assigned to Second AF, and equipped with B–17's. *Disbanded* on 20 Jun 1944.

SQUADRONS. *10th:* 1940–1943. *12th:* 1940–1944. *35th:* 1940–1944. *59th:* 1943–1944. *417th:* 1942–1944.

STATIONS. Langley Field, Va, 1 Feb–26 Oct 1940; Borinquen Field, PR, 1 Nov 1940; Edinburgh Field, Trinidad, 1 Nov 1942; Ft Amsterdam, Curacao, 1 Aug 1943; Borinquen Field, PR, 5 Oct 1943–24 Mar 1944; Alamogordo AAFld, NM, 6 Apr–20 Jun 1944.

COMMANDERS. Maj Theodore J Koenig, 1 Feb 1940; Maj William B Sousa, unkn; Lt Col Caleb V Haynes, 7 Jan 1941; Maj Alva L Harvey, 1 Jun 1941; Maj Neil B Harding, 10 Sep 1941; Maj Jasper N Bell, unkn; Lt Col Robert Alan, unkn; Maj Mathew J McKeever Jr, unkn; Maj Milton E Lipps, unkn; Maj Howard A Cheney, unkn; Col Charles F Born, 1942; Maj John J Mullen, unkn; Col Kenneth O Sanborn, 1 Aug 1943–7 Apr 1944; unkn, Apr–Jun 1944.

CAMPAIGNS. Antisubmarine, American Theater.

DECORATIONS. None.

INSIGNE. *Shield:* Azure, issuing out of sinister side an arm embowed grasping a trident bend sinisterwise prongs to base or, on and over the junction of the shaft and prongs a compass rose of the first on a background of the second. *Motto:* GUARD WITH POWER. (Approved 3 Oct 1940.)

25th BOMBARDMENT GROUP (RECONNAISSANCE)

Constituted as 25th Bombardment Group (Reconnaissance) on 17 Jul 1944. *Activated* in England on 9 Aug 1944. Served with Eighth AF until V–E Day. Used various aircraft, including B–17's B–24's, B–25's, B–26's, P–38's, and L–5's. Operations included reconnaissance over the waters adjacent to the British Isles and occasionally to the Azores to obtain meteorological data; flights over the Continent for weather information needed in planning operations; night photographic missions to detect enemy activity; and daylight photographic and mapping missions over the Continent. Occasionally engaged in scout missions to target areas for last-minute weather information that was furnished to approaching bomber formations, on-the-scene visual evaluation of bombardment strikes, and electronic-countermeasure missions in which chaff was spread to confuse enemy defenses during Allied attacks. Moved to the US, Jul–Aug 1945. *Inactivated* on 8 Sep 1945.

SQUADRONS. *652d:* 1944–1945. *653d:* 1944–1945. *654th:* 1944–1945.

STATIONS. Watton, England, 9 Aug 1944–23 Jul 1945; Drew Field, Fla, Aug–8 Sep 1945.

COMMANDERS. Lt Col Joseph A Stenglein, 9 Aug 1944; Col Leon W Gray, 23 Sep 1944; Lt Col John R Hoover, 14 Apr 1945; Maj Ernest H Patterson, 19 Jun 1945–unkn.

CAMPAIGNS. Northern France; Rhineland; Ardennes-Alsace; Central Europe.

DECORATIONS. None.

INSIGNE. None.

26th RECONNAISSANCE GROUP

Constituted as 26th Observation Group on 21 Aug 1941. *Activated* on 1 Sep 1941. Assigned to First and later to Third AF. *Redesignated* 26th Reconnaissance Group in Apr 1943, and 26th Tactical Reconnaissance Group in Aug 1943. Participated in the Carolina Maneuvers in the fall of 1941; flew antisubmarine patrols off the east coast after the US entered the war; took part in the Tennessee Maneuvers in the fall of 1942; later participated in exercises and provided air support for training ground forces. Aircraft: O–46's, O–47's, O–52's, L–4's, A–20's, B–25's, and P–39's. *Disbanded* on 11 Nov 1943.

Reconstituted, redesignated 26th Reconnaissance Group, and allotted to the reserve, on 27 Dec 1946. *Activated* on 23 Oct 1947. *Inactivated* on 27 Jun 1949.

SQUADRONS. *4th:* 1947–1949. *10th:* 1947–1949. *14th:* 1942–1943. *72d:* 1943. *91st:* 1943. *101st:* 1941–1943. *103d:* 1941–1943. *152d:* 1941–1943.

STATIONS. Ft Devens, Mass, 1 Sep 1941; Providence, RI, c. 12 Sep 1941; Quonset Point, RI, Jun 1942; Hyannis, Mass, Jul 1942; Harrisburg Mun Aprt, Pa, Sep 1942; Reading AAFld, Pa, Jun–11 Nov 1943. Niagara Falls Mun Aprt, NY, 23 Oct 1947; Buffalo, NY, c. 17 Feb 1948–27 Jun 1949.

COMMANDERS. Col Louis E Boutwell, c. 1 Sep 1941; Lt Col Paul D Myers, Aug 1942; Lt Col James R Gunn Jr, Jun 1943–unkn.

CAMPAIGNS. Antisubmarine, American Theater.

DECORATIONS. None.

INSIGNE. *Shield:* Bendy of eight azure tenne, a camera lens proper, ringed argent, superimposed on two electrical flashes in saltire of the last. *Motto:* INVENI ET RENUNTIATE—Reconnoiter and Report. (Approved 28 Oct 1942. This insigne was modified 4 Sep 1953.)

INVENI ET RENUNTIATE

27th FIGHTER GROUP

INTELLIGENT STRENGTH

Constituted as 27th Bombardment Group (Light) on 22 Dec 1939. *Activated* on 1 Feb 1940. Sailed for the Philippine Islands on 1 Nov 1941 and arrived at Manila on 20 Nov. The group's planes (A-24's), which had not arrived by 7 Dec, were diverted to Australia after the Japanese attack on the Philippines. The group's commander and 20 pilots who were flown from Luzon to Australia to get the aircraft did not return because of the deterioration of the situation in the Philippines; some of these pilots saw service in Java, Feb–May 1942, before they were assigned to another group. The men left on Luzon served as infantrymen in the battles of Bataan and Corregidor; though a few managed to escape, most were either killed or taken prisoners of war by the Japanese. The 27th group was transferred, without personnel and equipment, from Australia to the US in May 1942.

Remanned and equipped with A-20's. Trained in the US until Nov 1942. Moved to North Africa. Converted to A-36 aircraft. Began operations with Twelfth AF in Jun 1943 and served in the Mediterranean theater until the end of the war. Converted to P-40's in Jan 1944 and to P-47's in Jun 1944. *Redesignated* 27th Fighter-Bomber Group in Aug 1943, and 27th Fighter Group in May 1944. Participated in the reduction of Pantelleria and Lampedusa. Supported ground forces during the conquest of Sicily. Covered the landings at Salerno and received a DUC for preventing three German armored divisions from reaching the Salerno beachhead, 10 Sep 1943. Supported Fifth Army during the Allied drive toward Rome. Took part in the invasion of Southern France and assisted Seventh Army's advance up the Rhone Valley, receiving a DUC for helping to disrupt the German retreat, 4 Sep 1944. Took part in the interdiction of the enemy's communications in northern Italy, and assisted in the Allied drive from France into Germany during the last months of the war. Returned to the US, Oct–Nov 1945. *Inactivated* on 7 Nov 1945.

Activated in Germany on 20 Aug 1946. Assigned to United States Air Forces in Europe and equipped with P-47's. Transferred, without personnel and equipment, to the US in Jun 1947. Assigned to Strategic Air Command. Equipped with P-51's in 1947, F-82's in 1948, and F-84's in 1950. *Redesignated* 27th Fighter-Escort Group in Feb 1950. Moved to the Far East late in 1950 for temporary duty with Far East Air Forces during the Korean War. Operated first from a base in Korea and later from Japan, supporting ground forces, escorting bombers, and flying armed reconnaissance missions and counter-air patrols. Returned to the US in Jul 1951. *Inactivated* on 16 Jun 1952.

SQUADRONS. *15th:* 1940–1941. *465th:* 1942. *522d* (formerly 16th): 1940–1945; 1946–1952. *523d* (formerly 17th): 1940–1945; 1946–1952. *524th* (formerly 91st): 1941–1945; 1946–1952.

STATIONS. Barksdale Field, La, 1 Feb 1940; Hunter Field, Ga, 7 Oct 1940–21 Oct 1941; Philippine Islands, 20 Nov 1941; Batchelor, Australia, Mar–4 May 1942; Hunter Field, Ga, 4 May 1942; Key Field, Miss, Jul 1942; Hattiesburg, Miss, 15 Aug 1942; Harding Field, La, 25 Oct–21 Nov 1942; Ste-Barbe-du-Tlelat, Algeria, 26 Dec 1942; Nouvion, Algeria, Jan 1943; Ras el Ma, French Morocco, Apr 1943; Korba, Tunisia, Jun 1943; Sicily, Jul 1943; Italy, Sep 1943; Corsica, Jul 1944; Southern France, Aug 1944; Italy, c. Sep 1944; St-Dizier, France, 22 Feb 1945; Toul/Ochey, France, Mar 1945; Biblis, Germany, Apr 1945; Sandhofen, Germany, Jun 1945; Echterdingen, Germany, 15 Sep–20 Oct 1945; Camp Shanks, NY, 6–7 Nov 1945. Fritzlar, Germany, 20 Aug 1946; Bad Kissingen, Germany, 25 Jun 1947; Andrews Field, Md, 25 Jun 1947; Kearney AAFld, Neb, 16 Jul 1947; Bergstrom AFB, Tex, 16 Mar 1949–16 Jun 1952.

COMMANDERS. Col Clarence L Tinker, 1 Feb 1940; Lt Col W Wright, unkn; Col Guy L McNeil, Jul 1941; Col John H Davies, unkn–c. Apr 1942; Lt Col Harry F Van Leuven, 14 Jul 1942; Lt Col John D Stevenson, 11 Apr 1943; Col Dorr E Newton Jr, 6 Aug 1943; Col Stephen B Mack, 22 Apr 1944; Lt Col William R Nevitt, 10 Sep 1944–c. Nov 1945. Col Clarence T Edwinson, c. 20 Aug 1946; Col Robert P Montgomery, Nov 1946; Col Clarence T Edwinson, Feb 1947; Col Edwin A Doss, 15 Aug 1947; Col Ashley B Packard, 21 Jan 1948; Col Cy Wilson, c. Mar 1948; Col Donald J M Blakeslee, 7 Dec 1950; Lt Col William E Bertram, 3 Mar 1951–16 Jun 1952.

CAMPAIGNS. *World War II:* Philippine Islands; Air Combat, EAME Theater; Sicily; Naples-Foggia; Anzio; Rome-Arno; Northern France; Southern France; North Apennines; Rhineland; Central Europe. *Korean War:* CCF Intervention; 1st UN Counteroffensive; CCF Spring Offensive.

DECORATIONS. Distinguished Unit Citations: Philippine Islands, 7 Dec 1941–10 May 1942; Philippine Islands, 8–22 Dec 1941; Philippine Islands, 6 Jan–8 Mar 1942; Italy, 10 Sep 1943; France, 4 Sep 1944; Korea, 26 Jan–21 Apr 1951. Philippine Presidential Unit Citation. Republic of Korea Presidential Unit Citation: [Dec] 1950–31 May 1951.

INSIGNE. *Shield:* Per bend azure and or, in sinister chief a right clenched fist couped at the wrist in dexter base a magnolia blossom leaved all argent, fimbriated sable. *Motto:* INTELLIGENT STRENGTH. (Approved 12 Sep 1940.)

28th BOMBARDMENT GROUP

GUARDIAN OF THE NORTH

Constituted as 28th Composite Group on 22 Dec 1939. *Activated* on 1 Feb 1940. *Redesignated* 28th Bombardment Group (Composite) in Dec 1943. Aircraft included P-38's, P-39's, P-40's, B-26's and LB-30's during 1941–1943, and B-24's and B-25's during 1944–1945.

Operated in Alaska from Feb 1941 until after the war. Trained for Arctic warfare in 1941 and served as part of the defense system for the region. Helped to force the withdrawal of Japanese ships that attacked Dutch Harbor in Jun 1942. Flew missions against Kiska until the Japanese evacuated that island in Aug 1943. Bombed and strafed shipping, harbor facilities, canneries, fisheries, and military installations in the Kurils. Also flew photographic reconnaissance missions to obtain material for planning operations. Received a DUC for the period Apr 1944–Aug 1945 when the group's attacks on the Kurils caused Japan to divert some of her air power to that northern area, thus weakening Japanese opposition to Allied forces in the south. Flew its last bombing mission on 13 Aug 1945 but continued reconnaissance operations in the Kurils after the war. *Inactivated* in Alaska on 20 October 1945.

Redesignated 28th Bombardment Group (Very Heavy). *Activated* in the US on 4 Aug 1946 as part of Strategic Air Command. Equipped with B-29 aircraft. Was stationed in Alaska from Oct 1946 to Apr 1947. *Redesignated* 28th Bombardment Group (Medium) in May 1948. *Redesignated* 28th Bombardment Group (Heavy) in May 1949 and equipped with RB-36's in Jul. *Redesignated* 28th Strategic Reconnaissance Group in Apr 1950, and 28th Strategic Reconnaissance Group (Heavy) in Jul 1950. *Inactivated* on 16 Jun 1952.

SQUADRONS. *11th* Pursuit: 1942. *18th* Pursuit: 1941–1942. *34th* Pursuit: 1940. *36th:* 1940–1943. *37th:* 1940–1941. *73d:* 1941–1943. *77th:* 1942–1945; 1946–1952. *404th:* 1942–1945. *717th:* 1946–1952. *718th:* 1946–1952.

STATIONS. March Field, Calif, 1 Feb 1940; Moffett Field, Calif, 10 Dec 1940–12 Feb 1941; Elmendorf Field, Alaska, 23 Feb 1941; Adak, 14 Mar 1943; Shemya, 26 Feb 1944–20 Oct 1945. Grand Island AAFld, Neb, 4 Aug–6 Oct 1946; Elmendorf Field, Alaska, 20 Oct 1946–24 Apr 1947; Rapid City AAFld, SD, 3 May 1947–16 Jun 1952.

COMMANDERS. Col William H Crom, 1 Feb 1940; Lt Col Lotha A Smith, 12 Feb 1940; Maj William O Eareckson, 1 Sep 1940; Maj Donald W Titus, 20 Oct 1940; Maj William O Eareckson, 26 May 1941; Maj Norman D Sillin, 7 Nov 1941; Col Earl H DeFord, 23 Jan 1943; Maj Robert C Orth, 19 Mar 1943; Lt Col Jack N Donohew, 27 Mar 1943; Lt Col Ralph W Rodieck, 18 Apr 1943; Lt Col John W Massion, 27 Oct 1943; Lt Col Alexander W Bryant, 4 Jan 1944; Col Robert H Herman, 1 Apr 1944; Col Walter L Wheeler, 21 Jul 1945; Lt Col John C Larson, 27 Sep–20 Oct 1945. Col Richard M Montgomery, 4 Aug 1946; Col Thomas J Gent Jr, 23 Aug 1946; Lt Col Donald W Lang, 15 Aug 1947; Lt Col Everett W Best, 24 Dec 1947; Lt Col Frank W Iseman Jr, 16 Apr 1948; Lt Col Solomon Cutcher, 27 Jun 1948; Col John B Henry Jr, 10 Jul 1948; Lt Col Everett W Best, 25 Apr 1949; Col William P Brett, 2 May 1949; Lt Col Solomon Cutcher, 21 Mar 1950; Col Donald W Eisenhart, 3 Apr 1950; Col Frank W Iseman Jr, 24 Jul 1950; Col Bertram C Harrison, 18 Oct 1950; Col Richard E Ellsworth, 10 Feb 1951–16 Jun 1952.

CAMPAIGNS. Air Offensive, Japan; Aleutians.

DECORATIONS. Distinguished Unit Citation: Kuril Islands, 1 Apr 1944–13 Aug 1945.

INSIGNE. *Shield:* Per pale nebuly or and azure. *Crest:* On a wreath of the colors, or and azure, a fleur-de-lis vert the outer leaves terminated in the form of wings or. *Motto:* GUARDIAN OF THE NORTH. (Approved 14 Nov 1941.)

29th BOMBARDMENT GROUP

Constituted as 29th Bombardment Group (Heavy) on 22 Dec 1939. *Activated* on 1 Feb 1940. Equipped with B–17's and B–18's. Trained and took part in aerial reviews. Flew patrol missions in the Caribbean area, Dec 1941–Jun 1942. Equipped with B–24's in 1942. Functioned as an operational training and later as a replacement training unit. *Inactivated* on 1 Apr 1944.

Redesignated 29th Bombardment Group (Very Heavy). *Activated* on 1 Apr 1944. Prepared for overseas duty with B–29's. Moved to Guam, Dec 1944–Feb 1945, and assigned to Twentieth AF. Flew its first mission against Japan with an attack on Tokyo on 25 Feb 1945. Conducted a number of missions against strategic targets in Japan, operating in daylight and at high altitude to bomb factories, refineries, and other objectives. Beginning in Mar 1945, carried out incendiary raids on area targets, flying at night and at low altitude to complete the assignments. S/Sgt Henry E Erwin was awarded the Medal of Honor for action that saved his B–29 during a mission over Koriyama, Japan, on 12 Apr 1945. When a phosphorous smoke bomb exploded in the launching chute and shot back into the plane, Sgt Erwin picked up the burning bomb, carried it to a window, and threw it out. During the Allied assault on Okinawa, the group bombed airfields from which the enemy was sending out suicide planes against the invasion force. Received a DUC for an attack on an airfield at Omura, Japan, on 31 Mar 1945. Received second DUC for strikes on the industrial area of Shizuoka, the Mitsubishi aircraft plant at Tamashima, and the Chigusa arsenal at Nagoya, in Jun 1945. After the war, dropped food and supplies to Allied prisoners and participated in several show-of-force missions over Japan. *Inactivated* on Guam on 20 May 1946.

SQUADRONS. *6th:* 1940–1944; 1944–1946. *43d* (formerly 29th): 1940–1944; 1944–1946. *52d:* 1940–1944; 1944–1946. *411th:* 1942–1944. *761st* (later 9th Reconnaissance): 1945–1946.

STATIONS. Langley Field, Va, 1 Feb 1940; MacDill Field, Fla, 21 May 1940; Gowen Field, Idaho, 25 Jun 1942–1 Apr 1944. Pratt AAFld, Kan, 1 Apr–7 Dec 1944; North Field, Guam, 17 Jan 1945–20 May 1946.

COMMANDERS. Maj Vincent J Meloy, 1 Feb 1940; Maj Charles W Lawrence, 15 Jan 1941; Lt Col James P Hodges, 1 Feb 1941; Maj Frank H Robinson, 1 Oct 1941; Lt Col James M Fitzmaurice, 1 Dec 1941; Lt Col Robert F Travis, 30 Mar 1942; Lt Col William B David, 28 Aug 1942; Maj Henry H Covington, 2 Feb 1943; Lt Col Walter E Arnold Jr, 20 Feb 1943; Lt Col Horace M Wade, 20 Sep 1943–1 Apr 1944. 2d Lt Philip J Lamm, 21 Apr 1944; Capt Samuel W Bright, 28 Apr 1944; Maj Quinn L Oldaker, 2 May 1944; Col Carl R Storrie, 28 May 1944; Col Robert L Mason, 23 Jul 1945; Lt Col Loran D Briggs, 9 Oct 1945–unkn; Col Vincent M Miles Jr, 1946.

CAMPAIGNS. Antisubmarine, American Theater; Air Offensive, Japan; Western Pacific.

DECORATIONS. Distinguished Unit Citations: Japan, 31 Mar 1945; Japan, 19–26 Jun 1945.

INSIGNE. *Shield:* Azure, a drop bomb and lightning flash saltirewise or. *Motto:* POWER FOR PEACE. (Approved 14 Oct 1940.)

30th BOMBARDMENT GROUP

Constituted as 30th Bombardment Group (Heavy) on 20 Nov 1940. *Activated* on 15 Jan 1941. Trained with B–18's and A–29's. Equipped with B–24's for operations. Patrolled the west coast, 1942–1943, and trained crews for other organizations. Moved to Hawaii in Oct 1943, assigned to Seventh AF, and sailed for the

Central Pacific in Nov. Began operations from the Ellice Islands in Nov 1943. Assisted the invasion of the Gilberts by attacking enemy installations on those islands and by raiding airfields in the Marshalls to help prevent the launching of Japanese planes against the amphibious assault on Tarawa. After moving to the Gilberts in Jan 1944, bombed installations in the Marshall Islands in preparation for the invasion. Moved to Kwajalein in Mar 1944 and raided airfields and navy bases in the Truk Islands to keep them neutralized before and during the amphibious attack on the Marianas; also bombed Wake Island, Guam, and Saipan. Moved to Saipan in Aug 1944 and attacked airfields and shipping in the Bonin and Volcano Islands until Iwo Jima was occupied early in 1945. Struck bypassed islands in the Carolines and Marianas. Returned to Oahu in Mar 1945. Trained and flew patrol missions. *Inactivated* in Hawaii on 25 Jun 1946.

SQUADRONS. *21st:* 1941–1943. *27th:* 1941–1946. *38th:* 1941–1946. *392d:* 1942–1945. *819th:* 1943–1945.

STATIONS. March Field, Calif, 15 Jan 1941; New Orleans, La, c. Jun 1941; Muroc, Calif, 24 Dec 1941; March Field, Calif, 7 Feb 1942–28 Sep 1943; Hickam Field, TH, 20 Oct 1943; Nanumea, Ellice Islands, 12 Nov 1943; Abemama, 4 Jan 1944; Kwajalein, c. 20 Mar 1944; Saipan, 4 Aug 1944; Wheeler Field, TH, Mar 1945; Kahuku, TH, 29 Sep 1945; Wheeler Field, TH, Feb–25 Jun 1946.

COMMANDERS. Capt Budd J Peaslee, 15 Jan 1941; Maj Thomas W Steed, 10 Feb 1941; Lt Col Newton Longfellow, 1941; Maj Thomas W Steed, c. Dec 1941; Lt Col Jack Wood, 21 Aug 1942; Col Robert O Cork, May 1943; Col Edwin B Miller Jr, 30 Aug 1943; Col John J Morrow, c. 2 Nov 1944; Lt Col Elliott T Pardee, Mar 1945; Col Elder Patteson, 1 Jul 1945–unkn.

CAMPAIGNS. Antisubmarine, American Theater; Central Pacific; Air Offensive, Japan; Eastern Mandates; Western Pacific.

DECORATIONS. None.

INSIGNE. None.

31st FIGHTER GROUP

Constituted as 31st Pursuit Group (Interceptor) on 22 Dec 1939. *Activated* on 1 Feb 1940. Trained with P–39's and participated in maneuvers. *Redesignated* 31st Fighter Group in May 1942. Moved to England, May–Jun 1942. Assigned to Eighth AF and equipped with Spitfires. Entered combat in Aug 1942. Supported

RETURN WITH HONOR

a raid made by Canadian, British, American, and French forces at Dieppe on 19 Aug. Escorted bombers and flew patrol and diversionary missions until Oct. Assigned to Twelfth AF for the invasion of North Africa, the pilots of the group flying Spitfires from Gibraltar to Algeria on 8 Nov 1942 and the ground echelon landing at Arzeu beach the same day. Attacked motor transports, gun positions, and troop concentrations during the three-day campaign for Algeria and French Morocco. Helped to defeat Axis forces in Tunisia by supporting ground troops and providing cover for bomber and fighter aircraft. During May and Jun 1943, provided escort for bombers on raids to Pantelleria and cover for naval convoys in the Mediterranean. Supported the landings on Sicily in July and took part in the conquest of that island. Covered the landings at Salerno early in Sep 1943 and at Anzio in Jan 1944. Also operated in close support of Allied ground forces in Italy and flew patrol and escort missions.

Assigned to Fifteenth AF in Apr 1944, converted to P–51's, and thereafter engaged primarily in escort work. Received a DUC for a mission on 21 Apr 1944 when the group, despite the severe weather that was encountered, provided cover for a force of heavy bombers during a raid on production centers in Rumania. On numerous other occasions escorted bombers that attacked objectives in Italy, France, Germany, Poland, Czechoslovakia, Austria, Hungary, Bulgaria, Rumania, Yugoslavia, and Greece. In addition provided escort for reconnaissance aircraft and for C–47's engaged in the airborne operation connected with the invasion of Southern France. Also flew strafing missions against airdromes and communications targets. Took part in an operation in which a task force from Fifteenth AF attacked targets in Rumania while flying to Russia on 22 Jul 1944 and while returning to Italy on 26 Jul; on 25 Jul, after escorting P–38's from a base in Russia for a raid on an airdrome in Poland, the 31st group made attacks on a convoy of German trucks and on a force of German fighter-bombers, being awarded a DUC for its performance. Strafed rail and highway traffic in northern Italy in Apr 1945 when Allied forces were engaged in their final offensive in that area. Returned to the US in Aug. *Inactivated* on 7 Nov 1945.

Activated in Germany on 20 Aug 1946. Assigned to United States Air Forces in Europe. Transferred, without personnel and equipment, to the US in Jun 1947. Assigned to Tactical Air Command and equipped with P–51's. Converted to F–84's in 1948. *Redesignated* 31st Fighter-Bomber Group in Jan 1950. Assigned to Strategic Air Command in Jul 1950. *Redesignated* 31st Fighter-Escort Group. *Inactivated* on 16 Jun 1952.

SQUADRONS. *39th:* 1940–1942. *40th:* 1940–1942. *41st:* 1940–1942. *307th:* 1942–

1945; 1946–1952. *308th:* 1942–1945; 1946–1952. *309th:* 1942–1945; 1946–1952.

STATIONS. Selfridge Field, Mich, 1 Feb 1940; Baer Field, Ind, 6 Dec 1941; New Orleans AB, La, Feb–19 May 1942; Atcham, England, 11 Jun 1942; Westhampnett, England, 1 Aug 1942; Tafaraoui, Algeria, 8 Nov 1942; La Senia, Algeria, c. 12 Nov 1942; Thelepte, Tunisia, c. 7 Feb 1943; Tebessa, Algeria, 17 Feb 1943; Youks-les-Bains, Algeria, 21 Feb 1943; Kalaa Djerda, Tunisia, c. 25 Feb 1943; Thelepte, Tunisia, 11 Mar 1943; Djilma, Tunisia, 7 Apr 1943; Le Sers, Tunisia, 12 Apr 1943; Korba, Tunisia, 15 May 1943; Gozo, c. 30 Jun 1943; Ponte Olivo, Sicily, c. 13 Jul 1943; Agrigento, Sicily, 21 Jul 1943; Termini, Sicily, 2 Aug 1943; Milazzo, Sicily, 2 Sep 1943; Montecorvino, Italy, 20 Sep 1943; Pomigliano, Italy, 14 Oct 1943; Castel Volturno, Italy, 19 Jan 1944; San Severo, Italy, 2 Apr 1944; Mondolfo, Italy, 3 Mar 1945; Triolo Airfield, Italy, 15 Jul–Aug 1945; Drew Field, Fla, Aug–7 Nov 1945. Giebelstadt, Germany, 20 Aug 1946; Kitzingen, Germany, 30 Sep 1946; Langley Field, Va, 25 Jun 1947; Turner Field, Ga, 4 Sep 1947–16 Jun 1952.

COMMANDERS. Lt Col Harold H George, Feb 1940; Col John R Hawkins, 1 Jul 1941; Col Fred M Dean, 5 Dec 1942; Lt Col Frank A Hill, c. Jul 1943; Col Charles M McCorkle, c. Sep 1943; Col Yancey S Tarrant, 4 Jul 1944; Col William A Daniel, 4 Dec 1944–unkn. Lt Col Horace A Hanes, Aug 1946–unkn; Lt Col Frederick H LeFebre, Jan 1947; Maj Arland Stanton, Feb 1947; Col Dale D Fisher, Mar 1947; Lt Col Donald J M Blakeslee, May 1947; Maj Leonard P Marks, 22 Oct 1947; Col Carroll W McColpin, 1 Nov 1947; Col Earl H Dunham, c. Dec 1949; Col David C Schilling, 1 Jun 1951–16 Jun 1952.

CAMPAIGNS. Air Combat, EAME Theater; Air Offensive, Europe; Algeria-French Morocco; Tunisia; Sicily; Naples-Foggia; Anzio; Rome-Arno; Normandy; Northern France; Southern France; North Apennines; Rhineland; Central Europe; Po Valley.

DECORATIONS. Distinguished Unit Citations: Rumania, 21 Apr 1944; Poland, 25 Jul 1944.

INSIGNE. *Shield:* Per bend nebule or and azure, in chief a wyvern, sans legs, wings endorsed of the second. *Motto:* RETURN WITH HONOR. (Approved 28 Jun 1941.)

32d FIGHTER GROUP

Constituted as 32d Pursuit Group on 22 Nov 1940. *Activated* in Panama on 1 Jan 1941. *Redesignated* 32d Fighter Group in May 1942. Trained and served as part of the defense force for the Panama Canal, using P–26, P–36, P–38, P–39, and P–40 aircraft. *Disbanded* in the Canal Zone on 1 Nov 1943.

Reconstituted and *redesignated* 32d Fighter Group (Air Defense), on 11 Dec 1956. *Activated* in the US on 8 Feb 1957. Assigned to Air Defense Command.

SQUADRONS. *51st:* 1941–1943. *52d:* 1941–1943. *53d:* 1941–1943.

STATIONS. Rio Hato, Panama, 1 Jan 1941; France Field, CZ, 9 Dec 1941–1 Nov 1943. Minot AFB, ND, 8 Feb 1957–.

COMMANDERS. Capt Roger J Browne, 1 Jan 1941; Capt James B Buck, 16 Apr 1941; Lt Col Roger J Browne, 4 Aug 1941; Lt Col William R Robertson Jr, 23 Aug 1943–unkn. Maj Joe E Roberts, 1957–.

CAMPAIGNS. American Theater.

DECORATIONS. None.

INSIGNE. None.

33d FIGHTER GROUP

Constituted as 33d Pursuit Group (Interceptor) on 20 Nov 1940. *Activated* on 15 Jan 1941. Began training with P–39's but soon changed to P–40's. Served as part of the defense force for the east coast after the Japanese attack on Pearl Harbor. *Redesignated* 33d Fighter Group in May

1942. Moved to North Africa, part of the group (including the pilots and their planes) arriving with the invasion force on 8 Nov 1942, and the remainder arriving shortly afterwards. Operated with Twelfth AF in the Mediterranean theater until Feb 1944. Provided close support for ground forces and flew bombing and strafing missions against personnel concentrations, port installations, fuel dumps, bridges, highways, and rail lines during the campaigns in North Africa. Received a DUC for action on 15 Jan 1943: when enemy aircraft attempted to knock out the group's base in Tunisia, the 33d drove off the enemy's escort and destroyed most of the bombers. Took part in the reduction of Pantelleria and flew patrol missions while Allied troops landed after the enemy's garrison had surrendered. Participated in the invasion and conquest of Sicily. Supported landings at Salerno, Allied operations in southern Italy, and the beachhead at Anzio.

Moved to India in Feb 1944. Assigned to Tenth AF. Trained with P–38 and P–47 aircraft. Moved to China in Apr, became part of Fourteenth AF, continued training, and flew some patrol and interception missions. Returned to India in Sept 1944 and, as part of Tenth AF, flew dive-bombing and strafing missions in Burma until the Allied campaigns in that area had been completed. Returned t the US, Nov–Dec 1945. *Inactivated* on 8 Dec 1945.

Activated in Germany on 20 Aug 1946. Assigned to United States Air Forces in

Europe and equipped with P–51's. Transferred, less personnel and equipment, to the US in 1947. Remanned and equipped with P–51's; converted to F–84's in Jun 1948 and F–86's in Feb 1949. *Redesignated* 33d Fighter-Interceptor Group in Jan 1950. *Inactivated* on 6 Feb 1952.

Redesignated 33d Fighter Group (Air Defense). *Activated* on 18 Aug 1955. Assigned to Air Defense Command.

SQUADRONS. *58th:* 1941–1945; 1946–1952; 1955–. *59th:* 1941–1945; 1946–1952. *60th:* 1941–1945; 1946–1952; 1955–.

STATIONS. Mitchel Field, NY, 15 Jan 1941; Philadelphia, Pa, 13 Dec 1941–Oct 1942; Port Lyautey, French Morocco, 10 Nov 1942; Casablanca, French Morocco, c. 13 Nov 1942; Telergma, Algeria, 24 Dec 1942; Thelepte, Tunisia, 7 Jan 1943; Youks-les-Bains, Algeria, 8 Feb 1943; Telergma, Algeria, c. 20 Feb 1943; Berteaux, Algeria, c. 2 Mar 1943; Ebba Ksour, Tunisia, c. 12 Apr 1943; Menzel Temime, Tunisia, 20 May 1943; Sousse, Tunisia, 9 Jun 1943; Pantelleria, 19 Jun 1943; Licata, Sicily, c. 18 Jul 1943; Paestum, Italy, 13 Sep 1943; Santa Maria, Italy, 18 Nov 1943; Cercola, Italy, c. 1 Jan–Feb 1944; Karachi, India, c. 20 Feb 1944; Shwangliu, China, c. 18 Apr 1944; Pungchacheng, China, 9 May 1944; Nagaghuli, India, 3 Sep 1944; Sahmaw, Burma, 26 Dec 1944; Piardoba, India, 5 May–c. 15 Nov 1945; Camp Shanks, NY, 7–8 Dec 1945. Neubiberg, Germany, 20 Aug 1946; Bad Kissingen, Germany, Jul–25 Aug 1947; Andrews Field, Md, 25 Aug 1947; Roswell AAFld, NM, 16 Sep 1947; Otis AFB, Mass, 16 Nov 1948–6 Feb 1952. Otis AFB, Mass, 18 Aug 1955–.

COMMANDERS. Maj Minthorne W Reed, c. Jan 1941; Col Elwood R Quesada, 7 Oct 1941; Col William W Momyer, 29 Jun 1942; Col Loring F Stetson Jr, 17 Oct 1943; Lt Col Oliver G Cellini, 7 Jun 1944; Col David D Terry Jr, 9 Sep 1944; Col Frank L Dunn, 2 Mar 1945–unkn. Col Barton M Russell, 20 Aug 1946; Lt Col Albert A Cory, unkn; Col Gwen G Atkinson, Jan 1948; Lt Col Woodrow W Korges, c. May 1949; Col Charles H MacDonald, c. Aug 1949; Col Harrison R Thyng, 15 Jun 1950; Lt Col Willard W Millikan, c. Aug 1951–6 Feb 1952. Col Fred G Hook Jr, 1955–.

CAMPAIGNS. Air Combat, EAME Theater; Algeria-French Morocco; Tunisia; Sicily; Naples-Foggia; Anzio; Rome-Arno; India-Burma; China Defensive; Central Burma.

DECORATIONS. Distinguished Unit Citation: Central Tunisia, 15 Jan 1943.

INSIGNE. *Shield:* Azure, on a pale nebuly or a sword point to chief in pale of the field, flammant gules, all within a border of the second. *Motto:* FIRE FROM THE CLOUDS. (Approved 21 Feb 1942.)

34th BOMBARDMENT GROUP

Constituted as 34th Bombardment Group (Heavy) on 20 Nov 1940. *Activated* on 15 Jan 1941. Using B–17's, trained and participated in maneuvers until Dec 1941. Flew patrol missions

VALOR TO VICTORY

along the east coast after the Japanese attacked Pearl Harbor. Later became part of the defense force for the west coast. Served as a replacement training unit from mid–1942 until the end of 1943, and then began preparing for overseas duty with B–24's. Moved to England in Apr 1944 for operations with Eighth AF.

Entered combat in May 1944. Helped to prepare for the invasion of Normandy by bombing airfields in France and Germany, and supported the landing in Jun by attacking coastal defenses and communications. Continued to take part in the campaign in France by supporting ground forces at St Lo, 24–25 Jul, and by striking V-weapon sites, gun emplacements, and supply lines throughout the summer of 1944. Converted to B–17's and engaged primarily in bombardment of strategic objectives from Oct 1944 to Feb 1945. Targets included marshalling yards in Ludwigshaven, Hamm, Osnabruck, and Darmstadt; oil centers in Bielefeld, Merseburg, Hamburg, and Misburg; factories in Berlin, Dalteln, and Hannover; and air-

fields in Munster, Neumunster, and Frankfurt. During this period the group also supported ground forces during the Battle of the Bulge, Dec 1944–Jan 1945. In Mar 1945, with few industrial targets remaining and with Allied armies advancing across Germany, the 34th turned almost solely to interdicting enemy communications and supporting Allied ground forces. After V–E Day it carried food to flooded areas of Holland and transported prisoners of war from German camps to Allied centers. Returned to the US in the summer of 1945. *Inactivated* on 28 Aug 1945.

SQUADRONS. *4th:* 1941–1945. *7th:* 1941–1945. *18th:* 1941–1945. *391st:* 1942–1945.

STATIONS. Langley Field, Va, 15 Jan 1941; Westover Field, Mass, 29 May 1941; Pendleton Field, Ore, c. 27 Jan 1942; Davis-Monthan Field, Ariz, c. 13 May 1942; Geiger Field, Wash, 4 Jul 1942; Ephrata, Wash, 1 Dec 1942; Blythe, Calif, 15 Dec 1942–Apr 1944; Mendlesham, England, c. 26 Apr 1944–c. 25 Jul 1945; Sioux Falls AAFld, SD, Aug–28 Aug 1945.

COMMANDERS. Maj John W Monahan, 15 Jan 1941; Lt Col Harold D Smith, c. 1 Mar 1941; Maj Ford J Lauer, 9 Jan 1942; Col Ralph E Koon, 12 Feb 1942; Maj Irvine A Rendel, 21 Jul 1942; Maj John A Rouse, 24 Feb 1943; Lt Col John E Carmack, 15 Sep 1943; Col Ernest F Wackwitz Jr, c. 5 Jan 1944; Col William E Creer, Sep 1944; Lt Col Eugene B Lebailly, 29 May–c. Aug 1945.

CAMPAIGNS. Antisubmarine, American Theater; Air Offensive, Europe; Normandy; Northern France; Rhineland; Ardennes-Alsace; Central Europe.

DECORATIONS. None.

INSIGNE. *Shield:* Azure, a compass rose or. *Motto:* VALOR TO VICTORY. (Approved 4 Nov 1941.)

35th FIGHTER GROUP

Constituted as 35th Pursuit Group (Interceptor) on 22 Dec 1939. *Activated* on 1 Feb 1940. Trained with P–35, P–36, P–39, and P–40 aircraft. Two squadrons (21st and 34th) moved to the Philippines in Nov 1941. Headquarters and another squadron (70th) sailed for Manila on 5 Dec but because of the Japanese attack on Pearl Harbor they returned to the US where the squadron flew some patrols. Headquarters and the 70th squadron sailed for Australia on 12 Jan 1942. Three days later all the combat squadrons were relieved and three others, still in the US, were assigned. Headquarters reached Australia in Feb 1942 and moved on to India. Meanwhile the squadrons had

~ ATTACK TO DEFEND ~

moved from the US to Australia and were training for combat with P–39's. Headquarters was transferred back to Australia, without personnel and equipment, in May 1942.

Redesignated 35th Fighter Group. Served in combat with Fifth AF, operating successively from bases in Australia, New Guinea, Owi, Morotai, and the Philippines. First used P–38's and P–39's; equipped with P–47's late in 1943 and with P–51's in Mar 1945. Helped to halt the Japanese advance in Papua and took part in the Allied offensive that recovered the rest of New Guinea, flying protective patrols over Port Moresby, escorting bombers and transports, attacking Japanese airfields and supply lines, and providing cover for Allied landings. In 1944 began long-range missions against enemy airfields and installations in the southern Philippines, Halmahera, and Borneo, preparatory to the US invasion of the Philippines. Beginning in Jan 1945, operated in support of ground forces on Luzon. Also escorted bombers and completed some fighter sweeps to Formosa and China. Bombed and strafed railways and airfields in Kyushu and Korea after moving to Okinawa in Jun 1945. Moved to Japan in Oct 1945 and, as part of Far East Air Forces, trained, took part in maneuvers, and flew surveillance patrols over Honshu. *Redesignated* 35th Fighter-Interceptor Group in Jan 1950. Equipped with F–80's.

Entered combat in the Korean War in Jul 1950 and almost immediately began converting from F–80's to F–51's. Operated from bases in Japan and Korea in support of UN ground forces, bombing and strafing enemy supply lines, troop concentrations, and communications. Transferred without personnel and equipment to Japan in May 1951. Remanned and equipped with F–51's and F–80's. Provided air defense for Japan. Converted to F–86 aircraft in 1955.

SQUADRONS. *18th:* 1940. *20th:* 1940. *21st:* 1940–1942. *34th:* 1940–1942. *39th:* 1942–. *40th:* 1942–. *41st:* 1942–. *70th:* 1941–1942.

STATIONS. Moffett Field, Calif, 1 Feb 1940; Hamilton Field, Calif, 10 Sep 1940–5 Dec 1941 and 9 Dec 1941–12 Jan 1942; Brisbane, Australia, 1 Feb 1942; New Delhi, India, Mar 1942; Sydney, Australia, 4 May 1942; Port Moresby, New Guinea, 22 Jul 1942; Tsili Tsili, New Guinea, 15 Aug 1943; Nadzab, New Guinea, 5 Oct 1943; Gusap, New Guinea, 7 Feb 1944; Owi, Schouten Islands, 22 Jul 1944; Morotai, 27 Sep 1944; Mangaldan, Luzon, c. 20 Jan 1945; Lingayen, Luzon, c. 10 Apr 1945; Clark Field, Luzon, 19 Apr 1945; Okinawa, 28 Jun 1945; Irumagawa, Japan, Oct 1945; Yokota, Japan, 16 Mar 1950; Ashiya, Japan, 8 Jul 1950; Pohang, Korea, 14 Jul 1950; Tsuiki, Japan, 13 Aug 1950; Pohang, Korea, 3 Oct 1950; Yonpo, Korea, 18 Nov 1950; Pusan, Korea, c. 3 Dec 1950; Johnson AB, Japan, 25 May 1951; Yokota, Japan, 14 Aug 1954–.

COMMANDERS. Maj O R Strickland, 1940; Col George P Tourtellot, 1940–unkn; Col Richard A Legg, 12 Mar 1942; Lt Col Malcolm A Moore, 26 Jul 1943; Lt Col Edwin A Doss, 23 Oct 1943; Lt Col Furlo S Wagner, 12 Feb 1944; Col Edwin A Doss, 4 May 1944; Col Harney Estes Jr, 27 Jul 1945; Col Raymond P Todd, 22 Mar 1946; Lt Col Richard D Dick, c. 13 Sep 1946; Col James R Gunn Jr, c. 11 Feb 1947; Col Ford J Lauer, 28 Apr 1947; Col Ray W Clifton, 1 Sep 1947; Col Edgar M Scattergood Jr, 21 Jun 1948; Lt Col Bert W Marshall Jr, Aug 1948; Lt Col Archie M Burke, 13 May 1949; Lt Col Jack D Dale Jr, Nov 1949; Col William P McBride, 22 Feb 1951; Lt Col Homer M Cox, May 1951; Col John C Habecker, 25 Jun 1951; Col John R Propst, 6 Jun 1952; Lt Col Albert S Aiken, Feb 1955; Col Maurice L Martin, Jun 1955; Col Raymond M Gehrig, Aug 1955–.

CAMPAIGNS. *World War II:* East Indies; Air Offensive, Japan; China Defensive; Papua; New Guinea; Bismarck Archipelago; Western Pacific; Leyte; Luzon; Ryukyus; China Offensive. *Korean War:* UN Defensive; UN Offensive; CCF Intervention; 1st UN Counteroffensive; CCF Spring Offensive.

DECORATIONS. Distinguished Unit Citation: Papua, 23 Jul 1942–23 Jan 1943. Philippine Presidential Unit Citation. Republic of Korea Presidential Unit Citation: 7 Sep 1950–7 Feb 1951.

INSIGNE. *Shield:* Azure, a dexter cubit arm or grasping a dagger point to base gules. *Motto:* ATTACK TO DEFEND (Approved 21 Feb 1941.)

36th FIGHTER GROUP

Constituted as 36th Pursuit Group (Interceptor) on 22 Dec 1939. *Activated* on 1 Feb 1940. Trained with P-36's. Moved to Puerto Rico in Jan 1941. Equipped with P-39 and P-40 aircraft. Served as part of the defense force for the Caribbean area and Panama Canal, and flew antisubmarine patrols. *Redesignated* 36th Fighter Group in May 1942. Returned to the US, May-Jun 1943. Trained with P-47's.

Moved to England, Mar-Apr 1944. Assigned to Ninth AF. Served in combat in the European theater from May 1944 to May 1945. Operated primarily as a fighter-bomber organization, strafing and dive-bombing armored vehicles, trains, bridges, buildings, factories, troop concentrations, gun emplacements, airfields, and other targets. Also flew some escort missions. Began operations from England in May 1944 with armed reconnaissance, escort, and interdictory missions in preparation for the invasion of Normandy. Participated in the invasion in Jun 1944 by patrolling the air over the landing zone and by flying close-support and interdictory missions. Moved to France, Jul-Aug 1944. Supported the breakthrough at St Lo in Jul and the thrust of Third Army toward Germany in Aug and Sep. Received a DUC for operations on 1 Sep 1944 when, in a series of missions, the group attacked German columns south of the Loire in order to disrupt the enemy's retreat across central France to Dijon. Moved to Belgium in Oct and supported Ninth Army. Participated in the Battle of the Bulge, Dec 1944-Jan 1945, by flying armed reconnaissance and close-support missions. Aided First Army's push across the Roer River in Feb 1945. Supported operations at the Remagen bridgehead and during the airborne assault across the Rhine in Mar. Received second DUC for performance on 12 Apr 1945 when the group, operating through intense antiaircraft fire, relentlessly attacked airfields in southern Germany, destroying a large hangar and numerous aircraft. Remained in Europe for several months after V-E Day.

Transferred, without personnel and equipment, to the US in Feb 1946, the group's squadrons being inactivated in Mar. Headquarters was transferred, without personnel and equipment, to the Panama Canal Zone in Sep, and the squadrons were activated in Oct. Equipped with P-47's; converted to F-80's in Dec 1947. Moved to Germany, Jul-Aug 1948, and became part of United States Air Forces in Europe. *Redesignated* 36th Fighter-Bomber Group in Jan 1950, and 36th Fighter-Day Group in Aug 1954. Equipped successively with F–80, F–84, F–86, and F–100 aircraft after arriving in Europe in 1948.

SQUADRONS. *22d:* 1940–1946, 1946–. *23d:* 1940–1946, 1946–. *32d:* 1940–1943; 1955–. *53d:* 1943–1946, 1946–.

STATIONS. Langley Field, Va, 1 Feb 1940–2 Jan 1941; Losey Field, PR, Jan 1941–May 1943; Morrison Field, Fla, May 1943; Mitchel Field, NY, c. 3 Jun 1943; Charleston, SC, 23 June 1943; Alamogordo AAFld, NM, Sep 1943; Scribner AAFld, Neb, Nov 1943–Mar 1944; Kingsnorth, England, Apr 1944; Brucheville, France, Jul 1944; Le Mans, France, c. 23 Aug 1944; Athis, France, Sep 1944; Juvincourt, France, c. 1 Oct 1944; Le Culot, Belgium, c. 23 Oct 1944; Aachen, Germany, 28 Mar 1945; Niedermennig, Germany, c. 8 Apr 1945; Kassel/Rothwesten, Germany, c. 21 Apr 1945–15 Feb 1946; Bolling Field, DC, 15 Feb–Sep 1946; Howard Field, CZ, Oct 1946–Jul 1948; Furstenfeldbruck AFB, Germany, Aug 1948; Bitburg AB, Germany, 17 Nov 1952–.

COMMANDERS. Lt Col Ned Schramm, c. 1 Feb 1940; Maj Charles A Harrington, c. 15 Jul 1941; Lt Col Glenn O Barcus, c. 1 Nov 1941; Maj Richard P Klocko, c. 20 Feb 1942; Maj James B League Jr, c. 18 Jul 1942; Maj William L Curry, c. 1 Sep 1942; Maj [Earl H(?)] Dunham, c. 1 Oct 1942; Lt Col William L Curry, c. 14 Jan 1943; Lt Col Van H Slayden, 12 Jan 1944; Lt Col Paul P Douglas Jr, Apr 1945; Lt Col John L Wright, 30 Jun 1945; Maj Arthur W Holderness Jr, c. 25 Sep 1945; Lt Col William T McBride, 9 Nov 1945– unkn; Col Henry R Spicer, c. 15 Oct 1946– unkn; Col Hubert Zemke, 1949; Col William A Daniel, c. 1 Dec 1949; Lt Col George F Ceuleers, Dec 1950; Col George T Lee, Mar 1951; Col Seth J McKee, Dec 1951; Col Marvin E Childs, May 1953; Col Edward A McGough III, Dec 1954–.

CAMPAIGNS. Antisubmarine, American Theater; Air Offensive, Europe; Normandy; Northern France; Rhineland; Ardennes-Alsace; Central Europe.

DECORATIONS. Distinguished Unit Citations: France, 1 Sep 1944; Germany, 12 Apr 1945. Cited in the Order of the Day, Belgian Army: 1 Oct 1944–; 18 Dec 1944– 15 Jan 1945. Belgian Fourragere.

INSIGNE. *Shield:* Or, an arrow point palewise gules on a chief azure a wing argent. (Approved 19 Jun 1940.)

37th FIGHTER GROUP

Constituted as 37th Pursuit Group (Interceptor) on 22 Dec 1939. *Activated* in the Panama Canal Zone on 1 Feb 1940. *Redesignated* 37th Fighter Group in May 1942. Served as part of the defense force for the Panama Canal. Equipped first with P–26's, later with P–40's. *Disbanded* in the Canal Zone on 1 Nov 1943.

Reconstituted and *redesignated* 37th Fighter-Bomber Group, on 3 Mar 1953. *Activated* in the US on 8 Apr 1953. As-

signed to Tactical Air Command. *Inactivated* on 25 Jun 1953.

SQUADRONS. *28th:* 1940–1943; 1953. *30th:* 1940–1943; 1953. *31st:* 1940–1943. *33d:* 1953.

STATIONS. Albrook Field, CZ, 1 Feb 1940; Howard Field, CZ, 30 Sep–1 Nov 1943. Clovis AFB, NM, 8 Apr–25 Jun 1953.

COMMANDERS. Capt Russell E Randall, 1 Feb 1940; Maj Milo N Clark, 27 May 1940; Lt Col Morley F Slaght, 1942; Maj Ernest H Beverly, 2 Sep 1942–unkn. Col George W Larson, 1953.

CAMPAIGNS. American Theater.

DECORATIONS. None.

INSIGNE. *Shield:* Azure, a saltire or. *Crest:* On a wreath of the colors, or and azure, a griffin sejant azure armed and winged or. *Motto:* DEFENDERS OF THE CROSSROADS. (Approved 23 Jun 1941.)

38th BOMBARDMENT GROUP

Constituted as 38th Bombardment Group (Medium) on 20 Nov 1940. *Activated* on 15 Jan 1941. Trained with B–18, B–25, and B–26 aircraft. The ground echelon moved to Australia, Jan–Feb 1942, while the air echelon remained in the US for further training. Air echelons of two squadrons arrived in Hawaii in May 1942 and took part in the Battle of Midway; they did not rejoin the group and eventually were reassigned. Air echelons of the other squadrons arrived in Australia in Aug 1942. Assigned to Fifth AF and equipped with B–25's, the group operated from bases in Australia, New Guinea, and Biak, Sep 1942–Oct 1944, attacking Japanese airfields and shipping and supporting ground forces in New Guinea and the Bismarck Archipelago. Maj Ralph Cheli was awarded the Medal of Honor for action on 18 Aug 1943: while leading the 405th squadron to attack a heavily defended airdrome on New Guinea, his plane was severely hit by enemy fire;

rather than disrupt the formation, Maj Cheli remained in position and led the attack on the target before his bomber crashed into the sea. The group was awarded a DUC for bombing and strafing Japanese troops and fortifications on Cape Gloucester, New Britain, Dec 1943, preparatory to the Allied invasion. Received another DUC for two missions over New Guinea, 16 and 17 Jun 1944, against Japanese airfields, merchant ships, and naval vessels. Moved to the Moluccas in Oct 1944 and bombed airfields, ground installations, harbors, and shipping in the southern Philippines in support of the US invasion of Leyte. Struck a large enemy convoy in Ormoc Bay in Nov 1944 to prevent the landing of reinforcements, being awarded a DUC for the mission. After moving to the Philippines in Jan 1945, supported US ground forces on Luzon, bombed industries on Formosa, and attacked shipping along the China coast. Stationed temporarily on Palawan in Jun 1945 for participation in the preinvasion bombing of Japanese installations on Borneo. Moved to Okinawa in Jul 1945 and conducted several attacks on industries, railways, and shipping in southern Japan. Moved to Japan in Nov 1945 as part of Far East Air Forces. *Redesignated* 38th Bombardment Group (Light) in May 1946. Equipped with A–26 aircraft. *Inactivated* in the Far East on 1 Apr 1949.

Activated in France on 1 Jan 1953. Assigned to United States Air Forces in Europe. Equipped with B–26 and later with B–57 aircraft. *Redesignated* 38th

Bombardment Group (Tactical) in Oct 1955.

SQUADRONS. *69th:* 1941–1943. *70th:* 1941–1943. *71st:* 1941–1949; 1953–. *89th:* 1946–1949. *405th:* 1942–1949; 1953–. *822d:* 1943–1946; 1953–. *823d:* 1943–1946.

STATIONS. Langley Field, Va, 15 Jan 1941; Jackson AAB, Miss, c. 5 Jun 1941–18 Jan 1942; Doomben Field, Australia, 25 Feb 1942; Ballarat, Australia, 8 Mar 1942; Amberley Field, Australia, 30 Apr 1942; Eagle Farms, Australia, c. 10 Jun 1942; Breddan Field, Australia, 7 Aug 1942; Townsville, Australia, 30 Sep 1942; Port Moresby, New Guinea, Oct 1942; Nadzab, New Guinea, 4 Mar 1944; Biak, 1 Oct 1944; Morotai, 15 Oct 1944; Lingayen, Luzon, c. 29 Jan 1945; Okinawa, 25 Jul 1945; Itazuke, Japan, c. 22 Nov 1945; Itami, Japan, 26 Oct 1946–1 Apr 1949. Laon AB, France, 1 Jan 1953–.

COMMANDERS. Lt Col Robert D Knapp, 15 Jan 1941; Col Fay R Upthegrove, c. 18 Jan 1942–unkn; Lt Col Brian O'Neill, 19 Oct 1942; Lt Col Lawrence Tanberg, 1 Oct 1943; Lt Col Carl C Lausman, Jul 1944; Maj Howard M Paquin, 18 Aug 1944; Col Edward M Gavin, 9 Nov 1944; Lt Col Edwin H Hawes, 16 Mar 1945; Lt Col Vernon D Torgerson, 9 Aug 1945; Lt Col Bruce T Marston, 12 Sep 1945; Lt Col Joseph P Gentile, 17 Mar 1946; Lt Col John P Crocker, 16 May 1946; Col C J Bondley Jr, 2 Jul 1946; Col Dale D Brannon, 12 Nov 1946; Col C J Bondley Jr, 13 Dec 1946; Col John J Hutchison, 25 Jan 1947; Col Donald D Fitzgerald, 26 Feb 1948; Col Preston P Pender, 7 May 1948;

Lt Col Charles R Johnson, 18 Jul 1948–1 Apr 1949. Lt Col Max H Mortensen, 1 Jan 1953; Col Glen W Clark, 16 Mar 1953; Col Broadus B Taylor, 6 Jun 1955–.

CAMPAIGNS. Air Offensive, Japan; China Defensive; Papua; New Guinea; Bismarck Archipelago; Western Pacific; Leyte; Luzon; Southern Philippines; China Offensive.

DECORATIONS. Distinguished Unit Citations: Papua, [Sep] 1942–23 Jan 1943; New Britain, 24–26 Dec 1943; New Guinea, 16–17 Jun 1944; Leyte, 10 Nov 1944. Philippine Presidential Unit Citation.

INSIGNE. *Shield:* Azure a winged sword point downward argent, the hilt and pommel charged with a torteau, a pomeis, and a bezant, a fleur-de-lis fretting the blade or, between two cloud formations of the second issuing from dexter and sinister base. (Approved 16 Apr 1954.)

39th BOMBARDMENT GROUP

Constituted as 39th Bombardment Group (Heavy) on 20 Nov 1940. *Activated* on 15 Jan 1941. Assigned to Second AF. Equipped with B–17's. Patrolled the northwest coast of the US after the nation entered the war. Equipped with B–24's in 1942. Served as an operational training and later as a replacement training unit. *Inactivated* on 1 Apr 1944.

Redesignated 39th Bombardment Group (Very Heavy). *Activated* on 1 Apr 1944. Trained with B–29's. Moved to Guam early in 1945 for duty with Twentieth AF. Bombed enemy-held Maug early in Apr.

1945. Conducted its first mission against the Japanese home islands by hitting the Hodagaya chemical plant at Koriyama on 12 Apr. Supported the Allied invasion of Okinawa, Apr–May 1945, by attacking airfields that served as bases for kamikaze pilots. Bombed military and industrial targets in Japan and participated in incendiary raids on urban areas from mid-May until the end of the war. Received a DUC for an attack against the Otake oil refinery and storage area on Honshu in May 1945. Received second DUC for bombing industrial and dock areas in Yokohama and manufacturing districts in Tokyo, 23–29 May 1945. Dropped food and supplies to Allied prisoners and took part in show-of-force missions over Japan after V–J Day. Returned to the US, Nov–Dec 1945. *Inactivated* on 27 Dec 1945.

SQUADRONS. *60th:* 1941–1944; 1944–1945. *61st:* 1941–1944; 1944–1945. *62d:* 1941–1944; 1944–1945. *402d:* 1942–1944; 1944.

STATIONS. Ft Douglas, Utah, 15 Jan 1941; Geiger Field, Wash, 2 Jul 1941; Davis-Monthan Field, Ariz, 5 Feb 1942–1 Apr 1944. Smoky Hill AAFld, Kan, 1 Apr 1944–8 Jan 1945; North Field, Guam, 18 Feb–17 Nov 1945; Camp Anza, Calif, 15–27 Dec 1945.

COMMANDERS. Maj Newton Longfellow, 15 Jan 1941; Capt Maurice A Preston, 1 Feb 1941; Lt Col Elmer E Adler, 17 Mar 1941; Capt George W Hansen, 13 May 1941; Maj Charles B Overacker Jr, 12 Nov 1941; Lt Col George W Hansen, 25 Jan 1942; Col James H Wallace, 16 Feb 1942; Col Fay R Upthegrove, 12 Jul 1942; Lt

Col Samuel C Mitchell, 13 Sep 1942; Maj Marden M Munn, 17 Dec 1942; Lt Col Horace D Aynesworth, 1 Mar 1943; Lt Col Charles A Watt, 1 Jul 1943; Lt Col Frank R Pancake, 25 Nov 1943; Col Clyde K Rich, 1 Dec 1943–1 Apr 1944. Capt Claude J Hilton, 28 Apr 1944; Maj Gordon R Willis, 6 May 1944; Maj Campbell Weir, 11 May 1944; Lt Col Robert W Strong Jr, 10 Jun 1944; Col Potter B Paige, 15 Jun 1944; Col John G Fowler, 22 Feb 1945; Col George W Mundy, 16 Mar 1945; Col James E Roberts, 16 Aug 1945; Lt Col James C Thompson, 9 Oct 1945; Col Robert J Mason, 13 Oct 1945–unkn.

CAMPAIGNS. American Theater; Air Offensive, Japan; Western Pacific.

DECORATIONS. Distinguished Unit Citations: Japan, 10 May 1945; Tokyo and Yokohama, Japan, 23–29 May 1945.

INSIGNE. None.

40th BOMBARDMENT GROUP

Constituted as 40th Bombardment Group (Medium) on 22 Nov 1940. *Activated* in Puerto Rico on 1 Apr 1941. *Redesignated* 40th Bombardment Group (Heavy) in May 1942. Trained and patrolled the Caribbean area, using B–17 and B–26 aircraft. Operated first from Puerto Rico and later from the Panama Canal Zone.

Moved to the US in Jun 1943. *Redesignated* 40th Bombardment Group (Very Heavy) in Nov 1943. After training with B–29's, moved to India, via Africa, Mar–Jun 1944. Assigned to Twentieth AF in

Jun 1944. Transported supplies over the Hump to staging bases in China before entering combat with a strike on railroad shops at Bangkok, Thailand, on 5 Jun 1944. On 15 Jun participated in the first AAF attack on Japan since the Doolittle raid in 1942. Operating from bases in India, and at times staging through fields in China, the group struck such targets as transportation centers, naval installations, iron works, and aircraft plants in Burma, Thailand, China, Japan, Indonesia, and Formosa, receiving a DUC for bombing iron and steel works at Yawata, Japan, on 20 Aug 1944. From a staging field in Ceylon, it mined waters near the port of Palembang, Sumatra, in Aug 1944.

Moved to Tinian, Feb–Apr 1945, for further operations against Japan. Made daylight attacks from high altitude on strategic targets, participated in incendiary raids on urban areas, and dropped mines in Japanese shipping lanes. Received a DUC for attacking naval aircraft factories at Kure, oil storage facilities at Oshima, and the industrial area of Nagoya, in May

1945. Raided light metal industries in Osaka in Jul 1945, being awarded another DUC for this mission. After V–J Day, dropped food and supplies to Allied prisoners in Japan, Korea, and Formosa, and took part in show-of-force missions. Returned to the US in Nov 1945. Assigned to Strategic Air Command on 21 Mar 1946. *Inactivated* on 1 Oct 1946.

SQUADRONS. *25th:* 1943–1946. *29th:* 1941–1943. *44th:* 1941–1946. *45th:* 1941–1946. *74th:* 1942–1943. *343d:* 1945–1946. *395th:* 1942–1946.

STATIONS. Borinquen Field, PR, 1 Apr 1941; Howard Field, CZ, 16 Jun 1942; Albrook Field, CZ, 16 Sep 1942; Howard Field, CZ, 3–15 Jun 1943; Pratt AAFld, Kan, 1 Jul 1943–12 Mar 1944; Chakulia, India, 2 Apr 1944–25 Feb 1945; West Field, Tinian, 4 Apr–7 Nov 1945; March Field, Calif, 27 Nov 1945; Davis-Monthan Field, Ariz, 8 May–1 Oct 1946.

COMMANDERS. Lt Col William B Sousa, 1 Apr 1941; Maj George W McGregor, 29 Apr 1941; Col Ivan M Palmer, 26 Nov 1941; Col Vernon C Smith, 19 Jan 1943; Col Henry K Mooney, 16 May 1943; Col Lewis R Parker, 1 Jul 1943; Lt Col Louis E Coira, 24 Feb 1944; Col Leonard F Harman, 10 Apr 1944; Col William H Blanchard, 4 Aug 1944; Col Henry R Sullivan, 16 Feb 1945; Col William K Skaer, 27 Feb 1945; Lt Col Oscar R Schaaf, 21 Mar 1946; Col Alva L Harvey, 4 May 1946; Lt Col Oscar R Schaaf, 21 Aug 1946; 1st Lt William F Seith, 21 Sep–1 Oct 1946.

CAMPAIGNS. Antisubmarine, American Theater; India-Burma; Air Offensive, Japan; China Defensive; Western Pacific; Central Burma.

DECORATIONS. Distinguished Unit Citations: Yawata, Japan, 20 Aug 1944; Japan, 5–14 May 1945; Japan, 24 Jul 1945.

INSIGNE. *Shield:* Azure, on a bomb burst proper fimbriated argent four drop bombs in cross or. (Approved 28 Mar 1942. This insigne was replaced 6 Jan 1954.)

41st BOMBARDMENT GROUP

Constituted as 41st Bombardment Group (Medium) on 20 Nov 1940. *Activated* on 15 Jan 1941. Trained with B–18's and A–29's; later equipped with B–25's. Patrolled the west coast during 1942 and 1943. Moved to Hawaii in Oct 1943 and assigned to Seventh AF. Completed final training and moved to Tarawa in the Central Pacific in Dec 1943. Attacked enemy installations, airfields, and shipping in the Marshalls in preparation for the invasion by US forces, and after Feb 1944 staged through captured fields on Eniwetok to attack shipping in the Caroline Islands. In Apr 1944 moved to Makin where its missions were directed primarily against shipping and bypassed islands in the Marshalls and Carolines. Returned to Hawaii in Oct 1944 for training with rockets and new B–25's. Moved to Okinawa, May–Jun 1945. Bombed airfields, railways, and harbor facilities on Kyushu until Aug 1945. Also flew some missions against airfields in China. Moved to Manila in Dec 1945. *Inactivated* in the Philippines on 27 Jan 1946.

SQUADRONS. *46th:* 1941–1943. *47th:* 1941–1946. *48th:* 1941–1946. *76th:* 1943. *396th:* 1942–1946. *406th:* 1943. *820th:* 1943–1946.

STATIONS. March Field, Calif, 15 Jan 1941; Tucson, Ariz, May 1941; Muroc, Calif, c. 10 Dec 1941; Hammer Field, Calif, Feb 1942–29 Sep 1943; Hickam Field, TH, 16 Oct 1943; Tarawa, 17 Dec 1943; Makin, 24 Apr 1944; Wheeler Field, TH, 14 Oct 1944; Okinawa, 7 Jun 1945; Manila, Dec 1945–27 Jan 1946.

COMMANDERS. Capt Lawrence H Douthit, 15 Jan 1941; Lt Col Archibald Y Smith, 2 Jun 1941; Lt Col Charles B Dougher, 1942; Col Murray A Bywater, 18 Aug 1943–c. Nov 1945.

CAMPAIGNS. Antisubmarine, American Theater; Air Offensive, Japan; Eastern Mandates; Western Pacific; Ryukyus; China Offensive.

DECORATIONS. None.

INSIGNE. None.

42d BOMBARDMENT GROUP

Constituted as 42d Bombardment Group (Medium) on 20 Nov 1940. *Activated* on 15 Jan 1941. Trained with B–18, B–25, and B–26 aircraft. Patrolled the west coast during 1942. Moved to the Pacific theater, Mar–Apr 1943, and assigned to Thirteenth AF. Entered combat in Jun 1943, using B–25's and operating from bases in the Solomon Islands. Attacked Japanese airfields, personnel areas, gun positions, and shipping in the central Solomons. Engaged primarily in the neutralization of enemy airfields and harbor facilities on New Britain from Jan to Jul 1944, but also supported ground forces on Bougainville and attacked shipping in the northern Solomons and the Bismarcks. Later, beginning in Aug 1944, bombed airfields and installations on New Guinea, Celebes, and Halmahera, and flew photographic reconnaissance missions, while operating from bases in New Guinea and Morotai. Moved to the Philippines in Mar 1945. Attacked shipping along the China coast, struck targets in French Indochina, bombed airfields and installations in the Philippines, and supported ground operations on Mindanao. Also supported Australian forces on Borneo during May and Jun 1945, receiving a DUC for its pre-invasion bombing of Balikpapan, 23–30 Jun. Brought its combat service to an end, Jul and Aug 1945, by attacking isolated Japanese units on Luzon. Ferried troops and equipment to Manila after the war. Moved to Japan in Jan 1946 as part of the occupation force. *Inactivated* in Japan on 10 May 1946.

SQUADRONS. *69th:* 1943–1946. *70th:* 1943–1946. *75th:* 1941–1946. *76th:* 1941–1943. *77th:* 1941–1942. *100th:* 1945. *390th:* 1942–1946. *406th:* 1942–1943.

STATIONS. Ft Douglas, Utah, 15 Jan 1941; Boise, Idaho, c. 3 Jun 1941; Mc-Chord Field, Wash, c. 18 Jan 1942–15 Mar 1943; Fiji Islands, 22 Apr 1943; Guadalcanal, 6 Jun 1943; Russell Islands, Oct 1943; Sterling, Solomon Islands, 20 Jan 1944; Hollandia, Aug 1944; Sansapor, New Guinea, Sep 1944; Morotai, Feb 1945; Puerto Princesa, Palawan, Mar 1945; Itami, Japan, Jan–10 May 1946.

COMMANDERS. Col John V Hart, 15 Jan 1941; Col Harry E Wilson, Jul 1942; Maj Edwin J Latoszewski, 14 Dec 1942; Lt Col Guy L Hudson, Jan 1943; Col Harry E Wilson, 22 Apr 1943; Col Charles C Kegelman, 16 Nov 1944; Lt Col Harry C Harvey, 15 Mar 1945; Col Paul F Helmick, 10 May 1945; Lt Col Harry E Goldsworthy, Sep 1945; Maj Thomas B Waddel, Mar–10 May 1946.

CAMPAIGNS. Antisubmarine, American Theater; China Defensive; New Guinea; Northern Solomons; Bismarck Archipelago; Western Pacific; Leyte; Luzon; Southern Philippines; China Offensive.

DECORATIONS. Distinguished Unit Citation: Balikpapan, Borneo, 23–30 Jun 1945. Philippine Presidential Unit Citation.

INSIGNE. *Shield:* Azure, on a bend engrailed or, four annulets gules, between two aerial bombs palewise of the second. *Motto:* AETHERA NOBIS—The Skies for Us. (Approved 11 Mar 1942.)

43d BOMBARDMENT GROUP

WILLING, ABLE, READY

Constituted as 43d Bombardment Group (Heavy) on 20 Nov 1940. *Activated* on 15 Jan 1941. Trained with B–17, B–18, A–29, and LB–30 aircraft. Flew some antisubmarine patrols along the New England coast, Dec 1941–Feb 1942.

Moved to the Southwest Pacific, via Capetown, Feb–Mar 1942. Became part of Fifth AF. Equipped first with B–17's, but converted to B–24's, May–Sep 1943. Operated from Australia, New Guinea, and Owi Island, Aug 1942–Nov 1944, making numerous attacks on Japanese shipping in the Netherlands East Indies and the Bismarck Archipelago. Experimented with skip bombing and used this method for some shipping strikes, including attacks on Japanese vessels during the Battle of the Bismarck Sea, 2–4 Mar 1943; received a DUC for participation in this latter action in which repeated air attacks destroyed a large enemy convoy carrying reinforcements to New Guinea. Other operations during this period included support for ground forces on New Guinea; attacks on airfields and installations in New Guinea, the Bismarck Archipelago, Celebes, Halmahera, Yap, Palau, and the southern Philippines; and long-range raids against oil refineries on Ceram and Borneo. Capt Jay Zeamer Jr, pilot, and 2d Lt Joseph R Sarnoski, bombardier, each won the Medal of Honor for action during a photographic mapping mission over the Solomon Islands on 16 Jun 1943: when the mission was nearly completed, their aircraft was assaulted by about 20 interceptors; although painfully wounded, Lt Sarnoski remained at the nose guns and fired at the enemy until he died at his post; sustaining severe injuries, Capt Zeamer maneuvered the plane until the enemy had broken combat, then directed the flight to a base more than 500 miles away. After moving to the Philippines in Nov 1944, the group atttacked shipping along the Asiatic coast; struck industries, airfields, and installations in China and Formosa; and supported ground forces on Luzon. Moved to Ie Shima in Jul 1945 and conducted missions against airfields and railways in Japan and against shipping in the Inland Sea and the Sea of Japan. Returned to the Philippines in in Dec 1945. *Inactivated* on 29 Apr 1946.

Redesignated 43d Bombardment Group (Very Heavy). *Activated* in the US on 1 Oct 1946. Assigned to Strategic Air Command. *Redesignated* 43d Bombardment Group (Medium) in Jul 1948. Equipped first with B–29's, then with B–50's. Trained and conducted long-range test missions, including the first nonstop flight around the world (26 Feb–2 Mar 1949), accomplished in "Lucky Lady II," a B–50 commanded by Capt James G Gallagher. *Inactivated* on 16 Jun 1952.

SQUADRONS. *63d:* 1941–1946; 1946–1952. *64th:* 1941–1946; 1946–1952. *65th:* 1941–1946; 1946–1952. *403d:* 1942–1946.

STATIONS. Langley Field, Va, 15 Jan 1941; Bangor, Maine, 28 Aug 1941–17 Feb 1942; Sydney, Australia, 28 Mar 1942; Torrens Creek, Australia, c. 1 Aug 1942; Port Moresby, New Guinea, 14 Sep 1942; Dobodura, New Guinea, 10 Dec 1943; Nadzab, New Guinea, 4 Mar 1944; Owi, Schouten Islands, 2 Jul 1944; Tacloban, Leyte, c. 15 Nov 1944; Clark Field, Luzon, 16 Mar 1945; Ie Shima, 26 Jul 1945; Ft William McKinley, Luzon, 10 Dec 1945–29 Apr 1946. Davis-Monthan Field, Ariz, 1 Oct 1946–16 Jun 1952.

COMMANDERS. Lt Col Harold D Smith, 15 Jan 1941; Lt Col Francis B Valentine, 1 Mar 1941; Maj Conrad H Diehl Jr, 18 Feb 1942; Col Roger M Ramey, 21 Oct 1942; Lt Col John A Roberts, 30 Mar 1943; Col Harry J Hawthorne, 24 May 1943; Lt Col Edward W Scott Jr, 18 Nov 1943; Col Harry J Hawthorne, 8 Feb 1944; Col James T Pettus Jr, 18 Sep 1944; Maj Paul B Hansen, 8 Sep 1945–unkn. Col James C Selser

Jr, 5 Oct 1946; Col William E Eubank Jr, Apr 1948; Col Dalene Bailey, Jul 1948; Col Alvan N Moore, 3 Jan 1949–16 Jun 1952.

CAMPAIGNS. Antisubmarine, American Theater; Air Offensive, Japan; China Defensive; Papua; New Guinea; Bismarck Archipelago; Western Pacific; Leyte; Luzon; Southern Philippines; Ryukyus; China Offensive.

DECORATIONS. Distinguished Unit Citations: Papua, [Aug] 1942–23 Jan 1943; Bismarck Sea, 2–4 Mar 1943. Philippine Presidential Unit Citation.

INSIGNE. *Shield:* Per fess nebuly or and azure, a drop bomb counterchanged. *Motto:* WILLING, ABLE, READY. (Approved 31 Jan 1942.)

44th BOMBARDMENT GROUP

Constituted as 44th Bombardment Group (Heavy) on 20 Nov 1940. *Activated* on 15 Jan 1941. Trained with B–24's. Became an operational training unit in Feb 1942. Also served on anti-

submarine duty. In Jul 1942 began intensive preparations for combat. Moved to England, Aug–Oct 1942, for service with Eighth AF. Operations consisted primarily of assaults against strategic targets in France, Belgium, Holland, Germany, Italy Rumania, Austria, Poland, and Sicily. Pounded submarine installations, industrial establishments, airfields, harbors, shipyards, and other objectives in France and Germany, Nov 1942–Jun 1943. Received a DUC for an extremely hazardous mission against naval installations at Kiel on 14 May 1943: with its B–24's carrying incendiaries to be dropped after three B–17 groups had released high explosive bombs, the 44th flew in the wake of the main formation; thus the B–24's were particularly vulnerable because they had no protection from fire power of the main force, and this vulnerability increased when the group had to open its own formation for the attack; but the 44th blanketed the target with incendiaries in spite of the concentrated flak and continuous interceptor attacks it encountered. Late in Jun 1943 a large detachment moved to North Africa to help facilitate the invasion of Sicily by bombing airfields and marshalling yards in Italy. The detachment also participated in the famous low-level raid on the Ploesti oil fields on 1 Aug 1943. The group was awarded a DUC for its part in this raid and its commander, Col Leon Johnson, was awarded the Medal of Honor for his daring and initiative in leading his men into smoke, flame, and alerted fighter and antiaircraft opposition over the target, which already had been bombed in error by another group. Before returning to England at the end of Aug, the detachment bombed an aircraft factory in Austria and supported ground forces in Sicily. In Sep the group struck airfields in Holland and France and convoys in the North Sea. Also in Sep, a detachment was sent to North Africa to support the Salerno operations. The detachment returned to England in Oct and from Nov 1943 to Apr 1945, the entire group carried out operations against targets in western Europe, concentrating on airfields, oil installations, and marshalling yards. Took part in the intensive campaign of heavy bombers against the German aircraft industry during Big Week, 20–25 Feb 1944. Sometimes flew support and interdictory missions. Struck airfields, railroads, and V-weapon sites in preparation for the Normandy invasion; supported the invasion in Jun 1944 by attacking strong points in the beachhead area and transportation targets behind the front lines. Aided the Caen offensive and the St Lo breakthrough in Jul. Dropped food, ammunition, and other supplies to troops engaged in the airborne attack on Holland in Sep. Helped to check the enemy offensive during the Battle of the Bulge, Dec 1944–Jan 1945, by striking bridges, tunnels, choke points, rail and road junctions, and communications in the battle area. Attacked airfields and transportation in support of the advance into Germany, and flew a resupply mission during the airborne assault across the Rhine in Mar 1945. Flew

last combat mission on 25 Apr 1945. Returned to the US in Jun 1945. *Redesignated* 44th Bombardment Group (Very Heavy) in Aug 1945. Trained with B–29's. Assigned to Strategic Air Command on 21 Mar 1946. *Inactivated* on 12 Jul 1946.

Activated on 1 Jul 1947. Assigned to Strategic Air Command. Not manned during 1947 and 1948. *Inactivated* on 6 Sep 1948.

Redesignated 44th Bombardment Group (Medium). *Activated* on 2 Jan 1951. Assigned to Strategic Air Command and equipped with B–29's. *Inactivated* on 16 Jun 1952.

SQUADRONS. 66th: 1941–1946; 1947–1948; 1951–1952. 67th: 1941–1946; 1947–1948; 1951–1952. 68th: 1941–1946; 1947–1948; 1951–1952. 404th: 1942. 506th: 1943–1946.

STATIONS. MacDill Field, Fla, 15 Jan 1941; Barksdale Field, La, Feb 1942; Will Rogers Field, Okla, Jul–c. 28 Aug 1942; Shipham, England, Oct 1942–c. 15 Jun 1945; Sioux Falls AAFld, SD, c. 27 Jun 1945; Great Bend AAFld, Kan, 25 Jul 1945; Smoky Hill AAFld, Kan, 14 Dec 1945–12 Jul 1946. Andrews Field, Md, 1 Jul 1947–6 Sep 1948. March AFB, Calif, 2 Jan 1951; Lake Charles AFB, La, c. 1 Aug 1951–16 Jun 1952.

COMMANDERS. Lt Col Melvin B Asp, c. 15 Jan 1941; Lt Col Hugo P Rush, May 1941; Col F H Robinson, c. 1 Apr 1942; Col Leon W Johnson, c. 15 Jan 1943; Lt Col James T Posey, c. 3 Sep 1943; Col Frederick R Dent, Dec 1943; Col John H

Gibson, c. 1 Apr 1944; Col Eugene H Snavely, Aug 1944; Col Vernon C Smith, Apr 1945–unkn; Lt Col Henry C Coles, c. 6 Aug 1945; Col William J Cain Jr, c. 30 Aug 1945; Lt Col James F Starkey, c. 8 Jan 1946–unkn. Unkn, 1947–1948. Col Howell M Estes Jr, Feb 1951; Col Carlos J Cochrane, 7 Mar 1951–16 Jun 1952.

CAMPAIGNS. Antisubmarine, American Theater; Air Combat, EAME Theater; Air Offensive, Europe; Sicily; Naples-Foggia; Normandy; Northern France; Rhineland; Ardennes-Alsace; Central Europe.

DECORATIONS. Distinguished Unit Citations: Kiel, Germany, 14 May 1943; Ploesti, Rumania, 1 Aug 1943.

INSIGNE. *Shield:* Azure, a bomb, point downward, between eight stars, four and four, or, all bendwise. *Motto:* AGGRESSOR BEWARE. (Approved 15 May 1951.)

45th BOMBARDMENT GROUP

Constituted as 45th Bombardment Group (Light) on 20 Nov 1940. *Activated* on 15 Jan 1941. Trained with B–18's and A–20's. *Redesignated* 45th Bombardment Group (Medium) in Dec 1941. Flew patrol and search missions off the Atlantic and Gulf coasts, serving with First AF and later with AAF Antisubmarine Command. Used B–18, B–34, and DB–7 aircraft for operations. *Inactivated* on 8 Dec 1942.

SQUADRONS. *7th* Antisubmarine (formerly 78th Bombardment): 1941–1942.

8th Antisubmarine (formerly 79th Bombardment): 1941–1942. *9th* Antisubmarine (formerly 80th Bombardment): 1941–1942. *10th* Antisubmarine (formerly 433d Bombardment): 1941–1942.

STATIONS. Savannah, Ga, 15 Jan 1941; Manchester, NH, 18 Jun 1941; Dover, Del, 16 May 1942; Miami, Fla, 1 Aug–8 Dec 1942.

COMMANDERS. Lt Col James E Duke Jr, Jan 1941; Lt Col George A McHenry, 1 Apr 1941; Lt Col Charles W Haas, c. Sep–Dec 1942.

CAMPAIGNS. Antisubmarine, American Theater.

DECORATIONS. None.

INSIGNE. *Shield:* Azure, three aerial bombs or, a chief potentee of the last. *Motto:* DE ASTRA—From the Stars. (Approved 6 Jan 1942.)

46th BOMBARDMENT GROUP

Constituted as 46th Bombardment Group (Light) on 20 Nov 1940. *Activated* on 15 Jan 1941. Trained with A–20's and

CUSTOS LIBERTATE

participated in maneuvers. Flew some antisubmarine patrols over the Gulf of Mexico early in 1942. Assigned to Second AF in Aug 1942 and to Third AF in Nov 1942. Served as an operational training unit until late in 1943, then became a replacement training unit. *Disbanded* on 1 May 1944.

SQUADRONS. *50th:* 1941–1944. *51st:* 1941–1944. *53d:* 1941–1944. *87th:* 1941–1944.

STATIONS. Savannah, Ga, 15 Jan 1941; Bowman Field, Ky, 20 May 1941; Barksdale Field, La, Feb 1942; Galveston Mun Aprt, Tex, c. 1 Apr 1942; Blythe AAB, Calif, 23 May 1942; Will Rogers Field, Okla, Nov 1942; Drew Field, Fla, Oct 1943; Morris Field, NC, 6 Nov 1943–1 May 1944.

COMMANDERS. Maj Guy L McNeil, 15 Jan 1941; Maj Otto C George, 18 Apr 1941; Col Richard H Lee, 9 May 1941; Lt Col Robert D Gapen, 1 Nov 1942; Lt Col Martin P Crabtree, 11 Apr 1943; Lt Col Robert V DeShazo, 21 Jul 1943; Col

Harold L Mace, 13 Sep 1943; Lt Col Robert V DeShazo, 21 Oct 1943–1 May 1944.

CAMPAIGNS. Antisubmarine, American Theater.

DECORATIONS. None.

INSIGNE. *Shield:* Or, a bend invected azure. *Motto:* CUSTOS LIBERTATE—Guardians of Liberty. (Approved 14 Jul 1942.)

47th BOMBARDMENT GROUP

Constituted as 47th Bombardment Group (Light) on 20 Nov 1940. *Activated* on 15 Jan 1941. Patrolled the west coast for several weeks after Japan attacked Pearl Harbor, then trained for duty overseas. Moved to North Africa, Oct–Nov 1942. Assigned to Twelfth AF. Served in the Mediterranean theater until the end of the war, using A–20's and (after Jan 1945) some A–26's for support and interdictory operations in which the group attacked such targets as tanks, convoys, bivouac areas, troop concentrations, supply

47TH BOMBARDMENT GROUP L

dumps, roads, pontoon bridges, rail lines, and airfields. Also flew numerous night intruder missions after Jun 1944. Began operations by flying low-level missions against the enemy in North Africa during the period Dec 1942–May 1943. When Axis forces broke through at Kasserine Pass in Feb 1943, the 47th Group, though undermanned and undersupplied, flew eleven missions on 22 Feb to attack the advancing armored columns and thus to help stop the enemy's offensive—an action for which the group was awarded a DUC. Remained active in combat during Mar and Apr 1943 while training for medium-level bombardment. Participated in the reduction of Pantelleria and Lampedusa in Jun 1943 and the invasion of Sicily in Jul. Bombed German evacuation beaches near Messina in Aug. Supported British Eighth Army during the invasion of Italy in Sep. Assisted the Allied advance toward Rome, Sep 1943–Jun 1944. Supported the invasion of Southern France, Aug–Sep 1944. Attacked German communications in northern Italy, Sep 1944–Apr 1945. Received second DUC for performance from 21 to 24 Apr 1945 when, in bad weather and over rugged terrain, the group maintained operations for 60 consecutive hours, destroying enemy transportation in the Po Valley to prevent the organized withdrawal of German forces. Returned to the US in July 1945. Trained and participated in maneuvers. Equipped with B-45's in 1948. *Inactivated* on 2 Oct 1949.

Activated on 12 Mar 1951. Assigned to Tactical Air Command and equipped with B-45's. Moved to England, May–Jun 1952, and assigned to United States Air Forces in Europe. *Inactivated* on 8 Feb 1955.

SQUADRONS. *84th:* 1941–1949; 1951–1955. *85th:* 1941–1949; 1951–1955. *86th:* 1941–1949; 1954–1955. *97th:* 1941–1946. *422d:* 1953–1954.

STATIONS. McChord Field, Wash, 15 Jan 1941; Fresno, Calif, 14 Aug 1941; Will Rogers Field, Okla, c. 16 Feb 1942; Greensboro, NC, c. 16 Jul–18 Oct 1942; Mediouna, French Morocco, 18 Nov 1942; Youks-les-Bains, Algeria, 7 Jan 1943; Canrobert, Algeria, 6 Mar 1943; Thelepte, Tunisia, 30 Mar 1943; Souk-el-Arba, Tunisia, 13 Apr 1943; Soliman, Tunisia, c. 1 Jul 1943; Malta, 21 Jul 1943; Torrente Comunelli, Sicily, 9 Aug 1943; Gerbini, Sicily, 20 Aug 1943; Grottaglie, Italy, 24 Sep 1943; Vincenzo Airfield, Italy, 15 Oct 1943; Vesuvius Airfield, Italy, c. 10 Jan 1944; Capodichino, Italy, 22 Mar 1944; Vesuvius Airfield, Italy, 25 Apr 1944; Ponte Galeria, Italy, c. 10 Jun 1944; Ombrone Airfield, Italy, 27 Jun 1944; Corsica, 11 Jul 1944; Salon, France, 7 Sep 1944; Follonica, Italy, 18 Sep 1944; Rosignano Airfield, Italy, Oct 1944; Grosseto, Italy, 11 Dec 1944; Pisa, Italy, Jun–24 Jun 1945; Seymour Johnson Field, NC, 11 Jul 1945; Lake Charles AAFld, La, Sep 1945; Biggs Field, Tex, 20 Oct 1946; Barksdale AFB, La, 19 Nov 1948–2 Oct 1949. Langley AFB, Va, 12 Mar 1951–12 May 1952; Sculthorpe, England, 1 Jun 1952–8 Feb 1955.

COMMANDERS. Maj William A Schulgen, 15 Jan 1941; Lt Col Hilbert M Wittkop, unkn; Col Frederick R Terrell, Jan 1942; Col Malcolm Green Jr, 17 May 1943; Lt Col Kenneth S Wade, 1 Apr 1945; Col Marvin S Zipp, 28 Aug 1945; Col Robert J Hughey, 23 Nov 1945; Lt Col Broadus B Taylor, 27 Aug 1946; Col Gerald E Williams, 30 Aug 1946; Lt Col Stebbins W Griffith, 5 Jun 1947; Lt Col Frederick E Price, Aug 1947; Col Willis F Chapman, 10 Oct 1947–2 Oct 1949. Col Benjamin C Willis, 12 Mar 1951; Col David M Jones, Sep 1951; Col Galen B Price, 20 Feb 1952; Lt Col Hubert M Blair, unkn; Col Galen B Price, 1954–c. Feb 1955.

CAMPAIGNS. American Theater; Algeria-French Morocco; Tunisia; Sicily; Naples-Foggia; Anzio; Rome-Arno; Southern France; North Apennines; Po Valley.

DECORATIONS. Distinguished Unit Citations: North Africa, 22 Feb 1943; Po Valley, 21–24 Apr 1945.

INSIGNE. *Shield:* Or, in chief, a bomb sable, point downward, winged gules, surmounting an arc, reversed and couped, azure, all above a stylized cloud indication, of the second, emitting four lightning flashes gules toward base. (Approved 26 Oct 1951.)

48th FIGHTER GROUP

Constituted as 48th Bombardment Group (Light) on 20 Nov 1940. *Activated* on 15 Jan 1941. *Redesignated* 48th Bombardment Group (Dive) in Sep 1942, and 48th Fighter-Bomber Group in Aug 1943. Used A-20's and B-18's during 1941, and

VULNERATUS · NON · VICTUS

A-20, A-24, A-31, A-35, A-36, P-39, P-40, and other aircraft between 1942 and 1944. Served as a replacement training unit, participated in maneuvers, and for a brief time engaged in coastal patrol work.

Moved overseas, arriving in England in Mar 1944. Assigned to Ninth AF. Trained with P-47's. Began operations on 20 Apr 1944 by making a fighter sweep over the coast of France. *Redesignated* 48th Fighter Group in May 1944. Flew escort and dive-bombing missions to help prepare for the invasion of Normandy. Bombed bridges and gun positions on 6 Jun and attacked rail lines and trains, motor transports, bridges, fuel dumps, and gun positions during the remainder of the Normandy campaign. Moved to France, Jun–Jul 1944. Helped Allied forces break through the German lines at St Lo in Jul, supported the Allied drive across France in Aug and Sep, and assisted the airborne attack on Holland in Sep. Cited by the Belgian Government for close cooperation with Allied armies during the period Jun–Sep 1944. Moved to Belgium and operated from there in the fall and winter of 1944–1945, being awarded second Belgian citation for operations during that time. Received a DUC for action on 6 Dec 1944: facing intense enemy fire while flying below a heavy overcast, the group struck buildings, entrenchments, and troop concentrations to assist the advance of ground forces against an enemy stronghold north of Julich. Supported ground operations during the Battle of the Bulge (Dec 1944–Jan 1945) and received third Belgian citation for relentless assaults against the enemy during that battle. Continued tactical air operations from bases on the Continent, supporting ground forces until the end of the war. During combat, also flew patrol, escort, weather-reconnaissance, and leaflet missions; on one occasion carried blood plasma that was dropped in belly tanks to ground troops. Moved to the US during Aug–Sep 1945. *Inactivated* on 7 Nov 1945.

Redesignated 48th Fighter-Bomber Group. *Activated* in France on 10 Jul 1952. Assigned to United States Air Forces in Europe. Equipped with F–84's and later with F–86 aircraft.

SQUADRONS. *492d* (formerly 55th): 1941–1945; 1952–. *493d* (formerly 56th): 1941–1945; 1952–. *494th* (formerly 57th): 1941–1945; 1952–. *495th* (formerly 88th): 1941–1944.

STATIONS. Savannah, Ga, 15 Jan 1941; Will Rogers Field, Okla, 22 May 1941; Savannah, Ga, 7 Feb 1942; Key Field, Miss, 28 Jun 1942; William Northern Field, Tenn, 20 Aug 1943; Waterboro AAFld, SC, 27 Jan–13 Mar 1944; Ibsley, England, 29 Mar 1944; Deux Jumeaux, France, 18 Jun 1944; Villacoublay, France, 29 Aug 1944; Cambrai/Niergnies, France, 15 Sep 1944; St Trond, Belgium, 30 Sep 1944; Kelz, Germany, 26 Mar 1945; Kassel, Germany, 17 Apr 1945; Illesheim, Germany, 29 Apr 1945; Laon, France, 5 Jul–Aug 1945; Seymour Johnson Field, NC, 9 Sep–7 Nov 1945. Chaumont AB, France, 10 Jul 1952–.

COMMANDERS. Lt Col Bernard S Thompson, 1941; Col Norman R Burnett, unkn; Lt Col Preston P Pender, c. 1943; Lt Col Charles C Kegelman, c. Apr 1943; Col Dixon M Allison, c. 8 Nov 1943; Col George L Wertenbaker Jr, 23 Apr 1944; Col James K Johnson, c. Oct 1944; Lt Col Harold L McNeely, 8 Jun 1945; Lt Col Paul P Douglas Jr, 28 Jun 1945–unkn. Col Chesley G Peterson, 10 Jul 1952; Lt Col Arthur D Thomas, c. 1 Jun 1953; Col Frank A Hill, c. Sep 1953; Col Arthur D Thomas, c. Jul 1954; Lt Col John D McFarlane, 1955–.

CAMPAIGNS. Antisubmarine, American Theater; Air Offensive, Europe; Normandy; Northern France; Rhineland; Ardennes-Alsace; Central Europe.

DECORATIONS. Distinguished Unit Citation: Germany, 6 Dec 1944. Cited in the Order of the Day, Belgian Army: 6 Jun–30 Sep 1944; 1 Oct 1944–; 18 Dec 1944–15 Jan 1945. Belgian Fourragere.

INSIGNE. *Shield:* Argent, on a pale engrailed azure a dexter hand couped at the wrist grasping a sword or. *Motto:* VUL-

NERATUS NON VICTUS—Unconquered even though Wounded. (Approved 12 Jan 1942.)

49th FIGHTER GROUP

TUTOR ET ULTOR

Constituted as 49th Pursuit Group (Interceptor) on 20 Nov 1940. *Activated* on 15 Jan 1941. Trained with P–35's. Moved to Australia, Jan–Feb 1942, and became part of Fifth AF. *Redesignated* 49th Fighter Group in May 1942. Received P–40's in Australia and, after training for a short time, provided air defense for the Northern Territory, being awarded a DUC for engaging the enemy in frequent and intense aerial combat while operating with limited materiel and facilities, Mar–Aug 1942.

Moved to New Guinea in Oct 1942 to help stall the Japanese drive southward from Buna to Port Moresby. Engaged primarily in air defense of Port Moresby; also escorted bombers and transports, and attacked enemy installations, supply lines, and troop concentrations in support of Allied ground forces. Participated in the Allied offensive that pushed the Japanese back along the Buna trail, took part in the Battle of the Bismarck Sea (Mar 1943), fought for control of the approaches to Huon Gulf, and supported ground forces during the campaign in which the Allies eventually recovered New Guinea. Covered landings on Noemfoor and had a part in the conquest of Biak. After having used P–38, P–40, and P–47 aircraft, was equipped completely in Sep 1944 with P–38's, which were used to fly long-range escort and attack missions to Mindanao, Halmahera, Ceram, and Borneo. Arrived in the Philippines in Oct 1944, shortly after the assault landings on Leyte. Engaged enemy fighters, attacked shipping in Ormoc Bay, supported ground forces, and covered the Allied invasion of Luzon. Maj Richard I Bong, who became AAF's top ace of World War II, was awarded the Medal of Honor for voluntarily flying in combat from 10 Oct to 15 Nov 1944, a period for which he was credited with the destruction of eight enemy aircraft in the air. For intensive operations against the Japanese on Leyte, the group was awarded a DUC. Other missions from the Philippines included strikes against industry and transportation on Formosa and against shipping along the China coast. Moved to Okinawa in Aug 1945 and to Japan in Sep. Trained, took part in maneuvers, and flew surveillance patrols, as part of Far East Air Forces. Equipped with P–51's in 1946, with F–80's being added in 1948. *Redes-*

ignated 49th Fighter-Bomber Group in Feb 1950.

Began operations in the Korean War in Jun 1950. Covered the evacuation of civilian personnel from Kimpo and Suwon. Then flew missions in support of UN ground forces, hitting gun positions, troop concentrations, and other objectives. Later, struck interdiction targets in North Korea. In combat, operated first from Japan and later from Korea, beginning operations with F-51's and F-80's and completing conversion to F-84's in Sep 1951. Remained in Korea for a time after the armistice. Returned to Japan in Nov 1953.

SQUADRONS. *7th:* 1941-. *8th:* 1941-. *9th:* 1941-.

STATIONS. Selfridge Field, Mich, 15 Jan 1941; Morrison Field, Fla, 25 May 1941-4 Jan 1942; Melbourne, Australia, 2 Feb 1942; Bankstown, Australia, 16 Feb 1942; Darwin, Australia, c. 16 Apr 1942; Port Moresby, New Guinea, 9 Oct 1942; Dobodura, New Guinea, Mar 1943; Gusap, New Guinea, 20 Nov 1943; Finschhafen, New Guinea, 19 Apr 1944; Hollandia, New Guinea, c. 17 May 1944; Biak, 3 Jan 1944; Tacloban, Leyte, 24 Oct 1944; San Jose, Mindoro, c. 30 Dec 1944; Lingayen, Luzon, c. 25 Feb 1945; Okinawa, 16 Aug 1945; Atsugi, Japan, 15 Sep 1945; Chitose, Japan, 18 Feb 1946; Misawa, Japan, 20 Mar 1948; Itazuke, Japan, 9 Jul 1950; Taegu, Korea, 1 Dec 1950; Kunsan, Korea, 1 Apr 1953; Komaki, Japan, 2 Nov 1953; Nagoya, Japan, 16 Sep 1954-.

COMMANDERS. Maj Glenn L Davasher, 16 Jan 1941; Maj John F Egan, 10 Feb 1941; Maj George McCoy Jr, 2 May 1941; Col Paul B Wurtsmith, 11 Dec 1941; Col Donald R Hutchinson, 11 Nov 1942; Lt Col Robert L Morrissey, 30 Jan 1943; Col James C Selman, Jul 1943; Lt Col David A Campbell, 25 Jan 1944; Lt Col Furlo S Wagner, 3 Jun 1944; Col George A Walker, 19 Jul 1944; Lt Col Gerald R Johnson, 10 Mar 1945; Lt Col Clay Tice Jr, 16 Jul 1945; Lt Col Wallace R Jordan, 4 Feb 1946; Lt Col Charles H Terhune Jr, c. 18 Feb 1946; Col Herbert L Grills, 25 Mar 1946; Col Merrill D Burnside, 20 Jul 1946; Lt Col Clay Tice Jr, 11 Sep 1946; Col Louis R Hughes, 1 Sep 1947; Lt Col Robert E Kirtley, 18 Aug 1948; Lt Col Niven K Cranfill, 11 Mar 1949; Lt Col John R Murphy, 1 Sep 1949; Lt Col James A Rippin, 31 Oct 1949; Col Wilbur H Stratton, 10 Nov 1949; Col Stanton T Smith Jr, 20 Jan 1950; Col John R Murphy, 21 Oct 1950; Col Wilbur J Grumbles, 20 May 1951; Col William L Mitchell, 4 Nov 1951; Lt Col Gordon F Blood, 20 May 1952; Col Charles G Teschner, 1952; Col Robert H Orr, Sep 1952; Col Richard N Ellis, 17 Jan 1953; Col Charles G Teschner, 1 Apr 1953; Col Gilbert L Pritchard, Aug 1953-.

CAMPAIGNS. *World War II:* East Indies; Air Offensive, Japan; China Defensive; Papua; New Guinea; Bismarck Archipelago; Western Pacific; Leyte; Luzon; China Offensive. *Korean War:* UN Defensive; UN Offensive; CCF Intervention; 1st UN Counteroffensive; CCF

Spring Offensive; UN Summer-Fall Offensive; Second Korean Winter; Korea Summer-Fall, 1952; Third Korean Winter; Korea Summer-Fall, 1953.

DECORATIONS. Distinguished Unit Citations: Australia, 14 Mar–25 Aug 1942; Papua, [Oct] 1942–23 Jan 1943; Philippine Islands, 27 Oct–7 Dec 1944; Korea [Jun]–25 Nov 1950; Korea, 9 Jul–27 Nov 1951. Philippine Presidential Unit Citation. Republic of Korea Presidential Unit Citations: [Jun] 1950–7 Feb 1951; 8 Feb 1951–31 Mar 1953.

INSIGNE. *Shield:* A gyronny of three gules, or and azure, a bolt of lightning, bend sinisterwise argent, in chief, a knight's helmet, winged of the last, in dexter chief, five stars (Southern Cross) argent, two on gules, and three on azure, in sinister base a covered wagon, trees and road scene, all proper. *Motto:* TUTOR ET ULTOR—I Protect and Avenge. (Approved 29 Dec 1951.)

50th FIGHTER GROUP

Constituted as 50th Pursuit Group (Interceptor) on 20 Nov 1940. *Activated* on 15 Jan 1941. *Redesignated* 50th Fighter Group in May 1942. Functioned as part of the Fighter Command School, testing equipment and conducting training in air defense operations; also trained pilots and furnished cadres to night fighter units. Later operated with AAF School of Applied Tactics, training personnel in fighter tactics under simulated combat conditions.

Used P–40's and P–47's, plus some DB–7's, P–51's, and P–70's.

Moved to England, Mar–Apr 1944. Assigned to Ninth AF and, using P–47's, began operations by making a fighter sweep over France on 1 May. Engaged primarily in escort and dive-bombing missions for the next month. Covered the beach during the invasion of Normandy on 6 and 7 Jun, and moved to the Continent late that month. Attacked bridges, roads, vehicles, railways, trains, gun emplacements, and marshalling yards during the Normandy campaign. Bombed targets in the St Lo region in Jul and supported the subsequent drive across France. Assisted in stemming the German offensive in the Saar-Hardt area early in Jan 1945, engaged in the offensive that reduced the Colmar bridgehead in Jan and Feb 1945, and supported the drive that breached the Siegfried Line and resulted in the movement of Allied forces into southern Germany in Mar and Apr 1945.

Received a DUC for close cooperation with Seventh Army in Mar during the assault on the Siegfried Line; in spite of the hazards of enemy opposition and difficult weather conditions, the group struck enemy defenses and isolated battle areas by destroying bridges, communications, supply areas, and ammunition dumps. Received second DUC for a mission on 25 Apr 1945 when, despite intense antiaircraft fire, the group destroyed or damaged many enemy aircraft on an airfield southeast of Munich. Ended operations in May 1945. Returned to the US in Aug. *Inactivated* on 7 Nov 1945.

Allotted to the reserve. *Activated* on 1 Jun 1949. *Redesignated* 50th Fighter-Interceptor Group in Mar 1950. Ordered into active service on 1 Jun 1951. *Inactivated* on 2 Jun 1951.

Redesignated 50th Fighter-Bomber Group. *Activated* on 1 Jan 1953. Assigned to Tactical Air Command. Equipped with F–51's; converted to F–86's early in 1953. Moved to Germany, Jul-Aug 1953, and assigned to United States Air Forces in Europe.

SQUADRONS. *10th:* 1941–1945; 1953–. *11th:* 1941–1942. *12th:* 1941–1942. *81st:* 1942–1945; 1949–1951; 1953–. *313th:* 1942–1945. *417th:* 1953–. *445th:* 1943–1944.

STATIONS. Selfridge Field, Mich, 15 Jan 1941; Key Field, Miss, 3 Oct 1941; Orlando AB, Fla, 22 Mar 1943; Alachua AAFld, Fla, 20 Nov 1943; Orlando AB, Fla, 1 Feb–13 Mar 1944; Lymington, England, 5 Apr 1944; Carentan, France, 25 Jun 1944; Meautis, France, 16 Aug 1944; Orly, France, 4 Sep 1944; Laon, France, 15 Sep 1944; Lyons/Bron, France, 28 Sep 1944; Toul/Ochey, France, 3 Nov 1944; Giebelstadt, Germany, 20 Apr 1945; Mannheim, Germany, 21 May–c. Jun 1945; La Junta AAFld, Colo, Aug–7 Nov 1945. Otis AFB, Mass, 1 Jun 1949–2 Jun 1951. Clovis AFB, NM, 1 Jan–22 Jul 1953; Hahn AB, Germany, 10 Aug 1953–.

COMMANDERS. Capt George McCoy Jr, 16 Jan 1941; Col Allen R Springer, 1 May 1941; Lt Col John C Crosthwaite, 1 Apr 1942; Lt Col Murray C Woodbury, 15 May 1942; Lt Col T Alan Bennett, 23 Jul 1942; Lt Col Walter B Putnam, 29 Jan 1943; Lt Col Robert S Quinn, 9 Nov 1943; Col William D Greenfield, 1 Dec 1943; Col Harvey L Case Jr, Nov 1944–1945. Col Gerald J Dix, 1 Jan 1953; Col Albert W Schinz, 1 Jun 1953; Lt Col Edward A McGough III, 2 Apr 1954; Col James F Hackler Jr, 23 Apr 1954; Lt Col Chester L VanEtten, May 1955–.

CAMPAIGNS. American Theater; Air Offensive, Europe; Normandy; Northern France; Rhineland; Ardennes-Alsace; Central Europe.

DECORATIONS. Distinguished Unit Citations: ETO, 13–20 Mar 1945; Germany, 25 Apr 1945. Cited in the Order of the Day, Belgian Army: 6 Jun–30 Sep 1944.

INSIGNE. *Shield:* Azure, an Opinicus passant argent. *Motto:* MASTER OF THE SKY. (Approved 9 Jan 1942. This insigne was replaced 23 Aug 1956.)

51st FIGHTER GROUP

DEFTLY AND SWIFTLY

Constituted as 51st Pursuit Group (Interceptor) on 20 Nov 1940. *Activated* on 15 Jan 1941. Assigned to Fourth AF and equipped with P-40's. *Redesignated* 51st Pursuit Group (Fighter) in Mar 1941. While training for combat, served as part of the defense force for the west coast. Left the US in Jan 1942, stopped in Australia and Ceylon, and arrived in India in Mar 1942. Assigned to Tenth AF. *Redesignated* 51st Fighter Group in May 1942. Defended the Indian terminus of the Hump route and airfields in that area. Flew strafing, bombing, reconnaissance, and patrol missions in support of Allied ground troops during a Japanese offensive in northern Burma in 1943. Moved to China in Oct 1943 and assigned to Fourteenth AF. Used P-38's, P-40's, and (in 1945) P-51's to defend the eastern end of the route over the Hump, guard air bases in the Kunming area, harass Japanese shipping in the Red River delta, and support

Chinese ground forces in their drive along the Salween River. Returned to India in the fall of 1945 and sailed for the US in Nov. *Inactivated* on 13 Dec 1945.

Activated on Okinawa on 15 Oct 1946. Assigned to Far East Air Forces. Equipped with P-47's and P-61's in 1946, and with F-80 and F-82 aircraft in 1948. Trained, served as part of the occupation force, and provided air defense for the Ryukyus. *Redesignated* 51st Fighter-Interceptor Group in Feb 1950. Moved to Japan in Sep 1950 and, operating from bases in Japan and Korea, served in combat against Communist forces until the end of the Korean War. Used F-80's until Nov 1951 and then converted to F-86 aircraft. Supported ground forces and flew patrol, escort, interdictory, and reconnaissance missions. Frequently engaged the enemy's jet (MIG) fighters and reported numerous victories in aerial combat, Capt Joseph McConnell Jr becoming the leading ace of the Korean War. Returned to Okinawa in Aug 1954.

SQUADRONS. *16th:* 1941–1945; 1946–. *25th:* 1941–1945; 1946–. *26th:* 1941–1945; 1946–. *449th:* 1943–1945.

STATIONS. Hamilton Field, Calif, 15 Jan 1941; March Field, Calif, 20 Jun 1941–11 Jan 1942; Karachi, India, 14 Mar 1942; Dinjan, India, 10 Oct 1942; Kunming, China, 2 Oct 1943; India, Sep–Nov 1945; Ft Lewis, Wash, 12–13 Dec 1945. Yontan, Okinawa, 15 Oct 1946; Naha, Okinawa, 22 May 1947; Itazuke, Japan, 22 Sep 1950; Kimpo, Korea, 24 Oct 1950; Itazuke, Japan, 3 Jan 1951; Tsuiki, Japan, 20 Jan 1951; Suwon, Korea, 27 Jul 1951; Naha, Okinawa, 1 Aug 1954–.

COMMANDERS. Col Homer L Sanders, 1941; Col John F Egan, 23 Mar 1943; Lt Col Samuel B Knowles Jr, 20 Sep 1943; Col Louis R Hughes Jr, 27 May 1944; Lt Col William E Blankenship, Feb–13 Dec 1945. Col Loring F Stetson Jr, 15 Oct 1946; Col Homer A Boushey, 12 Apr 1947; Lt Col James F McCarthy, 1 Aug 1947; Col Homer A Boushey, unkn; Lt Col Bruce D Biddlecome, Jun 1948; Lt Col Kenneth L Garrett, 7 Mar 1949; Lt Col Robert F Worley, 24 May 1949; Col John T Shields, 1 Jul 1949; Lt Col Irwin H Dregne, Jun 1950; Col Oliver G Cellini, 1950; Col Irwin H Dregne, 24 Apr 1951; Lt Col John M Thacker, 21 Jul 1951; Lt Col George L Jones, 13 Nov 1951; Lt Col William M Shelton, Mar 1952; Lt Col Albert S Kelly, Jun 1952; Col Robert P Baldwin, Jan 1953; Lt Col Harold C Gibson, Aug 1953; Col Malcolm E Norton, Oct 1953; Lt Col Harold G Shook, 23 Mar 1954; Lt Col William A Campbell, 9 Jul 1954; Col George V Williams, 10 Aug 1954–.

CAMPAIGNS. *World War II:* India-Burma; China Defensive; China Offensive. *Korean War:* UN Offensive; CCF Intervention; 1st UN Counteroffensive; CCF Spring Offensive; UN Summer-Fall Offensive; Second Korean Winter; Korea Summer-Fall, 1952; Third Korean Winter; Korea Summer-Fall, 1953.

DECORATIONS. Distinguished Unit Citation: Korea, 28 Nov 1951–30 Apr 1953. Republic of Korea Presidential Unit Citations: [Sep] 1950–30 Jun 1951; 1 Jul 1951–31 Mar 1953.

INSIGNE. *Shield:* Per fess nebuly abased azure and or, issuing from partition line a demi-pegasus argent with a machine gun in each wing bendwise sable, gun fire proper. *Motto:* DEFTLY AND SWIFTLY. (Approved 5 Feb 1942. This insigne was modified 2 May 1956.)

52d FIGHTER GROUP

Constituted as 52d Pursuit Group (Interceptor) on 20 Nov 1940. *Activated* on 15 Jan 1941. *Redesignated* 52d Fighter Group in May 1942. Trained with P–39 and P–40 aircraft, and participated in maneuvers. Moved to the British Isles, the air echelon arriving in Jul 1942 and the ground echelon in Aug. Received Spitfire aircraft and, as part of Eighth AF, flew missions from England to France during Aug and Sep. The pilots of the group flew Spitfires from Gibraltar to Algeria during the invasion of North Africa on 8 Nov 1942; the remainder of the group, moving by ship from England, arrived after the campaign for Algeria-French Morocco had ended. Assigned first to Twelfth AF and later (after May 1944) to Fifteenth, the group served in combat in the Mediterranean theater until the end of the war. Flew escort, patrol, strafing, and reconnaissance missions to help defeat Axis forces in Tunisia. Took part in the conquest of Sicily. Attacked railroads, highways, bridges, coastal shipping, and other targets to support Allied operations in Italy. Converted to P-51's during Apr–May 1944 and afterwards engaged primarily in escorting bombers that attacked objectives in Italy, France, Germany, Czechoslovakia, Austria, Hungary, Rumania, and Yugoslavia. Received a DUC for a mission of 9 Jun 1944 when the group protected bombers that struck aircraft factories, communications centers, and supply lines in Germany. In addition to escorting bombers of Fifteenth AF, the group made strafing attacks on important targets in Italy, France, central Europe, and the Balkans. Received second DUC for a strafing raid in which the group destroyed a great number of fighter and transport planes on a landing ground in Rumania on 31 Aug 1944. Returned to the US in Aug 1945. *Inactivated* on 7 Nov 1945.

Activated in Germany on 9 Nov 1946. Assigned to United States Air Forces in Europe and organized as an all-weather fighter group. Transferred, without personnel and equipment, to the US in Jun 1947. *Redesignated* 52d Fighter Group (All Weather) in May 1948, and 52d Fighter-Interceptor Group in May 1951. Equipped with P-61's in 1947, F-82's in 1948, and F-94's in 1950. *Inactivated* on 6 Feb 1952.

Redesignated 52d Fighter Group (Air Defense). *Activated* on 18 Aug 1955. Assigned to Air Defense Command and equipped with F-86 aircraft.

SQUADRONS. *2d:* 1941–1945; 1946–1952; 1955–. *4th:* 1941–1945. *5th:* 1941–1945; 1946–1952; 1955–.

STATIONS. Selfridge Field, Mich, 15 Jan 1941; Norfolk, Va, 18 Dec 1941; Selfridge Field, Mich, Jan 1942; Florence, SC, 18 Feb 1942; Wilmington, NC, 27 Apr 1942; Grenier Field, NH, 14–24 Jun 1942; Northern Ireland, c. 13 Jul 1942; Goxhill, England, c. 26 Aug–Oct 1942; Tafaraoui, Algeria, 9 Nov 1942; La Senia, Algeria, 14 Nov 1942; Orleansville, Algeria, c. 1 Jan 1943; Telergma, Algeria, c. 17 Jan 1943; Youks-les-Bains, Algeria, c. 9 Mar 1943; Le Sers, Tunisia, 14 Apr 1943; La Sebala, Tunisia, 21 May 1943; Boccadifalco, Sicily, 30 Jul 1943; Corsica, 1 Dec 1943; Madna Airfield, Italy, 14 May 1944; Piagiolino Airfield, Italy, 21 Apr 1945; Lesina, Italy, 8 Jul–Aug 1945; Drew Field, Fla, 25 Aug–7 Nov 1945. Schweinfurt, Germany, 9 Nov 1946; Bad Kissingen, Germany, 5 May 1947–25 Jun 1947; Mitchel Field, NY, 25 Jun 1947; McGuire AFB, NJ, 10 Oct 1949–6 Feb 1952. Suffolk County AFB, NY, 18 Aug 1955–.

DEFENSE BY OFFENSE

COMMANDERS. Maj Earl W Barnes, 16 Jan 1941; Lt Col Robert L Schoenlein, 15 May 1941; Col Dixon M Allison, 27 Feb 1942; Lt Col Graham W West, 1 Mar 1943; Lt Col James S Coward, 24 Jun 1943; Lt Col Richard A Ames, 1 Sep 1943; Col Marvin L McNickle, 6 Sep 1943; Lt Col Robert Levine, 25 Feb 1944; Col Marion Malcolm, 27 Aug 1944–1945. Col Carroll W McColpin, c. 14 Dec 1946; Col Oliver G Cellini, unkn; Col Benjamin S Preston Jr, 6 Jul 1950; Col Royal N Baker, 1951–6 Feb 1952. Col James H Hancock, 1955–.

CAMPAIGNS. Air Combat, EAME Theater; Air Offensive, Europe; Algeria-French Morocco; Tunisia; Sicily; Naples-Foggia; Rome-Arno; Normandy; Northern France; Southern France; North Apennines; Rhineland; Central Europe; Po Valley.

DECORATIONS. Distinguished Unit Citations: Germany, 9 Jun 1944; Rumania, 31 Aug 1944.

INSIGNE. *Shield:* Quarterly per fess nebuly, first and fourth argent, each charged with a dagger in pale point downward gules, hilt and pommel of the same, grip or; second quarter azure; third quarter, sable. *Motto:* SEEK, ATTACK, DESTROY. (Approved 11 Jan 1951.)

53d FIGHTER GROUP

Constituted as 53d Pursuit Group (Interceptor) on 20 Nov 1940. *Activated* on 15 Jan 1941. *Redesignated* 53d Fighter Group in May 1942. Trained with P–35's and P–40's. Moved to the Panama Canal Zone in Dec 1941 and equipped with P–39's for operations as part of the defense force for the canal. Returned to the US in Nov 1942 and assigned to Third AF. Trained replacement pilots in P–39, P–47, and P–51 aircraft. *Disbanded* on 1 May 1944.

Reconstituted and *redesignated* 53d Fighter Group (Air Defense), on 20 Jun 1955. *Activated* on 18 Aug 1955. Assigned to Air Defense Command. Equipped first with F–86's, later with F–89's.

SQUADRONS. *13th:* 1941–1944; 1955–. *14th:* 1941–1944; 1955–. *15th:* 1941–1944. *438th:* 1943–1944.

STATIONS. MacDill Field, Fla, 15 Jan 1941; Tallahassee, Fla, 8 May–8 Dec 1941; Howard Field, CZ, 1 Jan–10 Nov 1942; Dale Mabry Field, Fla, 26 Nov 1942; Drew Field, Fla, 7 Jan 1943; Ft Myers, Fla, 5 Feb 1943–1 May 1944. Sioux City Mun Aprt, Iowa, 18 Aug 1955–.

COMMANDERS. Maj Hugo P Rush, 15 Jan 1941; Maj Eugene C Fleming, 9 May 1941; Col Earl W Barnes, 1 Jun 1941; Lt Col Don L Wilhelm Jr, 28 Jun 1942; Col

Morley F Slaght, 11 Apr 1943; Lt Col Anthony V Grossetta, 22 Sep 1943; Col Bryan B Harper, Oct 1943–1 May 1944. Col Malcolm A Moore, Aug 1955–.

CAMPAIGNS. American Theater.

DECORATIONS. None.

INSIGNE. *Shield:* Per bend azure and or, in chief an ancient Norse winged helmet argent, in base a palm tree proper. *Motto:* DEFENSE BY OFFENSE. (Approved 8 Jan 1943. This insigne was modified 26 Jul 1956.)

54th FIGHTER GROUP

Constituted as 54th Pursuit Group (Interceptor) on 20 Nov 1940. *Activated* on 15 Jan 1941. Trained with P–40's. Served as a part of the defense force for the northwest Pacific coast during the first few months of the war. *Redesignated* 54th Fighter Group in May 1942. The air echelon, equipped with P–39's, served in Alaska against the Japanese forces that invaded the Aleutian Islands during the summer of 1942, and for these operations the group received a DUC. The air echelon returned to the US in Dec 1942 and rejoined the group, which had been assigned to Third AF, and which became a replacement training unit for P–51 pilots. *Disbanded* on 1 May 1944.

Reconstituted and *redesignated* 54th Fighter Group (Air Defense), on 20 Jun 1955. *Activated* on 18 Aug 1955. Assigned to Air Defense Command and equipped with F–86's.

SQUADRONS. *42d:* 1941–1944; 1955–. *56th:* 1941–1944. *57th:* 1941–1944.

STATIONS. Hamilton Field, Calif, 15 Jan 1941; Everett, Wash, 26 Jun 1941; Harding Field, La, 31 Jan 1942; Bartow AAFld, Fla, 11 May 1943–1 May 1944. Greater Pittsburgh Aprt, Pa, 18 Aug 1955–.

COMMANDERS. Capt Harry A Hammond, 15 Jan 1941; Col Phineas K Morrill, Feb 1941; Col Charles M McCorkle, 12 Sep 1942; Lt Col George B Greene Jr, 11 Aug 1943; Lt Col Ward W Harker, 17 Sep 1943; Col Joseph S Holtoner, 6 Mar–1 May 1944. Col Edward F Roddy, 1955–.

CAMPAIGNS. American Theater.

DECORATIONS. Distinguished Unit Citation: Aleutian Islands, [Jun]–4 Nov 1942.

INSIGNE. *Shield:* Per bend of the light blue sky and azure, over a bomb, bend sinisterwise, a lightning flash, palewise, gules, fimbriated argent; a bend of the last superimposed over all and charged with a jet aircraft, in chief, sable, with vapor trail of the third; all between an increscent moon and a radiant sun in fess all of the fourth. (Approved 8 Mar 1957.)

55th FIGHTER GROUP

Constituted as 55th Pursuit Group (Interceptor) on 20 Nov 1940. *Activated* on 15 Jan 1941. Trained with P–43's. *Redesignated* 55th Fighter Group in May 1942. Converted to P–38's and prepared for combat. Moved to England, Aug–Sep 1943. Assigned to Eighth AF. Began operations with P–38's on 15 Oct 1943; converted to P–51's in Jul 1944. Engaged primarily in escorting bombers that attacked such targets as industries and marshalling yards in Germany, and airfields and V-weapon sites in France. Provided cover for B–17's and B–24's that bombed aircraft plants during Big Week in Feb 1944, gun emplacements during the St Lo breakthrough in Jul 1944, and transportation facilities during the Battle of the Bulge, Dec 1944–Jan 1945. Also patrolled the air over the Channel and bombed bridges in the Tours area during the invasion of the Continent in Jun 1944; patrolled the Arnhem sector to support the airborne invasion of Holland in Sep 1944; strafed trucks, locomotives, and oil depots near Wesel when the Allies crossed the Rhine in Mar 1945. Received a DUC for eight missions to Germany between 3 and 13 Sep 1944 when the group not only destroyed enemy fighters in the air to protect the bombers it was escorting, but also descended to low levels, in spite of intense antiaircraft fire, to strafe airdromes and to destroy enemy aircraft on the ground. Received second DUC for operations on 19 Feb 1945 when the organization flew a sweep over Germany to hit railway tracks, locomotives, oil cars, goods wagons, troop cars, buildings, and military vehicles. Flew last combat mission on 21 Apr 1945. Moved to Germany in Jul 1945 as part of the occupation forces. Assigned to United States Air Forces in Europe. Trained with P–51 and P–80 aircraft. *Inactivated* in Germany on 20 Aug 1946.

Redesignated 55th Reconnaissance Group (Very Long Range, Mapping). *Activated* in the US on 24 Feb 1947. Assigned to Strategic Air Command. *Redesignated* 55th Strategic Reconnaissance Group in Jun 1948. Aircraft included RB–17's and B– and RB–29's. *Inactivated* on 14 Oct 1949.

Redesignated 55th Strategic Reconnaissance Group (Medium). *Activated* in Puerto Rico on 1 Nov 1950. Assigned to

Strategic Air Command. Equipped with RB–29 and RB–50 aircraft. *Inactivated* on 16 Jun 1952.

SQUADRONS. *7th* Geodetic: 1949. *37th:* 1941–1943. *38th:* 1941–1946; 1949; 1950–1952. *54th:* 1941–1942. *338th:* 1942–1946; 1949; 1950–1952. *343d:* 1943–1946; 1947–1949; 1950–1952.

STATIONS. Hamilton Field, Calif, 15 Jan 1941; Portland, Ore, 21 May 1941; Paine Field, Wash, 10 Feb 1942; McChord Field, Wash, 22 Jul 1942–23 Aug 1943; Nuthampstead, England, 14 Sep 1943; Wormingford, England, 16 Apr 1944; Kaufbeuren, Germany, 22 Jul 1945; Giebelstadt, Germany, 29 Apr–20 Aug 1946. MacDill Field, Fla, 24 Feb 1947; Topeka AFB, Kan, 30 Jun 1948–14 Oct 1949. Ramey AFB, PR, 1 Nov 1950–16 Jun 1952.

COMMANDERS. Capt Kenneth S Wade, 15 Jan 1941; Maj James W McCauley, 1 May 1941; Lt Col Karl K Bowen, 1 May 1942; Maj Jack S Jenkins, 1 Aug 1942; Maj Ernest W Keating, 13 Nov 1942; Lt Col Frank B James, 15 May 1943; Col Jack S Jenkins, 6 Feb 1944; Col George T Crowell, 10 Apr 1944; Lt Col Elwyn C Righetti, 22 Feb 1945; Col Ben Rimerman, 22 Apr 1945; Lt Col Jack W Hayes Jr, 21 May 1945; Lt Col Horace A Hanes, Jul 1946–unkn. Capt Daniel W Burrows, 24 Feb 1947; Lt Col Albert M Welsh, 20 May 1947–unkn; Lt Col George Humbrecht, 26 Oct 1948–unkn; Col Herbert K Baisley, unkn–1949. Col Richard T King, 1 Nov 1950; Brig Gen Sydney D Grubbs Jr, 20 Dec 1950; Col Alfred K Kalberer, 18 Feb–16 Jun 1952.

CAMPAIGNS. American Theater; Air Offensive, Europe; Normandy; Northern France; Rhineland; Ardennes-Alsace; Central Europe.

DECORATIONS. Distinguished Unit Citations: ETO, 3–13 Sep 1944; Germany, 19 Feb 1945.

INSIGNE. *Shield:* Azure, on a fess indented or a similar bar gules. *Motto:* PURSUIT TO DEFEND. (Approved 18 Feb 1942. This insigne was replaced 4 Feb 1954.)

56th FIGHTER GROUP

Constituted as 56th Pursuit Group (Interceptor) on 20 Nov 1940. *Activated* on 15 Jan 1941. Equipped with P–39's and P–40's. Trained, participated in maneuvers, served as an air defense organization, and functioned as an operational training unit. *Redesignated* 56th Fighter Group in May 1942. Received P–47's in Jun and began training for combat. Moved to England, Dec 1942–Jan 1943. Assigned to

Eighth AF. Continued training for several weeks. Entered combat with a fighter sweep in the area of St Omer on 13 Apr 1943, and during the next two years destroyed more enemy aircraft in aerial combat than any other fighter group of Eighth AF. Flew numerous missions over France, the Low Countries, and Germany to escort bombers that attacked industrial establishments, V-weapon sites, submarine pens, and other targets on the Continent. Also strafed and dive-bombed airfields, troops, and supply points; attacked the enemy's communications; and flew counter-air patrols. Engaged in counter-air and interdictory missions during the invasion of Normandy in Jun 1944. Supported Allied forces for the breakthrough at St Lo in Jul. Participated in the Battle of the Bulge, Dec 1944–Jan 1945. Helped to defend the Remagen bridgehead against air attacks in Mar 1945. Received a DUC for aggressiveness in seeking out and destroying enemy aircraft and for attacking enemy air bases, 20 Feb–9 Mar 1944. Received another DUC for strikes against antiaircraft positions while supporting the airborne attack on Holland in Sep 1944. Flew last combat mission on 21 Apr 1945. Returned to the US in Oct. *Inactivated* on 18 Oct 1945.

Activated on 1 May 1946. Equipped with P–47 and P–51 aircraft; converted to F–80's in 1947. *Redesignated* 56th Fighter-Interceptor Group in Jan 1950. Converted to F–86 aircraft. *Inactivated* on 6 Feb 1952.

Redesignated 56th Fighter Group (Air Defense). *Activated* on 18 Aug 1955. Assigned to Air Defense Command and equipped with F–86's.

SQUADRONS. *61st:* 1941–1945; 1946–1952. *62d:* 1941–1945; 1946–1952; 1955–. *63d:* 1941–1945; 1946–1952; 1955–.

STATIONS. Savannah, Ga, 15 Jan 1941; Charlotte, NC, May 1941; Charleston, SC, Dec 1941; Bendix, NJ, Jan 1942; Bridgeport, Conn, c. 7 Jul–Dec 1942; Kings Cliffe, England, Jan 1943; Horsham St Faith, England, c. 6 Apr 1943; Halesworth, England, c. 9 Jul 1943; Boxted, England, c. 19 Apr 1944–Oct 1945; Camp Kilmer, NJ, c. 16–18 Oct 1945. Selfridge Field, Mich, 1 May 1946–6 Feb 1952. O'Hare Intl Aprt, Ill, 18 Aug 1955–.

COMMANDERS. Unkn, Jan–Jun 1941; Lt Col Davis D Graves, Jun 1941; Col John C Crosthwaite, c. 1 Jul 1942; Col Hubert A Zemke, Sep 1942; Col Robert B Landry, 30 Oct 1943; Col Hubert A Zemke, 19 Jan 1944; Col David C Schilling, 12 Aug 1944; Lt Col Lucian A Dade Jr, 27 Jan 1945; Lt Col Donald D Renwick, Aug 1945–unkn. Col David C Schilling, May 1946; Lt Col Thomas D DeJarnette, Aug 1948; Lt Col Irwin H Dregne, 1949; Lt Col Francis S Gabreski, 1950; Col Earnest J White Jr, 1951–unkn. Unkn, 1955–.

CAMPAIGNS. American Theater; Air Offensive, Europe; Normandy; Northern France; Rhineland; Ardennes-Alsace; Central Europe.

DECORATIONS. Distinguished Unit Citations: ETO, 20 Feb–9 Mar 1944; Holland, 18 Sep 1944.

INSIGNE. *Shield:* Tenne on a chevron azure fimbriated or two lightning flashes chevronwise of the last. *Motto:* CAVE TONITRUM—Beware of the Thunderbolt. (Approved 4 Apr 1942.)

57th FIGHTER GROUP

Constituted as 57th Pursuit Group (Interceptor) on 20 Nov 1940. *Activated* on 15 Jan 1941. Trained with P-40's. Served as part of the defense force on the east coast after the Japanese attack on Pearl Harbor. *Redesignated* 57th Fighter Group in May 1942. Moved to the Middle East, Jul–Aug 1942. Trained with RAF. Began operations in Oct 1942. Took part in the Battle of El Alamein and, as part of Ninth AF, supported British Eighth Army's drive across Egypt and Libya, escorting bombers and flying strafing and dive-bombing missions against airfields, communications, and troop concentrations until the defeat of Axis forces in Tunisia in May 1943. Re-

ceived a DUC for performance on 18 Apr 1943 when the group destroyed more than 70 of the enemy's transport and fighter planes in an aerial battle over the Gulf of Tunis. Participated in the reduction of Pantelleria (May–Jun 1943) and the conquest of Sicily (Jul–Aug 1943). Received another DUC for front-line operations in direct support of British Eighth Army from the Battle of El Alamein to the capitulation of enemy forces in Sicily. Assigned to Twelfth AF in Aug 1943 and continued operations in the Mediterranean theater until the end of the war. Supported British Eighth Army's landing at Termoli and subsequent operations in Italy (Oct 1943–Feb 1944) by flying dive-bombing, strafing, patrol, and escort missions. Converted to P-47's early in 1944 and used the new aircraft for interdictory operations in Italy, receiving a DUC for a series of devastating attacks on rail lines, trains, motor vehicles, bridges, and other targets in the Florence-Arezzo area on 14 Apr 1944. Participated in the French campaign against Elba in Jun 1944 and in the invasion of Southern France in Aug. Engaged in interdictory and support operations in northern Italy from Sep 1944 to May 1945. Returned to the US in Aug 1945. *Inactivated* on 7 Nov 1945.

Activated in Alaska on 15 Aug 1946. Assigned to Alaskan Air Command. *Redesignated* 57th Fighter-Interceptor Group in Jan 1950. Equipped successively with P-38, P-51, F-80, and F-94 aircraft. *Inactivated* in Alaska on 13 Apr 1953.

SQUADRONS. *64th:* 1941–1945; 1946–1953. *65th:* 1941–1945; 1946–1953. *66th:* 1941–1945; 1946–1953.

STATIONS. Mitchel Field, NY, 15 Jan 1941; Windsor Locks, Conn, 19 Aug 1941; Boston, Mass, 8 Dec 1941–c. 1 Jul 1942; Muqeibile, Palestine, c. 20 Jul 1942; Egypt, 16 Sep 1942; Libya, 12 Nov 1942; Tunisia, Mar 1943; Malta, Jun 1943; Sicily, Jul 1943; Southern Italy, Sep 1943; Gioia Airfield, Italy, c. 25 Sep 1943; Foggia, Italy, Oct 1943; Amendola, Italy, c. 27 Oct 1943; Cercola, Italy, Mar 1944; Corsica, Mar 1944; Ombrone Airfield, Italy, Sep 1944; Grosseto, Italy, Sep 1944; Villafranca di Verona, Italy, 29 Apr 1945; Grosseto, Italy, 7 May 1945; Bagnoli, Italy, 15 Jul–5 Aug 1945; Drew Field, Fla, 21 Aug–7 Nov 1945. Shemya, Alaska, 15 Aug 1946; Elmendorf AFB, Alaska, Mar 1947–13 Apr 1953.

COMMANDERS. Maj Reuben C Moffat, c. 15 Jan 1941; Maj Clayton B Hughes, unkn; Maj Minthorne W Reed, 12 Dec 1941; Lt Col Frank H Mears, 1942; Col Arthur G Salisbury, 20 Dec 1942; Col Archibald J Knight, 23 Apr 1944; Lt Col William J Yates, 23 May 1945–unkn. Maj Benjamin H King, 15 Aug 1946; Lt Col Gilmore V Norris, 26 Dec 1946; Lt Col Harry L Downing Jr, 10 Jan 1947; Col Morton D Magoffin, 14 Nov 1947; Col Bingham T Kleine, 22 Jan 1949; Col John W Mitchell, c. Nov 1950; Lt Col Ollie O Simpson, 19 Nov 1951; Col Thomas H Beeson, 21 Nov 1951; unkn, 1 Jul 1952–13 Apr 1953.

CAMPAIGNS. Air Combat, EAME Theater; Egypt-Libya; Tunisia; Sicily; Naples-Foggia; Rome-Arno; Southern France; North Apennines; Po Valley.

DECORATIONS. Distinguished Unit Citations: North Africa and Sicily, 24 Oct 1942–17 Aug 1943; Tunis and Cape Bon Area, 18 Apr 1943; Italy, 14 Apr 1944.

INSIGNE. *Shield:* Azure, on a chevron embattled or, between three pyramids of the last, as many mullets gules. *Motto:* FIRST IN THE BLUE. (Approved 2 Feb 1950.)

58th FIGHTER GROUP

Constituted as 58th Pursuit Group (Interceptor) on 20 Nov 1940. *Activated* on 15 Jan 1941. *Redesignated* 58th Fighter Group in May 1942. Used P–35, P–36, P–39, and P–40 aircraft while serving as a replacement training unit for pilots until 1943. Prepared for combat with P–47's. Moved to New Guinea, via Australia, Oct–Dec 1943. Assigned to Fifth AF. Began operations in Feb 1944, flying protective patrols over US bases and escorting transports. After that, covered bombers on raids over New Guinea, attacked Japanese airfields and installations, and escorted convoys to the Admiralty Islands. Moved to Noemfoor in Aug 1944, and until Nov bombed and strafed enemy airfields and installations on Ceram, Halmahera, and the Kai Islands. After moving to the Philippines in Nov 1944, conducted fighter sweeps against enemy airfields, supported ground forces, and flew patrols over convoy and transport routes. Received a DUC for strafing a Japanese naval force off Mindoro on 26 Dec 1944 to prevent destruction of the American base on that island. Moved to Okinawa in Jul 1945 and attacked railways, airfields, and installations in Korea and Kyushu before V-J Day. Remained in the theater after the war as part of Far East Air Forces. Flew some reconnaissance and surveillance missions over Japan. Moved to Japan in Oct and returned to the Philippines in Dec 1945. *Inactivated* on 27 Jan 1946.

Redesignated 58th Fighter-Bomber Group. *Activated* in Korea on 10 Jul 1952. Assigned to Tactical Air Command but attached to Far East Air Forces for operations in the Korean War. Using F-84's, bombed and strafed enemy airfields and installations and supported UN ground forces. Remained in Korea after the armistice. Equipped with F-86's in 1954.

SQUADRONS. *67th:* 1941-1942. *68th:* 1941-1942. *69th:* 1941-1946; 1952-. *310th:* 1942-1946; 1952-. *311th:* 1942-1946; 1952-.

STATIONS. Selfridge Field, Mich, 15 Jan 1941; Baton Rouge, La, 5 Oct 1941; Dale Mabry Field, Fla, 4 Mar 1942; Richmond AAB, Va, 16 Oct 1942; Philadelphia Mun Aprt, Pa, 24 Oct 1942; Bradley Field, Conn, c. 3 Mar 1943; Green Field, RI, 28 Apr 1943; Grenier Field, NH, 16 Sep-22 Oct 1943; Sydney, Australia, 19 Nov 1943; Brisbane, Australia, 21 Nov 1943; Dobodura, New Guinea, 28 Dec 1943; Saidor, New Guinea, c. 3 Apr 1944; Noemfoor, 30 Aug 1944; San Roque, Leyte, 18 Nov 1944; San Jose, Mindoro, c. 30 Dec 1944; Mangaldan, Luzon, 5 Apr 1945; Porac, Luzon, 18 Apr 1945; Okinawa, 10 Jul 1945; Japan, 26 Oct 1945; Ft William McKinley, Luzon, 28 Dec 1945-27 Jan 1946. Taegu, Korea, 10 Jul 1952; Osan-Ni, Korea, 15 Mar 1955-.

COMMANDERS. Capt John M Sterling, 15 Jan 1941-unkn; Maj Louis W Chick, Jr, unkn; Col Gwen G Atkinson, 8 Dec 1942; Lt Col Edward F Roddy, 12 Mar 1945-unkn. Col Charles E Jordan, 1952; Col Frederick J Nelander, 1953; Col George V Williams, 1954; Col William R Brown, 1954; Col Clifford D Nash, 1 Nov 1955-.

CAMPAIGNS. *World War II:* American Theater; Air Offensive, Japan; New Guinea; Bismarck Archipelago; Western Pacific; Leyte; Luzon; China Offensive. *Korean War:* Korea Summer-Fall, 1952; Third Korean Winter; Korea Summer-Fall, 1953.

DECORATIONS. Distinguished Unit Citations: Philippines, 26 Dec 1944; Korea, 1 May–27 Jul 1953. Philippine Presidential Unit Citation. Republic of Korea Presidential Unit Citation: 10 Jul 1952–31 Mar 1953.

INSIGNE. *Shield:* Azure, on clouds in base a representation of the Greek mythological goddess Artemis with quiver and bow, in her chariot drawn by the two deer, all or. *Motto:* NON REVERTAR INULTUS—I Will Not Return Unavenged. (Approved 10 Aug 1942.)

59th FIGHTER GROUP

Constituted as 59th Observation Group on 21 Aug 1941. *Activated* on 1 Sep 1941. Assigned to First AF. Participated in maneuvers and after the outbreak of war engaged in patrol activity along the east coast of the US. Used BC–1A, L–59, O–46, O–47, O–49, and O–52 aircraft. *Inactivated* on 18 Oct 1942.

Activated on 1 Mar 1943. Assigned to Third AF. *Redesignated* 59th Reconnaissance Group in Apr 1943, and 59th Fighter Group in Aug 1943. Trained pilots, using P–39 aircraft, with part of the group converting to P–40's in Apr 1944. *Disbanded* on 1 May 1944.

SQUADRONS. *34th* (formerly 126th): 1941–1942; 1943. *103d:* 1941–1942. *447th:* 1943–1944. *488th* (formerly 9th): 1942; 1943–1944. *489th* (formerly 104th): 1941–1942; 1943–1944. *490th* (formerly 119th): 1942; 1943–1944.

STATIONS. Newark, NJ, 1 Sep 1941; Pope Field, NC, c. Oct 1941; Ft Dix, NJ, Dec 1941–18 Oct 1942. Ft Myers, Fla, 1 Mar 1943; Thomasville AAFld, Ga, c. 30 Mar 1943–1 May 1944.

COMMANDERS. Lt Col Victor Dallin, 1941; Lt Col Chester A Charles, Jan 1942–unkn. Maj Leland S McGowan, c. 24 Mar 1943; Lt Col William R Clingerman Jr, 14 Apr 1943; Col James B League Jr, Oct 1943; Lt Col James Van G Wilson, 11 Mar–c. 1 May 1944.

CAMPAIGNS. Antisubmarine, American Theater.

DECORATIONS. None.

INSIGNE. *Shield:* Azure issuant fanwise from clouds in sinister base proper five rays, in dexter chief a mullet or. *Motto:* EXEMPLAR—An Example. (Approved 24 Nov 1942.)

60th TROOP CARRIER GROUP

Constituted as 60th Transport Group on 20 Nov 1940. *Activated* on 1 Dec 1940.

Prepared for duty overseas with C–47's. Moved to England in Jun 1942. *Redesignated* 60th Troop Carrier Group in Jul 1942. Received additional training in England, then assigned to Twelfth AF for operations in the Mediterranean theater. Flew its first mission on 8 Nov 1942, transporting paratroops from England and dropping them at Oran during the early hours of the invasion of North Africa. Operated from bases in Algeria, Tunisia, Sicily, and Italy until after V–E Day. Participated in the battle for Tunisia, dropping paratroops near the combat area on two occasions. Trained with gliders during Jun 1943, then towed gliders to Syracuse and dropped paratroops behind enemy lines at Catania when the Allies invaded Sicily in Jul. Dropped paratroops at Megava during the airborne invasion of Greece in Oct 1944. When not engaged in airborne operations, the group transported men and supplies and evacuated wounded personnel. Flew to north-ern Italy in Oct 1943 to drop supplies to men who had escaped from prisoner-of-war camps. Received a DUC for supporting the partisans in the Balkans, Mar–Sep 1944: flew at night, unarmed, over unfamiliar and mountainous enemy territory and landed on small, poorly-constructed airfields to provide guns, ammunition, clothing, food, medical supplies, gas, oil, jeeps, mail, and mules for underground forces in Yugoslavia, Albania, and Greece; evacuated wounded partisans and escaped prisoners; also dropped propaganda leaflets. Moved to Trinidad in Jun 1945 and assigned to Air Transport Command. *Inactivated* on 31 Jul 1945.

Activated in Germany on 30 Sep 1946. Assigned to United States Air Forces in Europe. Equipped first with C–47's, then (late in 1948) with C–54's. Participated in the Berlin airlift, Jun 1948–Sep 1949. *Redesignated* 60th Troop Carrier Group (Medium) in Jul 1948, 60th Troop Carrier Group (Heavy) in Nov 1948, and 60th Troop Carrier Group (Medium) in Nov 1949. Re-equipped with C–82 aircraft in 1949 and with C–119's in 1953.

SQUADRONS. *10th:* 1940–1945; 1946–. *11th:* 1940–1945; 1946–. *12th:* 1940–1945; 1946–. *28th:* 1942–1945.

STATIONS. Olmsted Field, Pa, 1 Dec 1940; Westover Field, Mass, c. 20 May 1941–Jun 1942; Chelveston, England, Jun 1942; Aldermaston, England, Aug 1942; Tafaraoui, Algeria, 8 Nov 1942; Relizane, Algeria, 27 Nov 1942; Thiersville, Algeria, May 1943; El Djem, Tunisia, Jun 1943; Gela, Sicily, c. 30 Aug 1943; Gerbini,

Sicily, 29 Oct 1943; Brindisi, Italy, 26 Mar 1944; Pomigliano, Italy, 8 Oct 1944–May 1945; Waller Field, Trinidad, 4 Jun–31 Jul 1945. Munich, Germany, 30 Sep 1946; Kaufbeuren AB, Germany, 14 May 1948; Wiesbaden AB, Germany, 15 Dec 1948; Rhein/Main AB, Germany, 26 Sep 1949; Dreux AB, France, 22 Sep 1955–.

COMMANDERS. Lt Col Samuel C Eaton Jr, 1 Dec 1940; Capt Arthur L Logan, 16 May 1941; Lt Col Russell L Maughan, 28 Jul 1941; Lt Col A J Kerwin Malone, 15 Apr 1942, Lt Col T J Schofield, 11 Oct 1942; Lt Col Julius A Kolb, 2 Dec 1942; Lt Col Frederick H. Sherwood, 29 Mar 1943; Col Clarence J Galligan, 26 Jul 1943; Lt Col Kenneth W Holbert, 8 Dec 1944; Lt Col Charles A Gibson Jr, 11 Jan 1945–unkn. Col Casper P West, 30 Sep 1946; Col Bertram C Harrison, Sep 1947; Col Theron H Coulter, Dec 1948; Lt Col Lawrence G Gilbert, Jan 1949; Col Robert D Forman, Mar 1949; Lt Col Reesor M Lawrence, 26 Aug 1950; Col Jay D Bogue, 5 Dec 1950; Col Donald J French, 29 Feb 1952; Lt Col John W Osborn, 14 Jun 1952; Col Lorris W Moomaw, 25 May 1953; Lt Col Robert L Olinger, 13 Jun 1954; Col Howard J Withycombe, 1 Jul 1954; Col Randolph E Churchill, c. 5 Jul 1955–.

CAMPAIGNS. Air Combat, EAME Theater; Algeria-French Morocco; Tunisia; Sicily; Naples-Foggia; Rome-Arno; Southern France; North Apennines; Po Valley.

DECORATIONS. Distinguished Unit Citation: MTO, 28 Mar–15 Sep 1944.

INSIGNE. *Shield:* Azure a pale of seven variegated pallets proper, black, yellow, red, white, blue, orange, and green, the pale fimbriated and surmounted by three symbols of flight or, in bend, all within a narrow border of the last. *Motto:* TERMINI NON EXISTENT—Boundaries Do Not Exist. (Approved 7 Sep 1955.)

61st TROOP CARRIER GROUP

Constituted as 61st Transport Group on 20 Nov 1940. *Activated* on 1 Dec 1940. *Redesignated* 61st Troop Carrier Group in Jul 1942. Used C–47's to prepare for operations with Twelfth AF. Moved to North Africa in May 1943 and, after a period of special training, began operations on the night of 9 Jul by dropping paratroops near Gela during the invasion of Sicily. Received a DUC for completing a reinforcement mission two nights later when the group sustained heavy attack by ground and naval forces. Moved to Sicily, Aug–Sep 1943, for participation in the invasion of Italy; dropped paratroops north of Agropoli on 13 Sep 1943 and flew a reinforcement mission to the same area on 14 Sep. Also transported cargo and evacuated patients while in the Mediterranean theater. Joined Ninth AF in England in Feb 1944 to prepare for the Normandy invasion. Received a DUC for dropping paratroops and supplies near Cherbourg on 6 and 7 Jun 1944. Dropped British paratroops at Arnhem on 17 Sep 1944 during the air attack on Holland; released gliders carrying reinforcements to that area on succeeding days. Moved to France in Mar 1945 for the airborne assault across the Rhine, dropping British paratroops near Wesel on 24 Mar. Also provided transport services in the European theater, hauling gasoline, ammunition, food, medicine, and other supplies, and evacuating wounded personnel. Moved to Trinidad in May 1945. Assigned to Air Transport Command. Used C–47's to transport troops returning to the US. *Inactivated* in Trinidad on 31 Jul 1945.

Activated in Germany on 30 Sep 1946. Assigned to United States Air Forces in Europe. *Redesignated* 61st Troop Carrier Group (Medium) in Jul 1948, and 61st Troop Carrier Group (Heavy) in Aug 1948. Participated in the Berlin Airlift from Jun 1948 to May 1949, using C–54's to ferry coal, flour, and other cargo into West Berlin. Moved to the US shortly after the outbreak of war in Korea for duty with Military Air Transport Service. Operated on the northern route to Japan,

transporting supplies for UN forces in Korea. Moved to Japan in Dec 1950, attached to Far East Air Forces, and engaged in transport operations between Japan and Korea. Returned to the US in Nov 1952 to join Tactical Air Command, to which the group had been assigned in Oct 1951. Converted from C–54 to C–124 aircraft.

SQUADRONS. *13th:* 1940–1942. *14th:* 1940–1945; 1946–. *15th:* 1940–1945; 1946–. *53d:* 1942–1945; 1946–. *59th:* 1942–1945.

STATIONS. Olmsted Field, Pa, 1 Dec 1940; Augusta, Ga, c. 9 Jul 1941; Pope Field, NC, 26 May 1942; Lubbock, Tex, 23 Sep 1942; Pope Field, NC, 26 Feb–4 May 1943; Lourmel, French Morocco, 15 May 1943; Kairouan, Tunisia, 21 Jun 1943; Licata, Sicily, 1 Sep 1943; Sciacca, Sicily, 6 Oct 1943–12 Feb 1944; Barkston, England, 18 Feb 1944–13 Mar 1945; Abbeville, France, 13 Mar–19 May 1945; Waller Field, Trinidad, 29 May–31 Jul 1945. Eschborn AB, Germany, 30 Sep 1946; Rhein/Main AB, Germany, 8 Feb 1947–21 Jul 1950; McChord AFB, Wash, 26 Jul–5 Dec 1950; Ashiya, Japan, 10 Dec 1950; Tachikawa, Japan, 26 Mar–18 Nov 1952; Larson AFB, Wash, 21 Nov 1952; Donaldson AFB, SC, 25 Aug 1954–.

COMMANDERS. Unkn, 1 Dec 1940–1 Feb 1941; Capt John Waugh, 1 Feb 1941; 1st Lt Thompson F Dow, c. 1 Jul 1941; Maj Lorin B Hillsinger, 11 Jul 1941; [1st(?)] Lt Charles A Inskip, unkn; [1st(?)] Lt Allen L Dickey, unkn; Capt John C Bennett, 26 May 1942; Lt Col Ralph J Moore, unkn; Maj Donald French, 6 Mar 1943; Col Willis W Mitchell, 11 Mar 1943; Col

Edgar W Hampton, 12 Apr 1945–unkn.
Maj Charles E Pickering, 30 Sep 1946; Lt
Col Henry J Lawrence, 6 Dec 1946; Maj
Richard C Brock, 13 Jan 1947; Maj Dace T
Garrison, 11 Apr 1947; Lt Col John C
Evers, c. 21 Apr 1948; Col Richard W
DaVania, 28 Aug 1948; Lt Col Jay D
Bogue, Aug 1949; Col Frank Norwood,
1 Oct 1949; Lt Col Hal E Ercanbrack Jr,
14 Feb 1952; Col Lionel F Johnson, 29 Jul
1953; Lt Col Jerome M Triolo, 7 Feb 1954;
Col Leland W Johnson, 1954; Col William
G Forwood, 13 Dec 1954–.

CAMPAIGNS. *World War II:* American
Theater; Sicily; Naples-Foggia; Rome-
Arno; Normandy; Northern France;
Rhineland; Central Europe. *Korean
War:* CCF Intervention; 1st UN Counter-
offensive; CCF Spring Offensive; UN
Summer-Fall Offensive; Second Korean
Winter; Korea Summer-Fall, 1952.

DECORATIONS. Distinguished Unit Citations: Sicily, 11 Jul 1943; France, [6–7]
Jun 1944; Korea, 13 Dec 1950–21 Apr 1951.
Republic of Korea Presidential Unit Citation: [1 Jul 1951–1952].

INSIGNE. *Shield:* Barry of six, or and
azure, a pale nebuly, all counterchanged.
(Approved 20 Aug 1951.)

62d TROOP CARRIER GROUP

Constituted as 62d Transport Group on
20 Nov 1940. *Activated* on 11 Dec 1940.
Transported military freight and supplies
in North and South America and trained
with C–47 and C–53 aircraft. *Redesignated* 62d Troop Carrier Group in Jul
1942. Moved to England, Aug–Sep 1942,
and engaged in further training. Assigned to Twelfth AF and moved to North
Africa to take part in the battle for Tunisia. Began operations on 29 Nov 1942
by dropping paratroops to attack enemy
airdromes in Tunisia. Trained with
gliders for several months, then towed
gliders to Syracuse and also dropped
paratroops behind enemy lines at Catania
during the Allied invasion of Sicily in Jul
1943. Operated from bases in Sicily and
Italy from Sep 1943 until after the war.
Dropped paratroops in northern Italy in
Jun 1944 to harass the retreating enemy
and to prevent the Germans from destroying bridges over which their forces had
withdrawn. Flew two missions in connection with the invasion of Southern France
in Aug 1944, releasing gliders and paratroops in the battle area. Transported
paratroops and towed gliders to Greece
during the Allied assault in Oct 1944. In

addition to the airborne operations, the group transported men and supplies in the Mediterranean theater and to the front lines during the campaigns for Tunisia, Italy, and southern France. Also evacuated wounded personnel and flew missions behind enemy lines in Italy and the Balkans to haul guns, ammunition, food, clothing, medical supplies, and other materials to the partisans and to drop propaganda leaflets. Aided in the redeployment of personnel after the war and also hauled freight and mail. *Inactivated* in Italy on 14 Nov 1945.

Activated in the US on 7 Sep 1946. *Redesignated* 62d Troop Carrier Group (Medium) in Jun 1948, and 62d Troop Carrier Group (Heavy) in Oct 1949. Used C–82, C–54, and C–124 aircraft. Carried out some special missions that included aiding flood-stricken areas in Oregon in 1948, dropping food to cattle snowbound in Nevada in 1949, flying to Japan with mail for troops in Korea in 1952, and participating in the airlift of medical supplies to flooded areas in Pakistan in 1954. Received the AFOUA for transporting French troops and equipment from France to Indochina, Apr–May 1954.

SQUADRONS. *4th:* 1940–1945; 1946–. *7th:* 1940–1945; 1946–. *8th:* 1940–1945; 1946–. *51st:* 1942–1945.

STATIONS. McClellan Field, Calif, 11 Dec 1940; Kellogg Field, Mich, c. 30 May 1942; Florence, SC, 1 Jul–14 Aug 1942; Keevil, England, Sep 1942; Tafaraoui, Algeria, 15 Nov 1942; Nouvion, Algeria, 24 Dec 1942; Matemore, Algeria, 16 May

1943; Tunisia, Jul 1943; Ponte Olivo, Sicily, 6 Sep 1943; Brindisi, Italy, Feb 1944; Ponte Olivo, Sicily, 20 Mar 1944; Gaudo Airfield, Italy, 8 May 1944; Galera Airfield, Italy, 30 Jun 1944; Malignano Airfield, Italy, 30 Sep 1944; Tarquinia, Italy, 8 Jan 1945; Rosignano Airfield, Italy, 25 May 1945; Naples, Italy, c. 17 Sep–14 Nov 1945. Bergstrom Field, Tex, 7 Sep 1946; McChord Field, Wash, c. Aug 1947; Kelly AFB, Tex, 9 May 1950; McChord AFB, Wash, 27 Jul 1950; Larson AFB, Wash, 9 May 1952–.

COMMANDERS. Lt Col Bernard J Tooher, 11 Dec 1940; Maj Donald E Shugart, unkn; Col Samuel J Davis, 1 Jul 1942; Lt Col Aubrey S Hurren, 27 Mar 1943; Col Gordon L Edris, 15 May 1944; Lt Col William M Massengale Jr, 13 Dec 1944; Col Gordon L Edris, 23 Feb 1945; Col Paul A Jones, 27 May 1945; Lt Col Riley B Whearty, 3 Jun 1945; Lt Col Oliver K Halderson, 20 Jul 1945–unkn. Col Donald J French, 7 Sep 1946; Col Adriel N Williams, 1 Mar 1948; Col George S Brown, c. Jul 1950; Col Richard Jones, c. Aug 1951–.

CAMPAIGNS. Air Combat, EAME Theater; Tunisia; Sicily; Naples-Foggia; Rome-Arno; Southern France; North Apennines; Po Valley.

DECORATIONS. Air Force Outstanding Unit Award: 19 Apr–5 May 1954.

INSIGNE. *Shield:* Medium blue, in chief, silhouetted land mass argent, in fess a sun, the rays radiating upward all proper, in base a golden winged sword, tip upward, in pale, hilt and pommel or, blade of the second, all between two branches of olive proper. *Motto:* IN OMNIA PARA-TUS—In All Things Ready. (Approved 18 Aug 1955.)

63d TROOP CARRIER GROUP

Constituted as 63d Transport Group on 20 Nov 1940. *Activated* on 1 Dec 1940. Trained with C-33, C-34, and C-50 aircraft; later equipped with C-47's and C-53's. Transported supplies, materiel, and personnel in the US and the Caribbean area. Became part of Air Transport Command (later I Troop Carrier Command) in Apr 1942. *Redesignated* 63d Troop Carrier Group in Jul 1942. Became a training organization, preparing cadres for troop carrier groups. Began training replacement crews in Jul 1943. *Disbanded* on 14 Apr 1944.

Reconstituted, allotted to the reserve, and *redesignated* 63d Troop Carrier Group (Medium), on 10 May 1949. *Activated* on 27 Jun 1949. Ordered to active service on 1 May 1951. *Inactivated* on 9 May 1951.

Redesignated 63d Troop Carrier Group (Heavy). *Activated* on 20 Jun 1953. Assigned to Tactical Air Command and equipped with C-124's. Trained, transported personnel and supplies, and participated in exercises and maneuvers with airborne troops. In 1955 transported construction equipment from bases in Canada to points north of the Arctic Circle for use in setting up a warning network in the Canadian Arctic; for this operation, accomplished in severe weather and without adequate navigational equipment, the group received an AFOUA.

SQUADRONS. *3d:* 1940–1944; 1949–1951; 1953–. *6th:* 1940–1942. *9th:* 1940–1943; 1949–1951; 1953–. *52d:* 1942–1944; 1949–1951; 1953–. *60th:* 1942–1944; 1949–1951.

STATIONS. Wright Field, Ohio, 1 Dec 1940; Patterson Field, Ohio, 17 Feb 1941; Brookley Field, Ala, 9 Sep 1941; Camp Williams, Wis, 24 May 1942; Dodd Field, Tex, c. 18 Sep 1942; Victorville, Calif, c. 18 Nov. 1942; Lawson Field, Ga, 7 May 1943; Grenada AAFld, Miss, c. 3 Jun 1943; Sedalia AAFld, Mo, 19 Jan–14 Apr 1944. Floyd Bennett NAS, NY, 27 Jun 1949–9 May 1951. Altus AFB, Okla, 20 Jun 1953; Donaldson AFB, SC, 15 Oct 1953–.

COMMANDERS. Capt James L Jackson, 1 Dec 1940; Maj Herman E Hurst, 30 Apr 1942; Lt Col Edward P Dimmick, 3 Oct 1942–14 Apr 1944. Col Kenneth L Johnson, 20 June 1953; Col Horace A Crosswell, 1955–.

CAMPAIGNS. American Theater.

DECORATIONS. Air Force Outstanding Unit Award: 2 Mar–31 May 1955.

INSIGNE. *Shield:* Light blue with a green embattled base, a red lightning flash striking from upper right corner and crossing the corner of one embattlement and a white parachute with shroud lines touching the tip of the flash; above the parachute three white aircraft, on the green base a circle of six yellow stars at the left and a triangle of three yellow stars. *Motto:* OMNIA, UBIQUE, SEMPER— Anything, Anywhere, Anytime. (Approved 2 Oct 1953.)

64th TROOP CARRIER GROUP

Constituted as 64th Transport Group on 20 Nov 1940. *Activated* on 4 Dec 1940. Used C–47's for training and flying transport missions in the US. *Redesignated* 64th Troop Carrier Group in Jul 1942. Moved to England in Aug 1942 and received additional training. Assigned to

FLYING SUPPORT

Twelfth AF. Moved to the Mediterranean theater, Nov–Dec 1942. Flew first mission on 11 Nov, landing paratroops at Maison Blanche. Dropped paratroops to capture airfields during the battle for Tunisia. Released paratroops near Gela and Catania when the Allies invaded Sicily in Jul 1943. Dropped paratroops near Avellino during the invasion of Italy in Sep 1943 to destroy a bridge on the enemy's supply line to Salerno. Participated in the assault on southern France in Aug 1944 by releasing gliders and paratroops in the battle zone. Supported the partisans in northern Italy early in 1945 by dropping paratroops, supplies, and propaganda leaflets behind enemy lines. When not engaged in airborne operations, the group continually transported men and supplies to the front lines and evacuated wounded personnel. Most of the group was on detached service in the CBI theater, Apr–Jun 1944, while a skeleton force remained in Sicily. With its squadrons operating from separate bases in India, the 64th group aided the Allied offensive in Burma, being awarded a DUC for flying unarmed over rugged enemy territory to carry food, clothing, medical supplies, guns, ammunition, and mules to the combat zone and to evacuate wounded personnel. Moved to Trinidad in Jun 1945. Assigned to Air Transport Command. *Inactivated* on 31 Jul 1945.

Activated in the US on 19 May 1947. Not manned during 1947–1948. *Inactivated* on 10 Sep 1948.

Redesignated 64th Troop Carrier Group (Medium). *Activated* on 14 Jul 1952. Assigned to Tactical Air Command. Used C–82 aircraft and later (after Jul 1953) C–119's. *Inactivated* on 21 Jul 1954.

SQUADRONS. *16th:* 1940–1945; 1947–1948. *17th:* 1940–1945; 1947–1948; 1952–1954. *18th:* 1940–1945; 1952–1954. *35th:* 1942–1945; 1952–1954. *54th:* 1942.

STATIONS. Duncan Field, Tex, 4 Dec 1940; March Field, Calif, c. 13 Jul 1941; Hamilton Field, Calif, c. 1 Feb 1942; Westover Field, Mass, c. 8 Jun–31 Jul 1942; Ramsbury, England, Aug–Nov 1942; Blida, Algeria, Dec 1942; Kairouan, Tunisia, 28 Jun 1943; El Djem, Tunisia, 26 Jul 1943; Comiso, Sicily, 29 Aug 1943; Ciampino, Italy, 10 Jul 1944; Rosignano Airfield, Italy, 10 Jan–23 May 1945; Waller Field, Trinidad, 4 Jun–31 Jul 1945. Langley Field, Va, 19 May 1947–10 Sep 1948. Donaldson AFB, SC, 14 Jul 1952–21 Jul 1954.

COMMANDERS. Lt Col Malcolm S Lawton, c. Dec 1940; Col Tracey K Dorsett, unkn; Lt Col Claire B Collier, c. 1 Mar 1943; Col John Cerny, 16 May 1943–1945. Col Steward H Nichols, c. Jul 1952; Col David E Kunkel Jr, c. Nov 1953; Lt Col William G Forwood, unkn–1954.

CAMPAIGNS. American Theater; Algeria-French Morocco; Tunisia; Sicily; Naples-Foggia; Rome-Arno; Southern France; North Apennines; Po Valley; India-Burma.

DECORATIONS. Distinguished Unit Citation: CBI Theater, 7 Apr–15 Jun 1944.

INSIGNE. *Shield:* Azure, an eagle's leg a la cuisse or charged with a mullet of the field. *Motto:* FLYING SUPPORT. (Approved 16 Jun 1942.)

65th RECONNAISSANCE GROUP

Constituted as 65th Observation Group on 21 Aug 1941. *Activated* on 1 Sep 1941. Equipped with O–47's, O–49's, O–52's, and other observation aircraft. Supported ground units during the Carolina Maneuvers in the fall and winter of 1941. Flew antisubmarine patrols off the east coast after Pearl Harbor. *Inactivated* on 18 Oct 1942.

Activated on 1 Mar 1943. *Redesignated* 65th Reconnaissance Group in Apr 1943. Served as a training organization for crews that changed from observation aircraft to B–25's. *Disbanded* on 15 Aug 1943.

Reconstituted, allotted to the reserve, and *activated,* on 27 Dec 1946. *Inactivated* on 27 Jun 1949.

Redesignated 65th Troop Carrier Group (Medium) and allotted to the reserve. *Activated* on 14 Jun 1952. Equipped with C–46's. *Inactivated* on 1 Apr 1953.

SQUADRONS. *2d:* 1947–1949; 1952–1953. *13th:* 1947–1949; 1952–1953. *14th:* 1947–1949; 1952–1953. *18th:* 1942; 1943. *105th:* 1941–1942; 1943. *112th:* 1941–1942. *121st:* 1941–1942.

STATIONS. Columbia, SC, 1 Sep 1941; Langley Field, Va, Dec 1941–18 Oct 1942. Columbia AAB, SC, 1 Mar 1943; Florence AAFld, SC, c. 15 Apr–15 Aug 1943.

Rome AAFld, NY, 27 Dec 1946–27 Jun 1949. Mitchel AFB, NY, 14 Jun 1952–1 Apr 1953.

COMMANDERS. Col Dache M Reeves, 1941; Lt Col Walter M Williams, c. 21 Feb–18 Oct 1942. Lt Col Blaine B Campbell, 1943.

CAMPAIGNS. Antisubmarine, American Theater.

DECORATIONS. None.

INSIGNE. None.

66th RECONNAISSANCE GROUP

OMNIA CONSPICIMUS

Constituted as 66th Observation Group on 21 Aug 1941. *Activated* on 1 Sep 1941. *Redesignated* 66th Reconnaissance Group in Apr 1943, and 66th Tactical Reconnaissance Group in Aug 1943. Equipped at various times with O–46, O–47, A–20, P–39, P–40, B–25, L–5, and L–6 aircraft. Supported ground units on maneuvers, including the Carolina Maneuvers of 1942, the Tennessee Maneuvers of 1942 and 1943, and the Second Army Maneuvers of 1943–1944. Trained personnel in aerial reconnaissance and artillery adjustment methods. Also flew antisubmarine patrols off the east coast, Jan–Aug 1942. *Disbanded* on 20 Apr 1944.

Reconstituted, redesignated 66th Reconnaissance Group, allotted to the reserve, and *activated,* on 27 Dec 1946. Equipped with RB–26's and RF–80's. *Redesignated* 66th Strategic Reconnaissance Group in Jun 1949. Called to active duty on 1 May 1951. *Inactivated* on 16 May 1951.

Redesignated 66th Tactical Reconnaissance Group. *Activated* on 1 Jan 1953. Assigned to Tactical Air Command. Equipped with RB–26's and RF–80's. Moved to Germany, Jun–Jul 1953, and assigned to United States Air Forces in Europe. Transitioned to RB–57's and RF–84's, 1954–1955.

SQUADRONS. *18th:* 1947–1949. *19th* Liaison: 1942–1943. *19th* Reconnaissance: 1947–1949. *20th:* 1947–1949, 1949–1951. *23d:* 1943. *30th:* 1947–1951; 1953–. *97th:* 1941–1943. *106th:* 1941–1943. *118th:* 1941–1943. *302d:* 1953–. *303d:* 1953–.

STATIONS. Jacksonville, Fla, 1 Sep 1941; Charleston, SC, Jan 1942; Jacksonville Mun Aprt, Fla, Mar 1942; Pope Field, NC, May 1942; Tullahoma, Tenn, Sep 1942; Morris Field, NC, Nov 1942; Camp Campbell, Ky, Apr 1943; Aiken AAFld, SC, Jun 1943; Lebanon, Tenn, Oct 1943–20 Apr 1944. Newark AAB, NJ, 27 Dec 1946; McGuire AFB, NJ, 27 Jun 1949; Barksdale AFB, La, 10 Oct 1949–16 May

1951. Shaw AFB, SC, 1 Jan–1 Jul 1953;
Sembach AB, Germany, c. 7 Jul 1953–.

COMMANDERS. Maj Harry W Generous,
4 Nov 1941; Lt Col Charles A Masson, c.
26 May 1942; Lt Col Theron Coulter, 6
Dec 1942; Maj Edward O McComas, c.
31 Aug 1943; Lt Col Frederick L Moore,
c. 16 Oct 1943–20 Apr 1944. Lt Col Stanley W Irons, Jan 1953; Col Harvey E Henderson, Jul 1953–.

CAMPAIGNS. Antisubmarine, American
Theater.

DECORATIONS. None.

INSIGNE. *Shield:* Per bend gules and
azure, a bend nebule argent between a
sprig of goldenrod or, and a sprig of mountain laurel vert, fimbriated of the fourth.
Motto: OMNIA CONSPICIMUS—We
Observe All. (Approved 5 Jan 1943.)

67th RECONNAISSANCE GROUP

Constituted as 67th Observation Group
on 21 Aug 1941. *Activated* on 1 Sep 1941.
Flew antisubmarine patrols along the east
coast of the US after the Japanese attacked
Pearl Harbor. Began training in Jan 1942
for duty overseas. Moved to the European
theater, Aug–Oct 1942. Assigned first to
Eighth and later (Oct 1943) to Ninth AF.
Redesignated 67th Reconnaissance Group
in May 1943, 67th Tactical Reconnaissance
Group in Nov 1943, and 67th Reconnaissance Group in Jun 1945. Trained in England for more than a year before beginning operations in Dec 1943. Used P–38's,
P–51's, and F–5's to fly artillery-adjustment, weather-reconnaissance, bomb-damage assessment, photographic-reconnaissance, and visual-reconnaissance missions.
Received a DUC for operations along
the coast of France, 15 Feb–20 Mar 1944,
when the group flew at low altitude in
the face of intense flak to obtain photographs that aided the invasion of the Continent. Flew weather missions, made
visual reconnaissance for ground forces,
and photographed enemy positions to support the Normandy campaign and later to
assist First Army and other Allied forces
in the drive to Germany. Took part in the
offensive against the Siegfried Line, Sep–
Dec 1944, and in the Battle of the Bulge,
Dec 1944–Jan 1945. From Jan to May
1945, photographed dams on the Roer
River in preparation for the ground offensive to cross the river, and aided the
Allied assault across the Rhine and into
Germany. Returned to the US, Jul–Sep
1945. *Inactivated* on 31 Mar 1946.

Activated on 19 May 1947. Assigned to
Tactical Air Command. Equipped with
RB–26's and RF–80's. *Redesignated* 67th

Tactical Reconnaissance Group in Jun 1948. *Inactivated* on 28 Mar 1949.

Activated in Japan on 25 Feb 1951. Assigned to Far East Air Forces. Moved to Korea in Mar 1951 and served in the Korean War until the armistice. Used RB–26, RF–51, RF–80, RF–86, and RF–84 aircraft. Made photographic reconnaissance of front lines, enemy positions, and installations; took pre-strike and bomb-damage assessment photographs; made visual reconnaissance of enemy artillery and naval gun positions; and flew weather missions. Received an AFOUA for the period 1 Dec 1952–30 Apr 1953 when, in the face of enemy opposition and adverse weather, the group performed reconnaissance missions on a 24-hour-a-day, 7-day-a-week basis to provide valuable intelligence for UN forces. Returned to Japan, Nov–Dec 1954.

SQUADRONS. *11th:* 1946; 1947–1949; 1953–. *12th:* 1942–1944; 1947–1949; 1951–. *15th* (formerly Observation): 1944; 1951–. *15th* (formerly Photographic): 1947. *30th:* 1944–1945. *33d:* 1944, 1945. *45th:* 1951–. *107th:* 1941–1945. *109th:* 1941–1945. *113th:* 1941–1942. *153d:* 1941–1944. *161st:* 1945.

STATIONS. Esler Field, La, 1 Sep 1941; Charleston, SC, Dec 1941; Esler Field, La, Jan–Aug 1942; Membury, England, Sep 1942; Middle Wallop, England, Dec 1943; Le Molay, France, Jul 1944; Toussus le Noble, France, Aug 1944; Gosselies, Belgium, Sep 1944; Vogelsang, Germany, Mar 1945; Limburg an der Lahn, Germany, c. 2 Apr 1945; Eschwege, Germany, c. 10 Apr–Jul 1945; Drew Field, Fla, c. 21 Sep 1945; MacDill Field, Fla, Dec 1945; Shaw Field, SC, Feb–31 Mar 1946. Langley Field, Va, 19 May 1947; March Field, Calif, c. 25 Jul 1947–28 Mar 1949. Komaki, Japan, 25 Feb 1951; Taegu, Korea, Mar 1951; Kimpo, Korea, Aug 1951; Itami, Japan, c. 1 Dec 1954–.

COMMANDERS. Unkn, Sep–Nov 1941; Lt Col Oliver H Stout, c. 21 Nov 1941; Col Frederick R Anderson, c. 4 May 1942; Col George W Peck, 6 Dec 1943; Lt Col Richard S Leghorn, 11 May 1945–unkn. Unkn, May–Jul 1947; Maj Edwin C Larson, 25 Jul 1947; Lt Col Arvis L Hilpert, 15 Aug 1947; Col Leon W Gray, 16 Aug 1947; Lt Col Royal B Allison, 20 Mar 1948; Col Horace A Hanes, 22 Mar 1948; Col Loren G McCollom, c. 16 Jan 1949–unkn. Col Jacob W Dixon, c. 28 Feb 1951; Lt Col [?] Stone, c. 29 Aug 1951; Col Charles C Andrews, Sep 1951; Col Robert R Smith, May 1952; Lt Col George T Prior, Oct 1952; Col John G Foster, 1952–unkn; Col John C Egan, c. 22 Oct 1953; Lt Col Hartwell C Lancaster, 8 May 1954; Col Loren G McCollom, 1 June 1954; Col Prescott M Spicer, 11 Aug 1954; Lt Col Joseph C Smith, 24 Nov 1954–unkn; Col John W Baer, 31 Aug 1955–.

CAMPAIGNS. *World War II:* Antisubmarine, American Theater; Air Offensive, Europe; Normandy; Northern France; Rhineland; Ardennes-Alsace; Central Europe. *Korean War:* 1st UN Counteroffensive; CCF Spring Offensive; UN Summer-Fall Offensive; Second Korean Winter; Korea Summer-Fall, 1952; Third

Korean Winter; Korea Summer-Fall, 1953.

DECORATIONS. Distinguished Unit Citations: Le Havre and Straits of Dover, 15 Feb–20 Mar 1944; Korea, 25 Feb–21 Apr 1951; Korea, 9 Jul–27 Nov 1951; Korea, 1 May–27 Jul 1953. Cited in the Order of the Day, Belgian Army: 6 Jun–30 Sep 1944; 16 Dec 1944–25 Jan 1945. Belgian Fourragere. Republic of Korea Presidential Unit Citation: [Mar] 1951–31 Mar 1953. Air Force Outstanding Unit Award: 1 Dec 1952–30 Apr 1953.

INSIGNE. *Shield:* Per bend sinister, sky proper (light blue) and azure between a lightning bolt gules, fimbriated sable, in bend sinister, the quarter section of a sun, issuing from the dexter chief, or, fimbriated sable, in sinister four stars argent, one, two and one, all the shield within a diminutive border sable. *Motto:* LUX EX TENEBRIS—Light from Darkness. (Approved 20 Mar 1952.)

68th RECONNAISSANCE GROUP

Constituted as 68th Observation Group on 21 Aug 1941. *Activated* on 1 Sep 1941. *Redesignated* 68th Reconnaissance Group in May 1943, and 68th Tactical Reconnaissance Group in Nov 1943. Flew patrols over the Gulf of Mexico and along the Mexican border after the Japanese attacked Pearl Harbor. Began training in Feb 1942 for duty overseas. Moved to the Mediterranean theater, Oct–Nov 1942, and assigned to Twelfth AF. Shortly after the group began operations most of its squadrons were detached for separate duty in order to carry out diverse activities over a wide area. Operating from bases in North Africa until Nov 1943, the group, or elements of the group, engaged in patrolling the Mediterranean; strafing trucks, tanks, gun positions, and supply dumps to support ground troops in Tunisia; training fighter pilots and replacement crews; and flying photographic and visual reconnaissance missions in Tunisia, Sicily, and Italy to provide information needed to adjust artillery fire. Moved to Italy and assigned to Fifteenth AF, in Nov 1943. Continued visual and photographic reconnaissance and began flying weather reconnaissance missions in Italy, France, Germany, Austria, Hungary, and the Balkans. Also engaged in electronic-countermeasure activities, investigating radar equipment captured from the enemy, flying ferret missions along the coasts of Italy and southern France, and accompanying bomber formations to detect approaching enemy fighters. Used P–38, P–39, P–40, P–51, A–20, A–36, B–17, and B–24 aircraft for operations. Returned to North Africa in Apr 1944. *Disbanded* on 15 Jun 1944.

Reconstituted, redesignated 68th Reconnaissance Group, and allotted to the reserve, on 10 Mar 1947. *Activated* in the US on 9 Apr 1947. *Inactivated* on 27 Jun 1949.

Redesignated 68th Strategic Reconnaissance Group (Medium). *Activated* on 10 Oct 1951. Assigned to Strategic Air Command. Trained with B–29's. *Inactivated* on 16 Jun 1952.

SQUADRONS. *16th:* 1942–1944. *24th:* 1947–1949; 1951–1952. *51st:* 1947–1949; 1951–1952. *52d:* 1947–1949; 1951–1952. *111th:* 1942–1944. *122d:* 1941–1944. *125th:* 1941–1942. *127th:* 1941–1942. *154th:* 1941–1944.

STATIONS. Brownwood, Tex, 1 Sep 1941; New Orleans AB, La, 17 Dec 1941; Daniel Field, Ga, 8 Feb 1942; Smith Reynolds Aprt, NC, 9 Jul 1942; Morris Field, NC, c. 17 Aug–18 Oct 1942; Casablanca, French Morocco, Nov 1942; Oujda, French Morocco, c. Nov 1942; Berrechid Airfield, French Morocco, 24 Mar 1943; Berteaux, Algeria, 5 Sep 1943; Massicault, Tunisia, Oct 1943; Manduria, Italy, Nov 1943; Blida, Algeria, c. Apr–15 Jun 1944. Hamilton Field, Calif, 9 Apr 1947–27 Jun 1949. Lake Charles AFB, La, 10 Oct 1951–16 Jun 1952.

COMMANDERS. Unkn, Sep–Dec 1941; Lt Col Guy L McNeil, 15 Dec 1941; Maj John R Fordyce, 30 Jun 1942; Lt Col Eu-gene C Woltz, 13 Mar 1943; Col Charles D Jones, 8 Aug 1943–c. 15 Jan 1944; Capt Harper L McGrady, unkn; Col [?] Smith, unkn; Col Monro MacCloskey, Mar–c. May 1944. Col Lowell G Sidling, 26 Oct 1951–c. 16 Jun 1952.

CAMPAIGNS. Antisubmarine, American Theater; Air Combat, EAME Theater; Algeria-French Morocco; Naples-Foggia; Rome-Arno.

DECORATIONS. None.

INSIGNE. *Shield:* Azure, an eye of the first surmounting a tuft of six feathers, imposed on a tuft of eight feathers, between and at the base of two wings conjoined in the form of a "V" or. *Motto:* VICTORIA PER OBSERVATIAM—Victory through Observation. (Approved 17 Sep 1942. This insigne was replaced 3 Oct 1952.)

69th RECONNAISSANCE GROUP

Constituted as 69th Observation Group on 21 Aug 1941. *Activated* on 3 Sep 1941. *Redesignated* 69th Reconnaissance Group in Apr 1943, and 69th Tactical Reconnaissance Group in Aug 1943. Used O–38, O–46, O–47, O–52, L–1, L–2, L–3, L–4, L–5, L–49, P–39, P–40, B–25, A–20, and other aircraft. Flew antisubmarine patrols along the Pacific coast after Pearl Harbor. Engaged primarily in air-ground training during 1943 and 1944. Began training with F–6's in Jan 1945 for duty overseas. Moved to France, Feb–Mar 1945. Assigned to Ninth AF. Flew visual-reconnaissance and photographic missions to provide intelligence for ground and air units. *Redesignated* 69th Reconnaissance Group in Jun 1945. Returned to the US, Jul–Aug 1945. Trained with F–6 and A–26 aircraft. *Inactivated* on 29 Jul 1946.

SQUADRONS. *10th:* 1942–1946. *22d:* 1945–1946. *31st:* 1942–1945, 1945–1946. *34th:* 1945. *37th:* 1943–1944. *39th:* 1946. *82d:* 1941–1942. *101st* (formerly 39th): 1944–1945. *102d:* 1942–1944. *111th:* 1945. *115th:* 1941–1943.

STATIONS. Paso Robles, Calif, 3 Sep 1941; Salinas, Calif, c. 3 Oct 1941; San Bernardino, Calif, Dec 1941; Ontario, Calif, ç. 1 Jun 1942; Laurel, Miss, Nov 1942; Esler Field, La, Mar 1943; Abilene AAFld, Tex, Sep 1943; Esler Field, La, Nov 1943; Key Field, Miss, Jan–Feb 1945; Nancy, France, c. 22 Mar 1945; Haguenau, France, c. 2 Apr–c. 30 Jun 1945; Drew Field, Fla, Aug 1945; Stuttgart AAFld, Ark, Nov 1945; Brooks Field, Tex, Dec 1945–29 Jul 1946.

COMMANDERS. Maj William C Sams, 3 Oct 1941; Col John N Jeffers, 9 Dec 1941; Col Kenneth R Crosher, 8 Nov 1942; Maj Cecil E West, 12 May 1943; Lt Col Eugene C Woltz, 29 Sep 1943; Lt Col Arthur Fite Jr, 26 Oct 1944; Col John T Shields, 21 Jan 1945; Lt Col Richard A Morehouse, c. 20 Feb 1946; Col Russell A Berg, c. 10 Mar–29 Jul 1946.

CAMPAIGNS. Antisubmarine, American Theater; Central Europe.

DECORATIONS. None.

INSIGNE. None.

70th RECONNAISSANCE GROUP

Constituted as 70th Observation Group on 21 Aug 1941. *Activated* on 13 Sep 1941. *Redesignated* 70th Reconnaissance Group in Apr 1943, and 70th Tactical Reconnaissance Group in Aug 1943. Aircraft: O–46's, O–47's, B–25's, A–20's, P–39's, L–2's, L–4's, L–5's, and L–6's. Provided artillery adjustment, reconnaissance, and fighter and bomber support to ground forces in training and on maneuvers along the west coast. Also flew antisubmarine patrols off the west coast from 7 Dec 1941 through Sep 1942. *Disbanded* on 30 Nov 1943.

Reconstituted, redesignated 70th Reconnaissance Group, and allotted to the reserve, on 10 Mar 1947. *Activated* on 26 Apr 1947. *Inactivated* on 27 Jun 1949.

SQUADRONS. *26th* Tactical Reconnaissance: 1942–1943. *26th* Photographic Reconnaissance: 1947–1949. *57th:* 1947–1949. *61st:* 1947–1949. *112th:* 1943. *116th:* 1941–1943. *123d:* 1941–1943.

STATIONS. Gray Field, Wash, 13 Sep 1941; Salinas AAB, Calif, Mar 1943; Redmond AAFld, Ore, 15 Aug 1943; Corvallis AAFld, Ore, Oct 1943; Will Rogers Field, Okla, c. 14–30 Nov 1943. Hill Field, Utah, 26 Apr 1947–27 Jun 1949.

COMMANDERS. Maj Hillford R Wallace, Sep 1941; Maj Wallace J O'Daniels, c. 1 Apr 1942; Maj G Robert Dodson, c. 3 May 1942; Col Don W Mayhue, c. 9 May 1942; Lt Col G Robert Dodson, c. 3 Nov 1942; Lt Col Stanley R Stewart, c. 3 Dec 1942; Lt Col G Robert Dodson, c. 3 Jan 1943–unkn.

CAMPAIGNS. Antisubmarine, American Theater.

DECORATIONS. None.

INSIGNE. *Shield:* Azure, on a bend nebuly between six billets or, two crowing cocks palewise gules. *Motto:* WE WATCH OUT FOR YOU. (Approved 5 Jan 1943.)

71st RECONNAISSANCE GROUP

Constituted as 71st Observation Group on 21 Aug 1941. *Activated* on 1 Oct 1941. Trained with B–25, P–38, P–39, and P–40 aircraft. Flew antisubmarine patrols off the west coast, Dec 1941–Jan 1943. *Redesignated* 71st Reconnaissance Group in Apr 1943, 71st Tactical Reconnaissance Group in May 1944, and 71st Reconnaissance Group in May 1945.

Moved to the Southwest Pacific, Sep-Nov 1943, and assigned to Fifth AF. Equipped with B–25, P–38, P–39, L–4, L–5, and later some L–6 aircraft. Based on New Guinea and Biak, flew reconnaissance missions over New Guinea, New Britain, and the Admiralties to provide target and damage-assessment photographs for air force units. Also bombed and strafed Japanese installations, airfields, and shipping; supported Allied forces on New Guinea and Biak; flew courier missions; participated in rescue operations; and hauled passengers and cargo. Moved to the Philippines in Nov 1944. Flew reconnaissance missions over Luzon to provide information for US forces as to Japanese troop movements, gun positions, and supply routes. Also supported ground forces on Luzon, photographed and bombed airfields in Formosa and China, and attacked enemy shipping off the Asiatic coast. Maj William A Shomo was awarded the Medal of Honor for action on 11 Jan 1945: sighting a formation of thirteen Japanese aircraft while leading a two-plane flight, Maj Shomo attacked the superior enemy force and destroyed seven planes. After moving to Ie Shima in Aug 1945, the group attacked transportation targets on Kyushu and flew over southern Japan to locate prisoner of war camps, to assess bomb damage, and to obtain information on Japanese military movements. Moved to Japan in Oct 1945. *Inactivated* on 1 Feb 1946.

Activated in Japan on 28 Feb 1947. Assigned to Far East Air Forces. Manned in Nov 1947 and equipped with RB–17, RB–29, RF–51, RF–61, and RF–80 aircraft. Photographed areas of Japan and South Korea. *Redesignated* 71st Tactical Reconnaissance Group in Aug 1948. *Inactivated* in Japan on 1 Apr 1949.

SQUADRONS. *8th:* 1947–1949. *17th:* 1942–1946. *25th* Liaison: 1942–1945. *25th* Reconnaissance: 1947–1949. *82d:* 1942–1946; 1947–1949. *102d:* 1941–1942. *110th:* 1941–1946. *128th:* 1941–1942.

STATIONS. Birmingham, Ala, 1 Oct 1941; Salinas AAB, Calif, 21 Dec 1941; Rice, Calif, 18 Aug 1942; Salinas AAB, Calif, 19 Oct 1942; Esler Field, La, 24 Jan 1943; Laurel AAFld, Miss, 31 Mar–24 Sep 1943; Port Moresby, New Guinea, 7 Nov 1943; Nadzab, New Guinea, 20 Jan 1944; Biak, 8 Aug 1944; Leyte, 5 Nov 1944; Binmaley, Luzon, 2 Feb 1945; Ie Shima, Aug 1945; Chofu, Japan, 6 Oct 1945; Tachikawa, Japan, 23 Oct 1945; Iruma-gawa, Japan, c. 15 Jan–1 Feb 1946. Itami, Japan, 28 Feb 1947; Johnson AAB, Japan, 15 Apr 1947; Yokota, Japan, 31 Oct 1947–1 Apr 1949.

COMMANDERS. Unkn, to Feb 1942; Col William C Sams, Feb 1942; Col Henry C Thompson, Oct 1944; Maj Jowell C Wise, 12 Oct 1945; 1st Lt Wilburn H Ohle, 21 Oct 1945–unkn. Lt Col William L Gray, 3 Nov 1947; Lt Col Ben K Armstrong, 23 Feb 1948; Lt Col Donald Lang, 25 Feb 1948; Col William E Basye, 5 Jun 1948; Lt Col Ben K Armstrong, 25 Mar–1 Apr 1949.

CAMPAIGNS. Antisubmarine, American Theater; Air Offensive, Japan; China Defensive; New Guinea; Bismarck Archipelago; Western Pacific; Leyte; Luzon; China Offensive.

DECORATIONS. Philippine Presidential Unit Citation.

INSIGNE. None.

72d RECONNAISSANCE GROUP

Constituted as 72d Observation Group on 21 Aug 1941. *Activated* on 26 Sep 1941. *Redesignated* 72d Reconnaissance Group in 1943. Used O–47, O–49, O–52, L–1, L–4, B–18, P–39, and other aircraft. Moved to the Panama Canal Zone, Dec 1941–Jan 1942. Flew patrol missions, carried mail, searched for missing aircraft, provided reconnaissance support to ground forces, and occasionally did photographic-mapping work. *Disbanded* in the Canal Zone on 1 Nov 1943.

Reconstituted and allotted to the reserve, on 13 May 1947. *Activated* on 12 Jul 1947. *Inactivated* on 27 Jun 1949.

SQUADRONS. *1st:* 1941–1943. *4th:* 1942–1943. *39th:* 1942–1943. *60th:* 1947–1949. *73d* Fighter: 1947–1949. *108th:* 1941–1943. *124th:* 1941.

STATIONS. Shreveport, La, 26 Sep 1941; Little Rock, Ark, Oct 1941; Marshall Field, Kan, 11–c. 27 Dec 1941; Howard Field, CZ, c. 18 Jan 1942–1 Nov 1943. Hamilton Field, Calif, 12 Jul 1947–27 Jun 1949.

COMMANDERS. Lt Col Jasper K McDuffie, Oct 1941; Col Perry B Griffin, c. 1 Feb 1942; Col Vernon C Smith, 19 May–1 Nov 1943.

CAMPAIGNS. American Theater.

DECORATIONS. None.

INSIGNE. None.

74th RECONNAISSANCE GROUP

Constituted as 74th Observation Group on 5 Feb 1942 and *activated* on 27 Feb. *Redesignated* 74th Reconnaissance Group in Apr 1943, and 74th Tactical Reconnaissance Group in Aug 1943. Equipped at various times with O–52's, L–1's, L–4's, L–5's, B–25's, A–20's, P–39's, P–40's, and P–51's. Flew reconnaissance, mapping, artillery adjustment, bombing, dive-bombing, and strafing missions to support ground units in training or on maneuvers; trained personnel in aerial reconnaissance, medium bombardment, and fighter techniques. *Inactivated* on 7 Nov 1945. *Redesignated* 74th Reconnaissance Group, allotted to the reserve, and *activated,* on 27 Dec 1946. *Inactivated* on 27 Jun 1949.

SQUADRONS. *5th:* 1943. *8th:* 1945. *11th:* 1942–1945. *13th:* 1942–1945. *21st:* 1947–1949. *22d Tactical Reconnaissance:* 1942–1945. *22d Photographic Reconnaissance:* 1947–1949. *33d* (formerly 31st): 1947–1949. *36th:* 1943–1944. *101st:* 1945.

STATIONS. Lawson Field, Ga, 27 Feb 1942; DeRidder, La, c. 10 Apr 1942; Esler Field, La, c. 13 Dec 1942; Desert Center, Calif, c. 28 Dec 1942; Morris Field, NC, Sep 1943; Camp Campbell AAFld, Ky, Nov 1943; DeRidder AAB, La, Apr 1944; Stuttgart AAFld, Ark, Feb–7 Nov 1945. Stewart Field, NY, 27 Dec 1946–27 Jun 1949.

COMMANDERS. Capt Austin H Burleigh, 1942; Maj George G Finch, c. 27 Mar 1942; Col Clarence D Wheeler, c. 7 Apr 1942; Lt Col James R Gunn Jr, 26 Oct 1943; Lt Col Herbert A Bott, c. 10 Nov 1943; Maj Woodrow W Ramsey, 23 Apr 1944; Lt Col Richard A Morehouse, 22 Sep 1944; Col Yancey S Tarrant, Aug 1945; Col John T Shields, 26 Sep–7 Nov 1945.

CAMPAIGNS. American Theater.

DECORATIONS. None.

INSIGNE. None.

75th RECONNAISSANCE GROUP

Constituted as 75th Observation Group on 5 Feb 1942 and *activated* on 27 Feb. *Redesignated* 75th Reconnaissance Group in Apr 1943, and 75th Tactical Reconnaissance Group in Aug 1943. Used B–25's, A–20's, L–1's, L–2's, L–4's, O–47's, O–52's, P–39's, P–40's, and P–51's. Until the fall of 1942 the group aided ground units with their training by flying reconnaissance, artillery adjustment, strafing, and dive-bombing missions; one squadron (124th) flew antisubmarine patrols over the Gulf of Mexico. In the fall of 1942 the group participated in the Louisiana Maneuvers.

Beginning early in 1943 it functioned primarily as a replacement training unit. *Disbanded* on 1 May 1944.

SQUADRONS. *21st:* 1942–1944.   *30th:* 1942–1944.   *124th:* 1942–1944.   *127th:* 1942–1943.

STATIONS.   Ellington Field, Tex, 27 Feb 1942; Birmingham, Ala, Mar 1942; Tullahoma, Tenn, Nov 1942; Key Field, Miss, Aug 1943–1 May 1944.

COMMANDERS. Col Frederick A Bacher, c. 30 Mar 1942; Col John E Bodle, 5 Apr 1943; Maj Delwin B Avery, 15 Sep 1943; Lt Col George C P Gifford, 17 Sep 1943; Lt Col John R Dyas, 1 Jan–1 May 1944.

CAMPAIGNS.   American Theater.

DECORATIONS.   None.

INSIGNE. *Shield:* Azure on a ship's crow's nest issuant from base an albatross sejant or, holding in its beak a mullet gules. *Motto:* APPERCEPTION. (Approved 23 Sep 1942.)

76th RECONNAISSANCE GROUP

Constituted as 76th Observation Group on 5 Feb 1942 and *activated* on 27 Feb. *Redesignated* 76th Reconnaissance Group in Apr 1943, and 76th Tactical Reconnaissance Group in Aug 1943. Aircraft included P–39's, P–40's, A–20's, B–25's, L–1's, L–4's, L–5's, and L–6's. Trained in aerial reconnaissance and air support techniques and aided ground units in their training, Feb 1942–May 1943; assisted Second Army on maneuvers, May–Sep 1943; participated

in maneuvers with ground forces in the California-Arizona desert training area beginning in Sep 1943. *Disbanded* on 15 Apr 1944.

SQUADRONS.   *20th:* 1942–1943.   *23d:* 1942–1943, 1943–1944.   *24th:* 1942–1943. *70th:* 1943.   *91st:* 1943.   *97th:* 1943–1944. *101st:* 1943–1944.   *102d:* 1944.   *106th:* 1943. *121st:* 1943.

STATIONS.   MacDill Field, Fla, 27 Feb 1942; Key Field, Miss, c. 3 Mar 1942; Pope Field, NC, c. 28 Mar 1942; Vichy, Mo, Dec 1942; Morris Field, NC, May 1943; Thermal AAFld, Calif, Sep 1943–15 Apr 1944.

COMMANDERS.   Lt Col H N Burkhalter, Mar 1942; Maj James E Ilgenfritz, c. 21 Jan 1943; Lt Col John T Shields, c. 18 Sep 1943–unkn; Maj Klem F Kalberer, 1944.

CAMPAIGNS.   American Theater.

DECORATIONS.   None.

INSIGNE. *Shield:* Azure a drop bomb argent surmounted by a pair of binoculars bendwise gules winged or. *Motto:* OUR OBSERVATION, YOUR SECURITY. (Approved 5 Nov 1942.)

77th RECONNAISSANCE GROUP

Constituted as 77th Observation Group on 5 Feb 1942. *Activated* on 2 Mar 1942. *Redesignated* 77th Reconnaissance Group in Apr 1943, and 77th Tactical Reconnaissance Group in Aug 1943. Aircraft included P-39's, P-40's, A-20's, B-25's, O-47's, O-52's, and L-5's. Supported ground units in training by flying reconnaissance, artillery adjustment, fighter, and bomber missions, and in the process trained reconnaissance personnel who later served overseas. One squadron (113th) flew antisubmarine patrols over the Gulf of Mexico from Mar until Jun 1942 when it was relieved by another squadron (128th). Still another squadron (120th) patrolled the Mexican border, Mar-Jul 1942. A detachment of the 77th served in India from Feb until Jul 1943. The group was *disbanded* on 30 Nov 1943.

SQUADRONS. *5th:* 1942-1943. *27th:* 1942-1943. *35th:* 1943. *113th:* 1942-1943. *120th:* 1942-1943. *125th:* 1942-1943. *128th:* 1942-1943.

STATIONS. Salinas AAB, Calif, 2 Mar 1942; Brownwood, Tex, c. 17 Mar 1942; DeRidder AAB, La, 25 Jul 1942; Alamo Airfield, Tex, 28 Sep 1942; Abilene AAFld, Tex, 6 Apr 1943; Esler Field, La, 13 Sep 1943; Birmingham AAFld, Ala, 14-30 Nov 1943.

COMMANDERS. Maj Harrison W Wellman, Mar 1942; Lt Col Christopher C Scott, c. 3 Apr 1942; Col J C Kennedy, 1942-unkn; Lt Col Joseph E Barzynski, c. 19 Apr 1943-unkn.

CAMPAIGNS. American Theater.

DECORATIONS. None.

INSIGNE. *Shield:* Or, a broad-winged hawk volant proper holding in its beak a mullet gules and emitting from its eyes seven flashes of the last, issuant from base a mountain range of seven peaks azure. *Motto:* ALL SEEING. (Approved 28 Feb 1943.)

78th FIGHTER GROUP

Constituted as 78th Pursuit Group (Interceptor) on 13 Jan 1942. *Activated* on 9 Feb 1942. *Redesignated* 78th Fighter Group in May 1942. Trained for combat with P-38's and served as part of the air defense organization. Moved to England, Nov-Dec 1942. Assigned to Eighth AF. Lost its P-38's and most of its pilots in Feb 1943 when they were assigned to Twelfth AF for service in North Africa. Began operations from England with P-47's in Apr 1943, converted to P-51's in Dec 1944, and continued combat until

ABOVE THE FOE

Apr 1945. Flew many missions to escort bombers that attacked industries, submarine yards and docks, V-weapon sites, and other targets on the Continent. Also engaged in counter-air activities and on numerous occasions strafed and dive-bombed airfields, trains, vehicles, barges, tugs, canal locks, barracks, and troops. In addition to other operations, participated in the intensive campaign against the German Air Force and aircraft industry during Big Week, 20–25 Feb 1944; helped to prepare the way for the invasion of France; supported landings in Normandy in Jun 1944; contributed to the breakthrough at St Lo in Jul 1944; participated in the Battle of the Bulge, Dec 1944–Jan 1945; and supported the airborne assault across the Rhine in Mar 1945. Received a DUC for activities connected with the airborne attack on Holland in Sep 1944 when the group covered troop carrier and bombard-

ment operations and carried out strafing and dive-bombing missions. Received second DUC for destroying numerous aircraft on five airfields near Prague and Pilsen on 16 Apr 1945. Returned to the US in Oct. *Inactivated* on 18 Oct 1945.

Activated in Germany on 20 Aug 1946. Assigned to United States Air Forces in Europe for duty with the occupation force. Transferred, without personnel and equipment, to the US in Jun 1947 and had few, if any, personnel assigned until Nov 1948. Equipped with F–84's in the spring of 1949. *Redesignated* 78th Fighter-Interceptor Group in Jan 1950. *Inactivated* on 6 Feb 1952.

Redesignated 78th Fighter Group (Air Defense). *Activated* on 18 Aug 1955. Assigned to Air Defense Command.

SQUADRONS. 82d: 1942–1945; 1946–1952. 83d: 1942–1945; 1946–1952; 1955–. 84th: 1942–1945; 1946–1952; 1955–.

STATIONS. Baer Field, Ind, 9 Feb 1942; Muroc, Calif, c. 30 Apr 1942; Hamilton Field, Calif, May–Nov 1942; Goxhill, England, Dec 1942; Duxford, England, Apr 1943–Oct 1945; Camp Kilmer, NJ, c. 16–18 Oct 1945. Straubing, Germany, 20 Aug 1946–Jun 1947; Mitchel Field, NY, Jun 1947; Hamilton AFB, Calif, Nov 1948–6 Feb 1952. Hamilton AFB, Calif, 18 Aug 1955–.

COMMANDERS. Col Arman Peterson, May 1942; Lt Col Melvin F McNickle, Jul 1943; Col James J Stone Jr, 31 Jul 1943; Col Frederic C Gray Jr, 22 May 1944; Lt Col Olin E Gilbert, 29 Jan 1945; Col John

D Landers, c. 22 Feb 1945; Lt Col Roy B Caviness, 1 Jul 1945–unkn. Col Robert P Montgomery, c. 20 Aug 1946–unkn; Col Earl H Dunham, 1946–unkn; Col John B Patrick, c. 1 Apr 1947; Col Earl H Dunham, c. 1 May 1947; Col Robert W Stephens, c. 1 Jun 1947–unkn; Col Barton M Russell, c. 8 Dec 1948; Col Brian O'Neill, Aug 1949–unkn; Col Jack W Hayes Jr, 1951–unkn. Col Wilton H Earle, 1955–.

CAMPAIGNS. Air Offensive, Europe; Normandy; Northern France; Rhineland; Ardennes-Alsace; Central Europe.

DECORATIONS. Distinguished Unit Citations: Holland, 17–23 Sep 1944; Czechoslovakia, 16 Apr 1945.

INSIGNE. *Shield:* Per pale indented azure and gules, in chief five chain lengths conjoined fesswise or. *Motto:* ABOVE THE FOE. (Approved 26 Sep 1942.)

79th FIGHTER GROUP

Constituted as 79th Pursuit Group (Interceptor) on 13 Jan 1942. *Activated* on 9 Feb 1942. *Redesignated* 79th Fighter Group in May 1942. Moved to the Middle East, Oct–Nov 1942, and became part of Ninth AF. Trained with P-40's while moving westward in the wake of the British drive across Egypt and Libya to Tunisia. Although many of the group's pilots flew combat missions with other organizations, the 79th group itself did not begin operations until Mar 1943. By escorting bombers, attacking enemy shipping, and supporting ground forces, the 79th took part in the Allied operations that defeated Axis forces in North Africa, captured Pantelleria, and conquered Sicily, the group being awarded a DUC for its support of British Eighth Army during that period, Mar–Aug 1943. Assigned to Twelfth AF in Aug 1943 and continued to support British Eighth Army by attacking troop concentrations, gun positions, bridges, roads, and rail lines in southern Italy. Operated in the area of the Anzio beachhead, Jan–Mar 1944. Participated in the drive on Rome, Mar–Jun 1944, and converted to P-47's during that time. Flew escort and strafing missions in southern France during Aug and Sep 1944, and afterward engaged in interdictory and close support operations in northern Italy. Received second DUC for numerous missions flown at minimum altitude in intense flak to help pierce the enemy line at the Santerno River in Italy, 16–20 Apr 1945. Remained overseas as part of United States Air Forces in Europe after the war. Transferred, without personnel and equipment, to the US in Jun 1947. *Inactivated* on 15 Jul 1947.

Redesignated 79th Fighter Group (Air Defense). *Activated* on 18 Aug 1955. Assigned to Air Defense Command.

SQUADRONS. *85th:* 1942–1947. *86th:* 1942–1947; 1955–. *87th:* 1942–1947.

STATIONS. Dale Mabry Field, Fla, 9 Feb 1942; Morris Field, NC, c. 1 May 1942; Hillsgrove, RI, c. 22 Jun 1942; Bedford, Mass, 2 Jul–28 Sep 1942; Egypt, 18 Nov 1942; Libya, c. 25 Jan 1943; Tunisia, c. 12 Mar 1943; Sicily, 16 Jul 1943; Southern

Italy, c. 15 Sep 1943; Foggia, Italy, c. 9 Oct 1943; Madna Airfield, Italy, 19 Nov 1943; Capodichino, Italy, Jan 1944; Pomigliano, Italy, 1 May 1944; Corsica, Jun 1944; Southern France, c. 25 Aug 1944; Iesi, Italy, Oct 1944; Fano, Italy, c. 5 Dec 1944; Cesenatico, Italy, c. 20 Mar 1945; Horsching, Austria, Jul 1945–25 Jun 1947; Langley Field, Va, 25 Jun–15 Jul 1947. Youngstown Mun Aprt, Ohio, 18 Aug 1955–.

COMMANDERS. 2d Lt Thomas G. Mitchell, 11 Feb 1942; Lt Col J Stanley Holtoner, 17 Feb 1942; Lt Col Peter Mc-Goldrick, 1942; Col Earl E Bates, Nov 1942; Col Charles W Stark, Apr 1944; Lt Col Melvin J Neilson, May 1944; Col Gladwyn E Pinkston, 28 Nov 1944; Lt Col John F Martin, 17 May 1945; Col German P Culver, May 1946; Lt Col Bascom A Brooks, 4 Feb 1947; Lt Col John M Thacker, Apr 1947–unkn. Col Benjamin H Emmert Jr, 1955–.

CAMPAIGNS. Air Combat, EAME Theater; Egypt-Libya; Tunisia; Sicily; Naples-Foggia; Anzio; Rome-Arno; Southern France; North Apennines; Po Valley.

DECORATIONS. Distinguished Unit Citations: North Africa and Sicily, Mar–17 Aug 1943; Italy, 16–20 Apr 1945.

INSIGNE. None.

80th FIGHTER GROUP

Constituted as 80th Pursuit Group (Interceptor) on 13 Jan 1942. *Activated* on 9 Feb 1942. *Redesignated* 80th Fighter Group in May 1942. Used P-47's to train

for combat and to serve as part of the defense force for the northeastern US. Sailed for India, via Brazil, Cape of Good Hope, and Ceylon, in May 1943. Assigned to Tenth AF. Began operations in Sep 1943 with P-38 and P-40 aircraft; later used P-47's. Supported Allied ground forces during the battle for northern Burma and the push southward to Rangoon, bombing and strafing troop concentrations, supply dumps, lines of communication, artillery positions, and other objectives. Defended the Indian terminus of the Hump route by striking Japanese airfields and by patrolling Allied airfields to safeguard them from attack. Received a DUC for intercepting a formation of enemy planes and preventing its attack on a large oil refinery in Assam, India, on 27 Mar 1944. Returned to the US in Oct 1945. *Inactivated* on 3 Nov 1945.

SQUADRONS. 88th: 1942–1945. 89th: 1942–1945. 90th: 1942–1945. 459th: 1943–1944.

STATIONS. Selfridge Field, Mich, 9 Feb 1942; Farmingdale, NY, 5 Jul 1942; Mitchel Field, NY, 9 Mar–30 Apr 1943; Karachi, India, 28 Jun 1943; Nagaghuli, India, Oct

1943; Tingkawk Sakan, Burma, 29 Aug 1944; Myitkyina, Burma, 20 Jan 1945; Dudhkundi, India, 24 May–6 Oct 1945; Camp Kilmer, NJ, 1–3 Nov 1945.

COMMANDERS. Unkn, Feb–May 1942; Col John C Crosthwaite, c. 20 May 1942; Maj Albert L Evans Jr, 1 Jul 1942; Col Ivan W McElroy, 14 Jul 1943; Col Albert L Evans Jr, 13 Apr 1944; Col Sydney D Grubbs Jr, 1 Feb 1945; Col Hiette S Williams Jr, c. 29 Apr 1945–unkn.

CAMPAIGNS. American Theater; India-Burma; Central Burma.

DECORATIONS. Distinguished Unit Citation: Assam, India, 27 Mar 1944.

INSIGNE. *Shield:* Per bend azure and sable a bend raguly or. *Motto:* ANGELS ON OUR WINGS. (Approved 14 Oct 1942.)

LE NOM LES ARMES LA LOYAUTE

81st FIGHTER GROUP

Constituted as 81st Pursuit Group (Intercepter) on 13 Jan 1942. *Activated* on 9 Feb 1942. *Redesignated* 81st Fighter Group in May 1942. Trained with P–39's. Moved overseas, Oct 1942–Feb 1943, the ground echelon arriving in French Morocco with the force that invaded North Africa on 8 Nov, and the air echelon, which had trained for a time in England, arriving in North Africa between late Dec 1942 and early Feb 1943. Began combat with Twelfth AF in Jan 1943. Supported ground operations during the Allied drive against Axis forces in Tunisia. Patrolled the coast of Africa and protected Allied shipping in the Mediterranean Sea, Apr–Jul 1943. Provided cover for the convoys that landed troops on Pantelleria on 11 Jun and on Sicily on 10 Jul 1943. Supported the landings at Anzio on 22 Jan 1944 and flew patrols in that area for a short time. Moved to India, Feb–Mar 1944, and began training with P–40 and P–47 aircraft. Moved to China in May and became part of Fourteenth AF. Continued training and on occasion flew patrol and escort missions before returning to full-time combat duty in Jan 1945. Attacked enemy airfields and installations, flew escort missions, and aided the operations of Chinese ground forces by attacking troop concentrations, ammunition dumps, lines of communications, and other targets to hinder Japanese efforts to move men and materiel to the front. *Inactivated* in China on 27 Dec 1945.

Activated in Hawaii on 15 Oct 1946. Equipped with P–51's; converted to F–47's early in 1948. Moved to the US in 1949 and converted to jet aircraft, receiving F–80's at first but changing to F–86's soon afterward.

Redesignated 81st Fighter-Interceptor Group in Jan 1950. Moved to England, Aug–Sep 1951. Assigned to United States Air Forces in Europe. *Redesignated* 81st Fighter-Bomber Group in Apr 1954. *Inactivated* in England on 8 Feb 1955.

SQUADRONS. *78th:* 1952–1955. *91st:* 1942–1945; 1946–1955. *92d:* 1942–1945; 1946–1955. *93d:* 1942–1945; 1946–1951. *116th:* 1951–1952.

STATIONS. Morris Field, NC, 9 Feb 1942; Dale Mabry Field, Fla, c. 1 May 1942; Muroc, Calif, c. 28 Jun–4 Oct 1942; Mediouna, French Morocco, c. 5 Jan 1943; Thelepte, Tunisia, 22 Jan 1943; Le Kouif Airfield, Algeria, 17 Feb 1943; Youks-les-Bains, Algeria, 22 Feb 1943; Le Kouif Airfield, Algeria, 24 Feb 1943; Thelepte, Tunisia, c. Mar 1943; Algeria, c. 3 Apr 1943; Monastir, Tunisia, c. 26 May 1943; Sidi Ahmed, Tunisia, 10 Aug 1943; Castelvetrano, Sicily, 12 Oct 1943; Montecorvino Airfield, Italy, c. Feb 1944; Karachi, India, c. 2 Mar 1944; Kwanghan, China, 12 May 1944; Fungwansham, China, Feb 1945; Huhsien, China, Aug–Dec 1945. Wheeler Field, TH, 15 Oct 1946–21 May 1949; Kirtland AFB, NM, 17 Jun 1949; Moses Lake AFB, Wash, c. 1 May 1950–21 Aug 1951; Bentwaters RAF Station, England, 3 Sep 1951–8 Feb 1955.

COMMANDERS. Unkn, Feb–May 1942; Capt Harry E Hammond, 5 May 1942; Capt John D Sureau, 10 May 1942; Lt Col Paul M Jacobs, 22 May 1942; Lt Col Kenneth S Wade, c. Jul 1942; Col Philip B Klein, May 1943; Lt Col Michael J Gordon, 2 Jul 1943; Maj Frederick S Hanson, 15 Jul 1943; Col Philip B Klein, 26 Aug 1943; Lt Col Fred G Hook Jr, 27 Sep 1944; Col Oliver G Cellini, 24 Oct 1944–unkn. Col Oswald W Lunde, [c. 1946]; Col Gladwyn E Pinkston, [c. 1948]; Lt Col Clay Tice Jr, c. Apr 1950; Lt Col Lucius D Clay Jr, 1950; Lt Col Clay Tice Jr, c. Feb 1951; Col Robert J Garrigan, c. Aug 1951; Col Benjamin B Cassiday Jr, c. Jul 1953; Col Walter L Moore, 1 Dec 1954–1955.

CAMPAIGNS. Air Combat, EAME Theater; Algeria-French Morocco; Tunisia; Sicily; Naples-Foggia; Anzio; Rome-Arno; China Defensive; China Offensive.

DECORATIONS. None.

INSIGNE. *Shield:* Or, a dragon salient wings displayed and addorsed azure, armed and langued gules, incensed proper, holding in its dexter claw a stylized boll weevil sable. *Motto:* LE NOM—LES ARMES—LA LOYAUTÉ—The Name, The Arms, and Loyalty. (Approved 2 Mar 1943.)

82d FIGHTER GROUP

Constituted as 82d Pursuit Group (Interceptor) on 13 Jan 1942. *Activated* on 9 Feb 1942. *Redesignated* 82d Fighter Group in May 1942. Trained with P–38's. Moved to Northern Ireland during Sep–Oct 1942 for further training. Moved to North Africa in Dec 1942 and served with Twelfth AF until Nov 1943. Took part in the defeat of Axis forces in Tunisia, the reduction of Pantelleria, the conquest of Sicily, and the invasion of Italy. Operated

against the enemy's air transports; flew dive-bombing and strafing missions; escorted medium bombers in their attacks on enemy shipping and their raids on Naples and Rome; and gave direct support to the ground forces during the invasion of Italy. Received a DUC for a low-level strafing raid against enemy aircraft concentrations at Foggia on 25 Aug 1943. Received second DUC for performance on 2 Sep 1943 when the group protected a formation of bombers that encountered strong opposition from enemy interceptors during an attack on marshalling yards near Naples.

Moved to Italy in Oct 1943. Assigned to Fifteenth AF in Nov. Continued to function occasionally as a fighter-bomber organization, supporting Allied armies, flying interdictory missions, and attacking strategic targets. Received third DUC for performance on 10 Jun 1944 when the 82d Group braved head-on attacks by hostile fighters to dive-bomb an oil refinery at

Ploesti and then strafed targets of opportunity while returning to base. Engaged primarily in escort work, however, from Oct 1943 to May 1945, covering the operations of heavy bombers that attacked aircraft industries, oil refineries, and other targets in France, Germany, Czechoslovakia, Austria, Hungary, Yugoslavia, Rumania, and Bulgaria. *Inactivated* in Italy on 9 Sep 1945.

Activated in the US on 12 Apr 1947. Assigned to Strategic Air Command and equipped with P–51's. Assigned to Continental Air Command in Aug 1949. *Inactivated* on 2 Oct 1949.

Redesignated 82d Fighter Group (Air Defense). *Activated* on 18 Aug 1955. Assigned to Air Defense Command and equipped with F–94 aircraft.

SQUADRONS. *95th:* 1942–1945; 1947–1949. *96th:* 1942–1945; 1947–1949; 1955–. *97th:* 1942–1945; 1947–1949; 1955–.

STATIONS. Harding Field, La, 9 Feb 1942; Muroc, Calif, 30 Apr 1942; Los Angeles, Calif, May 1942; Glendale, Calif, c. 16 Aug–16 Sep 1942; Northern Ireland, Oct 1942; Telergma, Algeria, Jan 1943; Berteaux, Algeria, 28 Mar 1943; Souk-el-Arba, Algeria, 13 Jun 1943; Grombalia, Tunisia, 3 Aug 1943; San Pancrazio, Italy, c. 3 Oct 1943; Lecce, Italy, 10 Oct 1943; Vincenzo Airfield, Italy, 11 Jan 1944; Lesina, Italy, c. 30 Aug–9 Sep 1945. Grenier Field, NH, 12 Apr 1947–2 Oct 1949. New Castle County Aprt, Del, 18 Aug 1955–.

COMMANDERS. 1st Lt Charles T Duke, Feb 1942; Col Robert Israel Jr, May 1942;

Lt Col William E Covington Jr, 17 Jun 1942; Col John W Weltman, 4 May 1943; Lt Col Ernest C Young, 2 Aug 1943; Lt Col George M MacNicol, 26 Aug 1943; Col William P Litton, Jan 1944; Lt Col Ben A Mason Jr, 4 Aug 1944; Col Clarence T Edwinson, 28 Aug 1944; Col Richard A Legg, 22 Nov 1944; Col Joseph S Holtoner, 4 Jun 1945; Lt Col Robert M Wray, 16 Jul 1945–unkn. Maj Leland R Raphun, c. Apr 1947; Lt Col Gerald W Johnson, 2 Jun 1947; Col Henry Viccellio, 14 Jun 1947; Col William M Banks, 5 Nov 1948–c. Oct 1949. Col Clay D Albright Jr, 1955–.

CAMPAIGNS. Air Combat, EAME Theater; Air Offensive, Europe; Tunisia; Sicily; Naples-Foggia; Rome-Arno; Normandy; Northern France; Southern France; North Apennines; Rhineland; Central Europe; Po Valley.

DECORATIONS. Distinguished Unit Citations: Italy, 25 Aug 1943; Italy, 2 Sep 1943; Ploesti, Rumania, 10 Jun 1944.

INSIGNE. *Shield:* Per bend or and azure a lightning bolt in bend throughout point to base, with two beviles, per bend argent, gules and or, between three fleurs-de-lis, two and one, of the second, and eleven stars in bend, six and five, of the first; over all in dexter chief a roundle per fess, wavy of two, sable and vert. *Motto:* ADORIMINI—"Up and at 'em!" (Approved 4 Nov 1957.)

83d FIGHTER GROUP

Constituted as 83d Fighter Group on 18 Sep 1943 and *activated* on 25 Sep. As-

signed to First AF. Served as a replacement training unit to train pilots for duty in P–47's. *Disbanded* on 10 Apr 1944.

Reconstituted, redesignated 83d Fighter-Day Group, and assigned to Tactical Air Command, on 24 Feb 1956. *Activated* on 8 Jul 1956.

(This group is not related to an 83d Pursuit Group (Interceptor) that was constituted on 13 Jan 1942; activated at New Orleans by Third AF on 9 Feb 1942; assigned the 301st, 302d, and 303d squadrons; and disbanded a few days later in order to bring AAF within the authorized number of pursuit groups.)

SQUADRONS. *448th:* 1943–1944. *532d:* 1943–1944; 1956–. *533d:* 1943–1944; 1956–. *534th:* 1943–1944; 1956–.

STATIONS. Richmond AAB, Va, 25 Sep 1943; Dover AAFld, Del, 22 Nov 1943–10 Apr 1944. Seymour-Johnson AFB, NC, 8 Jul 1956–.

COMMANDERS. Lt Col Woodrow W Korges, 25 Sep 1943; Lt Col Ernest H Beverly, 23 Feb–10 Apr 1944. Maj Amos H Domberger II, Jul 1956–.

CAMPAIGNS. None.

DECORATIONS. None.

INSIGNE. *Shield:* Per pile transposed azure and or; over all on an escutcheon per bend gules and medium blue, a bend embattled inverted, vert, fimbriated throughout argent; superimposed over the chief area of the escutcheon a stylized demi falcon bendwise, in profile, sable, his head and wings raised upward above the escutcheon; his eye gules, the falcon fimbriated throughout argent. (Approved 29 Mar 1957.)

84th FIGHTER GROUP

Constituted as 84th Bombardment Group (Light) on 13 Jan 1942. *Activated* on 10 Feb 1942. *Redesignated* 84th Bombardment Group (Dive) in Jul 1942, and 84th Fighter-Bomber Group in Aug 1943. Assigned to Third AF and later (Nov 1943) to Second AF. Aircraft included A-24's (1942–1943) and P-47's (1943–

1944). Served as an operational training and a replacement training unit. Also participated occasionally in demonstrations and maneuvers. *Disbanded* on 1 Apr 1944.

Reconstituted, redesignated 84th Fighter Group (All Weather), and allotted to the reserve, on 26 May 1949. *Activated* on 1 Jun 1949. Ordered into active service on 1 Jun 1951. *Inactivated* on 2 Jun 1951.

Redesignated 84th Fighter Group (Air Defense). *Activated* on 18 Aug 1955. Assigned to Air Defense Command. Equipped with F–86 aircraft.

SQUADRONS. *491st* (formerly 304th): 1942–1944. *496th* (formerly 301st): 1942–1944; 1949–1951. *497th* (formerly 302d): 1942–1944; 1955–. *498th* (formerly 303d): 1942–1944; 1955–.

STATIONS. Savannah AB, Ga, 10 Feb 1942; Drew Field, Fla, c. 7 Feb 1943; Harding Field, La, 4 Oct 1943–1 Apr 1944. Mitchel AFB, NY, 1 Jun 1949; McGuire AFB, NJ, 10 Oct 1949–2 Jun 1951. Geiger Field, Wash, 18 Aug 1955–.

COMMANDERS. Maj Augustus Nelson, 10 Feb 1942; Col Philo G Meisenholder, Mar 1942; Lt Col Harry R Melton Jr, Aug 1942; Lt Col John R Kelly, Dec 1942; Lt Col Paul A Zartman, 31 Jan 1943; Col Reginald F C Vance, 15 Aug 1943; Lt Col William D Gilchrist, Sep 1943–1944. Col Grover C Willcox Jr, 18 Aug 1955–.

CAMPAIGNS. American Theater.

DECORATIONS. None.

INSIGNE. *Shield:* Azure, a flash in pale between in dexter chief a gun sight and in sinister base a drop bomb palewise, all or. *Motto:* CURSUM PERFICIO—I Accomplish My Course. (Approved 22 Jan 1943.)

85th FIGHTER GROUP

COUP DE MAIN

Constituted as 85th Bombardment Group (Light) on 13 Jan 1942. *Activated* on 10 Feb 1942. *Redesignated* 85th Bombardment Group (Dive) in Jul 1942, and 85th Fighter-Bomber Group in Aug 1943. Assigned to Third AF, then to Second, and again to Third. Equipped first with V-72 aircraft; converted to A-24's in Aug 1942, A-36's early in 1943, and P-40's early in 1944, receiving a few P-47's in Mar 1944. Participated in maneuvers in California during fall and winter of 1942-1943 and in Kentucky in April 1943. Afterward served as a replacement training unit. *Disbanded* on 1 May 1944.

SQUADRONS. *499th* (formerly 305th): 1942-1944. *500th* (formerly 306th): 1942-1944. *501st* (formerly 307th): 1942-1944. *502d* (formerly 308th): 1942-1944.

STATIONS. Savannah AB, Ga, 10 Feb 1942; Bowman Field, Ky, c. 16 Feb 1942; Hunter Field, Ga, 9 Jun 1942; Waycross, Ga, 15 Aug 1942; Gillespie Field, Tenn, 3 Oct 1942; Blythe AAB, Calif, 2 Nov 1942; Rice, Calif, c. 11 Dec 1942; Harding Field, La, c. 9 Apr 1943; Waycross AAFld, Ga, c. 27 Aug 1943-1 May 1944.

COMMANDERS. 2d Lt Benson M Sherman, 18 Feb 1942; Capt Orren L Briggs, 23 Feb 1942; Capt Joseph Ralph Deming, 31 Mar 1942; Lt Col Arnold L Schroeder, 13 Jun 1942; Lt Col William R Clingerman Jr, 10 Oct 1943; Col James E Ellison, 13 Nov 1943; Col Joseph S Holtoner, 26 Jan 1944; Lt Col Thomas A Holdiman, 4 Mar 1944; Lt Col Robert C Bagby, 20 Mar 1944; Col Joseph S Holtoner, 1 Apr-1 May 1944.

CAMPAIGNS. American Theater.

DECORATIONS. None.

INSIGNE. *Shield:* Azure, five drop bombs or, arranged one large in pale, two to dexter bendwise in pale, and two to sinister bend sinisterwise in pale, a chief indented of eight points of the last. *Motto:* COUP DE MAIN—A Sudden (Unexpected) Attack. (Approved 6 Nov 1942.)

86th FIGHTER GROUP

Constituted as 86th Bombardment Group (Light) on 13 Jan 1942. *Activated* on 10 Feb 1942. *Redesignated* 86th Bombardment Group (Dive) in Sep 1942, 86th Fighter-Bomber Group in Aug 1943, and 86th Fighter Group in May 1944. Moved to North Africa, Mar-May 1943. Trained until Jul, then began combat with Twelfth

VIRTUS PERDURAT

AF. Engaged primarily in close support of ground forces, with the group moving forward to bases in Sicily, Italy, Corsica, France, and Germany as the battle line changed. Also flew patrol and interdictory missions. Used A–36, P–40, and P–47 aircraft to attack convoys, trains, ammunition dumps, troop and supply columns, shipping, bridges, rail lines, and other objectives. Participated in the softening up of Sicily and supported the invasion by Seventh Army in Jul 1943. Provided cover for the landings at Salerno in Sep 1943. Assisted the Allied advance toward Rome during Jan–Jun 1944. Supported the invasion of Southern France in Aug 1944. Operated against enemy communications in northern Italy from Sep 1944 to Apr 1945. Attacked enemy transportation in Germany during Apr and May 1945. Received two DUC's: for action on 25 May 1944 when the group repeatedly dived through intense flak to destroy enemy vehicles and troops as German forces tried to stop the Allies short of Rome; for activity against convoys and airfield installations in northern Germany on

20 Apr 1945 to disorganize the enemy's withdrawal from that area. Remained in Germany after the war as part of United States Air Forces in Europe. Transferred, without personnel and equipment, to the US in Feb 1946. *Inactivated* on 31 Mar 1946.

Activated in Germany on 20 Aug 1946. Assigned to United States Air Forces in Europe. *Redesignated* 86th Composite Group in May 1947, 86th Fighter Group in Jan 1948, 86th Fighter-Bomber Group in Jan 1950, and 86th Fighter-Interceptor Group in Aug 1954. Equipped successively with F–47, F–84, and F–86 aircraft.

SQUADRONS. *45th:* 1947–1948. *311th:* 1942–1943. *525th* (formerly 309th): 1942–1946; 1946–. *526th* (formerly 310th): 1942–1946; 1946–. *527th* (formerly 312th): 1942–1946; 1946–1947, 1948–.

STATIONS. Will Rogers Field, Okla, 10 Feb 1942; Hunter Field, Ga, c. 20 Jun 1942; Key Field, Miss, c. 7 Aug 1942–19 Mar 1943; La Senia, Algeria, c. 12 May 1943; French Morocco, 3 Jun 1943; Tafaraoui, Algeria, 11 Jun 1943; Korba, Tunisia, 30 Jun 1943; Gela, Sicily, 20 Jul 1943; Barcelona, Sicily, 27 Aug 1943; Sele Airfield, Italy, 22 Sep 1943; Serretella Airfield, Italy, 12 Oct 1943; Pomigliano, Italy, 19 Nov 1943; Marcianise, Italy, 30 Apr 1944; Ciampino, Italy, c. 12 Jun 1944; Orbetello, Italy, c. 19 Jun 1944; Corsica, c. 12 Jul 1944; Grosseto, Italy, c. 17 Sep 1944; Pisa, Italy, 23 Oct 1944; Tantonville, France, c. 20 Feb 1945; Braunschardt, Germany, c. 18 Apr 1945; Schweinfurt, Germany, 26

Sep 1945–15 Feb 1946; Bolling Field, DC, 15 Feb–31 Mar 1946. Nordholz, Germany, 20 Aug 1946; Lechfeld, Germany, c. 1 Dec 1946; Bad Kissingen, Germany, 5 Mar 1947; Neubiberg AB, Germany, 12 Jun 1947; Landstuhl AB, Germany, 9 Aug 1952–.

COMMANDERS. Unkn, Feb 1942–Feb 1943; Maj Clinton U True, 10 Feb 1943; Lt Col Robert C Paul, 7 Aug 1943; Col Harold E Hofahl, 4 Dec 1943; Col Earl E Bates Jr, 2 Aug 1944; Lt Col George T Lee, 14 Feb 1945; Maj John H Buckner, 23 Sep 1945–c. 14 Feb 1946. Col Adolphus R McConnell, 20 Aug 1946; Col Clarence T Edwinson, 15 Dec 1946; Col Maurice L Martin, Feb 1947; Maj John B England, c. Jul 1947; Col Clarence T Edwinson, c. Aug 1947; Col Michael J Ingelido, Jul 1948; Lt Col James G Thorsen, May 1949; Col William H Councill, Jun 1949; Col George T Lee, 25 Sep 1950; Col Richard O Hunziker, 6 Mar 1951; Col George Laven Jr, 18 Oct 1951; Col George R Bickell, 26 Apr 1952; Col George B Simler, 14 Jun 1952–1954; Col Robin Olds, Oct 1955–.

CAMPAIGNS. American Theater; Air Combat, EAME Theater; Sicily; Naples-Foggia; Anzio; Rome-Arno; Southern France; North Apennines; Rhineland; Central Europe.

DECORATIONS. Distinguished Unit Citations: Italy, 25 May 1944; Germany, 20 Apr 1945.

INSIGNE. *Shield:* Azure, on a pile or a drop bomb palewise gules. *Motto:* VIR-TUS PERDURAT—Courage Will Endure. (Approved 17 Oct 1942. This insigne was replaced 27 Jul 1956.)

87th FIGHTER GROUP

Constituted as 87th Fighter Group on 24 Sep 1943. *Activated* on 1 Oct 1943. Assigned to First AF. Trained replacement pilots, using P–47's. *Disbanded* on 10 Apr 1944.

Reconstituted on 16 May 1949 and allotted to the reserve. *Activated* on 27 Jun 1949. *Redesignated* 87th Fighter-Escort Group in Mar 1950. Ordered into active service on 1 May 1951. *Inactivated* on 25 Jun 1951.

Redesignated 87th Troop Carrier Group (Medium) and allotted to the reserve. *Activated* on 15 Jun 1952. *Inactivated* on 1 Feb 1953.

(This group is not related to an 87th Pursuit Group (Interceptor) that was constituted on 13 Jan 1942; activated at Selfridge Field by Third AF on 10 Feb 1942; assigned the 304th, 305th, and 306th squadrons; and disbanded a few days later in order to bring AAF within the authorized number of pursuit groups.)

SQUADRONS. *450th:* 1943–1944. *535th:* 1943–1944; 1949–1951; 1952–1953. *536th:* 1943–1944; 1952–1953. *537th:* 1943–1944; 1952–1953.

STATIONS. Richmond AAB, Va, 1 Oct 1943; Camp Springs AAFld, Md, 21 Jan–10 Apr 1944. Bergstrom AFB, Tex, 27 Jun

1949–25 Jun 1951. Atterbury AFB, Ind, 15 Jun 1952–1 Feb 1953.

COMMANDERS. Lt Col Robert N Maupin, Oct 1943–1944.

CAMPAIGNS. None.

DECORATIONS. None.

INSIGNE. None.

88th BOMBARDMENT GROUP

POWER TO SHATTER

Constituted as 88th Bombardment Group (Heavy) on 28 Jan 1942. *Activated* on 15 Jul 1942, but not manned until Sep. Equipped with B–17's. Served for a short time as an operational training unit and afterward as a replacement training unit. Assigned to Second and later to Third AF. *Inactivated* on 1 May 1944.

SQUADRONS. *316th:* 1942–1944. *317th:* 1942–1944. *318th:* 1942–1944. *399th:* 1942–1944.

STATIONS. Salt Lake City AAB, Utah, 15 Jul 1942; Geiger Field, Wash, 1 Sep 1942; Walla Walla, Wash, 21 Sep 1942;

Rapid City AAB, SD, c. 28 Oct 1942; Walla Walla, Wash, c. 28 Nov 1942; Avon Park AAFld, Fla, Nov 1943–1 May 1944.

COMMANDERS. Lt Col Edgar M Wittan, 1 Sep 1942; Lt Col Hewitt T Wheless, 1 Mar 1943; Lt Col William K Kincaid, 28 Oct 1943–1 May 1944.

CAMPAIGNS. American Theater.

DECORATIONS. None.

INSIGNE. *Shield:* Azure, a glass throughout shattered, argent. *Motto:* POWER TO SHATTER. (Approved 7 Jan 1943.)

89th TROOP CARRIER GROUP

PRIMIS CUM PLURIMIS

Constituted as 89th Transport Group on 19 Jan 1942. *Activated* on 1 Feb 1942. Assigned to Air Transport Command (later I Troop Carrier Command) in Apr 1942. *Redesignated* 89th Troop Carrier Group in Jul 1942. Provided transition training for pilots, using DC–3's and later C–47's. Began training replacement crews in Mar 1944. *Disbanded* on 14 Apr 1944.

Reconstituted, allotted to the reserve, and *redesignated* 89th Troop Carrier

Group (Medium), on 10 May 1949. *Activated* on 27 Jun 1949. Ordered to active service on 1 May 1951. *Inactivated* on 10 May 1951.

Redesignated 89th Fighter-Bomber Group and allotted to the reserve. *Activated* on 14 Jun 1952.

SQUADRONS. *24th:* 1942–1944; 1949–1951; 1952–. *25th:* 1942–1944; 1949–1951; 1952–. *26th:* 1942–1944; 1949–1951; 1952–. *27th:* 1942. *28th:* 1942. *30th:* 1942–1944; 1949–1951. *31st:* 1942–1944.

STATIONS. Daniel Field, Ga, 1 Feb 1942; Harding Field, La, 8 Mar 1942; Camp Williams, Wis, 20 Jun 1942; Sedalia, Mo, 8 Sep 1942; Del Valle, Tex, 14 Dec 1942–14 Apr 1944. Hanscom Aprt, Mass, 27 Jun 1949–10 May 1951. Laurence G Hanscom Field, Mass, 14 Jun 1952–.

COMMANDERS. Capt William C Allen, 1 Feb 1942; Col Julian M Chappell, 8 Apr 1942; Lt Col Ralph J Gibbons, 4 Apr 1943–14 Apr 1944.

CAMPAIGNS. American Theater.

DECORATIONS. None.

INSIGNE. *Shield:* Or, upon and over a bendlet gules a stylized radial motor azure, that portion over the second fimbriated of the field surmounted by a torteau fimbriated argent, and charged with a winged helmeted head of a soldier couped of the last. *Motto:* PRIMIS CUM PLURIMIS—First with the Most Men. (Approved 5 Jan 1943. This insigne became an element of a new insigne approved 12 Mar 1953.)

90th BOMBARDMENT GROUP

· IMPAVIDE ·

Constituted as 90th Bombardment Group (Heavy) on 28 Jan 1942. *Activated* on 15 Apr 1942. Prepared for combat with B–24's. Moved to Hawaii in Sep 1942 and assigned to Seventh AF. Completed training, moved to the Southwest Pacific in Nov 1942, and assigned to Fifth AF. Entered combat immediately, and from Nov 1942 to Jan 1945 operated from Australia, New Guinea, and Biak, attacking enemy airfields, troop concentrations, ground installations, and shipping in New Guinea, the Bismarck Archipelago, Palau, and the southern Philippines. Received a DUC for strikes, conducted through heavy flak and fighter opposition, on Japanese airfields at Wewak, New Guinea, in Sep 1943. Other operations included participation in the Battle of the Bismarck Sea in Mar 1943 and long-range raids on oil refineries at Balikpapan, Borneo, in Sep and Oct 1943. Moved to the Philippines in Jan 1945. Supported ground forces on Luzon, attacked industries on Formosa, and bombed railways, airfields, and harbor facilities on the Asiatic mainland. Moved to Ie Shima in Aug 1945, and after the war flew reconnaissance missions over Japan and ferried Allied prisoners from Okinawa to Manila. Returned to the Philippines in Dec 1945. *Inactivated* on 27 Jan 1946.

Redesignated 90th Bombardment Group (Very Heavy). *Activated* in the US on 1 Jul 1947. Assigned to Strategic Air Command. Probably not manned during 1947 and 1948. *Inactivated* on 6 Sep 1948.

Redesignated 90th Bombardment Group (Medium). *Activated* on 2 Jan 1951. Assigned to Strategic Air Command and equipped with B–29's. *Inactivated* on 16 Jun 1952.

SQUADRONS. *319th:* 1942–1946; 1947–1948; 1951–1952. *320th:* 1942–1946; 1947–1948; 1951–1952. *321st:* 1942–1946; 1947–1948; 1951–1952. *400th:* 1942–1946.

STATIONS. Key Field, Miss, 15 Apr 1942; Barksdale Field, La, 17 May 1942; Greenville AAB, SC, 21 Jun 1942; Ypsilante, Mich, 9–c. 18 Aug 1942; Hickam Field, TH, 12 Sep 1942; Iron Range, Australia, Nov 1942; Port Moresby, New Guinea, 10 Feb 1943; Dobodura, New Guinea, Dec 1943; Nadzab, New Guinea, 23 Feb 1944; Biak, 10 Aug 1944; San Jose, Mindoro, 26 Jan 1945; Ie Shima, c. 10 Aug 1945; Ft William McKinley, Luzon, Dec 1945–27 Jan 1946. Andrews Field, Md, 1 Jul 1947–6 Sep 1948. Fairchild AFB, Wash, 2 Jan 1951; Forbes AFB, Kan, 14 Mar 1951–16 Jun 1952.

COMMANDERS. 1st Lt Newman W Enloe, 17 Apr 1942; Lt Col Eugene P Mussett, 17 May 1942; Col Roger M Ramey, 14 Sep 1942; Lt Col Eugene P Mussett, 16 Oct 1942; Col Arthur Meehan, 21 Oct 1942; Lt Col Arthur H Rogers, 16 Nov 1942; Col Ralph E Koon, 18 Nov 1942; Col Arthur H Rogers, 11 Jul 1943; Lt Col Harry J Bullis, c. 20 Dec 1943; Col Carl A Brandt, 16 Mar 1944; Col Edward W Scott Jr, 10 Jun 1944; Lt Col Wilson H Banks, 8 Dec 1944; Col Ellis L Brown, 24 Feb 1945–unkn. Unkn, 1947–1948. Lt Col William L Gray, Jan 1951; Col Conrad F Necrason, Feb 1951–16 Jun 1952.

CAMPAIGNS. Air Offensive, Japan; China Defensive; Papua; New Guinea; Bismarck Archipelago; Western Pacific; Leyte; Luzon; China Offensive.

DECORATIONS. Distinguished Unit Citations: Papua, [Nov] 1942–23 Jan 1943; New Guinea, 13 and 15 Sep 1943. Philippine Presidential Unit Citation.

INSIGNE. *Shield:* Azure, a pterodactyl (Dimorphodon Macronyx) volant or langued gules, eyed vert. *Motto:* IMPAVIDE—Undauntedly. (Approved 22 Sep 1942.)

91st BOMBARDMENT GROUP

Constituted as 91st Bombardment Group (Heavy) on 28 Jan 1942. *Activated* on 15 Apr 1942. Trained with B–17's. Moved to England, Aug–Oct 1942, and assigned to Eighth AF. Operated primarily as a strategic bombardment organization

throughout the war. Entered combat in Nov 1942 and concentrated its attacks on submarine pens, ship-building yards, harbors, and dock facilities until mid-1943. During this period, also struck airdromes, factories, and communications. Attacked the navy yard at Wilhelmshaven on 27 Jan 1943 when heavy bombers of Eighth AF first penetrated Germany. Received a DUC for bombing marshalling yards at Hamm on 4 Mar 1943 in spite of adverse weather and heavy enemy opposition. From the middle of 1943 until the war ended, engaged chiefly in attacks on aircraft factories, airdromes, and oil facilities. Specific targets included airfields at Villacoublay and Oldenburg, aircraft factories in Oranienburg and Brussels, chemical industries in Leverkusen and Peenemunde, ball-bearing plants in Schweinfurt, and other industries in Ludwigshafen, Berlin, Frankfurt, and Wilhelmshaven. On 11 Jan 1944 organizations of Eighth AF went into central Germany to attack vital aircraft factories; participating in this operation, the 91st group successfully bombed its targets in spite of bad weather, inadequate fighter cover, and severe enemy attack, being awarded a DUC for the performance. Expanding its operations to include interdictory and support missions, the group contributed to the Normandy invasion by bombing gun emplacements and troop concentrations near the beachhead area in Jun 1944; aided the St Lo breakthrough by attacking enemy troop positions, 24–25 Jul 1944; supported troops on the front lines near Caen in Aug 1944; attacked communications near the battle area during the Battle of the Bulge, Dec 1944–Jan 1945; and assisted the push across the Rhine by striking airfields, bridges, and railroads near the front lines in the spring of 1945. Evacuated prisoners from German camps after the war ended. Returned to the US, Jun–Jul 1945. *Inactivated* on 7 Nov 1945.

Redesignated 91st Reconnaissance Group. *Activated* on 1 Jul 1947. Assigned to Strategic Air Command. *Redesignated* 91st Strategic Reconnaissance Group in Nov 1948. Used a variety of aircraft, including B– and RB–17's, B– and RB–29's, and B–50's. *Redesignated* 91st Strategic Reconnaissance Group (Medium) in Jul 1950. Equipped with RB–45's. *Inactivated* on 28 May 1952.

SQUADRONS. *7th* Geodetic: 1949–1950. *91st:* 1949–1950. *322d:* 1942–1945; 1947–1948, 1949–1952. *324th:* 1942–1945; 1947–1952. *401st:* 1942–1945.

STATIONS. Harding Field, La, 15 Apr 1942; MacDill Field, Fla, 16 May 1942; Walla Walla, Wash, c. 26 Jun–24 Aug 1942; Kimbolton, England, Sep 1942; Bassingbourn, England, c. 14 Oct 1942–23 Jun 1945; Drew Field, Fla, 3 Jul–7 Nov 1945. Andrews Field, Md, 1 Jul 1947; McGuire AFB, NJ, 20 Jul 1948; Barksdale AFB, La, 1 Oct 1949; Lockbourne AFB, Ohio, c. 5 Sep 1950–28 May 1952.

COMMANDERS. 1st Lt Edward R Eckert, 15 Apr 1942; Col Stanley T Wray, 15 May 1942; Lt Col Baskin R Lawrence Jr, c. 25 May 1943; Lt Col Clemens L Wurzbach, 25 Jun 1943; Col Claude E Putnam, Dec 1943; Col Henry W Terry, 17 May 1944; Lt Col Donald E Sheeler, 30 May 1945–unkn. Col Frank L Dunn, 1948; Lt Col Robert S Kittel, 10 Nov 1948; Col Charles R Greening, 24 Jun 1949; Maj James I Cox, 23 Aug 1949; Col Jean R Byerly, 1 Oct 1949; Col Lewis E Lyle, 25 Nov 1950–c. Aug 1951; Col Joseph A Preston, c. Aug 1951–28 May 1952.

CAMPAIGNS. Air Offensive, Europe; Normandy; Northern France; Rhineland; Ardennes-Alsace; Central Europe.

DECORATIONS. Distinguished Unit Citations: Hamm, Germany, 4 Mar 1943; Germany, 11 Jan 1944.

INSIGNE. Shield: Azure (sky blue), a lightning flash issuing from dexter base and pointing to an eye proper on a cloud issuing from the sinister chief, on the flash in dexter base a sphere proper in an orbit argent; over all a bend azure fimbriated argent. (Approved 23 Dec 1952.)

92d BOMBARDMENT GROUP

HIGHER · STRONGER · FASTER

Constituted as 92d Bombardment Group (Heavy) on 28 Jan 1942. *Activated* on 1 Mar 1942. Trained with B–17's and performed antisubmarine duty. Moved to England, Jul–Aug 1942, and assigned to Eighth AF. Flew a few combat missions in Sep and Oct 1942, then trained replacement crews. Began bombardment of strategic objectives in May 1943 and engaged primarily in such operations throughout the war. Targets from May 1943 to Feb 1944 included shipyards at Kiel, ball-bearing plants at Schweinfurt, submarine installations at Wilhelmshaven, a tire plant at Hannover, airfields near Paris, an aircraft factory at Nantes, and a magnesium mine and reducing plant in Norway. Flight Officer John C Morgan, co-pilot, received the Medal of Honor for action aboard a B–17 during a mission over Europe, [26] Jul 1943: when the aircraft was attacked by enemy fighters, the pilot suffered a brain injury which left him in a crazed condition; for two hours Morgan flew in formation with one hand at the controls and the other holding off the struggling pilot who was attempting to fly the plane; finally another crew member was able to relieve the situation and the B–17 made a safe landing at its base. Although handicapped by weather conditions, enemy fire, and insufficient fighter protection, the group bombed aircraft factories in central Germany on 11 Jan 1944 and received a DUC for the mission. Took part in the intensive campaign of heavy bombers against the German aircraft industry during Big Week, 20–25 Feb 1944. After that, attacked V-weapon sites in France; airfields in France, Germany, and the Low Countries; and industrial targets in France, Germany, and Belgium, making concentrated strikes on oil and transportation facilities after Oct 1944. In addition to strategic missions, performed some interdictory and support operations. Assisted the Normandy invasion in Jun 1944 by hitting gun emplacements, junctions, and marshalling yards in the beachhead area. Supported ground forces at St Lo during the breakthrough in Jul 1944. Bombed gun positions and bridges to aid the airborne assault on Holland in Sep 1944. Participated in the Battle of the Bulge, Dec 1944–Jan 1945, by attacking bridges and marshalling yards in and near the battle area. Bombed airfields near the landing zone to cover the airborne assault across the Rhine in Mar 1945. Moved to France in Jun 1945 and transported troops from Marseilles to Casablanca for return to the US. *Inactivated* in France on 28 Feb 1946.

Redesignated 92d Bombardment Group (Very Heavy). *Activated* in the US on 4 Aug 1946. Assigned to Strategic Air Command and equipped with B–29's. *Redesignated* 92d Bombardment Group (Medium) in May 1948. Temporarily stationed in Japan and attached to Far East Air Forces for duty in the Korean War. Served in combat against the communist forces from 12 Jul to 20 Oct 1950. Bombed strategic and interdictory targets, including factories, refineries, iron works, airfields, bridges, tunnels, troop concentrations, barracks, marshalling yards, road junctions, rail lines, supply dumps, docks, and vehicles. Returned to the US, Oct–Nov 1950. *Redesignated* 92d Bombardment Group (Heavy) in Jun 1951. Converted to B–36 aircraft. *Inactivated* on 16 Jun 1952.

SQUADRONS. *325th:* 1942–1946; 1946–1952. *326th:* 1942–1946; 1946–1952. *327th:* 1942–1946; 1946–1952. *407th:* 1942–1946.

STATIONS. Barksdale Field, La, 1 Mar 1942; MacDill Field, Fla, c. 26 Mar 1942; Sarasota, Fla, May–Jul 1942; Bovingdon, England, Aug 1942; Alconbury, England, Jan 1943; Podington, England, Sep 1943; Istres, France, Jun 1945–28 Feb 1946. Ft Worth AAFld, Tex, 4 Aug 1946; Smoky Hill AAFld, Kan, Oct 1946; Spokane AAFld, Wash, Jun 1947–16 Jun 1952.

COMMANDERS. Col James S Sutton, c. 27 Mar 1942; Lt Col Baskin R Lawrence Jr, c. 2 May 1943; Col William M Reid, c. 23 May 1943; Col James W Wilson, 27 Sep 1944; Lt Col Albert L Cox, Aug 1945; Lt

Col James A Smyrl, c. 12 Oct 1945; Maj Victor A Cherbak Jr, c. 18 Oct 1945–unkn. Col John G Eriksen, 4 Aug 1946; Col Brooks A Lawhon, Oct 1946; Capt William M Carrithers, Dec 1946–unkn; Lt Col Frank A Sharp, 14 Jul 1947; Col Albert J Shower, Jul 1947; Lt Col Richard J Fry, 18 Nov 1947; Col George A Blakey, Apr 1948; Col Salvatore E Manzo, c. 1 Jul 1948; Col Claude E Putnam Jr, 3 Oct 1949; Col Conrad F Necrason, c. Feb 1951; Col Claude E Putnam Jr, c. 14 Apr 1951; Col Kenneth B Hobson, c. Jun 1951; Col David Wade, c. 9 Feb–16 Jun 1952.

CAMPAIGNS. *World War II:* Antisubmarine, American Theater; Air Offensive, Europe; Normandy; Northern France; Rhineland; Ardennes-Alsace; Central Europe. *Korean War:* UN Defensive; UN Offensive.

DECORATIONS. Distinguished Unit Citation: Germany, 11 Jan 1944.

INSIGNE. *Shield:* Azure, a pterodactyl (pteranodon) volant, in bend or, langued gules, eyed vert. *Motto:* HIGHER—STRONGER—FASTER. (Approved 9 Mar 1943. This insigne was replaced 21 Nov 1957.)

93d BOMBARDMENT GROUP

Constituted as 93d Bombardment Group (Heavy) on 28 Jan 1942. *Activated* on 1 Mar 1942. Prepared for combat with B-24's. Engaged in antisubmarine operations over the Gulf of Mexico and the Caribbean Sea, May–Jul 1942.

Moved to England, Aug–Sep 1942, and assigned to Eighth AF. Entered combat on 9 Oct 1942 by attacking steel and engineering works at Lille. Until Dec 1942, operated primarily against submarine pens in the Bay of Biscay. A large detachment was sent to North Africa in Dec 1942, the group receiving a DUC for operations in that theater, Dec 1942–Feb 1943, when, with inadequate supplies and under the most difficult desert conditions, the detachment struck heavy blows at enemy shipping and communications. The detachment returned to England, Feb–Mar 1943, and until the end of Jun the group bombed engine repair works, harbors, power plants, and other targets in France, the Low Countries, and Germany. A detachment returned to the Mediterranean theater, Jun–Jul 1943, to support the invasion of Sicily and to participate in the famous low-level attack on enemy oil installations at Ploesti on 1 Aug. Having followed another element of the formation along the wrong course to Ploesti, the

93d hit targets that had been assigned to other groups, but it carried out its bombing of the vital oil installations despite heavy losses inflicted by attacks from the fully-alerted enemy and was awarded a DUC for the operation. Lt Col Addison E Baker, group commander, and Maj John L Jerstad, a former member of the group who had volunteered for this mission, were posthumously awarded the Medal of Honor for action in the Ploesti raid: refusing to make a forced landing in their damaged B–24, these men, as pilot and co-pilot of the lead plane, led the group to bomb the oil facilities before their plane crashed in the target area. After the detachment returned to England in Aug 1943, the group flew only two missions before the detachment was sent back to the Mediterranean to support Fifth Army at Salerno during the invasion of Italy in Sep 1943. The detachment rejoined the group in Oct 1943, and until Apr 1945 the 93d concentrated on bombardment of strategic targets such as marshalling yards, aircraft factories, oil refineries, chemical plants, and cities in Germany. In addition it bombed gun emplacements, choke points, and bridges near Cherbourg during the Normandy invasion in Jun 1944; attacked troop concentrations in northern France during the St Lo breakthrough in Jul 1944; transported food, gasoline, water, and other supplies to the Allies advancing across France, Aug–Sep 1944; dropped supplies to airborne troops in Holland on 18 Sep 1944; struck enemy transportation and other targets during the Battle of the

Bulge, Dec 1944–Jan 1945; and flew two missions on 24 Mar 1945 during the airborne assault across the Rhine, dropping supplies to troops near Wesel and bombing a night-fighter base at Stormede. Ceased operations in Apr 1945. Returned to the US, May–Jun 1945.

Redesignated 93d Bombardment Group (Very Heavy) in Jul 1945. Assigned to Strategic Air Command on 21 Mar 1946. Trained with B–29's. *Redesignated* 93d Bombardment Group (Medium) in May 1948. Converted to B–50 aircraft in 1949. *Inactivated* on 16 Jun 1952.

SQUADRONS. *328th:* 1942–1952. *329th:* 1942–1952. *330th:* 1942–1952. *409th:* 1942–1946.

STATIONS. Barksdale Field, La, 1 Mar 1942; Ft Myers, Fla, 15 May–2 Aug 1942; Alconbury, England, 7 Sep 1942; Hardwick, England, 6 Dec 1942–19 May 1945; Sioux Falls AAFld, SD, Jun 1945; Pratt AAFld, Kan, 24 Jul 1945; Clovis AAFld, NM, 13 Dec 1945; Castle Field, Calif, 21 Jun 1946–16 Jun 1952.

COMMANDERS. 1st Lt Robert M Tate, 1 Mar 1942; Col Edward J Timberlake Jr, 26 Mar 1942; Lt Col Addison E Baker, 17 May 1943; Col Leland G Fiegel, 9 Aug 1943; Lt Col Harvey P Barnard Jr, 27 Sep 1944; Col William R Robertson Jr, 5 Dec 1944; Lt Col Therman D Brown, 6 Apr 1945; Maj Jacob A Herrmann, 29 Jul 1945; Lt Col William W Amorous, 6 Aug 1945; Col Henry W Dorr, c. 5 Oct 1945–unkn; Lt Col Kenneth Grunewald, 1946; Maj Arthur R Pidgeon, 1946; Maj Loyd D Griffin, 1946; CWO Steve Stanowich,

1946; Capt Joe W Moore Jr, Oct 1946; Capt Allen Milnes, 1946–unkn; Lt Col John C Thrift, Aug 1947; Col Glendon P Overing, 1 Sep 1948; Lt Col Colin E Anderson, 3 Nov 1949; Col John E Dougherty, 1 Dec 1949; Brig Gen Robert H Terrill, Feb 1951; Col Richard H Carmichael, 16 Apr 1951; Col John E Dougherty, 19 Oct 1951–16 Jun 1952.

CAMPAIGNS. Antisubmarine, American Theater; Air Combat, EAME Theater; Egypt-Libya; Air Offensive, Europe; Tunisia; Sicily; Naples-Foggia; Normandy; Northern France; Rhineland; Ardennes-Alsace; Central Europe.

DECORATIONS. Distinguished Unit Citations: North Africa, 17 Dec 1942–20 Feb 1943; Ploesti, Rumania, 1 Aug 1943.

INSIGNE. *Shield:* Azure, in front of a bend parti per bend sable and argent between two globes of the last with latitude and longitude lines of the second, the one in chief bearing a wreath vert and the one in base bearing a cross of four arrows, points out of the first, gules, or and of the fifth, a lightning flash bend sinisterwise or. (Approved 4 Sep 1953.)

94th BOMBARDMENT GROUP

Constituted as 94th Bombardment Group (Heavy) on 28 Jan 1942. *Activated* on 15 Jun 1942. Trained for duty overseas with B–17's. Moved to England, Apr–May 1943, and assigned to Eighth AF. Served chiefly as a strategic bombardment organization throughout the war. Flew its first mission on 13 Jun 1943, bombing an airdrome at St Omer. After that, attacked such strategic objectives as the port of St Nazaire, shipyards at Kiel, an aircraft component parts factory at Kassel, a synthetic rubber plant at Hannover, a chemical factory at Ludwigshafen, marshalling yards at Frankfurt, oil facilities at Merseburg, and ball-bearing works at Eberhausen. Withstood repeated assaults by enemy interceptors to bomb an aircraft factory at Regensburg on 17 Aug 1943, being awarded a DUC for the mission. Braving adverse weather, heavy flak, and savage fighter attacks, the group completed a strike against an aircraft parts factory in Brunswick on 11 Jan 1944 and received another DUC for this operation. Took part in the campaign of heavy bombers against the enemy aircraft industry during Big Week, 20–25 Feb 1944. Sometimes operated in support of ground forces and flew interdictory missions. Prior to D–Day in Jun 1944, helped to neutralize V-weapon sites, airdromes, and other military installations along the coast of France. On 6 Jun bombed enemy positions in the battle area to support the invasion of Normandy. Struck troops and gun batteries to aid the advance of the Allies at St Lo in Jul and at Brest in Aug. Covered the airborne attack on Holland in Sep. Hit marshalling yards, airfields, and strong points near the combat area during the Battle of the Bulge, Dec 1944–Jan 1945. Bombed transportation, communications, and oil targets in the final push over the Rhine and across Germany. After V–E Day, dropped leaflets to displaced persons and German civilians. Returned to the US in Dec 1945. *Inactivated* on 21 Dec 1945.

Redesignated 94th Bombardment Group (Very Heavy). Allotted to the reserve. *Activated* on 29 May 1947. *Redesignated* 94th Bombardment Group (Light) in Jun 1949. Called to active duty on 10 Mar 1951. *Inactivated* on 20 Mar 1951.

Redesignated 94th Tactical Reconnaissance Group. Allotted to the reserve. *Activated* on 14 Jun 1952. *Redesignated* 94th Bombardment Group (Tactical) in May 1955.

SQUADRONS. *331st:* 1942–1945; 1947–1951; 1952–. *332d:* 1942–1945; 1947–1951; 1952–. *333d:* 1942–1945; 1947–1951; 1952–1955. *410th:* 1942–1945; 1947–1951.

STATIONS. MacDill Field, Fla, 15 Jun 1942; Pendleton Field, Ore, c. 1 Jul 1942; Davis-Monthan Field, Ariz, Aug 1942; Biggs Field, Tex, 1 Nov 1942; Pueblo AAB, Colo, Jan–Apr 1943; Earls Colne, England, May 1943; Bury St Edmunds, England, 15 Jun 1943–c. 12 Dec 1945; Camp Kilmer, NJ, c. 20–21 Dec 1945. Marietta AAFld, Ga, 29 May 1947–20 Mar 1951. Dobbins AFB, Ga, 14 Jun 1952; Scott AFB, Ill, 18 May 1955–.

COMMANDERS. Col John G Moore, 1942; Col Frederick W Castle, Jun 1943; Col Charles B Dougher, 17 Apr 1944; Col Nicholas T Perkins, 16 Mar 1945; Lt Col Ernest B Maxwell, 3 Jun 1945–unkn.

CAMPAIGNS. Air Offensive, Europe; Normandy; Northern France; Rhineland; Ardennes-Alsace; Central Europe.

DECORATIONS. Distinguished Unit Citations: Germany, 17 Aug 1943; Germany, 11 Jan 1944.

INSIGNE. *Shield:* On a shield azure, over a cloud formation argent, a chimerical creature, with the body of a panther, the head of a buffalo all sable, horns, talons, and eyes proper, and eagle's wings or, crouching over the top of a sphere of the last, lined of the third, the creature snorting fire proper. *Motto:* CUNNING—RUGGED—COURAGEOUS. (Approved 6 Apr 1956.)

95th BOMBARDMENT GROUP

Constituted as 95th Bombardment Group (Heavy) on 28 Jan 1942. *Activated* on 15 Jun 1942. Used B-17's in preparing for duty overseas. Moved to England, Mar–May 1943, and assigned to Eighth AF. Entered combat on 13 May 1943 by attacking an airfield at St Omer. During the next two months, made repeated attacks against V-weapon sites and

JUSTICE WITH VICTORY

airfields in France. Began bombing strategic objectives in Germany in Jul 1943 and engaged primarily in such operations until V–E Day. Targets included harbors, industries, marshalling yards, and cities. Received a DUC for maintaining a tight defensive formation in spite of severe assault by enemy fighters and bombing the aircraft assembly plant at Regensburg on 17 Aug 1943. Withstanding concentrated attacks by fighters during the approach to the target and intense antiaircraft fire directly over the objective, the group effectively bombarded marshalling yards at Munster on 10 Oct 1943, being awarded a DUC for the performance. Participated in the intensive campaign of heavy bombers against the German aircraft industry during Big Week, 20–25 Feb 1944. Received another DUC for action during an attack by AAF bombers on Berlin on 4 Mar 1944: while many participating organizations, because of weather conditions, either abandoned the operation or struck other targets, the 95th proceeded to Berlin and successfully bombed a suburb of the German capital despite snowstorms,

dense clouds, and severe enemy attack. The group interrupted its strategic operations to strike coastal defenses and communications during the invasion of Normandy in Jun 1944; hit enemy troop concentrations and thus assist the Allied breakthrough at St Lo in Jul 1944; drop ammunition, food, and medical supplies to Polish troops in Warsaw on 18 Sep 1944; attack enemy transportation during the Battle of the Bulge, Dec 1944–Jan 1945; and bomb airdromes in support of the Allied assault across the Rhine in Mar 1945. Flew its last combat mission, an attack on marshalling yards at Oranienburg, on 20 Apr 1945. Dropped food to the Dutch during the first week in May. After V–E Day, transported liberated prisoners and displaced persons from Austria to France and England. Returned to the US, Jun–Aug 1945. *Inactivated* on 28 Aug 1945.

Redesignated 95th Bombardment Group (Very Heavy). Allotted to the reserve. *Activated* on 29 May 1947. *Inactivated* on 27 Jun 1949.

SQUADRONS. *334th:* 1942–1945; 1947–1949. *335th:* 1942–1945; 1947–1949. *336th:* 1942–1945; 1947–1949. *412th:* 1942–1945; 1947–1949.

STATIONS. Barksdale Field, La, 15 Jun 1942; Pendleton Field, Ore, 26 Jun 1942; Geiger Field, Wash, 28 Aug 1942; Ephrata, Wash, 31 Oct 1942; Geiger Field, Wash, 24 Nov 1942; Rapid City AAB, SD, 14 Dec 1942–11 Mar 1943; Framlingham, England, 12 May 1943; Horham, England, 15 Jun 1943–19 Jun 1945; Sioux Falls

AAFld, SD, 14–28 Aug 1945. Memphis Mun Aprt, Tenn, 29 May 1947–27 Jun 1949.

COMMANDERS. Col Alfred A Kessler Jr, 23 Oct 1942; Col John K Gerhart, 22 Jun 1943; Col Chester P Gilger, c. 29 Jan 1944; Col Karl Truesdell Jr, 10 May 1944; Col Jack E Shuck, Dec 1944; Lt Col Robert H Stuart, 28 Apr 1945–unkn.

CAMPAIGNS. Air Offensive, Europe; Normandy; Northern France; Rhineland; Ardennes-Alsace; Central Europe.

DECORATIONS. Distinguished Unit Citations: Germany, 17 Aug 1943; Munster, Germany, 10 Oct 1943; Berlin, Germany, 4 Mar 1944.

INSIGNE. *Shield:* Azure, a Justin cross throughout or, over all a feather in bend gules. *Motto:* JUSTICE WITH VICTORY. (Approved 26 Feb 1943. This insigne was modified 3 Sep 1957.)

96th BOMBARDMENT GROUP

Constituted as 96th Bombardment Group (Heavy) on 28 Jan 1942. *Activated* on 15 Jul 1942. Trained with B–17's and also served as an operational training unit. Moved to England, Apr–May 1943, for duty with Eighth AF. Entered combat in May 1943 and functioned primarily as a strategic bombardment organization throughout the war. Attacked shipyards, harbors, railroad yards, airdromes, oil refineries, aircraft factories, and other industrial targets in Germany, France, Holland, Belgium, Norway, Poland, Hungary, and Czechoslovakia. Received a DUC for

· E SEMPRE L'ORA ·

withstanding severe assault by enemy fighters to bomb the vital aircraft factories at Regensburg on 17 Aug 1943. Received another DUC for leading the 45th Wing a great distance through heavy clouds and intense antiaircraft fire to raid important aircraft component factories in Poland on 9 Apr 1944. Other significant targets included airdromes in Bordeaux and Augsburg; marshalling yards in Kiel, Hamm, Brunswick, and Gdynia; aircraft factories in Chemnitz, Hannover, and Diosgyor; oil refineries in Merseburg and Brux; and chemical works in Weisbaden, Ludwigshafen, and Neunkirchen. In addition to strategic operations, missions included bombing coastal defenses, railway bridges, gun emplacements, and field batteries in the battle area prior to and during the invasion of Normandy in Jun 1944; attacking enemy positions in support of the breakthrough at St Lo in Jul 1944; aiding the campaign in France in Aug by striking roads and road junctions, and by dropping supplies to the Maquis; and attacking, during the early months of 1945, the communications supplying German armies on the western front. After V–E Day, flew food to Holland and hauled redeployed personnel to French Morocco, Ireland, France, and Germany. Returned to the US in Dec. *Inactivated* on 21 Dec 1945.

Redesignated 96th Bombardment Group (Very Heavy). Allotted to the reserve. *Activated* on 29 May 1947. *Inactivated* on 27 Jun 1949.

SQUADRONS. *337th:* 1942–1945; 1947–1949. *338th:* 1942–1945; 1947. *339th:* 1942–1945; 1947. *413th:* 1942–1945; 1947–1949. *546th:* 1947–1949. *547th:* 1947–1949.

STATIONS. Salt Lake City AAB, Utah, 15 Jul 1942; Gowen Field, Idaho, 6 Aug 1942; Walla Walla, Wash, 14 Aug 1942; Rapid City AAB, SD, 30 Sep 1942; Pocatello, Idaho, 30 Oct 1942; Pyote AAB, Tex, Jan–Mar 1943; Great Saling, England, May 1943; Snetterton Heath, England, 12 Jun 1943–12 Dec 1945; Camp Kilmer, NJ, 20–21 Dec 1945. Gunter Field, Ala, 29 May 1947–27 Jun 1949.

COMMANDERS. Col Archie J Old Jr, 6 Aug 1942; Col James L Travis, c. 6 Sep 1943; Col Robert W Warren, Jun 1944; Lt Col Robert J Nolan, c. 27 May 1945–unkn.

CAMPAIGNS. Air Offensive, Europe; Normandy; Northern France; Rhineland; Ardennes-Alsace; Central Europe.

DECORATIONS. Distinguished Unit Citations: Germany, 17 Aug 1943; Poznan, Poland, 9 Apr 1944.

INSIGNE. *Shield:* Azure a falcon's head erased or, holding in its beak a drop bomb bendwise gules, that portion over the first fimbriated of the second. *Motto:* E SEMPRE L'ORA—It Is Always the Hour. (Approved 18 Feb 1943.)

97th BOMBARDMENT GROUP

Constituted as 97th Bombardment Group (Heavy) on 28 Jan 1942. *Activated* on 3 Feb 1942. Trained with B–17's; also flew some antisubmarine patrols. Moved to England, May–Jul 1942, for duty with Eighth AF. Entered combat on 17 Aug 1942 by bombing a marshalling yard at Rouen, the first mission flown by AAF's heavy bombers based in England. After that, attacked airfields, marshalling yards, industries, naval installations, and other targets in France and the Low Countries. Moved to the Mediterranean theater in Nov 1942, being assigned first to Twelfth and later (Nov 1943) to Fifteenth AF. Struck shipping in the Mediterranean and airfields, docks, harbors, and marshalling yards in North Africa, southern France, Sardinia, Sicily, and southern Italy, Nov 1942–May 1943, in the campaign to cut supply lines to German forces in North

Africa. Helped to force the capitulation of Pantelleria in Jun 1943. Bombed in preparation for and in support of the invasions of Sicily and southern Italy in the summer and fall of 1943. From Nov 1943 to Apr 1945, engaged chiefly in long-range missions to targets in Italy, France, Germany, Czechoslovakia, Austria, Hungary, Rumania, Bulgaria, Yugoslavia, and Greece, attacking oil refineries, aircraft factories, marshalling yards, and other strategic objectives. Received a DUC for leading a strike against an aircraft factory at Steyr on 24 Feb 1944 during Big Week, the intensive air campaign against the German aircraft industry. 2d Lt David R Kingsley, bombardier, was awarded the Medal of Honor for saving the life of a wounded gunner on 23 Jun 1944: during a mission to Ploesti, Kingsley's B-17 was seriously crippled and the tail gunner was injured; when the crew was ordered to bail out, Kingsley gave his parachute to the gunner, whose own had been damaged, and assisted him in bailing out; Kingsley died a few moments later when his bomber crashed and burned. The group received its second DUC for a devastating raid against one of the Ploesti refineries on 18 Aug 1944. Other operations of the 97th included pounding enemy communications, transportation, and airfields in support of Allied forces at Anzio and Cassino; bombing coastal defenses in preparation for the invasion of Southern France; and assisting US Fifth and British Eighth Army in their advance through the Po Valley. *Inactivated* in Italy on 29 Oct 1945.

Redesignated 97th Bombardment Group (Very Heavy). *Activated* in the US on 4 Aug 1946. Assigned to Strategic Air Command. Equipped with B-29's. *Redesignated* 97th Bombardment Group (Medium) in May 1948. Converted to B-50's in 1950. *Inactivated* on 16 Jun 1952.

SQUADRONS. *340th:* 1942–1945; 1946–1952. *341st:* 1942–1945; 1946–1952. *342d:* 1942–1945; 1946–1952. *414th:* 1942–1945.

STATIONS. MacDill Field, Fla, 3 Feb 1942; Sarasota, Fla, 29 Mar–c. 16 May 1942; Polebrook, England, c. 13 Jun–c. 9 Nov 1942; Maison Blanche, Algeria, c. 13 Nov 1942; Tafaraoui, Algeria, c. 22 Nov 1942; Biskra, Algeria, c. 25 Dec 1942; Chateaudun-du-Rhumel, Algeria, c. 8 Feb 1943; Pont-du-Fahs, Tunisia, c. 1 Aug 1943; Depienne, Tunisia, c. 15 Aug 1943; Cerignola, Italy, c. 20 Dec 1943; Amendola, Italy, 16 Jan 1944; Marcianise, Italy, c. 1–29 Oct 1945. Smoky Hill AAFld, Kan, 4 Aug 1946; Biggs AFB, Tex, 17 May 1948–16 Jun 1952.

COMMANDERS. Col Cornelius W Cousland, Feb 1942; Col James H Walsh, c. Jul 1942; Col Frank A Armstrong Jr, c. 2 Aug 1942; Brig Gen Joseph H Atkinson, c. 27 Sep 1942; Col Stanley J Donovan, 5 Jan 1943; Col Leroy A Rainey, 29 Jun 1943; Col Frank Allen, Nov 1943; Col Jacob E Smart, 7 Apr 1944; Col Frank Allen, 11 May 1944; Col Elmer J Rogers Jr, Jun 1944; Col Nils O Ohman, 22 Aug 1944; Col Wil-

liam K Kincaid, May 1945–unkn. Col
Walter S Lee, c. 4 Aug 1946; Lt Col Wil-
liam D Bacon, c. 27 Aug 1946; Col William
E McDonald, 9 Oct 1946; Col George L
Robinson, 10 Sep 1947–unkn; Col George
L Robinson, 30 Sep 1948; Col Dalene E
Bailey, 20 Apr 1949; Col Harvey C Dor-
ney, Feb 1951; Col John D Ryan, 16 Jul
1951–16 Jun 1952.

CAMPAIGNS. Antisubmarine, American
Theater; Air Combat, EAME Theater;
Air Offensive, Europe; Tunisia; Sicily;
Naples-Foggia; Anzio; Rome-Arno; Nor-
mandy; Northern France; Southern
France; North Apennines; Rhineland;
Central Europe; Po Valley.

DECORATIONS. Distinguished Unit Citations: Steyr, Austria, 24 Feb 1944; Ploesti,
Rumania, 18 Aug 1944.

INSIGNE. *Shield:* Azure, a spear in pale
or, point to base flammant and embrued
proper. *Motto:* VENIT HORA—The
Hour Has Come. (Approved 5 Mar
1943.)

98th BOMBARDMENT GROUP

Constituted as 98th Bombardment
Group (Heavy) on 28 Jan 1942. *Activated* on 3 Feb 1942. Trained with B–24's.
Moved to the Mediterranean theater, Jul–
Aug 1942, and served in that area until the
end of the war. Assigned to Ninth AF in
Nov 1942, to Twelfth AF in Sep 1943, and
to Fifteenth AF in Nov 1943. Entered
combat in Aug 1942. Bombed shipping
and harbor installations in Libya, Tunisia,
Sicily, Italy, Crete, and Greece to cut

FORCE FOR FREEDOM

enemy supply lines to Africa. Also hit airdromes and rail facilities in Sicily and
Italy. Received a DUC for action against
the enemy in the Middle East, North
Africa, and Sicily from Aug 1942 to Aug
1943. Awarded another DUC for participation in the low-level assault on oil refineries at Ploesti on 1 Aug 1943: although
its target had already been attacked by another group, the 98th proceeded through
dense smoke and intense flak to bomb its
assigned objective. Col John R Kane,
group commander, received the Medal of
Honor for leading the 98th to complete
this attack despite the hazards of oil fires,
delayed-action bombs, and alerted defenses. Afterward the group flew many
long-range missions to Italy, France, Germany, Austria, Czechoslovakia, Hungary,
and the Balkans to bomb such strategic
targets as industries, airdromes, harbors,
and communications, and engaged primarily in such operations until Apr 1945.
1st Lt Donald D Pucket, one of the group's
pilots, was awarded the Medal of Honor
for action during a mission against oil re-

fineries at Ploesti on 9 Jul 1944: just after bombing the target, Lt Pucket's plane was crippled by antiaircraft fire and crew members were wounded; he calmed the crew, administered first aid, surveyed the damage, and, realizing it was impossible to reach friendly territory, gave the order to abandon ship; refusing to desert three men who were unable to leave the bomber, Lt Pucket stayed with the plane that a few moments later crashed on a mountainside. In addition to strategic operations, the 98th also flew interdictory and support missions. Aided Allied forces at Anzio and Cassino. Participated in the invasion of Southern France. Assisted the Russian advance in the Balkans. Returned to the US, Apr–May 1945. *Redesignated* 98th Bombardment Group (Very Heavy) in May. *Inactivated* on 10 Nov 1945.

Activated on 1 Jul 1947. Assigned to Strategic Air Command. Trained with B–29's. *Redesignated* 98th Bombardment Group (Medium) in May 1948. Moved to Japan in Aug 1950 and attached to Far East Air Forces for duty in the Korean War. Engaged primarily in interdicting enemy communications but also operated in support of UN ground forces. Targets included marshalling yards, oil centers, rail facilities, bridges, roads, troop concentrations, airfields, and military installations. *Inactivated* on 16 Jun 1952 while on temporary duty in Japan.

SQUADRONS. *343d:* 1942–1945; 1947–1952. *344th:* 1942–1945; 1947–1952. *345th:* 1942–1945; 1947–1952. *415th:* 1942–1945.

STATIONS. MacDill Field, Fla, 3 Feb 1942; Barksdale Field, La, Feb 1942; Ft Myers, Fla, 30 Mar 1942; Drane Field, Fla, c. 15 May–3 Jul 1942; Ramat David, Palestine, 25 Jul 1942; Fayid, Egypt, c. 11 Nov 1942; Benina, Libya, c. 9 Feb 1943; Hergla, Tunisia, c. 21 Sep 1943; Brindisi, Italy, c. 18 Nov 1943; Manduria, Italy, 19 Dec 1943; Lecce, Italy, 17 Jan 1944–19 Apr 1945; Fairmont AAFld, Neb, c. 6 May 1945; McCook AAFld, Neb, 25 Jun–10 Nov 1945. Andrews Field, Md, 1 Jul 1947; Spokane AAFld, Wash, 24 Sep 1947–16 Jun 1952.

COMMANDERS. Lt Col Frank H Robinson, c. Feb 1942; Col Hugo P Rush, 1942; Col John R Kane, c. 29 Dec 1942; Lt Col Julian M Bleyer, 1 Nov 1943; Col William E Karnes, 18 Nov 1943; Lt Col Marshall R Gray, 13 Jan 1944; Col Salvatore E Manzo, c. Jul 1944–unkn; Col John G Eriksen, 25 Jun–c. Sep 1945; unkn, Sep–Nov 1945. Unkn, Jul–Oct 1947; Lt Col Joseph D White, 20 Oct 1947; Col William D Cairnes, 12 Apr 1948; Col Richard D Dick, 20 Jan 1949; Col Richard H Carmichael, c. Apr 1950; Col David Wade, c. 31 Mar 1951; Col Edwin F Harding Jr, Sep 1951; Col Lewis A Curtis, Nov 1951; Col Winton R Close, May–16 Jun 1952.

CAMPAIGNS. *World War II:* Air Combat, EAME Theater; Egypt-Libya; Air Offensive, Europe; Tunisia; Sicily; Naples-Foggia; Anzio; Rome-Arno; Normandy; Northern France; Southern France; North Apennines; Rhineland; Central Europe; Po Valley. *Korean War:* UN Defensive; UN Offensive; CCF Intervention; 1st UN Counteroffensive; CCF

Spring Offensive; UN Summer-Fall Offensive; Second Korean Winter; Korea Summer-Fall, 1952.

DECORATIONS. Distinguished Unit Citations: North Africa and Sicily, Aug 1942–17 Aug 1943; Ploesti, Rumania, 1 Aug 1943. Republic of Korea Presidential Unit Citation: [Aug 1950–Jun 1952].

INSIGNE. *Shield:* Azure, a bend indented between a dexter mailed hand couped at the wrist, in bend, grasping a drop bomb and an olive wreath, all or. *Motto:* FORCE FOR FREEDOM. (Approved 29 Jul 1942.)

99th BOMBARDMENT GROUP

Constituted as 99th Bombardment Group (Heavy) on 28 Jan 1942. *Activated* on 1 Jun 1942. Trained with B–17's. Moved to North Africa, Feb–May 1943, and assigned to Twelfth AF. Entered combat in Mar 1943 and bombed such targets as airdromes, harbor facilities, shipping, railroads, viaducts, and bridges in Tunisia, Sardinia, Sicily, Pantelleria, and Italy until Dec 1943. Received a DUC for performance on 5 Jul 1943 when the group helped to neutralize fighter opposition prior to the invasion of Sicily by penetrating enemy defenses to bomb planes, hangars, fuel supplies, and ammunition dumps at the Gerbini airfield. Assigned to Fifteenth AF in Nov 1943 and moved to Italy in Dec. Flew long-range missions to attack such strategic objectives as oil refineries, marshalling yards, aircraft factories, and steel plants in Italy, France, Germany, Poland, Czechoslovakia, Austria, Hungary, Rumania, Bulgaria, Yugoslavia, and Greece. Received another DUC for withstanding severe fighter assaults to bomb the vital aircraft factory and facilities at Wiener Neustadt on 23 Apr 1944. Other operations included assisting ground forces at Anzio and Cassino, Feb–Mar 1944; participating in the pre-invasion bombing of southern France, Aug 1944; and supporting the Allied offensive in the Po Valley, Apr 1945. *Inactivated* in Italy on 8 Nov 1945.

Redesignated 99th Bombardment Group (Very Heavy). Allotted to the reserve. *Activated* on 29 May 1947. *Inactivated* on 27 Jun 1949.

SQUADRONS. *346th:* 1942–1945; 1947–1949. *347th:* 1942–1945; 1947–1949. *348th:* 1942–1945; 1947–1949. *416th:* 1942–1945; 1947–1949.

STATIONS. Orlando AB, Fla, 1 Jun 1942; MacDill Field, Fla, 1 Jun 1942; Pendleton Field, Ore, 29 Jun 1942; Gowen Field, Idaho, 28 Aug 1942; Walla Walla, Wash, c. 30 Sep 1942; Sioux City AAB, Iowa, 17 Nov 1942–3 Jan 1943; Navarin, Algeria, c. 23 Feb 1943; Oudna, Tunisia, 4 Aug 1943; Tortorella Airfield, Italy, c. 11 Dec 1943; Marcianise, Italy, Oct–8 Nov 1945. Birmingham Mun Aprt, Ala, 29 May 1947–27 Jun 1949.

COMMANDERS. Unkn, Jun–Sep 1942; Col Fay R Upthegrove, c. Sep 1942; Lt Col Wayne E Thurman, 24 Nov 1943; Col Charles W Lawrence, 19 Dec 1943; Lt Col Wayne E Thurman, 26 Jan 1944; Col Ford J Lauer, 15 Feb 1944; Col Trenholm J Meyer, Jul 1944; Lt Col James A Barnett, Aug 1944; Col Ford J Lauer, Sep 1944; Col Raymond V Schwanbeck, Jan 1945; Lt Col Robert E Guay, 8 Oct 1945; Maj Joseph D Russell, 11 Oct 1945; Maj John S Giegel, 16 Oct 1945–unkn.

CAMPAIGNS. Air Combat, EAME Theater; Air Offensive, Europe; Tunisia; Sicily; Naples-Foggia; Anzio; Rome-Arno; Normandy; Northern France; Southern France; North Apennines; Rhineland; Central Europe; Po Valley.

DECORATIONS. Distinguished Unit Citations: Sicily, 5 Jul 1943; Austria, 23 Apr 1944.

INSIGNE. *Shield:* Azure, issuant from sinister chief a cloud argent emitting a lightning flash to dexter base or between an eye of the second with pupil sable represented as a radar scope of the third with eyelid of the like, and a globe of the last with lines of the fifth encircled by a motion picture film silver. *Motto:* SIGHT WITH MIGHT. (Approved 3 Nov 1943. This insigne was replaced 7 Feb 1958.)

100th BOMBARDMENT GROUP

Constituted as 100th Bombardment Group (Heavy) on 28 Jan 1942. *Activated* on 1 Jun 1942. Used B–17's to prepare for duty overseas. Moved to England, May–Jun 1943, and assigned to Eighth AF. Operated chiefly as a strategic bombardment organization until the war ended. From Jun 1943 to Jan 1944, concentrated its efforts against airfields in France and naval facilities and industries in France and Germany. Received a DUC for seriously disrupting German fighter-plane production with an attack on an aircraft factory at Regensburg on 17 Aug 1943. Bombed airfields, industries, marshalling yards, and missile sites in western Europe, Jan–May 1944. Operations in this period included participation in the Allied campaign against enemy aircraft factories during Big Week, 20–25 Feb 1944. Completed a series of attacks against Berlin in Mar 1944 and received a DUC for the missions. Beginning in the summer of 1944, oil installations became major targets. In addition to strategic operations, the group engaged in support and interdictory missions, hitting bridges and gun positions in support of the Normandy invasion in Jun 1944; bombing enemy positions at St Lo in Jul and at Brest in Aug and Sep; striking transportation and ground defenses in the drive against the Siegfried Line, Oct–Dec 1944; attacking marshalling yards, defended villages, and communications in the Ardennes sector during the Battle of the Bulge, Dec 1944–Jan 1945; and covering the airborne assault across the Rhine in Mar 1945. Received the French Croix de Guerre with Palm for attacking heavily defended installations in Germany and for dropping supplies to French Forces of the Interior, Jun–Dec 1944. Returned to the US in Dec 1945. *Inactivated* on 21 Dec 1945.

Redesignated 100th Bombardment Group (Very Heavy). Allotted to the reserve. *Activated* on 29 May 1947. *Inactivated* on 27 Jun 1949.

SQUADRONS. *349th:* 1942–1945; 1947–1949. *350th:* 1942–1945; 1947–1949. *351st:* 1942–1945; 1947–1949. *418th:* 1942–1945; 1947–1949.

STATIONS. Orlando AB, Fla, 1 Jun 1942; Barksdale Field, La, c. 18 Jun 1942; Pendleton Field, Ore, c. 26 Jun 1942; Gowen Field, Idaho, 28 Aug 1942; Walla Walla, Wash, c. 1 Nov 1942; Wendover Field, Utah, c. 30 Nov 1942; Sioux City AAB, Iowa, c. 28 Dec 1942; Kearney AAFld, Neb, c. 30 Jan–May 1943; Thorpe Abbotts, England, 9 Jun 1943–Dec 1945; Camp Kilmer, NJ, c. 20–21 Dec 1945. Miami AAFld, Fla, 29 May 1947–27 Jun 1949.

COMMANDERS. Unkn, Jun–Nov 1942; Col Darr H Alkire, c. 14 Nov 1942; Col Howard M Turner, c. 28 Apr 1943; Col Harold Q Huglin, Jun 1943; Col Neil B Harding, c. Jul 1943; Col Robert H Kelly, 19 Apr 1944; Col Thomas S Jeffery, c. 9 May 1944; Col Frederick J Sutterlin, 2 Feb 1945; Lt Col John B Wallace, 23 Jun 1945–unkn.

CAMPAIGNS. Air Offensive, Europe; Normandy; Northern France; Rhineland; Ardennes-Alsace; Central Europe.

DECORATIONS. Distinguished Unit Citations: Germany, 17 Aug 1943; Berlin, Germany, 4, 6, 8 Mar 1944. French Croix de Guerre with Palm, 25 Jun–31 Dec 1944.

INSIGNE. *Shield:* Gray, issuing from a base nebuly azure bearing in fess arched reversed six mullets argent, nine billets in chevron sable, surmounted by two lions respectant or langued gules, grasping in saltire a palm branch bend sinisterwise vert and a lightning flash of the sixth. *Motto:* PEACE THROUGH STRENGTH. (Approved 22 Nov 1957.)

301st BOMBARDMENT GROUP

WHO FEARS?

Constituted as 301st Bombardment Group (Heavy) on 28 Jan 1942. *Activated* on 3 Feb 1942. Trained with B–17's. Moved to England, Jul–Aug 1942, and assigned to Eighth AF. Began combat in Sep 1942 and attacked submarine pens, airfields, railroads, bridges, and other targets on the Continent, primarily in France. Operated with Twelfth AF after moving to North Africa in Nov 1942. Bombed docks, shipping facilities, airdromes, and railroad yards in Tunisia, Sicily, and Sardinia. Attacked enemy shipping between Tunisia and Sicily. Received a DUC for action on 6 Apr 1943 when the group withstood intense antiaircraft fire from shore defenses and nearby vessels to attack a convoy of merchant ships off Bizerte and thus destroy supplies essential to the Axis defense of Tunisia. Assaulted gun positions on Pantelleria during May–Jun 1943. Flew numerous missions to Italy, Jul–Oct 1943. Assigned to Fifteenth AF in Nov 1943, moved to Italy in Dec, and afterward directed most of its attacks against such strategic targets as oil centers, communications, and industrial areas in Italy, France, Germany, Poland, Czechoslovakia, Austria, Hungary, Rumania, Bulgaria, Yugoslavia, and Greece. Received another DUC for a mission to Germany on 25 Feb 1944 when, in spite of vicious encounters with enemy fighters, the group bombed aircraft production centers at Regensburg. Other operations for the group during 1944–1945 included flying missions in support of ground forces in the Anzio and Cassino areas, supporting the invasion of Southern France, knocking out targets to assist the Russian advance in the Balkans, and aiding the Allied drive through the Po Valley. Returned to the US in July 1945. *Redesignated* 301st Bombardment Group (Very Heavy) in Aug. *Inactivated* on 15 Oct 1945.

Activated on 4 Aug 1946. Assigned to Strategic Air Command. Equipped with B–29's. *Redesignated* 301st Bombardment Group (Medium) in May 1948. *Inactivated* on 16 Jun 1952.

SQUADRONS. *32d:* 1942–1945; 1946–1952. *352d:* 1942–1945; 1946–1952. *353d:* 1942–1945; 1946–1952. *354th:* 1942. *419th:* 1942–1945.

STATIONS. Geiger Field, Wash, 3 Feb 1942; Alamogordo, NM, 27 May 1942; Richard E Byrd Field, Va, 21 Jun–19 Jul 1942; Chelveston, England, 9 Aug 1942; Tafaraoui, Algeria, c. 26 Nov 1942; Maison Blanche, Algeria, 5 Dec 1942; Biskra, Algeria, c. 16 Dec 1942; Ain M'lila, Algeria, c. 17 Jan 1943; St-Donat, Algeria, 6 Mar

1943; Oudna, Tunisia, 6 Aug 1943; Cerignola, Italy, c. 7 Dec 1943; Lucera, Italy, 1 Feb 1944–1945; Sioux Falls AAFld, SD, 28 Jul 1945; Pyote AAFld, Tex, 23 Aug–15 Oct 1945. Clovis AAFld, NM, 4 Aug 1946; Smoky Hill AAFld, Kan, 16 Jul 1947; Barksdale AFB, La, 7 Nov 1949–16 Jun 1952.

COMMANDERS. Col Ronald R Walker, Feb 1942; Lt Col Samuel J Gormly Jr, c. Feb 1943; Col John K Brown Jr, 3 Sep 1943; Col Jean R Byerly, 24 Nov 1943; Lt Col Karl T Barthelmess, 25 Dec 1943; Col John F Batjer, 3 Mar 1944; Lt Col John D Moorman, Sep 1944; Col Ernest S Holmes Jr, 8 Dec 1944; Lt Col Robert H Allyn, 1945; Col Raymond L Winn, 31 Aug 1945– unkn. Unkn, Aug 1946–Aug 1947; Col George L Robinson, 1 Aug 1947; Lt Col Frank W Ellis, Sep 1947; Lt Col Thomas J Classen, 20 Jun 1949; Col Harris E Rogner, 21 Jul 1949; Col Chester C Cox, 15 Dec 1950; Col Horace M Wade, Mar 1951–16 Jun 1952.

CAMPAIGNS. Air Combat, EAME Theater; Air Offensive, Europe; Tunisia; Sicily; Naples-Foggia; Anzio; Rome-Arno; Normandy; Northern France; Southern France; North Apennines; Rhineland; Central Europe; Po Valley.

DECORATIONS. Distinguished Unit Citations: Tunisia, 6 Apr 1943; Germany, 25 Feb 1944.

INSIGNE. Shield: Azure, three ravens pendent from a spear fessways or. Motto: WHO FEARS? (Approved 11 Aug 1942.)

302d BOMBARDMENT GROUP

JUSTUM ET TENACEM

Constituted as 302d Bombardment Group (Heavy) on 28 Jan 1942. Activated on 1 Jun 1942. Assigned to Second AF, later (Dec 1943) to First AF. Using B-24's, served first as an operational training and later as a replacement training unit. Inactivated on 10 Apr 1944.

Redesignated 302d Troop Carrier Group (Medium) and allotted to the reserve. Activated on 27 Jun 1949. Redesignated 302d Troop Carrier Group (Heavy) in Jan 1950. Ordered to active duty on 1 Jun 1951. Inactivated on 8 Jun 1951.

Redesignated 302d Troop Carrier Group (Medium) and allotted to the reserve. Activated on 14 Jun 1952.

SQUADRONS. 355th: 1942–1944; 1949–1951; 1952–. 356th: 1942–1944; 1949–1951; 1952–. 357th: 1942–1944; 1949–1951; 1952–. 420th: 1942.

STATIONS Geiger Field, Wash, 1 Jun 1942; Davis-Monthan Field, Ariz, 23 Jun 1942; Wendover Field, Utah, 30 Jul 1942; Pueblo AAB, Colo, 30 Sep 1942; Davis-Monthan Field, Ariz, 1 Dec 1942; Clovis, NM, 29 Jan 1943; Langley Field, Va, 17

Dec 1943–10 Apr 1944. McChord AFB, Wash, 27 Jun 1949–8 Jun 1951. Clinton County AFB, Ohio, 14 Jun 1952–.

COMMANDERS. Lt Col Joseph J Nazzaro, 1 Jun 1942; Col Eugene H Beebe, 12 Jul 1942; Lt Col Joseph J Nazzaro, 15 Sep 1942; Lt Col William K Martin, 1 Jan 1943; Maj Horace S Carswell, 15 Oct 1943; Lt Col Thomas J Gent Jr, 2 Nov 1943; Lt Col Carlos J Cochrane, 3 Jan–Apr 1944.

CAMPAIGNS. American Theater.

DECORATIONS. None.

INSIGNE. *Shield:* Azure, a thunderbolt in pale irradiated or, inflamed proper, winged, gules. *Motto:* JUSTUM ET TENACEM—Just and Resolute. (Approved 27 Feb 1943.)

303d BOMBARDMENT GROUP

MIGHT IN FLIGHT

Constituted as 303d Bombardment Group (Heavy) on 28 Jan 1942. *Activated* on 3 Feb 1942. Prepared for combat with B-17's. Moved to England, Aug–Sep 1942, and assigned to Eighth AF. Entered combat in Nov 1942 and raided targets such as airdromes, railroads, and submarine pens in France until 1943. Began bombardment of industries, marshalling yards, cities, and other strategic objectives in Germany in Jan 1943, and engaged primarily in such operations until V–E Day. Took part in the first penetration into Germany by heavy bombers of Eighth AF by striking the U-boat yard at Wilhelmshaven on 27 Jan 1943. Other targets included ball-bearing plants at Schweinfurt, shipbuilding yards at Bremen, a synthetic rubber plant at Huls, an aircraft engine factory at Hamburg, industrial areas of Frankfurt, an airdrome at Villacoublay, and a marshalling yard at Le Mans. Flying through intense antiaircraft fire during an attack on Vegesack on 18 Mar 1943, 1st Lt Jack W Mathis, the leading bombardier of his squadron, was knocked from his bombsight; although mortally wounded, he returned to his position and released the bombs; for this action, which ensured an accurate attack against the enemy, Lt Mathis was posthumously awarded the Medal of Honor. T/Sgt Forrest L Vosler, radio operator and gunner, received the Medal of Honor for a mission to Bremen on 20 Dec 1943: after bombing the target, Sgt Vosler's plane was hit by antiaircraft fire that knocked out two engines, damaged the radio equipment, seriously injured the tail gunner, and wounded Sgt Vosler in the legs and thighs; the burst of another 20-mm shell nearly blinded the sergeant; nevertheless, he maintained a steady stream of fire to protect the tail of the aircraft; when the pilot announced that the plane would ditch, Sgt Vosler, working entirely by touch, repaired the radio and sent out distress signals; after the plane went down in the Channel, the sergeant secured the tail gunner and himself on the wing; Sgt Vosler's radio signals brought help, and the entire crew was rescued. The organization received a DUC for an operation on 11 Jan 1944 when, in spite of continuous attacks by enemy fighters in weather that prevented effective fighter cover from reaching the group, it successfully struck an aircraft assembly plant at Oschersleben. Sometimes the group engaged in support and interdictory missions. Attacked gun emplacements and bridges in the Pas de Calais area during the invasion of Normandy in Jun 1944. Bombed enemy troops to support the breakthrough at St Lo in Jul 1944. Struck airfields, oil depots, and other targets during the Battle of the Bulge, Dec 1944–Jan 1945. Bombed military installations in the Wesel area to aid the Allied assault across the Rhine in Mar 1945. Flew last combat mission, an attack on armament works in Pilsen, on 25 Apr 1945. Moved to French Morocco, May–Jun 1945. *Inactivated* on 25 Jul 1945.

Redesignated 303d Bombardment Group (Very Heavy). *Activated* in the US on 1 Jul 1947. Assigned to Strategic Air Command. There is no evidence that the group was manned during 1947 and 1948. *Inactivated* on 6 Sep 1948.

Redesignated 303d Bombardment Group (Medium). *Activated* on 4 Sep 1951. Assigned to Strategic Air Command and equipped with B–29's. *Inactivated* on 16 Jun 1952.

SQUADRONS. *358th:* 1942–1945; 1947–1948; 1951–1952. *359th:* 1942–1945; 1947–1948; 1951–1952. *360th:* 1942–1945; 1947–1948; 1951–1952. *427th:* 1942–1945.

STATIONS. Pendleton Field, Ore, 3 Feb 1942; Gowen Field, Idaho, 11 Feb 1942; Alamogordo, NM, 17 Jun 1942; Biggs Field, Tex, 7–23 Aug 1942; Molesworth, England, 12 Sep 1942; Casablanca, French Morocco, c. 31 May–25 Jul 1945. Andrews Field, Md, 1 Jul 1947–6 Sep 1948. Davis-Monthan AFB, Ariz, 4 Sep 1951–16 Jun 1952.

COMMANDERS. Col Ford J Lauer, Feb 1942; Col Warren H Higgins, c. 29 May 1942; Col James H Wallace, c. 14 Jul 1942; Col Charles E Marion, c. 12 Feb 1943; Col Kermit D Stevens, Jul 1943; Col William S Raper, Oct 1944; Lt Col William C Sipes, 19 Apr 1945; Capt Bernard Thompson, Jun–25 Jul 1945. Unkn, 1947–1948. Maj Joe Maddalena Jr, Sep 1951; Col David Wade, 9 Oct 1951; Col John K Hester, Jan–16 Jun 1952.

CAMPAIGNS. Air Offensive, Europe; Normandy; Northern France; Rhineland; Ardennes-Alsace; Central Europe.

DECORATIONS. Distinguished Unit Citation: Germany, 11 Jan 1944.

INSIGNE. *Shield:* Azure, a diminutive pile between four flashes of lightning, two issuant palewise from chief and one from dexter and sinister chief sides chevronwise inverted, issuant from base a burst of five rays, all or. *Motto:* MIGHT IN FLIGHT. (Approved 9 Jan 1943.)

304th BOMBARDMENT GROUP

Constituted as 304th Bombardment Group (Heavy) on 28 Jan 1942. *Activated* on 15 Jul 1942. Assigned to Second AF. Received personnel in Sep and began training on the west coast. Later, operated with AAF Antisubmarine Command, using such planes as B–17's, B–18's, B–24's, B–34's, and A–20's to fly patrols along the east coast. Also trained crews for duty overseas. *Inactivated* on 30 Dec 1942.

SQUADRONS. *1st* Antisubmarine (formerly 361st Bombardment): 1942. *18th* Antisubmarine (formerly 362d Bombardment): 1942. *19th* Antisubmarine (formerly 363d Bombardment): 1942. *421st* Bombardment: 1942.

STATIONS. Salt Lake City AAB, Utah, 15 Jul 1942; Geiger Field, Wash, 15 Sep 1942; Ephrata, Wash, 1 Oct 1942; Langley Field, Va, 29 Oct–30 Dec 1942.

COMMANDERS. Col Ford J Lauer, 24 Sep 1942; Lt Col Dale O Smith, c. 29 Oct 1942; Maj Francis H Matthews, Nov–Dec 1942.

CAMPAIGNS. Antisubmarine, American Theater.

DECORATIONS. None.

INSIGNE. *Shield:* Azure, seme of drop bombs or. *Motto:* AQUILA NON CAPTAT MUSCAS—The Eagle Does Not Catch Flies. (Approved 7 Nov 1942.)

305th BOMBARDMENT GROUP

Constituted as 305th Bombardment Group (Heavy) on 28 Jan 1942. *Activated* on 1 Mar 1942. Trained for duty overseas with B–17's. Moved to England, Aug–Oct 1942, and assigned to Eighth AF. Began combat on 17 Nov 1942 and operated chiefly as a strategic bombardment organization until Apr 1945. Until mid-1943, attacked such targets as submarine pens, docks, harbors, shipyards, motor works, and marshalling yards in France, Germany, and the Low Countries. Bombed the navy yards at Wilhelmshaven on 27 Jan 1943 when heavy bombers of Eighth AF made their first penetration into Germany. Received a DUC for a mission on 4 Apr 1943 when an industrial target in Paris was bombed with precision in spite of pressing enemy fighter attacks and heavy flak. During the second half of 1943, began deeper penetration into enemy territory to strike heavy industry. Significant objectives included aluminum, magnesium, and nitrate works in Norway, industries in Berlin, oil plants at Merseburg, aircraft factories at Anklam, shipping at Gdynia, and ball-bearing works at Schweinfurt. Received another DUC for withstanding severe opposition to bomb aircraft factories in central Germany on 11 Jan 1944. Participated in the intensive campaign of heavy bombers against the German aircraft industry during Big Week, 20–25 Feb 1944. 1st Lt William R Lawley Jr, and 1st Lt Edward S Michael, pilots, each received the Medal of Honor for similar performances on 20 Feb and 11 Apr 1944, respectively; in each case a B–17 was severely damaged by fighters after it had bombed a target in Germany, crew members were wounded, and the pilot himself was critically injured; recovering in time to pull his aircraft out of a steep dive, and realizing that the wounded men would be unable to bail out, each pilot flew his plane back to England and made a successful crash landing. In addition to bombardment of strategic targets, the group often flew interdictory missions and supported infantry units. Prior to the Normandy invasion in Jun 1944, it helped to neutralize enemy installations such as V-weapon sites, airfields, and repair shops; and on D-Day, 6 Jun, bombed enemy strongholds near the battle area. Attacked enemy positions in advance of ground forces at St Lo in Jul 1944. Struck antiaircraft batteries to cover the airborne invasion of Holland in Sep. Took part in the Battle of the Bulge, Dec 1944–Jan 1945, by bombing military installations in the battle zone. Supported the airborne assault across the Rhine in Mar 1945. Sometimes flew missions at night to bomb enemy installations or to drop propaganda leaflets. Flew its last combat mission on 25 Apr 1945. Remained in the theater as part of United States Air Forces in Europe after V–E Day; and, from stations in Belgium and Germany, engaged in photographic mapping missions over parts of Europe and North Africa. *Inactivated* in Germany on 25 Dec 1946.

Redesignated 305th Bombardment Group (Very Heavy). *Activated* in the US on 1 Jul 1947. Assigned to Strategic Air Command. Few, if any, personnel were assigned. *Inactivated* on 6 Sep 1948.

Redesignated 305th Bombardment Group (Medium). *Activated* on 2 Jan 1951. Assigned to Strategic Air Command and equipped with B–29's. *Inactivated* on 16 Jun 1952.

SQUADRONS. *364th:* 1942–1946; 1947–1948; 1951–1952. *365th:* 1942–1946; 1947–1948; 1951–1952. *366th:* 1942–1946; 1947–1948; 1951–1952. *422d:* 1942–1946.

STATIONS. Salt Lake City, Utah, 1 Mar 1942; Geiger Field, Wash, c. 10 Jun 1942; Muroc, Calif, c. 31 Jun–Aug 1942; Grafton Underwood, England, Sep 1942; Chelveston, England, Dec 1942; St Trond, Belgium, Jul 1945; Lechfeld, Germany, Dec 1945–25 Dec 1946. Andrews Field, Md, 1 Jul 1947–6 Sep 1948. MacDill AFB, Fla, 2 Jan 1951–16 Jun 1952.

COMMANDERS. Capt John H deRussy, c. 15 Mar 1942; Lt Col Ernest H Lawson, c. 1 Apr 1942; Lt Col Fay R Upthegrove, c. 27 May 1942; Col Curtis E LeMay, c. 2 Jun 1942; Lt Col Donald K Fargo, 18 May 1943-unkn; Col Ernest H Lawson, Nov 1943; Col Anthony Q Mustoe, Jun 1944; Col Henry G MacDonald, Oct 1944; Col Paul L Barton, 22 Apr 1946; Col G M Palmer, Sep 1946–unkn. Unkn, 1947–1948. Lt Col James B Irwin, c. 2 Jan 1951; Col Elliot Vandevanter Jr, c. 1 Feb 1951–16 Jun 1952.

CAMPAIGNS. Air Offensive, Europe; Normandy; Northern France; Rhineland; Ardennes-Alsace; Central Europe.

DECORATIONS. Distinguished Unit Citations: France, 4 Apr 1943; Germany, 11 Jan 1944.

INSIGNE. *Shield:* Azure, in pale a bomb proper, winged or, in base a target proper, all within a bordure of the second. *Motto:* CAN DO. (Approved 23 Apr 1951.)

306th BOMBARDMENT GROUP

Constituted as 306th Bombardment Group (Heavy) on 28 Jan 1942. *Activated* on 1 Mar 1942. Trained for combat with B-17's. Moved to England, Aug–Sep 1942, and assigned to Eighth AF. Dur-

ABUNDANCE OF STRENGTH

ing combat, Oct 1942–Apr 1945, operated primarily against strategic targets, striking locomotive works at Lille, railroad yards at Rouen, submarine pens at Bordeaux, shipbuilding yards at Vegesack, ball-bearing works at Schweinfurt, oil plants at Merseburg, marshalling yards at Stuttgart, a foundry at Hannover, a chemical plant at Ludwigshafen, aircraft factories at Leipzig, and other objectives on the Continent. Took part in the first penetration into Germany by heavy bombers of Eighth AF on 27 Jan 1943 by attacking U-boat yards at Wilhelmshaven. Sgt Maynard H Smith received the Medal of Honor for his performance on 1 May 1943: when the aircraft on which he was a gunner was hit by the enemy and fires were ignited in the radio compartment and waist sections, the sergeant threw exploding ammunition overboard, manned a gun until the German fighters were driven off, administered first aid to the wounded tail gunner, and extinguished the fire. Without fighter escort and in the face of powerful opposition, the 306th completed an assault against aircraft factories in central Germany on 11 Jan 1944, being awarded a DUC for the mission. Received another DUC for action during Big Week, the intensive campaign against the German aircraft industry, 20–25 Feb 1944: although hazardous weather forced supporting elements to abandon the mission, the group effectively bombarded an aircraft assembly plant at Bernberg on 22 Feb. Often supported ground forces and attacked interdictory targets in addition to its strategic operations. Helped to prepare for the invasion of Normandy by striking airfields and marshalling yards in France, Belgium, and Germany; backed the assault on 6 Jun 1944 by raiding railroad bridges and coastal guns. Assisted ground forces during the St Lo breakthrough in Jul. Covered the airborne invasion of Holland in Sep. Helped stop the advance of German armies in the Battle of the Bulge, Dec 1944–Jan 1945, by attacking airfields and marshalling yards. Bombed enemy positions in support of the airborne assault across the Rhine in Mar 1945. Remained in the theater after V–E Day as part of United States Air Forces in Europe, and engaged in special photographic mapping duty in western Europe and North Africa. *Inactivated* in Germany on 25 Dec 1946.

Redesignated 306th Bombardment Group (Very Heavy). *Activated* in the US on 1 Jul 1947. Assigned to Strategic Air Command. Not manned until Aug 1948. *Redesignated* 306th Bombardment Group (Medium) in Aug 1948. Equipped with B–29's and later with B–50's. *Inactivated* on 16 Jun 1952.

SQUADRONS. *367th:* 1942–1946; 1947–1952. *368th:* 1942–1946; 1947–1952. *369th:* 1942–1946; 1947–1952. *423d:* 1942–1946.

STATIONS. Gowen Field, Idaho, 1 Mar 1942; Wendover Field, Utah, c. 6 Apr–1 Aug 1942; Thurleigh, England, Sep 1942; Giebelstadt, Germany, Dec 1945; Istres, France, Feb 1946; Furstenfeldbruck, Germany, 16 Aug 1946; Lechfeld, Germany, 13 Sep–25 Dec 1946. Andrews Field, Md, 1 Jul 1947; MacDill AFB, Fla, Aug 1948–16 Jun 1952.

COMMANDERS. Col Charles B Overacker Jr, c. 16 Mar 1942; Col Frank A Armstrong Jr, 3 Jan 1943; Col Claude E Putnam, 17 Feb 1943; Col George L Robinson, c. 20 Jun 1943; Col James S Sutton, Sep 1944; Col Hudson H Upham, c. 16 Apr 1945; Col Robert F Harris, May 1946; Lt Col Earl W Kesling, Jun 1946–unkn. Lt Col Charles R Heffner, 13 Aug 1948; Lt Col Loran D Briggs, c. 1 Nov 1948; Col John A Hilger, 1 Sep 1949; Col Michael N W McCoy, Mar 1950–16 Jun 1952.

CAMPAIGNS. Air Offensive, Europe; Normandy; Northern France; Rhineland; Ardennes-Alsace; Central Europe.

DECORATIONS. Distinguished Unit Citations: Germany, 11 Jan 1944; Germany, 22 Feb 1944.

INSIGNE. *Shield:* Per fess enhanced dancette azure and or, in base the Indian idiogram for the jaws of a rattlesnake gules. *Motto:* ABUNDANCE OF STRENGTH. (Approved 6 Jan 1943. This insigne became an element of a new insigne approved 2 Oct 1951.)

307th BOMBARDMENT GROUP

Constituted as 307th Bombardment Group (Heavy) on 28 Jan 1942. *Activated* on 15 Apr 1942. Trained and flew patrols off the west coast, first in B–17's and later in B–24's. Moved to Hawaii, Oct–Nov 1942, and assigned to Seventh AF. Trained and flew patrol and search missions. Attacked Wake Island, Dec 1942–Jan 1943, by staging through Midway. Moved to Guadalcanal in Feb 1943 and assigned to Thirteenth AF. Served in combat, primarily in the South and Southwest Pacific, until the war ended. Attacked Japanese airfields, installations, and shipping in the Solomons and Bismarcks. Helped to neutralize enemy bases on Yap and in the Truk and Palau Islands. Received a DUC for an unescorted, daylight attack on heavily defended airfields in the Truk Islands on 29 Mar 1944. Supported operations in the Philippines by striking Japanese shipping in the southern Philippines and by bombing airfields on Leyte, Luzon, Negros, Ceram, and Halmahera. Also took part in Allied air operations against the Netherlands Indies by hitting airfields, shipping, and installations. Received a DUC for an unescorted mission against vital oil refineries at Balikpapan, Borneo, on 3 Oct 1944. Supported Australian forces on Borneo and bombed targets in French Indochina during the last three months of the war. Flew patrol missions along the Asiatic mainland and ferried liberated prisoners from Okinawa to Manila after V–J Day. Returned to the US, Dec 1945–Jan 1946. *Inactivated* on 18 Jan 1946.

Redesignated 307th Bombardment Group (Very Heavy). *Activated* on 4 Aug 1946. Assigned to Strategic Air Command. Equipped with B–29's. Trained and developed antisubmarine tactics. *Redesignated* 307th Bombardment Group (Medium) in May 1948. Based temporarily on Okinawa and attached to Far East Air Forces for operations during the Korean War. Attacked strategic objectives in North Korea, Aug–Sep 1950. After that, struck interdictory targets, including communications and supply centers, and supported UN ground forces by hitting gun emplacements and troop concentrations. *Inactivated* on 16 Jun 1952.

SQUADRONS. *370th:* 1942–1946; 1946–1952. *371st:* 1942–1946; 1946–1952. *372d:* 1942–1945; 1946–1952. *424th:* 1942–1945.

STATIONS. Geiger Field, Wash, 15 Apr 1942; Ephrata, Wash, 28 May 1942; Sioux City AAB, Iowa, 30 Sep–20 Oct 1942; Hickam Field, TH, 1 Nov 1942; Guadalcanal, Feb 1943; New Georgia, 28 Jan 1944;

Los Negros, c. 29 Apr 1944; Wakde, 24 Aug 1944; Morotai, c. 18 Oct 1944; Clark Field, Luzon, Sep–Dec 1945; Camp Stoneman, Calif, 16–18 Jan 1946. MacDill Field, Fla, 4 Aug 1946–16 Jun 1952.

COMMANDERS. Capt Bill Jarvis, 1 May 1942; Col William A Matheny, 22 May 1942; Col Oliver S Picher, 19 Aug 1943; Col Glen R Birchard, 27 Oct 1943; Col Robert F Burnham, 28 Mar 1944; Col Clifford H Rees, Nov 1944–unkn. Col Richard T King Jr, 4 Aug 1946; Lt Col Clyde G Gillespie, 25 Aug 1946; Lt Col Frank L Davis, Sep 1946; Col John G Eriksen, 13 Jan 1947; Col Clifford J Heflin, 12 Aug 1947; Lt Col John P Proctor, 15 Feb 1950; Col John A Hilger, 13 Mar 1950; Col John M Reynolds, Mar 1951; Col William H Hanson, Aug 1951; Col John C Jennison Jr, 14 Feb 1952; Col Raymond L Winn, May–16 Jun 1952.

CAMPAIGNS. *World War II:* Central Pacific; Guadalcanal; New Guinea; Northern Solomons; Eastern Mandates; Bismarck Archipelago; Western Pacific; Leyte; Luzon; Southern Philippines; China Offensive. *Korean War:* UN Defensive; UN Offensive; CCF Intervention; 1st UN Counteroffensive; CCF Spring Offensive; UN Summer-Fall Offensive; Second Korean Winter; Korea Summer-Fall, 1952.

DECORATIONS. Distinguished Unit Citations: Truk, 29 Mar 1944; Borneo, 3 Oct 1944. Philippine Presidential Unit Citation. Republic of Korea Presidential Unit Citation: [Aug] 1950– [Jun 1952].

INSIGNE. *Shield:* Azure, a four-petalled dogwood bloom slipped or. (Approved 21 Dec 1942.)

308th BOMBARDMENT GROUP

Constituted as 308th Bombardment Group (Heavy) on 28 Jan 1942. *Activated* on 15 Apr 1942. Trained with B-24's. Moved to China early in 1943, with the air echelon flying its planes by way of Africa, and the ground echelon traveling by ship across the Pacific. Assigned to Fourteenth AF. Made many trips over the Hump to India to obtain gasoline, oil, bombs, spare parts, and other items the group needed to prepare for and then to sustain its combat operations. The 308th Group supported Chinese ground forces; attacked airfields, coalyards, docks, oil refineries, and fuel dumps in French Indochina; mined rivers and ports; bombed shops and docks at Rangoon; attacked Japanese shipping in the

East China Sea, Formosa Strait, South China Sea, and Gulf of Tonkin. Received a DUC for an unescorted bombing attack, conducted through antiaircraft fire and fighter defenses, against docks and warehouses at Hankow on 21 Aug 1943. Received second DUC for interdiction of Japanese shipping during 1944–1945. Maj Horace S Carswell Jr was awarded the Medal of Honor for action on 26 Oct 1944 when, in spite of intense antiaircraft fire, he attacked a Japanese convoy in the South China Sea; his plane was so badly damaged that when he reached land he ordered the crew to bail out; Carswell, however, remained with the plane to try to save one man who could not jump because his parachute had been ripped by flak; before Carswell could attempt a crash landing, the plane struck a mountainside and burned. The group moved to India in Jun 1945. Ferried gasoline and supplies over the Hump. Sailed for the US in Dec 1945. *Inactivated* on 6 Jan 1946.

Redesignated 308th Reconnaissance Group (Weather). *Activated* on 17 Oct 1946. Assigned to Air Weather Service and equipped with B–29's. *Inactivated* on 5 Jan 1951.

Redesignated 308th Bombardment Group (Medium). *Activated* on 10 Oct 1951. Assigned to Strategic Air Command and equipped with B–29 aircraft. *Inactivated* on 16 Jun 1952.

SQUADRONS. *53d:* 1946–1947. *59th:* 1946–1947. *373d:* 1942–1945; 1951–1952. *374th:* 1942–1946; 1947–1950; 1951–1952. *375th:* 1942–1946; 1951–1952. *425th:*

1942–1946. *512th:* 1947–1948, 1949. *513th:* 1947–1948, 1949–1950.

STATIONS. Gowen Field, Idaho, 15 Apr 1942; Davis-Monthan Field, Ariz, 20 Jun 1942; Wendover Field, Utah, 1 Oct–28 Nov 1942; Kunming, China, 20 Mar 1943; Hsinching, China, 10 Feb 1945; Rupsi, India, 27 Jun–15 Oct 1945; Camp Kilmer, NJ, 5–6 Jan 1946. Morrison Field, Fla, 17 Oct 1946; Fairfield-Suisun AAFld, Calif, 1 Jul 1947; Tinker AFB, Okla, 10 Nov 1949–5 Jan 1951. Forbes AFB, Kan, 10 Oct 1951; Hunter AFB, Ga, 11 Apr–16 Jun 1952.

COMMANDERS. Capt Harris K McCauley, 11 May 1942; Col Fay R Upthegrove, 5 Jun 1942; Maj Leroy A Rainey, 15 Jul 1942; Col Eugene H Beebe, 16 Sep 1942; Col William P Fisher, c. 3 Nov 1943; Col John G Armstrong, 19 Oct 1944; Col William D Hopson, 1 Jul 1945–unkn. Col Richard E Ellsworth, 17 Oct 1946–unkn; Col Hervey H Whitfield, Apr 1949–unkn. Col George L Newton Jr, 5 Nov 1951; Col Maurice A Preston, 10 May–16 Jun 1952.

CAMPAIGNS. India-Burma; China Defensive; New Guinea; Western Pacific; China Offensive.

DECORATIONS. Distinguished Unit Citations: China, 21 Aug 1943; East and South China Seas, Straits of Formosa, and Gulf of Tonkin, 24 May 1944–28 Apr 1945.

INSIGNE. *Shield:* Azure, between a pale argent thereon three pallets gules, on the dexter a star of twelve points white, charged with an annulet azure; on the sinister a thundercloud proper with three lightning flashes or; in chief per chevron, inverted and enhanced sable, three bombs points downward or, between a semee of fifteen stars argent. *Motto:* NON SIBI, SED ALIIS—Not for Self, But for Others. (Approved 29 Aug 1952.)

309th BOMBARDMENT GROUP

Constituted as 309th Bombardment Group (Medium) on 28 Jan 1942. *Activated* on 15 Mar 1942. Assigned to Third AF. Trained medium bombardment groups and later trained replacement crews, using B–25 aircraft in both the operational and the replacement training programs. *Disbanded* on 1 May 1944.

Reconstituted, redesignated 309th Troop Carrier Group (Medium), and allotted to the reserve, on 16 May 1949. *Activated* on 26 Jun 1949. *Inactivated* on 20 Feb 1951.

Redesignated 309th T r o o p Carrier Group (Assault, Fixed Wing). *Activated* on 8 Jul 1955. Assigned to Tactical Air Command. Using C–122 and C–123 aircraft, the group trained to airlift troops, equipment, and supplies for assault landings.

SQUADRONS. *376th:* 1942–1944; 1949–1951; 1955–. *377th:* 1942–1944; 1949–1950; 1955–. *378th:* 1942–1944; 1955–. *426th:* 1942–1944.

STATIONS. Davis-Monthan Field, Ariz, 15 Mar 1942; Jackson AAB, Miss, 15 Mar 1942; Key Field, Miss, c. 26 Apr 1942; Columbia AAB, SC, 16 May 1942–1 May 1944. Smyrna AFB, Tenn, 26 Jun 1949–

20 Feb 1951. Ardmore AFB, Okla, 8 Jul 1955–.

COMMANDERS. Maj Henry G Silleck, 1942; Lt Col Flint Garrison Jr, 2 June 1942; Col William C Mills, 26 Jun 1942; Col John L Nedwed, 3 Aug 1942; Lt Col Milton E Lipps, 2 Feb–c. 1 May 1944. Col William C Bentley, 8 Jul 1955–.

CAMPAIGNS. American Theater.

DECORATIONS. None.

INSIGNE. None.

310th BOMBARDMENT GROUP

Constituted as 310th Bombardment Group (Medium) on 28 Jan 1942. *Activated* on 15 Mar 1942. Used B–25's in preparing for duty overseas. Moved to the Mediterranean theater, Oct–Dec 1942, and assigned to Twelfth AF. Engaged primarily in support and interdictory operations in Tunisia, Sicily, Italy, Corsica, Sardinia, and southern France; also flew some missions to Austria and Yugoslavia. Attacked harbors and shipping to help defeat Axis forces in North Africa, Dec 1942–May 1943. Bombed airdromes, landing grounds, and gun emplacements on Pantelleria, Lampedusa, and Sicily, May–Jul 1943. Supported the Allied landing at Salerno, Sep 1943. Assisted the drive toward Rome, Jan–Jun 1944. Supported the invasion of Southern France, Aug 1944. Struck G e r m a n communications—bridges, rail lines, marshalling yards, viaducts, tunnels, and road junctions—in Italy, Aug 1943–Apr 1945. Also dropped propaganda leaflets behind enemy lines. Received a DUC for a mission to Italy on 27 Aug 1943 when, in spite of persistent attacks by enemy interceptors and antiaircraft artillery, the group effectively bombed marshalling yards at Benevento and also destroyed a number of enemy planes. Received second DUC for another mission in Italy on 10 Mar 1945 when the group, maintaining a compact formation in the face of severe antiaircraft fire, bombed the railroad bridge at Ora, a vital link in the German supply line. *Inactivated* in Italy on 12 Sep 1945.

Redesignated 310th B o m b a r dment Group (Light). Allotted to the reserve. *Activated* in the US on 27 Dec 1946. *Inactivated* on 27 Jun 1949.

SQUADRONS. *379th:* 1942–1945; 1947–1949. *380th:* 1942–1945; 1947–1949.

381st: 1942–1945; 1947–1949. *428th:* 1942–1945.

STATIONS. Davis-Monthan Field, Ariz, 15 Mar 1942; Jackson AAB, Miss, 15 Mar 1942; Key Field, Miss, Apr 1942; Columbia AAB, SC, 16 May 1942; Walterboro, SC, 14 Aug 1942; Greenville AAB, SC, 18 Sep–17 Oct 1942; Mediouna, French Morocco, c. 18 Nov 1942; Telergma, Algeria, 21 Dec 1942; Berteaux, Algeria, 1 Jan 1943; Dar el Koudia, Tunisia, c. 6 Jun 1943; Menzel Temime, Tunisia, c. 5 Aug 1943; Philippeville, Algeria, 10 Nov 1943; Corsica, c. 10 Dec 1943; Fano, Italy, 7 Apr 1945; Pomigliano, Italy, c. Aug–12 Sep 1945. Bedford AAFld, Mass, 27 Dec 1946–27 Jun 1949.

COMMANDERS. Lt Col William E Lee, 15 Mar 1942; Lt Col Flint Garrison Jr, 21 Apr 1942; Capt James A Plant, 19 May 1942; Col Anthony G Hunter, c. 17 Jun 1942; Col Peter H Remington, c. 7 Oct 1944; Col William M Bower, Jul–c. Sep 1945.

CAMPAIGNS. Air Combat, EAME Theater; Tunisia; Sicily; Naples-Foggia; Rome-Arno; Southern France; North Apennines; Central Europe; Po Valley.

DECORATIONS. Distinguished Unit Citations: Italy, 27 Aug 1943; Ora, Italy, 10 Mar 1945.

INSIGNE. *Shield:* On a blue shield between two yellow 45° triangles with the long sides facing each other and placed diagonally from upper right to lower left, three white stars; in the upper triangle a white mailed right hand grasping a red lightning flash and in the lower triangle a white dove in flight to base carrying a green and black olive branch in its beak, hand and dove outlined in black; in a row across the bottom of shield ten small white stars; the shield and triangles bordered with black, edged with white against the blue. (Approved 7 Jan 1954.)

311th FIGHTER GROUP

FULMINAT

Constituted as ·311th Bombardment Group (Light) on 28 Jan 1942. *Activated* on 2 Mar 1942. *Redesignated* 311th Bombardment Group (Dive) in Jul 1942, 311th Fighter-Bomber Group in Sep 1943, and 311th Fighter Group in May 1944. Trained with V–72 aircraft. Moved to India, via Australia, Jul–Sep 1943. Assigned to Tenth AF. Operating from India and using A–36's and P–51's, the group supported Allied ground forces in northern Burma; covered bombers that attacked Rangoon, Insein, and other targets; bombed enemy airfields at Myitkyina and Bhamo; and conducted patrol and reconnaissance missions to help protect transport planes that flew the Hump route between India and China. Moved to Burma in Jul 1944 and continued to support ground forces, including Merrill's Marauders; also flew numerous sweeps over enemy airfields in central and southern Burma. Moved to China in Aug 1944 and assigned to Fourteenth AF. Escorted bombers, flew interception missions, struck the enemy's communications, and supported ground operations, serving in combat until the end of the war. Ferried P–51's from India for Chinese Air Force in Nov 1945. Returned to the US in Dec 1945. *Inactivated* on 6 Jan 1946.

Redesignated 101st Fighter Group. Allotted to ANG (Maine) on 24 May 1946. Extended federal recognition on 4 Apr 1947. Ordered to active service on 1 Feb 1951. Assigned to Air Defense Command. *Redesignated* 101st Fighter-Interceptor Group in Feb 1951. *Inactivated* on 6 Feb 1952. Relieved from active service, returned to ANG (Maine), and *activated,* on 1 Nov 1952. ANG allotment changed in 1954 (withdrawn from Maine on 30 Apr and allotted to Vt on 1 Jun). Extended federal recognition on 1 Jun 1954.

SQUADRONS. *136th:* 1951–1952. *385th:* 1942–1943. *528th* (formerly 382d, later 132d): 1942–1946; 1951–1952. *529th* (formerly 383d, later 133d): 1942–1946; 1951–1952. *530th* (formerly 384th, later 134th): 1942–1946; 1951–1952.

STATIONS. Will Rogers Field, Okla, 2 Mar 1942; Hunter Field, Ga, 4 Jul 1942;

Waycross, Ga, 22 Oct 1942–18 Jul 1943; Nawadih, India, 14 Sep 1943; Dinjan, India, 11 Oct 1943; Tingkawk Sakan, Burma, 6 Jul 1944; Pungchacheng, China, 28 Aug 1944–14 Dec 1945; Ft Lawton, Wash, 5–6 Jan 1946. Dow AFB, Maine, 1 Feb 1951; Grenier AFB, NH, 23 Apr 1951; Larson AFB, Wash, 2 Aug 1951–6 Feb 1952.

COMMANDERS. Lt Col Clinton U True, 1942; Lt Col John R Kelly, 10 Aug 1942; Col Harry R Melton Jr, 26 Nov 1942; Col Charles G Chandler Jr, 25 Nov 1943; Col John S Chennault, 12 Feb 1945; Col Gabriel P Disosway, 24 May 1945; Col Allen R Springer, 5 Aug 1945–unkn. Col George J Labreche, 1951–1952.

CAMPAIGNS. American Theater; India-Burma; China Defensive; China Offensive.

DECORATIONS. None.

INSIGNE. *Shield:* Or a tornado issuant from base throughout azure, a demi-Indian issuant from chief proper, with war bonnet of the like and shooting from a bow sable a drop bomb gules. *Motto:* FULMINAT—It (He) Strikes as Lightning. (Approved 13 Nov 1942.)

312th BOMBARDMENT GROUP

Constituted as 312th Bombardment Group (Light) on 28 Jan 1942. *Activated* on 15 Mar 1942. *Redesignated* 312th Bombardment Group (Dive) in Jul 1942. Trained with A–24, A–31, A–36, and P–40 aircraft. Moved to the Southwest Pacific,

Oct–Dec 1943, and assigned to Fifth AF. *Redesignated* 312th Bombardment Group (Light) in Dec 1943. Began operations in New Guinea, flying patrol and escort missions with P–40's. Completed conversion to A–20's in Feb 1944. Until Nov 1944, attacked airfields, troop concentrations, gun positions, bridges, and warehouses on the northern and western coasts of New Guinea, and also supported amphibious operations on that island and in Palau. After moving to the Philippines in Nov 1944, provided support for ground troops and struck airfields and transportation facilities. Received a DUC for completing eight strikes against butanol plants on Formosa from 25 Mar to 4 Apr 1945. Began transition to B–32's, and made test flights over Luzon and Formosa in Jun 1945. *Redesignated* 312th Bombardment Group (Heavy) in Jul 1945. Moved to Okinawa in Aug 1945 and sailed for the US in Dec. *Inactivated* on 6 Jan 1946.

Redesignated 312th Bombardment Group (Very Heavy). Allotted to the reserve. *Activated* on 30 Jul 1947. *In-activated* on 27 Jun 1949.

Redesignated 312th Fighter-Bomber Group. *Activated* on 1 Oct 1954. Assigned to Tactical Air Command. Equipped with F–84's. Converted to F–86's in 1955.

SQUADRONS. *386th:* 1942–1945; 1947–1949; 1954–. *387th:* 1942–1946; 1947–1949; 1954–. *388th:* 1942–1946; 1947–1949; 1954–. *389th:* 1942–1945; 1947–1949.

STATIONS. Bowman Field, Ky, 15 Mar 1942; Will Rogers Field, Okla, Jun 1942; Hunter Field, Ga, Aug 1942; DeRidder AAB, La, 20 Feb 1943; Rice AAFld, Calif, 13 Apr 1943; Salinas AAB, Calif, 15 Aug–24 Oct 1943; Gusap, New Guinea, c. 1 Jan 1944; Hollandia, New Guinea, Jun 1944; Tanauan, Leyte, 19 Nov 1944; Mangaldan, Luzon, 10 Feb 1945; Floridablanca, Luzon, 19 Apr 1945; Okinawa, 13 Aug–13 Dec 1945; Vancouver, Wash, 3–6 Jan 1946. Ellington Field, Tex, 30 Jul 1947–27 Jun 1949. Clovis AFB, NM, 1 Oct 1954–.

COMMANDERS. Col Robert H Strauss, 1 Sep 1942; Lt Col Selmon W Wells, 10 Mar 1945; Col Frank R Cook, c. 25 Aug 1945–unkn. Lt Col Charles A Appel, 1954; Lt Col John E Vogt, 2 Feb 1955; Col Emmett S Davis, 8 Jul 1955–.

CAMPAIGNS. American Theater; Air Offensive, Japan; New Guinea; Western Pacific; Leyte; Luzon.

DECORATIONS. Distinguished Unit Citation: Formosa, 25 Mar–4 Apr 1945. Philippine Presidential Unit Citation.

INSIGNE. *Shield:* Azure an eagle volant or, carrying with his talons a futuramic bomb argent, fire exhaust proper, and a branch of olive vert. (Approved 30 Nov 1956.)

313th TROOP CARRIER GROUP

Constituted as 313th Transport Group on 28 Jan 1942. *Activated* on 2 Mar 1942. *Redesignated* 313th Troop Carrier Group in Jul 1942. Trained for overseas duty with C–47's and C–53's. Moved to North Africa, Apr–May 1943, and assigned to Twelfth AF. Trained for the invasion of Sicily and entered combat on the night of 9 Jul 1943 by dropping paratroops near Gela. Although attacked by ground and naval forces while carrying reinforcements to Sicily on the night of 11 Jul, the group completed the mission and received a DUC for the performance. Transported supplies and evacuated wounded in the Mediterranean area until late in Aug when the group moved to Sicily for the invasion of Italy. Dropped paratroops of 82d Airborne Division south of Salerno on the night of 13 Sep 1943 and flew a reinforcement mission the following night. Resumed transport activities in the theater until Feb 1944, and then joined Ninth AF in England. Prepared for the invasion of France and on D-Day 1944, released paratroops near Picauville; dropped reinforcements over the same area on 7 Jun, being awarded second DUC for its part in the invasion. Dropped paratroops near Arnheim and Nijmegen on 17 Sep during the airborne attack on Holland and released gliders carrying reinforcements to that area on 18 and 23 Sep. Moved to France, Feb–Mar 1945, and received C-46's for the airborne assault across the Rhine; dropped paratroops of 17th Airborne Division near Wesel on 24 Mar. When not engaged in airborne operations the group evacuated wounded personnel and ex-prisoners of war, and also transported cargo such as ammunition, gasoline, medical supplies, and food until after V–E Day. Returned to the US, Aug–Sep 1945. *Inactivated* on 15 Nov 1945.

Activated in Austria on 30 Sep 1946. Assigned to United States Air Forces in Europe and equipped with C–47 and C–54 aircraft. Transferred, without personnel and equipment, to the US on 25 Jun 1947 and assigned to Tactical Air Command. Trained with gliders and C–82's. *Redesignated* 313th Troop Carrier Group, (Heavy) in Jul 1948. Moved to Germany, Oct–Nov 1948, and joined United States Air Forces in Europe for participation in the Berlin airlift. Transported cargo such as coal, food, and medicine into West Berlin from Nov 1948 to Sep 1949. *Redesignated* 313th Troop Carrier Group (Special) in Feb 1949. *Inactivated* in Germany on 18 Sep 1949.

Redesignated 313th Troop Carrier Group (Medium). *Activated* in the US on 1 Feb 1953. Assigned to Tactical Air Command. Trained with C–119's. *Inactivated* on 8 Jun 1955.

SQUADRONS. *29th:* 1942–1945; 1946–1949; 1953–1955. *47th:* 1942–1945; 1946–1949; 1953–1955. *48th:* 1942–1945; 1946–1949; 1953–1955. *49th:* 1942–1945.

STATIONS. Daniel Field, Ga, 2 Mar 1942; Bowman Field, Ky, 21 Jun 1942; Florence, SC, 4 Aug 1942; Maxton, NC, 13 Dec 1942–24 Apr 1943; Oujda, French Morocco, 9 May 1943; Kairouan, Tunisia, 16 Jun 1943; Sciacca, Sicily, 23 Aug 1943; Trapani/Milo Airfield, Sicily, 3 Oct 1943; Folkingham, England, 4 Feb 1944; Achiet, France, 28 Feb–5 Aug 1945; Baer Field, Ind, 14 Sep–15 Nov 1945. Tulln AB, Austria, 30 Sep 1946–25 Jun 1947; Langley Field, Va, 25 Jun 1947; Bergstrom Field, Tex, 15 Jul 1947–22 Oct 1948; Fassberg, Germany, 9 Nov 1948–18 Sep 1949. Mitchel AFB, NY, 1 Feb 1953; Sewart AFB, Tenn, 2 Oct 1953–8 Jun 1955.

COMMANDERS. Capt Fred W Nelson, 7 Mar 1942; Col James J Roberts Jr, 26 Jun 1942; Lt Col William A Filer, 18 Mar 1945; Lt Col Paul W Stephens, 26 Mar 1945; Lt Col Carl W Campbell, c. Aug–15 Nov 1945. Col Clinton W Davies, 30 Sep 1946; Lt Col Walter R Washburn Jr, 15 Aug 1947; Col Frank P Bostrom, 3 Dec 1947; Lt Col Conway S Hall, unkn–Sep 1949. Col Benton R Baldwin, Feb 1953; Col Steward H Nichols, 1 Oct 1953–1955.

CAMPAIGNS. American Theater; Sicily; Naples-Foggia; Rome-Arno; Normandy;

Northern France; Rhineland; Central Europe.

DECORATIONS. Distinguished Unit Citations: Sicily, 11 Jul 1943; France, [6–7] Jun 1944.

INSIGNE. *Shield:* Per bend azure and gules, the silhouette of a stylized winged aircraft or, charged with a mullet of the first between six mullets, three and three of the third. (Approved 3 Feb 1943.)

314th TROOP CARRIER GROUP

Constituted as 314th Transport Group on 28 Jan 1942. *Activated* on 2 Mar 1942. *Redesignated* 314th Troop Carrier Group in Jul 1942. Used C–47's and C–53's in preparing for duty overseas. Moved to the Mediterranean theater in May 1943 and assigned to Twelfth AF for participation in two airborne operations. Flew two night missions during the invasion of Sicily in Jul 1943: released paratroops of 82d Airborne Division near Gela on 9 Jul; dropped reinforcements in the area on 11 Jul, receiving a DUC for carrying out this second mission in spite of bad weather and heavy attack by ground and

naval forces. Took part in the invasion of Italy by dropping paratroops and supplies near Salerno on 14 and 15 Sep 1943. Moved to England in Feb 1944 for operations with Ninth AF. Trained for the invasion of western Europe. Dropped paratroops in Normandy on 6 Jun 1944 and flew a resupply and reinforcement mission the following day, receiving a DUC for these operations. Released paratroops over Holland during the airborne attack in Sep and flew follow-up missions to provide reinforcements and supplies. Moved to France, Feb–Mar 1945. Released gliders carrying troops and equipment to the Wesel area on 24 Mar 1945 when the Allies launched the airborne assault across the Rhine. Continually transported freight in the Mediterranean and European theaters, when neither training for, nor participating in airborne operations; hauled supplies such as food, clothing, gasoline, aircraft parts, and ammunition. Also carried wounded personnel to rear-zone hospitals. After V–E Day, evacuated Allied prisoners from Germany, and later made scheduled flights to transport freight and personnel in Europe. Transferred, without personnel and equipment, to the US in Feb 1946.

Moved to the Canal Zone, Sep–Oct 1946, and assigned to Caribbean Air Command. Operated air terminals in the Panama and Antilles areas. *Redesignated* 314th Troop Carrier Group (Heavy) in Jun 1948. Returned to the US in Oct 1948 and assigned to Tactical Air Command. *Redesignated* 314th Troop Carrier Group (Medium) in

Nov 1948. Trained with C–47, C–82, and C–119 aircraft.

Moved to Japan, Aug–Sep 1950, and attached to Far East Air Forces for duty in the Korean War. Operated primarily with C–119 aircraft. Transported troops and supplies from Japan to Korea and evacuated wounded personnel. Participated in two major airborne operations: dropped paratroops and equipment over Sunchon in Oct 1950 in support of the UN assault on Pyongyang; dropped paratroops over Munsan-ni during the airborne attack across the 38th Parallel in Mar 1951. Remained in Japan after the armistice to transport supplies to Korea and evacuate prisoners of war.

Transferred, without personnel and equipment, to the US in Nov 1954. Manned, and equipped with C–119's. Received an AFOUA for an airborne exercise, Jan–Feb 1955, when the group transported elements of a regimental combat team from Tennessee to Alaska, dropped paratroops over the exercise area, and completed the return airlift.

SQUADRONS. *20th:* 1946–1949. *30th:* 1942. *31st:* 1942. *32d:* 1942–1945. *50th:* 1942–1946, 1949–. *61st:* 1943–1945, 1949–. *62d:* 1943–1946, 1949–. *301st:* 1945–1946. *302d:* 1945–1946. *321st:* 1945–1946, 1955–. *323d:* 1945–1946. *334th:* 1946–1949.

STATIONS. Drew Field, Fla, 2 Mar 1942; Bowman Field, Ky, 24 Jun 1942; Knobnoster, Mo, 4 Nov 1942; Lawson Field, Ga, c. 20 Feb–4 May 1943; Berguent, French Morocco, May 1943; Kairouan, Tunisia, 26 Jun 1943; Castelvetrano, Sicily, 24 Aug 1943–13 Feb 1944; Saltby, England, Feb 1944; Poix, France, Feb 1945; Villacoublay, France, 15 Oct 1945–15 Feb 1946; Bolling Field, DC, 15 Feb–Sep 1946; Albrook Field, CZ, 1 Oct 1946; Curundu Heights, CZ, 10 Mar–Oct 1948; Smyrna AFB, Tenn, 21 Oct 1948–Aug 1950; Ashiya, Japan, Sep 1950–15 Nov 1954; Sewart AFB, Tenn, 15 Nov 1954–.

COMMANDERS. 2d Lt L C Lillie, 2 Mar 1942; 2d Lt J W Blakeslee, 14 May 1942; Maj Leonard M Rohrbough, 26 Jun 1942; Col Clayton Stiles, 9 Apr 1943; Lt Col Halac G Wilson, 22 Aug 1945; Col Charles W Steinmetz, 29 Nov 1945–c. Feb 1946; Col Richard W Henderson, 8 Oct 1948; Col William H DeLacey, 27 Aug 1951; Col David E Daniel, 28 Sep 1951; Lt Col Harold L Sommers, 1 May 1952; Col William H DeLacey, Nov 1954–.

CAMPAIGNS. *World War II:* American Theater; Sicily; Naples-Foggia; Rome-Arno; Normandy; Northern France; Rhineland; Central Europe. *Korean War:* UN Defensive; UN Offensive; CCF Intervention; 1st UN Counteroffensive; CCF Spring Offensive; UN Summer-Fall Offensive; Second Korean Winter; Korea Summer-Fall, 1952; Third Korean Winter; Korea Summer-Fall, 1953.

DECORATIONS. Distinguished Unit Citations: Sicily, 11 Jul 1943; France, [6–7] Jun 1944; Korea, 28 Nov–10 Dec 1950. Republic of Korea Presidential Unit Citation: 1 Jul 1951–27 Jul 1953. Air Force Outstanding Unit Award: 11 Jan–14 Feb 1955.

INSIGNE. *Shield:* Or, on clouds in fess, azure, two boots passant of the field, ornamented, gules. *Motto:* VIRI VENIENTE—Men Will Come. (Approved 17 Aug 1942. This insigne was replaced 17 Jun 1954.)

315th TROOP CARRIER GROUP

ADVENIAM

Constituted as 315th Transport Group on 2 Feb 1942 and *activated* on 14 Feb. *Redesignated* 315th Troop Carrier Group in Jul 1942. Trained for combat operations with C–47's and C–53's. Departed the US, Oct–Nov 1942, for assignment to Eighth AF in England. Encountering bad weather while flying the North Atlantic route, the air echelon was detained for about a month in Greenland, where it searched for missing aircraft along the east coast and dropped supplies to crews. After the air and ground echelons were united in England in Dec, the group began ferrying cargo in the British Isles and training with airborne troops and gliders. A detachment was sent to Algeria in May 1943, and although not participating in the airborne phase of the invasions of Sicily and Italy, it did support those operations by transporting supplies in the theater. In Mar 1944 the detachment returned to England and rejoined the group, which had been assigned to Ninth AF in Oct 1943. Prepared for the invasion of the Continent, and dropped paratroops near Cherbourg early on D-Day in Jun 1944, receiving a DUC for its action in the Normandy invasion. Dropped paratroops of 82d Airborne Division on 17 Sep 1944 when the Allies launched the air attack on Holland; flew reinforcement missions on succeeding days, landing at Grave on 26 Sep to unload paratroops and supplies. Released British paratroops near Wesel during the airborne assault across the Rhine in Mar 1945. Following each airborne operation, the group resumed transport activities, hauling cargo such as medical supplies, signal equipment, rations, and gasoline, and evacuating wounded personnel. Moved to France in Apr 1945. Transported cargo and evacuated prisoners of war until after V–E Day. Moved to Trinidad in May 1945 and assigned to Air Transport Command. Used C–47's to transport troops returning to the US. *Inactivated* in Trinidad on 31 Jul 1945.

Activated in the US on 19 May 1947. Apparently was not manned. *Inactivated* on 10 Sep 1948.

Redesignated 315th Troop Carrier Group (Medium). *Activated* in Japan on

10 Jun 1952. Assigned to Far East Air Forces for operations in the Korean War. Used C-46 aircraft to participate in the airlift between Japan and Korea. Transported cargo such as vegetables, clothing, ordnance supplies, and mail; evacuated patients and other personnel. Remained in the theater after the armistice and continued to fly transport missions until 1955. *Inactivated* in Japan on 18 Jan 1955.

SQUADRONS. *19th:* 1952–1955. *33d:* 1942. *34th:* 1942–1945; 1947–1948; 1952–1955. *35th:* 1942. *43d:* 1942–1945; 1947–1948; 1952–1955. *54th:* 1942. *309th:* 1944–1945. *310th:* 1944–1945. *344th:* 1952–1955.

STATIONS. Olmsted Field, Pa, 14 Feb 1942; Bowman Field, Ky, 17 Jun 1942; Florence, SC, 3 Aug–11 Oct 1942; Aldermaston, England, c. 1 Dec 1942; Welford, England, 6 Nov 1943; Stanhoe, England, 7 Feb 1944; Amiens, France, 6 Apr–May 1945; Waller Field, Trinidad, May–31 Jul 1945. Langley Field, Va, 19 May 1947–10 Sep 1948. Brady AB, Japan, 10 Jun 1952–18 Jan 1955.

COMMANDERS. Capt Thomas J Schofield, 14 Feb 1942; Col Hamish McLelland, 17 Apr 1942; Col Howard B Lyon, 27 Sep 1944; Lt Col Robert J Gibbons, 27 Mar 1945–unkn. Unkn, May 1947–Sep 1948. Lt Col Jack L Crawford, 10 Jun 1952; Lt Col Gene I Martin, 5 Dec 1952; Col Kenneth L Glassburn, 11 Aug 1953; Lt Col Jacob P Sartz Jr, 9 Nov 1954–18 Jan 1955.

CAMPAIGNS. *World War II:* American Theater; Sicily; Naples-Foggia; Normandy; Northern France; Rhineland; Central Europe. *Korean War:* Korea Summer-Fall, 1952; Third Korean Winter; Korea Summer-Fall, 1953.

DECORATIONS. Distinguished Unit Citation: France, [6] Jun 1944. Republic of Korea Presidential Unit Citation: [10 Jun 1952]–27 Jul 1953.

INSIGNE. *Shield:* Azure, a winged packing box bend sinisterwise or. *Motto:* ADVENIAM—I Will Arrive. (Approved 22 May 1942.)

316th TROOP CARRIER GROUP

Constituted as 316th Transport Group on 2 Feb 1942 and *activated* on 14 Feb. *Redesignated* 316th Troop Carrier Group in Jul 1942. Trained with C-47 and C-53 aircraft. Moved to the Mediterranean theater, assigned to Ninth AF, and began operations, in Nov 1942. Transported supplies and evacuated casualties in support of the Allied drive across North Africa. In May 1943 began training for the invasion of Sicily; dropped paratroops over the assault area on the night of 9 Jul. Carried reinforcements to Sicily on 11 Jul and received a DUC for carrying out that mission although severely attacked by ground and naval forces. Received another DUC for supporting aerial and ground operations in Egypt, Libya, Tunisia, and Sicily, 25 Nov 1942–25 Aug 1943, by transporting reinforcements and supplies. Assigned to Twelfth AF and moved to Sicily to take part in the invasion of Italy; dropped paratroops over the beachhead south of the Sele River on the night of 14 Sep 1943. Transported cargo in the theater until Feb 1944, then joined Ninth AF in England and prepared for the invasion of France. Dropped paratroops near Ste-Mere-Eglise on D–Day 1944 and flew a reinforcement mission on 7 Jun, receiving a third DUC for these operations. During the air attack on Holland in Sep 1944, dropped paratroops and released gliders carrying reinforcements. Dropped paratroops near Wesel on 24 Mar 1945 when the Allies made the airborne assault across the Rhine. Also provided transport services in Europe while not engaged in airborne operations. Hauled supplies such as ammunition, gasoline, water, and rations; evacuated wounded personnel to rear-zone hospitals.

Returned to the US in May 1945. Trained with C–82 and C–119 aircraft. *Redesignated* 316th Troop Carrier Group (Medium) in Jun 1948, 316th Troop Carrier Group (Heavy) in Oct 1949, and 316th Troop Carrier Group (Medium) in Jan 1950. Transferred, without personnel and equipment, to Japan on 15 Nov 1954. Assigned to Far East Air Forces, manned, and equipped with C–119's.

SQUADRONS. *16th:* 1950–1954. *36th:* 1942–. *37th:* 1942–. *38th:* 1942. *44th:* 1942–1945. *45th:* 1942–1945. *75th:* 1945–1949, 1952–. *77th:* 1945–1946.

STATIONS. Patterson Field, Ohio, 14 Feb 1942; Bowman Field, Ky, 17 Jun 1942; Lawson Field, Ga, 9 Aug 1942; Del Valle, Tex, 29 Sep–12 Nov 1942; Deversoir, Egypt, 23 Nov 1942; El Adem, Egypt, 10 Dec 1942; Fayid, Egypt, Jan 1943; Nouvion, Algeria, 9 May 1943; Guercif, French Morocco, 29 May 1943; Enfidaville, Tunisia, 21 Jun 1943; Mazzara, Sicily, 3 Sep 1943; Borizzo, Sicily, 18 Oct 1943–12 Feb 1944; Cottesmore, England, 15 Feb 1944–May 1945; Pope Field, NC, 25 May 1945; Greenville AAB, SC, 25 Aug 1947; Smyrna AFB, Tenn, 4 Nov 1949–15 Nov 1954; Ashiya, Japan, 15 Nov 1954–.

COMMANDERS. Col Jerome B McCauley, 14 Feb 1942; Lt Col Burton R Fleet, 12 Aug 1943; Col Harvey A Berger, c. 13 May 1944; Lt Col Walter R Washburn, 2 Sep 1945; Lt Col Leonard C Fletcher, 17 Sep 1945; Col Jerome B McCauley, 5 Oct 1945; Col Clarence J Galligan, 2 Feb 1946; Lt Col Leroy M Stanton, 31 Sep 1946; Col Clarence J Galligan, 1 Nov 1946; Col John H Lackey Jr, c. Apr 1947; Col Edgar W Hampton, 20 Sep 1947; Col Norton H Van Sicklen III, 1 Aug 1950; Maj Dwight E Maul, 31 Aug 1950; Maj Gordon F Blood, 6 Sep 1950; Col Norton H Van Sicklen III, 28 Dec 1950; Col William H DeLacey,

1 Jun 1952; Col Richard P Carr, Nov 1954; Col William C Lindley, 19 Mar 1955–.

CAMPAIGNS. American Theater; Egypt-Libya; Tunisia; Sicily; Naples-Foggia; Rome-Arno; Normandy; Northern France; Rhineland; Central Europe.

DECORATIONS. Distinguished Unit Citations: Egypt, Libya, Tunisia, Sicily, 25 Nov 1942–25 Aug 1943; Sicily, 11 Jul 1943; France, [6–7] Jun 1944.

INSIGNE. *Shield:* Azure, nine parachutes argent, three, two, three, and one, all within a bordure per bend or and gules. *Motto:* VALOR WITHOUT ARMS. (Approved 17 Aug 1951.)

317th TROOP CARRIER GROUP

Constituted as 317th Transport Group on 2 Feb 1942 and *activated* on 22 Feb. *Redesignated* 317th Troop Carrier Group in Jul 1942. Trained with C–47's. Moved to Australia, Dec 1942–Jan 1943, and assigned to Fifth AF. Operated in New Guinea for a short time early in 1943. Received a DUC for making numerous flights in unarmed planes over the Owen Stanley Range, 30 Jan–1 Feb 1943, to trans-

port reinforcements and supplies to Wau, New Guinea, where enemy forces were threatening a valuable Allied airdrome. Exchanged its new C–47's for old C–39's, C–47's, C–49's, C–60's, B–17's, and LB–30's in New Guinea and began operating from Australia, where the group had maintained its headquarters. Flew troops and equipment to New Guinea, established courier and passenger routes in Australia, and trained with airborne troops. Equipped with C–47's and moved to New Guinea in Sep 1943. Took part in the first airborne operation in the Southwest Pacific on 5 Sep, dropping paratroops at Nadzab, New Guinea, to cut supply lines and seize enemy bases. Until Nov 1944, transported men and cargo to Allied bases on New Guinea, New Britain, Guadalcanal, and in the Admiralty Islands. Also dropped reinforcements and supplies to US forces on Noemfoor, 3–4 Jul 1944. After moving to the Philippines in Nov 1944, transported supplies to ground forces on Luzon, Leyte, and Mindoro, and supplied guerrillas on Mindanao, Cebu, and Panay. Participated in two airborne operations during Feb 1945: on 3 and 4 Feb dropped paratroops south of Manila to seize highway routes to the city, and on 16 and 17 Feb dropped the 502d Regiment on Corregidor to open Manila Bay to US shipping; received a DUC for the latter operation, performed at low altitude over small drop zones in a heavily defended area. Completed two unusual missions on 12 and 15 Apr 1945 when this troop carrier organization bombed Carabao

Island with drums of napalm. Dropped part of 511th Regiment near Aparri on 23 Jun 1945 to split Japanese forces in the Cagayen Valley and prevent a retreat to the hills in northern Luzon. Remained in the theater as part of Far East Air Forces after the war; used C-46 and C-47 aircraft, the latter being replaced in 1947 with C-54's. Flew courier and passenger routes to Japan, Guam, Korea, and the Philippines, and transported freight and personnel in the area. *Redesignated* 317th Troop Carrier Group (Heavy) in May 1948. Moved, via the US, to Germany in Sep 1948 and became part of United States Air Forces in Europe for service in the Berlin airlift. Used C-54's to transport coal, food, and other supplies to the block-aded city. *Inactivated* in Germany on 14 Sep 1949.

Redesignated 317th Troop Carrier Group (Medium). *Activated* in Germany on 14 Jul 1952. Assigned to United States Air Forces in Europe and equipped with C-119's.

SQUADRONS. *39th*: 1942–1949; 1952–. *40th*: 1942–1949; 1952–. *41st*: 1942–1949; 1952–. *46th*: 1942–1949.

STATIONS. Duncan Field, Tex, 22 Feb 1942; Bowman Field, Ky, 19 Jun 1942; Lawson Field, Ga, 11 Oct 1942; Maxton, NC, 3–12 Dec 1942; Townsville, Australia, 23 Jan 1943; Port Moresby, New Guinea, c. 30 Sep 1943; Finschhafen, New Guinea, Apr 1944; Hollandia, New Guinea, Jun 1944; Leyte, 17 Nov 1944; Clark Field, Luzon, c. 17 Mar 1945; Okinawa, 24 Aug 1945; Kimpo, Korea, 31 Oct 1945; Tachi-kawa, Japan, c. 15 Jan 1946–c. 21 Sep 1948; Wiesbaden AB, Germany, c. 30 Sep 1948; Celle RAF Station, Germany, 15 Dec 1948–14 Sep 1949. Rhein-Main AB, Germany, 14 Jul 1952; Neubiberg AB, Germany, 21 Mar 1953–.

COMMANDERS. Col Samuel V Payne, 22 Feb 1942; Col Robert L Olinger, 21 Jun 1944; Col John H Lackey Jr, 2 Oct 1944; Lt Col Robert I Choate, 31 Aug 1945; Col Dwight B Schannep, Oct 1945–unkn; Col Marshall S Roth, Jan 1946; Col Othel R Deering, Jan 1947; Col Thomas K Hampton, 19 May 1948; Lt Col James M Johnson, 18 Aug 1948; Col Bertram C Harrison, Oct 1948; Lt Col James M Johnson, 24 Nov 1948; Lt Col Walter E Chambers, 11 Mar 1949; Lt Col Robert J DuVal, 13 Jun 1949–unkn. Col Lucion N Powell, 14 Jul 1952; Lt Col James E Bauley, 1 Mar 1954; Col Harry M Pike, May 1954–.

CAMPAIGNS. Air Offensive, Japan; New Guinea; Northern Solomons; Bismarck Archipelago; Western Pacific; Leyte; Luzon.

DECORATIONS. Distinguished Unit Citations: New Guinea, 30 Jan–1 Feb 1943; Philippine Islands, 16–17 Feb 1945. Philippine Presidential Unit Citation.

INSIGNE. *Shield*: Or issuant from chief a dexter arm, fist clenched inflamed proper, in base a fire of seven tongues of the last, on a chief nebuly azure, three piles of the first. *Motto*: I GAIN BY HAZARD. (Approved 22 Dec 1942.)

318th FIGHTER GROUP

Constituted as 318th Pursuit Group (Interceptor) on 2 Feb 1942. *Redesignated* 318th Fighter Group in May 1942. *Activated* in Hawaii on 15 Oct 1942. Assigned to Seventh AF. Trained and flew patrols, using P–39, P–40, and P–47 aircraft. Moved to the Marianas in Jun 1944. Supported ground forces on Saipan, Tinian, and Guam; attacked enemy airfields; flew protective patrols over US bases; and, using some P–38's acquired in Nov 1944, flew missions to the Volcano and Truk Islands to escort bombers and to attack Japanese bases. Moved to the Ryukyu Islands in Apr 1945. Used P–47's to bomb and strafe airfields, railroad bridges, and industrial plants in Japan, escort bombers to China, and provide air defense for US bases in the Ryukyus. Assigned to Eighth AF in Aug 1945, shortly after V–J Day. Moved to the US, Dec 1945–Jan 1946. *Inactivated* on 12 Jan 1946.

Redesignated 102d Fighter Group. Allotted to ANG (Mass) on 24 May 1946. Extended federal recognition on 22 Oct 1946. *Redesignated* 102d Fighter-Interceptor Group in Aug 1952.

SQUADRONS. *19th:* 1943–1946. *44th:* 1942–1943. *72d:* 1942–1944. *73d:* 1942–1946. *333d:* 1943–1946.

STATIONS. Hickam Field, TH, 15 Oct 1942; Bellows Field, TH, 9 Feb 1943; Saipan, Jun 1944; Ie Shima, c. 30 Apr 1945; Okinawa, Nov–Dec 1945; Ft Lewis, Wash, 11–12 Jan 1946.

COMMANDERS. Col Lorry N Tindal, 20 Oct 1942; Lt Col Charles B Stewart, 3 Mar 1943; Col Lewis M Sanders, 21 Aug 1943; Lt Col Harry C McAfee, 31 Jul 1945; Maj Glen H Kramer, 5 Oct 1945; Maj Burton M Woodward, 22 Oct 1945–unkn.

CAMPAIGNS. Air Offensive, Japan; Eastern Mandates; Western Pacific; Ryukyus; China Offensive.

DECORATIONS. None.

INSIGNE. *Shield:* The upper part blue, with one small aircraft gray with white trail; the center part a portion of the globe showing the Northeastern portion of the Western Hemisphere in green and light blue with the North Pole in white and across it the front part of a gray aircraft with white outline and cockpit, firing three black rockets, tail flashes red, trails white, all headed toward upper right; in lower part on a bank of white clouds two small black aircraft climbing vertically, all within a red border. *Motto:* OMNIS VIR TIGRIS—Every Man a Tiger. (Approved 11 Jan 1954.)

319th BOMBARDMENT GROUP

Constituted as 319th Bombardment Group (Medium) on 19 Jun 1942 and *activated* on 26 Jun. Trained with B–26's. Moved via England to the Mediterranean theater, Aug–Nov 1942, with part of the group landing at Arzeu beach during the invasion of North Africa on 8 Nov. Operated with Twelfth AF until Jan 1945, except for a brief assignment to Fifteenth, Nov 1943–Jan 1944. Began combat in Nov 1942, attacking airdromes, harbors, rail facilities, and other targets in Tunisia until Feb 1943. Also struck enemy shipping to prevent supplies and reinforcements from reaching the enemy in North Africa. After a period of reorganization and training, Feb–Jun 1943, the group resumed combat and participated in the reduction of Pantelleria and the campaign for Sicily. Directed most of its attacks against targets in Italy after the fall of Sicily in Aug 1943. Hit bridges, airdromes, marshalling yards, viaducts, gun sites, defense positions, and other objectives. Supported forces at Salerno in Sep 1943 and at Anzio and Cassino during Jan–Mar 1944. Carried out interdictory operations in central Italy to aid the advance to Rome, being awarded a DUC for a mission on 3 Mar 1944 when the group, carefully avoiding religious and cultural monuments, bombed rail facilities in the capital. Received another DUC for striking marshalling yards in Florence on 11 Mar 1944 to disrupt rail communications between that city and Rome. Received the French Croix de Guerre with Palm for action in preparation for and in support of the Allied offensive in Italy, Apr–Jun 1944. From Jul to Dec 1944, bombed bridges in the Po Valley, supported the invasion of Southern France, hit targets in northern Italy, and flew some missions to Yugoslavia, converting in the meantime, in Nov, to B–25 aircraft. Returned to the US in Jan 1945. *Redesignated* 319th Bombardment Group (Light) in Feb. Trained with A–26 aircraft. Moved to Okinawa, Apr–Jul 1945, and assigned to Seventh AF. Flew missions to Japan and China, attacking airdromes, shipping, marshalling yards, industrial centers, and other objectives. Returned to the US, Nov–Dec 1945. *Inactivated* on 18 Dec 1945.

Allotted to the reserve. *Activated* on 27 Dec 1946. *Inactivated* on 2 Sep 1949.

Allotted to the reserve. *Activated* on 10 Oct 1949. Ordered to active duty on 10 Mar 1951. *Inactivated* on 22 Mar 1951.

Redesignated 319th Fighter-Bomber Group. Allotted to the reserve. *Activated* on 18 May 1955.

SQUADRONS. *46th:* 1947–1949; 1949–1951; 1955–. *50th:* 1947–1949; 1949–1951. *51st:* 1947–1949; 1949–1951. *59th:* 1947–1949; 1949–1951. *437th:* 1942–1945. *438th:* 1942–1945. *439th:* 1942–1945. *440th:* 1942–1945.

STATIONS. Barksdale Field, La, 26 Jun 1942; Harding Field, La, 8–27 Aug 1942; Shipdham, England, 12 Sep 1942; Horsham St Faith, England, c. 4 Oct 1942; St-Leu, Algeria, c. 11 Nov 1942; Tafaraoui, Algeria, 18 Nov 1942; Maison Blanche, Algeria, 24 Nov 1942; Telergma, Algeria, c. 12 Dec 1942; Oujda, French Morocco, 3 Mar 1943; Rabat Sale, French Morocco, 25 Apr 1943; Sedrata, Algeria, 1 Jun 1943; Djedeida, Tunisia, 26 Jun 1943; Sardinia, c. 1 Nov 1943; Corsica, c. 21 Sep 1944–1 Jan 1945; Bradley Field, Conn, 25 Jan 1945; Columbia AAB, SC, c. 28 Feb–27 Apr 1945; Kadena, Okinawa, c. 2 Jul 1945; Machinato, Okinawa, 21 Jul–21 Nov 1945; Ft Lewis, Wash, 17–18 Dec 1945. Mitchel Field, NY, 27 Dec 1946; Reading Mun Aprt, Pa, 27 Jun–2 Sep 1949. Birmingham Mun Aprt, Ala, 10 Oct 1949–22 Mar 1951. Memphis Mun Aprt, Tenn, 18 May 1955–.

COMMANDERS. Lt Col Alvord Rutherford, 26 Jun 1942; Lt Col Sam W Agee Jr, 27 Nov 1942; Maj Joseph A Cunningham, 5 Dec 1942; Lt Col Wilbur W Aring, c. 11 Jan 1943; Col Gordon H Austin, 6 Jul 1943; Col Joseph R Holzapple, 13 Aug 1943–1945.

CAMPAIGNS. Air Combat, EAME Theater; Algeria-French Morocco; Tunisia; Sicily; Naples-Foggia; Anzio; Rome-Arno; Southern France; North Apennines; Air Offensive, Japan; Ryukyus; China Offensive.

DECORATIONS. Distinguished Unit Citations: Rome, Italy, 3 Mar 1944; Florence, Italy, 11 Mar 1944. French Croix de Guerre with Palm: Apr, May, and Jun 1944.

INSIGNE. None.

320th BOMBARDMENT GROUP

FOREVER BATTLING

Constituted as 320th Bombardment Group (Medium) on 19 Jun 1942 and *activated* on 23 Jun. Trained with B–26 aircraft. Most of the group moved to North Africa via England, Aug–Dec 1942; crews flew their planes over the South Atlantic route and arrived in North Africa, Dec 1942–Jan 1943. Began combat with Twelfth AF in Apr 1943 and operated from bases in Algeria, Tunisia, Sardinia, and Corsica until Nov 1944. During the period Apr–Jul 1943, flew missions against enemy shipping in the approaches to Tunisia, attacked installations in Sardinia, participated in the reduction of Pantelleria, and supported the invasion of Sicily. Then bombed marshalling yards, bridges, airdromes, road junctions, viaducts, harbors, fuel dumps, defense positions, and other targets in Italy. Supported forces at Salerno and knocked out targets to aid the seizure of Naples and the crossing of the Volturno River. Flew missions to Anzio and Cassino and engaged in interdictory operations in central Italy in preparation for the advance toward Rome. Received the French Croix de Guerre with Palm for action in preparation for and in support of Allied offensive operations in central Italy, Apr–Jun 1944. Received a DUC for a mission on 12 May 1944 when, in the face of an intense anti-aircraft barrage, the group bombed enemy troop concentrations near Fondi in support of Fifth Army's advance toward Rome. From Jun to Nov 1944 operations included interdictory missions in the Po Valley, support for the invasion of Southern France, and attacks on enemy communications in northern Italy. Moved to France in Nov 1944 and bombed bridges, rail lines, gun positions, barracks, supply points, ammunition dumps, and other targets in France and Germany until V–E Day. Received a DUC for operations on 15 Mar 1945 when the group bombed pillboxes, trenches, weapon pits, and roads within the Siegfried Line to enable a breakthrough by Seventh Army. Moved to Germany in Jun 1945 and participated in the disarmament program. Returned to the US, Nov–Dec. *Inactivated* on 4 Dec 1945.

Redesignated 320th Bombardment Group (Light). Allotted to the reserve. *Activated* on 9 Jul 1947. *Inactivated* on 27 Jun 1949.

SQUADRONS. *441st:* 1942–1945; 1947–1949. *442d:* 1942–1945; 1947–1949. *443d:* 1942–1945; 1947–1949. *444th:* 1942–1945; 1947–1949.

STATIONS. MacDill Field, Fla, 23 Jun 1942; Drane Field, Fla, 8–28 Aug 1942; Hethel, England, 12 Sep 1942; La Senia, Algeria, c. 2 Dec 1942; Tafaraoui, Algeria, 28 Jan 1943; Montesquieu, Algeria, 9 Apr 1943; Massicault, Tunisia, 29 Jun 1943; El Bathan, Tunisia, 28 Jul 1943; Sardinia, c. 1 Nov 1943; Corsica, c. 18 Sep 1944; Dijon/Longvic, France, 11 Nov 1944; Dole/Tavaux, France, 1 Apr 1945; Herzogenaurach, Germany, 18 Jun 1945; Clastres, France, c. Oct–Nov 1945; Camp Myles Standish, Mass, 3–4 Dec 1945. Mitchel Field, NY, 9 Jul 1947–27 Jun 1949.

COMMANDERS. Maj John F Batjer, 1 Jul 1942; Col John A Hilger, c. 5 Aug 1942; Col Flint Garrison Jr, 25 Oct 1942; Lt Col John Fordyce, 15 Feb 1943; Col Karl E Baumeister, 25 May 1943; Lt Col Stanford Gregory, 25 Sep 1943; Col Eugene B Fletcher, 25 Oct 1943; Col Ashley E Woolridge, 2 Nov 1944; Lt Col Blaine B Campbell, 28 May 1945–unkn.

CAMPAIGNS. Air Combat, EAME Theater; Tunisia; Sicily; Naples-Foggia; Anzio; Rome-Arno; Southern France; North Apennines; Rhineland; Central Europe.

DECORATIONS. Distinguished Unit Citations: Italy, 12 May 1944; ETO, 15 Mar 1945. French Croix de Guerre with Palm: Apr, May, and Jun 1944.

INSIGNE. *Shield:* Azure, an alligator volant in bend or, winged and armed gules, speed lines sinisterward of the second. *Motto:* FOREVER BATTLING. (Approved 3 Mar 1943. This insigne was replaced 22 Jan 1953.)

321st BOMBARDMENT GROUP

Constituted as 321st Bombardment Group (Medium) on 19 Jun 1942 and *activated* on 26 Jun. Prepared for overseas duty with B-25's. Moved to the Mediterranean theater, Jan–Mar 1943, and assigned to Twelfth AF. Engaged primarily in support and interdictory operations, bombing marshalling yards, rail lines, highways, bridges, viaducts, troop concentrations, gun emplacements, shipping, harbors, and other objectives in North Africa, France, Sicily, Italy, Bulgaria, Yugoslavia, and Greece. Sometimes dropped propaganda leaflets behind enemy lines. Took part in the Allied operations against Axis forces in North Africa during Mar–May 1943, the reduction of Pantelleria and Lampedusa in Jun, the invasion of Sicily in Jul, the landing at Salerno in Sep, the Allied advance toward Rome during Jan–Jun 1944, the invasion of Southern France in Aug 1944, and the Allied operations in northern Italy from Sep 1944 to Apr 1945. Received two DUC's: for completing a raid on an airdrome near Athens, 8 Oct 1943, in spite of intense flak and attacks by numerous enemy interceptors; and for bombing a battleship, a cruiser, and a submarine in Toulon harbor on 18 Aug 1944 to assist the Allied invasion of Southern France. *Inactivated* in Italy on 12 Sep 1945.

Redesignated 321st Bombardment Group (Light). Allotted to the reserve. *Activated* in the US on 29 Jun 1947. *Inactivated* on 27 Jun 1949.

SQUADRONS. *445th:* 1942–1945; 1947–1949. *446th:* 1942–1945; 1947–1949. *447th:* 1942–1945; 1947–1949. *448th:* 1942–1945; 1947–1949.

STATIONS. Barksdale Field, La, 26 Jun 1942; Columbia AAB, SC, c. 1 Aug 1942; Walterboro, SC, Sep 1942; DeRidder AAB, La, c. 1 Dec 1942–21 Jan 1943; Ain M'lila, Algeria, 12 Mar 1943; Souk-el-Arba, Tunisia, c. 1 Jun 1943; Soliman, Tunisia, 8 Aug 1943; Grottaglie, Italy, 3 Oct 1943; Amendola, Italy, c. 20 Nov 1943; Vincenzo Airfield, Italy, 14 Jan 1944; Gaudo Airfield, Italy, Feb 1944; Corsica, 23 Apr 1944; Falconara, Italy, c. 1 Apr 1945; Pomigliano, Italy, c. Sep–12 Sep 1945. Mansfield, Ohio, 29 Jun 1947–27 Jun 1949.

COMMANDERS. Unkn, Jun–Aug 1942; Col William C Mills, 3 Aug 1942; Col Robert D Knapp, Sep 1942; Lt Col Charles

T Olmsted, 5 Dec 1943; Lt Col Peter H Remington, 18 Mar 1944; Col Richard H Smith, 26 Mar 1944; Lt Col Charles F Cassidy Jr, 28 Jan 1945–unkn.

CAMPAIGNS. Air Combat, EAME Theater; Tunisia; Sicily; Naples-Foggia; Rome-Arno; Southern France; North Apennines; Central Europe; Po Valley.

DECORATIONS. Distinguished Unit Citations: Athens, Greece, 8 Oct 1943; France, 18 Aug 1944.

INSIGNE. *Shield:* Azure, six drop bombs, three, two, and one or. *Motto:* PERSEVERANCE, VISION, AND DUTY. (Approved 7 Nov 1942. This insigne was replaced 30 Aug 1954.)

322d BOMBARDMENT GROUP

RECTE FACIENDO NEMINEM TIMEO

Constituted as 322d Bombardment Group (Medium) on 19 Jun 1942. *Activated* on 17 Jul 1942. Trained with B–26 aircraft. Part of the group moved overseas, Nov–Dec 1942; planes and crews followed, Mar–Apr 1943. Operated with Eighth AF until assignment to Ninth in Oct 1943. Served in combat, May 1943–Apr 1945, operating from England, France, and Belgium. Began combat on 14 May when it dispatched 12 planes for a minimum-level attack on a power plant in Holland. Sent 11 planes on a similar mission three days later: one returned early; the others, with 60 crewmen, were lost to flak and interceptors. Trained for medium-altitude operations for several weeks and resumed combat on 17 Jul 1943. Received a DUC for the period 14 May 1943–24 Jul 1944, during which its combat performance helped to prove the effectiveness of the medium bombers. Enemy airfields in France, Belgium, and Holland provided the principal targets from Jul 1943 through Feb 1944, but the group also attacked power stations, shipyards, construction works, marshalling yards, and other targets. Beginning in Mar the 322d bombed railroad and highway bridges, oil tanks, and missile sites in preparation for the invasion of Normandy; on 6 Jun 1944 it hit coastal defenses and gun batteries; afterward, during the Normandy campaign, it pounded fuel and ammunition dumps, bridges, and road junctions. Supported the Allied offensive at Caen and the breakthrough at St Lo in Jul. Aided the drive of Third Army across France in Aug and Sep. Bombed bridges, road junctions, defended villages, and ordnance depots in the assault on the Siegfried Line, Oct–Dec 1944. Flew a number of missions against railroad bridges during the Battle of the Bulge, Dec 1944–Jan 1945. Then concentrated on communications, marshalling yards, bridges, and fuel dumps until its last mission on 24 Apr 1945.

Moved to Germany in Jun 1945. Engaged in inventorying and disassembling German Air Force equipment and facilities. Returned to the US, Nov–Dec 1945. *Inactivated* on 15 Dec 1945.

Redesignated 322d Bombardment Group (Light). Allotted to the reserve. *Activated* on 9 Aug 1947. *Inactivated* on 27 Jun 1949.

Redesignated 322d Fighter-Day Group. *Activated* on 1 Jul 1954. Assigned to Tactical Air Command. Equipped first with F–86 and later with F–100 aircraft.

SQUADRONS. *35th:* 1947–1949. *449th:* 1942–1945; 1947–1949. *450th:* 1942–1945; 1947–1949; 1954–. *451st:* 1942–1945; 1947–1949; 1954–. *452d:* 1942–1945; 1947–1949; 1954–.

STATIONS. MacDill Field, Fla, 17 Jul 1942; Drane Field, Fla, 22 Sep–Nov 1942; Rougham, England, c. 1 Dec 1942; Great Saling, England, Jan 1943; Beauvais/Tille, France, Sep 1944; Le Culot, Belgium, Mar 1945; Fritzlar, Germany, Jun–Sep 1945; Camp Kilmer, NJ, c. 14–15 Dec 1945. Reading AAFld, Pa, 9 Aug 1947–27 Jun 1949. Foster AFB, Tex, 1 Jul 1954–.

COMMANDERS. Lt Col Jacob J Brogger, c. 8 Aug 1942; Col Robert R Selway Jr, c. 21 Oct 1942; Lt Col John F Batjer, c. 22 Feb 1943; Lt Col Robert M Stillman, c. 17 Mar 1943; Col Glenn C Nye, c. 19 May 1943; Col John S Samuel, Jul 1944; Maj John L Egan, c. 12 Jul 1945–unkn. Col Carlos M Talbott, 1 Jul 1954–.

CAMPAIGNS. Air Offensive, Europe; Normandy; Northern France; Rhineland; Ardennes-Alsace; Central Europe.

DECORATIONS. Distinguished Unit Citation: ETO, 14 May 1943–24 Jul 1944.

INSIGNE. *Shield:* Tierce per fess azure and or, five piles, three conjoined between two transposed counterchanged. *Motto:* RECTO FACIENDO NEMINEM TIMEO—I Fear None in Doing Right. (Approved 9 Jan 1943.)

323d BOMBARDMENT GROUP

VINCAMUS SINE TIMORIS

Constituted as 323d Bombardment Group (Medium) on 19 Jun 1942. *Activated* on 4 Aug 1942. Trained with B–26's. Moved to England, Apr–Jun 1943. Assigned first to Eighth AF and, in Oct 1943, to Ninth AF. Began operations in Jul 1943, attacking marshalling yards, airdromes, industrial plants, military installations, and other targets in France, Belgium, and Holland. Then carried out numerous attacks on V-weapon sites along the coast of France. Attacked airfields at Leeuwarden and Venlo in conjunction with the Allied campaign against the German Air Force and aircraft industry during Big Week, 20–25 Feb 1944. Helped to prepare for the invasion of Normandy by bombing coastal defenses, marshalling yards, and airfields in France; struck roads and coastal batteries on 6 Jun 1944. Participated in the aerial barrage that assisted the breakthrough at St Lo in Jul. Flew its first night mission after moving to the Continent in Aug, striking enemy batteries in the region of St Malo. Carried out other night missions during the month to hit fuel and ammunition dumps. Eliminated strong points at Brest early in Sep and then shifted operations to eastern France to support advances against the Siegfried Line. Received a DUC for actions (24–27 Dec 1944) during the Battle of the Bulge when the group effectively hit transportation installations used by the enemy to bring reinforcements to the Ardennes. Flew interdictory missions into the Ruhr and supported the drive into Germany by attacking enemy communications. Ended combat in Apr 1945 and moved to Germany in May to participate in the disarmament program. Returned to the US in Dec. *Inactivated* on 12 Dec 1945.

Redesignated 323d Bombardment Group (Light). Allotted to the reserve. *Activated* on 9 Sep 1947. Ordered to active duty on 10 Mar 1951. *Inactivated* on 17 Mar 1951.

Redesignated 323d Fighter-Bomber Group. *Activated* on 8 Aug 1955. Assigned to Tactical Air Command.

SQUADRONS. *453d:* 1942–1945; 1949–1951; 1955–. *454th:* 1942–1945; 1949–1951; *455th:* 1942–1945; 1949–1951; 1955–. *456th:* 1942–1945; 1947–1951.

STATIONS. Columbia AAB, SC, 4 Aug 1942; MacDill Field, Fla, 21 Aug 1942; Myrtle Beach Bombing Range, SC, 2 Nov 1942–25 Apr 1943; Horham, England, 12 May 1943; Earls Colne, England, 14 Jun 1943; Beaulieu, England, 21 Jul 1944; Lessay, France, 26 Aug 1944; Chartres, France, 21 Sep 1944; Laon/Athies, France, 13 Oct 1944; Denain/Prouvy, France, 9 Feb 1945; Gablingen, Germany, 15 May 1945; Landsberg, Germany, 16 Jul 1945; Clastres, France, Oct–Dec 1945; Camp Myles Standish, Mass, 11–12 Dec 1945. Tinker Field, Okla, 9 Sep 1947–17 Mar 1951. Bunker Hill AFB, Ind, 8 Aug 1955–.

COMMANDERS. Col Herbert B Thatcher, Sep 1942; Col Wilson R Wood, c. 13 Nov 1943; Col Rollin M Winingham, 14 Feb 1945; Lt Col George O Commenator, Aug 1945–unkn. Col John C Haygood, 1955–.

CAMPAIGNS. Air Offensive, Europe; Normandy; Northern France; Rhineland; Ardennes-Alsace; Central Europe.

DECORATIONS. Distinguished Unit Citation: Belgium and Germany, 24–27 Dec 1944.

INSIGNE. *Shield:* Per bend gules and azure, a bend between a mailed dexter gauntlet grasping a dagger and the winged hat of Mercury argent. *Motto:* VINCAMUS SINE TIMORIS—Without Fear We Conquer. (Approved 16 Feb 1943. This insigne was replaced 21 Jun 1957.)

324th FIGHTER GROUP

Constituted as 324th Fighter Group on 24 Jun 1942. *Activated* on 6 Jul 1942. Moved to the Middle East, Oct–Dec 1942, for operations with Ninth AF. Trained for several weeks with P-40 aircraft. While headquarters remained in Egypt, squadrons of the group began operating with other organizations against the enemy in Tunisia. Reunited in Jun 1943, the 324th group engaged primarily in escort and patrol missions between Tunisia and Sicily until Jul 1943. Received a DUC for action against the enemy from Mar 1943 to the invasion of Sicily. Trained during Jul–Oct 1943 for operations with Twelfth AF. Resumed combat on 30 Oct 1943 and directed most of its attacks against roads, bridges, motor transports, supply areas, rolling stock, gun positions, troop concentrations, and rail facilities in Italy until Aug 1944. Patrolled the beach and protected convoys during the assault on Anzio in Jan 1944. Aided the Allied offensive in Italy during May 1944, receiving another DUC for action from 12 to 14 May when the group bombed an enemy position on Monastery Hill (Cassino), attacked troops massing on the hill for a counterattack, and hit a nearby stronghold to force the surrender of an enemy garrison. Continued to give close support to ground forces until the fall of Rome in Jun 1944. Converted to P-47's in Jul and supported the assault on southern France in Aug by dive-bombing gun positions, bridges, and radar facilities, and by patrolling the combat zone. Attacked such targets as motor transports, rolling stock, rail lines, troops, bridges, gun emplacements, and supply depots after the invasion, giving tactical support to Allied forces advancing through France. Aided the reduction of the Colmar bridgehead, Jan–Feb 1945, and supported Seventh Army's drive through the Siegfried defenses in Mar. Received the French Croix de Guerre with Palm for supporting French forces during the campaigns for Italy and France, 1944–1945. Moved to the US, Oct–Nov 1945. *Inactivated* on 7 Nov 1945.

Redesignated 103d Fighter Group. Allotted to ANG (Conn) on 24 May 1946. Extended federal recognition on 7 Aug 1946. Ordered to active duty on 1 Mar 1951. Assigned to Air Defense Command. *Redesignated* 103d Fighter-Interceptor Group in Mar 1951. Used F-47 aircraft. *Inactivated* on 6 Feb 1952. Returned to the control of ANG (Conn) on 1 Dec 1952.

SQUADRONS. *118th:* 1951–1952. *314th:* 1942–1945. *315th:* 1942–1945. *316th:* 1942–1945.

STATIONS. Mitchel Field, NY, 6 Jul 1942; Baltimore Mun Aprt, Md, 6 Jul–28 Oct 1942; El Amiriya, Egypt, Dec 1942; El Kabrit, Egypt, 2 Feb 1943; Kairouan, Tunisia, 2 Jun 1943; El Haouaria, Tunisia, c. 18 Jun 1943; Menzel Heurr, Tunisia, 3 Oct 1943; Cercola, Italy, 25 Oct 1943; Pignataro Maggiore, Italy, 6 May 1944; Le Banca Airfield, Italy, 6 Jun 1944; Montalto Di Castro, Italy, 14 Jun 1944; Corsica, 19 Jul 1944; Le Luc, France, 25 Aug 1944; Istres, France, 2 Sep 1944; Amberieu, France, 6 Sep 1944; Tavaux, France, 20 Sep 1944; Luneville, France, 4 Jan 1945; Stuttgart, Germany, 8 May–20 Oct 1945; Camp Shanks, NY, 6–7 Nov 1945. Bradley Field, Conn, 1 Mar 1951; Suffolk County Aprt, NY, 1 Jun 1951–6 Feb 1952.

COMMANDERS. Col William K McNown, c. Jul 1942; Col Leonard C Lydon, 25 Dec 1943; Lt Col Franklin W Horton, 23 May–Nov 1945. Col Glenn T Eagleston, 1951–c. Feb 1952.

CAMPAIGNS. Tunisia; Sicily; Naples-Foggia; Anzio; Rome-Arno; Northern France; Southern France; Rhineland; Central Europe.

DECORATIONS. Distinguished Unit Citations: North Africa and Sicily, Mar–[Jul] 1943; Cassino, 12–14 May 1944. French Croix de Guerre with Palm.

INSIGNE. *Shield:* Or, a representation of a Connecticut colonial secretary running with the Colony's Charter in his left hand proper (hat, coat, and breeches—blue; hair, vest, tie, shoes, and stockings—black; face, hands, shirt collar, shoe buckles, and charter—white); all within a diminished bordure tri-parted black, white, and black, the white part separated to chief to form in code the letters FEA. (Approved 1 May 1953.)

325th FIGHTER GROUP

Constituted as 325th Fighter Group on 24 Jun 1942. *Activated* on 3 Aug 1942. Trained with P-40's. Moved to North Africa during Jan–Feb 1943. Assigned to Twelfth AF. Entered combat on 17 Apr. Escorted medium bombers, flew strafing missions, and made sea sweeps from bases in Algeria and Tunisia. Participated in the defeat of Axis forces in Tunisia, the reduction of Pantelleria, and the conquest of Sicily. Received a DUC for action over Sardinia on 30 Jul 1943 when the group, using diversionary tactics, forced a superior number of enemy planes into the air and destroyed more than half of them. Flew no combat missions from the end of Sep to mid-Dec 1943, a period in which the group changed aircraft and moved to Italy. Began operations with Fifteenth AF on 14 Dec, and afterward engaged primarily in escort operations, using P–47's until they were replaced by P–51's in May 1944. Escorted heavy bombers during long-range missions to attack the Messerschmitt factory at Regensburg, the Daimler-Benz tank factory at Berlin, oil refineries at Vienna, and other targets, such as airfields, marshalling yards, and communications in Italy, France, Germany, Czechoslovakia, Austria, Hungary, Rumania, and Yugoslavia. Also covered operations of reconnaissance aircraft and strafed such targets as trains, vehicles, and airfields. Received second DUC for a mission on 30 Jan 1944 when the group flew more than 300 miles at very low altitude to surprise the enemy fighters that were defending German airdromes near Villaorba; by severely damaging the enemy's force, the 325th group enabled heavy bombers to strike vital targets in the area without encountering serious opposition. Continued combat operations until May 1945. Returned to the US in Oct. *Inactivated* on 28 Oct 1945.

Activated on 21 May 1947. Organized as an all-weather fighter group. *Redesignated* 325th Fighter Group (All Weather) in May 1498, and 325th Fighter-Interceptor Group in May 1951. Equipped with P–

61's in 1947, F–82's in 1948, and F–94's in 1950. *Inactivated* on 6 Feb 1952.

Redesignated 325th Fighter Group (Air Defense). *Activated* on 18 Aug 1955. Assigned to Air Defense Command and equipped with F–86 aircraft.

SQUADRONS. *317th:* 1942–1945; 1947–1952; 1955–. *318th:* 1942–1945; 1947–1952; 1955–. *319th:* 1942–1945; 1947–1952.

STATIONS. Mitchel Field, NY, 3 Aug 1942; Hillsgrove, RI, c. 31 Aug 1942–23 Jan 1943; Tafaraoui, Algeria, 28 Feb 1943; Montesquieu, Algeria, 5 Apr 1943; Souk-el-Khemis, Tunisia, 3 Jun 1943; Mateur, Tunisia, 19 Jun 1943; Soliman, Tunisia, 4 Nov 1943; Foggia, Italy, 11 Dec 1943; Lesina, Italy, 29 Mar 1944; Rimini, Italy, c. 5 Mar 1945; Mondolfo, Italy, Apr 1945; Vincenzo Airfield, Italy, Jul–9 Oct 1945; Camp Kilmer, NJ, 26–28 Oct 1945. Mitchel Field, NY, 21 May 1947; Hamilton Field, Calif, 2 Dec 1947; Moses Lake AFB, Wash, 26 Nov 1948; McChord AFB, Wash, 23 Apr 1950–6 Feb 1952. McChord AFB, Wash, 18 Aug 1955–.

COMMANDERS. Maj Leonard C Lydon, 3 Aug 1942; Lt Col Gordon H Austin, 10 Dec 1942; Lt Col Robert L Baseler, 5 Jul 1943; Col Chester L Sluder, 1 Apr 1944; Lt Col Ernest H Beverly, 11 Sep 1944; Col Felix L Vidal, 2 Mar 1945; Lt Col Wyatt P Exum, 6 Jun 1945; Lt Col Wilhelm C Freudenthal, c. 30 Aug 1945–unkn. Unkn, May–Dec 1947; Lt Col Gordon D Timmons, 2 Dec 1947; Col Harold E Kofahl, c. Jan 1948; Lt Col Walter C Hearne, 1948; Lt Col Kermit A Tyler, 6 Mar 1950;

Col George W Prentice, 27 Mar 1950–unkn; Col Raymond K Gallagher, 1951–c. Feb 1952. Unkn, 1955–.

CAMPAIGNS. Air Combat, EAME Theater; Air Offensive, Europe; Tunisia; Sicily; Naples-Foggia; Anzio; Rome-Arno; Normandy; Northern France; Southern France; North Apennines; Rhineland; Central Europe; Po Valley.

DECORATIONS. Distinguished Unit Citations: Sardinia, 30 Jul 1943; Italy, 30 Jan 1944.

INSIGNE. *Shield:* Per fess, sable and azure, a fess arched, argent, upper line nebuly, over all a lightning flash or, issuing from dexter chief. *Motto:* LOCARE ET LIQUIDARE—Locate and Liquidate. (Approved 1 Oct 1951.)

326th FIGHTER GROUP

FORTITER ET SINCERE

Constituted as 326th Fighter Group on 24 Jun 1942. *Activated* on 19 Aug 1942. Assigned to First AF. Became part of the air defense force and also served as an operational training unit. Later became a replacement training unit, preparing

pilots for combat duty in P-47's. *Disbanded* on 10 Apr 1944.

Reconstituted and *redesignated* 326th Fighter Group (Air Defense), on 20 Jun 1955. *Activated* on 18 Aug 1955. Assigned to Air Defense Command. Equipped with F-86's.

SQUADRONS. *320th:* 1942–1943. *321st:* 1942–1944; 1955–. *322d:* 1942–1944. *442d:* 1943. *538th:* 1943–1944. *539th:* 1943–1944.

STATIONS. Mitchel Field, NY, 19 Aug 1942; Bradley Field, Conn, 1 Sep 1942; Westover Field, Mass, 1 Nov 1942; Seymour Johnson Field, NC, 13 Oct 1943–10 Apr 1944. Paine AFB, Wash, 18 Aug 1955–.

COMMANDERS. Lt Col Gilbert L Meyers, c. 24 Aug 1942; Lt Col William S Steele, c. 14 Jun 1943–10 Apr 1944. Col Ira F Wintermute, 1955–.

CAMPAIGNS. American Theater.

DECORATIONS. None.

INSIGNE. *Shield:* Azure, a cockatrice volant or crested and beaked gules. *Motto:* FORTITER ET SINCERE—Boldly and Sincerely. (Approved 31 Dec 1942.)

327th FIGHTER GROUP

Constituted as 327th Fighter Group on 24 Jun 1942. *Activated* on 25 Aug 1942. Assigned to First AF. Became part of the air defense force and also served as an operational training unit, using P-40's until Feb 1943 when they were replaced

328th FIGHTER GROUP

by P–47's. In 1944 began training replacement pilots for combat duty. *Disbanded* on 10 Apr 1944.

Reconstituted and *redesignated* 327th Fighter Group (Air Defense), on 20 Jun 1955. *Activated* on 18 Aug 1955. Assigned to Air Defense Command and equipped with F–86's.

SQUADRONS. *323d:* 1942–1944; 1955–. *324th:* 1942–1944. *325th:* 1942–1944; 1955–. *443d:* 1943–1944.

STATIONS. Mitchel Field, NY, 25 Aug 1942; Philadelphia Mun Aprt, Pa, 27 Aug 1942; Richmond AAB, Va, c. 22 Sept 1942–10 Apr 1944. Truax Field, Wis, 18 Aug 1955–.

COMMANDERS. Col Nelson P Jackson, unkn; Lt Col Frederick J Nelander, unkn. Col Oris B Johnson, 1955–.

CAMPAIGNS. American Theater.

DECORATIONS. None.

INSIGNE. *Shield:* Or, the head of the mythical Gorgon Medusa affronte azure, armed gules. *Motto:* NE DEFICIT ANIMUS—Courage Does Not Fail Me. (Approved 27 Feb 1943. This insigne was replaced 16 May 1958.)

Constituted as 328th Fighter Group on 24 Jun 1942. *Activated* on 10 Jul 1942. Assigned to Fourth AF. Served as part of the air defense force and also trained replacement pilots in P–39 aircraft. *Disbanded* on 31 Mar 1944.

Reconstituted and *redesignated* 328th Fighter Group (Air Defense), on 20 Jun 1955. *Activated* on 18 Aug 1955. Assigned to Air Defense Command. Equipped with F–86's.

SQUADRONS. *326th:* 1942–1944; 1955–. *327th:* 1942–1944. *329th:* 1942–1944. *444th:* 1943–1944.

STATIONS. Hamilton Field, Calif, 10 Jul 1942–31 Mar 1944. Grandview AFB, Mo, 18 Aug 1955–.

COMMANDERS. Maj Frederick D Granbo, 10 Jul 1942; Lt Col Harry N Renshaw, 11 Jan 1943; Lt Col Milton B Adams, 7 Jul 1943; Lt Col Kyle L Riddle, 13 Nov 1943; Col J C Crosthwaite, 4 Jan 1944; Col John W Weltman, 31 Jan–31 Mar 1944. Col Richard F Weltzin, 1955–.

CAMPAIGNS. American Theater.

DECORATIONS. None.

INSIGNE. *Shield:* Azure, a natural panther rampant affronte or, incensed proper. *Motto:* FAST AND FURIOUS. (Approved 23 Feb 1943. This insigne was replaced 24 Nov 1958.)

329th FIGHTER GROUP

Constituted as 329th Fighter Group on 24 Jun 1942. *Activated* on 10 Jul 1942. Assigned to Fourth AF. Used P–38's to train replacement pilots. Also provided cadres for fighter groups. *Disbanded* on 31 Mar 1944.

Reconstituted and *redesignated* 329th Fighter Group (Air Defense), on 20 Jun 1955. *Activated* on 18 Aug 1955. Assigned to Air Defense Command and equipped with F–86's.

SQUADRONS. *330th:* 1942–1944; 1955–. *331st:* 1942–1944; 1955–. *332d:* 1942–1944. *337th:* 1942–1944.

STATIONS. Hamilton Field, Calif, 10 Jul 1942; Paine Field, Wash, 14 Jul 1942; Glen-dale, Calif, 11 Sep 1942; Ontario AAFld, Calif, 27 Feb–31 Mar 1944. Stewart AFB, NY, 18 Aug 1955–.

COMMANDERS. Maj Ernest W Keating, 12 Jul 1942; Maj Harold E Kofahl, 8 Nov 1942; Maj Leo F Dusard, 18 Dec 1942; Lt Col Paul W Blanchard, c. 14 Feb 1943; Lt Col Leo F Dusard, 11 May 1943; Lt Col John P Randolph, 26 Oct 1943–31 Mar 1944. Col Emil L Sluga, 1955–.

CAMPAIGNS. American Theater.

DECORATIONS. None.

INSIGNE. *Shield:* On a background of the sky proper, a sinister arm embowed, fessways, issuing from sinister, habited azure, with leather falconer's glove proper, a falcon or, perched for flight on the gloved hand. (Approved 25 Jul 1957.)

330th BOMBARDMENT GROUP

Constituted as 330th Bombardment Group (Heavy) on 1 Jul 1942 and *activated* on 6 Jul. Assigned to Second AF. Functioned as an operational training and later as a replacement training unit, using B–24 aircraft. *Inactivated* on 1 Apr 1944.

Redesignated 330th Bombardment Group (Very Heavy). *Activated* on 1 Apr 1944. Prepared for combat with B–29's. Moved to Guam, Jan-Apr 1945, and assigned to Twentieth AF. Entered combat on 12 Apr 1945 with an attack on the Hodogaya chemical plant at Koriyama, Japan. From Apr to May 1945, struck airfields from which the Japanese were launching suicide planes against the invasion force at Okinawa. After that, operations were principally concerned with incendiary attacks against urban-industrial areas of Japan. Received a DUC for incendiary raids on the industrial sections of Tokushima and Gifu and for a strike against the hydro-electric power center at Kofu, Japan, in Jul 1945. Received another DUC for attacking the Nakajima-Musashino aircraft engine plant near Tokyo in Aug 1945. Dropped food and supplies to Allied prisoners and participated in several show-of-force missions over Japan after the war. Returned to the US, Nov-Dec 1945. *Inactivated* on 3 Jan 1946.

Redesignated 330th Bombardment Group (Medium). Allotted to the reserve. *Activated* on 27 Jun 1949. Ordered to active duty on 1 May 1951. *Inactivated* on 16 Jun 1951.

Redesignated 330th Troop Carrier Group (Medium) and allotted to the reserve. *Activated* on 14 Jun 1952. *Inactivated* on 14 Jul 1952.

SQUADRONS. *457th:* 1942–1944; 1944–1945; 1949–1951; 1952. *458th:* 1942–1944; 1944–1945; 1952. *459th:* 1942–1944; 1944–1945; 1952. *460th:* 1942–1944; 1944.

STATIONS. Salt Lake City AAB, Utah, 6 Jul 1942; Alamogordo, NM, 1 Aug 1942; Biggs Field, Tex, 5 Apr 1943–1 Apr 1944. Walker AAFld, Kan, 1 Apr 1944–7 Jan 1945; North Field, Guam, 18 Feb–15 Nov 1945; Camp Stoneman, Calif, unkn–3 Jan 1946. March AFB, Calif, 27 Jun 1949–16 Jun 1951. Greater Pittsburgh Aprt, Pa, 14 Jun–14 Jul 1952.

COMMANDERS. Maj Leroy A Rainey, 1 Aug 1942; Lt Col John R Sutherland, 15 Sep 1942; Lt Col John A Way, 1 Dec 1942; Lt Col Samuel C Mitchell, 6 Mar 1943; Lt Col Frank P Bostrom, 15 May 1943; Lt Col Troy W Crawford, 27 Jul 1943; Col Frank P Bostrum, 11 Nov 1943; Lt Col Troy W Crawford, 27 Nov 1943–1 Apr 1944. 1st Lt James J Shaffner, 29 Apr 1944; Maj John G Reiber, 3 May 1944; Lt Col Estley R Farley, 26 May 1944; Col Elbert D Reynolds, 23 Jun 1944; Col Douglas C Polhamus, 12 Aug 1944–unkn. Unkn, 1 May–16 Jun 1951.

CAMPAIGNS. American Theater; Air Offensive, Japan; Western Pacific.

DECORATIONS. Distinguished Unit Citations: Japan, 3–9 Jul 1945; Tokyo, Japan, 8 Aug 1945.

INSIGNE. None.

331st BOMBARDMENT GROUP

IMPARIDO PECTURE

Constituted as 331st Bombardment Group (Heavy) on 1 Jul 1942 and *activated* on 6 Jul. Assigned to Second AF. Equipped with B-17's and B-24's for duty as a replacement training unit. *Inactivated* on 1 Apr 1944.

Redesignated 331st Bombardment Group (Very Heavy). *Activated* on 12 Jul 1944. Assigned to Second AF. Trained for combat with B-29's. Moved to Guam, Apr-Jun 1945, and assigned to Twentieth AF. Bombed Japanese-held Truk late in Jun 1945. Flew first mission against the Japanese home islands on 9 Jul 1945 and afterward operated principally against the enemy's petroleum industry on Honshu. Despite the hazards of bad weather, fighter attacks, and heavy flak, the 331st bombed the coal liquefaction plant at Ube, the Mitsubishi-Hayama petroleum complex at Kawasaki, and the oil refinery and storage facilities at Shimotsu, in Jul 1945, and received a DUC for the missions. After the war the group dropped food and supplies to Allied prisoners of war in Japan. *Inactivated* on Guam on 15 Apr 1946.

SQUADRONS. *355th:* 1944-1946. *356th:* 1944-1946. *357th:* 1944-1946. *461st:* 1942-1944. *462d:* 1942-1944. *463d:* 1942-1944. *464th:* 1942-1944.

STATIONS. Salt Lake City AAB, Utah, 6 Jul 1942; Casper AAFld, Wyo, 15 Sep 1942-1 Apr 1944. Dalhart AAFld, Tex, 12 Jul 1944; McCook AAFld, Neb, 14 Nov 1944-6 Apr 1945; Northwest Field, Guam, 12 May 1945-15 Apr 1946.

COMMANDERS. Unkn, Jul-Sep 1942; 2d Lt William B Moeser, 17 Sep 1942; Lt Col Frank P Hunter Jr, 29 Sep 1942; Lt Col William Lewis Jr, 5 Mar 1943; Lt Col Marcus A Mullen, 1 Feb-1 Apr 1944. Maj

Willard W Wilson, 26 Jul 1944; Lt Col Hadley V Saehlenou, 30 Jul 1944; Col Hoyt L Prindle, 19 Aug 1944; Col James N Peyton, 24 Jan 1945; Lt Col Roland J Barnick, Oct 1945-15 Apr 1946.

CAMPAIGNS. American Theater; Air Offensive, Japan; Eastern Mandates; Western Pacific.

DECORATIONS. Distinguished Unit Citation: Japan, 22-29 Jul 1945.

INSIGNE. *Shield:* Azure, three sea gulls volant or, on a chief of the last a thunderbolt gules, irradiated of the field. *Motto:* IMPARIDO PECTORE—With Undaunted Heart. (Approved 22 Dec 1942.)

332d FIGHTER GROUP

Constituted as 332d Fighter Group on 4 Jul 1942. *Activated* on 13 Oct 1942. Trained with P-39 and P-40 aircraft. Moved to Italy, arriving early in Feb 1944. Began operations with Twelfth AF on 5 Feb. Used P-39's to escort convoys, protect harbors, and fly armed reconnaissance missions. Converted to P-47's during Apr-May and changed to P-51's in Jun. Operated with Fifteenth AF from May

1944 to Apr 1945, being engaged primarily in protecting bombers that struck such objectives as oil refineries, factories, airfields, and marshalling yards in Italy, France, Germany, Poland, Czechoslovakia, Austria, Hungary, Yugoslavia, Rumania, Bulgaria, and Greece. Also made strafing attacks on airdromes, railroads, highways, bridges, river traffic, troop concentrations, radar facilities, power stations, and other targets. Received a DUC for a mission on 24 Mar 1945 when the group escorted B-17's during a raid on a tank factory at Berlin, fought the interceptors that attacked the formation, and strafed transportation facilities while flying back to the base in Italy. Returned to the US in Oct 1945. *Inactivated* on 19 Oct 1945.

Activated on 1 Jul 1947. Equipped with P-47's. *Inactivated* on 1 Jul 1949.

SQUADRONS. *99th:* 1944-1945; 1947-1949. *100th:* 1942-1945; 1947-1949. *301st:* 1942-1945; 1947-1949. *302d:* 1942-1945.

STATIONS. Tuskegee, Ala, 13 Oct 1942; Selfridge Field, Mich, 29 Mar 1943; Oscoda, Mich, 12 Apr 1943; Selfridge Field, Mich, 9 Jul-22 Dec 1943; Montecorvino, Italy, 3 Feb 1944; Capodichino, Italy, 15 Apr 1944; Ramitelli Airfield, Italy, 28 May 1944; Cattolica, Italy, c. 4 May 1945; Lucera, Italy, c. 18 Jul-Sep 1945; Camp Kilmer, NJ, 17-19 Oct 1945. Lockbourne AAB, Ohio, 1 Jul 1947-1 Jul 1949.

COMMANDERS. Lt Col Sam W Westbrook Jr, 19 Oct 1942; Col Robert R Selway Jr, 16 May 1943; Col Benjamin O Davis Jr, 8 Oct 1943; Maj George S Roberts, 3 Nov 1944; Col Benjamin O Davis Jr, 24 Dec 1944; Maj George S Roberts, 9 Jun 1945-unkn. Unkn, 1 Jul-28 Aug 1947; Maj William A Campbell, 28 Aug 1947-1 Jul 1949.

CAMPAIGNS. American Theater; Air Combat, EAME Theater; Rome-Arno; Normandy; Northern France; Southern France; North Apennines; Rhineland; Central Europe; Po Valley.

DECORATIONS. Distinguished Unit Citation: Germany, 24 Mar 1945.

INSIGNE. *Shield:* Azure on a fess nebule or, a panther passant sable armed and incensed gules. *Motto:* SPIT FIRE. (Approved 15 Jan 1943.)

333d BOMBARDMENT GROUP

Constituted as 333d Bombardment Group (Heavy) on 9 Jul 1942 and *activated* on 15 Jul. Assigned to Second AF and equipped with B-17's. Served first as an operational training and later as a replacement training unit. *Inactivated* on 1 Apr 1944.

Redesignated 333d Bombardment Group (Very Heavy). *Activated* on 7 Jul 1944. Assigned to Second AF. Trained for combat with B-29 aircraft. Moved to the Pacific theater, Jun-Aug 1945, and assigned to Eighth AF. AAF operations against Japan terminated before the group could enter combat. For a time after the war the group ferried Allied prisoners of war from Japan to the Philippine Islands. *Inactivated* on Okinawa on 28 May 1946.

SQUADRONS. *435th:* 1944–1946. *460th:* 1944–1946. *466th:* 1942–1944. *467th:* 1942–1944. *468th:* 1942–1944. *469th:* 1942–1944. *507th:* 1944–1946.

STATIONS. Topeka, Kan, 15 Jul 1942; Dalhart AAFld, Tex, 22 Feb 1943–1 Apr 1944. Dalhart AAFld, Tex, 7 Jul 1944; Great Bend AAFld, Kan, 13 Jan–18 Jun 1945; Kadena, Okinawa, 5 Aug 1945–28 May 1946.

COMMANDERS. Unkn, Jul–Aug 1942; Col Leo W De Rosier, c. 25 Aug 1942; Lt Col Ted Faulkner, 1943; Lt Col Donald W Saunders, Sep 1943; Maj Walter D Atkins, 3 Jan 1944–unkn. Capt Harry J Whelchel, 26 Jul 1944; Col Milton F Summerfelt, 11 Aug 1944; Lt Col Ray H Martin, 15 Aug 1945–unkn.

CAMPAIGNS. American Theater; Asiatic-Pacific Theater.

DECORATIONS. None.

INSIGNE. None.

334th BOMBARDMENT GROUP

Constituted as 334th Bombardment Group (Medium) on 9 Jul 1942 and *activated* on 16 Jul. Assigned to Third AF.

Equipped with B–25's. Trained replacement crews for combat. *Disbanded* on 1 May 1944.

SQUADRONS. *470th:* 1942–1944. *471st:* 1942–1944. *472d:* 1942–1944. *473d:* 1942–1944.

STATIONS. Greenville AAB, SC, 16 Jul 1942–1 May 1944.

COMMANDERS. 1st Lt Francis M Whitlock Jr, 18 Jul 1942; Col A J Bird Jr, 5 Aug 1942–Apr 1944.

CAMPAIGNS. American Theater.

DECORATIONS. None.

INSIGNE. *Shield:* Azure, on a fess or between in chief three drop-bombs and in base four of the like of the second, three similar bombs of the first. *Motto:* AUXILIAM AB ALTO—Aid from Above. (Approved 18 Feb 1943.)

335th BOMBARDMENT GROUP

Constituted as 335th Bombardment Group (Medium) on 9 Jul 1942 and *activated* on 17 Jul. Assigned to Third AF. Equipped with B–26's. Served as a replacement training unit. *Disbanded* on 1 May 1944.

SQUADRONS. *474th:* 1942–1944. *475th:* 1942–1944. *476th:* 1942–1944. *477th:* 1942–1944.

STATIONS. Barksdale Field, La, 17 Jul 1942–1 May 1944.

COMMANDERS. Col Millard Lewis, 17 July 1942; Col Roland O S Akre, 10 Feb 1943; Lt Col Joe R Brabson, 12 May 1943; Col Joe W Kelly, 26 Jun 1943; Lt Col George R Anderson, 6 Nov 1943–1 May 1944.

CAMPAIGNS. American Theater.

DECORATIONS. None.

INSIGNE. *Shield:* Azure, from a fess nebuly a demi lion rampant issuant or. *Motto:* FIDUS ET FORTIS—Faithful and Brave. (Approved 19 Nov 1942.)

336th BOMBARDMENT GROUP

Constituted as 336th Bombardment Group (Medium) on 9 Jul 1942 and *activated* on 15 Jul. Assigned to Third AF. Served as a replacement training unit for B–26 crews. *Disbanded* on 1 May 1944.

SQUADRONS. *478th:* 1942–1944. *479th:* 1942–1944. *480th:* 1942–1944. *481st:* 1942–1944.

STATIONS. MacDill Field, Fla, 15 Jul 1942; Ft Myers, Fla, 10 Aug 1942; Avon Park, Fla, 13 Dec 1942; MacDill Field, Fla, 13 Oct 1943; Lake Charles AAFld, La, 6 Nov 1943–1 May 1944.

COMMANDERS. Lt Col Joshua T Winstead, 8 Aug 1942; Col Guy L McNeil, 3 Sep 1942; Lt Col Joshua T Winstead, 7 Oct 1942; Lt Col Hugh B Manson, 10 Dec 1943–1 May 1944.

CAMPAIGNS. American Theater.

DECORATIONS. None.

INSIGNE. None.

337th FIGHTER GROUP

Constituted as 337th Fighter Group on 16 Jul 1942 and *activated* on 23 Jul. Assigned to Third AF. Equipped with a variety of aircraft, primarily P–40's (1942–1943) and P–51's (1944). Trained replacement crews for duty overseas. *Disbanded* on 1 May 1944.

Reconstituted and *redesignated* 337th Fighter Group (Air Defense), on 20 Jun 1955. *Activated* on 18 Aug 1955. Assigned to Air Defense C o m m a n d. Equipped with F–86's.

SQUADRONS. *98th:* 1942–1944. *303d:* 1942–1944. *304th:* 1942–1944. *440th:* 1943–1944. *460th:* 1955–.

STATIONS. Morris Field, NC, 23 Jul 1942; Drew Field, Fla, 7 Aug 1942; Sarasota, Fla, c. 3 Jan 1943–1 May 1944. Portland Intl Aprt, Ore, 18 Aug 1955–.

COMMANDERS. Lt Col James Ferguson, 27 Jul 1942; Col Charles Kegelman, 12 Nov 1943–1 May 1944. Col George F Ceuleers, 1955–.

CAMPAIGNS. American Theater.

DECORATIONS. None.

INSIGNE. *Shield:* Per fess abaisse embattled, and per pale, in the first quarter two stylized delta wing aircraft flying in close formation, noses to dexter chief, a contrail from the two aircraft, bendwise across the shield to the embattlement; four stars arched over the sinister chief, all colors counterchanged, or and sable. (Approved 26 Jun 1957.)

338th FIGHTER GROUP

AD METAM

Constituted as 338th Fighter Group on 16 Jul 1942 and *activated* on 22 Jul. Assigned to Third AF. Trained replacement crews, using a variety of aircraft (P–39's, P–40's, P–47's, and P–51's) during the first year and P–47's after Sep 1943. *Disbanded* on 1 May 1944.

Reconstituted, redesignated 338th Bombardment Group (Very Heavy), and allotted to the reserve, on 5 May 1947.

Activated on 12 Jun 1947. *Inactivated* on 27 Jun 1949.

SQUADRONS. *42d:* 1947–1949. *305th:* 1942–1944. *306th:* 1942–1944. *312th:* 1942–1944. *441st:* 1943–1944. *560th:* 1947–1949. *561st:* 1947–1949. *562d:* 1947–1949. *563d:* 1947–1949.

STATIONS. Dale Mabry Field, Fla, 22 Jul 1942–1 May 1944. Orchard Place Aprt, Ill, 12 Jun 1947–27 Jun 1949.

COMMANDERS. 2d Lt Alfred T Bishop, 23 Jul 1942; Maj Robert B Richard, 7 Sep 1942; Col Lee Q Wasser, 18 Sep 1942; Lt Col Robert B Richard, 5 May 1943; Lt Col Oswald W Lunde, 10 Aug 1943; Lt Col Dale D Brannon, 11 Jan–1 May 1944.

CAMPAIGNS. American Theater.

DECORATIONS. None.

INSIGNE. *Shield:* Azure, issuing from a fess nebuly debased, a winged lion rampant or. *Motto:* AD METAM—To the Goal. (Approved 14 Nov 1942.)

339th FIGHTER GROUP

Constituted as 339th Bombardment Group (Dive) on 3 Aug 1942 and *activated* on 10 Aug. Equipped with A–24's and A–25's; converted to P–39's in Jul 1943. *Redesignated* 339th Fighter-Bomber Group in Aug 1943. Trained and participated in maneuvers. Moved to England, Mar–Apr 1944. Assigned to Eighth AF and equipped with P–51's. Began operations with a fighter sweep on 30 Apr. *Redesignated* 339th Fighter Group in May 1944. Engaged primarily in escort duties during its first five weeks of operations,

STRENGTH ALERTNESS THROUGH

and afterwards flew many escort missions to cover the operations of medium and heavy bombers that struck strategic objectives, interdicted the enemy's communications, or supported operations on the ground. Frequently strafed airdromes and other targets of opportunity while on escort missions. Received a DUC for operations on 10 and 11 Sep 1944. On the first of those days, when it escorted bombers to a target in Germany and then attacked an airdrome near Erding, the group destroyed or damaged many enemy planes despite the intense fire it encountered from antiaircraft guns and small arms. The following day the bomber formation being escorted to Munich was attacked by enemy fighters, but members of the 339th group destroyed a number of the interceptors and drove off the others; at the same time, other members of the 339th were attacking an airdrome near Karlsruhe, where they en-

countered heavy fire but were able to destroy or damage many of the aircraft parked on the field. The group provided fighter cover over the Channel and the coast of Normandy during the invasion of France in Jun 1944. Strafed and dive-bombed vehicles, locomotives, marshalling yards, antiaircraft batteries, and troops while Allied forces fought to break out of the beachhead in France. Attacked transportation targets as Allied armies drove across France after the breakthrough at St Lo in Jul. Flew area patrols during the airborne attack on Holland in Sep. Escorted bombers to, and flew patrols over the battle area during the German counterattack in the Ardennes (Battle of the Bulge), Dec 1944–Jan 1945. Provided area patrols during the assault across the Rhine in Mar 1945. Among all these varied activities, the outstanding feature of this group's combat record is the large number of enemy aircraft it destroyed in the air or on the ground during its one year of operations. Returned to the US in Oct. *Inactivated* on 18 Oct 1945.

Redesignated 107th Fighter Group. Allotted to ANG (NY) on 24 May 1946. Extended federal recognition on 8 Dec 1948. *Redesignated* 107th Fighter-Interceptor Group in Sep 1952.

SQUADRONS. *485th:* 1942–1943. *503d* (formerly 482d): 1942–1945. *504th* (formerly 483d): 1942–1945. *505th* (formerly 484th): 1942–1945.

STATIONS. Hunter Field, Ga, 10 Aug 1942; Drew Field, Fla, Feb 1943; Walterboro AAFld, SC, Jul 1943; Rice AAFld,

Calif, Sep 1943–Mar 1944; Fowlmere, England, 4 Apr 1944–Oct 1945; Camp Kilmer, NJ, c. 16–18 Oct 1945.

COMMANDERS. 2d Lt Harold Garret, c. 18 Aug 1942–unkn; Lt Col Marvin S Zipp, Feb 1943; Maj Harry L Galusha, 19 Feb 1943; Col John B Henry Jr, Aug 1943; Lt Col Harold W Scruggs, c. 1 Oct 1944; Lt Col Carl T Goldenberg, 24 Dec 1944; Col John B Henry Jr, 29 Dec 1944; Lt Col William C Clark, 14 Apr 1945–unkn.

CAMPAIGNS. American Theater; Air Offensive, Europe; Normandy; Northern France; Rhineland; Ardennes-Alsace; Central Europe.

DECORATIONS. Distinguished Unit Citation: Germany, 10–11 Sep 1944.

INSIGNE. *Shield:* Per fess enhanced embattled light blue and azure (dark blue) fimbriated argent in sinister base a mailed fist proper grasping a lance bendwise or, enfiling a cockatrice proper (light green) armed, combed, wattled, and scaled or, all between two clouds of the third. *Crest:* A dexter hand proper, grasping a winged torch or, flamed proper, above a wreath of the colors, argent and arzure. *Motto:* STRENGTH THROUGH ALERTNESS. (Approved 30 Jul 1954.)

340th BOMBARDMENT GROUP

Constituted as 340th Bombardment Group (Medium) on 10 Aug 1942 and *activated* on 20 Aug. Trained with B–25's for duty overseas. Arrived in the Mediterranean theater in Mar 1943. Assigned first to Ninth AF and later (in

Aug 1943) to Twelfth. Served in combat from Apr 1943 to Apr 1945. Engaged chiefly in support and interdictory missions, but sometimes bombed strategic objectives. Targets included airfields, railroads, bridges, road junctions, supply depots, gun emplacements, troop concentrations, marshalling yards, and factories in Tunisia, Sicily, Italy, France, Austria, Bulgaria, Albania, Yugoslavia, and Greece. Also dropped propaganda leaflets behind enemy lines. Participated in the reduction of Pantelleria and Lampedusa in Jun 1943, the bombing of German evacuation beaches near Messina in Jul, the establishment of the Salerno beachhead in Sep, the drive for Rome during Jan–Jun 1944, the invasion of Southern France in Aug, and attacks on the Brenner Pass and other German lines of communication in northern Italy from Sep 1944 to Apr 1945. Received a DUC for the period Apr–Aug 1943 when, although handicapped by difficult living conditions and unfavorable weather, the group supported British

Eighth Army in Tunisia and Allied forces in Sicily. Received second DUC for the destruction of a cruiser in the heavily defended harbor of La Spezia on 23 Sep 1944 before the ship could be used by the enemy to block the harbor's entrance. Returned to the US, Jul–Aug 1945. *Inactivated* on 7 Nov 1945.

Redesignated 340th Bombardment Group (Light). Allotted to the reserve. *Activated* on 31 Oct 1947. *Inactivated* on 19 Aug 1949.

SQUADRONS. *486th:* 1942–1945; 1947–1949. *487th:* 1942–1945; 1947–1949. *488th:* 1942–1945; 1947–1949. *489th:* 1942–1945; 1947–1949.

STATIONS. Columbia AAB, SC, 20 Aug 1942; Walterboro, SC, 30 Nov 1942–30 Jan 1943; El Kabrit, Egypt, Mar 1943; Medenine, Tunisia, Mar 1943; Sfax, Tunisia, Apr 1943; Hergla, Tunisia, 2 Jun 1943; Comiso, Sicily, c. 2 Aug 1943; Catania, Sicily, 27 Aug 1943; San Pancrazio, Italy, c. 15 Oct 1943; Foggia, Italy, 19 Nov 1943; Pompeii, Italy, c. 2 Jan 1944; Paestum, Italy, 23 Mar 1944; Corsica, c. 14 Apr 1944; Rimini, Italy, c. 2 Apr–27 Jul 1945; Seymour Johnson Field, NC, 9 Aug 1945; Columbia AAB, SC, 2 Oct–7 Nov 1945. Tulsa Mun Aprt, Okla, 31 Oct 1947–19 Aug 1949.

COMMANDERS. Lt Col Adolph E Tokaz, 3 Sep 1942; Col William C Mills, 21 Sep 1942; Lt Col Adolph E Tokaz, 7 May 1943; Col Charles D Jones, 8 Jan 1944; Col Willis F Chapman, 16 Mar 1944–7 Nov 1945.

CAMPAIGNS. Air Combat, EAME Theater; Tunisia; Sicily; Naples-Foggia; Anzio; Rome-Arno; Southern France; North Apennines; Central Europe; Po Valley.

DECORATIONS. Distinguished Unit Citations: North Africa and Sicily, [Apr]–17 Aug 1943; Italy, 23 Sep 1944.

INSIGNE. *Shield:* Per fess nebuly, azure and argent, in chief two cloud formations proper, one issuing from the dexter and one issuing from the sinister, in base three stars of five points, of the first, two and one, all surmounted in fess, with an ear of wheat proper and a lightning flash, gules in saltire, an edge around the shield sable. *Motto:* ANYWHERE—ANYTIME. (Approved 12 Sep 1955.)

341st BOMBARDMENT GROUP

Constituted as 341st Bombardment Group (Medium) on 14 Aug 1942. *Activated* in India on 15 Sep 1942. Equipped with B–25's. Entered combat early in 1943 and operated chiefly against enemy transportation in central Burma until 1944. Bombed bridges, locomotives, railroad yards, and other targets to delay movement of supplies to the Japanese troops fighting in northern Burma. Moved to China in Jan 1944. Engaged primarily in sea sweeps and attacks against inland shipping. Also bombed and strafed such targets as trains, harbors, and railroads in French Indochina and the Canton-Hong Kong area of China. Received a DUC for developing and using a special (glip) bombing technique against enemy bridges in French Indochina. Moved to the US in Oct 1945. *Inactivated* on 2 Nov 1945.

Redesignated 341st Bombardment Group (Light). Allotted to the reserve. *Activated* on 27 Dec 1946. *Inactivated* on 27 Jun 1949.

SQUADRONS. *10th:* 1947–1949. *11th:* 1942–1945. *12th:* 1947–1949. *22d:* 1942–1945. *490th:* 1942–1945; 1947–1949. *491st:* 1942–1945; 1947–1949.

STATIONS. Karachi, India, 15 Sep 1942; Chakulia, India, 30 Dec 1942; Kurmitola, India, Jun 1943; Kunming, China, 7 Jan 1944; Yangkai, China, 13 Dec 1944–unkn; Camp Kilmer, NJ, 1–2 Nov 1945. Westover Field, Mass, 27 Dec 1946–27 Jun 1949.

COMMANDERS. Col Torgils G Wold, 15 Sep 1942; Col James A Philpott, 21 Sep 1943; Col Torgils G Wold, 2 Nov 1943; Col Morris F Taber, 23 Nov 1943; Col Joseph B Wells, 11 Apr 1944; Col Donald L Clark, c. 1 Dec 1944; Col James W Newsome, 16 Apr 1945–unkn.

CAMPAIGNS. India-Burma; China Defensive; China Offensive.

DECORATIONS. Distinguished Unit Citation: French Indochina, 11 Dec 1944–12 Mar 1945.

INSIGNE. *Shield:* Per fess nebuly azure and argent a semee of stars in chief of the last, over all in pale a sheathed sword proper (white, silver gray shading and deep gray outlines), the rim of the sheath and winged hilt and pommel or (outlines and detail deep gray); the blade entwined with a girdle of the last; the sword point downward between two bolts of lightning radiating upward gules; over all, in base a branch of olive vert, detail vein lines or. *Motto:* PAX ORBIS PER ARMA AERIA—World Peace through Air Strength. (Approved 5 Jun 1957.)

342d COMPOSITE GROUP

Constituted as 342d Composite Group on 29 Aug 1942. *Activated* on 11 Sep 1942 in Iceland. Equipped with P–38's, P–39's, P–40's, and a B–18, the group served as part of the island's defense force, intercepting and destroying some of the German planes that on occasion attempted to attack Iceland or that appeared in that area on reconnaissance missions. Also conducted antisubmarine patrols in the North Atlantic and provided cover for convoys on the run to Murmansk. *Disbanded* on 18 Mar 1944.

Reconstituted and *redesignated* 342d Fighter-Day Group, on 7 May 1956. *Activated* on 25 Jul 1956. Assigned to Tactical Air Command.

SQUADRONS. *33d* Fighter: 1942–1944; 1956–. *50th* Fighter: 1942–1944. *337th* Fighter: 1942. *572d:* 1956–. *573d:* 1956–.

STATIONS. Iceland, 11 Sep 1942–18 Mar 1944. Myrtle Beach AFB, SC, 25 Jul 1956–.

COMMANDERS. Lt Col J S Holtoner, 11 Sep 1942; Lt Col W W Korges, 2 Jun 1943; Lt Col Cy Wilson, 10 Aug 1943–unkn. Maj Charles S Boster, Jul 1956–.

CAMPAIGNS. Air Combat, EAME Theater.

DECORATIONS. None.

INSIGNE. None.

343d FIGHTER GROUP

Constituted as 343d Fighter Group on 3 Sep 1942 and *activated* in Alaska on 11 Sep. Assigned to Eleventh AF. Began operations immediately. Provided air defense for the Aleutians; bombed and strafed Japanese camps, antiaircraft emplacements, hangars, and radio stations on Kiska; escorted bombers that struck enemy airfields, harbor facilities, and shipping. Flew its last combat mission in Oct 1943, but carried out patrol and reconnaissance assignments in the area until the end of the war. Later trained, carried mail, and served as part of the defense force for Alaska. Used P–38's and P–40's, and later (1946) P–51's. *Inactivated* in Alaska on 15 Aug 1946.

Redesignated 343d Fighter Group (Air Defense) on 20 Jun 1955. *Activated* in the US on 18 Aug 1955. Assigned to Air Defense Command and equipped with F–89's.

SQUADRONS. *11th:* 1942–1946; 1955–. *18th:* 1942–1946. *54th:* 1942–1946. *344th:* 1942–1946.

STATIONS. Elmendorf Field, Alaska, 11 Sep 1942; Ft Glenn, Alaska, Sep 1942; Elmendorf Field, Alaska, 3 Dec 1942; Adak, 7 Mar 1943; Amchitka, 25 Jul 1943; Alexai Point, Alaska, 22 Jan 1944; Shemya, 5 Oct 1945–15 Aug 1946. Duluth Mun Aprt, Minn, 18 Aug 1955–.

COMMANDERS. Lt Col John S Chennault, 11 Sep 1942; Lt Col Edgar A Boadway, 16 Nov 1942; Maj Edgar A Romberg, 10 Dec 1942; Lt Col Anthony V Grossetta, 19 Mar 1943; Lt Col James R Watt, 19 Apr 1943; Maj Edgar A Romberg, 25 May 1943; Lt Col William E Elder, 3 Jun 1943; Col Robert H Jones, 17 Oct 1943; Lt Col Dean Davenport, 18 Oct 1945; Maj Benjamin H King, 19 Jul–15 Aug 1946. Col George L Hicks III, 18 Aug 1955–.

CAMPAIGNS. Aleutian Islands.

DECORATIONS. None.

INSIGNE. *Shield:* Azure, fimbriated argent, within a diminutive border gules, an Indian arrow issuing from base, in pale, the shaft or, the arrowhead proper, markings and outline black, the thong fastening of the third, superimposed over the arrowhead a missile, in bend sinister, the power stream swirling upward to dexter chief all of the second, a sound barrier symbol in sinister chief sable. (Approved 3 Feb 1956.)

344th BOMBARDMENT GROUP

WE WIN OR DIE

Constituted as 344th Bombardment Group (Medium) on 31 Aug 1942. *Activated* on 8 Sep 1942. Equipped with B–26's and served as a replacement training unit. Moved to England, Jan–Feb 1944. Began operations with Ninth AF in Mar, attacking airfields, missile sites, marshalling yards, submarine shelters, coastal defenses, and other targets in France, Belgium, and Holland. Beginning in May, helped prepare for the Normandy invasion by striking vital bridges in France. On D–Day 1944 attacked coastal batteries at Cherbourg; during the remainder of Jun, supported the drive that resulted in the seizure of the Cotentin Peninsula. Bombed defended positions to assist British forces in the area of Caen. Received a DUC for three-day action against the enemy, 24–26 Jul 1944, when the group struck troop concentrations, supply dumps, a bridge, and a railroad viaduct to assist advancing ground forces at St Lo. Knocked out bridges to hinder the enemy's withdrawal through the Falaise gap, and bombed vessels and strong points at Brest, Aug–Sep 1944. Attacked bridges, rail lines, fortified areas, supply dumps, and ordnance depots in Germany, Oct–Nov 1944. Supported Allied forces during the Battle of the Bulge, Dec 1944–Jan 1945, and continued to strike such targets as supply points, communications centers, bridges, marshalling yards, roads, and oil storage tanks until Apr 1945. Made training flights and participated in air demonstrations after the war. Moved to Germany in Sep 1945 and, as part of United States Air Forces in Europe, served with the army of occupation. Began training in A–26 but continued to use B–26 aircraft. *Redesignated* 344th Bombardment Group (Light) in Dec 1945. Transferred, without personnel and equipment, to the US on 15 Feb 1946. *Inactivated* on 31 Mar 1946.

Redesignated 126th Bombardment Group (Light). Allotted to ANG (Ill) on 24 May 1946. Extended federal recognition on 29 Jun 1947. *Redesignated* 126th Composite Group in Nov 1950, and 126th

Bombardment Group (Light) in Feb 1951. Ordered to active service on 1 Apr 1951 and assigned to Tactical Air Command. Moved to France, Nov–Dec 1951, and assigned to United States Air Forces in Europe. Used B–26's for training and maneuvers. Relieved from active duty and transferred, without personnel and equipment, to the control of ANG (Ill), on 1 Jan 1953. *Redesignated* 126th Fighter-Bomber Group.

SQUADRONS. *108th:* 1951–1953. *115th:* 1951. *168th:* 1951–1953. *180th:* 1951–1953. *494th:* 1942–1946. *495th:* 1942–1946. *496th:* 1942–1946. *497th:* 1942–1945.

STATIONS. MacDill Field, Fla, 8 Sep 1942; Drane Field, Fla, 28 Dec 1942; Hunter Field, Ga, 19 Dec 1943–26 Jan 1944; Stansted, England, 9 Feb 1944; Cormeilles-en-Vexin, France, 30 Sep 1944; Florennes/Juzaine, Belgium, 5 Apr 1945; Schleissheim, Germany, c. 15 Sep 1945–15 Feb 1946; Bolling Field, DC, 15 Feb–31 Mar 1946. O'Hare Intl Aprt, Ill, 1 Apr 1951; Langley AFB, Va, 25 Jul–19 Nov 1951; Bordeaux AB, France, 7 Dec 1951; Laon AB, France, c. 25 May 1952–1 Jan 1953.

COMMANDERS. Lt Col Jacob J Brogger, 10 Oct 1942; Col Guy L McNeil, 2 Nov 1942; Col John A Hilger, 7 Nov 1942; Lt Col Vernon L Stintzi, 20 Jul 1943; Maj Robert W Witty, c. 6 Aug 1943; Col Reginald F C Vance, 19 Sep 1943; Col Robert W Witty, 7 Nov 1944; Lt Col Lucius D Clay Jr, 18 Aug 1945–15 Feb 1946. Col Russell B Daniels, 1 Apr 1951; Lt Col Carl R Norton, 25 Jun 1951; Lt Col Max H Mortensen, 21 Jul 1952; Col Glen W Clark, 5 Aug 1952; Lt Col Max H Mortensen, 18 Nov 1952–c. 1 Jan 1953.

CAMPAIGNS. American Theater; Air Offensive, Europe; Normandy; Northern France; Rhineland; Ardennes-Alsace; Central Europe.

DECORATIONS. Distinguished Unit Citation: France, 24–26 Jul 1944.

INSIGNE. *Shield:* Azure, a bend nebule or, between four spears, points to base, two and two of the last, inflamed proper. *Motto:* WE WIN OR DIE. (Approved 9 Jan 1943.)

345th BOMBARDMENT GROUP

Constituted as 345th Bombardment Group (Medium) on 3 Sep 1942 and *activated* on 8 Sep. Trained for overseas duty with B–25's. Moved to New Guinea, via Australia, Apr–Jun 1943, and assigned to Fifth AF. Entered combat on 30 Jun 1943. Operations until Jul 1944 included bombing and strafing Japanese airfields and installations in New Guinea and the Bismarck Archipelago; attacking shipping in the McCluer Gulf, Ceram Sea, and Bismarck Sea; supporting ground forces in the Admiralties; dropping supplies to ground troops; and flying courier and reconnaissance missions in the area. Received a DUC for a series of attacks against flak positions, shore installations, and barracks at Rabaul, New Britain, on 2 Nov 1943. Operated from Biak, Jul–Nov 1944, striking airfields and shipping in the southern Philippines and the Celebes. In Nov 1944 moved to the Philippines where targets included Japanese airfields and communications on Luzon, industries and communications on Formosa, and shipping along the China coast. After moving to Ie Shima in Jul 1945, flew some missions over Kyushu and the Sea of Japan. Returned to the US in Dec 1945. *Inactivated* on 29 Dec 1945.

Redesignated 345th Bombardment Group (Tactical). *Activated* on 19 Jul 1954. Assigned to Tactical Air Command. Equipped with B–26's and later with B–57's.

SQUADRONS. *498th:* 1942–1945; 1954–. *499th:* 1942–1945; 1954–. *500th:* 1942–1945; 1954–. *501st:* 1942–1945.

STATIONS. Columbia AAB, SC, 8 Sep 1942; Walterboro AAFld, SC, 6 Mar–16 Apr 1943; Port Moresby, New Guinea, 5 Jun 1943; Dobodura, New Guinea, 18 Jan 1944; Nadzab, New Guinea, c. 16 Feb 1944; Biak, Jul 1944; Leyte, 12 Nov 1944; Dulag, Leyte, Dec 1944; Tacloban, Leyte,

c. 1 Jan 1945; San Marcelino, Luzon, 13 Feb 1945; Clark Field, Luzon, 12 May 1945; Ie Shima, 25 Jul–10 Dec 1945; Camp Stoneman, Calif, 27–29 Dec 1945. Langley AFB, Va, 19 Jul 1954–.

COMMANDERS. Col Jarred V Crabb, 11 Nov 1942; Col Clinton U True, 19 Sep 1943; Col Chester A Coltharp, 24 Jun 1944; Col Glenn A Doolittle, 28 Jun 1945– unkn. Col John G Napier, 19 Jul 1954–.

CAMPAIGNS. Air Offensive, Japan; China Defensive; New Guinea; Bismarck Archipelago; Western Pacific; Leyte; Luzon; Southern Philippines; China Offensive.

DECORATIONS. Distinguished Unit Citation: Rabaul, New Britain, 2 Nov 1943. Philippine Presidential Unit Citation.

INSIGNE. On a disc azure, an orle argent, surmounting all the head, in profile, of an Apache, proper, wearing a feathered headdress of the second, with markings gules, and a string of animal's teeth of the second. *Motto*: AIR APACHES. (Approved 21 May 1954.)

346th BOMBARDMENT GROUP

Constituted as 346th Bombardment Group (Heavy) on 3 Sep 1942 and *activated* on 7 Sep. Assigned to Second AF. Equipped with B–17's and B–24's. Served first as an operational training and later as a replacement training unit. *Inactivated* on 1 Apr 1944.

Redesignated 346th Bombardment Group (Very Heavy). *Activated* on 18

Aug 1944. Assigned to Second AF. Prepared for combat with B–29's. Moved to the Pacific theater, Jun–Aug 1945, and assigned to Eighth AF. The war ended before the group could begin combat operations. After the war the group participated in several show-of-force missions over Japan and for a time ferried Allied prisoners of war from Okinawa to the Philippine Islands. *Inactivated* on Okinawa on 30 Jun 1946.

SQUADRONS. *461st:* 1944–1946. *462d:* 1944–1946. *463d:* 1944–1946. *502d:* 1942–1944. *503d:* 1942–1944. *504th:* 1942–1944. *505th:* 1942–1944.

STATIONS. Salt Lake City AAB, Utah, 7 Sep 1942; Smoky Hill AB, Kan, 3 Oct 1942; Dyersburg AAFld, Tenn, 26 Feb 1943–1 Apr 1944. Dalhart AAFld, Tex, 18 Aug 1944; Pratt AAFld, Kan, 18 Jan–29 Jun 1945; Kadena, Okinawa, 7 Aug 1945–30 Jun 1946.

COMMANDERS. Col Budd J Peaslee, 6 Oct 1942; Lt Col Samuel C Mitchell, 20 Dec 1942–1943; Lt Col John D Moorman, Mar 1943; Col Samuel C Gurney Jr, Oct 1943–1 Apr 1944. Maj James A Gibb Jr, 21 Aug 1944; Lt Col Charles E Dewey, 23 Aug 1944; Col William M Canterbury, 13 Sep 1944; Col Ben I Funk, 3 Jan 1945; Col Joseph F Carroll, 30 Nov 1945–30 Jun 1946.

CAMPAIGNS. American Theater; Asiatic-Pacific Theater.

DECORATIONS. None.

INSIGNE. None.

347th FIGHTER GROUP

Constituted as 347th Fighter Group on 29 Sep 1942. *Activated* in New Caledonia on 3 Oct 1942. Detachments of the group, which was assigned to Thirteenth AF in Jan 1943, were sent to Guadacanal, where they used P–39 and P–400 aircraft to fly protective patrols, support ground forces, and attack Japanese shipping. When the Allied campaign to recover the central and northern Solomons began in Feb 1943, the detachments, still operating from Guadalcanal and using P–38 and P–39 aircraft, escorted bombers and attacked enemy bases on New Georgia, the Russell Islands, and Bougainville. Headquarters moved up from New Caledonia at the end of 1943, and the following month the group moved from Guadalcanal to Stirling Island to support ground forces on Bougainville, assist in neutralizing enemy bases at Rabaul, and fly patrol and search missions in the northern Solomons. Moved to New Guinea in Aug 1944. Equipped completely with P–38's. Escorted bombers to oil refineries on Borneo; bombed and strafed airfields and installations on Ceram, Amboina, Boeroe, Celebes, and Halmahera. Received a DUC for a series of long-range bombing and strafing raids, conducted through intense flak and fighter defense, on the airfield and shipping at Makassar, Celebes, in Nov 1944. Moved to the Philippines in Feb 1945. Supported landings on Mindanao in Mar 1945, bombed and strafed enemy installations and supported Australian forces on Borneo, attacked Japanese positions in northern Luzon, and flew escort missions to the Asiatic mainland. Moved to the US in Dec 1945. *Inactivated* on 1 Jan 1946.

Redesignated 347th Fighter Group (All Weather). *Activated* in Japan on 20 Feb 1947. Assigned to Far East Air Forces. Equipped with F-61's and later with F-82's. *Inactivated* on 24 Jun 1950.

SQUADRONS. *4th:* 1947-1950. *67th:* 1942-1945. *68th:* 1942-1945; 1947-1950. *70th:* 1942-1943, 1945. *339th:* 1942-1946; 1947-1950.

STATIONS. New Caledonia, 3 Oct 1942; Guadalcanal, 29 Dec 1943; Stirling, Treasury Islands, 15 Jan 1944; Sansapor, New Guinea, 15 Aug 1944; Middleburg, New Guinea, 19 Sep 1944; San Jose, Mindoro, 22 Feb 1945; Puerto Princesa, Palawan, 6 Mar-Dec 1945; Camp Stoneman, Calif, 30 Dec 1945-1 Jan 1946. Nagoya, Japan, 20 Feb 1947; Itazuke, Japan, 25 Sep 1947; Bofu, Japan, 15 Oct 1948; Ashiya, Japan, 6 May 1949; Nagoya, Japan, 1 Apr-24 Jun 1950.

COMMANDERS. Lt Col George M McNeese, 3 Oct 1942; Col Leo F Dusard Jr, Jan 1944; Lt Col Leonard Shapiro, 25 Jun 1945-unkn. Unkn, Feb 1947-Aug 1948; Maj Elmer G DaRosa, Aug 1948; Maj Alden E West, Sep 1948; Lt Col John L McGinn, Oct 1948-unkn; Lt Col Clyde A Thompson, unkn-Jun 1950.

CAMPAIGNS. China Defensive; Guadalcanal; New Guinea; Northern Solomons; Bismarck Archipelago; Western Pacific; Leyte; Luzon; Southern Philippines; China Offensive.

DECORATIONS. Distinguished Unit Citation: Netherlands East Indies, 7, 20, and 22 Nov 1944. Philippine Presidential Unit Citation.

INSIGNE. None.

348th FIGHTER GROUP

Constituted as 348th Fighter Group on 24 Sep 1942 and *activated* on 30 Sep. Prepared for combat with P-47's. Moved to the Southwest Pacific, May-Jun 1943, and assigned to Fifth AF. Operated from New Guinea and Noemfoor until Nov 1944. Flew patrol and reconnaissance missions and escorted bombers to targets in New Guinea and New Britain. Col Neel E Kearby was awarded the Medal of Honor for action over New Guinea on 11 Oct 1943: after leading a flight of four fighters to reconnoiter the enemy base at Wewak, Col Kearby sighted a Japanese bomber formation escorted by more than 30 fighters; despite the heavy odds and a low fuel supply, and although his mission had been accomplished, Kearby ordered an attack, personally destroying six of the enemy planes. For covering Allied landings and supporting ground forces on New Britain, 16–31 Dec 1943, the group was awarded a DUC. In 1944 began to attack airfields, installations, and shipping in western New Guinea, Ceram, and Halmahera to aid in neutralizing those areas preparatory to the US invasion of the Philippines. After moving to the Philippines in Nov 1944, provided cover for convoys, flew patrols, escorted bombers, attacked enemy airfields, and supported ground forces. Received a DUC for withstanding assaults by enemy fighters to cover bombers raiding Clark Field on 24 Dec 1944. Also attacked shipping along the China coast and escorted bombers to Formosa and the Asiatic mainland. Moved to the Ryukyus in Jul 1945 and completed some escort and attack missions to Kyushu before the war ended. Moved to Japan in Oct 1945 as part of Far East Air Forces. *Inactivated* on 10 May 1946.

Redesignated 108th Fighter Group. Allotted to ANG (NJ) on 24 May 1946. Extended federal recognition on 16 Oct 1946. Called to active duty on 1 Mar 1951. *Redesignated* 108th Fighter-Bomber Group. Assigned first to Strategic Air Command and later to Tactical Air Command. Equipped with F–47's. Relieved from active service on 1 Dec 1952 and returned to the control of ANG (NJ).

SQUADRONS. *149th:* 1951–1952. *153d:* 1951–1952. *340th:* 1942–1946. *341st* (later 141st): 1942–1946; 1951–1952. *342d:* 1942–1946. *460th:* 1944–1946.

STATIONS. Mitchel Field, NY, 30 Sep 1942; Bradley Field, Conn, 4 Oct 1942; Westover Field, Mass, 29 Oct 1942; Providence, RI, c. 3 Jan 1943; Westover Field, Mass, 28 Apr–9 May 1943; Port Moresby, New Guinea, 23 Jun 1943; Finschhafen, New Guinea, 16 Dec 1943; Saidor, New Guinea, 29 Mar 1944; Wakde, 22 May 1944; Noemfoor, 26 Aug 1944; Leyte, 16 Nov 1944; San Marcelino, Luzon, 4 Feb 1945; Floridablanca, Luzon, 15 May 1945; Ie Shima, 9 Jul 1945; Itami, Japan, Oct 1945–10 May 1946. Newark Mun Aprt, NJ, 1 Mar 1951; Turner AFB, Ga, 14 Mar 1951; Godman AFB, Ky, 9 Dec 1951–1 Dec 1952.

COMMANDERS. Col Neel E Kearby, Oct 1942; Col Robert R Rowland, 17 Nov 1943; Lt Col William M Banks, 8 Jun 1945; Maj Walter G Benz, 26 Nov 1945–unkn. Maj J D Zink, Mar 1951; Col Alvan C Gillem II, Jun 1951; Col Carl W Stapleton, c. Nov 1951; Col Donald J Strait, 14 Jan 1952; Col George Laven Jr, 4 Aug–1 Dec 1952.

CAMPAIGNS. Air Offensive, Japan; China Defensive; New Guinea; Bismarck Archipelago; Western Pacific; Leyte; Luzon; China Offensive.

DECORATIONS. Distinguished Unit Citations: New Britain, 16–31 Dec 1943; Philippine Islands, 24 Dec 1944. Philippine Presidential Unit Citation.

INSIGNE. *Shield:* Azure, within a bordure dimidiated, gules, hand gauntleted in armour proper, encircled with wreath of laurel, vert, grasping a torch argent, flamant proper. *Motto:* PER CAELUM VICTORIAE—Through the Skies to Victory. (Approved 15 Aug 1951.)

349th TROOP CARRIER GROUP

Constituted as · 349th Troop Carrier Group on 23 Oct 1943. *Activated* on 1 Nov 1943. Equipped successively with C-53, C-47, and C-46 aircraft. Trained and participated in various maneuvers. Moved to the European theater, Mar–Apr 1945, and assigned to IX Troop Carrier Command. Used C-46's to transport vehicles, gasoline, and other supplies in western Europe and to evacuate patients and prisoners of war. Ceased operations on 15 Jun 1945. Returned to the US, Jul–Aug 1945. Trained Chinese crews to operate C-46 aircraft. *Inactivated* on 7 Sep 1946.

Redesignated 349th Troop Carrier Group (Medium). Allotted to the reserve. *Activated* on 27 Jun 1949. Ordered to active duty on 1 Apr 1951. *Inactivated* on 2 Apr 1951.

Redesignated 349th Fighter-Bomber Group. Allotted to the reserve. *Activated* on 13 Jun 1952.

SQUADRONS. *23d:* 1944–1946. *311th:* 1943–1944; 1949–1951. *312th:* 1943–1946; 1949–1951; 1952–. *313th:* 1943–1946; 1949–1951; 1952–. *314th:* 1943–1946; 1949–1951; 1952–.

STATIONS. Sedalia AAFld, Mo, 1 Nov 1943; Alliance AAFld, Neb, 19 Jan 1944; Pope Field, NC, 8 Mar 1944; Baer Field, Ind, 4–15 Mar 1945; Barkston, England, 30 Mar 1945; Roye/Amy Airfield, France, 18 Apr–13 Jul 1945; Bergstrom Field, Tex, 17 Sep 1945–7 Sep 1946. Hamilton AFB, Calif, 27 Jun 1949–2 Apr 1951. Hamilton AFB, Calif, 13 Jun 1952–.

COMMANDERS. Maj Elmer F Estrumse, 1 Nov 1943; Col Leonard J Barrow Jr, 26 Nov 1943; Lt Col Benjamin M Tarver Jr, 29 Aug–7 Sep 1946.

CAMPAIGNS. American Theater; EAME Theater.

DECORATIONS. None.

INSIGNE. *Shield:* Per bend sky blue and azure; in bend a lightning bolt gules, fimbriated argent, between three aircraft in flight, and a representation of the golden gate bridge or; the shield edged of the last. *Motto:* FACTA, NON VERBA—

Deeds, Not Words. (Approved 26 Jul 1956.)

350th FIGHTER GROUP

Activated in England on 1 Oct 1942 by special authority granted to Eighth AF prior to *constitution* as 350th Fighter Group on 2 Oct 1942. The air echelon moved from England to North Africa, Jan–Feb 1943; the ground echelon, which had been formed in the US, arrived in North Africa about the same time. The group operated with Twelfth AF from Jan 1943 until the end of the war, flying patrol and interception missions, protecting convoys, escorting aircraft, flying reconnaissance missions, engaging in interdictory operations, and providing close support for ground forces. Used P–39's, P–400's, and a few P–38's before converting to P–47's during Aug–Sep 1944. Operated against targets in Tunisia until the end of that campaign. Defended the coast of Algeria during the summer and fall of 1943. Afterward, operated primarily in support of Allied forces in Italy until the end of the war, bombing and strafing rail facilities, shipping docks, radar and transformer stations, power lines, bridges, motor transports, and military installations. Received a DUC for action in western Italy on 6 Apr 1944 when, despite intense flak and attacks by numerous enemy interceptors, the group flew ten missions, hitting troops, bridges, vehicles, barracks, and air warning installations. Also covered Allied landings on Elba in Jun 1944 and supported the invasion of Southern France in Aug. 1st Lt Raymond L Knight was awarded the Medal of Honor for missions on 24 and 25 Apr 1945: voluntarily leading attacks, through intense antiaircraft fire, against enemy airdromes in northern Italy, Lt Knight was responsible for eliminating more than 20 German planes intended for assaults on Allied forces; attempting to return his shattered plane to base after an attack on 25 Apr, Lt Knight crashed in the Apennines. The group moved to the US, Jul–Aug 1945. *Inactivated* on 7 Nov 1945.

Redesignated 112th Fighter Group. Allotted to ANG (Pa) on 24 May 1946. Extended federal recognition on 22 Apr 1949. *Redesignated* 112th Fighter-Interceptor Group in Oct 1952, and 112th Fighter-Bomber Group in Dec 1952.

SQUADRONS. 345th: 1942–1945. 346th: 1942–1945. 347th: 1942–1945.

STATIONS. Bushey Hall, England, 1 Oct 1942; Duxford, England, Oct 1942; Oujda,

French Morocco, 6 Jan 1943; Oran, Algeria, 14 Feb 1943; Maison Blanche, Algeria, May 1943; Rerhaia, Algeria, c. 17 Jul 1943; Sardinia, 5 Nov 1943; Corsica, 6 Feb 1944; Tarquinia, Italy, 8 Sep 1944; Pisa, Italy, 2 Dec 1944–14 Jul 1945; Seymour Johnson Field, NC, 25 Aug–7 Nov 1945.

COMMANDERS. Lt Col Richard P Klocko, 14 Oct 1942; Maj Ariel W Nielsen, 24 Feb 1943; Lt Col Marvin L McNickle, 1 Mar 1943; Lt Col Ariel W Nielsen, c. Sep 1943; Lt Col John C Robertson, 22 Oct 1944; Col Ariel W Nielsen, c. Feb 1945; Col John C Robertson, 20 Jun 1945–unkn.

CAMPAIGNS. Air Combat, EAME Theater; Tunisia; Sicily; Naples-Foggia; Rome-Arno; Southern France; North Apennines; Po Valley.

DECORATIONS. Distinguished Unit Citation: Italy, 6 Apr 1944.

INSIGNE. *Shield:* Per bend azure and or, on a bend sable between a Pegasus salient argent and a keystone charged with a ruffed grouse proper, a group of four vols with upper edges of wings parallel to the edge of the ordinary, each vol overlapping the next from dexter to sinister alternating of the fourth and second, a diminished border of the third. *Motto:* IN COMMON CAUSE. (Approved 10 Sep 1954.)

351st BOMBARDMENT GROUP

Constituted as 351st Bombardment Group (Heavy) on 25 Sep 1942. *Activated* on 1 Oct 1942. Trained for duty overseas with B–17's. Moved to England,

Apr–May 1943. Served in combat with Eighth AF from May 1943 to Apr 1945. Operated primarily against strategic objectives in Germany, striking such targets as ball-bearing plants at Schweinfurt, communications at Mayen, marshalling yards at Koblenz, a locomotive and tank factory at Hannover, industries at Berlin, bridges at Cologne, an armaments factory at Mannheim, and oil refineries at Hamburg. Also struck harbor facilities, submarine installations, airfields, V-weapon sites, and power plants in France, Belgium, Holland, and Norway. Received a DUC for performance of 9 Oct 1943 when an aircraft factory in Germany was accurately bombed in spite of heavy flak and pressing enemy interceptors. Received another DUC for its part in the successful attack of 11 Jan 1944 on aircraft factories in central Germany. Participated in the intensive air campaign against the German aircraft industry during Big Week, 20–25 Feb 1944. 2d Lt Walter E Truemper, navigator, and Sgt Archibald Mathies, engineer, were each awarded the Medal of Honor for action on 20 Feb 1944: when their aircraft received a direct hit that killed the co-pilot and wounded the pilot, Truemper and Mathies managed to fly the plane until other crew members could bail out; on the third attempt to land the plane in an effort to save the pilot, the B–17 crashed and the men were killed. In addition to its strategic missions, the group often operated in support of ground forces and attacked interdictory targets. Bombed in support of the Normandy invasion in Jun 1944 and the St Lo break-through in Jul. Hit enemy positions to cover the airborne attack on Holland in Sep 1944. Struck front-line positions, communications, and airfields to help stop the German counteroffensive in the Battle of the Bulge, Dec 1944–Jan 1945. Flew missions in support of the airborne assault across the Rhine in Mar 1945. Returned to the US soon after V–E Day. *Inactivated* on 28 Aug 1945.

Redesignated 351st Bombardment Group (Very Heavy). Allotted to the reserve. *Activated* on 9 Apr 1947. *Inactivated* on 27 Jun 1949.

SQUADRONS. *508th:* 1942–1945; 1947–1949. *509th:* 1942–1945; 1947–1948. *510th:* 1942–1945; 1947–1948. *511th:* 1942–1945; 1947–1949. *434th:* 1948–1949.

STATIONS. Salt Lake City AAB, Utah, 1 Oct 1942; Geiger Field, Wash, Nov 1942; Biggs Field, Tex, Dec 1942; Pueblo AAB, Colo, c. 1 Mar–c. 12 Apr 1943; Polebrook, England, c. 1 May 1943–Jun 1945; Sioux Falls AAFld, SD, Jul–28 Aug 1945. Scott Field, Ill, 9 Apr 1947–27 Jun 1949.

COMMANDERS. Col William A Hatcher Jr, Nov 1942; Col Eugene A Romig, c. 1 Jan 1944; Col Robert W Burns, Oct 1944; Col Merlin I Carter, 30 Mar 1945–unkn.

CAMPAIGNS. Air Offensive, Europe; Normandy; Northern France; Rhineland; Ardennes-Alsace; Central Europe.

DECORATIONS. Distinguished Unit Citations: Germany, 9 Oct 1943; Germany, 11 Jan 1944.

INSIGNE. None.

352d FIGHTER GROUP

Constituted as 352d Fighter Group on 29 Sep 1942. *Activated* on 1 Oct 1942. Served as part of the air defense force for the US while training with P–47's for duty overseas. Moved to England, Jun–Jul 1943. Assigned to Eighth AF. Operated against the enemy in air combat over Europe from Sep 1943 to May 1945, using P–47's before converting to P–51's in Apr 1944. Flew numerous escort missions to cover the operations of bombers that attacked factories, V-weapon sites, submarine pens, and other targets on the Continent. Escorted bombers that struck German aircraft factories during Big Week, 20–25 Feb 1944. Received a DUC for performance in Germany on 8 May 1944: while escorting bombers to targets in Brunswick, the group routed an attack by a numerically superior force of German interceptors and then continued the battle against the enemy planes until lack of ammunition and shortage of fuel forced the group to withdraw and return to its base. Also flew counter-air patrols, and on many occasions strafed and dive-bombed airfields, locomotives, vehicles, troops, gun positions, and various other targets. Supported the invasion of Normandy in Jun 1944 by strafing and dive-bombing enemy communications, assisted the Allies in breaking through the German line at St Lo in Jul, and participated in the airborne attack on Holland in Sep. After the Germans launched a counteroffensive in the Ardennes in Dec 1944, the group's planes and pilots were sent to Belgium and placed under the control of Ninth AF for operations in the Battle of the Bulge (Dec 1944–Jan 1945). During that battle, on 1 Jan 1945, action by the detachment earned for the group the French Croix de Guerre with Palm: just as 12 of the detachment's planes were taking off for an area patrol, the airdrome was attacked by about 50 German fighters; in the aerial battle that followed, the 352d shot down almost half the enemy planes without losing any of its own. In Feb 1945 the remainder of the group joined the detachment in Belgium for operations under the control of Eighth AF. While based on the Continent, the group participated in the airborne assault across the Rhine (Mar 1945). Returned to England in Apr and continued operations until a few days before V–E Day. Returned to the US in Nov. *Inactivated* on 10 Nov 1945.

Redesignated 113th Fighter Group. Allotted to ANG (DC) on 24 May 1946.

Extended federal recognition on 2 Nov 1946. Ordered to active duty on 1 Feb 1951. Assigned to Air Defense Command. *Redesignated* 113th Fighter-Interceptor Group. Used F–84's during 1951; converted to F–94 aircraft in 1952. *Inactivated* on 6 Feb 1952. Relieved from active duty, returned to control of ANG (DC), and *activated,* on 1 Nov 1952. *Redesignated* 113th Fighter-Bomber Group in Dec 1952.

SQUADRONS. *121st*: 1951–1952. *142d*: 1951–1952. *148th*: 1951–1952. *328th*: 1942–1945. *486th* (formerly 21st): 1942–1945. *487th* (formerly 34th): 1942–1945.

STATIONS. Mitchel Field, NY, 1 Oct 1942; Bradley Field, Conn, Oct 1942; Westover Field, Mass, Nov 1942; Trumbull Field, Conn, c. 15 Jan 1943; Republic Field, NY, c. 9 Mar–Jun 1943; Bodney, England, 7 Jul 1943; Chievres, Belgium, c. 27 Jan 1945; Bodney, England, c. 14 Apr–3 Nov 1945; Camp Kilmer, NJ, c. 9–10 Nov 1945. Andrews AFB, Md, 1 Feb 1951; New Castle County Aprt, Del, 16 Feb 1951–6 Feb 1952.

COMMANDERS. Lt Col Edwin M Ramage, c. Oct 1942; Col Joe L Mason, 17 May 1943; Col James D Mayden, 17 Nov 1944– unkn. Col Joseph Myers, 1951–unkn.

CAMPAIGNS. Air Offensive, Europe; Normandy; Northern France; Rhineland; Ardennes-Alsace; Central Europe.

DECORATIONS. Distinguished Unit Citation: Brunswick, Germany, 8 May 1944. French Croix de Guerre with Palm: 1 Jan 1945.

INSIGNE. *Shield:* Azure, a stylized aircraft bendwise above and between two clouds issuing from dexter and sinister base all argent, the dexter cloud pierced by two lightning flashes saltirewise or; in chief two mullets gules, fimbriated of the second and in base three of the like. *Motto*: CUSTODES PRO DEFENSIONE—Guardians for Defense. (Approved 9 Mar 1954.)

353d FIGHTER GROUP

VINCET AMOR PATRIAE

Constituted as 353d Fighter Group on 29 Sep 1942. *Activated* on 1 Oct 1942. Trained for duty overseas and at the same time served as an air defense organization. Moved to England, May–Jun 1943. Assigned to Eighth AF. Operated against the enemy in combat over Europe from Aug 1943 to Apr 1945, using P–47's until conversion to P–51's in Oct 1944. Regularly escorted bombers that attacked industrial establishments, marshalling yards, submarine installations, V-weapon sites, and other targets; frequently strafed and dive-bombed buildings, troops, flak batteries, barges and tug boats, locomotives and rail lines, vehicles, bridges, and airfields; also flew numerous counter-air missions. From Aug 1943 to Feb 1944, provided escort for bombers that attacked targets in western Europe, made counter-air sweeps over France and the Low Countries, and dive-bombed targets in France. Participated in the intensive campaign against the German Air Force and aircraft industry during Big Week, 20–25 Feb 1944. Increased its fighter-bomber activities, Mar–May 1944. Provided cover over the beachhead and close support for the Normandy invasion in Jun 1944. Supported the breakthrough at St Lo in Jul. Received a DUC for supporting the airborne attack on Holland, when the group contributed to the operation by protecting bombers and troop carriers and by strafing and dive-bombing ground targets during the period 17–23 Sep 1944. Continued its fighter-bomber, escort, and counter-air activities, participating in the Battle of the Bulge (Dec 1944–Jan 1945) and the airborne attack across the Rhine (Mar 1945). Remained in the theater until Oct. *Inactivated* in the US on 18 Oct 1945.

Redesignated 116th Fighter Group. Allotted to ANG (Ga) on 24 May 1946. Extended federal recognition on 9 Sep 1946. Ordered to active duty on 10 Oct 1950. *Redesignated* 116th Fighter-Bomber Group in Nov 1950. Assigned to Tactical Air Command. Trained with F–80's and converted to F–84 aircraft in the spring of 1951. Moved to Japan in Jul 1951 and attached to Far East Air Forces for operations in the Korean War. Flew interdictory and close-support missions, strafing and dive-bombing power plants, buildings, mine entrances, gun positions, bunkers, troops, rail lines, trains, bridges, and vehicles. During the same period, also provided air defense for Japan. Relieved from active duty, returned to control of ANG (Ga) without personnel and equipment, and *redesignated* 116th Fighter-Interceptor Group, on 10 Jul 1952. *Redesignated* 116th Fighter-Bomber Group in Dec 1952.

SQUADRONS. *196th:* 1950–1952. *350th:* 1942–1945. *351st* (later 158th): 1942–1945; 1950–1952. *352d* (later 159th): 1942–1945; 1950–1952.

STATIONS. Mitchel Field, NY, 1 Oct 1942; Richmond AAB, Va, c. 7 Oct 1942; Baltimore, Md, c. 26 Oct 1942–c. 27 May 1943; Goxhill, England, Jun 1943; Metfield, England, 3 Aug 1943; Raydon, England, Apr 1944–Oct 1945; Camp Kilmer, NJ, c. 16–18 Oct 1945. Dobbins AFB, Ga, 10 Oct 1950; George AFB, Calif, c. 25 Oct 1950–Jul 1951; Misawa, Japan, c. 25 Jul 1951–10 Jul 1952.

COMMANDERS. Lt Col Joseph A Morris, c. 15 Oct 1942; Lt Col Loren G McCollom, 18 Aug 1943; Col Glenn E Duncan, 25 Nov 1943; Col Ben Rimerman, 7 Jul 1944; Col Glenn E Duncan, 22 Apr 1945; Lt Col William B Bailey, 9 Sep 1945; Lt Col Robert A Elder, 24 Sep 1945–unkn. Col Charles M Ford Jr, 10 Oct–1 Nov 1950; Lt Col Howard L Galbreath, 11 Nov 1950; Lt Col Ralph G Kuhn, 8 May 1951–unkn;

Lt Col Daniel F Sharp, c. 31 Jan 1952–unkn.

CAMPAIGNS. *World War II:* Air Offensive, Europe; Normandy; Northern France; Rhineland; Ardennes-Alsace; Central Europe. *Korean War:* UN Summer-Fall Offensive; Second Korean Winter; Korea Summer-Fall, 1952.

DECORATIONS. Distinguished Unit Citation: Holland, 17–23 Sep 1944.

INSIGNE. *Shield:* Per fess embattled debased azure and argent, three chevronels reversed of the second, the base chevronel fimbriated, forming a frazure at its apex over the embattlement azure; in chief four darts of the second in formation chevronwise points downward, one in fess point, two in sinister, all within a diminutive border argent. *Motto:* VINCET AMOR PATRIAE—Love of Country Shall Conquer. (Approved 6 Jun 1952.)

354th FIGHTER GROUP

Constituted as 354th Fighter Group on 12 Nov 1942 and *activated* on 15 Nov. Trained with P-39's and served as part of the air defense force. Moved to England, Oct–Nov 1943. Assigned to Ninth AF and engaged in combat from Dec 1943 to May 1945, using P-51's except for the period from Nov 1944 to Feb 1945 when the group operated with P-47's. Received a DUC for its activities up to mid-May 1944, a period in which the 354th was instrumental in the development and execution of long-range missions to escort heavy bombers on raids deep into enemy terri-

VALOR IN COMBAT

tory. During that same period Maj James H Howard won the Medal of Honor for his single-handed efforts to defend a bomber formation that was attacked by a large force of enemy planes while on a mission over Germany on 11 Jan 1944. In addition to its escort work, the group began fighter-bomber operations, strafing and dive-bombing enemy airfields, gun positions, marshalling yards, and vehicles in France, Belgium, and Holland. Supporting the Normandy invasion in Jun 1944 by escorting gliders on D–Day and by dive-bombing and strafing bridges and railways near the front lines for the next few days. Moved to the Continent in Jun and assisted the Allied drive across France by flying close-support, armed-reconnaissance, fighter-sweep, dive-bombing, strafing, and escort missions. Received second DUC for a series of fighter sweeps in which the group destroyed a large number of enemy aircraft in the air and on the ground on 25 Aug 1944. Flew missions to support the airborne attack on Holland in Sep 1944. Attacked and destroyed many enemy barges, locomotives, vehicles, buildings, and troops to assist the Allied assault on the Siegfried Line. Participated in the Battle of the Bulge, Dec 1944–Jan 1945, by supporting ground forces and by conducting armed reconnaissance operations to destroy enemy troops, tanks, artillery, and rail lines. Assisted ground forces in their advance to and across the Rhine, Feb–May 1945. After V–E Day, served with the army of occupation, being assigned to United States Air Forces in Europe. Transferred, without personnel and equipment, to the US in Feb 1946. *Inactivated* on 31 Mar 1946.

(NOTE: The 354th Fighter Group was redesignated 117th Fighter Group and allotted to ANG (Ala), on 24 May 1946. The redesignation and the allotment were, however, revoked and nullified on 26 Sep 1956; at the same time the 117th group was constituted and allotted to ANG, effective 24 May 1946. Thus the 117th group is not related in any way to the 354th group.)

Redesignated 354th Fighter-Day Group. *Activated* on 19 Nov 1956. Assigned to Tactical Air Command.

SQUADRONS. *353d:* 1942–1946; 1956–. *355th:* 1942–1946; 1956–. *356th:* 1942–1946; 1956–.

STATIONS. Hamilton Field, Calif, 15 Nov 1942; Tonopah, Nev, c. 18 Jan 1943; Santa Rosa AAFld, Calif, c. 1 Mar 1943; Portland AAB, Ore, c. 2 Jun–Oct 1943; Greenham Common, England, c. 4 Nov 1943; Boxted, England, c. 13 Nov 1943;

Lashenden, England, Apr 1944; Criqueville, France, Jun 1944; Gael, France, Aug 1944; Orconte, France, Sep 1944; Meurthe-et-Moselle, France, c. 1 Dec 1944; Ober Olm, Germany, c. 8 Apr 1945; Ansbach, Germany, c. 30 Apr 1945; Herzogenaurach, Germany, May 1945–15 Feb 1946; Bolling Field, DC, 15 Feb–31 Mar 1946. Myrtle Beach AFB, SC, 19 Nov 1956–.

COMMANDERS. Col Kenneth R Martin, c. 26 Nov 1942; Col James H Howard, 12 Feb 1944; Col George R Bickell, Apr 1944; Lt Col Jack T Bradley, May 1945; Maj Robert A Ackerly, Nov 1945; Lt Col David L Lewis, Dec 1945–1946. Col James F Hackler Jr, 19 Nov 1956–.

CAMPAIGNS. Air Offensive, Europe; Normandy; Northern France; Rhineland; Ardennes-Alsace; Central Europe.

DECORATIONS. Distinguished Unit Citations: ETO, [Dec] 1943–15 May 1944; France, 25 Aug 1944. French Croix de Guerre with Palm: 1 Dec 1943–31 Dec 1944.

INSIGNE. *Shield:* Argent, four bendlets light blue, azure, gules and vert between a demi-horse rampant of the fourth and two swords saltirewise proper grip and guard of the third fimbriated or. *Motto:* VALOR IN COMBAT. (Approved 18 Oct 1957.)

355th FIGHTER GROUP

Constituted as 355th Fighter Group on 12 Nov 1942 and *activated* the same day. Prepared for combat with P–47's. Moved

OUR MIGHT ALWAYS

to England in Jul 1943 and assigned to Eighth AF. Flew its first combat mission, a fighter sweep over Belgium, on 14 Sep 1943 and afterward served primarily as escort for bombers that attacked industrial areas of Berlin, marshalling yards at Karlsruhe, an airfield at Neuberg, oil refineries at Misburg, synthetic oil plants at Gelsenkirchen, locks at Minden, and other objectives. Also flew fighter sweeps, area patrols, and bombing missions, striking such targets as air parks, locomotives, bridges, radio stations, and armored cars. On 5 Apr 1944, shortly after converting from P–47's to P–51's, the group successfully bombed and strafed German airdromes during a snow squall, a mission for which the group was awarded a DUC. Provided fighter cover for Allied forces landing in Normandy on 6 Jun 1944, and afterward hit transportation facilities to cut enemy supply lines. Hit fuel dumps, locomotives, and other targets in support of ground forces during the breakthrough at St Lo in Jul. Continued operations until 25 Apr 1945 and remained in the theater after the war for duty with United States Air Forces in Europe. Moved to Germany in Jul 1945 as part of the army of

occupation. Transferred, without personnel and equipment, to the US on 1 Aug
1946. *Inactivated* on 20 Nov 1946.

Redesignated 355th Fighter Group (Air
Defense). *Activated* on 18 Aug 1955.
Assigned to Air Defense Command and
equipped with F–86 aircraft.

SQUADRONS. *354th:* 1942–1946; 1955–.
357th: 1942–1946. *358th* (later 56th):
1942–1946. *469th:* 1955–.

STATIONS. Orlando AB, Fla, 12 Nov
1942; Richmond AAB, Va, 17 Feb 1943;
Philadelphia Mun Aprt, Pa, 4 Mar–16 Jun
1943; Steeple Morden, England, 9 Jul
1943; Gablingen, Germany, 3 Jul 1945;
Schweinfurt, Germany, 15 Apr 1946;
Mitchel Field, NY, 1 Aug–20 Nov 1946.
McGhee-Tyson Aprt, Tenn, 18 Aug 1955–.

COMMANDERS. Col William J Cum-
mings Jr, 12 Nov 1942; Lt Col Everett W
Stewart, 4 Nov 1944; Lt Col Claiborne H
Kinnard Jr, 21 Feb 1945; Lt Col William
D Gilchrist, 7 Jun 1945; Lt Col John L
Elder, Oct 1945; Col Carroll W McColpin,
14 Mar 1946–unkn. Col William A Lan-
ford, 18 Aug 1955–.

CAMPAIGNS. Air Offensive, Europe;
Normandy; Northern France; Rhineland;
Ardennes-Alsace; Central Europe.

DECORATIONS. Distinguished Unit Citation: Germany, 5 Apr 1944.

INSIGNE. *Shield:* Azure on a pile issuant from sinister throughout or, flames of
fire proper charged with a dagger fesswise
point to dexter of the second. *Motto:*
OUR MIGHT ALWAYS. (Approved
16 Mar 1943.)

356th FIGHTER GROUP

Constituted as 356th Fighter Group on
8 Dec 1942 and *activated* on 12 Dec.
Moved to England, Aug–Sep 1943, and
assigned to Eighth AF. Served in combat from Oct 1943 to May 1945, participating in operations that prepared for the
invasion of the Continent, and supporting
the landings in Normandy and the subsequent Allied drive across France and
Germany. Used P–47's until they were
replaced by P–51's in Nov 1944. From Oct
1943 until Jan 1944, operated as escort for
bombers that attacked such objectives as
industrial areas, missile sites, airfields, and
communications. Engaged primarily in
bombing and strafing missions after 23
Jan 1944, with its targets including U-boat
installations, barges, shipyards, airdromes,
hangars, marshalling yards, locomotives,
trucks, oil facilities, flak towers, and radar
stations. Bombed and strafed in the

Arnheim area on 17, 18, and 23 Sep 1944 to neutralize enemy gun emplacements; received a DUC for this contribution to the airborne attack on Holland. Flew its last combat mission, escorting B–17's dropping propaganda leaflets, on 7 May 1945. Returned to the US in Nov. *Inactivated* on 10 Nov 1945.

Redesignated 118th Fighter Group. Allotted to ANG (Tenn) on 24 May 1946. Extended federal recognition on 2 Oct 1947. *Redesignated* 118th Composite Group in Nov 1950, and 118th Tactical Reconnaissance Group in Feb 1951. Ordered to active duty on 1 Apr 1951 and assigned to Tactical Air Command. Used RF–47, RF–51, RF–80, and RB–26 aircraft for training and maneuvers. Relieved from active service and returned, without personnel and equipment, to control of ANG (Tenn) on 1 Jan 1953.

SQUADRONS. *106th*: 1951–1953. *185th*: 1951–1953. *359th* (later 155th): 1942–1945; 1951–1953. *360th*: 1942–1945. *361st*: 1942–1945.

STATIONS. Westover Field, Mass, 12 Dec 1942; Groton AAFld, Conn, 12 Mar 1943; Mitchel Field, NY, 30 May 1943; Grenier Field, NH, 4 Jul–15 Aug 1943; Goxhill, England, 27 Aug 1943; Martlesham, England, 5 Oct 1943–4 Nov 1945; Camp Kilmer, NJ, 9–10 Nov 1945. Berry Field, Tenn, 1 Apr 1951; Memphis Mun Aprt, Tenn, 12 Apr 1951; Shaw AFB, SC, 15 Jan 1952–1 Jan 1953.

COMMANDERS. 2d Lt Joseph Moris Jr, 28 Dec 1942; Capt Harold J Lister, 29 Dec 1942; Lt Col Harold J Rau, 9 Feb 1943;

Col Einar A Malmstrom, 28 Nov 1943; Lt Col Philip E Tukey Jr, 24 Apr 1944; Lt Col Donald A Baccus, 3 Nov 1944; Col Philip E Tukey Jr, 11 Jan 1945–unkn. Lt Col Enoch B Stephenson, 1 Apr 1951; Lt Col William J Johnson Jr, May 1951; Lt Col Ralph F Newman, 16 Aug 1951; Col James L Rose, Jan 1952; Lt Col Stanley W Irons, 2 Jun 1952; Col Robert R Smith, Nov 1952–unkn.

CAMPAIGNS. Air Offensive, Europe; Normandy; Northern France; Rhineland; Ardennes-Alsace; Central Europe.

DECORATIONS. Distinguished Unit Citation: Holland, 17, 18, and 23 Sep 1944.

INSIGNE. On a blue oval with a yellow border an aerial camera supporting binoculars and a torch, the whole group winged, all yellow with flame proper and lenses blue and white, above the torch and between the tips of the wings three white stars. (Approved 5 Jan 1954.)

357th FIGHTER GROUP

Constituted as 357th Fighter Group on 1 Dec 1942 and *activated* the same day. Used P–39's in preparing for duty overseas. Moved to England in Nov 1943 and became part of Eighth AF. Trained with P–51's and began operations on 11 Feb 1944 by making a fighter sweep over Rouen. Served primarily as an escort organization, providing penetration, target, and withdrawal support for bombers that attacked strategic objectives on the Continent. Participated in the assault against the German Air Force and aircraft indus-

SEMPER OMNIA

try during Big Week, 20–25 Feb 1944. Received a DUC for two escort missions in which heavy opposition was encountered from enemy fighters: on 6 Mar 1944 provided target and withdrawal support during the first attack that heavy bombers of Eighth AF made on Berlin; on 29 Jun 1944 protected bombers that struck targets at Leipzig. Received second DUC for operations on 14 Jan 1945 when the group, covering bombers on a raid to Derben, broke up an attack by a large force of interceptors and in the ensuing aerial battle destroyed a number of the enemy planes. In addition to escort the group conducted counter-air patrols, made fighter sweeps, and flew strafing and dive-bombing missions in which it attacked airdromes, marshalling yards, locomotives, bridges, barges, tugboats, highways, vehicles, fuel dumps, and other targets. Participated in the invasion of Normandy in Jun 1944; the breakthrough at St Lo in Jul; the Battle of the Bulge, Dec 1944–

Jan 1945; and the airborne assault across the Rhine in Mar 1945. Flew its last mission, an escort operation, on 25 Apr 1945. Moved to Germany in Jul and assigned to United States Air Forces in Europe for duty with the army of occupation. *Inactivated* in Germany on 20 Aug 1946.

Redesignated 121st Fighter Group. Allotted to ANG (Ohio) on 21 Aug 1946. Extended federal recognition on 26 Jun 1948. *Redesignated* 121st Fighter-Bomber Group on 16 Oct 1952.

SQUADRONS. *362d:* 1942–1946. *363d:* 1942–1946. *364th* (later 166th): 1942–1946.

STATIONS. Hamilton Field, Calif, 1 Dec 1942; Tonopah AAFld, Nev, 4 Mar 1943; Santa Rosa AAFld, Calif, 3 Jun 1943; Oroville AAFld, Calif, 18 Aug 1943; Casper AAFld, Wyo, 7 Oct–9 Nov 1943; Raydon, England, 30 Nov 1943; Leiston, England, 31 Jan 1944–8 Jul 1945; Neubiberg, Germany, 21 Jul 1945–20 Aug 1946.

COMMANDERS. Lt Col Loring F Stetson Jr, 1 Dec 1942; Lt Col Edwin S Chickering, 7 Jul 1943; Col Henry R Spicer, 17 Feb 1944; Col Donald W Graham, 7 Mar 1944; Lt Col John D Landers, 11 Oct 1944; Col Irwin H Dregne, 2 Dec 1944; Lt Col Andrew J Evans Jr, 21 Jul 1945; Lt Col Wayne E Rhynard, c. 20 Nov 1945; Col Barton M Russell, Apr 1946–unkn.

CAMPAIGNS. Air Offensive, Europe; Normandy; Northern France; Rhineland; Ardennes-Alsace; Central Europe.

DECORATIONS. Distinguished Unit Citations: Germany, 6 Mar and 29 Jun 1944; Derben, Germany, 14 Jan 1945. French

Croix de Guerre with Palm: 11 Feb 1944–15 Jan 1945.

INSIGNE. *Shield:* Per fess nebuly azure and or, in chief a chaplet azure and argent winged or, in base a cubit arm in armor brandishing a sword proper hilted bronze. *Motto:* SEMPER OMNIA—All Things at All Times. (Approved 27 May 1953.)

358th FIGHTER GROUP

Constituted as 358th Fighter Group on 20 Dec 1942. *Activated* on 1 Jan 1943. Trained with P-47's. Moved to England during Sep–Oct 1943. Began operations on 20 Dec 1943 and served in combat with Eighth and, later, Ninth AF until V-E Day. Engaged in escort work until Apr 1944 to cover the operations of bombers that the AAF sent against targets on the Continent. Dive-bombed marshalling yards and airfields during Apr to help prepare for the invasion of Normandy. Continued attacks on enemy communications and flew escort missions during May. Escorted troop carriers over the Cotentin Peninsula on 6 and 7 Jun, and attacked bridges, rail lines and trains, vehicles, and troop concentrations during the remainder of the month. Moved to the Continent in Jul and took part in operations that resulted in the Allied breakthrough at St Lo. Continued to fly escort, interdictory, and close-support missions during the Allied drive across France and into Germany, earning four citations before the end of the war. Received first DUC for operations from 24 Dec 1944 to 2 Jan 1945 when the group not only supported Seventh Army by attacking rail lines and rolling stock, vehicles, buildings, and artillery, but also destroyed numerous fighter planes during a major assault by the German Air Force against Allied airfields. Received second DUC for 19–20 Mar 1945, a period in which the 358th destroyed and damaged large numbers of motor transports and thus hampered the evacuation of German forces that were withdrawing from the area west of the Rhine. Received third DUC for performance between 8 and 25 Apr 1945 when the group attacked enemy airfields in the region of Munich and Ingolstadt, engaged the enemy in aerial combat, and supported advancing ground forces by attacking such targets as motor transports, tanks, locomotives, guns, and buildings. Received fourth citation, the French Croix de Guerre with Palm, for assisting in the liberation of France. Returned to the US in Jul 1945. *Inactivated* on 7 Nov 1945.

Redesignated 122d Fighter Group. Allotted to ANG (Ind) on 24 May 1946.

Extended federal recognition on 9 Dec 1946. Ordered into active service on 1 Feb 1951. Assigned to Air Defense Command. *Redesignated* 122d Fighter-Interceptor Group. Trained with F–51 and F–84 aircraft. *Inactivated* on 7 Feb 1952. Relieved from active service, returned to ANG (Ind), *redesignated* 122d Fighter-Bomber Group, and *activated,* on 1 Nov 1952.

SQUADRONS. *113th:* 1951–1952. *166th:* 1951–1952. *365th* (later 163d): 1943–1945; 1951–1952. *366th:* 1943–1945. *367th:* 1943–1945.

STATIONS. Richmond AAB, Va, 1 Jan 1943; Baltimore, Md, 28 Apr 1943; Camp Springs AAFld, Md, 28 May 1943; Philadelphia Mun Aprt, Pa, 16 Jun 1943; Richmond AAB, Va, 13 Aug–25 Sep 1943; Goxhill, England, 20 Oct 1943; Leiston, England, 29 Nov 1943; Raydon, England, 31 Jan 1944; High Halden, England, 13 Apr 1944; Cretteville, France, 3 Jul 1944; Pontorson, France, 14 Aug 1944; Vitry-le-Francois, France, 14 Sep 1944; Mourmelon, France, 16 Oct 1944; Toul, France, 9 Nov 1944; Sandhofen, Germany, 2 Apr 1945; Reims, France, c. 23 Jun–Jul 1945; La Junta AAFld, Colo, 3 Aug–7 Nov 1945. Stout Field, Ind, 1 Feb 1951; Baer Field, Ind, 10 Mar 1951–7 Feb 1952.

COMMANDERS. Col Cecil L Wells, 1 Jan 1943; Col James B Tipton, 20 Sep 1944–unkn; Lt Col John M Thacker, 1945. Col John A Carey, 1951–c. Feb 1952.

CAMPAIGNS. American Theater; Air Offensive, Europe; Normandy; Northern France; Rhineland; Ardennes-Alsace; Central Europe.

DECORATIONS. Distinguished Unit Citations: Ardennes, 24 Dec 1944–2 Jan 1945; ETO, 19–20 Mar 1945; Germany, 8–25 Apr 1945. French Croix de Guerre with Palm.

INSIGNE. *Shield:* Azure (light blue) a bordure or (Air Force yellow), overall and saltirewise an escutcheon in prospect, (per bend or and sable, in chief four mullets of the last) and a jet type aircraft with exhaust fire all proper. *Motto:* CONQUER ABOVE. (Approved 28 Jul 1954.)

359th FIGHTER GROUP

Constituted as 359th Fighter Group on 20 Dec 1942. *Activated* on 15 Jan 1943. Apparently not manned until Mar 1943. Moved to England in Oct 1943 and became part of Eighth AF. Entered combat in mid-Dec, after some of the pilots had already flown combat missions with another fighter group. Began operations with P-47's; converted to P-51's in Apr 1944. In combat, Dec 1943–May 1945, flew escort, patrol, strafing, dive-bombing, and weather-reconnaissance missions. At first, engaged primarily in escort activities to cover bombers that attacked airfields in France. Expanded area of operations in May 1944 to provide escort for bombers that struck rail centers in Germany and oil targets in Poland. Supported the invasion of Normandy (Jun 1944), patrolling the English Channel, escorting bombardment formations to the French coast, and dive-bombing and strafing bridges, locomotives, and rail lines near the battle area. During the period Jul 1944–Feb 1945, engaged chiefly in escorting bombers to oil refineries, marshalling yards, and other targets in such cities as Ludwigshafen, Stuttgart, Frankfurt, Berlin, Merseburg, and Brux. Received a DUC for operations over Germany on 11 Sep 1944 when the group protected a formation of heavy bombers against large numbers of enemy fighters. In addition to its escort duties, the group supported campaigns in France during Jul and Aug 1944, bombed enemy positions to support the airborne invasion of Holland in Sep, and participated in the Battle of the Bulge (Dec 1944–Jan 1945). Flew missions to support the assault across the Rhine in Mar 1945, and escorted medium bombers that attacked various communications targets, Feb–Apr 1945. Returned to the US in Nov 1945. *Inactivated* on 10 Nov 1945.

Redesignated 123d Fighter Group. Allotted to ANG (Ky) on 24 May 1946. Extended federal recognition on 20 Sep 1947. Ordered into active service on 10 Oct 1950. *Redesignated* 123d Fighter-Bomber Group. Assigned to Tactical Air Command. Trained with F-51's until late in 1951. Converted to F-84's in Nov and moved to England to become part of United States Air Forces in Europe. Transferred to the US without personnel and equipment, relieved from active duty, returned to control of ANG (Ky), and *redesignated* 123d Fighter-Interceptor Group, on 10 Jul 1952. *Redesignated* 123d Fighter-Bomber Group in Jan 1953.

SQUADRONS. *156th:* 1950–1952. *368th* (later 165th): 1943–1945; 1950–1952. *369th* (later 167th): 1943–1945; 1950–1952. *370th:* 1943–1945.

STATIONS. Westover Field, Mass, 15 Jan 1943; Grenier Field, NH, 7 Apr 1943; Republic Field, NY, 11 Jul 1943; Westover Field, Mass, 23 Aug–2 Oct 1943; East Wretham, England, Oct 1943–Nov 1945; Camp Kilmer, NJ, 9–10 Nov 1945. Standiford Mun Aprt, Ky, 10 Oct 1950; Godman AFB, Ky, c. 20 Oct 1950–15 Nov 1951; Manston RAF Station, England, 10 Dec 1951–10 Jul 1952.

COMMANDERS. Col Avelin P Tacon Jr, Jan 1943; Col John P Randolph, 12 Nov 1944; Lt Col Donald A Baccus, 8 Apr 1945; Lt Col Daniel D McKee, c. 16 Sep 1945–unkn. Col Philip P Ardery, 10 Oct 1950; Lt Col William J Payne, 26 Oct 1950; Lt Col Chesley G Peterson, 20 Apr 1951; Lt

Col Delynn E Anderson, 4 Aug 1951–Jul 1952.

CAMPAIGNS. Air Offensive, Europe; Normandy; Northern France; Rhineland; Ardennes-Alsace; Central Europe.

DECORATIONS. Distinguished Unit Citation: Germany, 11 Sep 1944.

INSIGNE. *Shield*: Per chevron, azure and or; in base a star argent over a hurt, between a bar voided per roundle azure; three rays issuing from the hurt to three winged plates argent, over three billets or, in chief; over all a chevron, per chevron, of the last and gules; the shield edged in chief or. *Motto*: FORTES FORTUNA JUVAT—Fortune Assists the Brave. (Approved 20 Dec 1951.)

360th FIGHTER GROUP

Constituted as 360th Fighter Group on 20 Dec 1942. *Activated* on 15 Jan 1943. Assigned to Fourth AF. Used P–38's to train replacement crews for combat. *Disbanded* on 31 Mar 1944.

SQUADRONS. *371st:* 1943–1944. *372d:* 1943–1944. *373d:* 1943–1944. *446th:* 1943–1944.

STATIONS. Glendale, Calif, 15 Jan 1943; Muroc AAB, Calif, 14 Apr 1943; Salinas AAB, Calif, 22 Sep 1943; Santa Maria AAFld, Calif, 11 Jan–31 Mar 1944.

COMMANDERS. Maj Frederick C Grambo, 19 Jan 1943; Lt Col John S Chennault, May 1943–31 Mar 1944.

CAMPAIGNS. American Theater.

DECORATIONS. None.

INSIGNE. None.

361st FIGHTER GROUP

Constituted as 361st Fighter Group on 28 Jan 1943. *Activated* on 10 Feb 1943. Joined Eighth AF in England in Nov 1943. Entered combat with P–47 aircraft on 21 Jan 1944 and converted to P–51's in May 1944. Operated from England during 1944 but sent a detachment to France for operations in the Battle of the Bulge (Dec 1944–Jan 1945), moved to Belgium in Feb 1945, and returned to England in Apr 1945. Served primarily as an escort organization, covering the penetration, attack, and withdrawal of bomber formations that the AAF sent against targets on the Continent. Also engaged in counter-air patrols, fighter sweeps, and strafing and dive-bombing missions. Attacked such targets as airdromes, marshalling yards, missile sites, industrial areas, ordnance depots, oil refineries, trains, and highways. During its operations, participated in the assault against the German Air Force and aircraft industry during Big Week, 20–25 Feb 1944; the Normandy invasion, Jun 1944;

the St Lo breakthrough, Jul 1944; the airborne attack on Holland, Sep 1944; and the airborne assault across the Rhine, Mar 1945. Flew last combat mission on 20 Apr 1945. Returned to the US in Nov. *Inactivated* on 10 Nov 1945.

Redesignated 127th Fighter Group. Allotted to ANG (Mich) on 24 May 1946. Extended federal recognition on 29 Sep 1946. Ordered into active service on 1 Feb 1951. Assigned to Air Training Command. *Redesignated* 127th Pilot Training Group in Mar 1951. Used F-51, F-80, and F-84 aircraft while serving as a training organization. Relieved from active duty and returned to ANG (Mich), on 1 Nov 1952. *Redesignated* 127th Fighter-Bomber Group.

SQUADRONS. *107th:* 1951-1952. *197th:* 1951-1952. *374th* (later 171st): 1943-1945; 1951-1952. *375th:* 1943-1945. *376th:* 1943-1945.

STATIONS. Richmond AAB, Va, 10 Feb 1943; Langley Field, Va, 26 May 1943; Millville AAFld, NJ, 20 Jul 1943; Camp Springs AAFld, Md, 28 Aug 1943; Richmond AAB, Va, 20 Sep-11 Nov 1943; Bottisham, England, 30 Nov 1943; Little Walden, England, 26 Sep 1944; Chievres, Belgium, 1 Feb-Apr 1945; Little Walden, England, 9 Apr-3 Nov 1945; Camp Kilmer, NJ, 9-10 Nov 1945; Detroit-Wayne Major Aprt, Mich, 1 Feb 1951; Luke AFB, Ariz, 23 Feb 1951-1 Nov 1952.

COMMANDERS. Col Thomas J J Christian Jr, 10 Feb 1943; Col Ronald F Fallows, 14 Aug 1944; Lt Col Roy B Caviness, 31 Aug 1944; Lt Col Joseph J Kruzel, 20 Sep 1944; Lt Col Roy B Caviness, 3 Nov 1944; Col Junius W Dennison Jr, 2 Dec 1944; Lt Col Roy B Caviness, 15 Apr 1945; Col John D Landers, 29 Jun 1945-unkn. Col David T McKnight, 1951; Col Maurice L Martin, 6 Aug 1951-unkn.

CAMPAIGNS. Air Offensive, Europe; Normandy; Northern France; Rhineland; Ardennes-Alsace; Central Europe.

DECORATIONS. None.

INSIGNE. *Shield:* Gules (scarlet) a bendlet divided per bend into five equal parts, the center azure, and the outer two or, and of the first (dark red), between in chief three fleur-de-lis in pale, of the third, and in base a giant (Saguaro) cactus footed to the sinister by an apple blossom stemmed both proper. *Motto:* PARATI STAMUS—We Stand Ready. (Approved 30 Jul 1954.)

362d FIGHTER GROUP

Constituted as 362d Fighter Group on 11 Feb 1943. *Activated* on 1 Mar 1943. Trained for combat with P-47's. Moved to England in Nov 1943. Assigned to Ninth AF. Flew first mission, escorting B-24's that attacked V-weapon launching sites near Pas de Calais, on 8 Feb 1944. Until Apr 1944, engaged chiefly in escorting bombers that struck factories, railroads, airfields, and other targets on the Continent. Repeatedly attacked communications in northern France and in Belgium during Apr and May, in preparation for the invasion of Normandy. Escorted C-47's that dropped paratroops

SURSUM PRORSUSQUE

over Normandy on 6 and 7 Jun. After-ward, engaged primarily in interdictory and close-support activities, flying strafing and dive-bombing missions designed to assist the operations of ground forces. Moved to the Continent early in Jul 1944 and bombed enemy troops to aid the Allied breakthrough at St Lo later that month. Supported the subsequent advance of ground forces toward the Rhine by attacking railroads, trucks, bridges, power stations, fuel dumps, and other facilities. Received a DUC for a mission against the harbor at Brest on 25 Aug 1944 when, in spite of heavy overcast and intense enemy fire, the group attacked at low altitude, hitting naval installations, cruisers, troop transports, merchant vessels, and other objectives. Bombed and strafed such targets as flak positions, armored vehicles, and troop concentrations during the Battle of the Bulge, Dec 1944–Jan 1945. Received second DUC for action over the Moselle-Rhine River triangle:

despite the intense antiaircraft fire encountered while flying armed reconnaissance in close cooperation with infantry forces in that area on 16 Mar 1945, the group hit enemy forces, equipment, and facilities, its targets including motor transports, armored vehicles, railroads, railway cars, and gun emplacements. Continued operations until 1 May 1945. Returned to the US, Aug–Sep 1945. Trained with P–51's. *Inactivated* on 1 Aug 1946.

Redesignated 128th Fighter Group. Allotted to ANG (Wis) on 2 Aug 1946. Extended federal recognition on 29 Jun 1948. Ordered to active duty on 1 Feb 1951. Assigned to Air Defense Command. *Redesignated* 128th Fighter-Interceptor Group. *Inactivated* on 6 Feb 1952. Relieved from active duty, returned to ANG (Wis), and *activated,* on 1 Nov 1952.

SQUADRONS. *126th:* 1951–1952. *172d:* 1951–1952. *176th:* 1951–1952. *377th:* 1943–1946. *378th:* 1943–1946. *379th:* 1943–1946.

STATIONS. Westover Field, Mass, 1 Mar 1943; Bradley Field, Conn, 22 Jun 1943; Groton Field, Conn, 2 Aug 1943; Mitchel Field, NY, 19 Oct–12 Nov 1943; Wormingford, England, 30 Nov 1943; Headcorn, England, 13 Apr 1944; Lignerolles, France, 2 Jul 1944; Rennes, France, 10 Aug 1944; Prosnes, France, 19 Sep 1944; Rouvres, France, 5 Nov 1944; Frankfurt, Germany, 8 Apr 1945; Furth, Germany, 30 Apr 1945; Illesheim, Germany, 3 May 1945; Straubing, Germany, 12 May–Aug 1945; Seymour Johnson Field, NC, 5 Sep

1945; Biggs Field, Tex, 3 Dec 1945–1 Aug 1946. General Billy Mitchell Field, Wis, 1 Feb 1951; Truax Field, Wis, 16 Feb 1951–6 Feb 1952.

COMMANDERS. Col Morton D Magoffin, 1 Mar 1943; Col Joseph L Laughlin, 10 Aug 1944–1 Aug 1946. Col Paul Fojtik, 1951–Feb 1952.

CAMPAIGNS. American Theater; Air Offensive, Europe; Normandy; Northern France; Rhineland; Ardennes-Alsace; Central Europe.

DECORATIONS. Distinguished Unit Citations: Brest, France, 25 Aug 1944; Moselle-Rhine River Triangle, 16 Mar 1945.

INSIGNE. *Shield:* Azure, a bend or between in chief, two barbs (triple pronged) of the last and a cumulo nimbus cloud proper issuing from base. Over all from dexter base, two parallel piles point to sinister chief, gules, points, sable. *Motto:* SURSUM PRORSUSQUE—Upward and Onward. (Approved 21 Apr 1954.)

363d RECONNAISSANCE GROUP

Constituted as 363d Fighter Group on 11 Feb 1943. *Activated* on 1 Mar 1943. Trained with P-39's and served as part of the air defense force. Moved to England in Dec 1943 for duty with Ninth AF. Equipped with P-51's in Jan 1944 and entered combat in Feb. Escorted bombers and fighter-bombers to targets in France, Germany, and the Low Countries; strafed and dive-bombed trains, marshalling yards, bridges, vehicles, airfields, troops, gun

positions, and other targets on the Continent. Supported the invasion of Normandy in Jun 1944 by escorting troop carriers and gliders and by attacking enemy positions near the front lines, and moved to the Continent at the end of Jun to take part in the Allied drive to the German border.

Redesignated 363d Tactical Reconnaissance Group in Sep 1944. Equipped with F-5 and F-6 aircraft. Flew photographic missions to support both air and ground operations; directed fighter-bombers to railway, highway, and waterway traffic, bridges, gun positions, troop concentrations, and other opportune targets; adjusted artillery fire; and took photographs to assess results of Allied bombardment operations. Received two Belgian citations for reconnaissance activities, including the group's support of the assault on the Siegfried Line and its participation in the Battle of the Bulge (Dec 1944–Jan 1945). Assisted Ninth Army's drive across the Rhine and deep into Germany during the period from Feb 1945 to V–E Day. *Redesignated* 363d Reconnaissance Group in Jun 1945. Returned to the US in Dec. *Inactivated* on 11 Dec 1945.

Activated on 29 Jul 1946. Equipped initially with RF–80 and RB–26 aircraft, and later with RF–84 and RB–57 aircraft. *Redesignated* 363d Tactical Reconnaissance Group in Jun 1948.

SQUADRONS. *9th:* 1953–. *12th:* 1946–1947. *17th:* 1951–. *31st:* 1945. *33d:* 1945. *39th:* 1945. *155th:* 1945. *160th* (formerly 380th, later 16th): 1943–1945; 1947–1949, 1950–. *161st* (formerly 381st, later 18th): 1943–1945; 1946–1949, 1951–. *162d* (formerly 382d): 1943–1944; 1946–1950.

STATIONS. Hamilton Field, Calif, 1 Mar 1943; Santa Rosa AAFld, Calif, Aug 1943; Sacramento, Calif, Oct–c. 3 Dec 1943; Keevil, England, c. 23 Dec 1943; Rivenhall, England, Jan 1944; Staplehurst, England, Apr 1944; Maupertuis, France, c. 1 Jul 1944; Azeville, France, Aug 1944; Le Mans, France, Sep 1944; Luxembourg, Luxembourg, c. 1 Oct 1944; Le Culot, Belgium, c. 29 Oct 1944; Venlo, Holland, Mar 1945; Gutersloh, Germany, c. 15 Apr 1945; Brunswick, Germany, c. 22 Apr 1945; Wiesbaden, Germany, May 1945; Eschwege, Germany, Aug 1945; Darmstadt, Germany, Sep–c. 2 Dec 1945; Camp Kilmer, NJ, c. 9–11 Dec 1945. Brooks Field, Tex, 29 Jul 1946; Langley Field, Va, Dec 1947; Shaw AFB, SC, c. 2 Apr 1951–.

COMMANDERS. Lt Col John R Ulricson, c. 1 Mar 1943; Capt Dave H Culberson, c. 8 Apr 1943; Maj Theodore C Bunker, c. 27 Apr 1943; Col John R Ulricson, 5 Jun 1943; Col James B Tipton, 7 May 1944; Col James M Smelley, c. 1 Sep 1944; Lt Col Seth A Mize, May 1945–unkn. Col Russell A Berg, 29 Jul 1946; Col John R Dyas, c. 23 Aug 1946; Col James M Smelley, 5 Nov 1947; Lt Col Walter W Berg, 30 Jun 1949; Col Willis F Chapman, 31 Oct 1949; Col Benjamin G Willis, 7 Sep 1950; Maj Charles N Keppler, c. 13 Mar 1951; Col Willie O Jackson Jr, 2 Apr 1951; Lt Col Robert R Smith, 1 Nov 1951; Lt Col Robert R Evans, 5 Mar 1952; Col John M McNabb, 17 Mar 1952; Col Robert R Smith, c. 4 Mar 1953; Col Paul A Pettigrew, c. 16 Mar 1955–.

CAMPAIGNS. Air Offensive, Europe; Normandy; Northern France; Rhineland; Ardennes-Alsace; Central Europe.

DECORATIONS. Cited in the Order of the Day, Belgian Army: 1 Oct 1944–; 18 Dec 1944–15 Jan 1945. Belgian Fourragere.

INSIGNE. *Shield:* Quarterly, first quarter checky, argent and gules; second and third quarters, azure; fourth quarter gules, a lion rampant or, armed and langued azure, all within a diminutive of the border or. Wreath of the colors, argent and gules. *Motto:* VOIR C'EST SAVOIR—To See is To Know. (Approved 16 Jun 1952.)

364th FIGHTER GROUP

Constituted as 364th Fighter Group on 25 May 1943. *Activated* on 1 Jun 1943. Trained with P–38's. Moved to England, Jan–Feb 1944. Began operations with

Eighth AF in Mar. Flew escort, dive-bombing, strafing, and patrol missions in France, Belgium, Holland, and Germany. At first, operated primarily as escort for heavy bombers. Patrolled the English Channel during the Normandy invasion in Jun 1944, and, while continuing escort operations, supported ground forces in France after the invasion by strafing and bombing locomotives, marshalling yards, bridges, barges, and other targets. Converted from P–38's to P–51's in the summer of 1944 and from then until the end of the war flew many long-range escort missions for B–17's that attacked oil refineries, industries, and other strategic objectives at Berlin, Regensburg, Merseburg, Stuttgart, Brussels, and elsewhere. Received a DUC for an escort mission on 27 Dec 1944 when the group dispersed a large force of German fighters that attacked the bomber formation the group was escorting on a raid to Frankfurt. Also flew air-sea rescue missions, engaged

in patrol activities, and continued to support ground forces as the battle line moved through France and into Germany. Took part in the effort to invade Holland by air, Sep 1944; the Battle of the Bulge, Dec 1944–Jan 1945; and the assault across the Rhine, Mar 1945. After the war, remained in England until Nov 1945. Returned to the US. *Inactivated* on 10 Nov 1945.

Redesignated 131st Fighter Group. Allotted to ANG (Mo) on 24 May 1946. Extended federal recognition on 15 Jul 1946. *Redesignated* 131st Composite Group in Nov 1950, and 131st Fighter Group in Feb 1951. Ordered into active service on 1 Mar 1951. Assigned to Strategic Air Command. *Redesignated* 131st Fighter-Bomber Group in Apr 1951. Assigned to Tactical Air Command in Nov 1951. Trained with F–51's. Relieved from active duty and returned to ANG (Mo), on 1 Dec 1952. *Redesignated* 131st Bombardment Group (Light).

SQUADRONS. *110th*: 1951–1952. *170th*: 1951–1952. *192d*: 1951–1952. *383d*: 1943–1945. *384th*: 1943–1945. *385th*: 1943–1945.

STATIONS. Glendale, Calif, 1 Jun 1943; Van Nuys, Calif, 12 Aug 1943; Ontario AAFld, Calif, 11 Oct 1943; Santa Maria AAFld, Calif, c. 7 Dec 1943–c. 11 Jan 1944; Honington, England, Feb 1944–c. Nov 1945; Camp Kilmer, NJ, 9–10 Nov 1945. Lambert Field, Mo, 1 Mar 1951; Bergstrom AFB, Tex, 10 Mar 1951; George AFB, Calif, 7 Aug 1951–1 Dec 1952.

COMMANDERS. Lt Col Frederick C Grambo, 12 Jun 1943; Col Roy W Osborn,

c. Mar 1944; Lt Col Joseph B McManus, c. 9 Sep 1944; Lt Col John W Lowell, c. 23 Oct 1944; Col Roy W Osborn, 2 Nov 1944; Lt Col Eugene P Roberts, 3 Jan–Nov 1945. Lt Col Val W Bollwerk, Mar 1951; Col Donald J M Blakeslee, c. Apr 1951; Col Woodrow W Ramsey, c. Dec 1951–1 Dec 1952.

CAMPAIGNS. Air Offensive, Europe; Normandy; Northern France; Rhineland; Ardennes-Alsace; Central Europe.

DECORATIONS. Distinguished Unit Citation: Frankfurt, Germany, 27 Dec 1944.

INSIGNE. *Shield:* Azure, on a pile issuing from sinister chief argent an aircraft rocket sable banded of the second leaving a trail gules between two general purpose aerial bombs in bend sinisterwise of the third. *Motto:* P A R A T I   A D   AGENDUM—Ready for Action. (Approved 29 Mar 1954.)

365th FIGHTER GROUP

Constituted as 365th Fighter Group on 27 Apr 1943. *Activated* on 15 May 1943. Trained with P–47's. Moved to England in Dec 1943. Began combat operations with Ninth AF in Feb 1944. Engaged in escort activities and flew dive-bombing missions to attack such targets as bridges, airdromes, rail facilities, gun positions, and V-weapon sites prior to the invasion of the Continent. Attacked rail targets and gun emplacements in France during the invasion on 6 Jun. Moved to the Continent late in Jun and continued to dive-bomb targets during the succeeding weeks of the

battle for Normandy. Bombed targets near St Lo in Jul to assist Allied forces in breaking through German lines at that point, and supported the subsequent drive across northern France during Aug–Sep. In Sep, also flew patrols in cooperation with airborne operations in Holland. Cited by the Belgian government for assisting Allied armies in the period from the invasion of Normandy through the initial phases of the liberation of Belgium. During the fall of 1944, operated in connection with the seizure of Aachen and aided ground troops in the offensive toward the Rhine, receiving a DUC for destroying and damaging numerous enemy fighters over the Bonn-Dusseldorf area in Germany on 21 Oct. Received second Belgian award for actions during the Battle of the Bulge when the group struck such targets as vehicles, rolling stock, marshalling yards, gun positions, factories, and towns. Provided cover during airborne operations across the Rhine in Mar 1945 and supported the drive into Germany. Awarded second DUC for operations on 20 Apr 1945 when the group attacked airfields, motor transports, and ammunition dumps to aid the Allied advance through southern Germany. Ended combat in May and took part in the disarmament program until Jun 1945. Moved to the US in Sep. *Inactivated* on 22 Sep 1945.

Redesignated 132d Fighter Group. Allotted to ANG (Iowa) on 24 May 1946. Extended federal recognition on 23 Aug 1946. Ordered into active service on 1 Apr 1951. Assigned to Strategic Air Command. *Redesignated* 132d Fighter-Bomber Group in Jun 1951. Assigned to Tactical Air Command in Nov 1951. Equipped with F–51's but with one squadron using F–84's until late in 1951. Relieved from active service and returned, less personnel and equipment, to ANG (Iowa), on 1 Jan 1953.

SQUADRONS. *124th:* 1951–1953. *173d:* 1951–1953. *386th* (later 174th): 1943–1945; 1951–1953. *387th:* 1943–1945. *388th:* 1943–1945.

STATIONS. Richmond AAB, Va, 15 May 1943; Langley Field, Va, 19 Jul 1943; Dover AAFld, Del, 11 Aug 1943; Richmond AAB, Va, 18 Nov–4 Dec 1943; Gosfield, England, 22 Dec 1943; Beaulieu, England, 5 Mar 1944; Azeville, France, 28 Jun 1944; Lignerolles, France, 15 Aug 1944; Bretigny, France, 3 Sep 1944; Juvincourt, France, 15 Sep 1944; Chievres, Belgium, 4 Oct 1944; Metz, France, 27 Dec 1944; Florennes/Juzaine, Belgium, 30 Jan 1945; Aachen, Germany, 16 Mar 1945; Fritzlar, Germany, 13 Apr 1945; Suippes,

France, c. 29 Jul 1945; Antwerp, Belgium, c. 22 Aug–11 Sep 1945; Camp Myles Standish, Mass, 20–22 Sep 1945. Des Moines Mun Aprt, Iowa, 1 Apr 1951; Dow AFB, Maine, 15 Apr 1951; Alexandria AFB, La, 19 Jun 1952–1 Jan 1953.

COMMANDERS. Col Lance Call, c. 15 May 1943; Col Ray J Stecker, 26 Jun 1944; Lt Col Robert C Richardson III, 26 Apr 1945–unkn. Col Charles G Teschner, c. 1 Apr 1951; Col Harold J Whiteman, 21 Jun 1952–c. 1 Jan 1953.

CAMPAIGNS. Air Offensive, Europe; Normandy; Northern France; Rhineland; Ardennes-Alsace; Central Europe.

DECORATIONS. Distinguished Unit Citations: Germany, 21 Oct 1944; Germany, 20 Apr 1945. Cited in the Order of the Day, Belgian Army: 6 Jun–30 Sep 1944; 16 Dec 1944–25 Jan 1945. Belgian Fourragere.

INSIGNE. *Shield:* Azure (sky blue), within a diminutive border or, a chevalier completely armed, in his dexter hand a tilting spear, with streamers; on his sinister arm an escutcheon charged with a tierce, in gyrons of two bendwise; the horse caparisoned and in full gallop, charging, all or, the horse's hind feet resting on a cloud proper, issuing from the base. (Approved 17 Oct 1952.)

366th FIGHTER GROUP

Constituted as 366th Fighter Group on 24 May 1943. *Activated* on 1 Jun 1943. Prepared for overseas duty with P–47's. Moved to England, Dec 1943–Jan 1944.

Assigned to Ninth AF. Entered combat on 14 Mar 1944 with a fighter sweep along the French coast, then took part in operations designed to prepare the way for the invasion of the Continent. Flew fighter sweeps over Normandy on 6 Jun 1944, attacking such targets as motor convoys and gun emplacements. Moved to the Continent soon after D-Day and engaged primarily in dive-bombing missions against enemy communications and fortifications until May 1945. Received a DUC for supporting ground forces on 11 Jul 1944: approaching the assigned target—pillboxes in the vicinity of St Lo—the group discovered an enemy tank column unknown to Allied infantry; despite driving rain and intense antiaircraft fire, the group not only attacked assigned objectives but also severely damaged the enemy's armored force. Among other operations, the group supported Allied armored columns during the breakthrough at St Lo in Jul 1944; attacked flak positions near Eindhoven during the airborne landing in Holland in Sep 1944; flew armed reconnaissance missions over the battle area during the Battle of the Bulge, Dec 1944–Jan 1945; and escorted bombers during the airborne assault across the Rhine in Mar 1945. The 366th frequently attacked such targets as railroads, highways, bridges, motor transports, gun emplacements, supply depots, and troops; often escorted bombers that hit airfields, factories, and marshalling yards; sometimes flew area patrols; and on occasion dropped leaflets. Flew last mission, attacking harbors at Kiel and Flensburg, on 3 May 1945. Remained in Germany after the war and, assigned to United States Air Forces in Europe, became part of the occupation force. *Inactivated* in Germany on 20 Aug 1946.

Redesignated 366th Fighter-Bomber Group. *Activated* in the US on 1 Jan 1953. Assigned to Tactical Air Command. Trained with F-51, F-84, and F-86 aircraft.

SQUADRONS. *389th:* 1943–1946; 1953–. *390th:* 1943–1946; 1953–. *391st:* 1943–1946; 1953–.

STATIONS. Richmond AAB, Va, 1 Jun 1943; Bluethenthal Field, NC, 9 Aug 1943; Richmond AAB, Va, 3–17 Dec 1943; Membury, England, 10 Jan 1944; Thruxton, England, 1 Mar–12 Jun 1944; St Pierre du Mont, France, 17 Jun 1944; Dreux/Vermouillet, France, 24 Aug 1944; Laon/Couvron, France, 8 Sep 1944; Assche, Belgium, 19 Nov 1944; Munster/Handorf, Germany, 11 Apr 1945; Bayreuth/Bindlach, Germany, 25 Jun 1945; Fritzlar, Germany, 14 Sep 1945–20 Aug 1946. Alexandria AFB, La, 1 Jan 1953–.

COMMANDERS. Maj Morris C Crossen, 1 Jun 1943; Col Dyke F Meyer, 11 Jul 1943; Lt Col James P Tipton, 19 Apr 1944; Lt Col Donald K Bennett, 30 Apr 1944; Col Harold N Holt, c. 22 May 1944; Lt Col Ansel J Wheeler, 28 Apr 1945; Col Clarence T Edwinson, May 1946–unkn. Col Harold J Whiteman, 1953; Lt Col Carroll B McElroy, 9 Jul 1953; Col Timothy F O'Keefe, 8 Aug 1953; Col Gerald J Dix, 1 Sep 1954; Col Clyde B Slocumb Jr, 16 Feb 1955–.

CAMPAIGNS. Air Offensive, Europe; Normandy; Northern France; Rhineland; Ardennes-Alsace; Central Europe.

DECORATIONS. Distinguished Unit Citation: Normandy, 11 Jul 1944. Cited in the Order of the Day, Belgian Army: 6 Jun–30 Sep 1944; 1 Oct 1944– ; 18 Dec 1944–15 Jan 1945. Belgian Fourragere.

INSIGNE. *Shield:* Vert, a tiger's face proper, armed and embrued gules. *Motto:* AUDENTES FORTUNA JUVAT—Fortune Favors the Bold. (Approved 6 Oct 1954.)

367th FIGHTER GROUP

Constituted as 367th Fighter Group on 26 May 1943. *Activated* on 15 Jul 1943. Trained with P–39's. Moved to England, Mar–Apr 1944, and assigned to Ninth AF. Equipped with P–38's in Apr 1944 and converted to P–47's in Feb 1945. Entered combat in May 1944, attacking rail-

roads, bridges, hangars, and other targets in western France, and escorting bombers that struck airfields, marshalling yards, and other facilities in the same area. From D–Day to 8 Jun 1944, provided cover for Allied forces crossing the Channel; during the remainder of Jun, bombed and strafed convoys, troops, flak towers, power stations, and other objectives behind the invasion beaches. Moved to the Continent in Jul 1944 and operated chiefly in support of ground forces until V–E Day. Struck railroads, marshalling yards, and trains to prevent enemy reinforcements from reaching the front during the Allied breakthrough at St Lo in Jul 1944. Received a DUC for a mission in France on 25 Aug: after attacking landing grounds at Clastres, Peronne, and Rosieries through an intense antiaircraft barrage, the group engaged a number of enemy planes and then, despite a low fuel supply, strafed a train and convoy after leaving the scene of battle; later the same day the 367th flew a fighter sweep of more than 800 miles, hitting landing grounds at Cognac, Bourges, and Dijon. Attacked German strong points to aid the Allied push against the Siegfried Line in the fall of 1944. On 26 Dec, during the Battle of the Bulge, escorted C–47's that dropped supplies to Allied troops encircled at Bastogne. Received another DUC for action on 19 Mar 1945: although its target was located in mountainous terrain, concealed by ground haze, and well-defended by antiaircraft artillery, the group descended to low altitude to bomb and strafe the headquarters of the German Commander-in-Chief, West, at Ziegenburg. Struck tanks, trucks, flak positions, and other objectives in support of the assault across the Rhine late in Mar and the final Allied operations in Germany. Flew last mission on V–E Day. Returned to the US, Jul–Aug 1945. *Inactivated* on 7 Nov 1945.

Redesignated 133d Fighter Group. Allotted to ANG (Minn) on 24 May 1946. Extended federal recognition on 28 Aug 1947. Ordered into active service on 1 Mar 1951. Assigned to Air Defense Command. *Redesignated* 133d Fighter-Interceptor Group. *Inactivated* on 6 Feb 1952. Relieved from active duty, returned to ANG (Minn), and *activated,* on 1 Dec 1952.

SQUADRONS. *109th:* 1951–1952. *175th:* 1951–1952. *392d:* 1943–1945. *393d* (later 179th): 1943–1945; 1951–1952. *394th:* 1943–1945.

STATIONS. Hamilton Field, Calif, 15 Jul 1943; Santa Rosa AAFld, Calif, 11 Oct 1943; Oakland Mun Aprt, Calif, 10 Dec 1943–8 Mar 1944; Stony Cross, England, 5 Apr 1944; Ibsley, England, 6 Jul 1944; Beuzeville, France, 22 Jul 1944; Criqueville, France, 14 Aug 1944; Peray, France, 4 Sep 1944; Clastres, France, 8 Sep 1944; Juvincourt, France, 28 Oct 1944; St-Dizier, France, 1 Feb 1945; Conflans, France, 14 Mar 1945; Frankfurt/Eschborn, Germany, 10 Apr–Jul 1945; Seymour Johnson Field, NC, Sep–7 Nov 1945. Holman Field, Minn, 1 Mar 1951; Ft Snelling, Minn, 21 Jan–6 Feb 1952.

COMMANDERS. Maj Tuevo A Ahola, 17 Jul 1943; Lt Col John R Alison, 11 Aug 1943; Maj Tuevo A Ahola, 22 Oct 1943; Maj Morris C Crossen, 25 Nov 1943; Col Charles M Young, 22 Jan 1944; Col Edwin S Chickering, 9 Nov 1944–unkn. Col John R Dohny, 1951–Feb 1952.

CAMPAIGNS. Air Offensive, Europe; Normandy; Northern France; Rhineland; Ardennes-Alsace; Central Europe.

DECORATIONS. Distinguished Unit Citations: France, 25 Aug 1944; Germany, 19 Mar 1945. Cited in the Order of the Day, Belgian Army: 6 Jun–30 Sep 1944; 16 Dec 1944–25 Jan 1945. Belgian Fourragere.

INSIGNE. *Shield:* Per bend azure and gules, throughout in bend between in chief the dominant constellation of the northern sky argent (the Big Dipper, Ursa Major, with the North Star in sinister chief) and in base a griffin sejant with left foreleg slightly raised or, wings, head and neck feathers of the first all highlighted white and outlined sable, a vol argent outlined gray. *Motto:* SPLENDENTES IN DE-

FENSIONE—Shining in Defense. (Approved 9 Jul 1954.)

368th FIGHTER GROUP

Constituted as 368th Fighter Group on 24 May 1943. *Activated* on 1 Jun 1943. Trained with P–47's. Moved to England, arriving in Jan 1944. Began operations with Ninth AF on 14 Mar when the group flew a fighter sweep over the coast of France. Made strafing and bombing attacks on airfields, rail and highway bridges, trains, vehicles, flak positions, and V-weapon sites to help prepare for the invasion of France. Supported the landings in Normandy early in Jun 1944 and began operations from the Continent later the same month. Aided in the taking of Cherbourg, participated in the air operations that prepared the way for the Allied breakthrough at St Lo on 25 Jul, and supported ground forces during their drive across France. Received a DUC for support operations in the vicinity of Mons on 3 Sep 1944 when the group, dispatch-ing seven missions against the enemy on that day, not only destroyed large numbers of motor transports, horse-drawn vehicles, and troops, but also attacked enemy positions that obstructed the progress of ground forces. Continued to support ground forces, participated in the assault against the Siegfried Line, and took part in the Battle of the Bulge (Dec 1944–Jan 1945) by attacking rail lines and trains, marshalling yards, roads and vehicles, armored columns, and gun positions. Operated with the Allied forces that pushed across the Rhine and into Germany. After V–E Day, served with the army of occupation, being assigned to United States Air Forces in Europe. *Inactivated* in Germany on 20 Aug 1946.

Redesignated 136th Fighter Group. Allotted to ANG (Tex) on 21 Aug 1946. Extended federal recognition on 27 Jan 1947. Ordered into active service on 10 Oct 1950. Assigned to Tactical Air Command. *Redesignated* 136th Fighter-Bomber Group. Used F–51's until early in 1951, then began conversion to F–84's. Moved to Japan, May–Jul 1951. Attached to Far East Air Forces for duty in the Korean War. Engaged primarily in interdiction but also flew close-support, escort, and armed-reconnaissance missions, operating first from Japan and later from Korea. Relieved from active duty, returned to ANG (Tex) without personnel and equipment, and *redesignated* 136th Fighter-Interceptor Group, on 10 Jul 1952. *Redesignated* 136th Fighter-Bomber Group on 1 Jan 1953.

SQUADRONS. *111th:* 1950–1952. *154th:* 1950–1952. *395th:* 1943–1946. *396th* (later 182d): 1943–1946; 1950–1952. *397th:* 1943–1946.

STATIONS. Westover Field, Mass, 1 Jun 1943; Farmingdale, NY, 23 Aug–20 Dec 1943; Greenham Common, England, 13 Jan 1944; Chilbolton, England, 15 Mar 1944; Cardonville, France, 20 Jun 1944; Chartres, France, 23 Aug 1944; Laon, France, 11 Sep 1944; Chievres, Belgium, 2 Oct 1944; Juvincourt, France, 27 Dec 1944; Metz, France, 5 Jan 1945; Frankfurt-am-Main, Germany, 15 Apr 1945; Buchschwabach, Germany, 13 May 1945; Straubing, Germany, 13 Aug 1945–20 Aug 1946. Hensley Field, Tex, 10 Oct 1950; Langley AFB, Va, 24 Oct 1950–13 May 1951; Itazuke, Japan, May 1951; Taegu, Korea, 19 Sep 1951–10 Jul 1952.

COMMANDERS. Col Gilbert L Meyers, c. 3 Jun 1943; Col Frank S Perego, 1 Nov 1944; Maj Dennis Crisp, 18 Oct 1945; Lt Col John L Locke, 2 Nov 1945; Col Robert P Montgomery, 22 Apr–20 Aug 1946. Col Albert C Prendergast, 10 Oct 1950; Lt Col William N Hensley, 26 Oct 1950; Lt Col Gerald E Montgomery, c. 9 May 1951; Col Dean Davenport, Jun 1951; Col William T Halton, c. 20 Sep 1951; Lt Col Daniel F Sharp, c. 21 Mar–c. Jul 1952.

CAMPAIGNS. *World War II:* Air Offensive, Europe; Normandy; Northern France; Rhineland; Ardennes-Alsace; Central Europe. *Korean War:* UN Summer-Fall Offensive; Second Korean Winter; Korea Summer-Fall, 1952.

DECORATIONS. Distinguished Unit Citation: Mons, France, 3 Sep 1944. Cited in the Order of the Day, Belgian Army: 6 Jun–30 Sep 1944; 16 Dec 1944–25 Jan 1945. Belgian Fourragere.

INSIGNE. *Shield:* Azure, a lightning bolt bendwise in front of a winged star or, on a chief argent a cluster of grapes and a Korean bell proper. *Motto:* NULLI SECUNDUS—Second to None. (Approved 22 Dec 1953.)

369th FIGHTER GROUP

Constituted as 369th Fighter Group on 26 May 1943. *Activated* on 1 Aug 1943. Assigned to Third AF, later (Mar 1944) to Fourth AF. *Redesignated* 369th Fighter-Bomber Group in Apr 1944, and 369th Fighter Group in Jun 1944. Trained replacement crews and participated in various maneuvers, such as the Louisiana Maneuvers in the summer of 1944. Aircraft included A-36's, P-39's, P-40's, and (in 1945) P-51's. *Inactivated* on 10 Aug 1945.

SQUADRONS. *398th:* 1943–1945. *399th:* 1943–1945. *400th:* 1943–1945.

STATIONS. Hamilton Field, Calif, 1 Aug 1943; Marysville AAFld, Calif, c. 5 Nov 1943; Oroville AAFld, Calif, 28 Jan 1944; Hamilton Field, Calif, 16 Mar 1944; De-Ridder AAB, La, 28 Mar 1944; Stuttgart AAFld, Ark, 8 Feb–10 Aug 1945.

COMMANDERS. Col Charles Young, 1 Aug 1943; Maj Paul M Brewer Jr, 12 Feb 1944; Lt Col Emmett S Davis, 27 Nov 1944; Lt Col Walter W Berg, 11 Jan 1945;

Lt Col Paul T O'Pizzi, 13 May 1945; Lt Col Harold G Lund, 19 May–10 Aug 1945.

CAMPAIGNS. American Theater.
DECORATIONS. None.
INSIGNE. None.

370th FIGHTER GROUP

MILITAT QUASI TIGRIS QUISQUE

Constituted as 370th Fighter Group on 25 May 1943. *Activated* on 1 Jul 1943. Trained with P-47's. Moved to England, Jan–Feb 1944. Assigned to Ninth AF. Equipped with P-38's in Feb and trained until 1 May 1944 when the group entered combat. Dive-bombed radar installations and flak towers, and escorted bombers that attacked bridges and marshalling yards in France as the Allies prepared for the invasion of the Continent. Provided cover for Allied forces that crossed the Channel on 6 Jun 1944, and flew armed reconnaissance missions over the Cotentin Peninsula until the end of the month. Moved to the Continent in Jul 1944 to sup-

port the drive of ground forces across France and into Germany. Hit gun emplacements, troops, supply dumps, and tanks near St Lo in Jul and in the Falaise-Argentan area in Aug 1944. Sent planes and pilots to England to provide cover for the airborne assault on Holland in Sep 1944. Struck pillboxes and troops early in Oct to aid First Army's capture of Aachen, and afterward struck railroads, bridges, viaducts, and tunnels in that area. Received a DUC for a mission in support of ground forces in the Hurtgen Forest area on 2 Dec 1944 when, despite bad weather and barrages of antiaircraft and small-arms fire, the group dropped napalm bombs on a heavily defended position in Bergstein, setting fire to the village and inflicting heavy casualties on enemy troops defending the area. Flew armed reconnaissance during the Battle of the Bulge, Dec 1944–Jan 1945, attacking warehouses, highways, railroads, motor transports, and other targets. Converted to P-51's, Feb–Mar 1945. Bombed bridges and docks in the vicinity of Wesel to prepare for the crossing of the Rhine, and patrolled the area as paratroops were dropped on the east bank on 24 Mar. Supported operations of 2d Armored Division in the Ruhr Valley in Apr. Flew last mission, a sweep over Dessau and Wittenberg, on 4 May 1945. Returned to the US, Sep–Nov 1945. *Inactivated* on 7 Nov 1945.

Redesignated 140th Fighter Group. Allotted to ANG (Colo) on 24 May 1946. Extended federal recognition on 1 Oct 1946. Ordered to active duty on 1

Apr 1951. Assigned to Tactical Air Command. *Redesignated* 140th Fighter-Bomber Group in May 1951. Trained with F–51's. Relieved from active service and returned, less personnel and equipment, to ANG (Colo), on 1 Jan 1953.

SQUADRONS. *120th:* 1951–1953. *191st:* 1951–1953. *401st:* 1943–1945. *402d* (later 187th): 1943–1945; 1951–1953. *485th:* 1943–1945.

STATIONS. Westover Field, Mass, 1 Jul 1943; Groton AAFld, Conn, 19 Oct 1943; Bradley Field, Conn, 5–20 Jan 1944; Aldermaston, England, 12 Feb 1944; Andover, England, 29 Feb–19 Jul 1944; Cardonville, France, 24 Jul 1944; La Vielle, France, 15 Aug 1944; Lonray, France, 6 Sep 1944; Roye/Amy, France, 11 Sep 1944; Florennes/Juxaine, Belgium, 26 Sep 1944; Zwartberg, Belgium, 27 Jan 1945; Gutersloh, Germany, 20 Apr 1945; Sandhofen, Germany, 27 Jun 1945; Fritzlar, Germany, 6 Aug–Sep 1945; Camp Myles Standish, Mass, c. 6–7 Nov 1945. Buckley Field, Colo, 1 Apr 1951; Clovis AFB, NM, 5 Dec 1951–1 Jan 1953.

COMMANDERS. Col Howard F Nichols, 1 Jul 1954; Lt Col Seth J McKee, 6 Nov 1944; Lt Col Morgan A Giffin, 22 Feb 1945; Col Seth J McKee, 10 May 1945–unkn. Col John H Lowell, 1 Apr 1951; Col Gerald J Dix, Dec 1952–1 Jan 1953.

CAMPAIGNS. Air Offensive, Europe; Normandy; Northern France; Rhineland; Ardennes-Alsace; Central Europe.

DECORATIONS. Distinguished Unit Citation: Hurtgen Forest, Germany, 2 Dec 1944. Cited in the Order of the Day,

Belgian Army: 6 Jun–30 Sep 1944; 1 Oct 1944–; 16 Dec 1944–25 Jan 1945. Belgian Fourragere.

INSIGNE. *Shield:* Per bend, argent and checky, sable and argent, over all a bend white. *Motto:* MILITAT QUASI TIGRIS QUISQUE—Each Fights Like a Tiger. (Approved 4 Jun 1952.)

371st FIGHTER GROUP

Constituted as 371st Fighter Group on 25 May 1943. *Activated* on 15 Jul 1943. Moved to the European theater during Feb–Mar 1944 and served in combat with Ninth AF from Apr 1944 to May 1945. Began operations, using P–47's, by making a fighter sweep over France. Flew fighter-sweep, dive-bombing, and escort missions prior to the invasion of the Continent. Attacked railroads, trains, vehicles, gun emplacements, and buildings in France during the invasion of 6 Jun 1944. Patrolled beachhead areas and continued its assaults against the enemy during the remainder of the Normandy campaign. Participated in the aerial barrage that prepared the way for the Allied breakthrough at St Lo on 25 Jul, and supported the subsequent drive across northern France. Operated in the area of northeastern France and southwestern Germany during the fall and winter of 1944–1945, attacking such targets as storage dumps, trains, rail lines, marshalling yards, buildings, factories, bridges, roads, vehicles, and strong points. Conducted operations that supported Allied ground action in the Battle of the Bulge, Dec 1944–Jan 1945. Launched a series of attacks against vehicles, factories, buildings, railroad cars, tanks, and gun emplacements during the period 15–21 Mar 1945, being awarded a DUC for this six-day action that contributed to the defeat of the enemy in southern Germany. Continued operations until May 1945. Returned to the US, Oct–Nov 1945. *Inactivated* on 10 Nov 1945.

Redesignated 142d Fighter Group. Allotted to ANG (Ore) on 24 May 1946. Extended federal recognition on 30 Aug 1946. Ordered into active service on 1 Mar 1951. Assigned to Air Defense Command. *Redesignated* 142d Fighter-Interceptor Group in Apr 1951. Supervised the training of attached squadrons that used F–51, F–84, and F–86 aircraft. *Inactivated* on 6 Feb 1952. Returned to ANG (Ore) and *activated,* on 1 Dec 1952.

SQUADRONS. *404th:* 1943–1945. *405th:* 1943–1945. *406th:* 1943–1945.

STATIONS. Richmond AAB, Va, 15 Jul 1943; Camp Springs AAFld, Md, 30 Sep 1943; Richmond AAB, Va, 18 Jan–14 Feb 1944; Bisterne, England, Mar 1944; Beuzeville, France, Jun 1944; Perthes, France, 18 Sep 1944; Dole/Tavaux, France, 1 Oct 1944; Tantonville, France, 20 Dec 1944; Metz, France, 15 Feb 1945; Frankfurt/Eschborn, Germany, 7 Apr 1945; Furth, Germany, 5 May 1945; Horsching, Austria, 16 Aug 1945; Stuttgart, Germany, Sep–Oct 1945; Camp Shanks, NY, 9–10 Nov 1945. Portland Mun Aprt, Ore, 1 Mar 1951; O'Hare Intl Aprt, Ill, 11 Apr 1951–6 Feb 1952.

COMMANDERS. Col Bingham T Kleine, 27 Jul 1943; Lt Col William P McBride, c. Sep 1945–unkn. Col Harold W Scruggs, 1951–c. Feb 1952.

CAMPAIGNS. Air Offensive, Europe; Normandy; Northern France; Rhineland; Ardennes-Alsace; Central Europe.

DECORATIONS. Distinguished Unit Citation: Germany, 15–21 Mar 1945. Cited in the Order of the Day, Belgian Army: 6 Jun–30 Sep 1944.

INSIGNE. *Shield:* Azure, issuing from a barrulet engrailed, argent, a demi sun in splendour, or; in chief a stylized futuramic aircraft gules, fimbriated of the second; issuing from base a mountain of three peaks vert, capped argent. *Motto:* SEMPER VIGILANS—A l w a y s on Guard. (Approved 24 Jul 1951.)

372d FIGHTER GROUP

Constituted as 372d Fighter Group on 12 Oct 1943 and *activated* on 28 Oct. Assigned to Fourth AF, and later (Mar 1944)

to Third AF. *Redesignated* 372d Fighter-Bomber Group in Apr 1944, and 372d Fighter Group in Jun 1944. Functioned as an operational training unit. Also provided air support for air-ground maneuvers and demonstrations, participating in the Louisiana Maneuvers in the summer of 1944 and in similar activities in the US until after V-J Day. Primary aircraft were P-40's until Jun 1945, then P-51's. *Inactivated* on 7 Nov 1945.

Redesignated 144th Fighter Group. Allotted to ANG (Calif) on 24 May 1946. Extended federal recognition on 2 Jun 1948. *Redesignated* 144th Fighter-Interceptor Group in Oct 1952, and 144th Fighter-Bomber Group in Dec 1952.

SQUADRONS. *407th:* 1943-1945. *408th:* 1943-1945. *409th:* 1943-1945.

STATIONS. Hamilton Field, Calif, 28 Oct 1943; Portland AAB, Ore, 7 Dec 1943; Esler Field, La, 29 Mar 1944; Pollock AAFld, La, 14 Apr 1944; Esler Field, La,

9 Feb 1945; Alexandria AAFld, La, 14 Sep-7 Nov 1945.

COMMANDERS. Maj Francis E Brenner, 28 Oct 1943; Maj Darrell G Welch, 21 Dec 1943; Maj Joseph S Wakefield, 4 Feb 1944; Maj John R Harrison, 16 Feb 1944; Lt Col Sam W Westbrook, 3 Mar 1944; Lt Col Robert W Stephens, 17 Mar 1945; Lt Col Jack J Oberhansly, 30 May 1945; Col George R Bickell, 6 Aug-7 Nov 1945.

CAMPAIGNS. American Theater.

DECORATIONS. None.

INSIGNE. *Shield:* Azure, three clouds two and one argent, issuing from the second cloud two lightning flashes one terminating on the first cloud and the other on the third cloud golden orange; in chief three mullets of the second. (Approved 10 Feb 1954.)

373d FIGHTER GROUP

Constituted as 373d Fighter Group on 25 May 1943. *Activated* on 15 Aug 1943. Trained for combat with P-47's. Moved to England, Mar-Apr 1944. Assigned to Ninth AF. Flew first combat mission, a fighter sweep over Normandy, on 8 May 1944, and then took part in preinvasion activities by escorting B-26's to attack airdromes, bridges, and railroads in France. Patrolled the air over the beachhead when the Allies launched the Normandy invasion on 6 Jun 1944, and hit troops, tanks, roads, fuel depots, and other targets in the assault area until the end of the month.

Moved to the Continent in Jul 1944; struck railroads, hangars, boxcars, warehouses, and other objectives to prevent enemy reinforcements from reaching the front at St Lo, where the Allies broke through on 25 Jul 1944. Bombed such targets as troops, gun emplacements, and armored vehicles to aid ground troops in the Falaise-Argentan area in Aug 1944. During the Battle of the Bulge, Dec 1944–Jan 1945, concentrated on the destruction of bridges, marshalling yards, and highways. Flew armed reconnaissance missions to support ground operations in the Rhine Valley in Mar 1945, hitting airfields, motor transports, and other objectives. Received a DUC for a mission, 20 Mar 1945, that greatly facilitated the crossing of the Rhine by Allied ground forces: without losing any planes, the group repeatedly dived through barrages of antiaircraft fire to bomb vital airfields east of the river; also attacked rail lines and highways leading to the Rhine, hitting rolling stock, motor transports, and other objectives. Con-

tinued tactical air operations until 4 May 1945. Returned to the US, Jul–Aug 1945. *Inactivated* on 7 Nov 1945.

Redesignated 146th Fighter Group. Allotted to ANG (Calif) on 24 May 1946. Extended federal recognition on 14 Sep 1946. *Redesignated* 146th Composite Group in Nov 1950, and 146th Fighter Group in Feb 1951. Ordered into active service on 1 Apr 1951 and assigned to Strategic Air Command. *Redesignated* 146th Fighter-Bomber Group in Jun 1951. Assigned to Tactical Air Command in Nov 1951. Trained with F–51's. Relieved from active duty on 1 Jan 1953 and returned, without personnel and equipment, to ANG (Calif).

SQUADRONS. *178th:* 1951–1953. *186th:* 1951–1953. *190th:* 1951–1953. *410th:* 1943–1945. *411th:* 1943–1945. *412th:* 1943–1945.

STATIONS. Westover Field, Mass, 15 Aug 1943; Norfolk, Va, 23 Oct 1943; Richmond AAB, Va, 15 Feb–15 Mar 1944; Woodchurch, England, 4 Apr–4 Jul 1944; Touren-Bassin, France, 19 Jul 1944; St-James, France, 19 Aug 1944; Reims, France, 19 Sep 1944; Le Culot, Belgium, 22 Oct 1944; Venlo, Holland, 11 Mar 1945; Lippstadt, Germany, 20 Apr 1945; Illesheim, Germany, 20 May–Jul 1945; Sioux Falls AAFld, SD, 4 Aug 1945; Seymour Johnson Field, NC, 20 Aug 1945; Mitchel Field, NY, 28 Sep–7 Nov 1945. Lockheed Air Terminal, Calif, 1 Apr 1951; Moody AFB, Ga, 10 May 1951; George AFB, Calif, 25 Oct 1951–1 Jan 1953.

COMMANDERS. Maj Ansel J Wheeler, 23 Aug 1943; Col William H Schwartz Jr, 25 Aug 1943; Col James C McGehee, 17 Nov 1944; Lt Col James F McCarthy, May 1945–unkn. Lt Col Jack D Blanchard, 1 Apr 1951; Col Cecil E West, Jun 1951; Col Earl H Dunham, 22 Jun 1951; Lt Col Jack D Blanchard, 7 Jan 1952; Col Amos F Riha, 4 Apr 1952; Col Paul P Douglas, 27 Oct 1952–1 Jan 1953.

CAMPAIGNS. Air Offensive, Europe; Normandy; Northern France; Rhineland; Ardennes-Alsace; Central Europe.

DECORATIONS. Distinguished Unit Citation: Rhine River, 20 Mar 1945. French Croix de Guerre with Palm: Aug 1944. Cited in the Order of the Day, Belgian Army: 1 Oct 1944–; 18 Dec 1944–15 Jan 1945. Belgian Fourragere.

INSIGNE. *Shield:* Azure (light blue), on a pale or, a futuristic interceptor aircraft sable, highlighted white, overall in saltire a sword piercing a vulture's wing both argent, detailed and outlined of the third. (Approved 21 Jun 1957.)

374th TROOP CARRIER GROUP

Constituted as 374th Troop Carrier Group on 7 Nov 1942 and *activated* in Australia on 12 Nov. Assigned to Fifth AF. Transported men and materiel in the theater from Nov 1942 until after the war, operating from Australia, New Guinea, Biak, and the Philippines. Used war-weary and worn-out aircraft, including B-18's, C-39's, C-49's, C-56's, C-60's, DC-3's, and DC-5's, until equipped with C-47's in Feb 1943. Engaged in supplying Allied forces in the Papuan Campaign, receiving one DUC for these missions, and being awarded another DUC for transporting troops and equipment to Papua and evacuating casualties to rear areas, Nov–Dec 1942. Received third DUC for transporting men and supplies over the Owen Stanley Range, 30 Jan–1 Feb 1943, to aid the small force defending the airdrome at Wau, New Guinea. Participated in the first airborne operation in the Southwest Pacific on 5 Sep 1943, dropping paratroops at Nadzab, New Guinea, to seize enemy bases and cut inland supply routes. Other operations included evacuating wounded personnel, flying courier routes, making passenger flights, and helping to move the 11th Division from Luzon to Okinawa in Aug 1945 for staging to Japan. From Sep 1945 to May 1946, hauled cargo to the occupation army in Japan and flew courier routes from the Philippines to Japan. *Inactivated* on Luzon on 15 May 1946.

Activated in the Philippines on 15 Oct 1946. Assigned to Far East Air Forces. Transferred, without personnel and equipment, to Guam on 1 Apr 1947. Remanned and equipped with C–46 and C–47 aircraft. Flew courier, passenger, and cargo routes in the western Pacific. *Redesignated* 374th Troop Carrier Group (Heavy) in May 1948. Began converting to C–54's. Moved to Japan in Mar 1949. Began operations in the Korea War in Jun 1950, using C–47 and C–54 aircraft, the C–47's being replaced with C–124's in 1952. Transported men and cargo to Korea and evacuated wounded personnel on return flights. Remained in Japan after the war.

SQUADRONS. *6th:* 1942–1946; 1946–. *19th:* 1946–1948. *21st:* 1942–1946; 1946–. *22d:* 1942–1946; 1946–. *33d:* 1942–1946.

STATIONS. Brisbane, Australia, 12 Nov 1942; Port Moresby, New Guinea, Dec 1942; Townsville, Australia, 7 Oct 1943; Nadzab, New Guinea, c. 1 Sep 1944; Biak, c. 14 Oct 1944; Nielson Field, Luzon, 28 May 1945–15 May 1946. Nichols Field, Luzon, 15 Oct 1946; Harmon Field, Guam, 1 Apr 1947; Tachikawa, Japan, 5 Mar 1949–.

COMMANDERS. Lt Col Erickson S Nichols, 12 Nov 1942; Maj Edgar H Hampton, 14 Dec 1942; Col Paul H Prentiss, 17 Dec 1942; Maj Fred M Adams, 22 May 1943; Lt Col Edgar H Hampton, 12 Jul 1943; Lt Col Fred M Adams, 2 Aug 1943; Col Edward T Imparato, c. 3 Aug 1944; Col John L Sullivan, Oct 1945–unkn. Col Audrin R Walker, 15 Oct 1946–unkn; Lt Col Forrest P Coons, 1947–unkn; Col Troy W Crawford, 1949; Lt Col Benjamin T Tarver Jr, Aug 1949; Col Herbert A Bott, 22 Jul 1950; Col Charles W Howe, Jul 1951; Col Edward H Nigro, Sep 1951; Lt Col James F Hogan, Apr 1952; Col Edward H Nigro, 11 Aug 1952; Lt Col Frederick C Johnson, 11 Sep 1952; Col Francis W Williams, 24 Apr 1953; Col Hollis B Tara, 15 Jun 1954–.

CAMPAIGNS. *World War II:* Air Offensive, Japan; Papua; New Guinea; Northern Solomons; Bismarck Archipelago; Western Pacific; Leyte; Luzon. *Korean War:* UN Defensive; UN Offensive; CCF Intervention; 1st UN Counteroffensive; CCF Spring Offensive; UN Summer-Fall Offensive; Second Korean Winter; Korea Summer-Fall, 1952; Third Korean Winter; Korea Summer-Fall, 1953.

DECORATIONS. Distinguished Unit Citations: Papua [Nov] 1942–23 Jan 1943; Papua, 12 Nov–22 Dec 1942; Wau, New Guinea, 30 Jan–1 Feb 1943; Korea, 27 Jun–15 Sep 1950. Philippine Presidential Unit Citation. Republic of Korea Presidential Unit Citation: 1 Jul 1951–27 Jul 1953.

INSIGNE. *Shield:* Per bend azure and or, in chief a hand couped in armour, holding a dagger, point upward, issuing from its handle an arrow and a wheat stalk or, in base a winged foot azure. *Motto:* CELERITER PUGNARE—Swiftly to Fight. (Approved 3 Jul 1951.)

375th TROOP CARRIER GROUP

Constituted as 375th Troop Carrier Group on 12 Nov 1942 and *activated* on

NOLLE SECUNDIS

18 Nov. Used C–47's in training for overseas duty. Moved to the Pacific theater, Jun–Jul 1943, and assigned to Fifth AF. Operated from New Guinea and Biak from Jul 1943 until Feb 1945, transporting men, supplies, and equipment to forward bases on New Guinea and New Britain and in the Solomon and Admiralty Islands. Used armed B–17's for the more hazardous missions that involved landing on fields that were under enemy attack. Took part in the first airborne operation in the Southwest Pacific, dropping paratroops to seize enemy bases and cut overland supply lines at Nadzab, New Guinea, on 5 Sep 1943. Converted to C–46 aircraft late in 1944. Moved to the Philippines in Feb 1945 and during the next few months most of its missions were supply flights to ground forces on Luzon and neighboring islands. Transported cargo to forces in the Ryukyus, Jun–Jul 1945. Moved to Okinawa in Aug, and after the war helped transfer troops from Luzon to the Ryukyus for staging to Japan. Also ferried liberated

prisoners from Okinawa to Luzon. Moved to Japan in Sep 1945. *Inactivated* on 25 Mar 1946.

Allotted to the reserve. *Activated* in the US on 3 Aug 1947. *Redesignated* 375th Troop Carrier Group (Medium) in Jun 1949. Called to active duty on 15 Oct 1950. Assigned to Tactical Air Command and equipped with C–82's. *Inactivated* on 14 Jul 1952.

Allotted to the reserve. *Activated* on 14 Jul 1952.

SQUADRONS. *14th:* 1947–1949. *55th:* 1942–1946; 1947–1952; 1952–. *56th:* 1942–1946; 1947–1952; 1952–. *57th:* 1942–1946; 1947–1952; 1952–. *58th:* 1942–1946; 1947–1950.

STATIONS. Bowman Field, Ky, 18 Nov 1942; Sedalia AAFld, Mo, 23 Jan 1943; Laurinburg-Maxton AAB, NC, 5 May 1943; Baer Field, Ind, 2–15 Jun 1943; Brisbane, Australia, 13 Jul 1943; Port Moresby, New Guinea, 31 Jul 1943; Dobodura, New Guinea, 19 Aug 1943; Port Moresby, New Guinea, 19 Dec 1943; Nadzab, New Guinea, 22 Apr 1944; Biak, 27 Sep 1944; San Jose, Mindoro, 17 Feb 1945; Porac, Luzon, 20 May 1945; Okinawa, Aug 1945; Tachikawa, Japan, Sep 1945–25 Mar 1946. Greater Pittsburgh Aprt, Pa, 3 Aug 1947; Donaldson AFB, SC, 15 Oct 1950–14 Jul 1952. Pittsburgh, Pa, 14 Jul 1952–.

COMMANDERS. Col Joel G Pitts, 20 Nov 1942; Lt Col Maurice W Wiley, 25 Dec 1944; Lt Col John L Ames Jr, Aug 1945; Lt Col Benjamin C King, Sep 1945; Col Marshall S Roth, Oct 1945–unkn. Capt Charles J Newell, 15 Oct 1950; Lt Col

Charles R Gianque, 7 Nov 1950; Col Kenneth L Johnson, 13 Nov 1951; Lt Col Arthur J Staveley, 1 Feb 1952; Col Stewart H Nichols, 17 Apr–14 Jul 1952.

CAMPAIGNS. Air Offensive, Japan; New Guinea; Northern Solomons; Bismarck Archipelago; Western Pacific; Leyte; Luzon; Ryukyus.

DECORATIONS. Philippine Presidential Unit Citation.

INSIGNE. *Shield:* Azure, between a bend, compony of seven or and azure, cottised argent, a Pegasus rampant argent, and a parachute between two wings of the last. *Motto:* NOLLE SECUNDIS—None but the Best. (Approved 12 Feb 1952.)

376th BOMBARDMENT GROUP

Constituted as 376th Bombardment Group (Heavy) on 19 Oct 1942 and *activated* in Palestine on 31 Oct. Began combat immediately, using B–24 aircraft. Operated with Ninth AF from bases in the Middle East, Nov 1942–Sep 1943, and with Twelfth AF from Tunisia, Sep–Nov 1943. Attacked shipping in the Mediterranean and harbor installations in Libya, Tunisia, Sicily, and Italy to cut enemy supply lines to Africa. Struck airdromes, marshalling yards, and other objectives in Sicily and Italy after the fall of Tunisia in May 1943. Received a DUC for action against the enemy in the Middle East, North Africa, and Sicily, Nov 1942–Aug 1943. Participated in the famed low-level assault on oil refineries at Ploesti and received another DUC: nearing Ploesti on 1 Aug 1943 and realizing that it was off course, the group attempted to reach its assigned objective from another direction; by this time, however, enemy defenses were thoroughly alerted and intense opposition forced the 376th to divert to targets of opportunity in the general target area. Moved to Italy in Nov 1943 and operated with Fifteenth AF until Apr 1945. Engaged primarily in long-range missions to targets in Italy, France, Germany, Czechoslovakia, Austria, Hungary, and the Balkans to bomb factories, marshalling yards, oil refineries, oil storage facilities, airdromes, bridges, harbors, and other objectives. Received a DUC for attacking the oil industry at Bratislava on 16 Jun 1944. Also flew support and interdictory missions, assisting Allied forces at Anzio and Cassino during Feb–Mar 1944, supporting the invasion of Southern France in Aug 1944, aiding the Russian sweep into the Balkans during the fall of 1944, and assisting Allied troops in northern Italy during Apr 1945. Moved to the US in Apr. *Redesignated* 376th Bombardment Group (Very Heavy) in May 1945. *Inactivated* on 10 Nov 1945.

Redesignated 376th Reconnaissance Group. *Activated* on 23 May 1947. Organized as a weather group. *Inactivated* on 20 Sep 1948.

Redesignated 376th Bombardment Group (Medium). *Activated* on 1 Jun 1951. Assigned to Strategic Air Command and equipped with B–29's. *Inactivated* on 16 Jun 1952.

SQUADRONS. *512th:* 1942–1945; 1947; 1951–1952. *513th:* 1942–1945; 1947; 1951–1952. *514th:* 1942–1945; 1951–1952. *515th:* 1942–1945.

STATIONS. Lydda, Palestine, 31 Oct 1942; Abu Sueir, Egypt, 8 Nov 1942; Gambut, Libya, c. Jan 1943; Soluch, Libya, 22 Feb 1943; Bengasi, Libya, c. 6 Apr 1943; Enfidaville, Tunisia, 26 Sep 1943; San Pancrazio, Italy, c. 17 Nov 1943–19 Apr 1945; Harvard AAFld, Neb, 8 May 1945; Grand Island AAFld, Neb, 25 Jun–10 Nov 1945. Gravelly Point, Va, 23 May 1947–20 Sep 1948. Forbes AFB, Kan, 1 Jun 1951; Barksdale AFB, La, c. 1 Oct 1951–16 Jun 1952.

COMMANDERS. Col George·F McGuire, 1 Nov 1942; Col Keith K Compton, 20 Feb 1943; Col Theodore Q Graff, c. 9 Jan 1944; Lt Col Richard W Fellows, 10 Jul 1944; Col Theodore Q Graff, 29 Sep 1944; Col Robert H Warren, 22 Feb 1945–unkn. Unkn, 23 May 1947–20 Sep 1948. Col Cecil E Combs, 1 Jun 1951; Col Frederick J Sutterlin, May–16 Jun 1952.

CAMPAIGNS. Air Combat, EAME Theater; Egypt-Libya; Air Offensive, Europe; Tunisia; Sicily; Naples-Foggia; Anzio; Rome-Arno; Normandy; Northern France; Southern France; North Apennines; Rhineland; Central Europe; Po Valley.

DECORATIONS. Distinguished Unit Citations: North Africa and Sicily, [Nov] 1942–17 Aug 1943; Ploesti, Rumania, 1 Aug 1943; Bratislava, Czechoslovakia, 16 Jun 1944.

INSIGNE. *Shield:* Azure, in base, a stylized winged sphinx or, shaded tenne, and fimbriated azure, on a terra cotta mound sanguine, in dexter chief, a bomb or, point downward, charged with a roundle and a lozenge, sanguine, a triangle azure and a square sanquine, all within a diminutive of a border or. *Motto:* LIBERANDOS. (Approved 8 Nov 1951.)

377th BOMBARDMENT GROUP

Constituted as 377th Bombardment Group (Heavy) on 13 Oct 1942 and *activated* on 18 Oct. Assigned to AAF Antisubmarine Command. Using O–47, O–52, and other aircraft, the group engaged in patrol activity along the east coast of the US. *Inactivated* on 9 Dec 1942.

SQUADRONS. *11th* Antisubmarine (formerly 516th Bombardment): 1942. *12th* Antisubmarine (formerly 517th Bombardment): 1942. *13th* Antisubmarine (formerly 518th Bombardment): 1942. *14th*

Antisubmarine (formerly 519th Bombardment): 1942.

STATIONS. Ft Dix, NJ, 18 Oct–9 Dec 1942.

COMMANDERS. Unkn.

CAMPAIGNS. Antisubmarine, American Theater.

DECORATIONS. None.

INSIGNE. None.

378th BOMBARDMENT GROUP

Constituted as 378th Bombardment Group (Heavy) on 13 Oct 1942 and *activated* on 18 Oct. Assigned to AAF Antisubmarine Command. Engaged in patrol work along the east coast of the US, operating primarily with O–46's and O–47's. *Inactivated* on 14 Dec 1942.

SQUADRONS. *15th* Antisubmarine (formerly 520th Bombardment): 1942. *17th* Antisubmarine (formerly 522d Bombardment): 1942. *521st* Bombardment: 1942. *523d* Bombardment: 1942.

STATIONS. Langley Field, Va, 18 Oct–14 Dec 1942.

COMMANDERS. Col Walter M Williams, 1942.

CAMPAIGNS. Antisubmarine, American Theater.

DECORATIONS. None.

INSIGNE. None.

379th BOMBARDMENT GROUP

Constituted as 379th Bombardment Group (Heavy) on 28 Oct 1942. *Activated* on 3 Nov 1942. Moved to England, with the air echelon flying B–17's via the North Atlantic route in Apr 1943 and the ground echelon crossing by ship in May. Began operations with Eighth AF on 19 May, and received a DUC for operations over Europe, May 1943–Jul 1944. Engaged primarily in bombardment of strategic targets such as industries, oil refineries, storage plants, submarine pens, airfields, and communications centers in Germany, France, Holland, Belgium, Norway, and Poland. Specific targets included a chemical plant in Ludwigshafen, an aircraft assembly plant in Brunswick, ball-bearing plants at Schweinfurt and Leipzig, synthetic oil refineries at Merseburg and Gelsenkirchen, marshalling yards at Hamm and Reims, and airfields in Mesnil au Val and Berlin. Received another DUC for flying without fighter protection into central Germany to attack vital aircraft factories on 11 Jan 1944. On several occasions attacked interdictory targets and operated in support of ground forces. Bombed V-weapon sites, airfields, radar stations, and other installations before the Normandy invasion in Jun 1944; bombed defended positions just ahead of the Allied landings on 6 Jun; and struck airfields, rail choke points, and gun emplacements during the campaign that followed. Bombed enemy positions to assist ground troops at St Lo during the breakthrough, 24–25 Jul 1944. Attacked German communications and fortifications during the Battle of the Bulge, Dec 1944–Jan 1945. Bombed bridges and viaducts in France and Germany to aid the Allied assault across the Rhine, Feb–Mar 1945. Moved to French Morocco in Jun 1945. *Inactivated* on 25 Jul 1945.

SQUADRONS. *524th:* 1942–1945. *525th:* 1942–1945. *526th:* 1942–1945. *527th:* 1942–1945.

STATIONS. Geiger Field, Wash, 3 Nov 1942; Wendover Field, Utah, 19 Nov 1942; Sioux City AAB, Iowa, 3 Feb–Apr 1943; Kimbolton, England, 21 May 1943–12 Jun 1945; Casablanca, French Morocco, 17 Jun–25 Jul 1945.

COMMANDERS. Col Maurice A Preston, 26 Nov 1942; Col Lewis E Lyle, 11 Oct 1944; Lt Col Lloyd C Mason, 6 May 1945; Lt Col Horace E Frink, 23 May–Jun 1945.

CAMPAIGNS. Air Offensive, Europe; Normandy; Northern France; Rhineland; Ardennes-Alsace; Central Europe.

DECORATIONS. Distinguished Unit Citations: Continental Europe, 29 May 1943–31 Jul 1944; Germany, 11 Jan 1944.

INSIGNE. *Shield:* Per bend azure and gules, on a lightning bolt per bend throughout, or, seven stars per bend argent; all between a dart, with three stars arched and an atomic symbol encircled by nine stars, all of the last. *Motto:* DILIGENTIA ET ACCURATIO—Precision and Accuracy. (Approved 23 Aug 1958.)

380th BOMBARDMENT GROUP

Constituted as 380th Bombardment Group (Heavy) on 28 Oct 1942. *Activated* on 3 Nov 1942. Used B–24's in preparing for overseas duty. Moved to the Asiatic-Pacific Theater, Apr–May 1943. Assigned to Fifth AF but attached to Royal Australian Air Force until Jan 1945. Trained Australian crews to operate B–24's. Began combat operations in May 1943 by flying armed reconnaissance patrols. Operated from Australian bases for a year and a half, striking enemy airfields, ground installations, shipping, and industries in the Netherlands Indies and the Bismarck Archipelago. Received a DUC for a series of long-range attacks on oil refineries, shipping, and dock facilities in Balikpapan, Borneo, in Aug 1943. Repeatedly bombed enemy airfields in western New Guinea during Apr and May 1944 in support of American landings in the Hollandia area, being awarded another DUC for this action. Moved in Feb 1945 to Mindoro where its missions included support for ground forces on Luzon and strikes on industries in Formosa, oil refineries in Borneo, railways and shipping in French Indochina, and ground installations on the China coast. Moved to Okinawa in Aug 1945, and after V–J Day flew reconnaissance missions over Japan and ferried liberated prisoners of war from Japan to Manila. Returned to the Philippines in Nov 1945. *Inactivated* on 20 Feb 1946.

Redesignated 380th Bombardment Group (Very Heavy). Allotted to the reserve. *Activated* in the US on 16 Jun 1947. *Redesignated* 380th Bombardment Group (Medium) in Jun 1949. Ordered to active duty on 1 May 1951. *Inactivated* on 16 May 1951.

SQUADRONS. *328th:* 1942–1946; 1947–1951. *329th:* 1942–1946; 1947–1949. *330th:* 1942–1946; 1947–1949. *331st:* 1942–1946; 1947–1951.

STATIONS. Davis-Monthan Field, Ariz, 3 Nov 1942; Biggs Field, Tex, 2 Dec 1942; Lowry Field, Colo, 4 Mar–c. 17 Apr 1943; Fenton, Australia, May 1943; Darwin, Australia, 9 Aug 1944; San Jose, Mindoro, 20 Feb 1945; Okinawa, c. 9 Aug 1945; Ft William McKinley, Luzon, 28 Nov

1945–20 Feb 1946. MacDill Field, Fla, 16 Jun 1947–16 May 1951.

COMMANDERS. Col William A Miller, 3 Nov 1942; Col Forrest L Brissey, 10 Feb 1944; Lt Col Gayle S Cox, 30 Aug 1945; Col David A Tate, 8 Sep 1945–unkn.

CAMPAIGNS. Air Offensive, Japan; China Defensive; New Guinea; Bismarck Archipelago; Western Pacific; Leyte; Luzon; Southern Philippines; China Offensive.

DECORATIONS. Distinguished Unit Citations: Borneo, 13, 15, and 17 Aug 1943; New Guinea, 20 Apr–17 May 1944. Philippine Presidential Unit Citation.

INSIGNE. *Shield:* Azure, two cloud formations argent, fesswise, one issuing from dexter enhanced, one from sinister abased surmounted by a sword in pale, point to base, or, hilt, grip and pommel gules, entwined with an olive branch vert. *Motto:* STRENGTH AND CONFIDENCE. (Approved 26 Nov 1956.)

381st BOMBARDMENT GROUP

Constituted as 381st Bombardment Group (Heavy) on 28 Oct 1942. *Activated* on 3 Nov 1942. Used B–17's in preparing for duty overseas. Moved to England, May–Jun 1943, and assigned to Eighth AF. Served in combat from Jun 1943 to Apr 1945, operating chiefly against strategic objectives on the Continent. Specific targets included an aircraft assembly plant at Villacoublay, an airdrome at Amiens, locks at St Nazaire, an aircraft engine factory at Le Mans, nitrate works in Norway, aircraft plants in Brussels, industrial areas of Munster, U-boat yards at Kiel, marshalling yards at Offenberg, aircraft factories at Kassel, aircraft assembly plants at Leipzig, oil refineries at Gelsenkirchen, and ball-bearing works at Schweinfurt. Received a DUC for performance on 8 Oct 1943 when shipyards at Bremen were bombed accurately in spite of persistent enemy fighter attacks and heavy flak. Received second DUC for similar action on 11 Jan 1944 during a mission against aircraft factories in central Germany. Participated in the intensive campaign of heavy bombers against enemy aircraft factories during Big Week, 20–25 Feb 1944. Often supported ground troops and attacked targets of interdiction when not engaged in strategic bombardment. Supported the Normandy invasion in Jun 1944 by bombing bridges and airfields near the beachhead. Attacked enemy positions in advance of ground forces at St Lo in Jul 1944. Assisted the airborne assault on Holland in Sep. Struck airfields and communications near the battle zone during the Battle of the Bulge, Dec 1944–Jan 1945. Supported the Allied crossing of the Rhine in Mar 1945 and then operated against communications and transportation in the final push through Germany. Returned to the US, Jun–Jul 1945. *Inactivated* on 28 Aug 1945.

Redesignated 381st Bombardment Group (Very Heavy). Allotted to the reserve. *Activated* on 24 Jul 1947. *Inactivated* on 27 Jun 1949.

SQUADRONS. *509th:* 1948–1949. *510th:* 1948–1949. *532d:* 1942–1945; 1947–1949. *533d:* 1942–1945. *534th:* 1942–1945; 1947–1948. *535th:* 1942–1945; 1947–1949.

STATIONS. Gowen Field, Idaho, 3 Nov 1942; Ephrata, Wash, c. 1 Dec 1942; Pyote AAB, Tex, c. 3 Jan 1943; Pueblo AAB, Colo, c. 5 Apr–c. 9 May 1943; Ridgewell, England, Jun 1943–Jun 1945; Sioux Falls AAFld, SD, Jul–28 Aug 1945. Offutt Field, Neb, 24 Jul 1947–27 Jun 1949.

COMMANDERS. Col Joseph J Nazzaro, Jan 1943; Col Harry P Leber Jr, c. 9 Jan 1944; Lt Col Conway S Hall, 6 Feb 1945–unkn.

CAMPAIGNS. Air Offensive, Europe; Normandy; Northern France; Rhineland; Ardennes-Alsace; Central Europe.

DECORATIONS. Distinguished Unit Citations: Germany, 8 Oct 1943; Germany, 11 Jan 1944.

INSIGNE. None.

382d BOMBARDMENT GROUP

Constituted as 382d Bombardment Group (Heavy) on 28 Oct 1942. *Activated* on 3 Nov 1942. Assigned to Second AF and equipped with B–24's. Served first as an operational training and later as a replacement training unit. *Inactivated* on 31 Mar 1944.

Redesignated 382d Bombardment Group (Very Heavy). *Activated* on 25 Aug 1944. Assigned to Second AF.

Trained for overseas duty with B–29's. Moved to the Pacific theater, Jul–Sep 1945, and assigned to Eighth AF. The war ended before the group could enter combat. Returned to the US in Dec 1945. *Inactivated* on 4 Jan 1946.

SQUADRONS. *420th:* 1944–1946. *464th:* 1944–1946. *536th:* 1942–1944. *537th:* 1942–1944. *538th:* 1942–1944. *539th:* 1942–1944. *872d:* 1944–1946.

STATIONS. Salt Lake City AAB, Utah, 3 Nov 1942; Davis-Monthan Field, Ariz, 23 Jan 1943; Pocatello AAFld, Idaho, 5 Apr 1943; Muroc AAFld, Calif, 6 Dec 1943–31 Mar 1944. Dalhart AAFld, Tex, 25 Aug 1944; Smoky Hill AAFld, Kan, 11 Dec 1944–8 Jul 1945; Guam, 8 Sep–16 Dec 1945; Camp Anza, Calif, 30 Dec 1945–4 Jan 1946.

COMMANDERS. Unkn, Nov 1942–Jan 1943; Maj Paul Schwartz, 23 Jan 1943; Lt Col George E Glober, 18 Jun 1943–31 Mar 1944. 2d Lt Melvin A Dilcherd, 29 Aug 1944; Col William W Jones, 19 Sep 1944; Col Audrin R Walker, 16 Feb 1945 unkn.

CAMPAIGNS. American Theater; Asiatic-Pacific Theater.

DECORATIONS. None.

INSIGNE. None.

383d BOMBARDMENT GROUP

Constituted as 383d Bombardment Group (Heavy) on 28 Oct 1942. *Activated* on 3 Nov 1942. Assigned to Second AF. Equipped with B–17's and B–24's. Served first as an operational training and later as a replacement training unit. *Inactivated* on 1 Apr 1944.

Redesignated 383d Bombardment Group (Very Heavy). *Activated* on 28 Aug 1944. Assigned to Second AF. Prepared for combat with B–29's. Moved to the Pacific theater, Aug–Sep 1945, and assigned to Eighth AF. The war ended before the group could enter combat. Returned to the US in Dec 1945. *Inactivated* on 3 Jan 1946.

SQUADRONS. *540th:* 1942–1944. *541st:* 1942–1944. *542d:* 1942–1944. *543d:* 1942–1944. *876th:* 1944–1946. *880th:* 1944–1946. *884th:* 1944–1946.

STATIONS. Salt Lake City AAB, Utah, 3 Nov 1942; Rapid City AAB, SD, 12 Nov 1942; Geiger Field, Wash, 20 Jun 1943; Peterson Field, Colo, 26 Oct 1943–1 Apr 1944. Dalhart AAFld, Tex, 28 Aug 1944; Walker AAFld, Kan, 14 Jan–11 Aug 1945; Tinian, 12 Sep–19 Dec 1945; Camp Anza, Calif, 2–3 Jan 1946.

COMMANDERS. Maj Elliot Vandevanter Jr, 27 Nov 1942–unkn. Lt Col John P Proctor, 1944; Col Richard M Montgomery, 8 Dec 1944–unkn.

CAMPAIGNS. American Theater; Asiatic-Pacific Theater.

DECORATIONS. None.

INSIGNE. None.

384th BOMBARDMENT GROUP

Constituted as 384th Bombardment Group (Heavy) on 25 Nov 1942. *Activated* on 1 Dec 1942. Trained for combat with B–17's. Moved to England, May–

KEEP THE SHOW ON THE ROAD

Jun 1943, and assigned to Eighth AF. Functioned primarily as a strategic bombardment organization, concentrating its attacks on airfields and industries in France and Germany. Targets included airdromes at Orleans, Bricy, and Nancy; motor works at Cologne; a coking plant at Gelsenkirchen; an aircraft component parts factory at Halberstadt; steel works at Magdeburg; and ball-bearing plants at Schweinfurt. Made a damaging raid on aircraft factories in central Germany on 11 Jan 1944 and received a DUC for the action. Took part in the campaign of heavy bombers against the German aircraft industry during Big Week, 20–25 Feb 1944. Received another DUC for the mission of 24 Apr 1944 when the group, although crippled by heavy losses of men and planes, led the 41st Wing through almost overwhelming opposition to attack an aircraft factory and airfield at Oberpfaffenhofen. The group also bombed ports, communications centers, oil facilities, and cities, attacking such targets as oil storage plants in Leipzig and Berlin, ports at Hamburg and Emden, and marshalling yards at Duren and Mannheim. At times it flew interdictory and support missions. Attacked installations along the coast of Normandy prior to and during the invasion in Jun 1944 and then bombed airfields and communications beyond the beachhead. Supported ground troops during the breakthrough at St Lo, 24–25 Jul, by bombing enemy strong points just beyond Allied lines. Hit tank and gun concentrations north of Eindhoven to assist the airborne assault on Holland in Sep. Struck enemy communications and fortifications during the Battle of the Bulge, Dec 1944–Jan 1945. Aided the Allied assault across the Rhine in Mar 1945 by attacking marshalling yards, railroad junctions, and bridges to cut off enemy supplies. Remained in the theater after the war as part of United States Air Forces in Europe. Carried American soldiers to Casablanca for return to the US, returned Greek soldiers to their homeland, and moved Allied troops to Germany. *Inactivated* in France on 28 Feb 1946.

Redesignated 384th Bombardment Group (Very Heavy). Allotted to the reserve. *Activated* on 16 Jul 1947. *Inactivated* on 27 Jun 1949.

SQUADRONS. 338th: 1947–1949. *339th:* 1947–1949. *544th:* 1942–1946; 1947–1949. *545th:* 1942–1946; 1947–1949. *546th:* 1942–1946. *547th:* 1942–1946.

STATIONS. Gowen Field, Idaho, 1 Dec 1942; Wendover Field, Utah, 2 Jan 1943;

Sioux City AAB, Iowa, c. 3 Apr–9 May 1943; Grafton Underwood, England, Jun 1943; Istres, France, c. Jun 1945–28 Feb 1946. Nashville Mun Aprt, Tenn, 16 Jul 1947–27 Jun 1949.

COMMANDERS. Col Budd J Peaslee, 2 Jan 1943; Col Lucius K Lacey, c. 6 Sep 1943; Col Dale O Smith, 23 Nov 1943; Lt Col Theodore E Milton, 24 Oct 1944; Lt Col Robert W Fish, 17 Jun 1945; Lt Col Lloyd D Chapman, 18 Oct 1945–Feb 1946.

CAMPAIGNS. Air Offensive, Europe; Normandy; Northern France; Rhineland; Ardennes-Alsace; Central Europe.

DECORATIONS. Distinguished Unit Citations: Germany, 11 Jan 1944; Germany, 24 Apr 1944.

INSIGNE. *Shield:* Azure, between two cloud formations in chief and one in base throughout proper, five stars, one, two, and two or, the one in chief emitting a ray to each star of the like voided azure, and a lightning flash palewise to base point gules fimbriated argent, all within a diminutive border of the last. *Motto:* KEEP THE SHOW ON THE ROAD. (Approved 9 Apr 1958.)

385th BOMBARDMENT GROUP

Constituted as 385th Bombardment Group (Heavy) on 25 Nov 1942. *Activated* on 1 Dec 1942. Trained with B-17's. Moved to England in Jun 1943 and assigned to Eighth AF. Operated primarily as a strategic bombardment organization until the war ended, striking such targets as industrial areas, air bases, oil refineries, and communications centers in Germany, France, Poland, Belgium, Holland, and Norway. Received a DUC for bombing an aircraft factory at Regensburg on 17 Aug 1943 after a long hazardous flight over enemy territory. Led the 4th Wing a great distance through heavy and damaging opposition for the successful bombardment of an aircraft repair plant at Zwickau on 12 May 1944, being awarded another DUC for this performance. Other strategic targets included aircraft factories in Oschersleben and Marienburg, battery works in Stuttgart, airfields in Beauvais and Chartres, oil refineries in Ludwigshafen and Merseburg, and marshalling yards in Munich and Oranienburg. Sometimes supported ground forces and struck interdictory targets. Attacked coastline defenses in Jun 1944 in preparation for the Normandy invasion and hit marshalling yards and choke points during the landing on D-Day. Bombed enemy positions in support of ground forces at St Lo in Jul 1944. Attacked German communications and fortifications during the Battle of the Bulge, Dec 1944–Jan 1945. Bombed troop concentrations and communications centers in Germany and France, Mar–Apr 1945, to assist the final thrust into Germany. After V-E Day, hauled prisoners of war from Germany to Allied centers and flew food to Holland. Returned to the US in Aug. *Inactivated* on 28 Aug 1945.

SQUADRONS. *548th:* 1942–1945. *549th:* 1942–1945. *550th:* 1942–1945. *551st:* 1942–1945.

STATIONS. Davis-Monthan Field, Ariz, 1 Dec 1942; El Paso, Tex, 21 Dec 1942; Geiger Field, Wash, 1 Feb 1943; Great Falls AAB, Mont, 11 Apr–Jun 1943; Great Ashfield, England, Jun 1943–Aug 1945; Sioux Falls AAFld, SD, Aug–28 Aug 1945.

COMMANDERS. Col Elliot Vandevanter Jr, 3 Feb 1943; Col George Y Jumper, 24 Aug 1944; Col William H Hanson, 2 Jun 1945; Maj Totton J Anderson, c. Jul 1945–unkn.

CAMPAIGNS. Air Offensive, Europe; Normandy; Northern France; Rhineland; Ardennes-Alsace; Central Europe.

DECORATIONS. Distinguished Unit Citations: Germany, 17 Aug 1943; Zwickau, Germany, 12 May 1944.

INSIGNE. None.

386th BOMBARDMENT GROUP

Constituted as 386th Bombardment Group (Medium) on 25 Nov 1942. *Activated* on 1 Dec 1942. Equipped with B–26's. Moved to England, arriving in Jun 1943. Operated with Eighth AF until assigned to Ninth in Oct 1943. Flew first mission in Jul 1943. Concentrated on airdromes but also bombed marshalling yards and gun positions during the first months of combat. Carried out an extensive campaign against V-weapon sites along the coast of France in the winter of 1943–1944, and bombed airfields in Holland and Belgium during Big Week, 20–25 Feb 1944. Hammered marshalling yards, gun positions, and airdromes preceding the invasion of Normandy and made numerous assaults on bridges of the Seine late in May. Struck coastal batteries on D-Day and hit bridges, supply and fuel stores, gun positions, and defended areas during the remainder of the Normandy campaign. Supported Allied forces at Caen, and participated in the massive blows against the enemy at St Lo on 25 Jul 1944. Knocked out targets to help clear the Falaise gap of German forces in Aug 1944 and hit strong points at Brest during Sep. After moving to the Continent in Oct 1944, attacked strong points at Metz, flew missions to Holland, and assaulted such objectives as defended areas, storage depots, and communications in Germany. Focused its attacks primarily on bridges during the Battle of the Bulge, Dec 1944–Jan 1945, in order to cut off enemy supplies and reinforcements. Converted to A–26's shortly after the Ardennes campaign and continued to strike German communications, transportation, and storage facilities until May 1945. *Redesignated* 386th Bombardment Group (Light) in Jun 1945. Returned to the US, Jul–Aug. *Inactivated* on 7 Nov 1945.

Redesignated 386th Fighter-Bomber Group. *Activated* on 8 Apr 1956. Assigned to Tactical Air Command.

SQUADRONS. *552d:* 1942–1945; 1956–. *553d:* 1942–1945; 1956–. *554th:* 1942–1945; 1956–. *555th:* 1942–1945.

STATIONS. MacDill Field, Fla, 1 Dec 1942; Lake Charles AAB, La, 9 Feb–8 May

1943; Snetterton Heath, England, 3 Jun 1943; Boxted, England, 10 Jun 1943; Great Dunmow, England, 24 Sep 1943; Beaumont-sur-Oise, France, 2 Oct 1944; St-Trond, Belgium, 9 Apr–Jul 1945; Seymour Johnson Field, NC, 7 Aug 1945; Westover Field, Mass 30 Sep–7 Nov 1945. Bunker Hill AFB, Ind, 8 Apr 1956–.

COMMANDERS. Col Lester J Maitland, c. 1 Dec 1942; Col Richard C Sanders, 18 Nov 1943; Col Joe W Kelly, 22 Jan 1944; Col Thomas G Corbin, c. 25 Aug 1944–1945. Capt Amos B Leighton, 8 Apr 1956–.

CAMPAIGNS. Air Offensive, Europe; Normandy; Northern France; Rhineland; Ardennes-Alsace; Central Europe.

DECORATIONS. Distinguished Unit Citation: ETO, 30 Jul 1943–30 Jul 1944.

INSIGNE. None.

387th BOMBARDMENT GROUP

Constituted as 387th Bombardment Group (Medium) on 25 Nov 1942. *Activated* on 1 Dec 1942. Trained with B–26 aircraft. Moved to England in Jun 1943. Served with Eighth AF until assigned to Ninth in Oct 1943. Began combat in Aug 1943 and concentrated its attacks on airdromes during the first months of operations. Made numerous strikes on V-weapon sites in France in the winter of 1943–1944. Hit airfields at Leeuwarden and Venlo during Big Week, 20–25 Feb 1944, the intensive campaign against the German Air Force and aircraft industry. Helped to prepare for the invasion of Normandy by attacking coastal batteries and bridges in France during May 1944. Bombed along the invasion coast on 6 Jun 1944 and supported ground forces throughout the month by raiding railroads, bridges, road junctions, defended areas, and fuel dumps. Moved to the Continent in Jul 1944 and participated in attacks on the enemy at St Lo in the latter part of the month and on German forces at Brest during Aug and Sep. Extended operations into Germany by fall of 1944. Received a DUC for action during the Battle of the Bulge when the group hit strongly defended transportation and communications targets at Mayen and Prum. Supported the Allied drive into the Reich by attacking bridges, communications centers, marshalling yards, storage installations, and other objectives. Ended combat operations in Apr 1945. Returned to the US in Nov. *Inactivated* on 17 Nov 1945.

SQUADRONS. *556th:* 1942–1945. *557th:* 1942–1945. *558th:* 1942–1945. *559th:* 1942–1945.

STATIONS. MacDill Field, Fla, 1 Dec 1942; Drane Field, Fla, 12 Apr 1943; Godman Field, Ky, c. 11 May–10 Jun 1943; Chipping Ongar, England, 25 Jun 1943; Stony Cross, England, 18 Jul 1944; Maupertuis, France, 22 Aug 1944; Chateaudun, France, 18 Sep 1944; Clastres, France, 30 Oct 1944; Beek, Holland, 29 Apr 1945; Rosieres-en-Santerre, France, 24 May–c. Nov 1945; Camp Kilmer, NJ, 14–17 Nov 1945.

COMMANDERS. Maj David S Blackwell, 20 Dec 1942; Col Carl R Storrie, c. 19 Jan

1943; Col Jack E Caldwell, 8 Nov 1943; Col Thomas M Seymour, 13 Apr 1944; Col Grover C Brown, c. 18 Jul 1944; Lt Col Richard R Stewart, 20 May 1945; Col Philip A Sykes, Jun 1945–unkn.

CAMPAIGNS. Air Offensive, Europe; Normandy; Northern France; Rhineland; Ardennes-Alsace; Central Europe.

DECORATIONS. Distinguished Unit Citation: Germany, 23 Dec 1944.

INSIGNE. None.

388th BOMBARDMENT GROUP

LIBERTAS VEL MORS

Constituted as 388th Bombardment Group (Heavy) on 19 Dec 1942 and *activated* on 24 Dec. Trained for combat with B–17's. Moved to England in Jun 1943 and assigned to Eighth AF. Began operations on 17 Jul 1943 by attacking an aircraft factory in Amsterdam. Functioned primarily as a strategic bombardment organization until the war ended.

Targets included industries, naval installations, oil storage plants, refineries, and communications centers in Germany, France, Poland, Belgium, Norway, Rumania, and Holland. Received a DUC for withstanding heavy opposition to bomb a vital aircraft factory at Regensburg on 17 Aug 1943. Received another DUC for three outstanding missions: an attack against a tire and rubber factory in Hannover on 26 Jul 1943; the bombardment of a synthetic oil refinery in Brux on 12 May 1944; and a strike against a synthetic oil refinery at Ruhland on 21 Jun 1944, during a shuttle raid from England to Russia. Attacked many other significant targets, including aircraft factories in Kassel, Reims, and Brunswick; airfields in Bordeaux, Paris, and Berlin; naval works at La Pallice, Emden, and Kiel; chemical industries in Ludwigshafen; ball-bearing plants in Schweinfurt; and marshalling yards in Brussels, Osnabruck, and Bielefeld. Operations also included support and interdictory missions. Helped prepare for the invasion of Normandy by attacking military installations in France, and on D–Day struck coastal guns, field batteries, and transportation. Continued to support ground forces during the campaign that followed, hitting such objectives as supply depots and troop concentrations. Bombed in support of ground forces at St Lo in Jul 1944 and at Caen in Aug. Covered the airborne assault on Holland in Sep 1944 by attacking military installations and airfields at Arnheim. Aided the final drive through Germany during the early months of 1945 by striking targets such as marshalling yards, rail bridges, and road junctions. After V–E Day, flew food to Holland to relieve flood-stricken areas. Returned to the US in Aug. *Inactivated* on 28 Aug 1945.

Redesignated 388th Fighter-Bomber Group. *Activated* on 23 Nov 1953. Assigned to Tactical Air Command. Trained with F–86 aircraft. Moved to France, Nov–Dec 1954, and became part of United States Air Forces in Europe.

SQUADRONS. *560th:* 1942–1945. *561st:* 1942–1945; 1953–. *562d:* 1942–1945; 1953–. *563d:* 1942–1945; 1953–.

STATIONS. Gowen Field, Idaho, 24 Dec 1942; Wendover Field, Utah, 1 Feb 1943; Sioux City AAB, Iowa, c. 29 Apr–10 Jun 1943; Knettishall, England, Jun 1943–Aug 1945; Sioux Falls AAFld, SD, 13–28 Aug 1945. Clovis AFB, NM, 23 Nov 1953–28 Nov 1954; Etain Rouvres AB, France, 12 Dec 1954–.

COMMANDERS. Col William B David, 1 Feb 1943; Col Chester C Cox, 7 Oct 1944–c. 28 Aug 1945. Maj Charles M Read, 23 Nov 1953; Col Clayton L Peterson, 11 Jan 1954–.

CAMPAIGNS. Air Offensive, Europe; Normandy; Northern France; Rhineland; Ardennes-Alsace; Central Europe.

DECORATIONS. Distinguished Unit Citations: Germany, 17 Aug 1943; Hannover, Germany (26 Jun 1943), Brux, Czechoslovakia (12 May 1944), and from England to Russia (21 Jun 1944).

INSIGNE. *Shield:* Per bend azure and gules, on a bend or, a lightning flash sable.

Supporters: The shield supported by two wings light blue, feathered and detail black. *Motto:* LIBERTAS VEL MORS—Liberty or Death. (Approved 11 Mar 1955.)

389th BOMBARDMENT GROUP

Constituted as 389th Bombardment Group (Heavy) on 19 Dec 1942 and *activated* on 24 Dec. Prepared for duty overseas with B–24's. Moved to England, Jun–Jul 1943, and assigned to Eighth AF. Almost immediately a detachment was sent to Libya, where it began operations on 9 Jul 1943. The detachment flew missions to Crete, Sicily, Italy, Austria, and Rumania. The group received a DUC for the detachment's participation in the famed low-level attack against oil refineries at Ploesti on 1 Aug 1943. For his action during the same operation, 2d Lt Lloyd H Hughes was awarded the Medal of Honor: refusing to turn back although gasoline was streaming from his flak-damaged plane, Lt Hughes flew at low altitude over the blazing target area and bombed the objective; the plane crashed before Hughes could make the forced landing that he attempted after the bomb run. The detachment returned to England in Aug and the group flew several missions against airfields in France and Holland. Operating temporarily from Tunisia, Sep–Oct 1943, the 389th supported Allied operations at Salerno and hit targets in Corsica, Italy, and Austria. Resumed operations from England in Oct

1943, and until Apr 1945 concentrated primarily on strategic objectives in France, the Low Countries, and Germany. Targets included shipbuilding yards at Vegesack, industrial areas of Berlin, oil facilities at Merseburg, factories at Munster, railroad yards at Sangerhausen, and V-weapon sites at Pas de Calais. Participated in the intensive air campaign against the German aircraft industry during Big Week, 20–25 Feb 1944. Also flew support and interdictory missions on several occasions, bombing gun batteries and airfields in support of the Normandy invasion in Jun 1944, striking enemy positions to aid the breakthrough at St Lo in Jul 1944, hitting storage depots and communications centers during the Battle of the Bulge (Dec 1944–Jan 1945), and dropping food, ammunition, gasoline, and other supplies to troops participating in the airborne assault across the Rhine in Mar 1945. Flew last combat mission late in Apr 1945. Returned to the US, May–Jun 1945. *Inactivated* on 13 Sep 1945.

SQUADRONS. *564th:* 1942–1945. *565th:* 1942–1945. *566th:* 1942–1945. *567th:* 1942–1945.

STATIONS. Davis-Monthan Field, Ariz, 24 Dec 1942; Biggs Field, Tex, 1 Feb 1943; Lowry Field, Colo, 19 Apr–8 Jun 1943; Hethel, England, 11 Jun 1943–30 May 1945; Charleston AAFld, SC, 12 Jun–13 Sep 1945.

COMMANDERS. Col David B Lancaster, 24 Dec 1942; Col Jack W Wood, 16 May 1943; Col Milton W Arnold, 30 Dec 1943; Col Robert B Miller, 29 Mar 1944; Col Ramsay D Potts Jr, 17 Aug 1944; Col John B Herboth Jr, 4 Dec 1944; Lt Col Jack G Merrell, 14 Apr 1945–unkn.

CAMPAIGNS. Air Combat, EAME Theater; Air Offensive, Europe; Sicily; Naples-Foggia; Normandy; Northern France; Rhineland; Ardennes-Alsace; Central Europe.

DECORATIONS. Distinguished Unit Citation: Ploesti, Rumania, 1 Aug 1943.

INSIGNE. None.

390th BOMBARDMENT GROUP

Constituted as 390th Bombardment Group (Heavy) on 15 Jan 1943 and *activated* on 26 Jan. Prepared for combat with B–17's. Moved to England in Jul 1943 and assigned to Eighth AF. Operated chiefly against strategic objectives, flying many missions with the aid of pathfinders. Began combat on 12 Aug 1943. Five days later, attacked the Messerschmitt aircraft complex at Regensburg and received a DUC for the mission. Received another DUC for a mission on 14 Oct 1943 when the group braved unrelenting assaults by enemy fighters to bomb the antifriction-bearing plants at Schweinfurt. Participating in the intensive Allied assault on the German aircraft industry during Big Week, 20–25 Feb 1944, the organization bombed aircraft factories, instrument plants, and air parks. Other strategic missions included attacks on marshalling yards at Frankfurt, bridges at Cologne, oil facilities at Zeitz, factories at Mannheim, naval installations at Bremen, and synthetic oil refineries at Merseburg. Sometimes flew interdictory and support missions. Bombed the coast near Caen fifteen minutes before the landings in Normandy on 6 Jun 1944. Attacked enemy artillery in support of ground forces during the breakthrough at St Lo in Jul. Cut German supply lines during the Battle of the Bulge, Dec 1944–Jan 1945. Hit airfields in support of the airborne assault across the Rhine in Mar 1945. Flew last combat mission on 20 Apr 1945. Dropped food supplies to the Dutch during the week prior to V–E Day. Returned to the US in Aug. *Inactivated* on 28 Aug 1945.

SQUADRONS. *568th:* 1943–1945. *569th:* 1943–1945. *570th:* 1943–1945. *571st:* 1943–1945.

STATIONS. Geiger Field, Wash, 26 Jan 1943; Great Falls AAB, Mont, 6 Jun–4 Jul 1943; Framlingham, England, Jul 1943–4 Aug 1945; Sioux Falls AAFld, SD, 12–28 Aug 1945.

COMMANDERS. Col Edgar M Whittan, 26 Jan 1943; Col Frederick W Ott, 21 Apr 1944; Col Joseph A Miller, 17 Sep 1944; Lt Col George W Von Arb Jr, 23 May 1945; Maj John A Angotti, 26 Jun–Aug 1945.

CAMPAIGNS. Air Offensive, Europe; Normandy; Northern France; Rhineland; Ardennes-Alsace; Central Europe.

DECORATIONS. Distinguished Unit Citations: Germany, 17 Aug 1943; Germany, 14 Oct 1943.

INSIGNE. None.

391st BOMBARDMENT GROUP

Constituted as 391st Bombardment Group (Medium) on 15 Jan 1943 and *activated* on 21 Jan. Trained with B–26's for duty in Europe with Ninth AF. Moved to England, Jan–Feb 1944. Entered combat on 15 Feb 1944 and during the ensuing weeks bombed targets such as airfields, marshalling yards, bridges, and V-weapon sites in France and the Low Countries to help prepare for the invasion of Normandy. Attacked enemy defenses along the invasion beaches on 6 and 7 Jun 1944. From Jun to Sep, continued cross-Channel operations, which included attacks on fuel dumps and troop concentrations in support of Allied forces during the breakthrough at St Lo in Jul 1944, and strikes on transportation and communications to block the enemy's retreat to the east. Began flying missions from bases on the Continent in Sep 1944, extending its area of operations into Germany and continuing its attacks against enemy railroads, highways, troops, bridges, ammunition dumps, and other targets. Contributed vital assistance to ground forces during the Battle of the Bulge by attacking heavily defended positions such as bridges and viaducts, 23–26 Dec 1944; for these missions, performed without fighter escort in the face of intense flak and overwhelming attacks by enemy aircraft, the group was awarded a DUC. From Jan to May 1945, and using A–26's beginning in Apr, the group concentrated its attacks on the German transportation and communications system. Flew its last mission on 3 May. *Redesignated* 391st Bombardment Group (Light) in Jul. Returned to the US in Oct. *Inactivated* on 25 Oct 1945.

Redesignated 111th Bombardment Group (Light). Allotted to ANG (Pa) on 24 May 1946. Extended federal recognition on 20 Dec 1948. *Redesignated* 111th Composite Group in Nov 1950, and 111th Bombardment Group (Light) in Feb 1951. Ordered to active service on 1 Apr 1951. Assigned to Strategic Air Command. Trained with B–26 and B–29 aircraft. *Redesignated* 111th Strategic Reconnaissance Group (Medium) in Aug 1951. Converted to RB–29's. *Inactivated* on 16 Jun 1952. Returned to ANG (Pa), *redesignated* 111th Fighter-Bomber Group, and *activated,* on 1 Jan 1953.

SQUADRONS. *103d:* 1951–1952. *117th:* 1951. *122d:* 1951. *129th:* 1951–1952. *130th:* 1951–1952. *572d:* 1943–1945. *573d:* 1943–1945. *574th:* 1943–1945. *575th:* 1943–1945.

STATIONS. MacDill Field, Fla, 21 Jan 1943; Myrtle Beach Bombing Range, SC, 24 May 1943; Godman Field, Ky, 4 Sep–31 Dec 1943; Matching, England, 25 Jan 1944; Roye/Amy, France, 19 Sep 1944; Assche, Belgium, 16 Apr 1945; Vitry-en-Artois, France, 27 May–27 Jul 1945; Camp Shanks, NY, Oct–25 Oct 1945. Philadelphia Intl Aprt, Pa, 1 Apr 1951; Fairchild AFB, Wash, 10 Apr 1951–16 Jun 1952.

COMMANDERS. Col Gerald E Williams, 23 Jan 1943–1945. Col Joseph B McManus, 1 Apr 1951; Col Edward D Edwards, 24 Jun 1951; Col S E Manzo, 8 Nov 1951–16 Jun 1952.

CAMPAIGNS. Air Offensive, Europe; Normandy; Northern France; Rhineland; Ardennes-Alsace; Central Europe.

DECORATIONS. Distinguished Unit Citation: Germany, 23–26 Dec 1944.

INSIGNE. *Shield:* Per bend or and azure, a bend counter compony sable and argent between in chief a Pegasus of the second and in base a cluster of three feathers of the first surmounted by a mullet of the fourth and third. *Motto:* VIRTUTE ALISQUE—With Wings and Courage. (Approved 11 Jan 1954.)

392d BOMBARDMENT GROUP

Constituted as 392d Bombardment Group (Heavy) on 15 Jan 1943 and *activated* on 26 Jan. Trained with B–24's.

Moved to England, Jul–Aug 1943, and assigned to Eighth AF. Began combat on 9 Sep 1943 and engaged primarily in bombardment of strategic objectives on the Continent until Apr 1945. Attacked such targets as an oil refinery at Gelsenkirchen, a marshalling yard at Osnabruck, a railroad viaduct at Bielefeld, steel plants at Brunswick, a tank factory at Kassel, and gas works at Berlin. Took part in the intensive campaign of heavy bombers against the German aircraft industry during Big Week, 20–25 Feb 1944, being awarded a DUC for bombing an aircraft and component parts factory at Gotha on 24 Feb. Sometimes supported ground forces or carried out interdictory operations. Bombed airfields and V-weapon sites in France prior to the Normandy invasion in Jun 1944 and struck coastal defenses and choke points on D-Day. Hit enemy positions to assist ground forces at St Lo during the breakthrough in Jul 1944. Bombed railroads, bridges, and highways to cut off German supply lines during the Battle of the Bulge, Dec 1944–Jan 1945. Dropped supplies to Allied troops during the air attack on Holland in Sep 1944 and during the airborne assault across the Rhine in Mar 1945. Flew last combat mission on 25 Apr 1945, then carried food to the Dutch. Returned to the US in Jun. *Inactivated* on 13 Sep 1945.

Redesignated 392d Bombardment Group (Very Heavy). Allotted to the reserve. *Activated* on 30 Jul 1947. *Redesignated* 392d Bombardment Group (Light) in Jun 1949. *Inactivated* on 10 Nov 1949.

SQUADRONS. *576th:* 1943–1945; 1947–1949. *577th:* 1943–1945; 1947–1949. *578th:* 1943–1945; 1947–1949. *579th:* 1943–1945; 1947–1949.

STATIONS. Davis-Monthan Field, Ariz, 26 Jan 1943; Biggs Field, Tex, 1 Mar 1943; Alamogordo AAB, NM, 18 Apr–18 Jul 1943; Wendling, England, Jul 1943–15 Jun 1945; Charleston AAFld, SC, 25 Jun–13 Sep 1945. Barksdale Field, La, 30 Jul 1947–10 Nov 1949.

COMMANDERS. Col Irvine A Rendle, 26 Jan 1943; Col Lorin L Johnson, 21 Jun 1944; Lt Col Lawrence G Gilbert, 27 May 1945–unkn.

CAMPAIGNS. Air Offensive, Europe; Normandy; Northern France; Rhineland; Ardennes-Alsace; Central Europe.

DECORATIONS. Distinguished Unit Citation: Gotha, Germany, 24 Feb 1944.

INSIGNE. None.

393d BOMBARDMENT GROUP

Constituted as 393d Bombardment Group (Heavy) on 29 Jan 1943. *Activated* on 16 Feb 1943. Assigned to Second AF. Equipped with B-17's. Served as an operational training unit until Aug 1943, then became a replacement training unit. *Inactivated* on 1 Apr 1944.

SQUADRONS. *580th:* 1943–1944. *581st:* 1943–1944. *582d:* 1943–1944. *583d:* 1943–1944.

STATIONS. Geiger Field, Wash, 16 Feb 1943; Gowen Field, Idaho, 3 Mar 1943;

Wendover Field, Utah, Apr 1943; Sioux City AAB, Iowa, 11 Jun 1943; Kearney AAFld, Neb, 1 Aug 1943; Sioux City AAB, Iowa, 7 Nov 1943–1 Apr 1944.

COMMANDERS. Col Chester P Gilger, Feb 1943; Lt Col George A Blakey, 15 Sep 1943–1 Apr 1944.

CAMPAIGNS. American Theater.

DECORATIONS. None.

INSIGNE. None.

394th BOMBARDMENT GROUP

READINESS LIBERTY STRENGTHENS

Constituted as 394th Bombardment Group (Medium) on 15 Feb 1943. *Activated* on 5 Mar 1943. Trained with B–26's. Moved to England, Feb–Mar 1944, and assigned to Ninth AF. Entered combat in Mar 1944 and helped to prepare for the invasion of Normandy by hitting V-weapon sites, marshalling yards, bridges, airdromes, and gun emplacements. On D–Day, 6 Jun, bombed gun positions at Cherbourg; afterward, struck communications,

fuel supplies, and strong points in support of the Normandy campaign. Aided the breakthrough at St Lo by bombing targets in the area on 25 Jul 1944. Received a DUC for operations from 7 to 9 Aug 1944 when the group made five attacks against strongly fortified targets in northern France, knocking out an ammunition dump and four railroad bridges. Capt Darrell R Lindsey was awarded the Medal of Honor for leading a formation of B–26's over one of these bridges on 9 Aug. During the flight, Lindsey's plane was hit and the right engine burst into flames. Knowing that the gasoline tanks could explode at any moment, he continued to lead the formation until the bomb run had been made, then ordered his crew to bail out. The bombardier, the last man to leave the plane, offered to lower the wheels so that Lindsey might escape through the nose of the aircraft, but realizing that this could throw the plane into a spin and hinder the bombardier's chances to escape, Lindsey refused the offer and remained with his B–26 until it crashed. After moving to the Continent late in Aug 1944, the group hit strong points at Brest and then began to operate against targets in Germany. Took part in the Battle of the Bulge, Dec 1944—Jan 1945, by hitting communications to deprive the enemy of supplies and reinforcements. Bombed transportation, storage facilities, and other objectives until the war ended; also dropped propaganda leaflets. Remained in the theater to serve with United States Air Forces in Europe as part of the army of occupation. *Redesignated* 394th Bombardment Group (Light) in Dec 1945. Began training with A-26's. Transferred, without personnel and equipment, to the US on 15 Feb 1946. *Inactivated* on 31 Mar 1946.

Redesignated 106th Bombardment Group (Light). Allotted to ANG (NY) on 24 May 1946. Extended federal recognition on 21 Mar 1947. *Redesignated* 106th Composite Group in Nov 1950, and 106th Bombardment Group (Light) in Feb 1951. Ordered to active service on 1 Mar 1951. Assigned to Strategic Air Command. *Redesignated* 106th Bombardment Group (Medium) in May 1951. Equipped with B-29's. *Inactivated* on 16 Jun 1952. Returned to ANG (NY) on 1 Dec 1952. *Redesignated* 106th Bombardment Group (Light).

SQUADRONS. *102d:* 1951-1952. *114th:* 1951-1952. *135th:* 1951-1952. *584th:* 1943-1946. *585th:* 1943-1946. *586th:* 1943-1946. *587th:* 1943-1945.

STATIONS. MacDill Field, Fla, 5 Mar 1943; Ardmore AAFld, Okla, 12 Jul 1943; Kellogg Field, Mich, 19 Aug 1943-15 Feb 1944; Boreham, England, c. 11 Mar 1944; Holmsley, England, 24 Jul 1944; Tour-en-Bassin, France, 25 Aug 1944; Bricy, France, 18 Sep 1944; Cambrai/Niergnies, France, 8 Oct 1944; Venlo, Holland, 2 May 1945; Kitzingen, Germany, Sep 1945-15 Feb 1946; Bolling Field, DC, 15 Feb-31 Mar 1946. Floyd Bennett Field, NY, 1 Mar 1951; March AFB, Calif, 28 Mar 1951-16 Jun 1952.

COMMANDERS. Lt Col Joe W Kelly, c. 20 Mar 1943; Col Thomas B Hall, 6 Apr 1943; Col Gove C Celio Jr, c. 24 Jan 1945-c. Feb 1946. Unkn, Mar-Aug 1951; Col Howell M Estes Jr, 4 Aug 1951; Col Loran D Briggs, 1 Mar-16 Jun 1952.

CAMPAIGNS. American Theater; Air Offensive, Europe; Normandy; Northern France; Rhineland; Ardennes-Alsace; Central Europe.

DECORATIONS. Distinguished Unit Citation: France, 7-9 Aug 1944. French Croix de Guerre with Palm: France, 6 Jun-14 Sep 1944.

INSIGNE. *Shield:* Azure, a clenched fist terminating in displayed dexter demi-wing of an eagle, the first grasping a torch, all sable fimbriated argent, flames gules fimbriated of the last. *Motto:* READINESS STRENGTHENS LIBERTY. (Approved 15 Apr 1954.)

395th BOMBARDMENT GROUP

Constituted as 395th Bombardment Group (Heavy) on 29 Jan 1943. *Activated* on 16 Feb 1943. Assigned to Second AF. Equipped with B-17's. Served first as an operational training unit, becoming a replacement training unit in Oct 1943. *Inactivated* on 1 Apr 1944.

SQUADRONS. *588th:* 1943-1944. *589th:* 1943-1944. *590th:* 1943-1944. *591st:* 1943-1944.

STATIONS. Ephrata AAB, Wash, 16 Feb 1943; Ardmore AAFld, Okla, 25 Oct 1943-1 Apr 1944.

COMMANDERS. Lt Col Luther J Fairbanks, Feb 1943; Lt Col Hugh D Wallace, 8 Apr 1943; Col Howard M Turner, 19 Apr 1943; Lt Col Hugh D Wallace, 24 Apr 1943; Col Allen W Reed, 2 Aug 1943; Lt Col Quentin T Quick, 23 Sep–Nov 1943; Unkn, Nov 1943–1 Apr 1944.

CAMPAIGNS. American Theater.

DECORATIONS. None.

INSIGNE. None.

396th BOMBARDMENT GROUP

Constituted as 396th Bombardment Group (Heavy) on 29 Jan 1943. *Activated* on 16 Feb 1943. Assigned to Second AF, later (Nov 1943) to Third AF. Equipped with B-17's. Served as an operational training unit until Aug 1943, then became a replacement training unit. *Inactivated* on 1 May 1944.

SQUADRONS. *592d:* 1943–1944. *593d:* 1943–1944. *594th:* 1943–1944. *595th:* 1943–1944.

STATIONS. Mountain Home AAFld, Idaho, 16 Feb 1943; Moses Lake AAB, Wash, 10 Apr 1943; Drew Field, Fla, 5 Nov 1943–1 May 1944.

COMMANDERS. Lt Col Frederick T Crimmins Jr, 1943–1 May 1944.

CAMPAIGNS. American Theater.

DECORATIONS. None.

INSIGNE. None.

397th BOMBARDMENT GROUP

Constituted as 397th Bombardment Group (Medium) on 20 Mar 1943. *Activated* on 20 Apr 1943. Trained with B-26's. Moved to England, Mar–Apr 1944, and assigned to Ninth AF. Participated in operations preparatory to the Normandy invasion by attacking V-weapon sites, bridges, coastal defenses, marshalling yards, and airfields, Apr–Jun 1944. Hit strong points in France on D-Day and assisted ground forces throughout the remainder of the Normandy campaign by bombing fuel dumps, defended areas, and other objectives. Engaged in bombardment of German forces in the region of St Lo during the Allied breakthrough in Jul. After moving to the Continent in Aug, struck enemy positions at St Malo and Brest and bombed targets in the Rouen area as Allied armies swept across the Seine and advanced to the Siegfried Line. Began flying missions into Germany in Sep, attacking such targets as bridges, defended areas, and storage depots. Struck the enemy's communications during the Battle of the Bulge (Dec 1944–Jan 1945) and received a DUC for a mission on 23 Dec 1944 when the group withstood heavy flak and fighter attack to sever a railway bridge at Eller, a vital link in the enemy's supply line across the Moselle. Continued to support the Allied drive into Germany until Apr 1945. Returned to the US, Dec 1945–Jan 1946. *Inactivated* on 6 Jan 1946.

SQUADRONS. *596th:* 1943–1945. *597th:* 1943–1946. *598th:* 1943–1945. *599th:* 1943–1945.

STATIONS. MacDill Field, Fla, 20 Apr 1943; Avon Park Bombing Range, Fla, 12

Oct 1943; Hunter Field, Ga, 1 Nov 1943–13 Mar 1944; Gosfield, England, 5 Apr 1944; Rivenhall, England, 15 Apr 1944; Hurn, England, 5 Aug 1944; Gorges, France, Aug 1944; Dreux, France, c. 11 Sep 1944; Peronne, France, 6 Oct 1944; Venlo, Holland, 25 Apr 1945; Peronne, France, c. 24 May–c. Dec 1945; Camp Kilmer, NJ, 5–6 Jan 1946.

COMMANDERS. Maj Rollin M Winingham, c. May 1943; Lt Col John F Batjer, 18 Jul 1943; Col Richard T Coiner Jr, 5 Oct 1943; Lt Col Jimmie W Britt, 23 Jul 1945–unkn.

CAMPAIGNS. Air Offensive, Europe; Normandy; Northern France; Rhineland; Ardennes-Alsace; Central Europe.

DECORATIONS. Distinguished Unit Citation: Eller, Germany, 23 Dec 1944.

INSIGNE. None.

398th BOMBARDMENT GROUP

Constituted as 398th Bombardment Group (Heavy) on 15 Feb 1943. *Activated* on 1 Mar 1943. Prepared for combat with B–17's, but interrupted these activities from Jul to Dec 1943 to train replacement crews for other organizations. Moved to England in Apr 1944 and assigned to Eighth AF. Entered combat in May 1944, and until V–E Day operated primarily against strategic objectives in Germany, attacking targets such as factories in Berlin, warehouses in Munich, marshalling yards in Saarbrucken, shipping facilities in Kiel, oil refineries in Merseburg, and aircraft plants in Munster. Temporarily suspended strategic missions to attack coastal defenses and enemy troops on the Cherbourg peninsula during the Normandy invasion in Jun 1944; strike gun positions near Eindhoven in support of the air attack on Holland in Sep 1944; raid power stations, railroads, and bridges during the Battle of the Bulge, Dec 1944–Jan 1945; and attack airfields to aid the Allied assault across the Rhine in Mar 1945. Flew last combat mission, attacking an airfield in Pilsen, Czechoslovakia, on 25 Apr 1945. Transported liberated prisoners from Germany to France after V–E Day. Returned to the US, May–Jun 1945. *Inactivated* on 1 Sep 1945.

SQUADRONS. *600th:* 1943–1945. *601st:* 1943–1945. *602d:* 1943–1945. *603d:* 1943–1945.

STATIONS. Ephrata AAB, Wash, 1 Mar 1943; Blythe AAFld, Calif, 5 Apr 1943; Geiger Field, Wash, 29 Apr 1943; Rapid City AAB, SD, 20 Jun 1943–4 Apr 1944; Nuthampstead, England, 22 Apr 1944–26 May 1945; Drew Field, Fla, 3 Jul–1 Sep 1945.

COMMANDERS. Col Frank P Hunter Jr, 1 Mar 1943; Lt Col Lewis P Ensign, 29 Jan 1945; Lt Col Arthur F Briggs, 18 Apr 1945–unkn.

CAMPAIGNS. American Theater; Air Offensive, Europe; Normandy; Northern France; Rhineland; Ardennes-Alsace; Central Europe.

DECORATIONS. None.

INSIGNE. None.

399th BOMBARDMENT GROUP

Constituted as 399th Bombardment Group (Heavy) on 15 Feb 1943. *Activated* on 1 Mar 1943. Assigned to Second AF; reassigned to Fourth AF in Dec 1943. Equipped with B–24's. Served first as an operational training unit and later (Aug 1943) became a replacement training unit. *Disbanded* on 31 Mar 1944.

SQUADRONS. *604th:* 1943–1944. *605th:* 1943–1944. *606th:* 1943–1944. *607th:* 1943–1944.

STATIONS. Davis-Monthan Field, Ariz, 1 Mar 1943; Gowen Field, Idaho, 10 Apr 1943; Wendover Field, Utah, 27 Apr 1943; March Field, Calif, 3 Dec 1943–31 Mar 1944.

COMMANDERS. Lt Col Luther J Fairbanks, Apr 1943; Lt Col James H Isbell, 1 Oct 1943; Lt Col John E Dougherty, 11 Nov 1943; Lt Col Eugene T Yarbrough, 15 Feb–31 Mar 1944.

CAMPAIGNS. American Theater.

DECORATIONS. None.

INSIGNE. None.

400th BOMBARDMENT GROUP

Constituted as 400th Bombardment Group (Heavy) on 15 Feb 1943. *Activated* on 1 Mar 1943. Equipped with B–24's. Functioned as an operational training unit of Second AF from May to Dec 1943. Reassigned to First AF to train replacement crews. *Disbanded* on 10 Apr 1944.

SQUADRONS. *608th:* 1943–1944. *609th:* 1943–1944. *610th:* 1943–1944. *611th:* 1943–1944.

STATIONS. Pyote AAB, Tex, 1 Mar 1943; Davis-Monthan Field, Ariz, Apr 1943; Pueblo AAB, Colo, c. 2 May 1943; Salina, Kan, 31 Jul 1943; Alamogordo AAFld, NM, 19 Sep 1943; Charleston AAFld, SC, 15 Dec 1943–10 Apr 1944.

COMMANDERS. Lt Col John A Way, c. Mar 1943–Apr 1944.

CAMPAIGNS. American Theater.

DECORATIONS. None.

INSIGNE. None.

401st BOMBARDMENT GROUP

Constituted as 401st Bombardment Group (Heavy) on 20 Mar 1943. *Activated* on 1 Apr 1943. Prepared for combat with B–17's. Moved to England, Oct-Nov 1943, and served in combat with Eighth AF, Nov 1943–Apr 1945. Operated chiefly against strategic targets, bombing industries, submarine facilities, shipyards, missile sites, marshalling yards, and airfields; beginning in Oct 1944, concentrated on oil reserves. Received a DUC for striking telling blows against German aircraft production on 11 Jan and 20 Feb 1944. In addition to strategic missions, operations included attacks on transportation, airfields, and fortifications prior to the Normandy invasion and on D-Day, Jun 1944; support for ground operations during the breakthrough at St Lo in Jul, the siege of Brest in Aug, and the airborne attack on Holland in Sep 1944; participation in the Battle of the Bulge, Dec 1944–Jan 1945, by assaulting transportation targets and communications centers in the battle area; and support for the airborne attack across the Rhine in Mar 1945. Returned to the US after V–E Day. *Inactivated* on 28 Aug 1945.

Redesignated 401st Bombardment Group (Very Heavy). Allotted to the reserve. *Activated* on 26 Jun 1947. *Redesignated* 401st Bombardment Group (Medium) in Jun 1949. Called to active service on 1 May 1951. Assigned to Strategic Air Command. *Inactivated* on 25 Jun 1951.

Redesignated 401st Fighter-Bomber Group. *Activated* on 8 Feb 1954. Assigned to Tactical Air Command and equipped with F–86's.

SQUADRONS. *612th:* 1943–1945; 1947–1951; 1954–. *613th:* 1943–1945; 1947–1949; 1954–. *614th:* 1943–1945; 1947–1949; 1954–. *615th:* 1943–1945; 1947–1949.

STATIONS. Ephrata AAB, Wash, 1 Apr 1943; Geiger Field, Wash, Jun 1943; Great Falls AAB, Mont, Jul–Oct 1943; Deenethorpe, England, c. 1 Nov 1943–May 1945; Sioux Falls AAFld, SD, c. 1–28 Aug 1945. Brooks Field, Tex, 26 Jun 1947; Biggs AFB, Tex, 27 Jun 1949–25 Jun 1951. Alexandria AFB, La, 8 Feb 1954–.

COMMANDERS. Col Neil B Harding, c. 1 Apr 1943; Col Harold W Bowman, Jun 1943; Col William T Seawell, Dec 1944–1945. Unkn, 1 May–25 Jun 1951. Col Walter G Benz Jr, 8 Feb 1954–.

CAMPAIGNS. Air Offensive, Europe; Normandy; Northern France; Rhineland; Ardennes-Alsace; Central Europe.

DECORATIONS. Distinguished Unit Citations: Germany, 11 Jan 1944; Germany, 20 Feb 1944.

INSIGNE. *Shield:* Azure, within a diminutive border argent a sheaf of four lances bend sinisterwise of the last, surmounted by a fess chequy sable and of the second overall a bend wavy vert, gules, or and of the first each fimbriated silver. *Motto:* CAELUM ARENA NOSTRA—The Sky is Our Arena. (Approved 9 Sep 1958. This insigne replaced an insigne approved 22 Apr 1955.)

402d FIGHTER GROUP

Constituted as 402d Bombardment Group (Medium) on 20 Apr 1943. *Activated* in China on 19 May 1943. Assigned to Fourteenth AF. No squadrons were assigned and headquarters apparently was never fully manned. *Disbanded* in China on 31 Jul 1943. *Reconstituted* (in Oct

1956) and *consolidated* with 402d Fighter Group.

402d Fighter Group was *constituted* on 24 Sep 1943. *Activated* in the US on 1 Oct 1943. Assigned to First AF. Trained replacement pilots for combat with P-47's. *Disbanded* on 10 Apr 1944.

Reconstituted and *redesignated* 402d Fighter-Day Group, on 4 Oct 1956. *Activated* on 15 Oct 1956. *Assigned* to Tactical Air Command.

SQUADRONS. *320th:* 1943–1944; 1956–. *442d:* 1943–1944; 1956–. *452d:* 1943–1944. *538th:* 1943. *539th:* 1943. *540th:* 1943–1944; 1956–.

STATIONS. Kunming, China, 19 May–31 Jul 1943. Westover Field, Mass, 1 Oct 1943; Seymour Johnson Field, NC, c. 13 Oct 1943; Bluethenthal Field, NC, c. 9 Dec 1943; Bradley Field, Conn, c. 11 Feb–10 Apr 1944. Greenville AFB, Miss, 15 Oct 1956–.

COMMANDERS. Unkn, 19 May–31 Jul 1943. Lt Col Joseph L Dickman, unkn–Apr 1944. Capt Charles E Burtner, 15 Oct 1956–.

CAMPAIGNS. Asiatic-Pacific Theater.

DECORATIONS. None.

INSIGNE. None.

403d TROOP CARRIER GROUP

Constituted as 403d Troop Carrier Group on 7 Dec 1942 and *activated* on 12 Dec. Trained for overseas duty with C-47's. Moved to the South Pacific, Jul–Sep 1943, and assigned to Thirteenth AF.

SPECTATE AD CAELUM

Transported men and supplies to forward areas in the Solomons and flew passenger and cargo routes to New Zealand, Australia, Fiji, and New Caledonia. Moved personnel of Thirteenth AF units to the Southwest Pacific. Supported the New Guinea and Philippines campaigns by transporting men and cargo to combat areas, evacuating casualties, and landing or dropping supplies for guerrilla forces. Dropped paratroops at Laguna de Bay, Luzon, on 23 Feb 1945, to free civilian internees held by the Japanese. Received a DUC for operations from Apr to Jun 1945 when it transported ammunition, food, and other supplies to Eighth Army forces in Mindanao and often landed on jungle airstrips to evacuate wounded personnel. Moved to Leyte in Jun 1945 and remained in the Philippines after the war as part of Far East Air Forces. Ferried occupation troops to Japan, evacuated prisoners who had been liberated, and flew cargo and passenger routes to Japan and Australia. *Inactivated* in Manila on 15 Oct 1946.

Redesignated 403d Troop Carrier Group (Medium). Allotted to the reserve. *Activated* in the US on 27 Jun 1949. Called to active duty on 1 Apr 1951. Assigned to Tactical Air Command. Trained with C-46 and C-47 aircraft. Moved to Japan, Mar–Apr 1952, and attached to Far East Air Forces for operations in the war against communist forces in Korea. Using C-119's, aided UN forces in Korea by dropping paratroops and supplies, transporting personnel and equipment, and evacuating casualties. Relieved from active duty and *inactivated* in Japan, on 1 Jan 1953.

Allotted to the reserve. *Activated* in the US on 1 Jan 1953.

SQUADRONS. *6th:* 1946. *9th:* 1946. *19th:* 1946. *63d:* 1942–1946; 1949–1953; 1953–. *64th:* 1942–1946; 1949–1953; 1953–. *65th:* 1942–1946; 1949–1953; 1953–. *66th:* 1942–1946; 1949–1951.

STATIONS. Bowman Field, Ky, 12 Dec 1942; Alliance, Neb, 18 Dec 1942; Pope Field, NC, 3 May 1943; Baer Field, Ind, 20 Jun-c. 15 Jul 1943; Espiritu Santo, 15 Sep 1943; Los Negros, 30 Aug 1944; Biak, 4 Oct 1944; Leyte, 25 Jun 1945; Clark Field, Luzon, Jan 1946; Manila, c. Jun–15 Oct 1946. Portland Mun Aprt, Ore, 27 Jun 1949–29 Mar 1952; Ashiya, Japan, 14 Apr 1952–1 Jan 1953. Portland Intl Aprt, Ore, 1 Jan 1953–.

COMMANDERS. Col Harry J Sands Jr, 12 Dec 1942; Lt Col Norton H Van Sicklen, 24 Aug 1945–unkn; Col Audrin R Walker, c. Jun–15 Oct 1946. Lt Col Robert B Asbury, 1 Apr 1951; Lt Col Henry C Althaus, 25 Jul 1951; Maj Wallace C Forsythe, 22 Apr 1952; Lt Col Ernest W Burton, Aug 1952–1 Jan 1953.

CAMPAIGNS. *World War II:* New Guinea; Northern Solomons; Bismarck Archipelago; Western Pacific; Leyte; Luzon; Southern Philippines. *Korean War:* Korea Summer-Fall, 1952; Third Korean Winter.

DECORATIONS. Distinguished Unit Citation: Philippine Islands, 17 Apr–30 Jun 1945. Philippine Presidential Unit Citation. Republic of Korea Presidential Unit Citation: [1952].

INSIGNE. *Shield:* Azure, two hands in bend sinister proper, the upper a dexter hand issuing from a cloud argent and holding an olive branch of the second, a lightning flash or and a sword sable, the lower sinister hand in profile issuing from a fan indented of seven sections (blue, white, orange, black, white, yellow and red) which in turn issues from base, above the cloud four mullets of four points of the third; all within a diminished bordure of the last. *Motto:* SPECTATE AD CAELUM—Look to the Skies. (Approved 9 Jan 1953.)

404th FIGHTER GROUP

Constituted as 404th Bombardment Group (Dive) on 25 Jan 1943. *Activated* on 4 Feb 1943. *Redesignated* 404th Fighter-Bomber Group in Aug 1943.

Trained with P-39, P-47, and other aircraft. Moved to England, Mar–Apr 1944. Assigned to Ninth AF. *Redesignated* 404th Fighter Group in May 1944. Became operational on 1 May 1944 and, using P-47's, helped to prepare for the Normandy invasion by bombing and strafing targets in France. Provided top cover for landings in Normandy on 6 and 7 Jun 1944 and continued operations from England until Jul 1944. Moved to the Continent and operated in close support of ground troops until the end of the war, supporting the Allied breakthrough at St Lo in Jul 1944, the drive through Holland in Sep 1944, Allied operations during the Battle of the Bulge (Dec 1944–Jan 1945), and the establishment of the Remagen bridgehead and the subsequent crossing of the Rhine in Mar 1945. Also flew interdictory and escort missions, strafing and bombing such targets as troop concentrations, railroads, highways, bridges, ammunition and fuel dumps, armored vehicles, docks, and tunnels, and covering

the operations of B-17's, B-24's, and B-26's that bombed factories, airdromes, marshalling yards, and other targets. Received a DUC for three armed reconnaissance missions flown on 10 Sep 1944 when, despite bad weather and antiaircraft fire, the group attacked enemy factories, rolling stock, and communications centers to aid the advance of ground forces. Received a French Croix de Guerre with Palm for assisting First Army at St Lo on 29, 30, and 31 Jul 1944 when the group, although suffering severe losses from flak, continuously provided cover for four armored divisions. Also cited by the Belgian government for operations contributing to the liberation of its people. After V-E Day, aided in disarming the German Air Force and in dismantling the enemy's aircraft industry. Returned to the US in Aug. *Inactivated* on 9 Nov 1945.

Redesignated 137th Fighter Group. Allotted to ANG (Okla) on 24 May 1946. Extended federal recognition on 18 Dec 1947. Ordered to active duty on 10 Oct 1950. *Redesignated* 137th Fighter-Bomber Group. Trained with F-84's. Moved to France in May 1952 and assigned to United States Air Forces in Europe. Relieved from active service and returned, without personnel and equipment, to the control of ANG (Okla), on 10 Jul 1952.

SQUADRONS. *125th:* 1950–1952. *127th:* 1950–1952. *128th:* 1950–1952. *455th:* 1943–1944. *506th* (formerly 620th): 1943–1945. *507th* (formerly 621st): 1943–1945. *508th* (formerly 622d): 1943–1945. *623d:* 1943.

STATIONS. Key Field, Miss, 4 Feb 1943; Congaree AAFld, SC, 5 Jul 1943; Burns AAFld, Ore, 4 Sep 1943; Myrtle Beach AAFld, SC, 13 Nov 1943–12 Mar 1944; Winkton, England, 4 Apr 1944; Chapelle, France, 6 Jul 1944; Bretigny, France, 29 Aug 1944; Juvincourt, France, 13 Sep 1944; St-Trond, Belgium, 1 Oct 1944; Keltz, Germany, 30 Mar 1945; Fritzlar, Germany, 12 Apr 1945; Stuttgart, Germany, 23 Jun–2 Aug 1945; Drew Field, Fla, 11 Sep–9 Nov 1945. Will Rogers Field, Okla, 10 Oct 1950; Alexandria Mun Aprt, La, 27 Nov 1950–4 May 1952; Chaumont, France, 13 May–10 Jul 1952.

COMMANDERS. Lt Col Lucius G Drafts, 4 Feb 1943; Lt Col James Van G Wilson, 6 May 1943; Col Carroll W McColpin, 27 Jan 1944; Lt Col Leo C Moon, 25 Nov 1944; Lt Col John R Murphy, 23 Apr 1945–unkn. Lt Col Joseph W Turner, 10 Oct 1950; Lt Col Roger B Ludeman, 27 Dec 1950; Col Chesley G Peterson, 8 Aug 1951–10 Jul 1952.

CAMPAIGNS. American Theater; Air Offensive, Europe; Normandy; Northern France; Rhineland; Ardennes-Alsace; Central Europe.

DECORATIONS. Distinguished Unit Citation: Germany, 10 Sep 1944. French Croix de Guerre with Palm: 29, 30, and 31 Jul 1944. Cited in the Order of the Day, Belgian Army: 6 Jun–30 Sep 1944; 1 Oct 1944–; 18 Dec 1944–15 Jan 1945. Belgian Fourragere.

INSIGNE. *Shield*: Azure, three lightning bolts, or, issuing from a cloud, proper, in dexter chief, all within a diminutive bordure, gules. *Motto*: TONITRUS E CAELO—Thunder from the Sky. (Approved 6 Jun 1952.)

405th FIGHTER GROUP

MOVERE ET AGGREDI

Constituted as 405th Bombardment Group (Dive) on 4 Feb 1943. *Activated* on 1 Mar 1943. *Redesignated* 405th Fighter-Bomber Group in Aug 1943, and 405th Fighter Group in May 1944. Trained with A–24, A–25, P–39, and finally P–47 aircraft, the latter being used in combat. Moved to England, Feb–Mar 1944. Entered combat with Ninth AF in Apr 1944. Until D-Day, engaged chiefly in bombing airdromes, marshalling yards, and bridges in France in preparation for the invasion of France. Flew patrols in the vicinity of Brest during the invasion and then flew armed reconnaissance missions to support operations in Normandy. Moved to the Continent at the end of Jun

1944 and engaged primarily in providing support for ground forces until May 1945. Bombed enemy vehicles and gun positions at St Lo in Jul 1944; attacked barges, troops, roads, and warehouses during the Battle of the Bulge, Dec 1944–Jan 1945; and struck airfields and marshalling yards when the Allies crossed the Rhine in Mar 1945. Received a DUC for a mission in France on 24 Sep 1944: answering a request from Third Army for support near Laneuveville-en-Saulnois, two squadrons, flying on instruments through rain and dense overcast, were directed by ground control toward a furious tank battle where, in spite of severe ground fire, one squadron repeatedly bombed and strafed enemy tanks; the second squadron, unable to find this target because of the weather, attacked a convoy of trucks and armored vehicles; later the same day, the third squadron hit warehouses and other buildings and silenced ground opposition in the area. For operations, Jun–Sep 1944, that aided the drive across Normandy and the liberation of Belgium, the group was cited by the Belgian government. Flew last mission on 8 May 1945. Returned to the US, Jul–Oct 1945. *Inactivated* on 29 Oct 1945. *Redesignated* 405th Fighter-Bomber Group. *Activated* on 1 Dec 1952. Assigned to Tactical Air Command and equipped with F–84's.

SQUADRONS. *509th* (formerly 624th): 1943–1945; 1952–. *510th* (formerly 625th): 1943–1945; 1952–. *511th* (formerly 626th): 1943–1945; 1952–. *627th:* 1943.

STATIONS. Drew Field, Fla, 1 Mar 1943; Walterboro AAFld, SC, 14 Sep 1943–14 Feb 1944; Christchurch, England, 7 Mar–22 Jun 1944; Picauville, France, 30 Jun 1944; St–Dizier, France, 14 Sep 1944; Ophoven, Belgium, 9 Feb 1945; Kitzingen, Germany, 30 Apr 1945; Straubing, Germany, 8 May–Jul 1945; Camp Patrick Henry, Va, Oct–29 Oct 1945. Godman AFB, Ky, 1 Dec 1952; Langley AFB, Va, 16 Apr 1953–.

COMMANDERS. Lt Col Marvin S Zipp, 1 Mar 1943; Lt Col Mark E Hubbard, 2 Jul 1943; Maj Fred G Hook Jr, 12 Jul 1943; Col James Ferguson, 5 Nov 1943; Col Robert L Delashaw, 26 Apr 1944; Lt Col J Garrett Jackson, 22 Oct 1944–unkn. Col George Laven Jr, 1 Dec 1952; Col Donald A Baccus, 16 Apr 1953; Col William S Cowart Jr, 6 Jul 1954; Col Robert D Johnston, c. 14 May 1955–.

CAMPAIGNS. Air Offensive, Europe; Normandy; Northern France; Rhineland; Ardennes-Alsace; Central Europe.

DECORATIONS. Distinguished Unit Citation: France, 24 Sep 1944. Cited in the Order of the Day, Belgian Army: 6 Jun–30 Sep 1944.

INSIGNE. *Shield:* Azure, a sphere argent, land marking and grid lines sable, surmounted by a bend gules, charged with a lightning flash or, between a fleur-de-lis of the last and two olive branches, in saltire, proper, all within a diminutive border of the second. *Motto:* MOVERE ET AGGREDI—Deploy and Attack. (Approved 10 Nov 1955.)

406th FIGHTER GROUP

ASCENDE ET DEFENDE

Constituted as 406th Bombardment Group (Dive) on 4 Feb 1943. *Activated* on 1 Mar 1943. *Redesignated* 406th Fighter-Bomber Group in Aug 1943, and 406th Fighter Group in May 1944. Trained with A–24, A–35, A–39, P–47, and other aircraft. Joined Ninth AF in England in Apr 1944 and entered combat with P–47's in May when the Allies were preparing for the invasion of the Continent. Provided area cover during the landings in Jun, and afterwards flew armed-reconnaissance and dive-bombing missions against the enemy, attacking such targets as motor transports, gun emplacements, ammunition dumps, rail lines, marshalling yards, and bridges during the campaign in Normandy. Helped prepare the way for the Allied breakthrough at St Lo on 25 Jul. Moved to the Continent early in Aug and continued to provide tactical air support for ground forces. Participated in the reduction of St Malo and Brest. Aided the Allied drive across France, receiving a DUC for operations on 7 Sep 1944 when the group destroyed a large column of armored vehicles and military transports that were attempting to escape from southeastern France through the Belfort Gap. Operated closely with ground forces and flew interdictory missions during the drive to the Moselle-Saar region. Shifted operations from the Saar basin to the Ardennes and assisted the beleaguered garrison at Bastogne after the Germans had launched the counteroffensive that precipitated the Battle of the Bulge. Operated almost exclusively within a ten-mile radius of Bastogne from 23–27 Dec 1944, a period for which the group received a second DUC for its attacks on tanks, vehicles, defended buildings, and gun positions. Flew escort, interdictory, and close-support missions in the Ruhr Valley early in 1945 and thus assisted Allied ground forces in their drive to and across the Rhine. Remained in Europe after V–E Day, being assigned to United States Air Forces in Europe for duty in Germany with the army of occupation. *Inactivated* on 20 Aug 1946.

Redesignated 406th Fighter-Bomber Group. *Activated* in England on 10 Jul 1952. Assigned to United States Air Forces in Europe. Equipped with F–84's; converted to F–86's late in 1953. *Redesignated* 406th Fighter-Interceptor Group in Apr 1954.

SQUADRONS. *512th* (formerly 628th): 1943–1946; 1952–. *513th* (formerly 629th): 1943–1946; 1952–. *514th* (formerly 630th): 1943–1946; 1952–. *631st:* 1943.

STATIONS. Key Field, Miss, 1 Mar 1943; Congaree AAFld, SC, c. 18 Sep 1943–13 Mar 1944; Ashford, England, 4 Apr 1944; Tour-en-Bassin, France, 5 Aug 1944; Cretteville, France, 17 Aug 1944; Le Mans, France, 4 Sep 1944; Mourmelon-le-Grand, France, 22 Sep 1944; Metz, France, 2 Feb 1945; Assche, Belgium, 8 Feb 1945; Handorf, Germany, 15 Apr 1945; Nordholz, Germany, 5 Jun 1945–20 Aug 1946. Manston, England, 10 Jul 1952–.

COMMANDERS. Lt Col Bryan B Harper, Mar 1943; Col Anthony V Grossetta, c. 6 Nov 1943; Lt Col Converse B Kelly, c. Jun 1945; Lt Col Robert C Brown, 27 Sep 1945; Lt Col Arvis L Hilpert, 17 Jan 1946; Col Earl H Dunham, 6 Apr–Aug 1946. Lt Col Delynn E Anderson, Jul 1952; Lt Col Arthur F Jeffrey, 1952; Lt Col Harry G Sanders, c. Mar 1953; Col William S Harrell, c. Jun 1954–.

CAMPAIGNS. American Theater; Air Offensive, Europe; Normandy; Northern France; Rhineland; Ardennes-Alsace; Central Europe.

DECORATIONS. Distinguished Unit Citations: France, 7 Sep 1944; Belgium, 23–27 Dec 1944.

INSIGNE. *Shield:* Azure, a bend gules fimbriated argent overall a dexter hand in spiked nail gauntlet palewise proper grasping a three-pronged lightning flash or and surmounted at the cuff by a chain of four links of the last. *Motto:* ASCEN-DE ET DEFENDE—Rise and Defend. (Approved 14 May 1953.)

407th FIGHTER GROUP

Constituted as 407th Bombardment Group (Dive) on 23 Mar 1943 and *activated* on 28 Mar. Assigned to Second and later (Nov 1943) to Third AF. Part of the group, the air echelon with A–24's, was stationed in Alaska during Jul and Aug 1943 for operations against the Japanese in the Aleutians. *Redesignated* 407th Fighter-Bomber Group in Aug 1943. Trained for combat and later functioned as a replacement training unit, using a variety of aircraft that included A–36's, P–47's, and P–51's. *Disbanded* on 1 Apr 1944.

SQUADRONS. *495th:* 1944. *515th* (formerly 632d): 1943–1944. *516th* (formerly 633d): 1943–1944. *517th* (formerly 634th): 1943–1944. *635th:* 1943.

STATIONS. Drew Field, Fla, 28 Mar 1943; Lakeland AAFld, Fla, 2 Oct 1943; Galveston AAFld, Tex, 9 Nov 1943–1 Apr 1944.

COMMANDERS. 1st Lt William E Garland, 28 Mar 1943; Lt Col Mark E Hubbard, 3 Jun 1943; Lt Col Carroll W McColpin, 8 Sep 1943; Maj Pat M DeBerry, 18 Jan 1944; Maj T W Rivers, 30 Mar–1 Apr 1944.

CAMPAIGNS. American Theater.

DECORATIONS. None.

INSIGNE. *Shield:* Azure (light blue), over an Indian bow and arrow proper, in saltire (the bow green, the arrow yellow, tipped red, feathered blue, yellow, and red, veins black) an Indian shield argent, edged black, charged with a war bird gules, markings sable, twelve feathers pendanted, from the base of the shield, proper. (Approved 1 Jun 1955.)

408th FIGHTER GROUP

Constituted as 408th Bombardment Group (Dive) on 23 Mar 1943. *Activated* on 5 Apr 1943. *Redesignated* 408th Fighter-Bomber Group in Aug 1943. As-

signed to Third AF, then to Second (Nov 1943), and again to Third (Feb 1944). Received A–24, A–26, P–40, and P–47 aircraft in Oct 1943 and began training. *Disbanded* on 1 Apr 1944.

Reconstituted and *redesignated* 408th Fighter Group (Air Defense), on 8 Jul 1955. *Activated* on 8 Apr 1956. Assigned to Air Defense Command.

SQUADRONS. *455th:* 1944. *518th* (formerly 636th): 1943–1944; 1956–. *519th* (formerly 637th): 1943–1944. *520th* (formerly 638th): 1943–1944. *639th:* 1943.

STATIONS. Key Field, Miss, 5 Apr 1943; Drew Field, Fla, 22 Sep 1943; Abilene AAFld, Tex, 10 Nov 1943; DeRidder AAB, La, 12 Feb 1944; Woodward AAFld, Okla, 26 Mar–1 Apr 1944. Klamath Falls Mun Aprt, Ore, 8 Apr 1956–.

COMMANDERS. 1st Lt Reynold H Ulick, 7 Apr 1943; Maj John R Reynolds, 22 Jun 1943; Maj Wyatt P Exum, 22 Sep 1943; Lt Col Thomas Hitchcock, 26 Dec 1943; Maj Wyatt P Exum, 1 Feb 1944; Lt Col Harry L Galusha, 18 Mar–1 Apr 1944. Lt Col Robert L Larson, Apr 1956–.

CAMPAIGNS. None.

DECORATIONS. None.

INSIGNE. *Shield:* Azure, a lightning bolt, bendwise, or, between two jet-like eagles volant proper with trailing speed vapor proper. *Motto:* DEFEND WITH VIGILANCE. (Approved 22 May 1957.)

409th BOMBARDMENT GROUP

Constituted as 409th Bombardment Group (Light) on 1 Jun 1943 and *acti-*

vated the same day. Used A–20's in preparing for duty overseas. Moved to England, Feb–Mar 1944, and assigned to Ninth AF. Bombed coastal defenses, V-weapon sites, airdromes, and other targets in France, Apr–Jun 1944, in preparation for the invasion of Normandy. Supported ground forces during the Normandy campaign by hitting gun batteries, rail lines, bridges, communications, and other objectives. During Jul 1944, aided the Allied offensive at Caen and the breakthrough at St Lo with attacks on enemy troops, flak positions, fortified villages, and supply dumps. Supported Third Army's advance toward Germany, Aug–Nov 1944, operating from bases in France beginning in Sep. Converted to A–26 aircraft in Dec and participated in the Battle of the Bulge (Dec 1944–Jan 1945) by attacking lines of communication and supply. Continued to operate against targets in Germany until May 1945. Flew last mission on 3 May, attacking an ammunition dump in Czechoslovakia. Returned to the US, Jun–Aug 1945. *Inactivated* on 7 Nov 1945.

SQUADRONS. *640th:* 1943–1945. *641st:* 1943–1945. *642d:* 1943–1945. *643d:* 1943–1945.

STATIONS. Will Rogers Field, Okla, 1 Jun 1943; Woodward AAFld, Okla, Oct 1943; DeRidder AAB, La, c. 10 Dec 1943–10 Feb 1944; Little Walden, England, 7 Mar 1944; Bretigny, France, Sep 1944; Laon/Couvron, France, Feb–Jun 1945; Seymour Johnson Field, NC, Aug 1945; Westover Field, Mass, c. 6 Oct–7 Nov 1945.

COMMANDERS. Col Preston P Pender, Jun 1943; Col Thomas R Ford, 4 Jul 1944–1945.

CAMPAIGNS. Air Offensive, Europe; Normandy; Northern France; Rhineland; Ardennes-Alsace; Central Europe.

DECORATIONS. None.

INSIGNE. None.

410th BOMBARDMENT GROUP

Constituted as 410th Bombardment Group (Light) on 16 Jun 1943. *Activated* on 1 Jul 1943. Trained with A–20's. Moved to England, Mar–Apr 1944, and assigned to Ninth AF. Entered combat in May 1944 and helped to prepare for the invasion of Normandy by assaulting coastal defenses, airfields, and V-weapon sites in France, and marshalling yards in France and Belgium. Supported the invasion in Jun by bombing gun positions and railway choke points. Assisted ground forces at Caen and St Lo in Jul and at Brest in Aug and Sep by attacking bridges, vehicles, fuel and ammunition dumps, and rail lines. Moved to France in Sep, and through mid-Dec struck defended villages, railroad bridges and overpasses, marshalling yards, military camps, and communications centers to support the Allied assault on the Siegfried Line. Participated in the Battle of the Bulge, Dec 1944–Jan 1945, by pounding marshalling yards, railheads, bridges, and vehicles in the battle area. Received a DUC for the effectiveness of its bombing in the Ardennes, 23–25 Dec 1944, when the group made numerous attacks on enemy lines of communications. Flew several night missions in Feb 1945, using B–26's as flare planes, an A–26 for target marking, and A–20's to bomb the objectives. Continued to fly support and interdictory missions, aiding the drive across the Rhine and into Germany, Feb–Apr 1945. Converted to A–26 aircraft, but the war ended before the group was ready to fly them in combat. Returned to the US, Jun–Aug 1945. *Inactivated* on 7 Nov 1945.

SQUADRONS. *644th:* 1943–1945. *645th:* 1943–1945. *646th:* 1943–1945. *647th:* 1943–1945.

STATIONS. Will Rogers Field, Okla, 1 Jul 1943; Muskogee AAFld, Okla, Oct 1943; Laurel AAFld, Miss, Jan 1944; Lakeland AAFld, Fla, c. 8 Feb–c. 13 Mar 1944; Birch, England, c. 4 Apr 1944; Gosfield, England, c. 16 Apr 1944; Coulommiers, France, Sep 1944; Juvincourt, France, Feb 1945; Beaumont-sur-Oise, France, May–Jun 1945; Seymour Johnson Field, NC, Aug 1945; Myrtle Beach AAFld, SC, c. 5 Oct–7 Nov 1945.

COMMANDERS. Unkn, 1 Jul–13 Aug 1943; Lt Col Clark L Miller, 13 Aug 1943; Col Ralph Rhudy, 17 Sep 1943; Col Sherman R Beaty, 3 Jul 1944; Col Robert J Hughey, Dec 1944–1945.

CAMPAIGNS. Air Offensive, Europe; Normandy; Northern France; Rhineland; Ardennes-Alsace; Central Europe.

DECORATIONS. Distinguished Unit Citation: Germany, 23–25 Dec 1944.

INSIGNE. None.

411th BOMBARDMENT GROUP

Constituted as 411th Bombardment Group (Light) on 14 Jul 1943. *Activated* on 1 Aug 1943. Assigned to Third AF. Functioned as a replacement training unit, using A–20 aircraft. *Disbanded* on 1 May 1944.

SQUADRONS. *648th:* 1943–1944. *649th:* 1943–1944. *650th:* 1943–1944. *651st:* 1943–1944.

STATIONS. Will Rogers Field, Okla, 1 Aug 1943; Florence AAFld, SC, 15 Aug 1943–1 May 1944.

COMMANDERS. Lt Col Blaine B Campbell, c. Aug 1943–1 May 1944.

CAMPAIGNS. None.

DECORATIONS. None.

INSIGNE. None.

412th FIGHTER GROUP

Constituted as 412th Fighter Group on 20 Nov 1943 and *activated* on 29 Nov. Assigned to Fourth AF. Conducted tests and engaged in experimental work with P–59A and P–80 jet aircraft. Also trained pilots and other personnel for duty with units using jet aircraft. *Inactivated* on 3 Jul 1946.

Redesignated 412th Fighter Group (Air Defense). *Activated* on 18 Aug 1955. Assigned to Air Defense Command.

SQUADRONS. *29th:* 1944–1946. *31st:* 1944–1946. *445th:* 1944–1946; 1955–.

STATIONS. Muroc, Calif, 29 Nov 1943; Palmdale AAFld, Calif, 1 Jun 1944; Bakersfield Mun Arpt, Calif, 11 Oct 1944; Santa Maria AAFld, Calif, 10 Jul 1945; March Field, Calif, c. 29 Nov 1945–3 Jul 1946. Wurtsmith AFB, Mich, 18 Aug 1955–.

COMMANDERS. Capt Brunner R Coke, 29 Nov 1943; Maj John W Mitchell, Dec 1943; Col Homer A Boushey, 11 Jan 1944; Col David L Hill, 29 Sep 1945; Col Bruce K Holloway, 30 Jan–3 Jul 1946. Col Ralph A Taylor Jr, 1955–.

CAMPAIGNS. American Theater.

DECORATIONS. None.

INSIGNE. *Shield:* Per bend azure and sable; a stylized jet aircraft, in bend, point to dexter chief, argent, with swirling jet stream moving to sinister base gules, streaked or, the end of the jet stream superimposed over a cloud formation issuing from sinister base of the third, shaded of the first; all between a star in sinister chief and a lightning bolt in dexter base of the fifth. (Approved 22 May 1957.)

413th FIGHTER GROUP

Constituted as 413th Fighter Group on 5 Oct 1944 and *activated* on 15 Oct. Trained for very-long-range operations with P–47's. Moved to the Asiatic-Pacific Theater, Apr–Jun 1945. Assigned to Twentieth AF; reassigned to the Eighth early in Aug 1945. Flew a few strafing missions from Saipan to the Truk Islands in May before beginning operations from Ie Shima in Jun. Engaged in dive-bombing and strafing attacks on factories, radar stations, airfields, small ships, and other targets in Japan. Made several attacks on shipping and airfields in China during Jul. Flew its only escort mission on 8 Aug 1945 when it covered B–29's during a raid against Yawata, Japan. Served as a part of the air defense and occupation

force for the Ryukyu Islands after the war. *Inactivated* on Okinawa on 15 Oct 1946.

Redesignated 413th Fighter-Day Group. *Activated* in the US on 11 Nov 1954. Assigned to Tactical Air Command. Equipped first with F–86's, later with F–100's.

SQUADRONS. *1st:* 1944–1946; 1954–. *21st:* 1944–1946; 1954–. *34th:* 1944–1946; 1954–.

STATIONS. Seymour Johnson Field, NC, 15 Oct 1944; Bluethenthal Field, NC, 9 Nov 1944–6 Apr 1945; Ie Shima, 19 May 1945; Kadena, Okinawa, 10 Nov 1945; Yontan, Okinawa, 29 Jan–15 Oct 1946. George AFB, Calif, 11 Nov 1954–.

COMMANDERS. Lt Col George H Hollingsworth, 15 Oct 1944; Col Harrison R Thyng, 1 Nov 1944; Lt Col John B Coleman, 14 Oct 1945; Col Loring F Stetson Jr, c. Jun–15 Oct 1946. Col George Laven Jr, 11 Nov 1954; Lt Col Maurice G Long, 4 Oct 1955–.

CAMPAIGNS. Air Offensive, Japan; Eastern Mandates; Western Pacific; Ryukyus; China Offensive.

DECORATIONS. None.

INSIGNE. *Shield:* Argent, within a diminutive border per border of the like and azure a sheaf of broad swords points upward gules of the second, vert and or, all with hilts of the first. *Motto:* SIVA. (Approved 26 Apr 1955.)

414th FIGHTER GROUP

Constituted as 414th Fighter Group on 5 Oct 1944 and *activated* on 15 Oct. Equipped with P–47's. Moved to the

Asiatic-Pacific Theater, Jun–Aug 1945. Assigned to Twentieth AF. The air echelon, based temporarily on Guam, attacked objectives in the Truk Islands on 13 and 22 Jul. The group began operations from Iwo Jima late that month with an attack against a radar station on Chichi Jima. Operations during Aug were directed primarily against enemy airfields in Japan, but the group also strafed hangars, barracks, ordnance dumps, trains, marshalling yards, and shipping. Moved to the Philippines late in Dec 1945. Assigned to Thirteenth AF. *Inactivated* in the Philippines on 30 Sep 1946.

Redesignated 414th Fighter Group (Air Defense). *Activated* in the US on 18 Aug 1955. Assigned to Air Defense Command. Equipped first with F–94's, later with F–89's.

SQUADRONS. *413th:* 1944–1946. *437th:* 1944–1946; 1955–. *456th:* 1944–1946.

STATIONS. Seymour Johnson Field, NC, 15 Oct 1944; Selfridge Field, Mich, 15 Nov 1944; Bluethenthal Field, NC, 19 Mar–11 May 1945; North Field, Iwo Jima, 7 Jul

1945; Clark Field, Luzon, 23 Dec 1945–30 Sep 1946. Oxnard AFB, Calif, 18 Aug 1955–.

COMMANDERS. Lt Col Robert C Bagby, 28 Oct 1944; Col Henry G Thorne Jr, 6 Dec 1944–unkn. Col Edwin F Carey Jr, 1955–.

CAMPAIGNS. Air Offensive, Japan; Eastern Mandates.

DECORATIONS. None.

INSIGNE. *Shield:* Azure, a bend or, between two martlets volant argent, lightning bolts gules streaming from each of their tails. (Approved 26 Jul 1956.)

415th BOMBARDMENT GROUP

Constituted as 415th Bombardment Group (Dive) on 12 Feb 1943 and *activated* on 15 Feb. Equipped with A–20's, A–24's, A–26's, B–25's, and P–39's. Served as a training and demonstration organization at AAF School of Applied Tactics and later as a replacement training unit of Second AF. *Disbanded* on 5 Apr 1944.

SQUADRONS. *465th:* 1943–1944. *521st* (formerly 667th): 1943–1944.

STATIONS. Alachua AAFld, Fla, 15 Feb 1943; Orlando AB, Fla, 25 Feb 1944; Dalhart AAFld, Tex, 19 Mar–5 Apr 1944.

COMMANDERS. 2d Lt Michael J Panek, 1 Mar 1943; Maj Wesley E Dickerson, 12 Mar 1943; Lt Col Robert K Martin, 29 Mar 1943; Col John R Kelly, 23 Oct 1943; Lt Col Steele R Patterson, 6 Mar–5 Apr 1944.

CAMPAIGNS. American Theater.

DECORATIONS. None.

INSIGNE. None.

416th BOMBARDMENT GROUP

Constituted as 416th Bombardment Group (Light) on 25 Jan 1943. *Activated* on 5 Feb 1943. Used A–20's in preparing for duty overseas. Moved to England, Jan–Feb 1944, and assigned to Ninth AF. Entered combat in Mar 1944, and during the next several weeks directed most of its attacks against V-weapon sites in France. Flew a number of missions against airfields and coastal defenses to help prepare for the invasion of Normandy. Supported the invasion in Jun 1944 by striking road junctions, marshalling yards, bridges, and railway overpasses. Assisted ground forces at Caen and St Lo in Jul and at Brest later in the summer, by hitting transportation facilities, supply dumps, radar installations, and other targets. In spite of intense resistance, the group bombed bridges, railways, rolling stock, and a radar station to disrupt the enemy's retreat through the Falaise gap, 6–9 Aug 1944, and received a DUC for the missions. Assisted the airborne attack on Holland in Sep. Supported the assault on the Siegfried Line by pounding transportation, warehouses, supply dumps, and defended villages in Germany. Converted to A–26 aircraft in Nov. Attacked transportation facilities, strong points, communications centers, and troop concentrations during the Battle of the Bulge, Dec 1944–Jan 1945. Aided the Allied thrust into Germany by continuing its strikes against transportation, communications, airfields, storage depots, and other objectives, Feb–May 1945. Bombed flak positions in support of the airborne assault across the Rhine in Mar 1945. Returned to the US, Jul–Oct 1945. *Inactivated* on 24 Oct 1945.

SQUADRONS. *668th:* 1943–1945. *669th:* 1943–1945. *670th:* 1943–1945. *671st:* 1943–1945.

STATIONS. Will Rogers Field, Okla, 5 Feb 1943; Lake Charles AAFld, La, 4 Jun 1943; Laurel AAFld, Miss, Nov 1943– c. 1 Jan 1944; Wethersfield, England, Feb 1944; Melun, France, Sep 1944; Laon/Athies, France, Feb 1945; Cormeilles-en-Vexin, France, May–Jul 1945; Camp Myles Standish, Mass, c. 23–24 Oct 1945.

COMMANDERS. Lt Col Richard D Dick, Feb 1943; Col Harold L Mace, Oct 1943; Col Theodore R Aylesworth, 3 Aug 1944–1945.

CAMPAIGNS. Air Offensive, Europe; Normandy; Northern France; Rhineland; Ardennes–Alsace; Central Europe.

DECORATIONS. Distinguished Unit Citation: France, 6–9 Aug 1944.

INSIGNE. None.

417th BOMBARDMENT GROUP

Constituted as 417th Bombardment Group (Light) on 23 Mar 1943 and *activated* on 28 Mar. Trained with A-20's. Moved to New Guinea, Dec 1943–Jan 1944, and assigned to Fifth AF. Began combat in Mar 1944, operating in support of ground forces on New Guinea and striking airfields, bridges, personnel concentra-tions, installations, and shipping in that area. Operated from Noemfoor, Sep–Dec 1944, attacking airfields and installations on Ceram, Halmahera, and western New Guinea. Moved to the Philippines in Dec 1944, and until Jun 1945 supported ground forces and attacked enemy airfields, transportation, and installations on Luzon, Cebu, Negros, and Mindanao. Received a DUC for attacking Japanese convoys at Lingayen, 30 Dec 1944–2 Jan 1945, action that not only impaired enemy shipping and supply strength, but also helped to clear the way for the American invasion of Luzon. Flew its last missions in Jul, dropping propaganda leaflets to Japanese troops on Luzon. Moved to Okinawa in Aug 1945 and to Japan in Nov. *Inactivated* on 15 Nov 1945.

SQUADRONS. *672d:* 1943–1945. *673d:* 1943–1945. *674th:* 1943–1945. *675th:* 1943–1945.

STATIONS. Will Rogers Field, Okla, 28 Mar 1943; DeRidder AAB, La, 4 Aug–10 Dec 1943; Cape Sudest, New Guinea, 28 Jan 1944; Dobodura, New Guinea, 7 Feb 1944; Saidor, New Guinea, 8 Apr 1944; Noemfoor, c. 9 Sep 1944; Tacloban, Leyte, 6 Dec 1944; San Jose, Mindoro, 22 Dec 1944; Okinawa, 17 Aug 1945; Itami, Japan, c. 1–15 Nov 1945.

COMMANDERS. Col Jack W Saunders, 31 Mar 1943; Lt Col Howard S Ellmore, 5 Jul 1944; Lt Col Milton W Johnson, 2 Jan 1945; Lt Col Charles W Johnson, 28 Apr 1945; Lt Col James E Sweeney, 10 Oct–15 Nov 1945.

CAMPAIGNS. New Guinea; Leyte; Luzon; Southern Philippines.

DECORATIONS. Distinguished Unit Citation: Philippine Islands, 30 Dec 1944–2 Jan 1945. Philippine Presidential Unit Citation.

INSIGNE. None.

418th BOMBARDMENT GROUP

Constituted as 418th Bombardment Group (Light) on 16 Jul 1943. *Activated* on 1 Aug 1943. Assigned to Third AF. *Disbanded* on 15 Sep 1943. *Consolidated* (in Apr 1958) with the 418th Bombardment Group (Very Heavy).

418th Bombardment Group (Very Heavy) was *constituted* on 28 Feb 1944. *Activated* on 11 Mar 1944. Assigned to Second AF as a replacement training unit but had no squadrons assigned. *Disbanded* on 1 Apr 1944.

SQUADRONS. *696th:* 1943. *697th:* 1943. *698th:* 1943. *699th:* 1943.

STATIONS. Lake Charles AAFld, La, 1 Aug–15 Sep 1943. Alamogordo AAFld, NM, 11 Mar–1 Apr 1944.

COMMANDERS. Unkn.

CAMPAIGNS. None.

DECORATIONS. None.

INSIGNE. None.

419th TROOP CARRIER GROUP

Constituted as 419th Troop Carrier Group on 1 Dec 1944. *Activated* on Guam on 31 Jan 1945. Assigned to Seventh AF.

No tactical squadrons or aircraft were assigned. The group's headquarters had detachments at Saipan, Tinian, and Anguar, the latter detachment moving to Iwo Jima in Mar 1945. These detachments operated transportation terminals that assisted in moving troops, equipment, food, and mail to, and in evacuating wounded personnel from, combat areas. *Inactivated* on Guam on 15 Feb 1946.

Allotted to the reserve. *Activated* in the US on 22 Mar 1947. *Redesignated* 419th Troop Carrier Group (Medium) in Jun 1949. Ordered to active service on 1 May 1951. *Inactivated* on 2 May 1951.

Redesignated 419th Troop Carrier Group (Assault, Fixed Wing). *Activated* on 9 Jul 1956. Assigned to Tactical Air Command and equipped with C–123's.

SQUADRONS. *12th* Rescue: 1947–1949. *15th* Fighter: 1947–1949. *63d:* 1947–1949. *64th:* 1947–1949. *65th:* 1947–1949. *66th:* 1947–1949. *79th:* 1948–1949. *339th:* 1949–

1951; 1956–. *340th:* 1949–1951; 1956–. *341st:* 1949–1951; 1956–. *342d:* 1949–1951.

STATIONS. Guam, 31 Jan 1945–15 Feb 1946. Richmond AAB, Va, 22 Mar 1947; Scott AFB, Ill, 27 Jun 1949–2 May 1951. Ardmore AFB, Okla, 9 Jul 1956–.

COMMANDERS. Capt Vernon C Dang, 1 Feb 1945; Maj Victor C Swearingen, 5 Mar 1945; Col Frank H Mears, 10 May 1945; Lt Col Victor C Swearingen, 6 Aug 1945; Maj John B Wakefield Jr, 19 Aug 1945; Capt Vernon C Dang, 10 Nov 1945; Capt John L Boggs, 21 Nov 1945–unkn. Maj Joseph C Hamilton Jr, 9 Jul 1956–.

CAMPAIGNS. Western Pacific.

DECORATIONS. None.

INSIGNE. *Shield:* Per pale azure and vert, on a pile argent a point in point reversed gules between the wings of an eagle volant, sable, his head and detail of the third, grasping with his talons the left hand of a Roman warrior and lowering him to base; the warrior holding a sword in his right hand; all between three stars, argent, one in chief, one in dexter base, one in sinister base. (Approved 25 Jun 1957.)

423d RECONNAISSANCE GROUP

Constituted as 423d Observation Group on 30 Mar 1943. *Activated* on 1 Apr 1943. Assigned to Third AF. *Redesignated* 423d Reconnaissance Group on 20 Apr 1943. Original mission of training replacements was changed in Jun 1943 to training pilot instructors for III Fighter Command. *Disbanded* on 15 Aug 1943.

SQUADRONS. *29th:* 1943. *32d:* 1943. *33d:* 1943. *34th:* 1943.

STATIONS. DeRidder AAB, La, 1 Apr–15 Aug 1943.

COMMANDERS. Unkn.

CAMPAIGNS. None.

DECORATIONS. None.

INSIGNE. None.

424th RECONNAISSANCE GROUP

Constituted as 424th Observation Group on 30 Mar 1943. *Activated* on 1 Apr 1943. Assigned to Third AF. *Redesignated* 424th Reconnaissance Group on 20 Apr 1943. Apparently was never fully organized. *Disbanded* on 15 Aug 1943.

SQUADRONS. *35th:* 1943. *36th:* 1943. *37th:* 1943. *38th:* 1943.

STATIONS. DeRidder AAB, La, 1 Apr–15 Aug 1943.

COMMANDERS. Unkn.

CAMPAIGNS. None.

DECORATIONS. None.

INSIGNE. None.

426th RECONNAISSANCE GROUP

Constituted as 426th Reconnaissance Group on 25 Jun 1943. *Activated* on 1 Jul 1943. Assigned to Third AF. Apparently was never fully organized. *Disbanded* on 15 Aug 1943.

SQUADRONS. *44th:* 1943. *45th:* 1943. *46th:* 1943. *47th:* 1943.

STATIONS. Gainesville AAFld, Tex, 1 Jul–15 Aug 1943.

COMMANDERS. Unkn.

CAMPAIGNS. None.

DECORATIONS. None.

INSIGNE. None.

432d RECONNAISSANCE GROUP

Constituted as 432d Observation Group on 18 Feb 1943 and *activated* on 22 Feb. Assigned to AAF School of Applied Tactics. *Redesignated* 432d Reconnaissance Group in Apr 1943, and 432d Tactical Reconnaissance Group in Aug 1943. Aircraft included P–39's and L–3's. Trained, and provided reconnaissance to assist fighter, bombardment, and ground units with their training. *Disbanded* on 1 Nov 1943.

Reconstituted on 14 Jan 1954. *Activated* on 18 Mar 1954. Assigned to Tactical Air Command. Equipped with RF–80's, RF–84's, RB–26's, RB–57's, and RB–66's.

SQUADRONS. *3d:* 1943. *20th:* 1954–. *29th:* 1954–. *41st:* 1954–. *43d:* 1954–.

STATIONS. Alachua AAFld, Fla, 22 Feb 1943; Keystone AAFld, Fla, Mar–1 Nov 1943. Shaw AFB, SC, 18 Mar 1954–.

COMMANDERS. 1st Lt Richard I Purnell, c. 1 Mar 1943; Capt John J Owen Jr, c. 17 Mar 1943; Capt William C Collins, c. 21 Mar 1943; Maj William B Merrill Jr, 23 Mar 1943; Lt Col Eugene H Rice, 18 Apr 1943–unkn. Col Frank A Sharp, 18 Mar 1954–unkn; Col John G Foster, 1955–.

CAMPAIGNS. None.

DECORATIONS. None.

INSIGNE. *Shield:* Gules, a stylized owl, holding in his dexter claws two lightning bolts in saltire, all sable, detail of the field. *Motto:* VICTORIA PER SCIENTIAM— Victory through Knowledge. (Approved 2 Jun 1955.)

433d TROOP CARRIER GROUP

Constituted as 433d Troop Carrier Group on 22 Jan 1943. *Activated* on 9 Feb 1943. Trained to tow gliders and to transport and drop supplies and paratroops. Moved to New Guinea, via Hawaii, the Fiji Islands, and Australia, Aug–Nov 1943. Assigned to Fifth AF. Operated from New Guinea and Biak until 1945, using C–47's and a few B–17's, plus C–46's that were acquired late in 1944. Transported troops; hauled such things as gasoline, ammunition, medicine, rations, communications equipment, and construction materials; and evacuated wounded personnel. Moved to the Philippines in Jan 1945. Operations included delivering ammunition, rations, and other items to Filipino guerrilla forces; evacuating prisoners of war and civilian internees; transporting combat units from New Guinea, the Netherlands Indies, and the Solomons, to the Philippines; and dropping rice to the leper colony on Culion Island. Transported organizations of Fifth AF to Okinawa, Jun–Aug 1945, and hauled occupation forces to Japan after V-J Day. Moved to Japan in Sep 1945. *Inactivated* on 15 Jan 1946.

Allotted to the reserve. *Activated* in the US on 6 Jul 1947. *Redesignated* 433d Troop Carrier Group (Medium) in Jun 1949. Equipped for a time with C–46 and C–47 aircraft; converted to C–119's in 1950. Ordered to active service on 15 Oct 1950. Assigned to Tactical Air Command. Moved to Germany, Jul–Aug 1951, and assigned to United States Air Forces in Europe. *Inactivated* in Germany on 14 Jul 1952.

Allotted to the reserve. *Activated* in the US on 18 May 1955.

SQUADRONS. *5th:* 1948–1949. *65th:* 1943–1945. *66th:* 1943–1945. *67th:* 1943– 1946; 1947–1952; 1955–. *68th:* 1943–1946; 1947–1952; 1955–. *69th:* 1943–1946; 1947– 1952. *70th:* 1943–1946; 1947–1950. *315th:* 1948–1949.

STATIONS. Florence AAFld, SC, 9 Feb 1943; Baer Field, Ind, 1–12 Aug 1943; Port Moresby, New Guinea, 25 Aug 1943; Biak, 17 Oct 1944; Tanauan, Leyte, 19 Jan 1945; Clark Field, Luzon, 31 May 1945; Tachikawa, Japan, 11 Sep 1945–15 Jan 1946. Akron, Ohio, 6 Jul 1947; Cleveland Mun Aprt, Ohio, 27 Jun 1949; Greenville AFB, SC, 16 Oct 1950–20 Jul 1951; Rhein-Main AB, Germany, 5 Aug 1951–14 Jul 1952. Brooks AFB, Tex, 18 May 1955–.

COMMANDERS. Col Cecil B Guile, 10 Feb 1943; Lt Col Marvin O Calliham, 17 Apr 1945; Lt Col James L Cole, Sep 1945– unkn. Lt Col Cornelius P Chima, 15 Oct 1950; Col Lucion N Powell, 24 Mar–14 Jul 1952.

CAMPAIGNS. Air Offensive, Japan; New Guinea; Northern Solomons; Bismarck Archipelago; Western Pacific; Leyte; Luzon; Southern Philippines; Ryukyus.

DECORATIONS. Philippine Presidential Unit Citation.

INSIGNE. None.

434th TROOP CARRIER GROUP

Constituted as 434th Troop Carrier Group on 30 Jan 1943. *Activated* on 9 Feb 1943. Trained with C–47's for operations in Europe with Ninth AF. Moved to England in Oct 1943 and entered a seven-month training period with 101st

Airborne Division in preparation for the invasion of northern France. Towed gliders carrying troops to Normandy on 6 Jun 1944 and flew follow-up missions later on D–Day and on 7 Jun to provide reinforcements of troops, vehicles, and ammunition. Received a DUC and the French Croix de Guerre with Palm for action in the invasion of Normandy. Dropped paratroops in the assault area and towed gliders with reinforcements during the airborne operation in Holland, 17–25 Sep 1944. Moved to France in Feb 1945. Participated in the airborne assault across the Rhine, dropping paratroops over the east bank on 24 Mar. In addition to these airborne operations, the group reinforced ground troops in the St Lo area during the breakthrough in Jul 1944; provided supplies for Third Army during its drive across France in Aug, an action for which the group was cited by the French Government; and resupplied troops at Bastogne in Dec 1944 in the effort to stop the German offensive in the Ardennes. Also engaged in numerous transport missions,

hauling mail, rations, clothing, and other supplies from England to bases in France and Germany, and evacuating the Allied wounded. After V–E Day, transported gasoline to Allied forces in Germany and evacuated prisoners of war to relocation centers in France and Holland. Returned to the US, Jul–Aug 1945. Trained with C–46's. *Inactivated* on 31 Jul 1946.

Allotted to the reserve. *Activated* on 15 Mar 1947. *Redesignated* 434th Troop Carrier Group (Medium) in Jul 1949. Ordered to active duty on 1 May 1951. Assigned to Tactical Air Command. Used C–47 aircraft. Relieved from active service and *inactivated,* on 1 Feb 1953.

Allotted to the reserve. *Activated* on 1 Feb 1953.

SQUADRONS. *71st:* 1943–1946; 1947–1953; 1953–. *72d:* 1943–1946; 1947–1953; 1953–. *73d:* 1943–1946; 1947–1948, 1949–1953; 1953–1954. *74th:* 1943–1946; 1947–1951. *80th:* 1948–1949. *81st:* 1948–1949.

STATIONS. Alliance AAFld, Neb, 9 Feb 1943; Baer Field, Ind, 5 Sep–Oct 1943; Fulbeck, England, 7 Oct 1943; Welford Park, England, 10 Dec 1943; Aldermaston, England, 3 Mar 1944–12 Feb 1945; Mourmelon-le-Grand, France, Feb–24 Jul 1945; Baer Field, Ind, 4 Aug 1945; Alliance AAFld, Neb, 15 Sep 1945; George Field, Ill, 1 Oct 1945; Greenville AAB, SC, 2 Feb–31 Jul 1946. Stout Field, Ind, 15 Mar 1947; Atterbury AFB, Ind, 1 Jul 1949; Lawson AFB, Ga, 23 Jan 1952–1 Feb 1953. Atterbury AFB, Ind, 1 Feb 1953–.

COMMANDERS. Maj Edward F Cullerton, 9 Feb 1943; Lt Col Fred D Stevers, 18

Aug 1943; Col William B Whitacre, 29 Nov 1943; Lt Col Ben A Garland, 17 Dec 1944; Lt Col Frank W Hansley, 15 Sep 1945; Col Adriel N Williams, 1 Oct 1945–31 Jul 1946. Col Wallace L Linn, 1 May 1951; Lt Col Jack F Linn, 20 Feb 1952–1 Feb 1953.

CAMPAIGNS. American Theater; Normandy; Northern France; Rhineland; Ardennes-Alsace; Central Europe.

DECORATIONS. Distinguished Unit Citation: France, [6–7] Jun 1944. French Croix de Guerre with Palm: 6–7 Jun 1944; 20–28 Aug 1944. French Fourragere.

INSIGNE. *Shield:* Or, in chief a pair of stylized wings erect and conjoined azure, between a chevronel reversed gules; issuing from base a demi-sphere with land markings azure, longitude and latitude lines argent, thereover a parachute of the last; the sphere surmounting the apex of the chevronel. (Approved 10 Oct 1952.)

435th TROOP CARRIER GROUP

Constituted as 435th Troop Carrier Group on 30 Jan 1943. *Activated* on 25 Feb 1943. Used C–47's and C–53's in preparing for duty overseas with Ninth AF. Moved to England, Oct–Nov 1943, and began training for participation in the airborne operation over Normandy. Entered combat on D–Day 1944 by dropping paratroops of 101st Airborne Division near Cherbourg; towed Waco and Horsa gliders carrying reinforcements to that area on the afternoon of D–Day and on the following morning; received a DUC for its part in the Normandy invasion. Began transport services following the landings in France and intermittently engaged in missions of this type until V–E Day; hauled supplies such as serum, blood plasma, radar sets, clothing, rations, and ammunition, and evacuated wounded personnel to Allied hospitals. Interrupted supply and evacuation missions to train for and participate in three major airborne assaults. A detachment that was sent to Italy in Jul 1944 for the invasion of Southern France dropped paratroops over the assault area on 15 Aug and released gliders carrying troops and equipment such as jeeps, guns, and ammunition; flew a resupply mission over France on 16 Aug; and then transported supplies to bases in Italy before returning to England at the end of the month. In Sep 1944 the group participated in the air attack on Holland, dropping paratroops of 82d and 101st Airborne Divisions and releasing gliders carrying reinforcements. Moved to France in Feb 1945 for the airborne assault across the Rhine; each aircraft towed two gliders in transporting troops and equipment to the east bank of the Rhine on 24 Mar; then the group flew resupply missions to Germany in support of ground forces. Transported supplies to occupation forces in Germany and evacuated Allied prisoners of war after V–E Day. Returned to the US in Aug. *Inactivated* on 15 Nov 1945.

Allotted to the reserve. *Activated* on 15 Jul 1947. *Redesignated* 435th Troop Carrier Group (Medium) in Jun 1949. Ordered to active service on 1 Mar 1951. Assigned to Tactical Air Command. Trained with C–119's. Relieved from active duty and *inactivated,* on 1 Dec 1952. Allotted to the reserve. *Activated* on 1 Dec 1952.

SQUADRONS. *75th:* 1943–1945. *76th:* 1943–1945; 1947–1952; 1952–. *77th:* 1943–1945; 1947–1952; 1952–. *78th:* 1943–1945; 1947–1952; 1952–1954, 1955–. *326th:* 1947–1949. *349th:* 1949–1951.

STATIONS. Bowman Field, Ky, 25 Feb 1943; Sedalia AAFld, Mo, 4 May 1943; Pope Field, NC, 2 Jul 1943; Baer Field, Ind, 6–13 Oct 1943; Langer, England, 3 Nov 1943; Welford Park, England, 25 Jan 1944; Bretigny, France, c. 13 Feb–25 Jun 1945; Baer Field, Ind, 5 Aug 1945; Kellogg Field, Mich, 13 Sep–15 Nov 1945. Morrison Field, Fla, 15 Jul 1947; Miami Intl Aprt, Fla, 26 Jun 1949–1 Dec 1952. Miami Intl Aprt, Fla, 1 Dec 1952–.

COMMANDERS. Col Frank J MacNees, 25 Feb 1943–15 Nov 1945. Lt Col Stanley N Simpson, 1 Mar 1951; Lt Col John R Pountnay, 1951; Maj Thomas L Morris, 20 Feb 1952; Col Leonard J Barrow Jr, 20 Mar–1 Dec 1952.

CAMPAIGNS. Rome-Arno; Normandy; Northern France; Southern France; Rhineland; Ardennes-Alsace; Central Europe.

DECORATIONS. Distinguished Unit Citation: France, [6–7] Jun 1944.

INSIGNE. *Shield:* Per fess wavy, or and azure, charged with two martlets, countervolant and counter-changed, between two flanches chequy sable and gules. *Motto:* CITUS ET CERTUS—Swift and Sure. (Approved 22 May 1952.)

436th TROOP CARRIER GROUP

Constituted as 436th Troop Carrier Group on 23 Mar 1943. *Activated* on 1 Apr 1943. Trained with C–47's for duty in Europe with Ninth AF. Moved overseas, Dec 1943–Jan 1944. Began operations in Jun 1944 and participated in four major airborne operations prior to the Allied victory in May 1945. Received a DUC for its first missions, which were flown during the Normandy invasion: dropped paratroops of 82d Airborne Division over the beachhead early on 6 Jun; released gliders with reinforcements of troops and supplies on the afternoon of D–Day and on the following morning. In Jul 1944 a detachment was sent to Italy to take part in the invasion of Southern France: released gliders carrying troops and dropped paratroops in the assault area on 15 Aug; flew several resupply missions to France and then dropped supplies to Allied forces in Italy. The detachment returned to England late in Aug, and in Sep the group carried out airborne operations over Holland, dropping paratroops of 101st Airborne Division and releasing gliders with reinforcements of troops and equipment. Towed gliders to Wesel on 24 Mar 1945 to provide troops for the airborne assault across the Rhine; carried gasoline to the front lines and evacuated patients, 30–31 Mar. Flew transport missions almost daily when not engaged in airborne operations; hauled such things as gasoline, ammunition, medical supplies, rations, and clothing; evacuated the wounded to hospitals in England and France. After V–E Day, evacuated patients and prisoners of war and flew practice missions with French paratroops. Returned to the US in Aug. *Inactivated* on 15 Nov 1945.

Allotted to the reserve. *Activated* on 15 Mar 1947. *Redesignated* 436th Troop Carrier Group (Medium) in Jun 1949. Ordered to active duty on 1 Apr 1951. *Inactivated* on 16 Apr 1951.

Allotted to the reserve. *Activated* on 18 May 1955.

SQUADRONS. *73d:* 1948–1949. *79th:* 1943–1945; 1949–1951; 1955–. *80th:* 1943–1945; 1947–1948, 1949–1951. *81st:* 1943–1945; 1947–1948, 1949–1951; 1955–. *82d:* 1943–1945; 1947–1951. *316th:* 1947–1949.

STATIONS. Baer Field, Ind, 1 Apr 1943; Alliance AAFld, Neb, 2 May 1943; Laurinburg-Maxton AAB, NC, 1 Aug 1943; Baer Field, Ind, 14–28 Dec 1943; Bottesford, England, Jan 1944; Membury, England, 3 Mar 1944–Feb 1945; Melun, France, 26 Feb–Jul 1945; Baer Field, Ind, 15 Aug 1945; Malden AAFld, Mo, 13 Sep–15 Nov 1945. Godman Field, Ky, 15 Mar 1947; Standiford Mun Aprt, Ky, 20 Oct 1950–16 Apr 1951. New York NAS, NY, 18 May 1955–.

COMMANDERS. Col Adriel N Williams, 1 Apr 1943–1 Oct 1945; unkn, 1 Oct–15 Nov 1945.

CAMPAIGNS. American Theater; Rome-Arno; Normandy; Northern France; Southern France; Rhineland; Ardennes-Alsace; Central Europe.

DECORATIONS. Distinguished Unit Citation: France, [6–7] Jun 1944.

INSIGNE. *Shield:* Gules, a sphere azure with longitude and latitude lines argent; the sphere issuing from four lightning bolts radiating upward from base of the last; a parachute, in pale, between the four bolts, two and two, argent, gores outlined of the second, all superimposed over the sphere; over all in chief an antique crown or, winged argent. *Motto:* PARATI,

VOLENTES, POTENTES—Ready, Willing and Able. (Approved 20 Jun 1957.)

437th TROOP CARRIER GROUP

Constituted as 437th Troop Carrier Group on 15 Apr 1943. *Activated* on 1 May 1943. Trained with C–46 and C–47 aircraft for duty overseas with Ninth AF. Moved to England, Jan–Feb 1944, and began preparing for the Normandy invasion. Released gliders near Cherbourg early on 6 Jun 1944; flew follow-up missions on 6 and 7 Jun, carrying reinforcements of troops, antiaircraft pieces, ammunition, rations, and other supplies for 82d Airborne Division; received a DUC for these actions in France. A detachment was sent to Italy in Jul 1944 for the invasion of Southern France in Aug; it dropped paratroops over the assault area on 15 Aug, flew a resupply mission on the following day, and then hauled freight to bases in Italy until it returned to England

on 24 Aug. During the airborne attack on Holland, 17–25 Sep 1944, the group released gliders carrying troops and equipment, and flew several resupply missions to provide reinforcements. Moved to France in Feb 1945 for action during the air assault across the Rhine; each aircraft towed two gliders over the east bank and released them near Wesel on 24 Mar 1945. Flew numerous missions in Mar and Apr to carry gasoline, food, medicine, and other supplies to ground forces pushing across Germany. When not participating in one of the major airborne operations, the organization continually transported ammunition, rations, clothing, and other supplies, and evacuated wounded personnel to rear-zone hospitals. Evacuated prisoners of war and displaced persons to relocation centers after V–E Day. Returned to the US in Aug 1945. *Inactivated* on 15 Nov 1945.

Redesignated 437th Troop Carrier Group (Medium). Allotted to the reserve. *Activated* on 27 Jun 1949. Ordered to active duty on 10 Aug 1950. Moved to Japan in Nov 1950 and assigned to Far East Air Forces for duty in the Korean War. Used C–119's and C–46's to participate in the airlift between Japan and Korea from Dec 1950 to Jun 1952, transporting ammunition, rations, aircraft parts, gasoline, and other items to Pusan, Taegu, Suwon, Kimpo, Pyongyang, and other bases in Korea, and evacuating wounded personnel to hospitals in Japan. Dropped paratroops of 187th Regimental Combat Team at Munsan-ni in Mar 1951 and flew resupply and reinforcement missions in Apr and May. Supported the advance of Eighth Army into North Korea in Jun 1951. From Jan to Jun 1952, engaged chiefly in evacuating personnel on leave and in transporting replacements to the battle area. Relieved from active duty and *inactivated* in Japan, on 10 Jun 1952. Allotted to the reserve. *Activated* in the US on 15 Jun 1952.

SQUADRONS. *83d:* 1943–1945; 1949–1952; 1952–. *84th:* 1943–1945; 1949–1952; 1952–. *85th:* 1943–1945; 1949–1952; 1952–. *86th:* 1943–1945; 1949–1950, 1951–1952.

STATIONS. Baer Field, Ind, 1 May 1943; Sedalia AAFld, Mo, 8 Jun 1943; Pope Field, NC, 10 Oct 1943; Baer Field, Ind, 29 Dec 1943–Jan 1944; Balderton, England, Jan 1944; Ramsbury, England, 5 Feb 1944; Coulommiers/Voisins, France, 25 Feb–Jul 1945; Baer Field, Ind, 15 Aug 1945; Marfa AAFld, Tex, 14 Sep–15 Nov 1945. Chicago-Orchard Aprt, Ill, 27 Jun 1949; Shaw AFB, SC, 14 Aug–16 Oct 1950; Brady AB, Japan, 8 Nov 1950–10 Jun 1952. O'Hare Intl Aprt, Ill, 15 Jun 1952–.

COMMANDERS. Col Cedric E Hudgens, 1 May 1943; Col Donald J French, 12 Jun 1944–1945. Col John R Roche, 1950; Lt Col Edward H Nigro, Jan 1951; Lt Col George W Sutcliffe, Mar 1951; Lt Col Jack L Crawford Jr, 5 Sep 1951–10 Jun 1952.

CAMPAIGNS. *World War II:* American Theater; Rome-Arno; Normandy; Northern France; Southern France; Rhineland; Ardennes-Alsace; Central Europe. *Korean War:* CCF Intervention; 1st UN Counteroffensive; CCF Spring Offensive; UN Summer-Fall Offensive; Second Korean Winter; Korea Summer-Fall, 1952.

DECORATIONS. Distinguished Unit Citation: France, [6–7] Jun 1944. Republic of Korea Presidential Unit Citation: 1 Jul 1951–[10 Jun 1952].

INSIGNE. On a yellow disk, within a narrow blue border and a narrow white border, a running "Minute Man" with rifle at high port, all in blue silhouette, in front of a pair of wings elevated and conjoined. (Approved 24 Nov 1953.)

438th TROOP CARRIER GROUP

Constituted as 438th Troop Carrier Group on 14 May 1943. *Activated* on 1 Jun 1943. Trained with C–47's. Moved to England in Feb 1944 and assigned to Ninth AF. Until Jun 1945, trained for and participated in airborne operations, flew resupply and reinforcement missions to combat zones, evacuated casualties, and hauled freight. Received a DUC for dropping paratroops in Normandy and towing gliders with reinforcements during the invasion of France in Jun 1944. A detachment went to Italy in Jul 1944 and participated in the invasion of Southern France in Aug by dropping paratroops and towing gliders that carried reinforcements; also hauled freight in Italy before returning to England late in Aug. In Sep the group helped to supply Third Army in its push across France, and transported troops and supplies when the Allies launched the airborne operation in Holland. Flew supply missions to battle areas, including two flights to Bastogne, during the Battle of the Bulge (Dec 1944–Jan 1945). Moved to France, Feb–Mar 1945. Dropped paratroops during the airborne attack across the Rhine in Mar. Evacuated Allied prisoners of war after V–E Day. Returned to the US, Aug–Sep 1945. *Inactivated* on 15 Nov 1945.

Redesignated 438th Troop Carrier Group (Medium). Allotted to the reserve. *Activated* on 27 Jun 1949. Called to active duty on 10 Mar 1951. *Inactivated* on 14 Mar 1951.

Redesignated 438th Fighter-Bomber Group. Allotted to the reserve. *Activated* on 15 Jun 1952.

SQUADRONS. *87th:* 1943–1945; 1949–1951; 1952–. *88th:* 1943–1945; 1949–1951; 1952–. *89th:* 1943–1945; 1949–1951; 1952–. *90th:* 1943–1945; 1949–1951.

STATIONS. Baer Field, Ind, 1 Jun 1943; Sedalia AAFld, Mo, c. 11 Jun 1943; Laurinburg-Maxton AAB, NC, Oct 1943; Baer Field, Ind, c. 15–c. 28 Jan 1944; Welford, England, Feb 1944; Greenham Common, England, Mar 1944; Prosnes, France, Feb 1945; Amiens/Glisy, France, May–c. 3 Aug 1945; Baer Field, Ind, c. 16 Sep 1945; Lawson Field, Ga, c. 1 Oct–15 Nov 1945. Offutt AFB, Neb, 27 Jun 1949–14 Mar 1951. General Billy Mitchell Field, Wis, 15 Jun 1952; Milwaukee, Wis, Jan 1953–.

COMMANDERS. Lt Col William F Stewart, c. 1 Jun 1943; Col John M Donalson, c. 13 Jul 1943; Col Lucion N Powell, 27 Dec 1944–1945.

CAMPAIGNS. Rome-Arno; Normandy; Northern France; Southern France; Rhineland; Ardennes-Alsace; Central Europe.

DECORATIONS. Distinguished Unit Citation: France, [6–7] Jun 1944.

INSIGNE. *Shield:* Per bend sinister purpure and argent, fimbriated or, a globe all elements counterchanged, the globe fimbriated or and purpure, surmounting a stylized lashing swirling spear of the first, second and third, the shield fimbriated purpure and or. *Motto:* NUNQUAM NON PARATUS—Never Unprepared. (Approved 10 Aug 1954.)

439th TROOP CARRIER GROUP

Constituted as 439th Troop Carrier Group on 14 May 1943. *Activated* on 1 June 1943. Trained with C–47's. Moved to England, Feb–Mar 1944, for duty with

Ninth AF. Prepared for the invasion of the Continent and began operations by dropping paratroops of 101st Airborne Division in Normandy on 6 Jun 1944 and releasing gliders with reinforcements on the following day, receiving a DUC and a French citation for these missions. After the Normandy invasion the group ferried supplies in the United Kingdom until the air echelon was sent to Italy in Jul to transport cargo to Rome and evacuate wounded personnel. The detachment dropped paratroops of 517th Parachute Infantry Regiment along the Riviera to aid the invasion of Southern France on 15 Aug 1944 and later towed gliders to provide reinforcements; for these missions the group was again cited by the French government. After the air echelon returned to England on 25 Aug, the group resumed its cargo missions. In Sep the group moved to France for further operations in support of the advancing Allies. Dropped paratroops of 82d Airborne Division near Nijmegen and towed gliders

carrying reinforcements during the airborne attack on Holland, 17–25 Sep 1944. Participated in the Battle of the Bulge by releasing gliders with supplies for 101st Airborne Division near Bastogne on 27 Dec 1944. Each aircraft of the group towed two gliders with troops of 17th Airborne Division and released them near Wesel when the Allies made the air assault across the Rhine on 24 Mar 1945. Continually hauled food, clothing, medicine, gasoline, ordnance equipment, and other supplies to the front lines and evacuated patients to rear-zone hospitals when not engaged in airborne operations. Converted from C–47's to C–46's, which were used to transport displaced persons from Germany to France and Belgium after V–E Day. Returned to the US, Jul–Sep 1945. Trained with C–46 aircraft. *Inactivated* on 10 Jun 1946.

Redesignated 439th Troop Carrier Group (Medium). Allotted to the reserve. *Activated* on 27 Jun 1949. Ordered to active duty on 1 Apr 1951. *Inactivated* on 3 Apr 1951.

Redesignated 439th Fighter-Bomber Group. Allotted to the reserve. *Activated* on 15 Jun 1952.

SQUADRONS. *91st:* 1943–1946; 1949–1951; 1952–1954. *92d:* 1943–1946; 1949–1951; 1952–1954. *93d:* 1943–1946; 1949–1951; 1952–. *94th:* 1943–1946; 1949–1951. *471st:* 1954–. *472d:* 1954–.

STATIONS. Alliance AAFld, Neb, 1 Jun 1943; Sedalia AAFld, Mo, 15 Jun 1943; Alliance AAFld, Neb, 2 Aug 1943; Laurinburg-Maxton AAB, NC, 16 Dec 1943; Baer

Field, Ind, 2–14 Feb 1944; Balderton, England, 21 Feb 1944; Upottery, England, 26 Apr 1944; Juvincourt, France, 8 Sep 1944; Lonray, France, 28 Sep 1944; Chateaudun, France, 4 Nov 1944–11 Jul 1945; Baer Field, Ind, Jul 1945; Sedalia AAFld, Mo, 7 Oct 1945–10 Jun 1946. Selfridge AFB, Mich, 27 Jun 1949–3 Apr 1951. Selfridge AFB, Mich, 15 Jun 1952–.

COMMANDERS. Lt Col Ralph L Zimmerman, 1 Jun 1943; Col Charles H Young, 21 Jan 1944; Col Gordon L Edris, 6 Oct 1945; Lt Col Lester C Messenger, 16 Apr 1946; Lt Col William M Massengale Jr, 28 May–10 Jun 1946.

CAMPAIGNS. American Theater; Rome-Arno; Normandy; Northern France; Southern France; Rhineland; Ardennes-Alsace; Central Europe.

DECORATIONS. Distinguished Unit Citation: France, [6–7] Jun 1944. French Croix de Guerre with Palm: [6–7] Jun 1944; 15 Aug 1944. French Fourragere.

INSIGNE. *Shield:* Azure, a beaver volant proper, holding a missile in his right paw, argent, markings gules and sable and supported in the air with aircraft wings of the third, tanks of the fourth, on the right wing the national aircraft marking in its proper colors. (Approved 20 Apr 1956.)

440th TROOP CARRIER GROUP

Constituted as 440th Troop Carrier Group on 25 May 1943. *Activated* on 1 Jul 1943. Prepared for duty overseas with C–47's. Moved to England, Feb–Mar 1944, and assigned to Ninth AF. Began

operations by dropping paratroops of 101st Airborne Division near Carentan on the Cotentin Peninsula on 6 Jun 1944 and by transporting gasoline, ammunition, food, and other supplies to the same area on 7 Jun, being awarded a DUC for completing these missions during the invasion of Normandy. Began flying supply and evacuation missions between England and France after the invasion of the Continent. In Jul 1944 part of the group was sent to Italy where it transported supplies to Rome until Aug. The detachment also participated in the invasion of Southern France, dropping paratroops of 517th Parachute Infantry Regiment near Le Muy on 15 Aug 1944 and towing gliders carrying reinforcements to that area later in the day. Meanwhile, the group in England continued to haul cargo, and on 10 Aug 1944 it dropped supplies to an infantry battalion encircled at Mortain in northern France. The detachment returned to England on 25 Aug and the group moved to France in Sep. During the attack on Holland the 440th dropped paratroops of 82d Airborne Division near Groesbeek on 17 Sep 1944 and released gliders with reinforcements on 18 and 23 Sep. On 26 Dec 1944, during the Battle of the Bulge, it hauled gliders filled with supplies for 101st Airborne Division encircled at Bastogne. In Mar 1945 it towed gliders with troops of 17th Airborne Division to the battle area near Wesel during the airborne assault across the Rhine. When not engaged in airborne operations the group transported food, clothing, medical supplies, gasoline, ammunition, and other cargo to the front lines and evacuated casualties to rear-zone hospitals. After the war the group transported liberated prisoners and displaced persons. *Inactivated* in Europe on 18 Oct 1945.

Allotted to the reserve. *Activated* in the US on 3 Sep 1947. *Redesignated* 440th Troop Carrier Group (Medium) in Jun 1949. Ordered to active duty on 1 May 1951. *Inactivated* on 4 May 1951.

Redesignated 440th Fighter-Bomber Group. Allotted to the reserve. *Activated* on 15 Jun 1952.

SQUADRONS. *95th:* 1943–1945; 1947–1951; 1952–. *96th:* 1943–1945; 1947–1951; 1952–. *97th:* 1943–1945; 1947–1951; 1952–. *98th:* 1943–1945; 1947–1951.

STATIONS. Baer Field, Ind, 1 Jul 1943; Sedalia AAFld, Mo, 9 Jul 1943; Alliance AAFld, Neb, 7 Sep 1943; Pope Field, NC, 4 Jan 1944; Baer Field, Ind, 14–21 Feb 1944; Bottesford, England, 11 Mar 1944; Exeter, England, 18 Apr 1944; Reims,

France, 11 Sep 1944; Le Mans, France, 30 Sep 1944; Orleans, France, 2 Nov 1944–18 Oct 1945. Wold-Chamberlain Field, Minn, 3 Sep 1947–4 May 1951. Ft Snelling, Minn, 15 Jun 1952; Minneapolis-St Paul Intl Aprt, Minn, 8 Jan 1953–.

COMMANDERS. Maj Charles H Young, 5 Jul 1943; Lt Col Frank X Krebs, 7 Jul 1943; Lt Col Loyd C Waldorf, 18 Sep 1944; Col Frank X Krebs, 29 Oct 1944–1945.

CAMPAIGNS. Rome-Arno; Normandy; Northern France; Southern France; Rhineland; Ardennes-Alsace; Central Europe.

DECORATIONS. Distinguished Unit Citation: France, [6–7] Jun 1944.

INSIGNE. *Shield:* Argent, on and over the upper edge of a targe azure bearing Polaris and Ursa Major of the field within an orle or, a winged viking helmet of the like, behind the targe a sword and spear in saltire of the last all detailed and fimbriated of the second; all within an orle of the last and a diminished border gold. *Motto:* NUNQUAM NON PARATUS— Never Unprepared. (Approved 14 Nov 1958.)

441st TROOP CARRIER GROUP

Constituted as 441st Troop Carrier Group on 25 May 1943. *Activated* on 1 Aug 1943. Used C–47's to train for overseas duty. Moved to England, Feb–Mar 1944, and assigned to Ninth AF. Trained and transported cargo in the United Kingdom until Jun 1944. Began operations during the invasion of Normandy, dropping paratroops of 101st Airborne Division near Cherbourg on D–Day and releasing gliders with reinforcements on 7 Jun, being awarded a DUC for carrying out these missions. Following the operations in Normandy, the organization transported cargo in France and the United Kingdom until part of the group went to Italy in Jul 1944. In Italy it made scheduled flights between Grosseto and Rome, transporting supplies and evacuating patients. When the Allies invaded southern France in Aug 1944 the detachment in Italy dropped troops of 509th Parachute Infantry Regiment along the Riviera on 15 Aug and hauled gliders with reinforcements later in the day. After the detached echelon returned to England on 25 Aug, the group resumed its cargo missions, then moved to the Continent in Sep 1944 for further operations in support of the advancing Allies. Dropped paratroops of 82d and 101st Airborne Divisions near Nijmegen on 17 Sep during the air attack on Holland, and towed gliders with reinforcements on 18 and 23 Sep. In Dec, transported ammunition, rations, medicine, and other supplies to troops of 101st Airborne Division surrounded by the enemy at Bastogne. Released gliders carrying troops of 17th Airborne Division near Wesel on 24 Mar 1945 when the Allies launched the airborne assault across the Rhine. Hauled gasoline to armored columns in Germany after the Allies crossed the Rhine. Continually transported freight and personnel in the theater when not participating in airborne operations. Evacuated casualties and prisoners who had been liberated. Remained overseas after the war as part of United States Air Forces in Europe. Continued to transport personnel and equipment, using C–46, C–47, and C–109 aircraft. *Inactivated* in Germany on 30 Sep 1946.

Redesignated 441st Troop Carrier Group (Medium). Allotted to the reserve. *Activated* in the US on 27 Jun 1949. Ordered to active service on 10 Mar 1951. *Inactivated* on 14 Mar 1951.

SQUADRONS. *32d:* 1945–1946. *61st:* 1945–1946. *99th:* 1943–1945; 1949–1951. *100th:* 1943–1946; 1949–1951. *301st:* 1943–1945; 1949–1951. *302d:* 1943–1945; 1949–1951. *306th:* 1945–1946.

STATIONS. Sedalia AAFld, Mo, 1 Aug 1943; Camp Mackall, NC, 18 Jan 1944; Baer Field, Ind, 22–29 Feb 1944; Langar, England, 17 Mar 1944; Merryfield, England, 25 Apr 1944; Villeneuve/Vetrus, France, 8 Sep 1944; St Marceau, France, 2 Oct 1944; Dreux, France, 3 Nov 1944; Frankfurt, Germany, c. 12 Aug 1945–30 Sep 1946. Chicago-Orchard Aprt, Ill, 27 Jun 1949–14 Mar 1951.

COMMANDERS. Col Theodore G Kershaw, 8 Aug 1943; Col William H Parkhill, 24 Nov 1944–unkn; Lt Col Roswell Freedman, unkn–1946; Col Hoyt L Prindle, 1946; Col James E Daniel Jr, unkn–Sep 1946.

CAMPAIGNS. Rome-Arno; Normandy; Northern France; Southern France; Rhineland; Ardennes-Alsace; Central Europe.

DECORATIONS. Distinguished Unit Citation: France, [6–7] Jun 1944.

INSIGNE. None.

442d TROOP CARRIER GROUP

Constituted as 442d Troop Carrier Group on 25 May 1943. *Activated* on 1 Sep 1943. Trained with C–47's and C–53's. Moved to England in Mar 1944 for duty with Ninth AF. Received additional training with C–47's and C–53's, and later used these aircraft for operations. Flew first missions during the invasion of the Continent, dropping paratroops near Ste-Mere-Eglise on 6 Jun 1944 and flying a resupply mission on 7 Jun, being awarded a DUC for its part in the Normandy invasion. Hauled freight and evacuated casualties during the remainder of the summer. In Jul, however, a detachment flew to Italy where it transported cargo, evacuated casualties, and took part in the invasion of Southern France on 15 Aug by dropping paratroops in the battle area and releasing gliders carrying reinforcements. The detachment returned to England late in Aug, and in Sep the group took part in the airborne attack in Holland by transporting paratroops and towing gliders with reinforcements. Moved to the Continent in Oct 1944, flying resupply missions, hauling freight, and evacuating casualties in support of the Allied effort to breach the Siegfried Line. Continued transport duties until V–E Day but also participated in the airborne assault across the Rhine in Mar 1945 by releasing gliders filled with troops, carried supplies to ground forces in Germany (Apr–May), and evacuated prisoners who had been liberated. Remained in the theater after the war as part of United States Air Forces in Europe. *Inactivated* in Germany on 30 Sep 1946.

Redesignated 442d Troop Carrier Group (Medium). Allotted to the reserve. *Activated* in the US on 27 Jun 1949. Called to active duty on 10 Mar 1951. *Inactivated* on 12 Mar 1951.

Allotted to the reserve. *Activated* on 15 Jun 1952.

SQUADRONS. *301st*: 1945. *303d*: 1943–1946; 1949–1951; 1952–. *304th*: 1943–1946; 1949–1951; 1952–. *305th*: 1943–1946; 1949–1951; 1952–1955. *306th*: 1943–1946; 1949–1951.

STATIONS. Sedalia AAFld, Mo, 1 Sep 1943; Alliance AAFld, Neb, Dec 1943; Pope Field, NC, Jan 1944; Baer Field, Ind, c. 2–c. 8 Mar 1944; Fulbeck, England, c. 29 Mar 1944; Weston Zoyland, England,

Jun 1944; Bonnetable, France, Oct 1944; St-Andre-de-L'Eure, France, Nov 1944; Munich/Riem, Germany, Sep 1945–30 Sep 1946. Fairfax Field, Kan, 27 Jun 1949; Olathe NAS, Kan, May 1950–12 Mar 1951. Olathe NAS, Kan, 15 Jun 1952; Grandview AFB, Mo, Apr 1955–.

COMMANDERS. Col Charles M Smith, Sep 1943; Col John C Kilborn, 25 Sep 1945; Lt Col Paul A Jones, 4 Oct 1945–1946; Col Bertram C Harrison, 1946–unkn.

CAMPAIGNS. Rome-Arno; Normandy; Northern France; Southern France; Rhineland; Central Europe.

DECORATIONS. Distinguished Unit Citation: France, [6–7] Jun 1944.

INSIGNE. *Shield:* Light blue, over a silhouetted parachute Air Force yellow, a target pattern, to base, red and white, charged with an elongated arrow red, standing on the target a silhouetted airman, head uplifted toward a stylized aircraft surmounting the upper section of the parachute all black, the aircraft highlighted white. *Motto:* SI JEUNESSE SAVAIT, SI VIELLESSE POUVAIT—If Youth Knew, If Age Were Able. (Approved 6 May 1955.)

443d TROOP CARRIER GROUP

Constituted as 443d Troop Carrier Group on 25 May 1943. *Activated* on 1 Oct 1943. Equipped with L–3, C–53, and C–47 aircraft. Transferred, without personnel and equipment, on 15 Feb 1944 to India, where the group was remanned and new squadrons were assigned. Operated in the CBI theater until after the war, using C–47's and sometimes gliders to transport Allied troops, evacuate wounded personnel, and haul supplies and materiel, including gasoline, oil, signal and engineering equipment, medicine, rations, and ammunition. The group's missions were concerned primarily with support for Allied forces that were driving southward through Burma, but the 443d also made many flights to China. It moved to China in Aug 1945 and received a DUC for transporting a Chinese army of more than 30,000 men from Chihkiang to Nanking in Sep 1945. Returned to the US in Dec. *Inactivated* on 26 Dec 1945.

Redesignated 443d Troop Carrier Group (Medium) and allotted to the reserve. *Activated* on 27 Jun 1949. Called to active duty on 1 May 1951. Assigned to Tactical Air Command. Equipped first with C–46's, later (in Feb 1952) with C–119's. *Inactivated* on 1 Feb 1953.

SQUADRONS. *1st:* 1944–1945. *2d:* 1944–1945. *27th:* 1944–1945. *309th:* 1943–1944; 1949–1953. *310th:* 1943–1944; 1949–1953. *315th:* 1944–1945. *343d:* 1949–1953. *344th:* 1949–1951.

STATIONS. Sedalia AAFld, Mo, 1 Oct 1943; Alliance AAFld, Neb, 19 Jan 1944–15 Feb 1944; Sylhet, India, 15 Feb 1944; Sookerating, India, 6 Jun 1944; Dinjan, India, 9 Jul 1944; Ledo, India, 8 Oct 1944; Dinjan, India, 11 May 1945; Chihkiang, China, 28 Aug 1945; Hankow, China, 25 Sep–30 Nov 1945; Camp Anza, Calif, 23–26 Dec 1945. Hensley Field, Tex, 27 Jun

1949; Donaldson AFB, SC, 9 Aug 1951–1 Feb 1953.

COMMANDERS. Maj Elmer F Estrumse, 5 Oct 1943; Lt Col Charles D Farr, 13 Mar 1944; Lt Col Loren Cornell, 16 May 1944; Col Thomas J Schofield, 1 Nov 1944; Col Herbert A Bott, 12 Apr 1945; Col Frederick L Moore, 11 Sep 1945; Lt Col Jack F Marr, Dec–c. 26 Dec 1945. Col James B Henson, 1 May 1951; Maj Clifford F Harris, c. 15 Dec 1952–1 Feb 1953.

CAMPAIGNS. India-Burma; China Defensive; Central Burma; China Offensive.

DECORATIONS. Distinguished Unit Citation: China, 5–30 Sep 1945.

INSIGNE. None.

444th BOMBARDMENT GROUP

Constituted as 444th Bombardment Group (Heavy) on 15 Feb 1943. *Activated* on 1 Mar 1943. *Redesignated* 444th Bombardment Group (Very Heavy) in Nov 1943. Trained with B–17, B–24, and B–26 aircraft, and later with B–29's. Moved to India, via Africa, Mar–Apr 1944. Assigned to Twentieth AF on 29 Jun 1944. Flew supplies over the Hump to Chinese bases that its B–29's were to use for staging attacks on Japan. On 15 Jun 1944 participated in the first AAF strike on the Japanese home islands since the Doolittle raid in 1942. Bombed transportation centers, naval installations, aircraft plants, and other targets in Burma, China, Thailand, Japan, and Formosa. Conducted a daylight raid against iron and steel works at Yawata, Japan, in Aug 1944, being awarded a DUC for the mission. Evacuated staging fields in China in Jan 1945 but continued operations from India, bombing targets in Thailand and mining waters around Singapore.

Moved to Tinian in the spring of 1945 for further operations against targets in Japan. Participated in bombardment of strategic objectives and in incendiary raids on urban areas for the duration of the war. Received a DUC for attacking oil storage facilities at Oshima, bombing an aircraft plant near Kobe, and dropping incendiaries on Nagoya, in May 1945. Struck light metal industries at Osaka in Jul 1945, receiving another DUC for this action. Returned to the US late in 1945. Assigned to Strategic Air Command on 21 Mar 1946. *Inactivated* on 1 Oct 1946.

SQUADRONS. *344th:* 1945–1946. *409th:* 1946. *676th:* 1943–1946. *677th:* 1943–1946. *678th* (later 10th): 1943–1946. *679th:* 1943–1944. *825th:* 1945.

STATIONS. Davis-Monthan Field, Ariz, 1 Mar 1943; Great Bend AAFld, Kan, 29 Jul 1943–12 Mar 1944; Charra, India, 11 Apr 1944; Dudhkundi, India, 1 Jul 1944–1 Mar 1945; West Field, Tinian, 7 Apr–28 Sep 1945; Merced AAFld, Calif, 15 Nov 1945; Davis-Monthan Field, Ariz, 6 May–1 Oct 1946.

COMMANDERS. Maj Arthur T[?] Snell, 28 Mar 1943; Maj Walter W Cross, 17 Apr 1943; Col Alva L Harvey, 5 Aug 1943; Col Henry R Sullivan, 22 Apr 1945; Col James C Selser Jr, 3 Jun 1945–1 Oct 1946.

CAMPAIGNS. American Theater; India-Burma; Air Offensive, Japan; China Defensive; Western Pacific; Central Burma.

DECORATIONS. Distinguished Unit Citations: Yawata, Japan, 20 Aug 1944; Japan, 10–14 May 1945; Japan, 24 Jul 1945.

INSIGNE. None.

445th BOMBARDMENT GROUP

THE BISON WING

Constituted as 445th Bombardment Group (Heavy) on 20 Mar 1943. *Activated* on 1 Apr 1943. Prepared for combat with B-24's. Moved to England, Oct–Dec 1943, for service with Eighth AF. Entered combat on 13 Dec 1943 by attacking U-boat installations at Kiel. Operated primarily as a strategic bombardment organization until the war ended, striking such targets as industries in Osnabruck, synthetic oil plants in Lutzkendorf, chemical works in Ludwigshafen, marshalling yards at Hamm, an airfield at Munich, an ammunition plant at Duneberg, underground oil storage facilities at Ehmen, and factories at Munster. Participated in the Allied campaign against the German aircraft industry during Big Week, 20–25 Feb 1944, being awarded a DUC for attacking an aircraft assembly plant at Gotha on 24 Feb. Occasionally flew interdictory and support missions. Helped to prepare for the invasion of Normandy by bombing airfields, V-weapon sites, and other targets; attacked shore installations on D-Day, 6 Jun 1944. Supported ground forces at St Lo by striking enemy defenses in Jul 1944. Bombed German communications during the Battle of the Bulge, Dec 1944–Jan 1945. Early on 24 Mar 1945 dropped food, medical supplies, and ammunition to troops that landed near Wesel during the airborne assault across the Rhine; that afternoon flew a bombing mission to the same area, hitting a landing ground at Stormede. On occasion dropped propaganda leaflets and hauled gasoline to France. Awarded the Croix de Guerre with Palm by the French government for operations in the theater from Dec 1943 to Feb 1945. Flew last combat mission on 25 Apr 1945. Returned to the US, May–Jun. *Inactivated* on 12 Sep 1945.

Redesignated 445th Bombardment Group (Very Heavy). Allotted to the reserve. *Activated* on 12 Jul 1947. *Inactivated* on 27 Jun 1949.

Redesignated 445th Fighter-Bomber Group. Allotted to the reserve. *Activated* on 8 Jul 1952.

SQUADRONS. *15th:* 1947–1949. *700th:* 1943–1945; 1947–1949; 1952–. *701st:* 1943–

1945; 1947–1949; 1952–. *702d:* 1943–1945; 1947–1949; 1952–. *703d:* 1943–1945; 1947–1948.

STATIONS. Gowen Field, Idaho, 1 Apr 1943; Wendover Field, Utah, 8 Jun 1943; Sioux City AAB, Iowa, 8 Jul–20 Oct 1943; Tibenham, England, 4 Nov 1943–28 May 1945; Ft Dix AAB, NJ, 9 Jun–12 Sep 1945. McChord Field, Wash, 12 Jul 1947–27 Jun 1949. Buffalo, NY, 8 Jul 1952; Niagara Falls Mun Aprt, NY, 15 Jun 1955–.

COMMANDERS. Col Robert H Terrill, 1 Apr 1943; Col William W Jones, 25 Jul 1944–12 Sep 1945.

CAMPAIGNS. Air Offensive, Europe; Normandy; Northern France; Rhineland; Ardennes-Alsace; Central Europe.

DECORATIONS. Distinguished Unit Citation: Gotha, Germany, 24 Feb 1944. French Croix de Guerre with Palm.

INSIGNE. *Shield:* Azure, a snorting bison, proper, winged argent, with streaks of fire proper, issuing from his horns and nostrils, in base three stars of the third. *Motto:* THE BISON WING. (Approved 7 Sep 1955.)

446th BOMBARDMENT GROUP

Constituted as 446th Bombardment Group (Heavy) on 20 Mar 1943. *Activated* on 1 Apr 1943. Trained for overseas duty with B–24's. Moved to England, Oct–Nov 1943, and assigned to Eighth AF. Operated chiefly against strategic objectives on the Continent from Dec 1943 until Apr 1945. Targets included U-boat installations at Kiel, the port at Bremen, a chemical plant at Ludwigshafen, ballbearing works at Berlin, aero-engine plants at Rostock, aircraft factories at Munich, marshalling yards at Coblenz, motor works at Ulm, and oil refineries at Hamburg. Besides strategic missions, the group often carried out support and interdictory operations. Supported the Normandy invasion in Jun 1944 by attacking strong points, bridges, airfields, transportation, and other targets in France. Aided ground forces at Caen and St Lo during Jul by hitting bridges, gun batteries, and enemy troops. Dropped supplies to Allied troops near Nijmegen during the airborne attack on Holland in Sep. Bombed marshalling yards, bridges, and road junctions during the Battle of the Bulge, Dec 1944–Jan 1945. Dropped supplies to airborne and ground troops near Wesel during the Allied assault across the Rhine in Mar 1945. Flew last combat mission on 25 Apr, attacking a bridge near Salzburg. Returned to the US, Jun–Jul. *Inactivated* on 28 Aug 1945.

Redesignated 446th Bombardment Group (Very Heavy). Allotted to the reserve. *Activated* on 26 Mar 1948. *Redesignated* 446th Bombardment Group (Heavy) in Jun 1949. Ordered to active duty on 1 May 1951. Assigned to Strategic Air Command. *Inactivated* on 25 Jun 1951.

Redesignated 446th Troop Carrier Group (Medium). Allotted to the reserve. *Activated* on 25 May 1955.

SQUADRONS *704th:* 1943–1945; 1948–1951; 1955–. *705th:* 1943–1945; 1948–

1951; 1955–. *706th:* 1943–1945; 1948–1949; 1955–. *707th:* 1943–1945; 1948–1949.

STATIONS. Davis-Monthan Field, Ariz, 1 Apr 1943; Lowry Field, Colo, c. 8 Jun–Oct 1943; Flixton, England, c. 4 Nov 1943–c. Jul 1945; Sioux Falls AAFld, SD, c. Jul–28 Aug 1945. Carswell AFB, Tex, 26 Mar 1948–25 Jun 1951. Ellington AFB, Tex, 25 May 1955–.

COMMANDERS. Lt Col Arthur Y Snell, 25 Apr 1943; Col Jacob J Brogger, 28 Sep 1943; Col Troy W Crawford, 23 Sep 1944; Lt Col William A Schmidt, 4 Apr 1945–unkn. Unkn, 1 May–25 Jun 1951.

CAMPAIGNS. Air Offensive, Europe; Normandy; Northern France; Rhineland; Ardennes-Alsace; Central Europe.

DECORATIONS. None.

INSIGNE. None.

447th BOMBARDMENT GROUP

Constituted as 447th Bombardment Group (Heavy) on 6 Apr 1943. *Activated* on 1 May 1943. Trained for combat with B-17's. Moved to England in Nov 1943 and assigned to Eighth AF. Entered combat in Dec 1943 and operated chiefly as a strategic bombardment organization. From Dec 1943 to May 1944, helped to prepare for the invasion of the Continent by attacking submarine pens, naval installations, and cities in Germany; ports and missile sites in France; and airfields and marshalling yards in France, Belgium, and Germany. During Big Week, 20–25 Feb 1944, took part in the intensive campaign of heavy bombers against the German aircraft industry. Supported the invasion of Normandy in Jun 1944 by bombing airfields and other targets near the beachhead. Aided the breakthrough at St Lo in Jul and the effort to take Brest in Sep. Pounded enemy positions to assist the airborne invasion of Holland in Sep. Also dropped supplies to Free French forces during the summer of 1944. Turned to strategic targets in Germany in Oct 1944, placing emphasis on sources of oil production until mid-Dec. 2d Lt Robert E Femoyer, navigator, won the Medal of Honor for action on 2 Nov 1944: while on a mission over Germany, his B-17 was damaged by flak and Femoyer was severly wounded by shell fragments; determined to navigate the plane out of danger and save the crew, he refused a sedative and, for more than two hours, directed the navigation of the bomber so effectively that it returned to base without further damage; Femoyer died shortly after being removed from the plane. During the Battle of the Bulge, Dec 1944–Jan 1945, the group assaulted marshalling yards, railroad bridges, and communications centers in the combat zone. Then resumed operations against targets in Germany, attacking oil, transportation, communications, and other objectives until the war ended. During this period, also supported the airborne assault across the Rhine (Mar 1945). Returned to the US in Aug 1945. *Inactivated* on 7 Nov 1945.

Redesignated 447th Bombardment Group (Very Heavy). Allotted to the reserve. *Activated* on 12 Aug 1947. Equipped with B–29's. *Redesignated* 447th Bombardment Group (Medium) in Jun 1949. Ordered to active duty on 1 May 1951. Assigned to Strategic Air Command. *Inactivated* on 16 Jun 1951.

SQUADRONS. *708th:* 1943–1945; 1947–1951. *709th:* 1943–1945; 1947–1949. *710th:* 1943–1945. *711th:* 1943–1945.

STATIONS. Ephrata AAB, Wash, 1 May 1943; Rapid City AAB, SD, c. 1 Jul 1943; Harvard AAFld, Neb, Aug–11 Nov 1943; Rattlesden, England, c. 29 Nov 1943–c. 1 Aug 1945; Drew Field, Fla, c. 14 Aug–7 Nov 1945. Bergstrom Field, Tex, 12 Aug 1947; Castle AFB, Calif, 26 Jun 1949–16 Jun 1951.

COMMANDERS. Lt Col Robert D McDonald, 10 May 1943; Col Hunter Harris Jr, 23 May 1943; Col William J Wrigglesworth, 25 Sep 1944; Lt Col Louis G Thorup, 31 Mar 1945; Lt Col Wilfred Beaver, 1 Jul 1945–unkn. Unkn, 1 May–16 Jun 1951.

CAMPAIGNS. Air Offensive, Europe; Normandy; Northern France; Rhineland; Ardennes-Alsace; Central Europe.

DECORATIONS. None.

INSIGNE. None.

448th BOMBARDMENT GROUP

Constituted as 448th Bombardment Group (Heavy) on 6 Apr 1943. *Activated* on 1 May 1943. Prepared for duty overseas with B–24's. Moved to England, Nov–Dec 1943, and assigned to Eighth AF. Entered combat on 22 Dec 1943, and until Apr 1945 served primarily as a strategic bombardment organization, hitting such targets as aircraft factories in Gotha, ball-bearing plants in Berlin, an airfield at Hanau, U-boat facilities at Kiel, a chemical plant at Ludwigshafen, synthetic oil refineries at Politz, aircraft engine plants at Rostock, marshalling yards at Cologne, and a buzz-bomb assembly plant at Fallersleben. Took part in the intensive campaign of heavy bombers against the German aircraft industry during Big Week, 20–25 Feb 1944. In addition to strategic operations, flew interdictory and support missions. Bombed V-weapon sites, airfields, and transportation facilities prior to the Normandy invasion in Jun 1944, and on D-Day attacked coastal defenses and choke points. Struck enemy positions to assist the Allied offensive at Caen and the breakthrough at St Lo in Jul. Dropped supplies to airborne troops near Nijmegen during the airborne attack on Holland in Sep. Bombed transportation and communications centers in the combat zone during the Battle of the Bulge, Dec 1944–Jan 1945. Dropped supplies to troops at Wesel during the airborne assault across the Rhine in Mar 1945. Flew last combat mission on 25 Apr, attacking a marshalling yard at Salzburg. Returned to the US in Jul 1945. *Redesignated* 448th Bombardment Group (Very Heavy) in Aug 1945. Equipped with B–29's. Assigned to

Strategic Air Command on 21 Mar 1946. *Inactivated* on 4 Aug 1946.

Allotted to the reserve. *Activated* on 19 Apr 1947. *Redesignated* 448th Bombardment Group (Light) in Jun 1949. Ordered to active duty on 17 Mar 1951. *Inactivated* on 21 Mar 1951.

Redesignated 448th Fighter-Bomber Group. Allotted to the reserve. *Activated* on 18 May 1955.

SQUADRONS. *41st:* 1947–1949. *711th:* 1949–1951; 1955–. *712th:* 1943–1946; 1947–1951. *713th:* 1943–1946; 1947–1951; 1955–. *714th:* 1943–1946; 1947–1951. *715th:* 1943–1946.

STATIONS. Gowen Field, Idaho, 1 May 1943; Wendover Field, Utah, c. 3 Jul 1943; Sioux City AAB, Iowa, c. Sep–Nov 1943; Seething, England, c. 1 Dec 1943–c. Jul 1945; Sioux Falls AAFld, SD, c. 15 Jul 1945; McCook AAFld, Neb, c. 8 Sep 1945; Ft Worth AAFld, Tex, c. Dec 1945–4 Aug 1946. Long Beach Mun Aprt, Calif, 19 Apr 1947–21 Mar 1951. Dallas NAS, Tex, 18 May 1955–.

COMMANDERS. Col James M Thompson, c. 25 May 1943; Col Gerry L Mason, 3 Apr 1944; Col Charles B Westover, 14 Nov 1944; Lt Col Lester F Miller, 27 May 1945–unkn; Col John G Ericksen, Sep 1945–4 Aug 1946.

CAMPAIGNS. American Theater; Air Offensive, Europe; Normandy; Northern France; Rhineland; Ardennes-Alsace; Central Europe.

DECORATIONS. None.

INSIGNE. None.

449th BOMBARDMENT GROUP

Constituted as 449th Bombardment Group (Heavy) on 6 Apr 1943. *Activated* on 1 May 1943. Prepared for combat with B–24's. Moved to Italy, Dec 1943–Jan 1944, and assigned to Fifteenth AF. Operated primarily as a strategic bombardment organization, attacking such targets as oil refineries, communications centers, aircraft factories, and industrial areas in Italy, Germany, Austria, Czechoslovakia, Hungary, Rumania, Bulgaria, Albania, and Greece. Received a DUC for a mission on 4 Apr 1944 when the group, flying without escort, raided marshalling yards in Bucharest; although heavily outnumbered by German fighters, the group succeeded not only in bombing the target but also in destroying many of the enemy interceptors. Received another DUC for action on 9 Jul 1944 when the group flew through heavy smoke and intense enemy fire to attack an oil refinery at Ploesti. Other operations of the group included bombing gun emplacements in southern France in preparation for the invasion in Aug 1944, and attacking troop concentrations, bridges, and viaducts in Apr 1945 to assist Allied forces in northern Italy. Returned to the US in May 1945. *Redesignated* 449th Bombardment Group (Very Heavy). Trained with B–17, B–25, and B–29 aircraft. Assigned to Strategic Air Command on 21 Mar 1946. *Inactivated* on 4 Aug 1946.

SQUADRONS. *716th*: 1943–1946. *717th*: 1943–1946. *718th*: 1943–1946. *719th*: (later 46th): 1943–1946.

STATIONS. Davis-Monthan Field, Ariz, 1 May 1943; Alamagordo AAFld, NM, 5 Jul 1943; Bruning AAFld, Neb, 12 Sep–3 Dec 1943; Grottaglie, Italy, c. 4 Jan 1944–16 May 1945; Sioux Falls AAFld, SD, 29 May 1945; Dalhart AAFld, Tex, 24 Jul 1945; Grand Island AAFld, Neb, 8 Sep 1945–4 Aug 1946.

COMMANDERS. Col A J Kerwin Malone, 1 May 1943; Col Darr H Alkire, 30 Jul 1943; Col Thomas J Gent Jr, 3 Feb 1944; Col Jack L Randolph, Oct 1944–c. Jun 1945; Capt Charles K Howell, c. Jul 1945; Maj Walter W Cross, 31 Jul 1945; Lt Col Leon Stann, 6 Aug 1945; Col William H Hanson, 15 Aug 1945; Col Richard M Montgomery, 16 Sep 1945–4 Aug 1946.

CAMPAIGNS. American Theater; Air Combat, EAME Theater; Air Offensive, Europe; Naples-Foggia; Anzio; Rome-Arno; Normandy; Northern France; Southern France; North Apennines; Rhineland; Central Europe; Po Valley.

DECORATIONS. Distinguished Unit Citations: Bucharest, Rumania, 4 Apr 1944; Ploesti, Rumania, 9 Jul 1944.

INSIGNE. None.

450th BOMBARDMENT GROUP

Constituted as 450th Bombardment Group (Heavy) on 6 Apr 1943. *Activated* on 1 May 1943. Trained with B–24's. Moved to Italy, arriving in Dec 1943. Began operations with Fifteenth AF in Jan 1944 and engaged chiefly in missions against strategic targets in Italy, France, Germany, Austria, Czechoslovakia, Hungary, and the Balkans until Apr 1945. Bombed aircraft factories, assembly plants, oil refineries, storage areas, marshalling yards, airdromes, and other objectives. Contributed to the intensive Allied campaign against the enemy aircraft industry during Big Week (20–25 Feb 1944) by attacking factories at Steyr and Regensburg, being awarded a DUC for braving the hazards of bad weather, enemy fighters, and flak to bombard a Messerschmitt factory at Regensburg on 25 Feb. Received second DUC for a mission on 5 Apr 1944 when the group fought its way through relentless attacks by enemy aircraft to bomb marshalling yards at Ploesti. Also struck such objectives as enemy defenses, troop concentrations, bridges, and marshalling yards in support of the invasion of Southern France, the advance of Russian troops in the Balkans, and the Allied effort in Italy. Returned to the US in May 1945. *Redesignated* 450th Bombardment Group (Very Heavy).

Trained with B–29's. *Inactivated* on 15 Oct 1945.

Redesignated 450th Fighter-Bomber Group. *Activated* on 1 Jul 1954. Assigned to Tactical Air Command. Used F–86 aircraft. *Redesignated* 450th Fighter-Day Group in Mar 1955. Converted to F–100's.

SQUADRONS. *720th:* 1943–1945. *721st:* 1943–1945; 1954–. *722d:* 1943–1945; 1954–. *723d:* 1943–1945; 1954–.

STATIONS. Gowen Field, Idaho, 1 May 1943; Clovis AAB, NM, c. 21 May 1943; Alamogordo AAFld, NM, c. 8 Jul–20 Nov 1943; Manduria, Italy, 20 Dec 1943–12 May 1945; Harvard AAFld, Neb, c. 26 Jul–15 Oct 1945. Foster AFB, Tex, Jul 1954–.

COMMANDERS. Col John S Mills, 12 Jun 1943; Col Robert R Gideon, 7 Jul 1944; Col Ellsworth R Jacoby, 17 Nov 1944–1945. Col Wallace E Hopkins, Jul 1954; Lt Col James P Hagerstrom, c. 17 May 1955–.

CAMPAIGNS. Air Combat, EAME Theater; Air Offensive, Europe; Naples-Foggia; Anzio; Rome-Arno; Normandy; Northern France; Southern France; North Apennines; Rhineland; Po Valley.

DECORATIONS. Distinguished Unit Citations: Regensburg, Germany, [25] Feb 1944; Ploesti, Rumania, 5 Apr 1944.

INSIGNE. *Shield:* Per bend sinister, argent and azure, a silhouetted eagle, displayed wings inverted gules, fimbriated argent on the azure, debruised by a ribbon bend sinisterwise charged with a diamond all or. (Approved 14 Sep 1955.)

451st BOMBARDMENT GROUP

Constituted as 451st Bombardment Group (Heavy) on 6 Apr 1943. *Activated* on 1 May 1943. Prepared for combat with B–24's. Moved to the Mediterranean theater, Nov 1943–Jan 1944, with the air echelon training in Algeria for several weeks before joining the remainder of the group in Italy. Operated with Fifteenth AF, Jan 1944–May 1945, functioning primarily as a strategic bombardment organization. Attacked such targets as oil refineries, marshalling yards, aircraft factories, bridges, and airfields in Italy, France, Germany, Czechoslovakia, Austria, Hungary, Rumania, Bulgaria, Albania, and Greece. Received a DUC for each of three missions: to an aircraft factory at Regensburg on 25 Feb 1944, to oil refineries and marshalling yards at Ploesti on 5 Apr 1944, and to an airdrome at Vienna on 23 Aug 1944; although encountering large numbers of enemy fighters and severe antiaircraft fire during each of these missions, the group fought its way through the opposition, destroyed many interceptors, and inflicted serious damage on the assigned targets. At times the group also flew support and interdictory missions. Helped to prepare the way for and participated in the invasion of Southern France in Aug 1944. Transported supplies to troops in Italy during Sep 1944. Supported the final advances of Allied armies in northern Italy in Apr 1945. Returned to the US in Jun. *Inactivated* on 26 Sep 1945.

SQUADRONS. *724th:* 1943–1945. *725th:* 1943–1945. *726th:* 1943–1945. *727th:* 1943–1945.

STATIONS. Davis-Monthan Field, Ariz, 1 May 1943; Dyersburg AAFld, Tenn, 3 Jun 1943; Wendover Field, Utah, c. 18 Jul 1943; Fairmont AAFld, Neb, 9 Sep–26 Nov 1943; Gioia del Colle, Italy, c. 20 Jan 1944; San Pancrazio, Italy, c. 5 Mar 1944; Castelluccio Airfield, Italy, c. 6 Apr 1944– Jun 1945; Dow Field, Maine, c. 19 Jun–26 Sep 1945.

COMMANDERS. Col Robert E L Eaton, c. 1 May 1943; Col James B Knapp, 19 Sep 1944; Col Leroy L Stefonowicz, Dec 1944; Maj William H McGuire, unkn–26 Sep 1945.

CAMPAIGNS. Air Combat, EAME Theater; Air Offensive, Europe; Rome-Arno; Normandy; Northern France; Southern France; North Apennines; Rhineland; Central Europe; Po Valley.

DECORATIONS. Distinguished Unit Citations: Regensburg, Germany, 25 Feb 1944; Ploesti, Rumania, 5 Apr 1944; Austria, 23 Aug 1944.

INSIGNE. None.

452d BOMBARDMENT GROUP

Constituted as 452d Bombardment Group (Heavy) on 14 May 1943. *Activated* on 1 Jun 1943. Trained with B–17's. Moved to England, Dec 1943–Jan 1944, and assigned to Eighth AF. Entered combat on 5 Feb 1944 with an attack against aircraft assembly plants at Brunswick.

Throughout combat, engaged primarily in bombardment of strategic targets, including marshalling yards at Frankfurt, aircraft assembly plants at Regensburg, aircraft component works at Kassel, the ball-bearing industry at Schweinfurt, a synthetic rubber plant at Hannover, and oil installations at Bohlen. 1st Lt Donald J Gott and 2d Lt William E Metzger Jr were each awarded the Medal of Honor for remaining with their aircraft (crippled during a mission over Germany on 9 Nov 1944) in an attempt to save a wounded crew member who was unable to bail out; the men were killed when the B–17 exploded in mid-air. In addition to strategic missions, the 452d supported ground forces and carried out interdictory operations. Helped prepare for the invasion of Normandy by hitting airfields, V-weapon sites, bridges, and other objectives in France; struck coastal defenses on D–Day, 6 Jun 1944. Bombed enemy positions in support of the breakthrough at St Lo in Jul and the offensive against Brest in Aug and Sep. Later in Sep, assisted the airborne attack on Holland. Hit enemy communications in and near the combat zone during the Battle of the Bulge, Dec 1944–Jan 1945. Bombed an airfield in support of the airborne assault across the Rhine in Mar 1945. Received a DUC for action on 7 Apr 1945 when, despite vigorous fighter attacks and heavy flak, it accurately bombed a jet-fighter base at Kaltenkirchen. Flew last combat mission of World War II on 21 Apr, striking marshalling yards at Ingolstadt. Returned to the US in Aug. *Inactivated* on 28 Aug 1945.

Redesignated 452d Bombardment Group (Very Heavy). Allotted to the reserve. *Activated* on 19 Apr 1947. *Redesignated* 452d Bombardment Group (Light) in Jun 1949. Ordered to active duty on 10 Aug 1950. Assigned to Tactical Air Command. Trained with B–26 aircraft for duty in the Korean War. Moved to Japan, Oct–Nov 1950, and assigned to Far East Air Forces. Entered combat against communist forces late in Oct, operating first from Japan and later from Korea. Flew armed reconnaissance, intruder, and interdictory missions, and provided support for ground troops. Bombed and strafed buildings, tunnels, rail lines, switching centers, bridges, vehicles, supply dumps, and airfields. Relieved from active duty and *inactivated* in Korea, on 10 May 1952.

Allotted to the reserve. *Redesignated* 452d Tactical Reconnaissance Group. *Activated* in the US on 13 Jun 1952. *Re-designated* 452d Bombardment Group (Tactical) in May 1955.

SQUADRONS. *703d:* 1948–1949. *728th:* 1943–1945; 1947–1952; 1952–. *729th:* 1943–1945; 1947–1952; 1952–. *730th:* 1943–1945; 1947–1952; 1952–. *731st:* 1943–1945; 1947–1951.

STATIONS. Geiger Field, Wash, 1 Jun 1943; Rapid City AAB, SD, c. 15 Jun 1943; Pendleton Field, Ore, c. 11 Oct 1943; Walla Walla AAFld, Wash, c. 4 Nov–c. 22 Dec 1943; Deopham Green, England, c. 3 Jan 1944–c. 6 Aug 1945; Sioux Falls AAFld, SD, c. 12–28 Aug 1945. Long Beach, Calif, 19 Apr 1947; George AFB, Calif, 10 Aug–Oct 1950; Itazuke, Japan, c. 22 Oct 1950; Miho, Japan, c. 8 Dec 1950; Pusan-East AB, Korea, c. 17 May 1951–10 May 1952. Long Beach Mun Aprt, Calif, 13 Jun 1952–.

COMMANDERS. Lt Col Herbert O Wangeman, c. 15 Jun 1943; Lt Col Robert B Satterwhite, 8 Feb 1944; Lt Col Marvin F Stalder, 28 Feb 1944; Col Thetus C Odom, 30 Mar 1944; Col Archibald Y Smith, c. 24 Jul 1944; Col William D Eckert, c. 1 Aug 1944; Lt Col Charles W Sherburne, 13 Sep 1944; Col Burnham L Batson, c. 25 Sep 1944; Col Jack E Shuck, c. 6 Jun 1945–unkn. Col Charles W Howe, 10 Aug 1950; Col Frank L Wood Jr, c. May 1951; Lt Col John A Herrington, c. Jun 1951; Lt Col Harry C Mailey, c. Dec 1951; Col James D Kemp, c. 28 Mar 1952–unkn.

CAMPAIGNS. *World War II:* Air Offensive, Europe; Normandy; Northern

France; Rhineland; Ardennes-Alsace; Central Europe. *Korean War:* UN Offensive; CCF Intervention; 1st UN Counteroffensive; CCF Spring Offensive; UN Summer-Fall Offensive; Second Korean Winter; Korea Summer-Fall, 1952.

DECORATIONS. Distinguished Unit Citations: Germany, 7 Apr 1945; Korea, 9 Jul-27 Nov 1951; Korea, 28 Nov 1951-30 Apr 1952. Republic of Korea Presidential Unit Citation: 27 Oct 1950-27 Oct 1951.

INSIGNE. *Shield:* Azure, a bomb, point downward, in pale, gules, highlighted and fimbriated argent, superimposed over two lightning flashes or, shaded of the second, highlighted and fimbriated of the third; the shield edged argent, gules and or. *Motto:* LABOR AD FUTURUM—Work for the Future. (Approved 8 Mar 1956.)

453d BOMBARDMENT GROUP

Constituted as 453d Bombardment Group (Heavy) on 14 May 1943. *Activated* on 1 Jun 1943. Trained with B-24's. Moved to England, Dec 1943-Jan 1944, and assigned to Eighth AF. Began combat on 5 Feb 1944 with an attack against an airfield at Tours. Throughout combat, served chiefly as a strategic bombardment organization. Targets included a fuel depot at Dulmen, marshalling yards at Paderborn, aircraft assembly plants at Gotha, railroad centers at Hamm, an ordnance depot at Glinde, oil refineries at Gelsenkirchen, chemical works at Leverkusen, an airfield at Neumunster, a canal at Minden, and a railroad viaduct at Altenbeken. Took part in the concentrated attack against the German aircraft industry during Big Week, 20-25 Feb 1944. Besides strategic operations, engaged in support and interdictory missions. Bombed V-weapon sites, airfields, and gun batteries in France prior to the invasion of Normandy in Jun 1944; on 6 Jun hit shore installations between Le Havre and Cherbourg and other enemy positions farther inland. Attacked enemy troops in support of the Allied breakthrough at St Lo in Jul. Bombed German communications during the Battle of the Bulge, Dec 1944-Jan 1945. Ferried cargo on two occasions: hauled gasoline, blankets, and rations to France in Sep 1944; dropped ammunition, food, and medical supplies near Wesel during the airborne assault across the Rhine in Mar 1945. Flew last combat mission in Apr. Returned to the US in May. *Inactivated* on 12 Sep 1945.

SQUADRONS. *732d:* 1943-1945. *733d:* 1943-1945. *734th:* 1943-1945. *735th:* 1943-1945.

STATIONS. Wendover Field, Utah, 1 Jun 1943; Pocatello AAFld, Idaho, 29 Jul 1943; March Field, Calif, 30 Sep-2 Dec 1943; Old Buckenham, England, 23 Dec 1943-9 May 1945; New Castle AAFld, Del, 25 May 1945; Fort Dix AAB, NJ, 18 Jun-12 Sep 1945.

COMMANDERS. Col Joseph A Miller, 29 Jun 1943; Col Ramsay D Potts Jr, 19 Mar 1944; Col Lawrence M Thomas, 7 Jul 1944; Lt Col Edward F Hubbard, 25 Jan 1945-unkn.

CAMPAIGNS. Air Offensive, Europe; Normandy; Northern France; Rhineland; Ardennes-Alsace; Central Europe.

DECORATIONS. None.

INSIGNE. None.

454th BOMBARDMENT GROUP

Constituted as 454th Bombardment Group (Heavy) on 14 May 1943. *Activated* on 1 Jun 1943. Trained for combat with B-24's. Moved to Italy, Dec 1943-Jan 1944, and operated with Fifteenth AF until Apr 1945. Flew some interdictory and support missions, bombing bridges, marshalling yards, troop concentrations, and rail lines. Participated in the drive to Rome, the invasion of Southern France, and the defeat of Axis forces in northern Italy. Engaged primarily, however, in long-range strikes against enemy oil refineries, aircraft and munition factories, industrial areas, harbors, and airfields in Italy, France, Germany, Czechoslovakia, Hungary, Austria, Yugoslavia, Rumania, and Greece. Received a DUC for a raid on an airdrome at Bad Voslau on 12 Apr 1944. Received second DUC for performance on 25 Jul 1944 when, despite severe opposition, the group led the wing formation in an attack against steel plants at Linz. Returned to the US in Jul 1945. *Redesignated* 454th Bombardment Group (Very Heavy) in Aug 1945. *Inactivated* on 17 Oct 1945.

Allotted to the reserve. *Activated* on 27 Apr 1947. *Redesignated* 454th Bombardment Group (Medium) in Jun 1949. Or-dered into active service on 1 May 1951. Assigned to Strategic Air Command. *Inactivated* on 16 Jun 1951.

Redesignated 454th Troop Carrier Group (Medium). Allotted to the reserve. *Activated* on 13 Jun 1952. *Inactivated* on 1 Jan 1953.

SQUADRONS. *81st:* 1947-1949. *736th:* 1943-1945; 1947-1951; 1952-1953. *737th:* 1943-1945; 1947-1949; 1952-1953. *738th:* 1943-1945; 1947-1949; 1952-1953. *739th:* 1943-1945; 1947-1949.

STATIONS. Alamogordo AAFld, NM, 1 Jun 1943; Davis-Monthan Field, Ariz, 1 Jul 1943; McCook AAFld, Neb, c. 31 Jul 1943; Charleston AAFld, SC, 3 Oct-Dec 1943; San Giovanni, Italy, Jan 1944-Jul 1945; Sioux Falls AAFld, SD, 1 Aug 1945; Pyote AAFld, Tex, 17 Aug-17 Oct 1945. McChord Field, Wash, 27 Apr 1947; Spokane AFB, Wash, 27 Jun 1949-16 Jun 1951. Portland Intl Aprt, Ore, 13 Jun 1952-1 Jan 1953.

COMMANDERS. Col Horace D Aynesworth, c. Jun 1943; Col John A Way, 22 Mar 1945; Lt Col William R Large Jr, 21 May 1945; Lt Col Edward R Casey, 24 May 1945-unkn. Unkn, 1 May-16 Jun 1951.

CAMPAIGNS. Air Combat, EAME Theater; Air Offensive, Europe; Rome-Arno; Normandy; Northern France; Southern France; North Apennines; Rhineland; Central Europe; Po Valley.

DECORATIONS. Distinguished Unit Citations: Bad Voslau, Austria, 12 Apr 1944; Linz, Austria, 25 Jul 1944.

INSIGNE. None.

455th BOMBARDMENT GROUP

Constituted as 455th Bombardment Group (Heavy) on 14 May 1943. *Activated* on 1 Jun 1943. Trained with B–24's. Moved to Italy, arriving in Jan and Feb 1944. Served in combat with Fifteenth AF from Feb 1944 to Apr 1945. Engaged primarily in bombardment of strategic targets such as factories, marshalling yards, oil refineries, storage areas, harbors, and airdromes in Italy, France, Germany, Poland, Czechoslovakia, Hungary, Austria, and the Balkans. Received a DUC for a mission on 2 Apr 1944 when the group contributed to Fifteenth AF's campaign against enemy industry by attacking a ball-bearing plant at Steyr. Although meeting severe fighter opposition and losing several of its bombers on 26 Jun 1944, the group proceeded to attack an oil refinery at Moosbierbaum, receiving another DUC for this performance. In addition to strategic missions in the Balkans, the group bombed troop concentrations, bridges, marshalling yards, and airdromes during the fall of 1944 to hamper the enemy's withdrawal from the region. The group also supported ground forces at Anzio and Cassino in Mar 1944; knocked out gun positions in preparation for the invasion of Southern France in Aug 1944; and assisted the final Allied drive through Italy in Apr 1945 by hitting such targets as bridges, gun positions, and troop concentrations. *Inactivated* in Italy on 9 Sep 1945.

Redesignated 455th Bombardment Group (Very Heavy). Allotted to the reserve. *Activated* in the US on 25 Mar 1947. *Inactivated* on 27 Jun 1949.

Redesignated 455th Fighter-Day Group. *Activated* on 25 Jul 1956. Assigned to Tactical Air Command.

SQUADRONS. *740th:* 1943–1945; 1947–1949; 1956–. *741st:* 1943–1945; 1947–1949; 1956–. *742d:* 1943–1945; 1947–1949; 1956–. *743d:* 1943–1945; 1947–1949.

STATIONS. Alamogordo AAFld, NM, 1 Jun 1943; Kearns, Utah, c. 6 Sep 1943; Langley Field, Va, c. 5 Oct–2 Dec 1943; San Giovanni, Italy, 15 Jan 1944–9 Sep 1945. Hensley Field, Tex, 25 Mar 1947–27 Jun 1949. Myrtle Beach AFB, SC, 25 Jul 1956–.

COMMANDERS. Col Kenneth A Cool, c. Jul 1943; Col William L Snowden, c. 26 Sep 1944; Lt Col William R Boutz, May 1945; Maj Jerome Hoss, Jul 1945–unkn. Maj John C Smith, 25 Jul 1956–.

CAMPAIGNS. Air Combat, EAME Theater; Air Offensive, Europe; Anzio; Rome-Arno; Normandy; Northern France; Southern France; North Apennines; Rhineland; Central Europe; Po Valley.

DECORATIONS. Distinguished Unit Citations: Steyr, Austria, 2 Apr 1944; Austria, 26 Jun 1944.

INSIGNE. None.

456th BOMBARDMENT GROUP

Constituted as 456th Bombardment Group (Heavy) on 14 May 1943. *Acti-*

vated on 1 Jun 1943. Trained with B–24's for duty overseas. Moved to Italy, Dec 1943–Jan 1944. Began combat with Fifteenth AF in Feb 1944, operating chiefly against strategic targets until late in Apr 1945. Early operations included attacks against such objectives as marshalling yards, aircraft factories, railroad bridges, and airdromes in Italy, Austria, and Rumania. Received a DUC for performance at Wiener Neustadt on 10 May 1944: when other groups turned back because of adverse weather, the 456th proceeded to the target and, withstanding repeated attacks by enemy interceptors, bombed the manufacturing center. Helped to prepare the way for and supported the invasion of Southern France during Jul and Aug 1944. At the same time, expanded previous operations to include attacks on oil refineries and storage facilities, locomotive works, and viaducts in France, Germany, Czechoslovakia, Hungary, Austria, and the Balkans. Received second DUC for a mission in Hungary on 2 Jul 1944 when the group braved severe fighter attacks and antiaircraft fire to bomb oil facilities at Budapest. In Apr 1945 bombed gun positions, bridges, roads, depots, and rail lines to support US Fifth and British Eighth Army in their advance through Italy. Transported supplies to airfields in northern Italy after V–E Day. Returned to the US in Jul 1945. *Redesignated* 456th Bombardment Group (Very Heavy) in Aug. *Inactivated* on 17 Oct 1945.

Allotted to the reserve. *Activated* on 12 Jul 1947. *Inactivated* on 27 Jun 1949.

Redesignated 456th Troop Carrier Group (Medium). *Activated* on 1 Dec 1952. Assigned to Tactical Air Command and equipped with C–119's. *Inactivated* on 1 Mar 1955.

SQUADRONS. *744th:* 1943–1945; 1947–1949; 1952–1955. *745th:* 1943–1945; 1947–1949; 1952–1955. *746th:* 1943–1945; 1947–1949; 1952–1955. *747th:* 1943–1945; 1947–1949.

STATIONS. Wendover Field, Utah, 1 Jun 1943; Gowen Field, Idaho, 14 Jul 1943; Bruning AAFld, Neb, c. 30 Jul 1943; Kearns, Utah, c. 11 Sep 1943; Muroc AAB, Calif, Oct–Dec 1943; Cerignola, Italy, Jan 1944; Stornara, Italy, Jan 1944–Jul 1945; Sioux Falls AAFld, SD, 1 Aug 1945; Smoky Hill AAFld, Kan, 17 Aug–17 Oct 1945. McChord Field, Wash, 12 Jul 1947–27 Jun 1949. Miami Intl Aprt, Fla, 1 Dec 1952; Charleston AFB, SC, 15 Aug 1953–1 Mar 1955.

COMMANDERS. Unkn, 1 Jun–14 Jul 1943; Col Thomas W Steed, 14 Jul 1943;

Lt Col Joseph G Russell, 16 Jul 1944; Col Thomas W Steed, Oct 1944; Lt Col Robert C Whipple, c. 19 May 1945–unkn; Col George E Henry, 31 Aug 1945; Col John W White, 4 Sep 1945–unkn. Col Leonard J Barrow Jr, c. Dec 1952; Lt Col Malcolm P Hooker, c. Feb 1953; Col Jay D Bogue, 1953–1 Mar 1955.

CAMPAIGNS. Air Combat, EAME Theater; Air Offensive, Europe; Rome-Arno; Normandy; Northern France; Southern France; North Apennines; Rhineland; Central Europe; Po Valley.

DECORATIONS. Distinguished Unit Citations: Wiener Neustadt, Austria, 10 May 1944; Budapest, Hungary, 2 Jul 1944.

INSIGNE. *Shield:* Azure, a bar gemel de-based argent over-all on a pile quarterly of the second and gules four stylized birds counterchanged. (Approved 7 Jul 1953.)

457th BOMBARDMENT GROUP

Constituted as 457th Bombardment Group (Heavy) on 19 May 1943. *Activated* on 1 Jul 1943. Trained for combat with B–17's. Moved to England, Jan–Feb 1944, and assigned to Eighth AF. Flew first mission on 21 Feb 1944 during Big Week, taking part in the concentrated attacks of heavy bombers on the German aircraft industry. Until Jun 1944, engaged primarily in bombardment of strategic targets, such as ball-bearing plants, aircraft factories, and oil refineries in Germany. Bombed targets in France during the first week of Jun 1944 in preparation for the Normandy invasion, and attacked coastal defenses along the Cherbourg peninsula on D–Day. Struck airfields, railroads, fuel depots, and other interdictory targets behind the invasion beaches throughout the remainder of the month. Resumed bombardment of strategic objectives in Jul 1944 and engaged chiefly in such operations until Apr 1945. Sometimes flew support and interdictory missions, aiding the advance of ground forces during the St Lo breakthrough in Jul 1944 and the landing of British 1 Airborne Division during the airborne attack on Holland in Sep 1944; and participating in the Battle of the Bulge, Dec 1944–Jan 1945, and the assault across the Rhine in Mar 1945. Flew last combat mission on 20 Apr 1945. Transported prisoners of war from Austria to France after V–E Day. Returned to the US in Jun 1945. *Inactivated* on 28 Aug 1945.

SQUADRONS. *748th:* 1943–1945. *749th:* 1943–1945. *750th:* 1943–1945. *751st:* 1943–1945.

STATIONS. Geiger Field, Wash, 1 Jul 1943; Rapid City AAB, SD, 9 Jul 1943; Ephrata AAB, Wash, 28 Oct 1943; Wendover Field, Utah, 4 Dec 1943–1 Jan 1944; Glatton, England, 22 Jan 1944–1 Jun 1945; Sioux Falls AAFld, SD, 20 Jul–28 Aug 1945.

COMMANDERS. Col Herbert E Rice, 24 Jul 1943; Lt Col Hugh D Wallace, 3 Sep 1943; Col James R Luper, 4 Jan 1944; Col Harris E Rogner, 11 Oct 1944–Aug 1945.

CAMPAIGNS. Air Offensive, Europe; Normandy; Northern France; Rhineland; Ardennes-Alsace; Central Europe.

DECORATIONS. None.

INSIGNE. None.

458th BOMBARDMENT GROUP

Constituted as 458th Bombardment Group (Heavy) on 19 May 1943. *Activated* on 1 Jul 1943. Prepared for combat with B-24's. Moved to England, Jan–Feb 1944, and assigned to Eighth AF. Flew diversionary missions on 24 and 25 Feb 1944 to draw enemy fighters from German targets being attacked by other AAF bombers. Began bombardment on 2 Mar 1944, and afterward operated primarily against strategic objectives in Germany. Hit such targets as the industrial area of Saarbrucken, oil refineries at Hamburg, an airfield at Brunswick, aircraft factories at Oschersleben, a fuel depot at Dulmen, a canal at Minden, aircraft works at Brandenburg, marshalling yards at Hamm, and an aircraft engine plant at Magdeburg. Carried out some interdictory and support operations in addition to the strategic missions. Helped to prepare for the invasion of Normandy by striking gun batteries, V-weapon sites, and airfields in France; hit coastal defenses in support of the assault on 6 Jun 1944; afterward, bombed bridges and highways to prevent the movement of enemy materiel to the beachhead. Attacked enemy troops to aid the Allied breakthrough at St Lo in Jul. Ceased bombardment during Sep 1944 to haul gasoline to airfields in France. Struck transportation lines during the Battle of the Bulge, Dec 1944–Jan 1945. Attacked enemy airfields to assist the Allied assault across the Rhine in Mar 1945. Flew last combat mission on 25 Apr 1945. Returned to the US, Jun–Jul 1945. *Redesignated* 458th Bombardment Group (Very Heavy) in Aug 1945. Trained with B-29's. *Inactivated* on 17 Oct 1945.

SQUADRONS. *752d:* 1943–1945. *753d:* 1943–1945. *754th:* 1943–1945. *755th:* 1943–1945.

STATIONS. Wendover Field, Utah, 1 Jul 1943; Gowen Field, Idaho, 28 Jul 1943; Kearns, Utah, 11 Sep 1943; Wendover Field, Utah, 15 Sep 1943; Tonopah AAFld, Nev, 31 Oct–29 Dec 1943; Horsham St Faith, England, Jan 1944–14 Jun 1945; Sioux Falls AAFld, SD, 12 Jul 1945; Walker AAFld, Kan, 25 Jul 1945; March Field, Calif, 21 Aug–17 Oct 1945.

COMMANDERS. Lt Col Robert F Hardy, 28 Jul 1943; Col James H Isbell, 16 Dec 1943; Col Allen F Herzberg, 10 Mar 1945; Capt Patrick Hays, 13 Aug 1945; Maj Bernard Carlos, 17 Aug 1945; Maj V R Woodward, 22 Aug 1945; Lt Col Wilmer C Hardesty, 3 Sep–17 Oct 1945.

CAMPAIGNS. Air Offensive, Europe; Normandy; Northern France; Rhineland; Ardennes-Alsace; Central Europe.

DECORATIONS. None.

INSIGNE. None.

459th BOMBARDMENT GROUP

Constituted as 459th Bombardment Group (Heavy) on 19 May 1943. *Activated* on 1 Jul 1943. Trained for combat with B-24's. Moved to Italy, Jan–Feb 1944, and assigned to Fifteenth AF. Engaged primarily in strategic bombardment, Mar 1944–Apr 1945, attacking such targets as oil refineries, munitions and aircraft factories, industrial areas, airfields, and communications centers in Italy, France, Germany, Poland, Czechoslovakia, Hungary, Austria, Rumania, Bulgaria, Yugoslavia, and Greece. ' Received a DUC for leading the 304th Wing through enemy interceptors and intense flak to raid an airfield and aircraft assembly plant at Bad Voslau on 23 Apr 1944. During combat the group also flew some support and interdictory missions. Struck railroads in Mar 1944 to cut enemy supply lines leading to the Anzio beachhead. Participated in the preinvasion bombing of southern France in Aug 1944. Hit railroad bridges,

depots, and marshalling yards during Apr 1945 to assist Allied forces in northern Italy. Returned to the US in Aug. *Inactivated* on 28 Aug 1945.

Redesignated 459th Bombardment Group (Very Heavy). Allotted to the reserve. *Activated* on 19 Apr 1947. *Redesignated* 459th Bombardment Group (Medium) in Jun 1949. Ordered to active duty on 1 May 1951. Assigned to Strategic Air Command. *Inactivated* on 16 Jun 1951.

Redesignated 459th Troop Carrier Group (Medium). Allotted to the reserve. *Activated* on 26 Jan 1955.

SQUADRONS. *57th:* 1947–1949. *756th:* 1943–1945; 1947–1949; 1955–. *757th:* 1943–1945; 1947–1949; 1955–. *758th:* 1943–1945; 1947–1949. *759th:* 1943–1945; 1947–1951.

STATIONS. Alamogordo AAFld, NM, 1 Jul 1943; Kearns, Utah, c. 31 Aug 1943; Davis-Monthan Field, Ariz, c. 20 Sep 1943; Westover Field, Mass, c. 1 Nov 1943–2 Jan 1944; Giulia Airfield, Italy, Feb 1944–c. Jul 1945; Sioux Falls AAFld, SD, c. 16–28 Aug 1945. Long Beach AAFld, Calif, 19 Apr 1947; Davis-Monthan AFB, Ariz, 27 Jun 1949–16 Jun 1951. Andrews AFB, Md, 26 Jan 1955–.

COMMANDERS. Col Marden M Munn, 28 Jul 1943; Col Henry K Mooney, 13 Aug 1944; Lt Col William R Boutz, 19 May 1945; Lt Col J C Bailey, 30 May 1945–unkn. Unkn, 1 May–16 Jun 1951.

CAMPAIGNS. Air Combat, EAME Theater; Air Offensive, Europe; Rome-Arno; Normandy; Northern France;

Southern France; North Apennines; Rhineland; Central Europe; Po Valley.

DECORATIONS. Distinguished Unit Citation: Bad Voslau, Austria, 23 Apr 1944.

INSIGNE. *Shield:* Azure, an American eagle proper flying over clouds in the base argent between two parachutes, one in chief transporting an airman, one in base transporting supplies all of the last; in chief a canton argent charged with the Capitol dome of the second. *Motto:* IN HONOR OF CONGRESS. (Approved 17 Jan 1956.)

460th BOMBARDMENT GROUP

Constituted as 460th Bombardment Group (Heavy) on 19 May 1943. *Activated* on 1 Jul 1943. Trained for combat with B–24's. Moved to Italy, Jan–Feb 1944, and became part of Fifteenth AF. Entered combat in Mar 1944 and operated primarily as a strategic bombardment organization until Apr 1945. Attacked oil refineries, oil storage facilities, aircraft factories, railroad centers, industrial areas, and other objectives in Italy, France, Germany, Poland, Czechoslovakia, Hungary, Austria, Rumania, Yugoslavia, and Greece. Received a DUC for leading the wing formation through adverse weather and heavy enemy fire to attack an airdrome and aircraft facilities in Zwolfaxing on 26 Jul 1944. Also flew some interdictory and support missions. Participated in the invasion of Southern France in Aug 1944 by striking submarine pens, marshalling yards, and gun positions in the assault area. Hit bridges, viaducts, ammunition dumps, railroads, and other targets to aid the advance of Allied forces in northern Italy. Moved to Trinidad and then to Brazil in Jun 1945, being assigned to Air Transport Command to assist in moving redeployed personnel from Europe to the US. *Inactivated* in Brazil on 26 Sep 1945.

SQUADRONS. *760th:* 1943–1945. *761st:* 1943–1945. *762d:* 1943–1945. *763d:* 1943–1945.

STATIONS. Alamogordo AAFld, NM, 1 Jul 1943; Kearns, Utah, 31 Aug 1943; Chatham AAFld, Ga, Oct 1943–3 Jan 1944; Spinazzola, Italy, Feb 1944–Jun 1945; Waller Field, Trinidad, 15 Jun 1945; Natal, Brazil, 30 Jun–26 Sep 1945.

COMMANDERS. Unkn, 1 Jul–12 Aug 1943; Col Robert T Crowder, 12 Aug 1943; Lt Col Bertram C Harrison, 16 Apr 1944; Lt Col Harold T Babb, Sep 1944; Col John M Price, 18 Oct 1944–1945.

CAMPAIGNS. American Theater; Air Combat, EAME Theater; Air Offensive, Europe; Rome-Arno; Normandy; Northern France; Southern France; North Apennines; Rhineland; Central Europe; Po Valley.

DECORATIONS. Distinguished Unit Citation: Austria, 26 Jul 1944.

INSIGNE. None.

461st BOMBARDMENT GROUP

Constituted as 461st Bombardment Group (Heavy) on 19 May 1943. *Activated* on 1 Jul 1943. Moved to the Mediterranean theater, Jan–Feb 1944, the air

echelon flying B–24's via the South Atlantic and stopping in North Africa before joining the ground echelon in Italy. Began combat with Fifteenth AF in Apr 1944. Engaged chiefly in bombardment of communications, industries, and other strategic objectives in Italy, France, Germany, Czechoslovakia, Hungary, Austria, Rumania, Yugoslavia, and Greece. Supported Fifteenth AF's counter-air operations by bombing enemy airdromes and aircraft centers, receiving a DUC for a mission on 13 Apr 1944 when the group battled its way through enemy defenses to attack an aircraft components plant in Budapest. Participated in the effort against the enemy's oil supply by flying missions to such oil centers as Brux, Blechhammer, Moosbierbaum, Vienna, and Ploesti. Received second DUC for a mission against oil facilities at Ploesti in Jul 1944 when, despite flak, clouds, smoke, and fighter attacks, the group bombed its objective. Also operated in support of ground forces and flew some interdictory missions. Hit artillery positions in sup-

port of the invasion of Southern France in Aug 1944 and flew supply missions to France in Sep. Aided the Allied offensive in Italy in Apr 1945 by attacking gun emplacements and troop concentrations. Dropped supplies to prisoner-of-war camps in Austria during May 1945. Returned to the US in Jul. *Inactivated* on 28 Aug 1945.

Redesignated 461st Bombardment Group (Light). *Activated* on 23 Dec 1953. Assigned to Tactical Air Command. Trained with B–26's and later converted to B–57's. *Redesignated* 461st Bombardment Group (Tactical) in Oct 1955.

SQUADRONS. *764th:* 1943–1945; 1953–. *765th:* 1943–1945; 1953–. *766th:* 1943–1945; 1953–. *767th:* 1943–1945.

STATIONS. Wendover Field, Utah, 1 Jul 1943; Gowen Field, Idaho, 29 Jul 1943; Kearns, Utah, 11 Sep 1943; Wendover Field, Utah, 30 Sep 1943; Hammer Field, Calif, 30 Oct 1943–Jan 1944; Torretto Airfield, Italy, c. 20 Feb 1944–Jul 1945; Sioux Falls AAFld, SD, 22 Jul–28 Aug 1945. Hill AFB, Utah, 23 Dec 1953–.

COMMANDERS. Unkn, 1 Jul–12 Aug 1943; Lt Col Willis G Carter, 12 Aug 1943; Col Frederic E Glantzberg, c. 25 Oct 1943; Col Philip R Hawes, 22 Sep 1944; Col Brooks A Lawhon, 20 Dec 1944; Col Craven C Rogers, 16 Apr 1945–unkn. Maj Gordon Baker, c. Dec 1953; Lt Col Donald F Blake, 4 Feb 1954; Lt Col Robert F Price, 20 Feb 1954; Col Maxwell W Roman, c. 14 Jul 1954; Lt Col John A McVey, c. 16 May 1955; Lt Col William F Furman, c. 1 Aug 1955–.

CAMPAIGNS. Air Combat, EAME Theater; Air Offensive, Europe; Rome-Arno; Normandy; Northern France; Southern France; North Apennines; Rhineland; Central Europe; Po Valley.

DECORATIONS. Distinguished Unit Citations: Budapest, Hungary, 13 Apr 1944; Ploesti, Rumania, 15 Jul 1944.

INSIGNE. *Shield:* Per bend azure and light blue, superimposed over the bend a thunderbolt, bendwise, or, piercing through a cloud formation proper, over an increscent moon to the sinister chief, and a sun to the dexter base of the third; on a chief argent, over a bar to base of chief, embattled gules, an olive branch and seven arrows in saltire, between two spheres all proper. (Approved 4 Aug 1955.)

462d BOMBARDMENT GROUP

Constituted as 462d Bombardment Group (Heavy) on 19 May 1943. *Activated* on 1 Jul 1943. *Redesignated* 462d Bombardment Group (Very Heavy) in Nov 1943. Prepared for combat with B-29's. Moved to the CBI theater, via Africa, Mar-Jun 1944. Assigned to Twentieth AF in Jun 1944. Transported supplies over the Hump to staging fields in China before entering combat with an attack on railroad shops at Bangkok, Thailand, on 5 Jun 1944. On 15 Jun 1944 took part in the first AAF strike on the Japanese home islands since the Doolittle raid in 1942. Operating from India and China, bombed transportation centers, naval in-

stallations, iron works, aircraft plants, and other targets in Japan, Thailand, Burma, China, Formosa, and Indonesia. From a staging base in Ceylon, mined the Moesi River on Sumatra in Aug 1944. Received a DUC for a daylight attack on iron and steel works at Yawata, Japan, in Aug 1944.

Moved to Tinian in the spring of 1945 for further operations against targets in Japan. Participated in mining operations, bombardment of strategic targets, and incendiary raids on urban areas. Bombed industrial areas in Tokyo and Yokohama in May 1945, being awarded a DUC for the action. Received another DUC for a daylight attack on an aircraft plant at Takarazuka on 24 Jul 1945. Returned to the US late in 1945. Assigned to Strategic Air Command on 21 Mar 1946. *Inactivated* on 31 Mar 1946.

SQUADRONS. *345th:* 1945-1946. *768th:* 1943-1946. *769th:* 1943-1946. *770th:* 1943-1946. *771st:* 1943-1944.

STATIONS. Smoky Hill AAFld, Kan, 1 Jul 1943; Walker AAFld, Kan, 28 Jul 1943-12 Mar 1944; Piardoba, India, 7 Apr 1944-26 Feb 1945; West Field, Tinian, 4 Apr-5 Nov 1945; MacDill Field, Fla, Nov 1945-31 Mar 1946.

COMMANDERS. Unkn, 1 Jul-5 Aug 1943; Col Alan D Clark, 5 Aug 1943; Col Richard H Carmichael, 26 Aug 1943; Col Alfred F Kalberer, 20 Aug 1944-unkn.

CAMPAIGNS. American Theater; India-Burma; Air Offensive, Japan; China Defensive; Western Pacific; Central Burma.

DECORATIONS. Distinguished Unit Citations: Yawata, Japan, 20 Aug 1944; Tokyo

and Yokohama, Japan, 23, 25, and 29 May 1945; Takarazuka, Japan, 24 Jul 1945.
INSIGNE. None.

463d BOMBARDMENT GROUP

Constituted as 463d Bombardment Group (Heavy) on 19 May 1943. *Activated* on 1 Aug 1943. Trained with B-17's for duty overseas. Moved to Italy, Feb–Mar 1944, and assigned to Fifteenth AF. Entered combat on 30 Mar 1944 and operated chiefly against strategic objectives. Attacked such targets as marshalling yards, oil refineries, and aircraft factories in Italy, Germany, Austria, Czechoslovakia, Rumania, Yugoslavia, and Greece. Received a DUC for bombing oil refineries at Ploesti on 18 May 1944: when clouds limited visibility to such an extent that other groups turned back, the 463d proceeded to Ploesti and, though crippled by opposition from interceptors and flak, rendered destructive blows to both the target and the enemy fighters. Received second DUC for leading the wing through three damaging enemy attacks to bomb tank factories in Berlin on 24 Mar 1945. Also engaged in interdictory and support missions. Bombed bridges during May and Jun 1944 in the campaign for the liberation of Rome. Participated in the invasion of Southern France in Aug 1944 by striking bridges, gun positions, and other targets. Hit communications such as railroad bridges, marshalling yards, and airdromes in the Balkans. Operated primarily against communications in northern Italy during Mar and Apr 1945. After V-E Day, transported personnel from Italy to Casablanca for return to the US. *Inactivated* in Italy on 25 Sep 1945.

Redesignated 463d Troop Carrier Group (Medium). *Activated* in the US on 16 Jan 1953. Assigned to Tactical Air Command and equipped with C-119's.

SQUADRONS. 772d: 1943–1945; 1953–. 773d: 1943–1945; 1953–. 774th: 1943–1945; 1953–. 775th: 1943–1945; 1955–.

STATIONS. Geiger Field, Wash, 1 Aug 1943; Rapid City AAB, SD, Aug 1943; MacDill Field, Fla, 5 Nov 1943; Lakeland AAFld, Fla, 3 Jan–2 Feb 1944; Celone Airfield, Italy, 9 Mar 1944–25 Sep 1945. Memphis Mun Aprt, Tenn, 16 Jan 1953; Ardmore AFB, Okla, 24 Aug 1954–.

COMMANDERS. Lt Col Elmer H Stambaugh, 9 Aug 1943; Col Frank A Kurtz, 27 Aug 1943; Col George W McGregor, 11 Sep 1944; Col Ephraim M Hampton,

Apr–c. Sep 1945. Col John R Roche, 16 Jan 1953; Col Woodrow T Merrill, 10 Aug 1953; Col Benjamin M Tarver Jr, 12 Aug 1954–.

CAMPAIGNS. Air Combat, EAME Theater; Air Offensive, Europe; Rome-Arno; Normandy; Northern France; Southern France; North Apennines; Rhineland; Central Europe; Po Valley.

DECORATIONS. Distinguished Unit Citations: Ploesti, Rumania, 18 May 1944; Germany, 24 Mar 1945.

INSIGNE. *Shield:* Azure, on a representation of a cloud argent a silhouette of mythical Pegasus drawing a chariot driven by Mars, the mythical Roman God of War, all sable. (Approved 30 Aug 1954.)

464th BOMBARDMENT GROUP

Constituted as 464th Bombardment Group (Heavy) on 19 May 1943. *Acti-*

CERTISSIMUS IN INCERTIS

vated on 1 Aug 1943. Trained for combat with B–24's. Moved to the Mediterranean theater, Feb–Apr 1944, with the air echelon training for a few weeks in Tunisia before joining the remainder of the group in Italy. Served with Fifteenth AF, Apr 1944–May 1945, operating primarily as part of the strategic bombardment force that disrupted German industry and communications. Flew long-range missions to attack such objectives as marshalling yards, oil refineries, oil storage facilities, aircraft factories, and chemical plants in Italy, France, Germany, Poland, Czechoslovakia, Hungary, Austria, Rumania, Yugoslavia, and Greece. Received a DUC for leading the 55th Wing in compact formation through heavy opposition to bomb marshalling yards and an oil refinery at Vienna on 8 Jul 1944. Received another DUC for a mission on 24 Aug 1944 when the group scored hits not only on the target, an oil refinery at Pardubice, but also on nearby railroad tracks. Sometimes engaged in support and interdictory operations. Supported Allied forces during the invasion of Southern France in Aug 1944. Hit railroad centers to assist the advance of Russian troops in southeastern Europe in Mar 1945. Bombed enemy supply lines to assist the advance of US Fifth and British Eighth Army in northern Italy in Apr 1945. Moved to Trinidad in Jun 1945. Assigned to Air Transport Command. *Inactivated* on 31 Jul 1945.

Redesignated 464th Troop Carrier Group (Medium). *Activated* in the US on 1 Feb 1953. Assigned to Tactical Air Command. Used C–46 and C–119 aircraft.

SQUADRONS. *776th:* 1943–1945; 1953–. *777th:* 1943–1945; 1953–. *778th:* 1943–1945; 1953–. *779th:* 1943–1945; 1955–.

STATIONS. Wendover Field, Utah, 1 Aug 1943; Gowen Field, Idaho, 22 Aug 1943; Pocatello AAFld, Idaho, 2 Oct 1943–9 Feb 1944; Pantanella Airfield, Italy, Mar 1944; Gioia, Italy, 21 Apr 1944; Pantanella Airfield, Italy, c. 1 Jun 1944–c. May 1945; Waller Field, Trinidad, Jun–31 Jul 1945. Lawson AFB, Ga, 1 Feb 1953; Pope AFB, NC, 16 Sep 1954–.

COMMANDERS. Unkn, 1 Aug–2 Sep 1943; Col Marshall Bonner, 2 Sep 1943; Col Arnold L Schroeder, 30 Jun 1944; Col A J Bird Jr, 13 Mar 1945–unkn. Col James A Evans, c. 1 Feb 1953; Col Charles F Franklin, 1954; Lt Col Adam A Reaves, 1955–.

CAMPAIGNS. American Theater; Air Combat, EAME Theater; Air Offensive, Europe; Rome-Arno; Normandy; Northern France; Southern France; North Apennines; Rhineland; Central Europe; Po Valley.

DECORATIONS. Distinguished Unit Citations: Vienna, Austria, 8 Jul 1944; Pardubice, Czechoslovakia, [24] Aug 1944.

INSIGNE. *Shield:* Azure, surmounting a cloud argent, an American eagle descendant, wings, endorsed proper, between his beak four lightning streaks, two and two gules, speed lines of the first all inclosed by two bendlets sinister vert, edged or. *Motto:* CERTISSIMUS IN INCERTIS—Most Certain (in the sense of unerring or dependable) in Uncertainties. (Approved 15 Apr 1954.)

465th BOMBARDMENT GROUP

Constituted as 465th Bombardment Group (Heavy) on 19 May 1943. *Activated* on 1 Aug 1943. Prepared for duty overseas with B–24's. Moved to the Mediterranean theater, Feb–Apr 1944; the air echelon received additional training in Tunisia before joining the ground echelon in Italy. Assigned to Fifteenth AF. Entered combat on 5 May 1944 and served primarily as a strategic bombardment organization until late in Apr 1945. Attacked marshalling yards, dock facilities, oil refineries, oil storage plants, aircraft factories, and other objectives in Italy, France, Germany, Czechoslovakia, Austria, Hungary, and the Balkans. On two different missions—to marshalling yards and an oil refinery at Vienna on 8 Jul 1944 and to steel plants at Friedrichshafen on 3 Aug 1944—the group bombed its targets despite antiaircraft fire and fighter opposition, being awarded a DUC for each of these attacks. Other operations included bombing troop concentrations and bivouac areas in May 1944 to aid the Partisans in Yugoslavia; attacking enemy troops and supply lines to assist the drive toward Rome, May–Jun 1944; striking bridges, rail lines, and gun emplacements prior to the invasion of Southern France in Aug 1944; bombing rail facilities and rolling stock in Oct 1944 to support the advance of Russian and Rumanian forces in the Balkans; and hitting troops, gun positions, bridges, and supply lines during Apr 1945 in support of Allied forces in northern Italy. Moved to the Caribbean area in Jun 1945. Assigned to Air Transport Command. *Inactivated* in Trinidad on 31 Jul 1945.

Redesignated 465th Troop Carrier Group (Medium). *Activated* in the US on 1 Feb 1953. Trained with C–119's. Moved to France in Dec 1953 to become part of United States Air Forces in Europe.

SQUADRONS. *780th:* 1943–1945; 1953–. *781st:* 1943–1945; 1953–. *782d:* 1943–1945; 1953–. *783d:* 1943–1945.

STATIONS. Alamogordo AAFld, NM, 1 Aug 1943; Kearns, Utah, Sep 1943; McCook AAFld, Neb, c. 5 Oct 1943–1 Feb 1944; Pantanella Airfield, Italy, Apr 1944–Jun 1945; Waller Field, Trinidad, 15 Jun–31 Jul 1945. Donaldson AFB, SC, 1 Feb–30 Nov 1953; Toul/Rosiere AB, France, Dec 1953; Evreux AB, France, c. 20 May 1955–.

COMMANDERS. Col Elmer J Rogers Jr, 24 Aug 1943; Col Charles A Clark Jr, 13 Mar 1944; Lt Col Joshua H Foster, 1 Dec 1944; Lt Col William F Day Jr, 26 Apr 1945–unkn. Maj Clifford F Harris, Feb 1953; Col Earl W Worley, c. Mar 1953; Lt Col James D Barlow, 10 May 1954; Col James A Evans Jr, 19 Sep 1954; Col James D Barlow, 7 Apr 1955–.

CAMPAIGNS. American Theater; Air Combat, EAME Theater; Air Offensive, Europe; Rome-Arno; Normandy; Northern France; Southern France; North Apennines; Rhineland; Central Europe; Po Valley.

DECORATIONS. Distinguished Unit Citations: Vienna, Austria, 8 Jul 1944; Germany, 3 Aug 1944.

INSIGNE. *Shield:* Per bend gules and vert, a bend argent charged with a bendlet azure, between a wing of the third and a compass proper (bezant, with diapering green, bordered argent, thereover a four-pointed star compass, gules and azure). *Motto:* ONUS FERENS VITAM—Cargo Carrying Life. (Approved 1 Jun 1955.)

466th BOMBARDMENT GROUP

Constituted as 466th Bombardment Group (Heavy) on 19 May 1943. *Activated* on 1 Aug 1943. Prepared for duty overseas with B–24's. Moved to England,

Feb–Mar 1944, and assigned to Eighth AF. Entered combat on 22 Mar 1944 by participating in a daylight raid on Berlin. Operated primarily as a strategic bombardment organization, attacking such targets as marshalling yards at Liege, an airfield at St Trond, a repair and assembly plant at Reims, an airdrome at Chartres, factories at Brunswick, oil refineries at Bohlen, aircraft plants at Kempten, mineral works at Hamburg, marshalling yards at Saarbrucken, a synthetic oil plant at Misburg, a fuel depot at Dulmen, and aero-engine works at Eisenach. Other operations included attacking pillboxes along the coast of Normandy on D-Day (6 Jun 1944), and afterward striking interdictory targets behind the beachhead; bombing enemy positions at St Lo during the Allied breakthrough in Jul 1944; hauling oil and gasoline to Allied forces advancing across France in Sep; hitting German communications and transportation during the Battle of the Bulge, Dec 1944–Jan 1945; and bombing the airfield at Nordhorn in support of the airborne assault across the Rhine on 24 Mar 1945. Flew last combat mission on 25 Apr 1945, striking a transformer station at Traunstein. Returned to the US in Jul. *Redesignated* 466th Bombardment Group (Very Heavy) in Aug 1945. Trained with B-29's. *Inactivated* on 17 Oct 1945.

SQUADRONS. *784th:* 1943–1945. *785th:* 1943–1945. *786th:* 1943–1945. *787th:* 1943–1945.

STATIONS. Alamogordo AAFld, NM, 1 Aug 1943; Kearns, Utah, 31 Aug 1943; Alamogordo AAFld, NM, 24 Nov 1943; Topeka AAFld, Kan, 5–13 Feb 1944; Attlebridge, England, 7 Mar 1944–6 Jul 1945; Sioux Falls AAFld, SD, 15 Jul 1945; Pueblo AAB, Colo, 25 Jul 1945; Davis-Monthan Field, Ariz, 15 Aug–17 Oct 1945.

COMMANDERS. Maj Beverly E Steadman, 23 Aug 1943; Maj Walter A Smith Jr, 29 Aug 1943; Col Walter G Bryte Jr, 2 Sep 1943; Col Arthur J Pierce, 17 Dec 1943; Col Luther J Fairbanks, 1 Aug 1944; Col William H Cleveland, 1 Nov 1944–1945.

CAMPAIGNS. Air Offensive, Europe; Normandy; Northern France; Rhineland; Ardennes-Alsace; Central Europe.

DECORATIONS. None.

INSIGNE. None.

467th BOMBARDMENT GROUP

Constituted as 467th Bombardment Group (Heavy) on 19 May 1943. *Activated* on 1 Aug 1943. Prepared for combat with B-24's. Moved to England, Feb–Mar 1944, and assigned to Eighth AF. Began operations on 10 Apr 1944 with an attack on an airfield at Bourges. Served chiefly as a strategic bombardment organization, attacking the harbor at Kiel, chemical plants at Bonn, textile factories at Stuttgart, power plants at Hamm, steel works at Osnabruck, the aircraft industry at Brunswick, and other objectives. In addition to strategic operations, engaged occasionally in support and interdictory missions. Bombed shore installations and bridges near Cherbourg on D-Day, 6 Jun 1944. Struck enemy troop and supply concentrations near Montreuil on 25 Jul 1944 to assist the Allied drive across France. Hauled gasoline to France in Sep for mechanized forces. Attacked German communications and fortifications during the Battle of the Bulge, Dec 1944–Jan 1945. Hit enemy transportation to assist the Allied assault across the Rhine in Mar 1945. Flew last combat mission on 25 Apr. Returned to the US, Jun–Jul. *Redesignated* 467th Bombardment Group (Very Heavy) in Aug 1945. Assigned to Strategic Air Command on 21 Mar 1946. Trained with B–17 and B–29 aircraft. *Inactivated* on 4 Aug 1946.

SQUADRONS. *788th:* 1943–1944, 1944–1946. *789th:* 1943–1946. *790th:* 1943–1946. *791st:* 1943–1946.

STATIONS. Wendover Field, Utah, 1 Aug 1943; Mountain Home AAFld, Idaho, 8 Sep 1943; Kearns, Utah, c. 17 Oct 1943; Wendover Field, Utah, 1 Nov 1943–12 Feb 1944; Rackheath, England, 11 Mar 1944–12 Jun 1945; Sioux Falls AAFld, SD, c. 15 Jul 1945; Fairmont AAFld, Neb, c. 25 Jul 1945; Alamogordo AAFld, NM, 25 Aug 1945; Harvard AAFld, Neb, 8 Sep 1945; Clovis AAFld, NM, Dec 1945–4 Aug 1946.

COMMANDERS. Capt Garnet B Palmer, 9 Sep 1943; Col Frederic E Glantzberg, 17 Sep 1943; Col Albert H Shower, 25 Oct 1943–1945; Maj Frank E McCarthy, 10 Sep 1945; Col Audrin R Walker, 16 Sep 1945; Lt Col William W Amorous, Mar 1946; Lt Col Kenneth S Steele, Apr 1946; Col Thomas J Gent Jr, 21 Jun–Aug 1946.

CAMPAIGNS. American Theater; Air Offensive, Europe; Normandy; Northern France; Rhineland; Ardennes-Alsace; Central Europe.

DECORATIONS. None.

INSIGNE. None.

468th BOMBARDMENT GROUP

Constituted as 468th Bombardment Group (Heavy) on 19 May 1943. *Activated* on 1 Aug 1943. *Redesignated* 468th Bombardment Group (Very Heavy) in Nov 1943. Equipped with B–29's. Moved, via Africa, to the CBI theater, Mar–Jun 1944. Assigned to Twentieth AF in Jun 1944. Flew over the Hump to carry supplies from India to staging fields in China before entering combat with an attack on railroad shops at Bangkok, Thailand, on 5 Jun 1944. On 15 Jun participated in the first AAF attack on Japan since the Doolittle raid in 1942. From bases in India, China, and Ceylon, mined shipping lanes near Saigon, French Indochina, and Shanghai, China, and struck Japanese installations in Burma, Thailand, French Indochina, Indonesia, Formosa, China, and Japan. Targets included iron works, aircraft factories, transportation centers, and naval installations. Received a DUC for participation in a daylight raid on the iron and steel works at Yawata, Japan, in Aug 1944. Evacuated advanced bases in China in Jan 1945 but continued operations from India, bombing storage areas in Rangoon, Burma, a railroad bridge at Bangkok, Thailand, railroad shops at Kuala Lumpur, Malaya, and the drydock in Singapore harbor. Flew additional missions against Japan after moving to Tinian during Feb–May 1945. Took part in mining operations, incendiary raids on area targets, and high-altitude missions against strategic objectives. Dropped incendiaries on Tokyo and Yokohama in May 1945, being awarded a DUC for the attacks. Received another DUC for a daylight strike on an aircraft plant at Takarazuka, Japan, in Jul 1945. After the war, dropped food and supplies to Allied prisoners and participated in show-of-force missions over Japan. Returned to the US in Nov 1945. Assigned to Strategic Air Command on 21 Mar 1946. *Inactivated* on 31 Mar 1946.

SQUADRONS. *512th*: 1945–1946. *792d*: 1943–1946. *793d*: 1943–1946. *794th* (later 6th): 1943–1946. *795th*: 1943–1946.

STATIONS. Smoky Hill AAFld, Kan, 1 Aug 1943–12 Mar 1944; Kharagpur, India, 13 Apr 1944–24 Feb 1945; West Field, Tinian, 6 Apr–15 Nov 1945; Ft Worth AAFld, Tex, 1 Dec 1945; Roswell AAFld, NM, 12 Jan–31 Mar 1946.

COMMANDERS. Col Howard E Engler, 8 Sep 1943; Col Ted S Faulkner, 3 Aug 1944; Col James V Edmundson, 5 Nov 1944–31 Mar 1946.

CAMPAIGNS. India-Burma; Air Offensive, Japan; China Defensive; Western Pacific; Central Burma.

DECORATIONS. Distinguished Unit Citations: Yawata, Japan, 20 Aug 1944; Tokyo and Yokohama, Japan, 23–29 May 1945; Takarasuka, Japan, 24 Jul 1945.

INSIGNE. None.

469th BOMBARDMENT GROUP

Constituted as 469th Bombardment Group (Heavy) on 22 Apr 1943. *Activated* on 1 May 1943. Assigned to Second AF. Equipped with B–17's. Served as a replacement training unit. *Disbanded* on 1 Apr 1944.

SQUADRONS. *796th*: 1943–1944. *797th*: 1943–1944. *798th*: 1943–1944. *799th*: 1943–1944.

STATIONS. Pueblo AAB, Colo, 1 May 1943; Alexandria, La, 7 May 1943–1 Apr 1944.

COMMANDERS. Maj Walter E Chambers, 7 May 1943; Lt Col William I Marsalis, 17 May 1943; Lt Col William E Creer, 21 Aug 1943; Lt Col Marshall R Gray, 5 Sep 1943; Lt Col Quentin T Quick, 12 Nov 1943–unkn.

CAMPAIGNS. None.

DECORATIONS. None.

INSIGNE. None.

470th BOMBARDMENT GROUP

Constituted as 470th Bombardment Group (Heavy) on 22 Apr 1943. *Activated* on 1 May 1943. Assigned to Second AF; reassigned to Fourth AF in Jan 1944. Equipped with B–24's. Served first as an operational training and later as a replacement training unit. *Disbanded* on 31 Mar 1944.

SQUADRONS. *800th*: 1943–1944. *801st*: 1943–1944. *802d*: 1943–1944. *803d*: 1943–1944.

STATIONS. Mountain Home AAFld, Idaho, 1 May 1943; Tonopah AAFld, Nev, 6 Jan–31 Mar 1944.

COMMANDERS. Maj Henry H Covington Jr, 7 Jul 1943; Lt Col Roland J Barnick, 12 Nov 1943–unkn.

CAMPAIGNS. None.

DECORATIONS. None.

INSIGNE. None.

471st BOMBARDMENT GROUP

Constituted as 471st Bombardment Group (Heavy) on 22 Apr 1943. *Activated* on 1 May 1943. Assigned to Second AF and later (Jan 1944) to First AF. Served as a replacement training unit, using B–24 aircraft. *Disbanded* on 10 Apr 1944.

SQUADRONS. *804th:* 1943–1944. *805th:* 1943–1944. *806th:* 1943–1944. *807th:* 1943–1944.

STATIONS. Alexandria, La, 1 May 1943; Pueblo AAB, Colo, 7 May 1943; Westover Field, Mass, 28 Jan–10 Apr 1944.

COMMANDERS. Lt Col Raymond L Cobb, 1 Jun 1943; Lt Col Wilson H Banks, 16 Oct 1943–unkn.

CAMPAIGNS. None.

DECORATIONS. None.

INSIGNE. None.

472d BOMBARDMENT GROUP

Constituted as 472d Bombardment Group (Heavy) on 19 May 1943. *Activated* on 1 Sep 1943. Assigned to Second AF. *Redesignated* 472d Bombardment Group (Very Heavy) on 1 Dec 1943. Trained crews for combat with B–29's. *Disbanded* on 1 Apr 1944.

SQUADRONS. *808th:* 1943–1944. *809th:* 1943–1944. *810th:* 1943–1944. *811th:* 1943–1944.

STATIONS. Smoky Hill AAFld, Kan, 1 Sep 1943; Clovis AAFld, NM, 7 Dec 1943–1 Apr 1944.

COMMANDERS. Maj Conrad H Diehl, 6 Oct 1943; Col Thomas H Chapman, 22 Oct 1943–unkn.

CAMPAIGNS. None.

DECORATIONS. None.

INSIGNE. None.

473d FIGHTER GROUP

Constituted as 473d Fighter Group on 12 Oct 1943. *Activated* on 1 Nov 1943. Assigned to Fourth AF. Equipped primarily with P–38 aircraft. Operated as a replacement training unit. *Disbanded* on 31 Mar 1944.

Reconstituted and *redesignated* 473d Fighter Group (Air Defense), on 8 Jul 1955. *Activated* on 8 Apr 1956. Assigned to Air Defense Command. Had no combat squadrons assigned.

SQUADRONS. *451st:* 1943–1944. *482d:* 1943–1944. *483d:* 1943–1944. *484th:* 1943–1944.

STATIONS. Grand Central Air Terminal, Calif, 1 Nov 1943; Ephrata AAB, Wash, 28–31 Mar 1944. K I Sawyer Mun Aprt, Mich, 8 Apr 1956–.

COMMANDERS. Lt Col Robert L Johnston, Nov 1943; Col Romulus W Puryear, 27 Nov 1943; Lt Col Milton H Ashkins, 20 Dec 1943–31 Mar 1944. Lt Col Robert L Brocklehurst, 1956–.

CAMPAIGNS. None.

DECORATIONS. None.

INSIGNE. None.

474th FIGHTER GROUP

Constituted as 474th Fighter Group on 26 May 1943. *Activated* on 1 Aug 1943. Trained for combat with P–38's. Moved to England, Feb–Mar 1944. Assigned to Ninth AF. Flew first combat mission, an area patrol along the coast of France, on 25 Apr 1944. Attacked bridges and railroads in France in preparation for the Normandy invasion. Provided cover for the invasion force that was crossing the Channel on the night of 5/6 Jun and flew bombing missions to support the landings on the following day. Began armed re-connaissance missions after D–Day to assist ground forces, and attacked highways and troops to aid the Allied breakthrough at St Lo, 25 Jul. Moved to the Continent in Aug 1944 for continued operations in support of ground forces. Bombed and strafed such targets as airfields, hangars, railroads, bridges, highways, barges, fuel dumps, ammunition depots, gun emplacements, and troop concentrations until the end of the war; also escorted bombers that struck marshalling yards, factories, cities, and other objectives. Received a DUC for a mission in France on 23 Aug 1944: participating in a joint air-ground attack against retreating enemy forces in the Falaise-Argentan area, the group discovered an immense quantity of enemy equipment massed along the Seine River; despite severe fire from small arms and from antiaircraft guns that the Germans had placed at two bridges to protect the materiel and cover the retreat, the group repeatedly bombed and strafed the enemy, knocking out motor transports, barges, bridges, and other objectives, thereby disrupting the evacuation and enabling Allied ground forces to capture German troops and equipment. Other operations included bombardment of flak positions near Eindhoven in advance of British 1 Airborne Division during the attack on Holland in Sep 1944; participation in the Battle of the Bulge, Dec 1944–Jan 1945; and patrols along the route of the airborne assault across the Rhine in Mar 1945. Continued operations until V–E Day.

Returned to the US, Nov–Dec 1945. *Inactivated* on 8 Dec 1945.

Redesignated 474th Fighter-Bomber Group. *Activated* in Japan on 10 Jul 1952. Assigned to Tactical Air Command but attached to Far East Air Forces for duty in the Korean War. Served in combat from Aug 1952 until the armistice in Jul 1953, operating from Korea and using F–84 aircraft. Bombed and strafed such targets as bunkers, troops, artillery positions, bridges, vehicles, airfields, and power plants, and sometimes escorted bombers that attacked munitions factories and other objectives. After the armistice, trained with F–84 and F–86 aircraft. Moved to the US, Nov–Dec 1954, and continued training with F–86's.

SQUADRONS. *428th:* 1943–1945; 1952–. *429th:* 1943–1945; 1952–. *430th:* 1943–1945; 1952–.

STATIONS. Glendale, Calif, 1 Aug 1943; Van Nuys Metropolitan Aprt, Calif, 11 Oct 1943; Oxnard Flight Strip, Calif, 5 Jan–6 Feb 1944; Moreton, England, 12 Mar 1944; Neuilly, France, 6 Aug 1944; St Marceau, France, 29 Aug 1944; Peronne, France, 6 Sep 1944; Florennes, Belgium, 1 Oct 1944; Strassfeld, Germany, 22 Mar 1945; Langensalza, Germany, 22 Apr 1945; Schweinfurt, Germany, 16 Jun 1945; Stuttgart, Germany, 25 Oct–21 Nov 1945; Camp Kilmer, NJ, 6–8 Dec 1945. Misawa, Japan, 10 Jul 1952; Kunsan, Korea, 10 Jul 1952; Taegu, Korea, 1 Apr 1953–22 Nov 1954; Clovis AFB, NM, 13 Dec 1954–.

COMMANDERS. Col Clinton C Wasem, 1 Aug 1943; Lt Col Earl C Hedlund, c. 17 Feb 1945; Lt Col David L Lewis, Apr 1945–unkn. Lt Col William L Jacobsen, 10 Jul 1952; Lt Col Francis J Vetort, 29 Aug 1952; Col Joseph Davis Jr, 16 Dec 1952; Col Richard N Ellis, 1953; Col John S Loisel, May 1953–unkn; Col Franklin H Scott, May 1954–.

CAMPAIGNS. *World War II:* Air Offensive, Europe; Normandy; Northern France; Rhineland; Ardennes-Alsace; Central Europe. *Korean War:* Korea Summer-Fall, 1952; Third Korean Winter; Korea Summer-Fall, 1953.

DECORATIONS. Distinguished Unit Citations: France, 23 Aug 1944; Korea, 1 Dec 1952–30 Apr 1953. Cited in the Order of the Day, Belgian Army: 6 Jun–30 Sep 1944; 16 Dec 1944–25 Jan 1945. Belgian Fourragere. Republic of Korea Presidential Unit Citation: 10 Jul 1952–30 Mar 1953.

INSIGNE. *Shield*: Per bend azure and or, in bend a lightning bolt throughout bendwise gules, fimbriated or, between a sphere argent, grid lines sable, and a stylized jet tail pipe vert, emitting eight fire blasts gules, the pipe charged with an annulet of the first, fimbriated or, a semee of stars of the fourth on the azure field. (Approved 22 Jun 1955.)

475th FIGHTER GROUP

Activated in Australia on 14 May 1943 by special authority granted to Fifth AF prior to *constitution* as 475th Fighter Group on 15 May 1943. Equipped with P–38's and trained to provide long-range

In Proelio Gaudete

escort for bombers during daylight raids on Japanese airfields and strongholds in the Netherlands Indies and the Bismarck Archipelago. Moved to New Guinea and began operations in Aug 1943. Received a DUC for missions in Aug 1943 when the group not only protected B–25's that were engaged in strafing attacks on airdromes at Wewak but also destroyed a number of the enemy fighter planes that attacked the formation. Received second DUC for intercepting and destroying many of the planes the Japanese sent against American shipping in Oro Bay on 15 and 17 Oct 1943. Covered landings in New Guinea, New Britain, and the Schouten Islands. After moving to Biak in Jul 1944, flew escort missions and fighter sweeps to the southern Philippines, Celebes, Halmahera, and Borneo. Moved to the Philippines in Oct 1944 and received another DUC for bombing and strafing enemy airfields and installations, escorting bombers, and engaging in aerial combat

during the first stages of the Allied campaign to recover the Philippines, Oct–Dec 1944. Maj Thomas B McGuire Jr was awarded the Medal of Honor: while voluntarily leading flights of P–38's escorting bombers that struck Mabalacat Airdrome on 25 Dec 1944 and Clark Field the following day, he shot down seven Japanese fighters; on 7 Jan 1944, while attempting to save a fellow flyer from attack during a fighter sweep over Los Negroes Island, Maj McGuire risked a hazardous maneuver at low altitude, crashed, and was killed. The group flew many missions to support ground forces on Luzon during the first part of 1945. Also flew escort missions to China and attacked railways on Formosa. Began moving to Ie Shima in Aug but the war ended before the movement was completed. Moved to Korea in Sep 1945 for occupation duty as part of Far East Air Forces. Converted to P–51's in 1946. Moved to Japan in 1948. *Inactivated* on 1 Apr 1949.

Redesignated 475th Fighter Group (Air Defense). *Activated* in the US on 18 Aug 1955. Assigned to Air Defense Command and equipped with F–89's.

SQUADRONS. *431st:* 1943–1949. *432d:* 1943–1949; 1955–. *433d:* 1943–1949.

STATIONS. Amberley Field, Australia, 14 May 1943; Dobodura, New Guinea, 14 Aug 1943; Nadzab, New Guinea, 24 Mar 1944; Hollandia, New Guinea, 15 May 1944; Biak, c. 14 Jul 1944; Dulag, Leyte, 28 Oct 1944; San Jose, Mindoro, 5 Feb 1945; Clark Field, Luzon, 28 Feb 1945; Lingayen, Luzon, c. 20 Apr 1945; Ie Shima, 8 Aug 1945; Kimpo, Korea, c. 23 Sep 1945; Itazuke, Japan, 28 Aug 1948; Ashiya, Japan, 25 Mar–1 Apr 1949. Minneapolis-St Paul Intl Aprt, Minn, 18 Aug 1955–.

COMMANDERS. Lt Col George W Prentice, 21 May 1943; Col Charles H MacDonald, 26 Nov 1943; Lt Col Meryl M Smith, Aug 1944; Col Charles H MacDonald, 13 Oct 1944; Lt Col John S Loisel, 15 Jul 1945; Col Henry G Thorne Jr, 18 Apr 1946; Col Ashley B Packard, 20 Jul 1946; Col Leland S Stranathan, c. 22 Mar 1947; Col Carl W Pyle, 7 Jun 1947; Col William O Moore, 19 Sep 1947; Lt Col Woodrow W Ramsey, 28 Aug 1948–25 Mar 1949. Col David Gould, Aug 1955–.

CAMPAIGNS. China Defensive; New Guinea; Bismarck Archipelago; Western Pacific; Leyte; Luzon; China Offensive.

DECORATIONS. Distinguished Unit Citations: New Guinea, 18 and 21 Aug 1943; New Guinea, 15 and 17 Oct 1943; Philippine Islands, 25 Oct–25 Dec 1944. Philippine Presidential Unit Citation.

INSIGNE. *Shield:* Azure, over a crossbow or, string argent, bow striped red and silver; a lightning bolt gules, highlighted of the third, surmounting the stock; a pair of wings argent, issuing from the end of the stock; between four seven-pointed stars and one five-pointed star, spattered over the field; all within a diminutive border per pale argent and gules. *Motto:* IN PROELIO GAUDETE—Be Joyful in Battle. (Approved 26 Nov 1956.)

476th FIGHTER GROUP

Constituted as 476th Fighter Group on 20 Apr 1943. Assigned to Fourteenth AF. *Activated* in China on 19 May 1943 with no squadrons assigned. *Disbanded* in China on 31 Jul 1943.

Reconstituted on 11 Oct 1943. *Activated* in the US on 1 Dec 1943. Assigned to First AF as a replacement training unit. *Disbanded* on 1 Apr 1944.

Reconstituted and *redesignated* 476th Fighter Group (Air Defense), on 11 Dec 1956. *Activated* on 8 Feb 1957. Assigned, without combat squadrons, to Air Defense Command.

SQUADRONS. *453d:* 1943–1944. *541st:* 1943–1944. *542d:* 1943–1944. *543d:* 1943–1944.

STATIONS. Kunming, China, 19 May–31 Jul 1943. Richmond AAB, Va, 1 Dec 1943; Pocatello AAFld, Idaho, 26 Mar–1 Apr 1944. Glasgow AFB, Mont, 8 Feb 1957–.

COMMANDERS. Unkn.

CAMPAIGNS. Asiatic-Pacific Theater.

DECORATIONS. None.

INSIGNE. None.

477th COMPOSITE GROUP

Constituted as 477th Bombardment Group (Medium) on 13 May 1943. *Activated* on 1 Jun 1943. Assigned to Third AF. Trained with B–26 aircraft. *Inactivated* on 25 Aug 1943.

Activated on 15 Jan 1944. Assigned to First AF. Trained with B–25's. *Redesignated* 477th Composite Group in Jun 1945. Equipped with B–25's and P–47's. *Inactivated* on 1 Jul 1947.

SQUADRONS. *99th* Fighter: 1945–1947. *616th* Bombardment: 1943; 1944–1945. *617th* Bombardment: 1943; 1944–1947. *618th* Bombardment: 1943; 1944–1945. *619th* Bombardment: 1943; 1944–1945.

STATIONS. MacDill Field, Fla, 1 Jun–25 Aug 1943. Selfridge Field, Mich, 15 Jan 1944; Godman Field, Ky, 6 May 1944; Lockbourne AAB, Ohio, 13 Mar 1946–1 Jul 1947.

COMMANDERS. Lt Col Andrew O Lerche, 1943. Col Robert R Selway Jr, 21 Jan 1944; Col Benjamin O Davis Jr, 21 Jun 1945–1 Jul 1947.

CAMPAIGNS. American Theater.

DECORATIONS. None.

INSIGNE. None.

478th FIGHTER GROUP

Constituted as 478th Fighter Group on 12 Oct 1943. *Activated* on 1 Dec 1943. Assigned to Fourth AF. After a delay in obtaining personnel and equipment, the group began operations in Mar 1944 as a replacement training unit, using P–39 aircraft. *Disbanded* on 31 Mar 1944.

Reconstituted and *redesignated* 478th Fighter Group (Air Defense), on 11 Dec 1956. *Activated* on 8 Feb 1957. Assigned to Air Defense Command.

SQUADRONS. *18th:* 1957–. *454th:* 1943–1944. *544th:* 1943–1944. *545th:* 1943–1944. *546th:* 1943–1944.

STATIONS. Hamilton Field, Calif, 1 Dec 1943; Santa Rosa AAFld, Calif, 12 Dec 1943; Redmond AAFld, Ore, 3 Feb–31 Mar 1944. Grand Forks AFB, ND, 8 Feb 1957–.

COMMANDERS. Col John W Weltman, 7 Dec 1943; Lt Col Ernest C Young, 31 Jan–31 Mar 1944. Unkn, 1957.

CAMPAIGNS. None.

DECORATIONS. None.

INSIGNE. None.

479th ANTISUBMARINE GROUP

Constituted as 479th Antisubmarine Group on 1 Jul 1943 and *activated* in England on 8 Jul. Assigned to AAF Antisubmarine Command. Began operations with B–24 aircraft on 13 Jul. The 479th's most effective antisubmarine patrols were in the Bay of Biscay from 18 Jul to 2 Aug 1943, the period in which the group made nearly all of its attacks on enemy U-boats. After that time the enemy avoided surfacing during daylight and adopted a policy of evasion, but the group continued its patrols, often engaging enemy aircraft in combat. Ended operations in Oct 1943. *Disbanded* in England on 11 Nov 1943.

SQUADRONS. *4th:* 1943. *6th:* 1943. *19th:* 1943. *22d:* 1943.

STATIONS. St Eval, England, 8 Jul 1943; Dunkeswell, England, 6 Aug 1943; Podington, England, Nov–11 Nov 1943.

COMMANDERS. Col Howard Moore, 8 Jul–c. Nov 1943.

CAMPAIGNS. Antisubmarine, EAME Theater; Air Offensive, Europe.

DECORATIONS. None.

INSIGNE. None.

479th FIGHTER GROUP

Constituted as 479th Fighter Group on 12 Oct 1943 and *activated* on 15 Oct. Equipped with P–38's. Trained for combat and served as an air defense organization. Moved to England, Apr–May 1944, and assigned to Eighth AF. From May 1944 to Apr 1945, escorted heavy bombers during operations against targets on the Continent, strafed targets of opportunity, and flew fighter-bomber, counter-air, and area-patrol missions. Engaged primarily in escort activities and fighter sweeps until the Normandy invasion in June 1944. Patrolled the beachhead during the invasion. Strafed and dive-bombed troops, bridges, locomotives, railway cars, barges, vehicles, airfields, gun emplacements, flak towers, ammunition dumps, power stations, and radar sites while on escort or fighter-bomber missions as the Allies drove across France during the summer and fall of 1944; flew area patrols to support the breakthrough at St Lo in Jul and the airborne attack on Holland in Sep. Received a DUC for the destruction of numerous aircraft on airfields in France on 18 Aug and 5 Sep and during an aerial battle near Munster on 26 Sep. Continued escort and fighter-bomber activities from Oct to mid-Dec 1944, converting to P–51's during this period. Participated in the Battle of the Bulge (Dec 1944–Jan 1945) by escorting bombers to and from targets in the battle area and by strafing transportation targets while on escort duty. Flew escort missions from Feb to Apr 1945, but also provided area patrols to support the airborne attack across the Rhine in Mar. Returned to the US in Nov 1945. *Inactivated* on 1 Dec 1945.

Redesignated 479th Fighter-Bomber Group. *Activated* on 1 Dec 1952. Assigned to Tactical Air Command. Equipped successively with F–51, F–86, and F–100 aircraft. *Redesignated* 479th Fighter-Day Group in Feb 1954.

SQUADRONS. *434th:* 1943–1945; 1952–. *435th:* 1943–1945; 1952–. *436th:* 1943–1945; 1952–.

STATIONS. Grand Central Air Terminal, Calif, 15 Oct 1943; Lomita Flight Strip, Calif, c. 6 Feb 1944; Santa Maria AAFld, Calif, c. 8–c. 12 Apr 1944; Wattisham, England, c. 15 May 1944–c. 23 Nov 1945;

Camp Kilmer, NJ, c. 29 Nov–1 Dec 1945. George AFB, Calif, 1 Dec 1952–.

COMMANDERS. Lt Col Leo F Dusard Jr, c. 28 Oct 1943; Maj Francis J Pope, c. 14 Nov 1943; Lt Col Kyle L Riddle, c. 26 Dec 1943; Col Hubert Zemke, 12 Aug 1944; Col Kyle L Riddle, 1 Nov 1944–unkn. Col Woodrow W Ramsey, 1952–unkn; Lt Col Verl D Luehring, 1953; Col Jacob W Dixon, c. 19 Aug 1953; Col William B Harris, c. 31 May 1955–.

CAMPAIGNS. Air Offensive, Europe; Normandy; Northern France; Rhineland; Ardennes-Alsace; Central Europe.

DECORATIONS. Distinguished Unit Citation: ETO, 18 Aug, 5 and 26 Sep 1944. French Croix de Guerre with Palm.

INSIGNE. *Shield:* Or, a broad sword gules in bend piercing a cloud proper, between a point sinister pointed gules, charged with six stars argent three, two and one, and a point in base vert, all within a diminutive border azure. *Motto:* PROTECTORES LIBERTATIS—Defenders of Liberty. (Approved 10 Sep 1954.)

480th ANTISUBMARINE GROUP

Constituted as 480th Antisubmarine Group on 19 Jun 1943 and *activated* in North Africa on 21 Jun. Assigned to AAF Antisubmarine Command. Using B–24's, the group had the primary mission of carrying out antisubmarine patrols in an area of the Atlantic extending north and west from Morocco. Its antisubmarine activity reached a peak in Jul 1943 when enemy U–boats concentrated off the coast of Portugal to intercept convoys bound for the Mediterranean; by destroying and damaging several submarines during the month, the group aided in protecting supply lines to forces involved in the campaign for Sicily. The group also covered convoys and engaged numerous enemy aircraft in combat. In Sep 1943 part of the group moved temporarily to Tunisia and operated in connection with the assault on Italy; missions included searching for enemy submarines, covering Allied convoys, and protecting the Italian fleet after the surrender of Italy. The group was awarded a DUC for actions that contributed to the winning of the Battle of the Atlantic. Moved to the US in Nov and Dec 1943. *Disbanded* on 29 Jan 1944.

SQUADRONS. *1st:* 1943–1944. *2d:* 1943–1944.

STATIONS. Port Lyautey, French Morocco, 21 Jun–Nov 1943; Langley Field, Va, c. 18 Nov 1943; Clovis AAFld, NM, c. 1–29 Jan 1944.

COMMANDERS. Col Jack Roberts, 21 Jun 1943–unkn.

CAMPAIGNS. Antisubmarine, EAME Theater; Air Combat, EAME Theater.

DECORATIONS. Distinguished Unit Citation: North African Theater of Operations [1943].

INSIGNE. None.

482d BOMBARDMENT GROUP

Constituted as 482d Bombardment Group (Pathfinder) on 10 Aug 1943 and *activated* in England on 20 Aug. Assigned to Eighth AF. Provided a pathfinder force of radar-equipped aircraft to precede bomber formations and indicate targets obscured by weather. Flew its first mission on 27 Sep 1943, leading bombers of 1st and 3d Bombardment Divisions to attack the port at Emden. Operated chiefly as a pathfinder organization until Mar 1944, detaching its B-17 and B-24 aircraft, with crews, to other stations in England to lead Eighth AF elements on specific missions to the Continent. Led attacks on factories at Gotha, Brunswick, Schweinfurt, and other industrial centers during Big Week, 20–25 Feb 1944. Also served as the pathfinder force for bombers attacking airfields, submarine installations, cities, marshalling yards, and other targets, primarily in Germany. Received a DUC for a mission on 11 Jan 1944 when it led organizations of Eighth AF into central Germany to attack aircraft industries; although weather conditions prevented effective fighter protection against severe attack by enemy aircraft, the group not only bombed the assigned targets, but also destroyed a number of enemy planes. Removed from combat status in Mar 1944 and after that operated a school for pathfinder crews with the objective of training a pathfinder squadron for each Eighth AF bombardment group; made radarscope photographs of France, the Low Countries, and Germany for use in training and briefing combat crews; and tested radar and other navigational equipment. Often bombed such targets as bridges, fuel depots, power plants, and railroad stations while on experimental flights; flew a pathfinder mission to assist the bombardment of coastal defenses in Normandy on 6 Jun 1944 and later that day led attacks on traffic centers behind the beachhead; sometimes dropped propaganda leaflets. *Redesignated* 482d Bombardment Group (Heavy) in Nov 1944. Continued its training and experimental work until V-E Day. Moved to the US, May–Jun 1945. *Inactivated* on 1 Sep 1945.

Redesignated 482d Bombardment Group (Very Heavy). Allotted to the reserve. *Activated* on 26 Jun 1947. *Inactivated* on 27 Jun 1949.

Redesignated 482d Troop Carrier Group (Medium). Allotted to the reserve. *Activated* on 14 Jun 1952. *Inactivated* on 1 Dec 1952.

Redesignated 482d Fighter-Bomber Group. Allotted to the reserve. *Activated* on 18 May 1955.

SQUADRONS. *6th:* 1947–1949. *812th:* 1943–1945; 1947–1949; 1952; 1955–. *813th:* 1943–1945; 1947–1949; 1952. *814th:* 1943–1945; 1947–1949; 1952.

STATIONS. Alconbury, England, 20 Aug 1943–21 May 1945; Victorville AAFld, Calif, c. 5 Jul–1 Sep 1945. New Orleans Mun Aprt, La, 26 Jun 1947–27 Jun 1949. Miami Intl Aprt, Fla, 14 Jun–1 Dec 1952. Dobbins AFB, Ga, 18 May 1955–.

COMMANDERS. Col Baskin R Lawrence Jr, 20 Aug 1943; Col Howard Moore, 1 Dec 1943; Lt Col Clement W Bird, 15 Dec 1944–1945.

CAMPAIGNS. Air Offensive, Europe; Normandy; Northern France; Rhineland; Ardennes-Alsace; Central Europe.

DECORATIONS. Distinguished Unit Citation: Germany, 11 Jan 1944.

INSIGNE. None.

483d BOMBARDMENT GROUP

EFFECTIVE AIRLIFT SUPPORT

Constituted as 483d Bombardment Group (Heavy) on 14 Sep 1943 and *activated* on 20 Sep. Trained with B–17's. Moved to Italy, Mar–Apr 1944, and assigned to Fifteenth AF. Began operations in Apr 1944 and served in combat until late in Apr 1945, hitting such targets as factories, oil refineries, marshalling yards, storage areas, airdromes, bridges, gun positions, and troop concentrations in Italy, France, Germany, Poland, Czechoslovakia, Austria, Hungary, Rumania, Yugoslavia,

and Greece. Received a DUC for action on 18 Jul 1944 when, without fighter escort, the group engaged numerous enemy aircraft in the target area and also bombed the objective, an airdrome and installations at Memmingen. Assisting the strategic bombardment of enemy industry, the group received another DUC for braving fighter assaults and antiaircraft fire to bomb tank factories at Berlin on 24 Mar 1945. Struck targets in southern France in preparation for the invasion in Aug 1944. Operated in suport of ground forces in northern Italy during the Allied offensive in Apr 1945. After V–E Day, transported personnel from Italy to North Africa for movement to the US. *Inactivated* in Italy on 25 Sep 1945.

Redesignated 483d Troop Carrier Group (Medium). *Activated* in Japan on 1 Jan 1953. Assigned to Tactical Air Command but attached to Far East Air Forces for duty in the Korean War. Used C–119's to transport personnel and supplies to Korea, receiving a Korean PUC for the missions. Received an AFOUA for operations during 1953–1954: while transporting supplies to UN forces in Korea and training with airborne troops, the group also assisted the French in Indochina by hauling supplies and training personnel for airlift operations in C–119's. Assigned to Far East Air Forces in 1954.

SQUADRONS. *815th:* 1943–1945; 1953–. *816th:* 1943–1945; 1953–. *817th:* 1943–1945; 1953–. *840th* (formerly 818th): 1943–1945.

STATIONS. Ephrata AAB, Wash, 20 Sep 1943; MacDill Field, Fla, 7 Nov 1943–2 Mar 1944; Tortorella, Italy, 30 Mar 1944; Sterparone Airfield, Italy, 22 Apr 1944; Pisa, Italy 15 May–25 Sep 1945. Ashiya AB, Japan, 1 Jan 1953–.

COMMANDERS. Col Paul L Barton, c. 26 Sep 1943; Col Joseph B Stanley, 8 May–c. Sep 1945. Lt Col Ernest W Burton, 1 Jan 1953; Col George M Foster, 1 Mar 1953; Lt Col Kenneth C Jacobs, Jul 1955; Col Horace W Patch, c. Aug 1955–.

CAMPAIGNS. *World War II:* Air Combat, EAME Theater; Air Offensive, Europe; Rome-Arno; Normandy; Northern France; Southern France; North Apennines; Rhineland; Central Europe; Po Valley. *Korean War:* Third Korean Winter; Korea Summer-Fall, 1953.

DECORATIONS. Distinguished Unit Citations: Germany, 18 Jul 1944; Germany, 24 Mar 1945. Republic of Korea Presidential Unit Citation: [Jan]–27 Jul 1953. Air Force Outstanding Unit Award: 6 May 1953–10 Sep 1954.

INSIGNE. *Shield:* Azure (sky blue), a sphere encircled with an orbit all or, latitude and longitude lines azure (deep blue), over the sphere a hand proper supporting a parachute proper, an aircraft proper, and artillery proper; encircling the upper section of the sphere, three clouds proper and an increscent moon and four stars of the second color; on a chief of the third, thirteen stars argent, the chief fimbriated or. *Motto:* EFFECTIVE AIRLIFT SUPPORT. (Approved 2 Feb 1956.)

484th BOMBARDMENT GROUP

Constituted as 484th Bombardment Group (Heavy) on 14 Sep 1943 and *activated* on 20 Sep. Trained for combat with B–24's. Moved to Italy, Mar–Apr 1944. Assigned to Fifteenth AF. *Redesignated* 484th Bombardment Group (Pathfinder) in May 1944 but did not perform pathfinder functions. *Redesignated* 484th Bombardment Group (Heavy) in Nov 1944. Operated primarily as a strategic bombardment organization, Apr 1944–Apr 1945. Attacked such targets as oil refineries, oil storage plants, aircraft factories, heavy industry, and communications in Italy, France, Germany, Austria, Czechoslovakia, Hungary, Rumania, and Yugoslavia. On 13 Jun 1944 a heavy smoke screen prevented the group from bombing marshalling yards at Munich; however, in spite of severe damage from flak and interceptors, and despite heavy gunfire encountered at the alternate target, the group bombed marshalling yards at Innsbruck and received a DUC for its persistent action. Received second DUC for performance on 21 Aug 1944 when, unescorted, the organization fought its way through intense opposition to attack underground oil storage installations in Vienna. In addition to strategic missions, the 484th participated in the drive toward Rome by bombing bridges, supply dumps, viaducts, and marshalling yards, Apr–Jun 1944; ferried gasoline and oil to Allied forces in southern France, Sep 1944; and supported the final advance through northern Italy, Apr 1945. Moved to Casablanca in May 1945. Assigned to Air Transport Command. *Inactivated* in French Morocco on 25 Jul 1945.

SQUADRONS. *824th*: 1943–1945. *825th*: 1943–1945. *826th*: 1943–1945. *827th*: 1943–1945.

STATIONS. Harvard AAFld, Neb, 20 Sep 1943–2 Mar 1944; Torretto Airfield, Italy, Apr 1944; Casablanca, French Morocco, c. 25 May–25 Jul 1945.

COMMANDERS. Col William B Keese, Oct 1943; Lt Col Chester C Busch, Apr 1945–unkn.

CAMPAIGNS. Air Combat, EAME Theater; Air Offensive, Europe; Rome-Arno; Normandy; Northern France; Southern France; North Apennines; Rhineland; Central Europe; Po Valley.

DECORATIONS. Distinguished Unit Citations: Munich, Germany, and Innsbruck, Austria, 13 Jun 1944; Vienna, Austria, 21 Aug 1944.

INSIGNE. None.

485th BOMBARDMENT GROUP

Constituted as 485th Bombardment Group (Heavy) on 14 Sep 1943 and *activated* on 20 Sep. Trained with B–24's. Moved to the Mediterranean theater, Mar–Apr 1944, with the air echelon receiving additional training in Tunisia before joining the ground echelon in Italy. Assigned to Fifteenth AF. Entered combat in May 1944 and engaged primarily in flying long-range missions to targets in Italy, France, Germany, Austria, Hungary, Rumania,

and Yugoslavia, bombing marshalling yards, oil refineries, airdrome installations, heavy industry, and other strategic objectives. Received a DUC for combating intense fighter opposition and attacking an oil refinery at Vienna on 26 Jun 1944. Also carried out some support and interdictory operations. Struck bridges, harbors, and troop concentrations in Aug 1944 to aid the invasion of Southern France. Hit communications lines and other targets during Mar and Apr 1945 to support the advance of British Eighth Army in northern Italy. Returned to the US in May 1945. *Redesignated* 485th Bombardment Group (Very Heavy) in Aug 1945. Equipped with B–29's. Assigned to Strategic Air Command on 21 Mar 1946. *Inactivated* on 4 Aug 1946.

SQUADRONS. *506th*: 1946. *828th*: 1943–1946. *829th*: 1943–1946. *830th*: 1943–1946. *831st*: 1943–1945.

STATIONS. Fairmont AAFld, Neb, 20 Sep 1943–11 Mar 1944; Venosa, Italy, Apr 1944–15 May 1945; Sioux Falls AAFld, SD, 30 May 1945; Sioux City AAB, Iowa, 24 Jul 1945; Smoky Hill AAFld, Kan, 8 Sep 1945–4 Aug 1946.

COMMANDERS. Col Walter E Arnold Jr, 27 Sep 1943; Col John P Tomhave, c. 29 Aug 1944; Col John B Cornett, 17 Feb 1945; Lt Col Douglas M Cairns, 23 Mar 1945–unkn; Lt Col Richard T Lively, 6 Aug 1945; Col John W White, 15 Sep 1945; Col Walter S Lee, 1946–Aug 1946.

CAMPAIGNS. American Theater; Air Combat, EAME Theater; Air Offensive,

Europe; Rome-Arno; Normandy; Northern France; Southern France; North Apennines; Rhineland; Central Europe; Po Valley.

DECORATIONS. Distinguished Unit Citation: Vienna, Austria, 26 Jun 1944.

INSIGNE. None.

486th BOMBARDMENT GROUP

Constituted as 486th Bombardment Group (Heavy) on 14 Sep 1943 and *activated* on 20 Sep. Moved to England in Mar 1944 and assigned to Eighth AF. Entered combat in May 1944 with B–24 aircraft but soon converted to B–17's. Operated chiefly against strategic objectives in Germany until May 1945. Targets included marshalling yards in Stuttgart, Cologne, and Mainz; airfields in Kassel and Munster; oil refineries and storage plants in Merseburg, Dollbergen, and Hamburg; harbors in Bremen and Kiel; and factories in Mannheim and Weimar. Other missions included bombing airfields, gun positions, V-weapon sites, and railroad bridges in France in preparation for or in support of the invasion of Normandy in Jun 1944; striking road junctions and troop concentrations in support of ground forces pushing across France, Jul-Aug 1944; hitting gun emplacements near Arnheim to minimize transport and glider losses during the airborne invasion of Holland in Sep 1944; and bombing enemy installations in support of ground troops during the Battle of the Bulge (Dec 1944–Jan 1945) and the assault across the Rhine (Mar-Apr 1945).

Returned to the US in Aug 1945. *Inactivated* on 7 Nov 1945.

SQUADRONS. *832d:* 1943–1945. *833d:* 1943–1945. *834th:* 1943–1945. *835th:* 1943–1945.

STATIONS. McCook AAFld, Neb, 20 Sep 1943; Davis-Monthan Field, Ariz, 9 Nov 1943–Mar 1944; Sudbury, England, Mar 1944–Aug 1945; Drew Field, Fla, 3 Sep–7 Nov 1945.

COMMANDERS. Col Glendon P Overing, 20 Sep 1943; Col William B Kieffer, c. 13 Apr 1945; Lt Col James J Grater, Jul 1945–unkn.

CAMPAIGNS. Air Offensive, Europe; Normandy; Northern France; Rhineland; Ardennes-Alsace; Central Europe.

DECORATIONS. None.

INSIGNE. None.

487th BOMBARDMENT GROUP

Constituted as 487th Bombardment Group (Heavy) on 14 Sep 1943 and *activated* on 20 Sep. Prepared for overseas duty with B–24's. Moved to England, Mar-Apr 1944, and assigned to Eighth AF. Began combat in May 1944, bombing airfields in France in preparation for the invasion of Normandy; then pounded coastal defenses, road junctions, bridges, and locomotives during the invasion. Attacked German troops and artillery positions to assist British forces near Caen in Jul; struck gun emplacements to support the Allied effort at Brest in Aug and to cover the airborne attack on Holland in Sep 1944. Flew a few missions against

German industries, refineries, and communications during the period May–Aug 1944, but operated almost solely against strategic targets from Aug 1944, when conversion to B–17's was completed, until Mar 1945. Attacked oil refineries in Merseburg, Mannheim, and Dulmen; factories in Nurnberg, Hannover, and Berlin; and marshalling yards in Cologne, Munster, Hamm, and Neumunster. Aided ground forces during the Battle of the Bulge, Dec 1944–Jan 1945, and turned again to support and interdictory operations in Mar 1945 as the Allies crossed the Rhine and made the final thrust into Germany. Returned to the US, Aug–Sep 1945. *Inactivated* on 7 Nov 1945.

SQUADRONS. *836th:* 1943–1945. *837th:* 1943–1945. *838th:* 1943–1945. *839th:* 1943–1945.

STATIONS. Bruning AAFld, Neb, 20 Sep 1943; Alamogordo AAFld, NM, 15 Dec 1943–c. 13 Mar 1944; Lavenham, England, 5 Apr 1944–c. 26 Aug 1945; Drew Field, Fla, 3 Sep–7 Nov 1945.

COMMANDERS. Lt Col Charles E Lancaster, 4 Oct 1943; Lt Col Beirne Lay Jr, 28 Feb 1944; Col Robert Taylor III, 12 May 1944; Col William K Martin, 28 Dec 1944; Lt Col Howard C Todt, May 1945; Col Nicholas T Perkins, 3 Jun 1945–unkn.

CAMPAIGNS. Air Offensive, Europe; Normandy; Northern France; Rhineland; Ardennes-Alsace; Central Europe.

DECORATIONS. None.

INSIGNE. None.

488th BOMBARDMENT GROUP

Constituted as 488th Bombardment Group (Heavy) on 14 Sep 1943. *Activated* on 1 Oct 1943. Assigned to Second AF; reassigned to Third AF in Nov 1943. Equipped with B–17's. Served as a replacement training unit. *Disbanded* on 1 May 1944.

SQUADRONS. *818th* (formerly 840th): 1943–1944. *841st:* 1943–1944. *842d:* 1943–1944. *843d:* 1943–1944.

STATIONS. Geiger Field, Wash, 1 Oct 1943; MacDill Field, Fla, 1 Nov 1943–1 May 1944.

COMMANDERS. Lt Col Rudolph B Robeck, 1 Oct 1943; Maj George H Goody, 12 Oct 1943; Lt Col Ansley Watson, 25 Oct 1943; Col Gerry L Mason, 11 Dec 1943; Lt Col Ansley Watson, 11 Feb 1944; Lt Col Robert K Martin, 15 Mar–1 May 1944.

CAMPAIGNS. None.

DECORATIONS. None.

INSIGNE. None.

489th BOMBARDMENT GROUP

Constituted as 489th Bombardment Group (Heavy) on 14 Sep 1943. *Activated* on 1 Oct 1943. Trained with B–24's. Moved to England, Apr–May 1944, and assigned to Eighth AF. Entered combat on 30 May 1944, and during the next few days concentrated on targets in France in preparation for the Normandy invasion.

In an attack against coastal defenses near Wimereaux on 5 Jun 1944, the group's lead plane was seriously crippled by enemy fire, its pilot was killed, and the deputy group commander, Lt Col Leon R Vance Jr, who was commanding the formation, was severely wounded; although his right foot was practically severed, Vance took control of the plane, led the group to a successful bombing of the target, and managed to fly the damaged aircraft to the coast of England, where he ordered the crew to bail out; believing a wounded man had been unable to jump, he ditched the plane in the Channel and was rescued. For his action during this mission, Vance was awarded the Medal of Honor. The group supported the landings in Normandy on 6 Jun 1944, and afterward bombed coastal defenses, airfields, bridges, railroads, and V-weapon sites in the campaign for France. Began flying missions into Germany in Jul, and engaged primarily in bombing strategic targets such as factories, oil refineries and storage plants, marshalling yards, and airfields in Ludwigshafen, Magdeburg, Brunswick, Saarbrucken, and other cities until Nov 1944. Other operations included participating in the saturation bombing of German lines just before the breakthrough at St Lo in Jul, dropping food to the liberated French and to Allied forces in France during Aug and Sep, and carrying food and ammunition to Holland later in Sep. Returned to the US, Nov–Dec 1944, to prepare for redeployment to the Pacific

theater. *Redesignated* 489th Bombardment Group (Very Heavy) in Mar 1945. Equipped with B–29's. Alerted for movement overseas in the summer of 1945, but war with Japan ended before the group left the US. *Inactivated* on 17 Oct 1945.

SQUADRONS. *844th:* 1943–1945. *845th:* 1943–1945. *846th:* 1943–1945. *847th:* 1943–1945.

STATIONS. Wendover Field, Utah, 1 Oct 1943–3 Apr 1944; Halesworth, England, c. 1 May–Nov 1944; Bradley Field, Conn, 12 Dec 1944; Lincoln AAFld, Neb, c. 17 Dec 1944; Great Bend AAFld, Kan, c. 28 Feb 1945; Davis-Monthan Field, Ariz, 3 Apr 1945; Fairmont AAFld, Neb, c. 13 Jul 1945; Ft Lawton, Wash, 23 Aug 1945; March Field, Calif, 2 Sep–17 Oct 1945.

COMMANDERS. Col Ezekiel W Napier, 20 Oct 1943; Lt Col Robert E Kollimer, 5 Feb 1945; Col Paul C Ashworth, 11 Apr 1945–unkn.

CAMPAIGNS. American Theater; Air Offensive, Europe; Normandy; Northern France; Rhineland.

DECORATIONS. None.

INSIGNE. None.

490th BOMBARDMENT GROUP

Constituted as 490th Bombardment Group (Heavy) on 14 Sep 1943. *Activated* on 1 Oct 1943. Trained for combat with B–24's. Moved to England in Apr 1944 for operations with Eighth AF. Entered combat in Jun 1944, bombing airfields and coastal defenses in France immediately preceding and during the invasion of Normandy. Then struck bridges, rail lines, vehicles, road junctions, and troop concentrations in France. Supported ground forces near Caen in Jul and near Brest in Sep 1944. After that, converted to B–17's and operated primarily against strategic targets until the end of Feb 1945. Mounted attacks against enemy oil plants, tank factories, marshalling yards, aircraft plants, and airfields in such cities as Berlin, Hamburg, Merseburg, Munster, Kassel, Hannover, and Cologne. Interrupted strategic missions to attack supply lines and military installations during the Battle of the Bulge, Dec 1944–Jan 1945. Beginning in Mar 1945, attacked interdictory targets and supported advancing ground forces. After V–E Day, carried food to flood-stricken areas of Holland and transported French, Spanish, and Belgian prisoners of war from Austria to Allied centers. Returned to the US, Aug–Sep 1945. *Inactivated* on 7 Nov 1945.

SQUADRONS. *848th:* 1943–1945. *849th:* 1943–1945. *850th:* 1943–1945. *851st:* 1943–1945.

STATIONS. Salt Lake City AAB, Utah, 1 Oct 1943; Mountain Home AAFld, Idaho, 4 Dec 1943–Apr 1944; Eye, England, c. 1 May 1944–Aug 1945; Drew Field, Fla, 3 Sep–7 Nov 1945.

COMMANDERS. Maj Lyle E Halstead, 11 Oct 1943; Lt Col Beirne Lay Jr, 28 Oct 1943; Lt Col James H Isbell, Nov 1943; Col Lloyd H Watnee, 30 Dec 1943; Col Frank P Bostrom, 26 Jun 1944; Col Gene

H Tibbets, c. 10 Jun 1945; Lt Col Clarence J Adams, c. 9 Jul 1945–unkn.

CAMPAIGNS. Air Offensive, Europe; Normandy; Northern France; Rhineland; Ardennes-Alsace; Central Europe.

DECORATIONS. None.

INSIGNE. None.

491st BOMBARDMENT GROUP

Constituted as 491st Bombardment Group (Heavy) on 14 Sep 1943. *Activated* on 1 Oct 1943. Trained for combat with B–24's. On 1 Jan 1944 the group, less the air echelon, was transferred without personnel and equipment to England, where personnel were assigned later. The air echelon continued to train in the US until it joined the group in England in May 1944. Served in combat with Eighth AF until the end of Apr 1945. Began operations early in Jun 1944 and attacked airfields, bridges, and coastal defenses both preceding and during the invasion of Normandy. Then concentrated its attacks on strategic objectives in Germany, striking communications centers, oil refineries, storage depots, industrial areas, shipyards, and other targets in such places as Berlin, Hamburg, Kassel, Cologne, Gelsenkirchen, Bielefeld, Hannover, and Magdeburg; on one occasion attacked the headquarters of the German General Staff at Zossen, Germany. While on a mission to bomb an oil refinery at Misburg on 26 Nov 1944, the group was attacked by large numbers of enemy fighters; although about one-half of its planes were destroyed, the remainder fought off the interceptors, successfully bombed the target, and won for the group a DUC. Although engaged primarily in strategic bombardment, the group also supported ground forces at St Lo in Jul 1944; assaulted V-weapon sites and communications lines in France during the summer of 1944; dropped supplies to paratroops on 18 Sep 1944 during the airborne attack in Holland; bombed German supply lines and fortifications during the Battle of the Bulge, Dec 1944–Jan 1945; supported Allied forces in the airborne drop across the Rhine in Mar 1945; and interdicted enemy communications during the Allied drive across Germany in Apr 1945. Returned to the US in Jul. *Inactivated* on 8 Sep 1945.

SQUADRONS. *852d:* 1943–1945. *853d:* 1943–1945. *854th:* 1943–1945. *855th:* 1943–1945.

STATIONS. Davis-Monthan Field, Ariz, 1 Oct 1943; El Paso, Tex, 11 Nov 1943; England, 1 Jan 1944; North Pickenham, England, Feb 1944; Metfield, England, Mar 1944; North Pickenham, England, 15 Aug 1944–Jun 1945; McChord Field, Wash, 17 Jul–8 Sep 1945.

COMMANDERS. Col Dwight O Morteith, 10 Oct 1943; Maj Jack G Merrell, 20 Dec 1943; Col Wilson H Banks, 5 Jan 1944; Maj Alex E Burleigh, 19 Jan 1944; Lt Col Jack G Merrell, 29 Jan 1944; Lt Col Carl T Goldenburg, 12 Feb 1944; Col F H Miller, 26 Jun 1944; Col Allen W Reed, c. 20 Oct 1944–1945.

CAMPAIGNS. Air Offensive, Europe; Normandy; Northern France; Rhineland; Ardennes-Alsace; Central Europe.

DECORATIONS. Distinguished Unit Citation: Misburg, Germany, 26 Nov 1944.

INSIGNE. None.

492d BOMBARDMENT GROUP

Constituted as 492d Bombardment Group (Heavy) on 14 Sep 1943. *Activated* on 1 Oct 1943. Trained for combat with B-24's. Moved to England in Apr 1944 and assigned to Eighth AF. Entered combat on 11 May 1944, and throughout the month operated primarily against industrial targets in central Germany. Attacked airfields and V-weapon launching sites in France during the first week in Jun. Bombed coastal defenses in Normandy on 6 Jun 1944 and attacked bridges, railroads, and other interdiction targets in France until the middle of the month. Resumed bombardment of strategic targets in Germany and, except for support of the infantry during the St Lo breakthrough on 25 Jul 1944, continued such operations until Aug 1944. Transferred, less personnel and equipment, to another station in England on 5 Aug 1944 and assumed personnel, equipment, and the CARPETBAGGER mission of a provisional group that was discontinued. Operated chiefly over southern France with B-24's and C-47's, engaging in CARPETBAGGER operations, that is, transporting agents, supplies, and propaganda leaflets to patriots. Ceased these missions on 16

Sep 1944 to haul gasoline to advancing mechanized forces in France and Belgium. Intermittently attacked airfields, oil refineries, seaports, and other targets in France, the Low Countries, and Germany until Feb 1945. Meanwhile, in Oct 1944, began training for night bombardment operations; concentrated on night bombing of marshalling yards and goods depots in Germany, Feb–Mar 1945. Ceased these missions on 18 Mar 1945 to engage in CARPETBAGGER operations over Germany and German-occupied territory, using B–24, A–26, and British Mosquito aircraft to drop leaflets, demolition equipment, and agents. Received a DUC for these operations, performed at night despite adverse weather and vigorous opposition from enemy ground forces, 20 Mar–25 Apr 1945. Also cited by the French government for similar operations over France in 1944. Flew its last CARPET-BAGGER mission in Apr 1945 and then ferried personnel and equipment to and from the Continent until Jul. Returned to the US, Jul–Aug 1945. *Redesignated* 492d Bombardment Group (Very Heavy) in Aug 1945. *Inactivated* on 17 Oct 1945.

SQUADRONS. *406th:* 1945. *856th:* 1943–1945. *857th:* 1943–1945. *858th:* 1943–1944, 1944–1945. *859th:* 1943–1945.

STATIONS. Alamogordo AAFld, NM, 1 Oct 1943–1 Apr 1944; North Pickenham, England, 18 Apr 1944; Harrington, England, 5 Aug 1944–8 Jul 1945; Sioux Falls AAFld, SD, 14 Aug 1945; Kirtland Field, NM, 17 Aug–17 Oct 1945.

COMMANDERS. Col Arthur J Pierce, 19 Oct 1943; Maj Louis C Adams, 17 Dec 1943; Col Eugene H Snavely, 26 Jan 1944; Col Clifford J Heflin, 13 Aug 1944; Lt Col Robert W Fish, 26 Aug 1944; Col Hudson H Upham, 17 Dec 1944; Lt Col Jack M Dickerson, c. 7 Jun 1945; Lt Col Dalson E Crawford, 30 Aug–Oct 1945.

CAMPAIGNS. Air Offensive, Europe; Normandy; Northern France; Southern France; Rhineland; Central Europe.

DECORATIONS. Distinguished Unit Citation: Germany and German-occupied territory, 20 Mar–25 Apr 1945. French Croix de Guerre with Palm.

INSIGNE. None.

493d BOMBARDMENT GROUP

Constituted as 493d Bombardment Group (Heavy) on 14 Sep 1943. *Activated* on 1 Nov 1943. On 1 Jan 1944 transferred, less the air echelon and without personnel and equipment, to England where personnel were assigned. Joined by the air echelon in May 1944. Served in combat with Eighth AF, May 1944–Apr 1945, using B–24's until they were replaced with B–17's in Sep 1944. Operated chiefly against industrial and military installations in Germany, attacking an ordnance depot at Magdeburg, marshalling yards at Cologne, synthetic oil plants at Merseburg, a railroad tunnel at Ahrweiler, bridges at Irlich, factories at Frankfurt, and other strategic objectives. Additional operations included striking airfields, bridges, and gun batteries prior to and during the invasion of Normandy in Jun 1944; hitting enemy positions to assist ground forces south of Caen and at St Lo in Jul 1944; bombing German fortifications to cover the airborne attack on Holland in Sep 1944; attacking enemy communications during the Battle of the Bulge, Dec 1944–Jan 1945; and assisting the airborne assault across the Rhine in Mar 1945. Flew last combat mission, an attack on marshalling yards at Nauen, on 20 Apr 1945. Returned to the US in Aug. *Inactivated* on 28 Aug 1945.

SQUADRONS. *860th:* 1943–1945. *861st:* 1943–1945. *862d:* 1943–1945. *863d:* 1943–1945.

STATIONS. McCook AAFld, Neb, 1 Nov 1943; Elveden Hall, England, 1 Jan 1944; Debach, England, Apr 1944–6 Aug 1945; Sioux Falls AAFld, SD, 12–28 Aug 1945.

COMMANDERS. Col Elbert Helton, 1 Nov 1943; Col Robert B Landry, 16 Feb 1945; Lt Col Shepler W Fitzgerald Jr, 5 Jun–28 Aug 1945.

CAMPAIGNS. Air Offensive, Europe; Normandy; Northern France; Rhineland; Ardennes-Alsace; Central Europe.

DECORATIONS. None.

INSIGNE. None.

•

494th BOMBARDMENT GROUP

Constituted as 494th Bombardment Group (Heavy) on 14 Sep 1943. *Activated* on 1 Dec 1943. Trained for combat with B–24's. Moved to Hawaii in Jun 1944 for additional training. Assigned to Seventh AF and moved to Palau late in

Sep. Helped to construct a base of operations on Angaur, then entered combat on 3 Nov 1944 with attacks against Japanese airfields on Yap and Koror. Conducted strikes on other bypassed enemy installations in the Pacific and against the Japanese in the Philippines. Late in 1944 hit gun emplacements, personnel areas, and storage depots on Corregidor and Caballo at the entrance to Manila Bay; bombed radio installations and power plants at Japanese bases in the Philippines; and attacked enemy-held airfields, including Clark Field on Luzon. Early in 1945 struck airfields on Mindanao and ammunition and supply dumps in the Davao Gulf and Illana Bay areas. Moved to Okinawa in Jun 1945. Engaged primarily in attacks against enemy airfields on Kyushu until V–J Day. Also participated in incendiary raids, dropped propaganda leaflets over urban areas of Kyushu, and struck airfields in China, in southern Korea, and around the Inland Sea of Japan. Transported personnel and supplies from Manila to Tokyo after the war. Returned to the US in Dec 1945. *Inactivated* on 4 Jan 1946.

SQUADRONS. *864th:* 1943–1946. *865th:* 1943–1946. *866th:* 1943–1946. *867th:* 1944–1946.

STATIONS. Wendover Field, Utah, 1 Dec 1943; Mountain Home AAFld, Idaho, 15 Apr–1 June 1944; Barking Sands, TH, 15 Jun 1944; Angaur, 30 Sep 1944; Yontan, Okinawa, 24 Jun–8 Dec 1945; Ft Lawton, Wash, 2–4 Jan 1946.

COMMANDERS. Unkn, Dec 1943–Feb 1944; Col Laurence B Kelly, 24 Feb 1944–unkn.

CAMPAIGNS. Air Offensive, Japan; Eastern Mandates; Western Pacific; Luzon; Southern Philippines; Ryukyus; China Offensive.

DECORATIONS. Philippine Presidential Unit Citation.

INSIGNE. None.

497th BOMBARDMENT GROUP

Constituted as 497th Bombardment Group (Very Heavy) on 19 Nov 1943 and *activated* on 20 Nov. Prepared for overseas duty with B–29's. Moved to Saipan, Jul–Oct 1944, and assigned to Twentieth AF. Began operations in Oct 1944 with attacks against Iwo Jima and the Truk Islands. Took part in the first attack (24 Nov 1944) on Japan by AAF planes based in the Marianas. Flew many missions against strategic objectives in Japan; on numerous raids, made its attacks in daylight and from high altitude. Received a DUC for a mission on 27 Jan 1945: although weather conditions prevented the group from bombing its primary objective, the unescorted B–29's withstood severe enemy attacks to strike an alternate target, the industrial area of Hamamatsu. Awarded second DUC for attacking strategic centers in Japan during Jul and Aug 1945. Assisted the assault on Okinawa in Apr 1945 by bombing enemy airfields to cut down air attacks against the invasion force. Beginning in Mar 1945

and continuing until the end of the war the group made incendiary raids against Japan, flying at night and at low altitude to bomb area targets. Returned to the US in Nov 1945. Assigned to Strategic Air Command on 21 Mar 1946. *Inactivated* on 31 Mar 1946.

SQUADRONS. *513th:* 1945–1946. *869th:* 1943–1946. *870th:* 1943–1946. *871st:* 1943–1946. *872d:* 1943–1946.

STATIONS. El Paso Mun Aprt, Tex, 20 Nov 1943; Clovis AAFld, NM, 1 Dec 1943; Pratt AAFld, Kan, 13 Apr–18 Jul 1944; Isley Field, Saipan, 17 Oct 1944–1 Nov 1945; Camp Stoneman, Calif, 14 Nov 1945; March Field, Calif, 26 Nov 1945; MacDill Field, Fla, 5 Jan–31 Mar 1946.

COMMANDERS. Lt Col John P Veerling, 10 Dec 1943; Col Karl Truesdell Jr, 6 Mar 1944; Col Stuart P Wright, 26 Apr 1944; Col Arnold T Johnson, 26 Feb 1945–31 Mar 1946.

CAMPAIGNS. Air Offensive, Japan; Eastern Mandates; Western Pacific.

DECORATIONS. Distinguished Unit Citations: Japan, 27 Jan 1945; Japan, 26 Jul–2 Aug 1945.

INSIGNE. None.

498th BOMBARDMENT GROUP

Constituted as 498th Bombardment Group (Very Heavy) on 19 Nov 1943 and *activated* on 20 Nov. Equipped with B–29's. Moved to Saipan, Jul–Nov 1944, for duty with Twentieth AF. Flew its first combat missions against Iwo Jima and the Truk Islands. On 24 Nov 1944 participated in the first assault on Japan by B-29's operating from the Marianas. Conducted numerous attacks against industrial targets in Japan, flying in daylight and at high altitude to carry out these missions. Received a DUC for striking an aircraft engine plant at Nagoya on 13 Dec 1944. Began flying missions at night in Mar 1945, operating from low altitude to drop incendiaries on area targets in Japan; received second DUC for incendiary raids on urban industries near Kobe and Osaka during Jun 1945. Operations also included strikes against Japanese airfields during the Allied invasion of Okinawa in Apr 1945. Returned to the US in Nov 1945. Assigned to Strategic Air Command on 21 Mar 1946. *Inactivated* on 4 Aug 1946.

SQUADRONS. *514th:* 1945–1946. *873d:* 1943–1946. *874th:* 1943–1946. *875th:* 1943–1946. *876th:* 1943–1944.

STATIONS. Clovis AAFld, NM, 20 Nov 1943; Great Bend AAFld, Kan, 13 Apr–13 Jul 1944; Isley Field, Saipan, 6 Sep 1944–2 Nov 1945; March Field, Calif, Dec 1945; MacDill Field, Fla, 5 Jan–4 Aug 1946.

COMMANDERS. Lt Col Joseph H West, 11 Dec 1943; Maj Crocker Snow, 20 Jan 1944; Col Wiley D Ganey, 14 Mar 1944; Col Donald W Saunders, 10 Aug 1945–unkn; Col Richard T King Jr, unkn–4 Aug 1946.

CAMPAIGNS. American Theater; Air Offensive, Japan; Eastern Mandates; Western Pacific.

DECORATIONS. Distinguished Unit Citations: Japan, 13 Dec 1944; Japan, 1–7 Jun 1945.

INSIGNE. None.

499th BOMBARDMENT GROUP

Constituted as 499th Bombardment Group (Very Heavy) on 19 Nov 1943 and *activated* on 20 Nov. Trained for combat with B-29's. Moved to Saipan, Jul–Nov 1944, and assigned to Twentieth AF. Began operations with attacks in the Truk Islands and on Iwo Jima, and took part on 24 Nov 1944 in the first strike against Japan by AAF planes stationed in the Marianas. Flew numerous missions in daylight, operating from high altitude to bomb strategic targets in Japan. Received a DUC for striking the Mitsubishi aircraft engine plant at Nagoya on 23 Jan 1945. In Mar 1945 began to conduct night attacks, flying at low altitude to drop incendiaries on area targets in Japan. Completed a series of attacks against enemy airfields on Kyushu to aid the Allied assault on Okinawa in Apr 1945 and received another DUC for this action. Also dropped propaganda leaflets on Japan, and after the war dropped food and supplies to Allied prisoners of war. Returned to the US in Nov 1945. *Inactivated* on 16 Feb 1946.

SQUADRONS. *877th:* 1943–1946. *878th:* 1943–1946. *879th:* 1943–1946. *880th:* 1943–1944.

STATIONS. Davis-Monthan Field, Ariz, 20 Nov 1943; Smoky Hill AAFld, Kan, 1

Dec 1943–22 Jul 1944; Isley Field, Saipan, 18 Sep 1944–9 Nov 1945; March Field, Calif, c. 25 Nov 1945–16 Feb 1946.

COMMANDERS. Unkn, Nov 1943–Jan 1944; Maj Douglas C Northrup, 22 Jan 1944; Col Thomas C Musgrave, 1 Feb 1944; Col Samuel R Harris, 4 Apr 1944; Col Morris J Lee, 17 Mar 1945; Lt Col Walter E Chambers, 13 Aug 1945–unkn.

CAMPAIGNS. Air Offensive, Japan; Eastern Mandates; Western Pacific.

DECORATIONS. Distinguished Unit Citations: Nagoya, Japan, 23 Jan 1945; Japan, 22–28 Apr 1945.

INSIGNE. None.

500th BOMBARDMENT GROUP

Constituted as 500th Bombardment Group (Very Heavy) on 19 Nov 1943 and *activated* on 20 Nov. Equipped first with B–17's; later trained for combat with B–29's. Moved to Saipan, Jul–Nov 1944, for service with Twentieth AF. Entered combat on 11 Nov 1944 with an attack against a submarine base in the Truk Islands. On 24 Nov participated in the first attack on Japan by B–29's based in the Marianas. After that, conducted many daylight raids, operating from high altitude to bomb strategic targets in Japan. Struck the Mitsubishi aircraft engine plant at Nagoya in Jan 1945 and received a DUC for the mission. Bombed enemy airfields and other installations on Kyushu in support of the Allied assault on Okinawa in Apr 1945. Beginning in Mar 1945, flew missions at night and at low altitude to drop incendiaries on area targets in Japan. Received second DUC for incendiary attacks on the urban-industrial section of Osaka, feeder industries at Hamamatsu, and shipping and rail targets on Kyushu, in Jun 1945. Released propaganda leaflets over the Japanese home islands, Jul–Aug 1945. Dropped food and supplies to Allied prisoners in Japan, Korea, China, and Formosa after the war. Returned to the US in Oct 1945. *Inactivated* on 17 Jan 1946.

SQUADRONS. *881st:* 1943–1946. *882d:* 1943–1946. *883d:* 1943–1946. *884th:* 1943–1944.

STATIONS. Gowen Field, Idaho, 20 Nov 1943; Clovis AAFld, NM, 12 Jan 1944; Walker AAFld, Kan, 16 Apr–23 Jul 1944; Isley Field, Saipan, 18 Sep 1944–21 Oct 1945; March Field, Calif, 24 Oct 1945–17 Jan 1946.

COMMANDERS. Unkn, Nov 1943–Jan 1944; Maj Ralph A Reeve, 28 Jan 1944; Maj John E Gay, 7 Feb 1944; Lt Col John E Dougherty, 8 Mar 1944; Col Richard T King Jr, 5 May 1944; Col John E Dougherty, 5 Dec 1944; Lt Col William L McDowell Jr, 4 Dec 1945; Maj James H Coats, 19 Dec 1945–17 Jan 1946.

CAMPAIGNS. Air Offensive, Japan; Eastern Mandates; Western Pacific.

DECORATIONS. Distinguished Unit Citations: Nagoya, Japan, 23 Jan 1945; Japan, 15–20 Jun 1945.

INSIGNE. None.

501st BOMBARDMENT GROUP

Constituted as 501st Bombardment Group (Very Heavy) on 25 May 1944. *Activated* on 1 Jun 1944. Moved to Guam, Mar–Apr 1945, and assigned to Twentieth AF. Entered combat on 19 Jun 1945 when its B–29's bombed Japanese fortifications in the Truk Islands. Flew its first mission against Japan on 27 Jun 1945, and afterward operated principally against the enemy's petroleum industry on Honshu. Received a DUC for attacks on the Maruzen oil refinery at Shimotsu, the Utsubo oil refinery at Yokkaichi, and the petroleum center at Kawasaki, in Jul 1945. After the war, dropped food and supplies to Allied prisoners in Japan, China, Korea, and Manchuria. *Inactivated* on Guam on 10 Jun 1946.

SQUADRONS. *21st:* 1944–1946. *41st:* 1944–1946. *485th:* 1944–1946.

STATIONS. Dalhart AAFld, Tex, 1 Jun 1944; Harvard AAFld, Neb, 22 Aug 1944–7 Mar 1945; Northwest Field, Guam, 14 Apr 1945–10 Jun 1946.

COMMANDERS. Capt Harry L Young, c. 27 Jun 1944; Lt Col Arch G Campbell Jr, 6 Jul 1944; Col Boyd Hubbard Jr, 11 Aug 1944; Col Vincent M Miles Jr, 15 Apr–20 May 1946.

CAMPAIGNS. Air Offensive, Japan; Eastern Mandates; Western Pacific.

DECORATIONS. Distinguished Unit Citation: Japan, 6–13 Jul 1945.

INSIGNE. None.

502d BOMBARDMENT GROUP

Constituted as 502d Bombardment Group (Very Heavy) on 25 May 1944. *Activated* on 1 Jun 1944. Trained for combat with B–29's. Moved to Guam, Apr–Jun 1945, and assigned to Twentieth AF. Entered combat on 30 Jun 1945 when the group bombed enemy installations on Rota. Bombed Japanese-held Truk early in Jul 1945. Flew its first mission against the Japanese home islands on 15 Jul 1945, and afterward operated principally against the enemy's petroleum industry. Awarded a DUC for attacks on the coal liquefaction plant at Ube, the tank farm at Amagasaki, and the Nippon oil refinery at Tsuchizaki, in Aug 1945. After the war, dropped food and supplies to Allied prisoners in Japan and participated in several show-of-force missions over Japan. *Inactivated* on Guam on 15 Apr 1946.

SQUADRONS. *402d:* 1944–1946. *411th:* 1944–1946. *430th:* 1944–1946.

STATIONS. Davis-Monthan Field, Ariz, 1 Jun 1944; Dalhart AAFld, Tex, 5 Jun 1944; Grand Island AAFld, Neb, 26 Sep 1944–7 Apr 1945; Northwest Field, Guam, 12 May 1945–15 Apr 1946.

COMMANDERS. Lt Col Estley R Farley, 9 Jul 1944; Lt Col Robert C McBride, 1 Aug 1944; Col Kenneth O Sanborn, 6 Oct 1944–15 Apr 1946.

CAMPAIGNS. Air Offensive, Japan; Eastern Mandates; Western Pacific.

DECORATIONS. Distinguished Unit Citation: Japan, 5–15 Aug 1945.

INSIGNE. None.

504th BOMBARDMENT GROUP

Constituted as 504th Bombardment Group (Very Heavy) on 28 Feb 1944. *Activated* on 11 Mar 1944. Equipped first with B-17's; later trained for combat with B-29's. Moved to the Asiatic-Pacific Theater late in 1944 for service with Twentieth AF. Began combat operations from Tinian in Jan 1945 with attacks on Japanese airfields and other installations on Maug and Iwo Jima and in the Truk Islands. Flew its first mission against the Japanese home islands early in Feb 1945 when the group bombed the industrial area of Kobe. Continued to attack strategic targets in Japan, operating in daylight and at high altitude to bomb such objectives as aircraft factories, chemical plants, harbors, and arsenals. Received a DUC for striking the industrial center at Yokohama late in May 1945. Began incendiary raids in Mar 1945, flying at night and at low altitude to strike area targets in Japan. Started mining operations against enemy shipping late in Mar, receiving a DUC for mining Korean shipping lanes, the Shimonoseki Strait, and harbors of the Inland Sea, Jul-Aug 1945. In Apr and May 1945 the group hit airfields from which the Japanese launched kamikaze planes against the invasion force during the assault on Okinawa. After the war it dropped food and supplies to Allied prisoners, participated in show-of-force missions, and flew over Japan to evaluate damage inflicted by bombardment operations. Moved to the Philippines in Mar 1946. *Inactivated* on Luzon on 15 Jun 1946.

SQUADRONS. *393d:* 1944. *398th:* 1944–1946. *421st:* 1944–1946. *507th:* 1944. *680th:* 1944–1946.

STATIONS. Dalhart AAFld, Tex, 11 Mar 1944; Fairmont AAFld, Neb, 12 Mar–5 Nov 1944; North Field, Tinian, 23 Dec 1944; Clark Field, Luzon, 6 Mar–15 Jun 1946.

COMMANDERS. Capt Basil D Murray, Mar 1944; Col James T Connally, 6 Apr 1944; Col Glen W Martin, 6 Feb 1945; Col Charles B Root, 18 Sep 1945; Col John P Kenny, 2 Apr–15 Jun 1946.

CAMPAIGNS. Air Offensive, Japan; Eastern Mandates; Western Pacific.

DECORATIONS. Distinguished Unit Citations: Yokohama, Japan, 28 May 1945; Japan and Korea, 27 Jul–14 Aug 1945.

INSIGNE. None.

505th BOMBARDMENT GROUP

Constituted as 505th Bombardment Group (Very Heavy) on 28 Feb 1944. *Activated* on 11 Mar 1944. Equipped first with B-17's; later trained for overseas duty with B-29's. Moved to Tinian late in 1944. Assigned to Twentieth AF. Entered combat in Feb 1945 with strikes on Iwo Jima and the Truk Islands. Then began daylight missions against Japan, operating at high altitude to bomb strategic objectives. Received a DUC for a strike against the Nakajima aircraft factory at Ota in Feb 1945. Conducted incendiary raids on area targets in Japan, carrying out these missions at night and at low altitude. Bombed in support of the Allied assault on Okinawa in Apr 1945. Engaged in mining operations against Japanese shipping, receiving second DUC for mining the Shimonoseki Strait and harbors of the Inland Sea, Jun–Jul 1945. After V–J Day, dropped supplies to Allied prisoners, participated in show-of-force missions, and flew over Japan to evaluate bombardment damage. Moved to the Philippine Islands in Mar 1946. *Inactivated* on Luzon on 30 Jun 1946.

SQUADRONS. *482d*: 1944–1946. *483d*: 1944–1946. *484th*: 1944–1946. *485th*: 1944.

STATIONS. Dalhart AAFld, Tex, 11 Mar 1944; Harvard AAFld, Neb, 1 Apr–6 Nov 1944; North Field, Tinian, 19 Dec 1944–5 Mar 1946; Clark Field, Luzon, 14 Mar–30 Jun 1946.

COMMANDERS. Maj George D Roberts, 15 Apr 1944; Col Robert A Ping, 3 May 1944; Lt Col Charles M Eisenhart, 1 Jul 1945; Col John P Kenny, c. Sep 1945–1946.

CAMPAIGNS. Air Offensive, Japan; Eastern Mandates; Western Pacific.

DECORATIONS. Distinguished Unit Citations: Ota, Japan, 10 Feb 1945; Japan, 17 Jun–1 Jul 1945.

INSIGNE. None.

506th FIGHTER GROUP

Constituted as 506th Fighter Group on 5 Oct 1944 and *activated* on 21 Oct. Equipped with P–51 aircraft. Moved to the Asiatic-Pacific Theater, Feb–Apr 1945,

the air echelon flying patrols from Tinian before joining the rest of the group on Iwo Jima. The group, assigned to Twentieth AF, flew its first mission from Iwo on 18 May when it bombed and strafed an airfield in the Bonin Islands. Afterward, attacked airfields, antiaircraft emplacements, shipping, barracks, radio and radar stations, railway cars, and other targets in the Bonin Islands or Japan. Also provided air defense for Iwo and escorted B–29's during bombardment missions from the Marianas to Japan. Received a DUC for defending B–29's against attacks by fighter aircraft during the period 7–10 Jun 1945. Returned to the US in Dec 1945. *Inactivated* on 16 Dec 1945.

SQUADRONS. *457th*: 1944–1945. *458th*: 1944–1945. *462d*: 1944–1945.

STATIONS. Lakeland AAFld, Fla, 21 Oct 1944–16 Feb 1945; North Field, Iwo Jima, 24 Apr–3 Dec 1945; Camp Anza, Calif, 15–16 Dec 1945.

COMMANDERS. Col Bryan B Harper, 25 Oct 1944–1945.

CAMPAIGNS. Air Offensive, Japan.

DECORATIONS. Distinguished Unit Citation: Japan, 7–10 Jun 1945.

INSIGNE. *Shield:* On a barry wavy of four argent and azure, second bar semee of stars of the first, over-all an escutcheon, per pale argent and or, a crest of a stylized wing of the first, fimbriated of the second, the escutcheon surmounting a sword bendwise, hilt and pommel or, blade of the last, shaded gules; on a chief of the second, a sphere argent, land areas vert, over two lightning flashes in saltire gules, fimbriated of the first. (Approved 21 Jul 1955.)

507th FIGHTER GROUP

Constituted as 507th Fighter Group on 5 Oct 1944 and *activated* on 12 Oct. Moved to the Asiatic-Pacific Theater, Apr–Jun 1945. Assigned to Twentieth AF; reas-signed to Eighth AF in Aug 1945. Entered combat on 1 Jul 1945, operating from Ie Shima with P–47's. Flew missions to Japan, Korea, and China to attack such targets as shipping, railroad bridges, airfields, factories, and barracks. Met little fighter opposition until 8 Aug 1945 when the group, flying its only B–29 escort mission of the war, encountered many enemy planes over Yawata, Japan. Received a DUC for its performance on 13 Aug 1945: while flying a long-range sweep to Korea, the group engaged a host of interceptors and destroyed a number of them. Moved to Okinawa in Jan 1946. *Inactivated* on 27 May 1946.

Redesignated 507th Fighter Group (Air Defense). *Activated* on 18 Aug 1955. Assigned to Air Defense Command and equipped with F–89's.

SQUADRONS. *438th:* 1955–. *463d:* 1944–1946. *464th:* 1944–1946. *465th:* 1944–1946.

STATIONS. Peterson Field, Colo, 12 Oct 1944; Bruning AAFld, Neb, 20 Oct 1944; Dalhart AAFld, Tex, 15 Dec 1944–24 Apr 1945; Ie Shima, 24 Jun 1945; Yontan, Okinawa, 29 Jan–27 May 1946. Kinross AFB, Mich, 18 Aug 1955–.

COMMANDERS. Col Loring F Stetson Jr, 27 Oct 1944; Lt Col Woodrow W Korges, 12 Sep 1945; Maj Byron H Foreman, 2 Nov 1945; Capt Franklin L Fisher, 20 Nov 1945–unkn. Col John L Locke, 1955–.

CAMPAIGNS. Air Offensive, Japan; Western Pacific; Ryukyus; China Offensive.

DECORATIONS. Distinguished Unit Citation: Korea, 13 Aug 1945.

INSIGNE. *Shield:* Azure, edged argent, over a point pointed in point bendwise and arched gules, fimbriated of the second, a falcon flying downward per bend argent; between two planets and a star in sinister chief, and the Great Dipper in dexter base all proper. *Motto:* DEFENDIMUS US- QUE AD ASTRA—We Defend Even to the Stars. (Approved 17 Aug 1956.)

508th FIGHTER GROUP

Constituted as 508th Fighter Group on 5 Oct 1944 and *activated* on 12 Oct. Trained with P-47 aircraft to provide very-long-range escort for bombardment units. Moved to Hawaii in Jan 1945 and served as part of the defense force for the islands. Also trained replacement pilots for other organizations, repaired P-47's and P-51's received from combat units, and ferried aircraft to forward areas. *Inactivated* in Hawaii on 25 Nov 1945.

SQUADRONS. *466th:* 1944–1945. *467th:* 1944–1945. *468th:* 1944–1945.

STATIONS. Peterson Field, Colo, 12 Oct 1944; Pocatello AAFld, Idaho, 25 Oct 1944; Bruning AAFld, Neb, 15 Nov–18 Dec 1944; Kahuku, TH, 6 Jan 1945; Mokuleia, TH, 25 Feb 1945; Bellows Field, TH, 16 Sep–25 Nov 1945.

COMMANDERS. Col Henry G Thorne Jr, 9 Nov 1944; Col Frank H Mears, 27 Nov 1944; Col Oswald W Lunde, 4 May–25 Nov 1945.

CAMPAIGNS. Asiatic-Pacific Theater.

DECORATIONS. None.

INSIGNE. *Shield:* Per bend engrailed azure and gules, in bend a chain or and in chief an atomic cloud argent issuing from a base gray, over-all three figures representing the "Spirit of '76" sable fimbriated of the fourth. *Motto:* KNOWL- EDGE AND COURAGE. (Approved 14 Sep 1953.)

509th COMPOSITE GROUP

Constituted as 509th Composite Group on 9 Dec 1944 and *activated* on 17 Dec. Became the first AAF group to be organized, equipped, and trained for atomic warfare. Moved to Tinian, Apr–Jun 1945. Assigned to Twentieth AF. Flew practice missions in Jun and Jul. On 6 Aug 1945 one of the group's B-29's, the "Enola Gay," piloted by the group commander, Col Paul W Tibbets Jr, dropped an atomic bomb on Hiroshima, Japan. Three days later a B-29, "Bock's Car," piloted by Maj Charles W Sweeney, dropped an atomic bomb on Nagasaki. These two bombs, the first atomic weapons ever employed,

(Medium) in Jul 1948. Converted from B–29 to B–50 aircraft, 1949–1950. *Inactivated* on 16 Jun 1952.

SQUADRONS. *320th* Troop Carrier: 1944–1946. *393d* Bombardment: 1944–1952. *715th*: 1946–1952. *830th*: 1946–1952.

STATIONS. Wendover Field, Utah, 17 Dec 1944–26 Apr 1945; North Field, Tinian, 29 May–17 Oct 1945; Roswell AAFld, NM, 6 Nov 1945–16 Jun 1952.

COMMANDERS. Col Paul W Tibbets Jr, 17 Dec 1944; Col William H Blanchard, 22 Jan 1946; Col John D Ryan, 15 Sep 1948; Col William H Blanchard, 21 Jul 1951–16 Jun 1952.

CAMPAIGNS. Air Offensive, Japan; Eastern Mandates; Western Pacific.

DECORATIONS. None.

INSIGNE. *Shield*: Or, in base a label of three points gules, surmounted by an atomic cloud proper, between a pair of wings conjoined in base azure. *Crest*: On a wreath of the colors, or and azure, an atomic cloud or, with broken pattern gules, between two lightning bolts gules. *Motto*: DEFENSOR VINDEX—Defender Avenger. (Approved 10 Jul 1952.)

quickly brought the war to an end. The group returned to the US, Oct–Nov 1945. Assigned to Strategic Air Command on 21 Mar 1946, providing the nucleus for the command's atomic striking force. *Redesignated* 509th Bombardment Group (Very Heavy) in Jul 1946. Participated in atomic tests (Operation CROSS-ROADS) in the Marshall Islands in 1946. *Redesignated* 509th Bombardment Group

WINGS

1st BOMBARDMENT WING

Organized as 1st Pursuit Wing in France on 6 Jul 1918. Served in combat, Jul–Nov 1918. Operated first in the defensive sector near Toul. During the St Mihiel offensive in Sep, flew reconnaissance sorties, protected observation aircraft, attacked enemy observation balloons, strafed enemy troops, flew counter-air patrols, and bombed towns, bridges, and railroad stations behind the enemy's lines. During the Meuse-Argonne offensive (26 Sep–11 Nov 1918) bombardment aircraft continued their attacks behind the lines while pursuit ships concentrated mainly on large-scale counter-air patrols. *Demobilized* in France in Dec 1918.

Reconstituted and *consolidated* (1936) with 1st Wing, which was *organized* in the US on 16 Aug 1919 and was engaged in border patrol activities until it became an advanced flying training wing in 1922. *Inactivated* on 26 Jun 1924.

Redesignated 1st Bombardment Wing in 1929. *Activated* on 1 Apr 1931. *Redesignated* 1st Pursuit Wing in 1933, 1st Wing in 1935, and 1st Bombardment Wing in 1940. Became one of the original wings of GHQAF in 1935 and conducted much of the Army's pursuit, bombardment, attack, and observation activities in the western part of the US until 1941. Moved to England, Jul–Aug 1942, and became a heavy bombardment wing of Eighth AF. *Redesignated* 1st Combat Bombardment Wing (Heavy) in Aug 1943, and 1st Bombardment Wing (Heavy) in Jun 1945. Served in combat in the European theater from Aug 1942 until 25 Apr 1945, receiving a DUC for an attack on aircraft factories in Germany on 11 Jan 1944. Returned to the US in Aug 1945. *Inactivated* on 7 Nov 1945.

GROUPS. *1st* Pursuit: 1919–1922; 1933–1935. *2d* (formerly 1st) Bombardment: 1918; 1919–1922. *2d* Pursuit: 1918. *3d* Pursuit: 1918. *3d* Attack (formerly 1st Surveillance): 1919–1924. *7th* Bombardment: 1931–1933, 1935–1941. *8th* Pursuit: 1933–1935. *17th* Bombardment: 1931–1941. *19th* Bombardment: 1935–1941. *20th* Pursuit: 1939–1941. *35th* Pursuit: 1940–1941. *41st* Bombardment: 1941. *91st* Bombardment: 1942–1945. *92d* Bombardment: 1942, 1943. *93d* Bombardment: 1942. *97th* Bombardment: 1942. *301st* Bombardment: 1942. *303d* Bombardment: 1942–1943. *305th* Bombardment: 1942–1943. *306th* Bombardment: 1942–1943. *351st* Bombardment: 1943. *379th*

Bombardment: 1943. *381st* Bombardment: 1943–1945. *384th* Bombardment: 1943. *398th* Bombardment: 1944–1945. *482d* Bombardment: 1943.

STATIONS. Toul, France, 6 Jul 1918; Chaumont-Sur-Aire, France, c. 24 Sep 1918–unkn. Kelly Field, Tex, 16 Aug 1919–26 Jun 1924. March Field, Calif, 1 Apr 1931; Tucson, Ariz, 27 May 1941–Jul 1942; Brampton Grange, England, c. 19 Aug 1942; Bassingbourn, England, Sep 1943; Alconbury, England, c. 26 Jun–c. 26 Aug 1945; McChord Field, Wash, c. 6 Sep–7 Nov 1945.

COMMANDERS. Lt Col Thomas DeW Milling, c. 6 Jul 1918; Lt Col Bert M Atkinson, c. 20 Aug 1918–unkn. Lt Col Henry B Clagett, 1919–unkn; Col Henry C Pratt, c. 1 Jun–c. 1 Sep 1920. Maj Carl Spaatz, c. 1 Nov 1931–c. Jun 1933; Brig Gen Henry H Arnold, Nov 1933–Jan 1936; Brig Gen Henry B Clagett, c. 1 Mar 1936; Brig Gen Delos C Emmons, 17 Jul 1936; Brig Gen Jacob E Fickel, c. 31 Mar 1939; Brig Gen Frank D Lackland, 1 Feb 1940–unkn; Maj Woodrow W Dunlop, Jul 1942–unkn; Col Claude E Duncan, c. 19 Aug 1942; Brig Gen Newton Longfellow, 21 Aug 1942; Brig Gen Laurence S Kuter, 1 Dec 1942; Brig Gen Haywood S Hansell Jr, 2 Jan 1943; Brig Gen Frank A Armstrong Jr, 15 Jun 1943; Brig Gen Robert B Williams, 1 Aug 1943; Brig Gen William M Gross, 17 Sep 1943–c. Oct 1945.

CAMPAIGNS. *World War I:* Lorraine; St Mihiel; Meuse-Argonne. *World War II:* Air Offensive, Europe; Normandy; Northern France; Rhineland; Ardennes-Alsace; Central Europe.

DECORATIONS. Distinguished Unit Citation: Germany, 11 Jan 1944.

INSIGNE. None.

2d BOMBARDMENT WING

Organized as 2d Wing on 4 Sep 1919. Served as an observation organization. *Inactivated* on 30 Sep 1921.

Activated on 8 Aug 1922. *Redesignated* 2d Bombardment Wing in 1929, 2d Wing in 1935, and 2d Bombardment Wing in 1940. Engaged primarily in bombardment activities for more than a decade. Became one of the original wings of GHQAF in 1935 and conducted much of the Army's pursuit, bombardment, and observation operations in the eastern part of the US. *Inactivated* on 5 Sep 1941.

Activated on 7 June 1942. Moved to England, Aug–Sep 1942, and became a heavy bombardment wing of Eighth AF. In the fall of 1942, helped to train bombardment groups assigned to Twelfth AF. Served in combat in the European theater from Nov 1942 to June 1943. Ceased combat temporarily during Jul–Aug 1943 when its groups were on detached duty in the Mediterranean theater. *Redesignated* 2d Combat Bombardment Wing (Heavy) in Aug. Served on detached duty in the Mediterranean theater during Sep–Oct 1943. Resumed combat in the European theater in Oct 1943 and continued operations until Apr 1945. *Redesignated* 2d Bombardment Wing (Heavy) in Jun 1945. Returned to the US in Aug. *Inactivated* on 7 Nov 1945.

GROUPS. *1st* Pursuit: 1935–1941. *2d* Bombardment: 1922–1941. *7th* Bombardment (formerly 1st Army Observation): 1919–1921; 1933–1935. *8th* Pursuit: 1932–1933, 1935–1941. *9th* Bombardment: 1935–1940. *22d* Bombardment: 1940–1941. *31st* Pursuit: 1940–1941. *44th* Bombardment: 1942–1943, 1943. *93d* Bombardment: 1942–1943. *389th* Bombardment: 1943–1945. *392d* Bombardment: 1943. *445th* Bombardment: 1943–1945. *453d* Bombardment: 1944–1945.

STATIONS. Langley Field, Va, 4 Sep 1919–30 Sep 1921. Langley Field, Va, 8 Aug 1922–5 Sep 1941. Detrick Field, Md, 7 Jun–15 Aug 1942; Old Catton, England, c. 7 Sep 1942; Hethel, England, 14 Sep 1943; Alconbury, England, c. 12 Jun–c. 25 Aug 1945; McChord Field, Wash, 6 Sep–7 Nov 1945.

COMMANDERS. Col Townsend F Dodd, 4 Sep–c. 5 Oct 1919; unkn, 1919–1921. Unkn, 1922–1924; Maj Oscar Westover, c. Sep 1924–c. Sep 1926; Lt Col Clarence C Culver, c. Sep 1926–unkn; Col Roy T Kirtland, Jul 1930–Jul 1932; Maj Byron Q Jones, 1934–unkn; Brig Gen Henry C Pratt, 1 Mar 1935; Brig Gen Gerald C Brant, 15 Mar 1937; Brig Gen Arnold N Krogstad, 31 Mar 1938–5 Sep 1941. Maj Justus K Hetsch, c. 13 Jul 1942; Col Harold D Smith, c. 10 Aug 1942; Brig Gen James P Hodges, 7 Sep 1942; Col Edward J Timberlake Jr, c. 15 Sep 1943; Brig Gen James P Hodges, 16 Sep 1943; Brig Gen Edward J Timberlake Jr, 4 Oct 1943; Col Milton J Arnold, 7 Aug 1944; Col James M Stewart, 10 May 1945; Col Eugene A Romig, 15 Jun 1945–unkn.

CAMPAIGNS. Air Offensive, Europe; Naples-Foggia; Normandy; Northern France; Rhineland; Ardennes-Alsace; Central Europe.

DECORATIONS. None.

INSIGNE. *Shield:* On a hurt a griffin segreant within a diminished border argent. (Approved 5 Jan 1933.)

4th BOMBARDMENT WING

Constituted as 4th Bombardment Wing on 19 Oct 1940. *Activated* on 18 Dec 1940. *Inactivated* on 1 Oct 1941.

Activated on 7 Jun 1942. Moved to England, Aug–Sep 1942. Assigned to Eighth AF. *Redesignated* 4th Combat Bombardment Wing (Heavy) in Aug 1943. Had

no groups assigned until the spring of 1943 and was not manned from 29 Sep 1942 to 19 Jan 1943. Began combat in May 1943 and received a DUC for a mission on 17 Aug 1943 when the wing attacked an aircraft factory at Regensburg. Brig Gen Frederick W Castle, wing commander, was posthumously awarded the Medal of Honor for action on 24 Dec 1944 when he kept a burning B–17 from crashing until other members of the crew had parachuted to safety. The wing remained in combat until Apr 1945. *Disbanded* in England on 18 Jun 1945.

Reconstituted, redesignated 4th Bombardment Wing (Light), and allotted to the reserve. *Activated* in the US on 20 Dec 1946. *Redesignated* 4th Air Division (Bombardment) in Apr 1948. *Inactivated* on 27 Jun 1949.

Redesignated 4th Air Division. *Organized* on 10 Feb 1951. Assigned to Strategic Air Command.

COMPONENTS. *Groups. 34th:* 1941. *43d:* 1941. *94th:* 1943–1945. *95th:* 1943. *96th:* 1943. *100th:* 1943. *319th:* 1946–1949. *320th:* 1947–1949. *385th:* 1943–1945. *388th:* 1943. *390th:* 1943. *447th:* 1943–1945. *486th:* 1945. *487th:* 1945. *Wings. 91st* Reconnaissance: 1951. *301st* Bombardment: 1951–. *376th* Bombardment: 1951–.

STATIONS. Mitchel Field, NY, 18 Dec 1940; Westover Field, Mass, 20 Mar–1 Oct 1941. Westover Field, Mass, 7 Jun 1942; Bolling Field, DC, c. 28 Jul–c. 28 Aug 1942; Camp Lynn, England, 12 Sep 1942; Marks Hall, England, 18 Jan 1943; Camp Blainey, England, Jun 1943; Bury St Edmunds, England, 13 Sep 1943–18 Jun 1945. Mitchel Field, NY, 20 Dec 1946–27 Jun 1949. Barksdale AFB, La, 10 Feb 1951–.

COMMANDERS. Brig Gen John B Brooks, c. 18 Dec 1940–c. 31 Jul 1941. Brig Gen James H Doolittle, c. Jun 1942; Col Charles T Phillips, c. 1 Aug 1942–unkn; Lt Col Thomas L Dawson, c. 19 Jan 1943; Lt Col Charles C Bye Jr, c. 27 Jan 1943; Brig Gen Frederick L Anderson, 19 Apr 1943; Col Curtis E LeMay, 18 Jun 1943; Brig Gen Russell A Wilson, 14 Sep 1943; Brig Gen Frederick W Castle, c. 6 Mar 1944; Col Charles B Dougher, 25 Dec 1944; Col Robert W Burns, 29 Jan 1945–unkn. Col Thomas W Steed, 10 Feb 1951; Brig Gen Henry K Mooney, 22 May 1951; Brig Gen Fay R Upthegrove, 22 Oct 1952; Maj Gen Frederic E Glantzberg, 6 Jan 1953; Brig Gen Maurice A Preston, 14 Jan 1954–.

CAMPAIGNS. Air Offensive, Europe; Normandy; Northern France; Rhineland; Ardennes-Alsace; Central Europe.

DECORATIONS. Distinguished Unit Citation: Germany, 17 Aug 1943.

INSIGNE. *Shield:* Per bend, or and azure a terrestrial globe sable, markings argent, winged proper, enfiled and interfretted with a chain of twelve links of the third; a hand bendwise, proper issuing from the sinister base grasping the chain. (Approved 18 Jun 1954.)

5th BOMBARDMENT WING

Constituted as 5th Bombardment Wing on 19 Oct 1940. *Activated* on 18 Dec 1940. Assigned to Second AF. *Inactivated* on 5 Sep 1941.

Activated on 10 Jul 1942. Moved to North Africa, Oct–Dec 1942, and began operations with Twelfth AF. Assigned to Fifteenth AF in Nov 1943. *Redesignated* 5th Bombardment Wing (Heavy) in Jan 1945. Served in combat until May 1945. *Inactivated* in Italy on 2 Nov 1945.

Redesignated 5th Air Division. *Activated* in the US on 14 Jan 1951. Assigned to Strategic Air Command. Transferred, without personnel and equipment, to French Morocco in May 1951. Had no combat elements assigned but operated with bombardment wings temporarily deployed from the US and attached for short periods of duty.

GROUPS. *1st* Fighter: 1943, 1943–1944. *2d* Bombardment: 1943–1945. *12th* Bombardment: 1941. *14th* Fighter: 1943–1944. *17th* Bombardment: 1941. *39th* Bombardment: 1941. *47th* Bombardment: 1942–1943. *68th* Reconnaissance: 1942–1943. *82d* Fighter: 1944. *97th* Bombardment: 1943–1945. *98th* Bombardment: 1943. *99th* Bombardment: 1943–1945. *301st* Bombardment: 1943–1945. *325th* Fighter: 1943–1944. *376th* Bombardment: 1943. *463d* Bombardment: 1944–1945. *483d* Bombardment: 1944–1945.

STATIONS. McChord Field, Wash, 18 Dec 1940; Ft George Wright, Wash, 9 Jan–5 Sep 1941. Bolling Field, DC, 10 Jul 1942; Westover Field, Mass, c. 31 Jul–Oct 1942; Casablanca, French Morocco, Nov 1942; Oujda, French Morocco, Dec 1942; Biskra, Algeria, c. Jan 1943; Chateaudun, Algeria, c. Mar 1943; Depienne, Tunisia, Aug 1943; Foggia, Italy, Dec 1943–2 Nov 1945. Offutt AFB, Neb, 14 Jan 1951; Rabat/Sale Airfield, French

Morocco, 25 May 1951; Sidi Slimane, French Morocco, 29 May 1954–.

COMMANDERS. Brig Gen Carlyle H Wash, c. Dec 1940–1941. Maj Charles R Simpson, 28 Jul 1942; Col John W Monahan, 11 Sep 1942; Brig Gen Joseph H Atkinson, 5 Jan 1943; Brig Gen Charles W Lawrence, 24 Jan 1944; Col Wallace E Whitson, c. 22 May 1945–unkn. Maj Gen Archie J Old Jr, 25 May 1951; Maj Gen David W Hutchison, 15 Jan 1953; Brig Gen Charles B Dougher, 5 Mar 1954; Brig Gen Joseph J Nazzaro, 6 Jul 1955–.

CAMPAIGNS. Air Combat, EAME Theater; Air Offensive, Europe; Tunisia; Sicily; Naples-Foggia; Rome-Arno; Normandy; Northern France; Southern France; North Apennines; Rhineland; Central Europe; Po Valley.

DECORATIONS. None.

INSIGNE. *Shield:* Gules, a stylized silhouetted aircraft volant, nose to the chief argent; on a chief per fess gules and argent, five stars argent in chief, and a ribbon of the firmament, sky blue, in base charged with semee of stars of the second. (Approved 3 Nov 1954.)

6th FIGHTER WING

Constituted as 6th Pursuit Wing on 19 Oct 1940. *Activated* on 18 Dec 1940. *Inactivated* on 7 Dec 1941.

Redesignated 6th Fighter Wing. *Activated* on 7 Jun 1942. No combat groups were assigned. Moved to England in Aug 1942 for duty with Eighth AF. Trained replacement pilots for fighter organiza-

tions. *Disbanded* in England in 13 Sep 1943.

Reconstituted on 5 Aug 1946 and *activated* in the Panama Canal Zone on 25 Aug. *Inactivated* in the Canal Zone on 28 Jul 1948.

Redesignated 6th Air Division. *Organized* in the US on 10 Feb 1951. Assigned to Strategic Air Command.

COMPONENTS. *Groups. 1st* Pursuit: 1940–1941. *31st* Pursuit: 1940–1941. *36th* Fighter: 1946–1948. *52d* Pursuit: 1941. *Wings. 305th* Bombardment: 1951–. *306th* Bombardment: 1951–. *307th* Bombardment: 1951–1953.

STATIONS. Selfridge Field, Mich, 18 Dec 1940–7 Dec 1941. Harrisburg Mun Aprt, Pa, 7 Jun–c. 4 Aug 1942; Bushey Hall, England, c. 16 Aug 1942; Atcham, England, c. 24 Aug 1942–13 Sep 1943. Howard Field, CZ, 25 Aug 1946–28 Jul 1948. MacDill AFB, Fla, 10 Feb 1951–.

COMMANDERS. Brig Gen Henry B Clagett, c. 16 Jan 1941–unkn; Col Lawrence P Hickey, c. 8 Apr–c. 7 Dec 1941. Lt

Col Paul M Jacobs, 13 Jul–14 Sep 1942;
Lt Col John W Ranson, c. 17 Sep 1942;
Lt Col Jack W Hickman, 13 Mar 1943;
Col Ross G Hoyt, 18 Mar 1943; Col Jack
W Hickman, c. 4 Jun 1943–unkn. Brig
Gen Morris R Nelson, Aug 1946; Col
William R Morgan, 29 Dec 1947; Col
Murray C Woodbury, 17 Feb 1948–unkn.
Col Thayer S Olds, 10 Feb 1951; Maj Gen
Frank A Armstrong Jr, May 1951; Brig
Gen Henry K Mooney, 16 Nov 1952;
Brig Gen Kenneth O Sanborn, 31 Jul
1954–.

CAMPAIGNS. European-African-Middle
Eastern Theater.

DECORATIONS. None.

INSIGNE. *Shield:* Per chevron argent
and gules, in chief, a stylized silhouetted
jet aircraft, issuing from chief, nose toward
base azure; in base a sphere with land
areas of the first and water areas of the
third, grid lines black, over a branch of
olive or, between two lightning bolts
argent; super-imposed over-all and flank-
ing the dexter and sinister, two stylized
arrows or. *Motto:* POWER FOR
PEACE. (Approved 5 Oct 1955.)

7th FIGHTER WING

Constituted as 7th Fighter Wing on 31
Mar 1944. *Activated* in Hawaii on 21 Apr
1944. Assigned to Seventh AF to provide
air defense for the Hawaiian Islands. *Redesignated* 7th Air Division in Dec 1947.
Inactivated in Hawaii on 1 May 1948.

Activated in England on 20 Mar 1951.
Assigned to Strategic Air Command. Op-
erated with components of Strategic Air
Command temporarily deployed to the
United Kingdom.

GROUPS. *15th* Fighter: 1945–1946. *21st*
Fighter: 1944. *30th* Bombardment: 1945–
1946. *81st* Fighter: 1946–1948. *508th*
Fighter: 1945.

STATIONS. Ft Shafter, TH, 21 Apr 1944;
Wheeler Field, TH, 18 Nov 1946–1 May
1948. South Ruislip, England, 20 Mar
1951–.

COMMANDERS. Col John M Weikert, 1
Jul 1944; Col Orrin L Grover, 24 Nov 1944;
Brig Gen John W Weikert, 15 Dec 1944;
Col Richard A Grussendorf, 22 Apr 1946;
Col Earl H Jacobsen, 10 Jun 1947; Col
Thomas W Blackburn, 26 Aug 1947–1 May
1948. Maj Gen Archie J Old Jr, 26 Apr
1951; Maj Gen John P McConnell, 23 May
1951; Maj Gen James C Selser Jr, 14 Mar
1953; Brig Gen Thomas C Musgrave Jr,

20 Jul 1954; Brig Gen James H Walsh, 10 Jul 1955–.

CAMPAIGNS. Asiatic-Pacific Theater.

DECORATIONS. None.

INSIGNE. *Shield:* Blue within a narrow yellow border, a vertical white sword partially sheathed, point down, the hilt in the shape of wings, the handle diagonally striped blue and yellow, the sword interlaced with a red seven terminating in a pointed foot between two smaller red flashes, all three outlined in white; interlaced with the flashes and behind the sword a spray of yellow laurel leaves. (Approved 16 Sep 1954.)

9th FIGHTER WING

Constituted as 9th Pursuit Wing on 19 Oct 1940. *Activated* on 18 Dec 1940. *Inactivated* on 1 Oct 1941.

Redesignated 9th Fighter Wing. *Activated* on 24 Jul 1942. Moved to the Middle East, Dec 1942–Feb 1943. Assigned to Ninth AF. Apparently no combat groups were assigned to the wing during 1942–1943. *Inactivated* on 31 Mar 1943.

GROUPS. *14th:* 1941. *51st:* 1941.

STATIONS. March Field, Calif, 18 Dec 1940–1 Oct 1941. Drew Field, Fla, 24 Jul–13 Dec 1942; El Kabrit, Egypt, 1 Feb–31 Mar 1943.

COMMANDERS. Unkn.

CAMPAIGNS. European-African-Middle Eastern Theater.

DECORATIONS. None.

INSIGNE. None.

10th FIGHTER WING

Constituted as 10th Pursuit Wing on 19 Oct 1940. *Activated* on 18 Dec 1940. *Inactivated* on 7 Dec 1941.

Redesignated 10th Fighter Wing. *Activated* on 1 Oct 1942. Assigned to Eighth AF but attached to Third AF for manning and training. No groups were assigned. *Inactivated* on 1 May 1943. *Disbanded* on 1 Dec 1943.

GROUPS. *20th:* 1940–1941. *35th:* 1940–1941.

STATIONS. Hamilton Field, Calif, 18 Dec 1940–7 Dec 1941. Drew Field, Fla, 1 Oct 1942–1 May 1943.

COMMANDERS. Col Michael F Davis, Dec 1940–1941. Maj William L Hayes Jr, Oct 1942–unkn.

CAMPAIGNS. None.

DECORATIONS. None.

INSIGNE. *Shield:* On an ultramarine blue disc a golden orange winged sunburst above two arrows of like color, crossed salterwise and with points down, in front of a white cloud. (Approved 1 Oct 1941.)

11th FIGHTER WING

Constituted as 11th Pursuit Wing on 19 Oct 1940. *Activated* on 18 Dec 1940. *Inactivated* on 1 Oct 1941.

Redesignated 11th Fighter Wing. *Activated* on 1 Nov 1942. Assigned to Eighth AF but attached to Third AF for manning and training. No groups were assigned. *Inactivated* in the US on 1 May 1943. *Disbanded* on 1 Dec 1943.

GROUPS. *54th:* 1941. *55th:* 1941.

STATIONS. Hamilton Field, Calif, 18 Dec 1940; Portland, Ore, Jun–1 Oct 1941. Drew Field, Fla, 1 Nov 1942–1 May 1943.

COMMANDERS. Unkn.

CAMPAIGNS. None.

DECORATIONS. None.

INSIGNE. None.

12th BOMBARDMENT WING

Constituted as 12th Pursuit Wing on 19 Oct 1940. *Activated* in the Panama Canal Zone on 20 Nov 1940. *Inactivated* on 6 Mar 1942.

Redesignated 12th Bombardment Wing. *Activated* in the US on 8 Sep 1942. No groups were assigned. Moved to England, Nov–Dec 1942. Assigned to Eighth AF. All personnel and equipment were withdrawn in Jan 1943. *Disbanded* in England on 9 Oct 1944.

THE OLD ONE TWO

Reconstituted, redesignated 12th Bombardment Wing (Light), and allotted to the reserve, on 3 Jul 1947. *Activated* in the US on 3 Aug 1947. *Redesignated* 12th Air Division (Bombardment) in Apr 1948. *Inactivated* on 27 Jun 1949.

Redesignated 12th Air Division. *Organized* on 10 Feb 1951. Assigned to Strategic Air Command.

COMPONENTS. *Groups. 16th:* 1940–1942. *32d:* 1941–1942. *37th:* 1940–1942. *53d:* 1941–1942. *321st:* 1947–1949. *322d:* 1947–1949. *Wings. 22d* Bombardment: 1951–. *44th* Bombardment: 1951. *106th* Bombardment: 1951–1952. *320th* Bombardment: 1952–.

STATIONS. Albrook Field, CZ, 20 Nov 1940–6 Mar 1942. MacDill Field, Fla, 8 Sep 1942–28 Nov 1943; Chelveston, England, c. 17 Dec 1942; Marks Hall, England, 12 Jan 1943–9 Oct 1944. Cleveland Mun Aprt, Ohio, 3 Aug 1947–27 Jun 1949. March AFB, Calif, 10 Feb 1951–.

COMMANDERS. Brig Gen Adlai H Gilkeson, 20 Nov 1940–c. 6 Mar 1942. 2d Lt Leonard B Flemmons Jr, c. 10 Sep 1942; Maj George M Green, c. 24 Sep 1942; Maj Henry G Silleck, c. 17 Nov 1942; Maj Thomas L Dawson, c. 25 Nov 1942–c. 19 Jan 1943. Brig Gen Wiley D Ganey, 10 Feb 1951; Brig Gen Howell M Estes Jr, 1 Mar 1952; Brig Gen Charles B Westover, 23 Jul 1953–.

CAMPAIGNS. American Theater; European-African-Middle Eastern Theater.

DECORATIONS. None.

INSIGNE. *Shield:* Azure (sky blue), in dexter chief a star argent, charged with a torteau, two fuzes of bomb or, encased with boxing gloves proper, in bend, gloves toward base, surrounded with indications of speed lines argent. *Motto:* THE OLD ONE TWO. (Approved 16 Apr 1952.)

13th BOMBARDMENT WING

Constituted as 13th Composite Wing on 2 Oct 1940 and *activated* on 10 Oct. Moved to Puerto Rico at the end of the same month. *Inactivated* on 25 Oct 1941.

Redesignated 13th Bombardment Wing. *Activated* in the US on 1 Oct 1942. Assigned to Eighth AF. *Redesignated* 13th Bombardment Wing (Medium) in Feb 1943. Moved to England, May–Jun 1943. *Redesignated* 13th Combat Bombardment Wing (Heavy) in Aug 1943. Groups were assigned in Sep 1943 and the wing served in combat in the European theater until Apr 1945. *Redesignated* 13th Bombard-

ment Wing (Heavy) in Jun 1945. Returned to the US in Aug 1945. *Redesignated* 13th Bombardment Wing (Very Heavy) in Aug 1945. *Inactivated* on 17 Oct 1945.

GROUPS. *25th* Bombardment: 1940–1941. *36th* Pursuit: 1941. *40th* Bombardment: 1941. *95th* Bombardment: 1943–1945. *100th* Bombardment: 1943–1945. *390th* Bombardment: 1943–1945. *490th* Bombardment: 1945. *493d* Bombardment: 1945.

STATIONS. Langley Field, Va, 10–26 Oct 1940; Borinquen Field, PR, 1 Nov 1940; San Juan, PR, c. 6 Jan 1941; Borinquen Field, PR, c. 1 May–25 Oct 1941. MacDill Field, Fla, 1 Oct 1942–c. 10 May 1943; Marks Hall, England, c. 2 Jun 1943; Camp Blainey, England, c. 13 Jun 1943; Horham, England, 13 Sep 1943–c. 6 Aug 1945; Sioux Falls AAFld, SD, c. 15 Aug 1945; Peterson Field, Colo, 17 Aug–17 Oct 1945.

COMMANDERS. Capt Kenneth O Sanborn, c. 10 Oct 1940; Brig Gen Follett Bradley, c. 1 Nov 1940; Lt Col Robert V Ignico, c. 4 Aug 1941; Brig Gen Douglas B Netherwood, c. 7 Sep–25 Oct 1941. Maj Henry G Silleck, 1942–unkn; Col Alfred A Kessler Jr, 16 Sep 1943; Col Harold Q Huglin, c. 9 Feb–c. 1 Apr 1944; Col Edgar M Wittan, 17 Apr 1944; Col Karl Truesdell Jr, 13 Sep 1944; Col Hunter Harris Jr, 25 Sep 1944; Brig Gen Alfred A Kessler Jr, 5 Nov 1944; Brig Gen Harold Q Huglin, 19 Nov 1944; Lt Col Clifton D Wright, 18 Jul 1945–unkn; Lt Col Paul C Hutchins, 31 Aug 1945–unkn.

CAMPAIGNS. Air Offensive, Europe; Normandy; Northern France; Rhineland; Ardennes-Alsace; Central Europe.

DECORATIONS. None.

INSIGNE. None.

14th BOMBARDMENT WING

Constituted as 14th Pursuit Wing on 19 Oct 1940. *Activated* in Hawaii on 1 Nov 1940. Suffered heavy losses during the Japanese attack on Pearl Harbor on 7 Dec 1941 but managed to shoot down several enemy aircraft. *Inactivated* in Hawaii on 23 Jan 1942.

Redesignated 14th Bombardment Wing. *Activated* in the US on 1 Oct 1942. *Redesignated* 14th Bombardment Wing (Heavy) in Feb 1943. Moved to England, May–Jun 1943. *Redesignated* 14th Combat Bombardment Wing (Heavy) in Aug 1943. Received groups in Sep 1943 and served in combat in the European theater until Apr 1945. *Redesignated* 14th Bombardment Wing (Heavy) in Jun 1945. Returned to the US in Aug. *Inactivated* on 7 Nov 1945.

Redesignated 14th Air Division. *Organized* on 10 Feb 1951. Assigned to Strategic Air Command.

COMPONENTS. *Groups. 15th* Pursuit: 1940–1942. *18th* Pursuit: 1940–1942. *44th* Bombardment: 1943, 1943–1945. *94th* Bombardment: 1945. *392d* Bombardment: 1943–1945. *447th* Bombardment: 1945. *486th* Bombardment: 1945. *487th* Bombardment: 1945. *491st* Bombardment: 1944–1945. *492d* Bombardment: 1944. *Wings. 5th* Bombardment: 1951–. *9th* Bombardment: 1951–1953.

STATIONS. Wheeler Field, TH, 1 Nov 1940–23 Jan 1942. MacDill Field, Fla, 1 Oct 1942–c. 9 May 1943; Camp Lynn, England, c. 4 Jun 1943; Hethel, England, c. 9 Jun 1943; Camp Thomas, England, c. 1 Jul 1943; Shipdham, England, 13 Sep 1943; Bury St Edmunds, England, 13 Jun–26 Aug 1945; McChord Field, Wash, 6 Sep–7 Nov 1945. Travis AFB, Calif, 10 Feb 1951–.

COMMANDERS. Col Harvey S Burwell, Nov 1940; Brig Gen Howard C Davidson, 7 May 1941–c. 23 Jan 1942. Maj Alan W Detweiler, 16 Dec 1942–unkn; Lt Col Roderick Ott, 1943; Brig Gen Leon W Johnson, c. 14 Sep 1943; Brig Gen Robert W Burns, c. 16 Jun 1945; Lt Col Charles D Birdsall, c. 24 Jul 1945–unkn. Brig Gen J W Kelly, 10 Feb 1951; Col John M Sterling, 16 Sep 1951; Brig Gen Richard H

Carmichael, 22 Oct 1951; Brig Gen Stanley J Donovan, 16 May 1953; Brig Gen Alfred F Kalberer, 1 Aug 1955–.

CAMPAIGNS. Central Pacific; Air Offensive, Europe; Normandy; Northern France; Rhineland; Ardennes-Alsace; Central Europe.

DECORATIONS. None.

INSIGNE. *Shield:* Quartered, azure and white; first quarter an atomic symbol of the second; second quarter, an olive branch vert and a sword proper, hilt and pommel or, in saltire; superimposed over the third and fourth quarter, a silhouetted stylized heavy bomber sable in fess, nose to the dexter, all within a diminutive border of the last. *Motto:* On a light pink scroll, edged and inscribed black, DAY AND NIGHT—PEACE OR WAR. (Approved 10 May 1957.)

15th BOMBARDMENT TRAINING WING

Constituted as 15th Bombardment Wing on 19 Oct 1940. *Activated* on 18 Dec 1940. Apparently never had sufficient personnel to carry out effectively its mission of light bombardment operations and training. *Inactivated* on 3 Sep 1941.

Activated on 23 Jun 1942. Assigned to Second AF. *Redesignated* 15th Bombardment Training Wing in Jan 1943, and 15th Bombardment Operational Training Wing in Apr 1943. Trained groups and heavy bombardment replacement crews until Feb 1945 when it ceased all activity.

Inactivated on 9 Apr 1946. *Disbanded* on 8 Oct 1948.

GROUPS. *47th:* 1941. *48th:* 1941. (Various groups assigned for training, 1942–1945.)

STATIONS. March Field, Calif, 18 Dec 1940; Fresno, Calif, c. 2 Aug–3 Sep 1941. Gowen Field, Idaho, 23 Jun 1942; Sioux City AAB, Iowa, Nov 1942; Gowen Field, Idaho, Jul 1943; Pueblo AAB, Colo, May 1944; Colorado Springs, Colo, 18 Sep 1944–9 Apr 1946.

COMMANDERS. Unkn, 1940–1941. Col Ford J Lauer, c. 23 Jun 1942; Brig Gen Robert F Travis, 3 Sep 1942; Col Hugo P Rush, Jul 1943; Col Henry K Mooney, Jan 1944; Lt Col Willis G Carter, Jul 1944; Col Harold A McGinnis, c. 1 Sep 1944; Col Brooke E Allen, c. Oct 1944; Brig Gen Julius K Lacey, c. Jul 1945–unkn.

CAMPAIGNS. American Theater.

DECORATIONS. None.

INSIGNE. *Shield:* On a light blue rectangle, long axis vertical, corners engrailed, a chevron inverted gold between a gold stylized wing in chief and fifteen gold stars in base, all within a border of gold. (Approved 26 Mar 1943.)

16th BOMBARDMENT TRAINING WING

Constituted as 16th Bombardment Wing on 19 Oct 1940. *Activated* on 18 Dec 1940. Apparently did not have sufficient personnel for effective training and operations. *Inactivated* on 1 Sep 1941.

Activated on 23 Jun 1942. Assigned to Second AF. *Redesignated* 16th Bombardment Training Wing in Jan 1943, 16th Bombardment Operational Training Wing in Apr 1943, and 16th Bombardment Operational Training Wing (Very Heavy) in May 1945. Began training heavy bombardment groups and personnel in Jun 1942; later changed to very heavy bombardment training, which lasted until operations ceased late in 1945. *Inactivated* on 9 Apr 1946. *Disbanded* on 8 Oct 1948.

GROUPS. *45th:* 1941. *46th:* 1941. (Various groups assigned for training, 1942–1945.)

STATIONS. Langley Field, Va, 18 Dec 1940; Bowman Field, Ky, Mar–1 Sep 1941. Wendover Field, Utah, 23 Jun 1942; Biggs Field, Tex, Nov 1942; Davis-Monthan Field, Ariz, c. 1 Jun 1943; Biggs Field, Tex, Oct 1943; Colorado Springs, Colo, Dec 1945–9 Apr 1946.

COMMANDERS. Brig Gen Junius W Jones, c. Apr–c. 1 Sep 1941. Col Ernest

H Lawson, 23 Jun 1942; Brig Gen Robert B Williams, 4 Apr 1943; Col Walter R Agee, May 1943; Brig Gen Newton Longfellow, 11 Oct 1943; Col Claude E Duncan, c. 25 Nov 1945–unkn.

CAMPAIGNS. American Theater.
DECORATIONS. None.
INSIGNE. None.

17th BOMBARDMENT TRAINING WING

Constituted as 17th Bombardment Wing on 3 Oct 1940. *Activated* on 18 Dec 1940. *Inactivated* on 1 Sep 1941.

Activated on 23 Jun 1942. Assigned to Second AF. *Redesignated* 17th Bombardment Training Wing in Jan 1943, and 17th Bombardment Operational Training Wing in Apr 1943. Trained a number of heavy bombardment groups; also trained heavy bombardment crews. *Inactivated* on 15 Nov 1943.

Redesignated 17th Bombardment Operational Training Wing (Very Heavy). *Activated* on 11 Mar 1944. Assigned to Second AF. Trained very heavy bombardment organizations and personnel. *Inactivated* on 9 Apr 1946. *Disbanded* on 8 Oct 1948.

GROUPS. *3d* Bombardment: 1940–1941. *27th* Bombardment: 1940–1941.

STATIONS. Savannah, Ga, 18 Dec 1940–1 Sep 1941. Rapid City, SD, 23 Jun 1942; Walla Walla AAFld, Wash, c. 1 Jul–15 Nov 1943. Smoky Hill AAFld, Kan, 11 Mar 1944; Colorado Springs, Colo, Apr 1944; Grand Island AAFld, Neb, May

1944; Sioux City AAB, Iowa, Feb 1945; Ft Worth AAFld, Tex, Dec 1945–9 Apr 1946.

COMMANDERS. Maj Gen Lewis H Brereton, Dec 1940–unkn; Col Asa N Duncan, c. 7 Aug–c. 1 Sep 1941. Brig Gen Walter R Peck, 5 Jul 1942; Col Allen W Reed, 14 Sep–c. 15 Nov 1943. Brig Gen Frank A Armstrong Jr, 12 Apr 1944; Brig Gen Robert F Travis, c. 7 Nov 1944; Col Kermit D Stevens, Aug 1945; Brig Gen Hugo P Rush, 7 Sep 1945; Brig Gen Robert F Travis, 5 Nov 1945–unkn.

CAMPAIGNS. American Theater.

DECORATIONS. None.

INSIGNE. None.

18th REPLACEMENT WING

Constituted as 18th Composite Wing on 8 May 1929. Activated in Hawaii on 1 May 1931. Served as part of the defense force for the Hawaiian Islands. Redesignated 18th Wing in 1937, and 18th Bombardment Wing in 1940. Inactivated in Hawaii on 29 Jan 1942.

Redesignated 18th Replacement Wing. Activated in the US on 23 Jun 1942. Assigned to Second AF. Processed personnel entering Second AF for assignments to units. Disbanded on 11 Apr 1944.

GROUPS. 5th Bombardment: 1931–1942. 11th Bombardment: 1940–1942. 18th Pursuit: 1931–1940.

STATIONS. Ft Shafter, TH, 1 May 1931; Hickam Field, TH, 30 Oct 1937–29 Jan 1942. Salt Lake City, Utah, 23 Jun 1942–11 Apr 1944.

COMMANDERS. Lt Col Gerald C Brant, May 1931; Lt Col Delos C Emmons, Aug 1934; Lt Col John C McDonnell, Jul 1936; Lt Col Hume Peabody, Jul 1936; Lt Col John C McDonnell, Jul 1936; Brig Gen Barton K Yount, Sep 1936; Col Millard F Harmon, Jul 1937; Brig Gen Barton K Yount, Jul 1937; Brig Gen Walter H Frank, Sep 1938; Col Shepler W FitzGerald, Jul 1940; Col Howard C Davidson, Oct 1940; Brig Gen Jacob H Rudolph, unkn; Brig Gen Willis H Hale, 20–29 Jan 1942. Col Henry W Harms, 23 Jun 1942; Col Frank W Wright, 30 Jan 1944; Col Henry W Harms, 27 Mar–11 Apr 1944.

CAMPAIGNS. American Theater; Central Pacific.

DECORATIONS. None.

INSIGNE. None.

20th BOMBARDMENT WING

Constituted as 20th Bombardment Wing on 19 Oct 1940. Activated on 18 Dec 1940. Inactivated on 1 Sep 1941.

Activated on 1 Nov 1942. Redesignated 20th Bombardment Wing (Heavy) in Feb 1943. Moved to England, May–Jun 1943, for duty with Eighth AF. Redesignated 20th Combat Bombardment Wing (Heavy) in Aug 1943. Received its first groups in Nov 1943 and served in combat in the European theater from Dec 1943 until Apr 1945. Redesignated 20th Bombardment Wing (Heavy) in Jun 1945. Returned to the US in Aug 1945. Redesignated 20th Bombardment Wing (Very Heavy) in Aug, and VIII Bomber Command (Very Heavy) in Oct 1945. Apparently had no combat components assigned after Aug 1945. *Inactivated* on 10 Nov 1946. *Disbanded* on 8 Oct 1948.

GROUPS. *7th:* 1940–1941. *34th:* 1945. *42d:* 1941. *93d:* 1943–1945. *385th:* 1945. *388th:* 1945. *446th:* 1943–1945. *448th:* 1943–1945. *452d:* 1945. *489th:* 1944.

STATIONS. Ft Douglas, Utah, 18 Dec 1940–1 Sep 1941. MacDill Field, Fla, 1 Nov 1942–c. 8 May 1943; Camp Lynn, England, c. 9 Jun 1943; Cheddington, England, c. 1 Jul 1943; Horsham St Faith, England, c. 14 Sep 1943; Hethel, England, 24 Sep 1943; Hardwick, England, c. 7 Nov 1943; Snetterton Heath, England, c. 13 Jun–6 Aug 1945; Sioux Falls AAFld, SD, c. 15 Aug 1945; Peterson Field, Colo, 17 Aug 1945; MacDill Field, Fla, 14 May–10 Nov 1946.

COMMANDERS. Col Shepler W Fitz-Gerald, 16 Jan 1941; Brig Gen Walter H Frank, 6 Feb 1941; Brig Gen Ralph Royce, 2 Mar 1941; Col Lowell H Smith, 6 May–c. 1 Sep 1941. Col John H Hayden, c. 30 Oct 1943; Col Jack W Wood, 29 Dec 1943; Brig Gen Edward J Timberlake Jr, 25 Sep 1944; Col Leland G Fiegel, 17 May 1945; Brig Gen Archie J Old Jr, 18 Jun 1945–unkn; Col Brooke E Allen, c. 18 Aug 1945; Col John W Warren, 22 Aug 1945; Brig Gen Hugo P Rush, 2 Nov 1945–unkn; Col Neil B Harding, 14 May 1946; Maj Gene A Nelson, 16 Aug 1946; Maj Leroy S English, 10 Sep 1946; Lt Col Ermanno D Grana, 3–c. 10 Nov 1946.

CAMPAIGNS. American Theater; Air Offensive, Europe; Normandy; Northern France; Rhineland; Ardennes-Alsace; Central Europe.

DECORATIONS. None.

INSIGNE. None.

21st BOMBARDMENT WING

Constituted as 21st Bombardment Wing on 16 Dec 1942 and *activated* on 22 Dec. Assigned to Second AF. Functioned throughout the war as a staging wing, processing heavy bombardment crews and aircraft to prepare them for overseas movement; in Apr 1944 began processing men returning to the US from combat zones. *Redesignated* I Staging Command in Sep 1945. Assigned to Fourth AF in Nov. *Inactivated* on 3 Apr 1946.

Redesignated 21st Bombardment Wing (Very Heavy). Allotted to the reserve. *Activated* on 20 Dec 1946. *Redesignated* 21st Air Division (Bombardment) in Apr 1948. *Inactivated* on 27 Jun 1949.

Redesignated 21st Air Division. *Activated* on 16 Feb 1951. Assigned to Strategic Air Command.

(This wing is not related to a 21st Bombardment Wing that was constituted on 19 Oct 1940, activated at Barksdale Field on 1 Nov 1940, inactivated on 1 Nov 1941, and disbanded on 15 Dec 1942.)

COMPONENTS. *Groups.* *95th:* 1947–1949. *384th:* 1947–1949. *Wings.* *44th* Bombardment: 1951–1952. *55th* Reconnaissance: 1952–. *90th* Reconnaissance: 1951–.

STATIONS. Smoky Hill AB, Kan, 22 Dec 1942; Topeka AAFld, Kan, May 1943; Merced AAFld, Calif, c. 7 Oct 1945–3 Apr 1946. Memphis Mun Aprt, Tenn, 20 Dec 1946–27 Jun 1949. Forbes AFB, Kan, 16 Feb 1951–.

COMMANDERS. Brig Gen Albert F Hegenberger, 22 Dec 1942; Col Henry W Harms, Feb 1944; Col Cornelius W Cousland, 26 Dec 1944; Col Wallace S Dawson, 21 Jan 1945; Col Ralph E Koon, 29 May 1945; Brig Gen James M Fitzmaurice, 19 Jul 1945–c. Apr 1946. Maj Gen David W Hutchison, 16 Mar 1951; Brig Gen Joseph D C Caldara, 4 Dec 1952; Brig Gen David Wade, 15 Apr 1954; Brig Gen Henry R Sullivan Jr, 25 Jul 1955–.

CAMPAIGNS. American Theater.

DECORATIONS. None.

INSIGNE. *Shield:* Per bend enhanced, azure and argent, in base a branch of olive proper, over all a sword bend sinisterwise proper, hilt and pommel or, point to dexter base, in chief five stars or, encircling the hilt and pommel of the sword, three and two. (Approved 17 Jul 1952.)

24th COMPOSITE WING

Constituted as 24th Composite Wing on 19 Nov 1942. *Activated* in Iceland on 25 Dec 1942. Served in the defense of Iceland. *Disbanded* on 15 Jun 1944.

Reconstituted on 5 Aug 1946 and *activated* in Puerto Rico on 25 Aug. Assigned to Caribbean Air Command. No tactical groups were assigned, but the wing supervised various air force units and bases in the Antilles. *Inactivated* in Puerto Rico on 28 Jul 1948.

GROUPS. *342d:* 1942–1944.

STATIONS. Iceland, 25 Dec 1942–15 Jun 1944. Borinquen Field, PR, 25 Aug 1946–28 Jul 1948.

COMMANDERS. Brig Gen George P Tourtellot, c. 25 Dec 1942; Brig Gen Early E W Duncan, c. 5–15 Jun 1944. Brig Gen John A Samford, c. Jan 1947–c. 28 Jul 1948.

CAMPAIGNS. Air Combat, EAME Theater.

DECORATIONS. None.

INSIGNE. None.

25th ANTISUBMARINE WING

Constituted as 25th Antisubmarine Wing on 17 Nov 1942 and *activated* on 20 Nov. Assigned to AAF Antisubmarine Command and later (Aug 1943) to First AF. Conducted patrols, primarily off the eastern coast of the US. *Disbanded* on 15 Oct 1943.

SQUADRONS. *1st:* 1942–1943. *2d* (formerly 523d Bombardment): 1942–1943. *3d:* 1942–1943. *4th:* 1942–1943. *5th:* 1942–1943. *6th:* 1942–1943. *11th:* 1942–1943. *12th:* 1942–1943. *13th:* 1942–1943. *14th:* 1942–1943. *16th* (formerly 521st Bombardment): 1942–1943. *18th:* 1942–1943. *19th:* 1942–1943. *20th:* 1943. *22d:* 1943. *24th:* 1943.

STATIONS. New York, NY, 20 Nov 1942–15 Oct 1943.

COMMANDERS. Col Howard Moore, 20 Nov 1942; Col Wallace E Whitson, 22 Dec 1942; Col Chester A Charles, 8 Jun 1943; Col Ephraim M Hampton, 20 Aug 1943–unkn.

CAMPAIGNS. Antisubmarine, American Theater.

DECORATIONS. None.

INSIGNE. None.

26th ANTISUBMARINE WING

Constituted as 26th Antisubmarine Wing on 17 Nov 1942 and *activated* on 20 Nov. Assigned to AAF Antisubmarine Command and later (Aug 1943) to First AF. Flew patrols in the Gulf of Mexico and the Caribbean Sea. *Disbanded* on 15 Oct 1943.

SQUADRONS. *7th:* 1942–1943. *8th:* 1942–1943. *9th:* 1942–1943. *10th:* 1942–1943. *15th:* 1942–1943. *17th:* 1942–1943. *21st:* 1943. *23d:* 1943. *25th:* 1943

STATIONS. Miami, Fla, 20 Nov 1942–15 Oct 1943.

COMMANDERS. Col Harry A Halverson, c. 20 Nov 1942–1943.

CAMPAIGNS. Antisubmarine, American Theater.

DECORATIONS. None.

INSIGNE. None.

40th BOMBARDMENT WING

Constituted as 40th Bombardment Wing on 15 Jan 1943 and *activated* on 21 Jan. *Redesignated* 40th Bombardment Wing (Heavy) in May 1943. Moved to England, May–Jun 1943, for duty with Eighth AF. *Redesignated* 40th Combat Bombardment Wing (Heavy) in Aug 1943, and 40th Bombardment Wing (Heavy) in Jun 1945. Served in combat in the European theater from Sep 1943 until Apr 1945, receiving a DUC for an attack on aircraft factories in central Germany on 11 Jan 1944. Remained in Europe after the war as part of United States Air Forces in Europe. *Inactivated* in Germany on 25 Dec 1946.

Redesignated 40th Air Division. *Organized* in the US on 14 Mar 1951. Assigned to Strategic Air Command.

COMPONENTS. *Groups. 2d:* 1945–1946. *92d:* 1943–1946. *305th:* 1943–1945, 1945–1946. *306th:* 1943–1945, 1945–1946. *384th:* 1945–1946. *492d:* 1944–1945. *Wings. 31st* Fighter: 1951–. *108th* Fighter: 1951. *146th* Fighter: 1951. *508th* Fighter: 1952–.

STATIONS. MacDill Field, Fla, 21 Jan–c. 17 May 1943; Brampton Grange, England, Jun 1943; Thurleigh, England, c. 16 Sep 1943; Istres, France, 26 Jun 1945; Erlangen, Germany, 15 Nov 1945–25 Dec 1946. Turner AFB, Ga, 14 Mar 1951–.

COMMANDERS. Maj Charles Normand, 1943–unkn; Brig Gen Howard M Turner, 16 Sep 1943; Col Anthony Q Mustoe, 22 Oct 1944; Brig Gen Emil C Kiel, 1 Mar–c. 1 Dec 1946. Col Eugene H Snavely, 14 Mar 1951; Brig Gen Thayer S Olds, 1 Jun 1951; Col Hubert Zemke, 11 Oct 1955–.

CAMPAIGNS. Air Offensive, Europe; Normandy; Northern France; Rhineland; Ardennes-Alsace; Central Europe.

DECORATIONS. Distinguished Unit Citation: Germany, 11 Jan 1944.

INSIGNE. *Shield:* Azure, in dexter chief a stylized comet gules, bordered argent, with tail of stripes, gules, argent, and gules curved toward base edge, overall four lightning flashes or, bend sinisterwise, one above the other. (Approved 14 Apr 1952.)

41st BOMBARDMENT WING

Constituted as 41st Bombardment Wing (Heavy) on 29 Jan 1943. *Activated* on 16 Feb 1943. Moved to England in Jul 1943 for duty with Eighth AF. *Redesignated* 41st Combat Bombardment Wing (Heavy) in Aug 1943. Served in the European theater from Sep 1943 to Apr 1945, receiving a DUC for a raid on aircraft factories in central Germany on 11 Jan 1944. *Disbanded* in England on 18 Jun 1945.

GROUPS. *303d:* 1943–1945. *379th:* 1943–1945. *384th:* 1943–1945.

STATIONS. Salt Lake City AAB, Utah, 16 Feb 1943; Rapid City AAB, SD, Mar–c. 4 Jul 1943; Brampton Grange, England, c. 26 July 1943; Molesworth, England, c. 16 Sep 1943–18 Jun 1945.

COMMANDERS. Lt Col Donald S Graham, 1943–unkn; Brig Gen Robert F Travis, 16 Sep 1943; Col Maurice A Preston, 11 Oct 1944; Col Lewis E Lyle, May 1945–unkn.

CAMPAIGNS. Air Offensive, Europe; Normandy; Northern France; Rhineland; Ardennes-Alsace; Central Europe.

DECORATIONS. Distinguished Unit Citation: Germany, 11 Jan 1944.

INSIGNE. None.

42d BOMBARDMENT WING

Constituted as 42d Bombardment Wing (Dive) on 8 Feb 1943 and *activated* on 16 Feb. *Redesignated* 42d Bombardment Wing (Medium), transferred overseas without personnel and equipment, and assigned to Twelfth AF, on 31 Jul 1943. Received groups in Aug 1943 and served in combat in the Mediterranean and European theaters until the end of the war. Returned to the US in Oct 1945. *Inactivated* on 25 Oct 1945.

Redesignated 42d Air Division. *Organized* on 10 Mar 1951. Assigned to Strategic Air Command.

COMPONENTS. *Groups. 1st* Fighter: 1943. *17th* Bombardment: 1943–1945. *319th* Bombardment: 1943–1944. *320th* Bombardment: 1943–1945. *325th* Fighter: 1943. *Wings. 1st* Fighter: 1951–. *27th* Fighter: 1951–. *131st* Fighter: 1951.

STATIONS. Birmingham AAB, Ala, 16 Feb–31 Jul 1943; North Africa, 31 Jul 1943; Ariana, Tunisia, 21 Aug 1943; El-mas, Sardinia, 15 Nov 1943; Borgo, Corsica, 21 Sep 1944; Dijon, France, 24 Nov 1944; Reims, France, Jul–c. Oct 1945; Camp Shanks, NY, 24–25 Oct 1945. Bergstrom AFB, Tex, 10 Mar 1951–.

COMMANDERS. Brig Gen Robert M Webster, 24 Aug 1943; Brig Gen John P Doyle, 1 Sep 1944–1945. Brig Gen Clarence T Edwinson, c. 15 Mar 1951–.

CAMPAIGNS. Naples-Foggia; Anzio; Rome-Arno; Southern France; North Apennines; Rhineland; Central Europe.

DECORATIONS. French Croix de Guerre with Palm: Apr–Jun 1944.

INSIGNE. None.

45th BOMBARDMENT WING

Constituted as 45th Bombardment Wing (Medium) on 15 Feb 1943. *Activated* on 1 Apr 1943. *Redesignated* 45th Bombardment Wing (Heavy). Moved to England in Aug 1943 for duty with Eighth AF. *Redesignated* 45th Combat Bombardment Wing (Heavy). Groups were assigned in Sep 1943 and the wing participated in combat in the European theater until Apr 1945. *Disbanded* in England on 18 Jun 1945.

Reconstituted and *redesignated* 45th Air Division, on 24 Sep 1954. *Activated* in the US on 8 Oct 1954. Assigned to Strategic Air Command.

COMPONENTS. *Groups. 34th:* 1945. *96th:* 1943–1945. *385th:* 1945. *388th:* 1943–1945. *452d:* 1944–1945. *Wings.* 42d Bombardment: 1954–.

STATIONS. MacDill Field, Fla, 1 Apr–c. 3 Aug 1943; Brampton Grange, England, c. 25 Aug 1943; Snetterton Heath, England, 13 Sep 1943–18 Jun 1945. Loring, AFB, Maine, 8 Oct 1954–.

COMMANDERS. Maj Carl L Liles, c. Apr 1943–unkn; Col Archie J Old Jr, 14 Sep 1943; Brig Gen Charles P Cabell, c. 1 Dec 1943; Brig Gen Archie J Old Jr, 12 Apr 1944–18 Jun 1945. Brig Gen Bertram C Harrison, 8 Oct 1954; Brig Gen William K Martin, 18 Jun 1955–.

CAMPAIGNS. Air Offensive, Europe; Normandy; Northern France; Rhineland; Ardennes-Alsace; Central Europe.

DECORATIONS. None.

INSIGNE. None.

47th BOMBARDMENT WING

Constituted as 7th Pursuit Wing on 19 Oct 1940. *Activated* on 18 Dec 1940. *Inactivated* on 31 Aug 1941.

Redesignated 7th Fighter Wing. *Activated* on 7 Jun 1942. Moved to North Africa, Oct–Nov 1942, to operate with Twelfth AF. *Redesignated* 47th Bom-

bardment Wing (Medium) in Feb 1943. Assigned to Fifteenth AF in Nov 1943 and afterward operated as a heavy bombardment organization until the war ended. *Redesignated* 47th Bombardment Wing (Heavy) in Apr 1945. Returned to the US in May. *Redesignated* 47th Bombardment Wing (Very Heavy) in Jun. *Inactivated* on 15 Oct 1945.

Redesignated 47th Air Division. *Organized* on 10 Feb 1951. Assigned to Strategic Air Command.

COMPONENTS. *Groups.* *8th* Pursuit: 1940–1941. *17th* Bombardment: 1943. *33d* Fighter: 1940–1941; 1942–1943, 1943. *57th* Pursuit: 1940–1941. *81st* Fighter: 1942–1943. *82d* Fighter: 1943–1944. *98th* Bombardment: 1943, 1943–1945. *310th* Bombardment: 1943. *319th* Bombardment: 1943. *320th* Bombardment: 1943. *321st* Bombardment: 1943. *325th* Fighter: 1943. *376th* Bombardment: 1943, 1943–1945. *449th* Bombardment: 1944–1945. *450th* Bombardment: 1944–1945. *451st* Bombardment: 1944. *489th* Bombard-

ment: 1945. *Wings.* *6th* Bombardment: 1951–. *509th* Bombardment: 1951–.

STATIONS. Mitchel Field, NY, 18 Dec 1940–31 Aug 1941. Harrisburg Mun Aprt, Pa, 7 Jun–Oct 1942; Casablanca, French Morocco, Nov 1942; Chateaudun, Algeria, Jan 1943; El Guerrah, Algeria, c. 1 Mar 1943; Souk-el-Arba, Tunisia, 8 Jun 1943; Hammamet, Tunisia, 7 Aug 1943; Manduria, Italy, 11 Nov 1943–May 1945; Sioux Falls, SD, May 1945; Sioux City AAB, Iowa, Jul–15 Oct 1945. Walker AFB, NM, 10 Feb 1951–.

COMMANDERS. Lt Col Edward M Morris, 1941. Maj Eugene Berglund, 7 Jun 1942; Col John C Crosthwaite, 14 Sep 1942; Brig Gen Carlyle H Ridenour, 14 Jan 1943; Brig Gen Joseph H Atkinson, 11 Feb 1944; Brig Gen Hugo P Rush, 5 Mar 1944–7 Oct 1945. Brig Gen Hunter Harris Jr, 10 Feb 1951; Col William H Blanchard, c. Dec 1951; Brig Gen Thomas C Musgrave Jr, 7 Apr 1952; Brig Gen Charles W Scott, 7 Jul 1954–.

CAMPAIGNS. Air Combat, EAME Theater; Air Offensive, Europe; Algeria-French Morocco; Tunisia; Sicily; Naples-Foggia; Rome-Arno; Normandy; Northern France; Southern France; North Apennines; Rhineland; Central Europe; Po Valley.

DECORATIONS. None.

INSIGNE. *Shield:* Sable, an atomic cloud proper (shades of red, orange and yellow) rising from base to chief, surmounted by a bend argent charged with a sword proper (blade silver, hilt and pommel gold), the blade entwined with a branch of olive vert. (Approved 6 Sep 1956.)

49th BOMBARDMENT WING

Constituted as 49th Bombardment Operational Training Wing (Medium) on 17 Mar 1943 and *activated* on 31 Mar. *Redesignated* 49th Bombardment Wing (Medium) in Oct 1943, and 49th Bombardment Wing (Heavy) in Dec. Moved to Italy (Feb–Apr 1944) where groups were assigned. Operated with Fifteenth AF in the Mediterranean and European theaters from Apr 1944 until May 1945. *Inactivated* in Italy on 16 Oct 1945.

Redesignated 49th Bombardment Wing (Very Heavy). Allotted to the reserve. *Activated* in the US on 20 Dec 1946. *Redesignated* 49th Air Division (Bombardment) in Apr 1948. *Inactivated* on 27 Jun 1949.

Redesignated 49th Air Division. *Activated* on 7 Nov 1951. Assigned to Tactical Air Command. *Redesignated* 49th Air Division (Operational) in Apr 1952.

Moved to England, May–Jun 1952, and assigned to United States Air Forces in Europe. No combat elements were assigned but wings were attached for operations.

GROUPS. *100th:* 1946–1949. *380th:* 1946–1949. *451st:* 1944–1945. *461st:* 1944–1945. *484th:* 1944–1945.

STATIONS. Columbia AAB, SC, 31 Mar 1943; Greenville AAB, SC, c. 28 Apr 1943–2 Feb 1944; Italy, Apr 1944–16 Oct 1945. Miami AAFld, Fla, 20 Dec 1946–27 Jun 1949. Langley AFB, Va, 7 Nov 1951–May 1952; Sculthorpe RAF Station, England, Jun 1952–.

COMMANDERS. Brig Gen William L Lee, c. 31 Mar 1943; Col Robert F Worden, 4 Aug–c. Oct 1945. Col James D Jones, 7 Nov 1951; Brig Gen John D Stevenson, Feb 1952; Brig Gen James F Whisenand, 26 Feb 1955–.

CAMPAIGNS. Air Combat, EAME Theater; Air Offensive, Europe; Rome-Arno; Normandy; Northern France; Southern France; North Apennines; Rhineland; Central Europe; Po Valley.

DECORATIONS. None.

INSIGNE. *Shield:* Quarterly argent and sable, rising from base the outline of an atomic cloud counterchanged, overall a lightning flash issuing from sinister chief and striking to dexter base or. (Approved 23 Dec 1953.)

50th TROOP CARRIER WING

Constituted as 50th Transport Wing on 8 Jan 1941 and *activated* on 14 Jan. Assigned to Office, Chief of the Air Corps.

Transported personnel, supplies, and materiel in the US, Alaska, and the Caribbean area. Assigned to Air Transport Command (later I Troop Carrier Command) in Apr 1942. *Redesignated* 50th Troop Carrier Wing in Jul 1942. Functioned as a training organization. Moved overseas, Sep–Oct 1943, and assigned to Ninth AF. Operated in the European and Mediterranean theaters until after the war. Transferred, without personnel and equipment, to the US in Sep 1945. Remanned and re-equipped. *Inactivated* on 31 Jul 1946.

GROUPS. *439th*: 1944–1945. *440th*: 1944–1945. *441st*: 1944–1945. *442d*: 1944–1945. (Numerous other groups assigned for training or operations, 1941–1944.)

STATIONS. Wright Field, Ohio, 14 Jan 1941; Camp Williams, Wis, 25 May 1942; Knobnoster, Mo, 9 Sep 1942; Camp Mackall, NC, 27 Apr 1943; Pope Field, NC, 28 Jul-29 Sep 1943; Cottesmore, England, 17 Oct 1943; Bottesford, England, 18 Nov 1943; Exeter, England, 26 Apr–1 Oct 1944; Le Mans, France, 1 Oct 1944; Chartres, France, 3 Nov 1944–29 Sep 1945; Pope Field, NC, 29 Sep 1945–31 Jul 1946.

COMMANDERS. Lt Col Fred S Borum, 14 Jan 1941; Lt Col P R Love, 8 Dec 1941; Col Harold L Clark, 29 May 1942; Lt Col Julian M Chappell, 2 Nov 1942; Col P R Love, 20 Nov 1942; Brig Gen Julian M Chappell, 4 Apr 1943–31 Jul 1946.

CAMPAIGNS. American Theater; Rome-Arno; Normandy; Northern France; Southern France; Rhineland; Ardennes-Alsace; Central Europe.

DECORATIONS. None.

INSIGNE. *Shield*: On a blue diamond edged in gold, a transport aircraft with stylized wing surmounting a pile voided of the second, issuing from sinister and extending to dexter base. *Motto*: NOBIS VOLANDUM EST—It will be flown by us. (Approved 22 Sep 1942.)

51st TROOP CARRIER WING

Constituted as 51st Transport Wing on 30 May 1942. *Activated* on 1 Jun 1942. *Redesignated* 51st Troop Carrier Wing in Jul 1942. Arrived in England in Sep 1942 and trained for the invasion of North Africa. Operated with Twelfth AF in North Africa and the Mediterranean area from Nov 1942 to May 1945. Moved to Germany in Sep 1945. Assigned to United States Air Forces in Europe. *Inactivated* in Germany on 5 Jan 1948.

GROUPS. *60th*: 1942–1945, 1946–1947. *61st*: 1942, 1946–1947. *62d*: 1942–1945.

64th: 1942–1945. *313th:* 1946–1947. *314th:* 1945–1946. *441st:* 1945–1946. *442d:* 1945–1946. *516th:* 1945–1946.

STATIONS. Pope Field, NC, 1 Jun–19 Jul 1942; Greenham Common, England, Sep–Nov 1942; Algiers, Algeria, 23 Nov 1942; La Senia, Algeria, 28 Mar 1943; Mascara, Algeria, 13 May 1943; Goubrine, Tunisia, 24 Jun 1943; Gela, Sicily, 29 Aug 1943; Catania, Sicily, 29 Sep 1943; Lido di Roma, Italy, 29 Jun 1944; Siena, Italy, 8 Jan 1945; Wiesbaden, Germany, Sep 1945–5 Jan 1948.

COMMANDERS. Col Russell L Maughan, 1 Jun 1942; Col Paul L Williams, 20 Oct 1942; Col Ralph B Bagby, 22 Jan 1943; Col Ray A Dunn, c. 22 Feb 1943; Col Samuel J Davis, 26 Mar 1943; Brig Gen Ray A Dunn, 22 May 1943; Brig Gen George H Beverley, 28 Sep 1943; Brig Gen Timothy J Manning, 20 Mar 1944; Lt Col Paul A Jones, 3 Jun–Aug 1945; Brig Gen Lucas V Beau, c. Sep 1945; Brig Gen James F Powell, 13 Aug 1947–5 Jan 1948.

CAMPAIGNS. Air Combat, EAME Theater; Algeria-French Morocco; Tunisia; Sicily; Naples-Foggia; Rome-Arno; Southern France; North Apennines; Po Valley.

DECORATIONS. None.

INSIGNE. None.

52d TROOP CARRIER WING

Constituted as 52d Transport Wing on 30 May 1942. *Activated* on 15 Jun 1942. *Redesignated* 52d Troop Carrier Wing in

Jul 1942. Moved to the Mediterranean theater, Apr–May 1943, and served with Twelfth AF until Feb 1944. Moved to England, Feb–Mar 1944, assigned to Ninth AF, and engaged in operations in the European theater until Jun 1945. Returned to the US, Jun–Jul 1945. *Inactivated* on 27 Aug 1946.

Redesignated 52d Fighter Wing. Allotted to ANG (NY) on 28 Aug 1946. Extended federal recognition on 3 Oct 1947. *Inactivated* on 31 Oct 1950.

GROUPS. *10th:* 1942–1943. *61st:* 1942, 1943–1945. *63d:* 1942. *64th:* 1943. *313th:* 1942, 1942–1945. *314th:* 1942, 1943–1945. *315th:* 1942, 1944–1945. *316th:* 1942, 1943–1946. *317th:* 1942. *349th:* 1945, 1946. *433d:* 1943. *434th:* 1945–1946. *439th:* 1945–1946.

STATIONS. Daniel Field, Ga, 15 Jun 1942; Bowman Field, Ky, 20 Jul 1942; Pope Field, NC, 3 Aug 1942–24 Apr 1943; Oujda, French Morocco, 8 May 1943; Kairouan, Tunisia, Jul 1943; Agrigento, Sicily, 1 Sep 1943–13 Feb 1944; Cottesmore,

England, 17 Feb 1944; Amiens, France, 5 Mar–20 Jun 1945; Baer Field, Ind, Jul 1945; Kellogg Field, Mich, Aug 1945; Sedalia AAFld, Mo, 1 Oct 1945; Bergstrom Field, Tex, 1 Mar–27 Aug 1946.

COMMANDERS. Lt Col Donald F Shugart, 1 Jul 1942; Brig Gen Harold L Clark, 10 Nov 1942; Lt Col James A Provan, c. Jul 1945; Maj Wilfred F Simmons, Sep 1945; Col Reed G Landis, 4 Oct 1945; Brig Gen Paul H Prentiss, 14 Jan 1946–unkn.

CAMPAIGNS. American Theater; Sicily; Naples-Foggia; Rome-Arno; Normandy; Northern France; Rhineland; Ardennes-Alsace; Central Europe.

DECORATIONS. None.

INSIGNE. *Shield:* On a blue rectangle edged in gold, long axis vertical, corners rounded, a stylized wing between five (5) mullets in chief and two of the like in base all gold. (Approved 22 Sep 1942.)

53d TROOP CARRIER WING

Constituted as 53d Troop Carrier Wing on 27 Jul 1942. *Activated* on 1 Aug 1942. Moved to England, Jan–Mar 1944. Assigned to Ninth AF. Operated in the European theater until after V–E Day. Returned to the US in Oct 1945. *Inactivated* on 11 Oct 1945.

Redesignated 53d Fighter Wing. Allotted to ANG (Pa) on 24 May 1946. Extended federal recognition on 17 Jan 1947. *Inactivated* on 31 Oct 1950.

GROUPS. *61st:* 1942–1943. *63d:* 1942–1943. *89th:* 1942. *313th:* 1942. *314th:* 1942. *316th:* 1942. *433d:* 1943. *434th:* 1943, 1944–1945. *435th:* 1943, 1944–1945. *436th:* 1943, 1944–1945. *437th:* 1943, 1944–1945. *438th:* 1943, 1944–1945. *439th:* 1943. *440th:* 1943.

STATIONS. General Billy Mitchell Field, Wis, 1 Aug 1942; Pope Field, NC, 26 Aug 1942; Ft Sam Houston, Tex, 15 Sep 1942; Bergstrom AAFld, Tex, 5 Nov 1942; Sedalia AAFld, Mo, 15 Apr 1943; Alliance AAFld, Neb, 25 Jul 1943; Laurinburg-Maxton AAB, NC, 19 Sep 1943; Pope Field, NC, 20 Dec 1943–19 Jan 1944; Greenham Common, England, 11 Mar 1944; Voisenon, France, 20 Feb–Oct 1945; Camp Shanks, NY, 10–11 Oct 1945.

COMMANDERS. Col Harold L Clark, 1 Aug 1942; Brig Gen Maurice M Beach, 22 Aug 1942–1945.

CAMPAIGNS. American Theater; Normandy; Northern France; Southern

France; Rhineland; Ardennes-Alsace; Central Europe.

DECORATIONS. None.

INSIGNE. *Shield:* Over and through an ultramarine blue disc, within a light blue annulet, piped gold, a torch of liberty fired proper, handle of torch formed of open parachute argent, surmounted by a C-47 transport plane or, in flight, in front of flames of torch; on the field eight mullets or, arranged five to dexter, three to sinister. (Approved 6 Apr 1943.)

54th TROOP CARRIER WING

Constituted as 54th Troop Carrier Wing on 26 Feb 1943. *Activated* in Australia on 13 Mar 1943. Assigned to Fifth AF. Engaged in troop carrier and transport operations from May 1943 until after the end of the war. *Inactivated* in the Philippines on 31 May 1946.

Redesignated 54th Fighter Wing. Allotted to ANG (Ga) on 1 Jun 1946. Extended federal recognition on 2 Oct 1946. Called to active service on 10 Oct 1950. *Inactivated* on 11 Oct 1950.

GROUPS. *2d* Combat Cargo: 1944–1946. *317th* Troop Carrier: 1943–1946. *374th* Troop Carrier: 1943. *375th* Troop Carrier: 1943–1946. *433d* Troop Carrier: 1943–1946.

STATIONS. Brisbane, Australia, 13 Mar 1943; Port Moresby, New Guinea, 3 May 1943; Nadzab, New Guinea, 18 Apr 1944; Biak, 5 Oct 1944; Leyte, 14 Feb 1945; Clark Field, Luzon, Jun 1945; Tachikawa, Japan, Sep 1945; Manila, Luzon, Jan–31 May 1946.

COMMANDERS. Brig Gen Paul H Prentiss, 20 May 1943; Brig Gen Warren R Carter, 30 Mar 1944; Brig Gen Paul H Prentiss, 19 Nov 1944; Brig Gen William D Old, c. Oct 1945–unkn.

CAMPAIGNS. Air Offensive, Japan; New Guinea; Bismarck Archipelago; Western Pacific; Leyte; Luzon; Southern Philippines; Ryukyus.

DECORATIONS. Philippine Presidential Unit Citation.

INSIGNE. None.

55th BOMBARDMENT WING

Constituted as 55th Bombardment Operational Training Wing (Medium) on 17 Mar 1943 and *activated* on 31 Mar. Various groups were attached for training prior to Oct 1943. *Redesignated* 55th Bombardment Wing (Medium) in Oct 1943, and 55th Bombardment Wing (Heavy) in Dec. Moved to Italy (Feb–Mar 1944) where combat elements were assigned. Operated with Fifteenth AF in the Mediterranean and European theaters from Mar 1944 until May 1945. *Inactivated* in Italy on 9 Sep 1945.

Redesignated 55th Fighter Wing. Allotted to ANG (Ohio) on 24 May 1946. Extended federal recognition on 7 Dec 1947. *Inactivated* on 31 Oct 1950.

GROUPS. *460th:* 1944–1945. *461st:* 1944. *464th:* 1944–1945. *465th:* 1944–1945. *485th:* 1944–1945.

STATIONS. MacDill Field, Fla, 31 Mar 1943–Feb 1944; Spinazzola, Italy, Mar 1944; Bari, Italy, c. Jul–9 Sep 1945.

COMMANDERS. Col Guy L McNeil, Apr 1943; Brig Gen George R Acheson, 11 Jun 1943–c. Jun 1945.

CAMPAIGNS. Air Combat, EAME Theater; Rome-Arno; Normandy; Northern France; Southern France; North Apennines; Rhineland; Central Europe; Po Valley.

DECORATIONS. None.

INSIGNE. None.

57th BOMBARDMENT WING

Constituted as 8th Pursuit Wing on 19 Oct 1940. *Activated* on 6 Nov 1940. *Inactivated* on 1 Nov 1941.

Redesignated 8th Fighter Wing. *Activated* on 24 Jul 1942. Moved to Egypt, Oct–Dec 1942, and served with Ninth AF in the Middle East and North Africa. *Redesignated* 57th Bombardment Wing in Apr 1943. Assigned to Twelfth AF in Aug 1943 and continued operations in the Mediterranean theater until the end of the war. *Inactivated* in Italy on 12 Sep 1945. *Redesignated* 57th Air Division. *Organized* on 16 Apr 1951. Assigned to Strategic Air Command.

COMPONENTS. *Groups. 12th* Bombardment: 1943–1944. *47th* Bombardment: 1943–1944. *49th* Pursuit: 1941. *57th* Fighter: 1943–1944. *79th* Fighter: 1943–1944. *310th* Bombardment: 1944–1945. *319th* Bombardment: 1944–1945. *321st* Bombardment: 1943–1944, 1944–1945. *340th* Bombardment: 1943–1944, 1944–1945. *Wings. 92d* Bombardment: 1951–. *98th* Bombardment: 1951–1953. *99th* Bombardment: 1953–. *111th* Reconnaissance: 1951–1953.

STATIONS. Maxwell Field, Ala, 6 Nov 1940; Morrison Field, Fla, 16 May–1 Nov 1941. Drew Field, Fla, 24 Jul–28 Oct 1942; Egypt, 23 Dec 1942; Tunisia, c. 29 Aug 1943; Lentini, Sicily, 4 Sep 1943; Naples, Italy, 7 Oct 1943; Foggia, Italy, 29 Oct 1943; Trocchia, Italy, 4 Jan 1944; Ghisonaccia, Corsica, 20 Apr 1944; Fano, Italy, 7 Apr 1945; Pomigliano, Italy, Aug–12 Sep 1945. Fairchild AFB, Wash, 16 Apr 1951–.

COMMANDERS. Capt Harold H Fulk, 6 Nov 1940–1941. Unkn, 1942–c. Mar 1943; Col Thomas C Darcy, c. Mar 1943–unkn; Capt John J Darmody, 1943; Col William S Gravely, 15 Oct 1943–1 Jan 1944; Brig Gen Robert D Knapp, 1 Mar 1944; Col Anthony G Hunter, 24 May 1945–unkn. Brig Gen Charles J Bondley Jr, 16 Apr 1951; Brig Gen David Wade, 1 Nov 1952;

Brig Gen James V Edmundson, 20 Mar 1954; Brig Gen Edwin B Broadhurst, 18 Jan 1955–.

CAMPAIGNS. Air Combat, EAME Theater; Tunisia; Naples-Foggia; Rome-Arno; Southern France; North Apennines; Central Europe; Po Valley.

DECORATIONS. None.

INSIGNE. *Shield:* Per bend azure and gules, a bend argent between in chief a globe of the third lined sable emitting three lightning flashes or and issuing from base a hand holding a torch of the fourth garnished of the fifth flammant of the second and silver. (Approved 7 Apr 1954.)

58th BOMBARDMENT WING

Constituted as 58th Bombardment Operational Training Wing (Heavy) on 22 Apr 1943. *Activated* on 1 May 1943. *Redesignated* 58th Bombardment Wing (Heavy) in Jul 1943, and 58th Bombardment Wing (Very Heavy) in Nov 1943. Moved to India in the spring of 1944. Assigned to Twentieth AF. Engaged in very-long-range bombardment operations from Jun to Oct 1944. *Disbanded* in India on 12 Oct 1944.

Reconstituted on 1 Feb 1945 and *activated* in India on 8 Feb. Assigned to Twentieth AF. Engaged in combat until the war ended. Returned to the US late in 1945. Assigned to Strategic Air Command on 21 Mar 1946. *Redesignated* 58th Air Division (Bombardment) in Apr 1948. *Inactivated* on 16 Oct 1948.

Redesignated 58th Air Division (Defense). *Activated* on 8 Sep 1955. Assigned to Air Defense Command. No combat elements were assigned to the division prior to 31 Dec 1955.

GROUPS. *40th:* 1943–1944; 1945–1946. *444th:* 1943–1944; 1945–1946. *462d:* 1943–1944; 1945–1946. *468th:* 1943–1944; 1945–1946. *472d:* 1943–1944.

STATIONS. Smoky Hill AAFld, Kan, 1 May 1943; Cobb County AAFld, Ga, 15 Jun 1943; Smoky Hill AAFld, Kan, 15 Sept 1943–12 Mar 1944; Chakulia, India, 2 Apr 1944; Kharagpur, India, 23 Apr–12 Oct 1944. Hijli Base Area, India, 8–24 Feb 1945; West Field, Tinian, 29 Mar–15 Nov 1945; March Field, Calif, 2 Dec 1945; Ft Worth AAFld, Tex, 9 May 1946; Andrews AFB, Md, 1 Mar–16 Oct 1948. Wright-Patterson AFB, Ohio, 8 Sep 1955–.

COMMANDERS. Brig Gen Kenneth B Wolfe, 21 Jun 1943; Col Leonard F Harman, 27 Nov 1943; Brig Gen LaVern G Saunders, Mar 1944–unkn. Col Dwight O

Monteith, 8 Feb 1945; Brig Gen Roger M Ramey, 24 Apr 1945–1 Nov 1946; unkn, 1 Nov 1946–16 Oct 1948. Col Von R Shores Jr, 8 Sep 1955–.

CAMPAIGNS. India-Burma; Air Offensive, Japan; China Defensive; Western Pacific; Central Burma.

DECORATIONS. None.

INSIGNE. *Shield:* Per bend argent, and checky of the first and sable, in chief an escutcheon gules, charged with a cross or between four stylized arrowheads, tips to center, of the last. *Motto:* PRIMUS INTER PARES—First Among Equals. (Approved 11 Jan 1956.)

60th TROOP CARRIER WING

Constituted as 60th Troop Carrier Wing on 5 Jun 1943 and *activated* on 12 Jun. Assigned to I Troop Carrier Command. Trained groups and glider crews and participated in several airborne maneuvers. *Inactivated* on 8 Oct 1945.

Redesignated 60th Fighter Wing. Allotted to ANG (Wash) on 24 May 1946. Extended federal recognition on 19 Apr 1948. *Inactivated* on 31 Oct 1950.

COMPONENTS. (Omitted because of large number and frequent changes.)

STATIONS. Sedalia AAFld, Mo, 12 Jun 1943; Pope Field, NC, c. 22 Jul 1943; Laurinburg-Maxton AAB, NC, c. 20 Dec 1943; Pope Field, NC, c. 8 Mar 1944–8 Oct 1945.

COMMANDERS. Col Maurice M Beach, Jun 1943; Col Julian M Chappell, c. 22 Jul 1943; Col Jerome B McCauley, c. 31 Aug 1943; Col Younger A Pitts, 23 Mar 1944–c. 8 Oct 1945.

CAMPAIGNS. American Theater.

DECORATIONS. None.

INSIGNE. None.

61st TROOP CARRIER WING

Constituted as 61st Troop Carrier Wing on 5 Jun 1943 and *activated* on 13 Jun. Assigned to I Troop Carrier Command. Trained groups, troop carrier replacement personnel, and glider crews. *Inactivated* on 4 Oct 1945.

Redesignated 61st Fighter Wing. Allotted to ANG (Calif) on 24 May 1946. Extended federal recognition on 4 Apr 1948. *Inactivated* on 31 Oct 1950.

COMPONENTS. (Omitted because of large number and frequent changes.)

STATIONS. Pope Field, NC, 13 Jun 1943; Sedalia AAFld, Mo, Jul 1943–4 Oct 1945.

COMMANDERS. Col Tracy K Dorsett, Jun 1943; Col Reed G Landis, Dec 1943–4 Oct 1945.

CAMPAIGNS. American Theater.

DECORATIONS. None.

INSIGNE. None.

62d FIGHTER WING

Constituted as 1st Air Defense Wing on 12 Dec 1942 and *activated* the same day. Moved to the Mediterranean theater in Jan 1943. *Redesignated* 62d Fighter Wing in Jul 1943. Served with Twelfth AF until the end of the war. *Inactivated* in Italy on 12 Sep 1945.

Allotted to ANG (Calif) on 24 May 1946. Extended federal recognition on 14 Sep 1946. *Inactivated* on 31 Oct 1950.

GROUPS. *52d*: 1943. *81st*: 1943, 1943–1944. *332d*: 1944. *350th*: 1944–1945.

STATIONS. Mitchel Field, NY, 12 Dec 1942–13 Jan 1943; Casablanca, French Morocco, 30 Jan 1943; Sousse, Tunisia, 14 May 1943; Palermo, Sicily, 25 Jul 1943; Naples, Italy, 20 Oct 1943; Antignano, Italy, c. 15 Sep 1944; Pomigliano, Italy, Aug–12 Sep 1945.

COMMANDERS. Brig Gen Elwood R Quesada, 12 Dec 1942; Col John N Stone, 18 Mar 1943; Brig Gen Robert S Israel Jr, 4 Sep 1943; Col John F Wadman, 11 May 1945–unkn.

CAMPAIGNS. Air Combat, EAME Theater; Sicily; Naples-Foggia; Rome-Arno; North Apennines; Po Valley.

DECORATIONS. None.

INSIGNE. None.

63d FIGHTER WING

Constituted as 2d Air Defense Wing on 12 Dec 1942 and *activated* the same day. Moved to North Africa in Jan 1943. *Redesignated* 63d Fighter Wing in Jul 1943. Operated with Twelfth AF until Nov 1944 when the wing moved to the European theater and lost its combat elements. Returned to the US in Dec 1945. *Inactivated* on 11 Dec 1945.

Allotted to ANG (Tex) on 24 May 1946. Extended federal recognition on 23 May 1948. Ordered into active service on 10 Oct 1950. *Inactivated* on 11 Oct 1950.

GROUPS. *52d*: 1943–1944. *350th*: 1943–1944.

STATIONS. Mitchel Field, NY, 12 Dec 1942–13 Jan 1943; Oran, Algeria, 27 Jan 1943; Maison Blanche, Algeria, c. May 1943; Rerhaia, Algeria, 8 Aug 1943; Bastia, Corsica, c. Oct 1943; San Pietro, Italy, c. 15 Oct 1944; Vittel, France, 22 Nov 1944; Heidelberg, Germany, c. 7 Apr 1945; Schwabisch-Hall, Germany, 14 Jun 1945; Darmstadt, Germany, 17 Jul 1945–unkn; Camp Kilmer, NJ, Dec–11 Dec 1945.

COMMANDERS. Brig Gen Davis D Graves, Dec 1942; Brig Gen Laurence C Craigie, 8 Mar 1944; Col Richard A Ames, 7 Oct 1944–unkn.

CAMPAIGNS. Air Combat, EAME Theater; Tunisia; Sicily; Naples-Foggia; Rome-Arno; Southern France.

DECORATIONS. None.

INSIGNE. None.

64th FIGHTER WING

Constituted as 3d Air Defense Wing on 12 Dec 1942 and *activated* the same day. Moved to Algeria in Feb 1943. *Redesignated* 64th Fighter Wing in Jul 1943. Served with Twelfth AF in the Mediterranean theater until Nov 1944. Moved to the European theater and continued operations until the war ended. Remained in Germany after the war as part of United States Air Forces in Europe. *Inactivated* on 5 Jun 1947.

Redesignated 64th Air Division (Defense). *Activated* in Newfoundland on 8

Apr 1952. Assigned to Northeast Air Command.

COMPONENTS. *Groups. 27th* Fighter: 1943, 1946–1947. *31st* Fighter: 1943. *33d* Fighter: 1943. *36th* Fighter: 1945–1946. *52d* Fighter: 1946–1947. *86th* Fighter: 1943, 1945–1946, 1946–1947. *324th* Fighter: 1943, 1945. *354th* Fighter: 1945–1946. *355th* Fighter: 1946. *363d* Reconnaissance: 1945. *366th* Fighter: 1945–1946. *370th* Fighter: 1945. *404th* Fighter: 1945. *406th* Fighter: 1945–1946. *Squadrons. 59th* Fighter: 1952–. *61st* Fighter: 1953–. *79th* Fighter: 1954–. *318th* Fighter: 1953–1954.

STATIONS. Mitchel Field, NY, 12 Dec 1942–c. 7 Feb 1943; Oran, Algeria, 23 Feb 1943; Tunisia, Mar 1943; Licata, Sicily, c. 10 Jul 1943; Gela, Sicily, c. Aug 1943; Milazzo, Sicily, 1 Sep 1943; Frattamaggiore, Italy, 7 Oct 1943; Orbetello, Italy, Jun 1944; Santa Maria di Capua, Italy, 19 Jul 1944; St Tropez, France, 15 Aug 1944; Dole, France, 19 Sep 1944; Ludres, France,

3 Nov 1944; Nancy, France, 15 Jan 1945; Edenkoben, Germany, 1 Apr 1945; Schwabisch-Hall, Germany, 29 Apr 1945; Darmstadt, Germany, 7 Jul 1945; Bad Kissingen, Germany, 1 Dec 1945–5 Jun 1947. Pepperrell AFB, Newfoundland, 8 Apr 1952–.

COMMANDERS. Col Robert S Israel Jr, 17 Dec 1942; Brig Gen John R Hawkins, 24 Jul 1943; Brig Gen Glenn O Barcus, 30 Apr 1944; Col Nelson P Jackson, 29 Jan 1945; Brig Gen Ned Schramm, Sep 1945; Col Henry W Dorr, c. 2 Jun 1946–c. Jun 1947. Col William S Magalhaes, 8 Apr 1952; Col Charles R Bond Jr, 12 Sep 1952; Col Charles B Downer, 20 May 1954; Col Joseph Myers, Feb 1955; Col Carroll W McColpin, 23 Jul 1955–.

CAMPAIGNS. Tunisia; Sicily; Naples-Foggia; Anzio; Rome-Arno; Northern France; Southern France; Rhineland; Ardennes-Alsace; Central Europe.

DECORATIONS. None.

INSIGNE. *Shield:* Or, issuing from base a demi-sphere with line markings azure, snow capped, surmounted with a radar antenna, proper; in front of a representation of the Aurora Borealis argent, edges gules, in chief, surmounting the Aurora Borealis a stylized aircraft azure, in bend, with trailing flames proper. (Approved 8 Aug 1952.)

65th FIGHTER WING

Constituted as 4th Air Defense Wing on 25 Mar 1943 and *activated* on 27 Mar.

Moved to England, May–Jun 1943, for duty with Eighth AF. *Redesignated* 65th Fighter Wing in Jul 1943. Served in combat in the European theater from Jul 1943 to late in Apr 1945. *Inactivated* in England on 21 Nov 1945.

Redesignated 65th Air Division (Defense). *Organized* in Iceland on 24 Apr 1952. Assigned to Military Air Transport Service. Served in the air defense of Iceland, its combat elements being fighter squadrons temporarily deployed from the US. *Discontinued* on 8 Mar 1954.

Activated in Spain on 8 Apr 1957. Assigned to Sixteenth AF. No combat elements were assigned at the time of activation.

GROUPS. *4th:* 1943–1945. *56th:* 1943–1945. *78th:* 1943. *355th:* 1943–1945. *356th:* 1943–1944. *361st:* 1944–1945, 1945. *479th:* 1944–1945.

STATIONS. Hamilton Field, Calif, 27 Mar–c. 6 May 1943; Debden, England, 4 Jun 1943; Saffron Walden, England, c. 17 Jun 1943; Elveden Hall, England, c. 1 Sep 1945; Troston, England, c. 25 Oct–21 Nov 1945. Keflavik Aprt, Iceland, 24 Apr 1952–8 Mar 1954. Madrid, Spain, 8 Apr 1957–.

COMMANDERS. Col Jesse Auton, Apr 1943; Brig Gen Ross G Hoyt, 4 Jun 1943; Brig Gen Jesse Auton, c. 6 Sep 1943; Col William L Curry, 29 Jul 1945–unkn. 1st Lt John J Brody, 24 Apr 1952; Col Meredith H Shade, 10 Oct 1952; Col Emmett S Davis, 5 Sep 1953–unkn. Capt Newell H Beaty, 8 Apr 1957–.

CAMPAIGNS. Air Offensive, Europe; Normandy; Northern France; Rhineland; Ardennes-Alsace; Central Europe.

DECORATIONS. None.

INSIGNE. None.

66th FIGHTER WING

Constituted as 5th Air Defense Wing on 25 Mar 1943 and *activated* on 27 Mar. Moved to England, May–Jun 1943, and assigned to Eighth AF. *Redesignated* 66th Fighter Wing in Jul 1943. Participated in combat in the European theater from Nov 1943 to late in Apr 1945. *Inactivated* in England on 21 Nov 1945.

Allotted to ANG (Ill) on 24 May 1946. Extended federal recognition on 26 Nov 1946. *Inactivated* on 31 Oct 1950.

GROUPS. *4th:* 1945. *55th:* 1943–1945. *56th:* 1945. *78th:* 1943–1945. *339th:* 1944–1945. *353d:* 1943–1945. *357th:* 1944–1945. *358th:* 1943–1944. *359th:* 1943. *361st:* 1943–1944, 1945. *479th:* 1945.

STATIONS. Norfolk Mun Aprt, Va, 27 Mar–c. 11 May 1943; Duxford, England, c. 3 Jun 1943; Sawston, England, 20 Aug 1943; Troston, England, c. 25 Oct–21 Nov 1945.

COMMANDERS. Brig Gen Murray C Woodbury, 1 Apr 1943; Col Glenn E Duncan, 9 Sep–c. 8 Oct 1945.

CAMPAIGNS. Air Offensive, Europe; Normandy; Northern France; Rhineland; Ardennes-Alsace; Central Europe.

DECORATIONS. None.

INSIGNE. None.

67th FIGHTER WING

Constituted as 6th Air Defense Wing on 14 Jun 1943 and *activated* on 15 Jun. *Redesignated* 67th Fighter Wing in Jul 1943. Moved to England in Aug 1943 and assigned to Eighth AF. Served in combat in the European theater from Dec 1943 until late in Apr 1945. *Inactivated* in England on 21 Nov 1945.

Allotted to ANG (Mass) on 24 May 1946. Extended federal recognition on 15 Oct 1946. *Inactivated* on 31 Oct 1950.

GROUPS. *20th*: 1943–1945. *352d*: 1943–1945. *356th*: 1944–1945. *359th*: 1943–1945. *361st*: 1944. *364th*: 1944–1945.

STATIONS. Bedford AAFld, Mass, 15 Jun–4 Aug 1943; Walcot Hall, England, c. 26 Aug 1943; Troston, England, c. 25 Oct–21 Nov 1945.

COMMANDERS. Lt Col Frank K Johnson, 15 Jun 1943; Lt Col Roy W Osborn, c. 28 Aug 1943; Brig Gen Edward W Anderson, 6 Sep 1943; Col Avelin P Tacon Jr, 17 Jul–c. 25 Sep 1945.

CAMPAIGNS. Air Offensive, Europe; Normandy; Northern France; Rhineland; Ardennes-Alsace; Central Europe.

DECORATIONS. None.

INSIGNE. None.

68th COMPOSITE WING

Constituted as 68th Fighter Wing on 9 Aug 1943. *Activated* in China on 3 Sep 1943. Assigned to Fourteenth AF. *Redesignated* 68th Composite Wing in Dec 1943. Served in combat from Dec 1943 until Aug 1945. *Inactivated* in China on 10 Oct 1945.

GROUPS. *23d* Fighter: 1943–1945.

STATIONS. Kunming, China, 3 Sep 1943; Kweilin, China, c. 23 Dec 1943; Liuchow, China, c. 15 Sep 1944; Luliang, China, c. 7 Nov 1944; Peishiyi, China, c. 19 Sep–10 Oct 1945.

COMMANDERS. Brig Gen Clinton D Vincent, c. 23 Dec 1943; Col Clayton B Claassen, c. 13 Dec 1944; Lt Col Frank N Graves, 1 Aug 1945; Lt Col Charles C Simpson Jr, 10 Aug 1945; Lt Col Oliver H Clayton, 22 Aug 1945; Maj Asa F Constable, 8 Sep 1945–unkn.

CAMPAIGNS. China Defensive; Western Pacific; China Offensive.

DECORATIONS. None.

INSIGNE. None.

69th COMPOSITE WING

Constituted as 69th Bombardment Wing on 9 Aug 1943. *Activated* in China on 3 Sep 1943. Assigned to Fourteenth AF. *Redesignated* 69th Composite Wing in Dec 1943. Served in combat from Dec 1943 until Aug 1945. Assigned to Tenth AF in Aug. Engaged in transport operations after V–J Day, being awarded a DUC for the period 1–30 Sep 1945 when the wing ferried troops and supplies in China, helped to evacuate prisoners of war, and flew mercy and other special missions to areas in China, French Indochina, and Manchuria. *Inactivated* in China on 26 Dec 1945.

Redesignated 69th Troop Carrier Wing. Allotted to the reserve. *Activated* in the US on 23 Mar 1947. *Redesignated* 69th Air Division (Troop Carrier) in Apr 1948. *Inactivated* on 27 Jun 1949.

GROUPS. *51st* Fighter: 1943–1945. *341st* Bombardment: 1943–1945. *375th* Troop Carrier: 1947–1949. *419th* Troop Carrier: 1947–1949. *433d* Troop Carrier: 1947–1949.

STATIONS. Kunming, China, 3 Sep 1943; Tsuyung, China, c. 12 Jan 1944; Kunming, China, Apr 1944–c. 26 Dec 1945. Greater Pittsburgh Aprt, Pa, 23 Mar 1947–27 Jun 1949.

COMMANDERS. Brig Gen John C Kennedy, c. 23 Dec 1943; Col Charles H Anderson, 1 Sep 1945; Maj James F Rhodes, c. 15 Nov 1945–unkn.

CAMPAIGNS. India-Burma; China Defensive; China Offensive.

DECORATIONS. Distinguished Unit Citation: China, French Indochina, Manchuria, 1–30 Sep 1945.

INSIGNE. None.

70th FIGHTER WING

Constituted as 70th Fighter Wing on 11 Aug 1943 and *activated* on 15 Aug. Moved to England in Nov 1943 and assigned to Ninth AF. Served in the European theater from Feb 1944 to May 1945, operating with various fighter groups assigned or attached for brief periods of time. Remained in Europe after the war as part of United States Air Forces in Europe. *Inactivated* in Germany on 25 Sep 1947.

COMPONENTS. (See narrative.)

STATIONS. Paine Field, Wash, 15 Aug–8 Nov 1943; Greenham Common, England, 29 Nov 1943; Boxted, England, 6 Dec 1943; Ibsley, England, 17 Apr–Jun 1944; Criqueville, France, 9 Jun 1944; Villedieu les Poeles, France, 4 Aug 1944; Le Teilleul, France, 16 Aug 1944; Aillieres, France, 22 Aug 1944; Versailles, France, 31 Aug 1944; Marchais, France, 10 Sep 1944; Liege, Belgium, 3 Oct 1944; Verviers, Belgium, 22 Jan 1945; Bruhl, Germany, 18 Mar 1945; Bad Wildungen, Germany, 30 May 1945; Furstenfeldbruck, Germany, 28 Jul 1945; Neubiberg, Germany, 10 Nov 1945–25 Sep 1947.

COMMANDERS. Lt Col Josiah M Towne, 23 Aug 1943; Brig Gen James W McCauley, 22 Oct 1943; Col Clinton C Wassem, c. 11 Jul 1945; Brig Gen Glenn O Barcus, 7 Dec 1945; Lt Col Earl C Hedlund, c. 9 Jan 1946; Col Glenn E Duncan, c. Apr 1946; Brig Gen James M Fitzmaurice, 3 Jun 1946; Col John B Patrick, 1 Apr 1947; Col Edward E Hildreth, 1 May 1947–unkn.

CAMPAIGNS. Air Offensive, Europe; Normandy; Northern France; Rhineland; Ardennes-Alsace; Central Europe.

DECORATIONS. Cited in the Order of the Day, Belgian Army: 6 Jun–30 Sep 1944; 16 Dec 1944–25 Jan 1945. Belgian Fourragere.

INSIGNE. None.

71st FIGHTER WING

Constituted as 71st Fighter Wing on 11 Aug 1943 and *activated* on 15 Aug. Moved to the European theater in Dec 1943. Assigned to Ninth AF. Served in combat from Mar to Aug 1944 when its combat elements were relieved of assignment. Returned to the US, Nov–Dec 1945. *Inactivated* on 3 Dec 1945.

Allotted to ANG (Mo) on 24 May 1946. Extended federal recognition on 3 Jul 1946. *Inactivated* on 31 Oct 1950.

GROUPS. *366th:* 1944. *368th:* 1944. *370th:* 1944.

STATIONS. March Field, Calif, 15 Aug–26 Nov 1943; Aldermaston, England, 23 Dec 1943; Greenham Common, England, 14 Jan 1944; Andover, England, 1 Mar–4 Jul 1944; Ecrammeville, France, 10 Jul 1944; St-Pierre-Eglise, France, 1 Aug 1944; Ecrammeville, France, 7 Aug 1944; Rennes, France, 20 Aug 1944; Versailles, France, 9 Sep 1944; Vittel, France, 23 Oct 1944; Heidelberg, Germany, 23 Apr 1945; Nancy, France, 21 May 1945; Nancy/Essey, France, 16 Jul 1945; Darmstadt, Germany, 25 Sep–Nov 1945; Camp Shanks, NY, 2–3 Dec 1945.

COMMANDERS. Lt Col Merrick Bayer, 6 Sep 1943; Lt Col Joseph C Smith, 18 Oct 1943; Brig Gen Ned Schramm, 18 Nov 1943; 2d Lt Gordon L Belsey, Sep 1945; Capt Augustus D Clemens, 26 Oct 1945–unkn.

CAMPAIGNS. Air Offensive, Europe; Normandy; Northern France.

DECORATIONS. Cited in the Order of the Day, Belgian Army: 6 Jun–[Aug] 1944.

INSIGNE. None.

72d FIGHTER WING

Constituted as 72d Bombardment Operational Training Wing (Heavy) on 12 Aug 1943 and *activated* on 20 Aug. Assigned to Second AF. *Redesignated* 72d Fighter Wing in Sep 1943. Trained fighter organizations and replacement crews. *Inactivated* on 9 Apr 1946.

GROUPS. *36th:* 1943–1944. *84th:* 1943–1944. *357th:* 1943. *407th:* 1943–1944. *408th:* 1943–1944. *476th:* 1944. *507th:* 1944–1945. *508th:* 1944.

STATIONS. Rapid City AAB, SD, 20 Aug 1943; Colorado Springs, Colo, 7 Oct 1943; Peterson Field, Colo, Nov 1943; Colorado Springs, Colo, Jan–9 Apr 1946.

COMMANDERS. Col Felix L Vidal, 10 Oct 1943; Brig Gen George P Tourtellot, 6 Jul 1944; Col Irving L Branch, 23 Jan 1945; Brig Gen John E Upston, 14 Mar 1945; Brig Gen Leonard D Weddington, 30 Sep 1945–unkn.

CAMPAIGNS. American Theater.

DECORATIONS. None.

INSIGNE. None.

73d BOMBARDMENT WING

Constituted as 5th Heavy Bombardment Processing Headquarters on 9 Feb 1943 and *activated* on 17 Feb. Assigned to Second AF. *Redesignated* 73d Bombardment

Operational Training Wing (Heavy) in Aug 1943. *Inactivated* on 15 Oct 1943.

Redesignated 73d Bombardment Wing (Very Heavy). *Activated* on 20 Nov 1943. Moved to Saipan, Jul–Sep 1944, and assigned to Twentieth AF. Engaged in very heavy bombardment operations from Oct 1944 to Aug 1945. Returned to the US late in 1945. Assigned to Strategic Air Command on 21 Mar 1946. *Inactivated* on 31 May 1946.

Allotted to the reserve. *Activated* on 12 Jun 1947. *Redesignated* 73d Air Division (Bombardment) in Apr 1948. *Inactivated* on 27 Jun 1949.

Redesignated 73d Air Division (Weapons). *Activated* on 8 Jul 1957. Assigned to Air Defense Command. No combat elements were assigned at the time of activation.

GROUPS. *338th:* 1947–1949. *381st:* 1947–1949. *497th:* 1943–1946. *498th:* 1943–1946. *499th:* 1943–1946. *500th:* 1943–1946.

STATIONS. Walker AAFld, Kan, 17 Feb 1943; Smoky Hill AAFld, Kan, 30 Jun–15 Oct 1943. Smoky Hill AAFld, Kan, 20 Nov 1943; Colorado Springs, Colo, 29 Feb–17 Jul 1944; Isley Field, Saipan, 24 Aug 1944–20 Oct 1945; MacDill Field, Fla, 15 Jan–31 May 1946. Orchard Place Aprt, Ill, 12 Jun 1947–27 Jun 1949. Tyndall AFB, Fla, 8 Jul 1957–.

COMMANDERS. Col Thomas H Chapman, 2 Jul–15 Oct 1943. Col Thomas H Chapman, 27 Nov 1943; Brig Gen Emmett O'Donnell Jr, 15 Mar 1944; Col Morris J Lee, 16 Sep 1945; Col Neil B Harding, 28 Jan–14 May 1946. Col Milton H Ashkins, 1957–.

CAMPAIGNS. American Theater; Air Offensive, Japan; Eastern Mandates; Western Pacific.

DECORATIONS. None.

INSIGNE. *Shield:* Azure, a diminished border argent, issuant from base and sinister two piles throughout bendwise the sinister overlapping the dexter and terminating upon the border of the last, each charged with an arrowhead sable garnished of the second and emitting a flight trail throughout or edged gules. *Motto:* MORS AGGRESSORIBUS—Death to Aggressors. (Approved 9 Apr 1958.)

84th FIGHTER WING

Constituted as 84th Fighter Wing on 4 Nov 1943 and *activated* on 10 Nov. Moved to the European theater in Jan 1944. Assigned to Ninth AF. Engaged in combat from Mar 1944 until May 1945, operating with various groups that were assigned or attached for short periods of time. *Disbanded* in Europe on 12 Aug 1945.

COMPONENTS.   (See narrative.)

STATIONS.   Bluethenthal Field, NC, 10 Nov 1943–1 Jan 1944; Keevil, England, 29 Jan 1944; Beaulieu, England, 4 Mar 1944; Houesville, France, 19 Jun 1944; Criqueville, France, 2 Aug 1944; Aillieres, France, 30 Aug 1944; St Quentin, France, 12 Sep 1944; Vermand, France, 17 Sep 1944; Arlon, Belgium, 1 Oct 1944; Maastricht, Holland, 22 Oct 1944; Munchen-Gladbach, Germany, 8 Mar 1945; Haltern, Germany, 3 Apr 1945; Gutersloh, Germany, 14 Apr 1945; Brunswick, Germany, 22 Apr 1945–unkn.

COMMANDERS.   Lt Col Joseph H Moore, 10 Nov 1943; Brig Gen Otto P Weyland, 24 Nov 1943; Col Randolph P Williams, 15 Feb 1944; Col Arthur G Salisbury, 8 May 1944; Col Dyke F Meyer, c. 14 Sep 1944–1945.

CAMPAIGNS.   Air Offensive, Europe; Normandy; Northern France; Rhineland; Ardennes-Alsace; Central Europe.

DECORATIONS.   Cited in the Order of the Day, Belgian Army: 6 Jun–30 Sep 1944; 1 Oct 1944–; Dec 1944–Jan 1945.   Belgian Fourragere.

INSIGNE.   None.

85th FIGHTER WING

Constituted as 85th Fighter Wing on 4 Nov 1943 and *activated* on 10 Nov. Moved to the Southwest Pacific, Jan–Feb 1944.

Served in combat with Fifth AF until May 1945 when the wing lost its tactical groups. Afterwards, operated an aircraft warning system for the Philippines. Remained on Luzon as part of Far East Air Forces after the war. Was not manned from late in 1945 until early in 1946 when the wing was given control of fighter groups on Luzon. Transferred, without personnel and equipment, to Japan in Jun 1947 and evidently was not remanned. *Inactivated* on 30 Jun 1948.

Redesignated 85th Air Division (Defense). *Activated* on 8 Sep 1955. Assigned to Air Defense Command. No combat elements were assigned prior to 31 Dec 1955.

GROUPS. *18th:* 1946–1947. *49th:* 1944. *348th:* 1944–1945. *414th:* 1946. *475th:* 1944–1945.

STATIONS.   Hamilton Field, Calif, 10 Nov 1943; San Francisco Mun Aprt, Calif, 10 Nov 1943–10 Jan 1944; Gusap, New Guinea, 25 Feb 1944; Hollandia, New

Guinea, 24 Jul 1944; Leyte, 24 Oct 1944; Ft William McKinley, Luzon, Jun 1945; Floridablanca, Luzon, Jul 1946; Nagoya, Japan, 1 Jun 1947–30 Jun 1948. Andrews AFB, Md, 8 Sep 1955–.

COMMANDERS. Col John M Bartella, 10 Nov 1943; Col Harlan T McCormick, 6 Dec 1943; Col Philip H Greasley, 11 Nov 1944; Col George A Walker, 23 Apr 1945; Brig Gen George P Tourtellot, 20 May 1945; Lt Col Vernon L Head, 2 Oct 1945–unkn; Col Raymond J Reeves, 1 Feb 1946; Brig Gen William M Morgan, 26 Feb 1946–1 May 1947. Brig Gen Emmett F Yost, 8 Sep 1955–.

CAMPAIGNS. New Guinea; Western Pacific; Leyte; Luzon; Southern Philippines.

DECORATIONS. Philippine Presidential Unit Citation.

INSIGNE. *Shield:* Per bend azure and of the sky proper, a sinister quarter pointed or; overall in chief, a silhouetted futuramic jet aircraft bendwise, volant, sable, with speed lines gules; in base a lightning bolt, bendwise of the third, over a checky grid throughout proper (red). (Approved 26 Dec 1956.)

86th FIGHTER WING

Constituted as 86th Fighter Wing on 19 Nov 1943. *Activated* on 1 Dec 1943. Moved to the Southwest Pacific, Mar–May 1944. Assigned to Fifth AF. Engaged in combat from May until early in 1945 when the wing became responsible for establishing and operating an aircraft warning sys-tem in the Philippine Islands. *Inactivated* in the Philippines on 15 Mar 1946.

Alotted to ANG (Colo) on 24 May 1946. Extended federal recognition on 3 Jul 1946. *Inactivated* on 31 Oct 1950.

(This wing is not related to an 86th Fighter Wing that was constituted on 1 Jul 1948 and activated in Germany the same day by United States Air Forces in Europe.)

GROUPS. *8th:* 1944–1945. *49th:* 1944–1945. *58th:* 1944–1945.

STATIONS. March Field, Calif, 1 Dec 1943–25 Mar 1944; Finschhafen, New Guinea, 1 May 1944; Toem, New Guinea, 4 Aug 1944; Sansapor, New Guinea, 19 Aug 1944; Luzon, 16 Jan 1945–15 Mar 1946.

COMMANDERS. Lt Col Robert L Johnston, 11 Dec 1943; Col Romulus W Puryear, 14 Dec 1943; Col Robert L Johnston, 16 Sep 1944; Col Norman D Sillin, 5 Nov 1944; Col James O Guthrie, 14 Dec 1944; Col Robert L Johnston, 11 Jun 1945–unkn.

CAMPAIGNS. New Guinea; Western Pacific; Leyte; Luzon.

DECORATIONS. Philippine Presidential Unit Citation.

INSIGNE. None.

87th FIGHTER WING

Constituted as 87th Fighter Wing on 14 Oct 1943 and *activated* on 25 Oct. Moved overseas, Dec 1943–Jan 1944, and operated with Twelfth AF in the Mediterranean theater from Apr 1944 until the wing's groups were reassigned in Sep 1944. *Disbanded* in Italy on 1 Apr 1945.

GROUPS. *57th:* 1944. *79th:* 1944. *86th:* 1944.

STATIONS. Mitchel Field, NY, 25 Oct–15 Dec 1943; Nouvion, Algeria, 11 Jan 1944; Caserta, Italy, 9 Feb 1944; Bastia, Corsica, 28 Mar 1944; Vescovato, Corsica, 9 May 1944; Furiani, Corsica, 13 Jul 1944; Caserta, Italy, 22 Sep 1944; Florence, Italy, 25 Dec 1944–1 Apr 1945.

COMMANDERS. Lt Col Gladwyn E Pinkston, 30 Oct 1943; Brig Gen Laurence C Craigie, 22 Nov 1943; Lt Col Gladwyn E Pinkston, 6 Mar 1944; Brig Gen Thomas C Darcy, 18 Apr 1944; Lt Col Theodore V Prochazka, c. 20 Sep 1944–c. 31 Mar 1945.

CAMPAIGNS. Rome-Arno; Southern France; North Apennines.

DECORATIONS. None.

INSIGNE. None.

90th RECONNAISSANCE WING

Constituted as 90th Photographic Wing (Reconnaissance) on 11 Oct 1943. *Activated* in North Africa on 22 Nov 1943. Provided photographic reconnaissance for both Twelfth AF and Fifteenth until the wing's groups were reassigned on 1 Oct 1944. Afterward, aided in establishing a photographic library for use in the European and Mediterranean theaters. Returned to the US in Apr 1945. *Redesignated* 90th Reconnaissance Wing in Jun. *Inactivated* on 23 Oct 1945.

Allotted to the reserve. *Activated* on 20 Dec 1946. *Redesignated* 90th Air Division (Reconnaissance) in Apr 1948. *Inactivated* on 27 Jun 1949.

GROUPS. *3d:* 1943–1944. *5th:* 1943–1944. *26th:* 1947–1949. *65th:* 1946–1949.

STATIONS. La Marsa, Tunisia, 22 Nov 1943; San Severo, Italy, 14 Dec 1943–c. 4 Apr 1945; Buckley Field, Colo, Apr–23 Oct 1945. Niagara Falls Mun Aprt, NY, 20 Dec 1946–27 Jun 1949.

COMMANDERS. Col Elliott Roosevelt, 22 Nov 1943; Col Karl L Polifka, 25 Jan 1944; Col George G Northrup, 30 Jan 1945; Lt Col James D Berry, 26 Jul 1945; Col Karl L Polifka, 8 Sep 1945; Maj Clair E Cheney, Oct–23 Oct 1945.

CAMPAIGNS. Air Combat, EAME Theater; Air Offensive, Europe; Naples-Foggia; Anzio; Rome-Arno; Southern France; North Apennines.

DECORATIONS. None.

INSIGNE. None.

91st RECONNAISSANCE WING

Constituted as 91st Photographic Wing (Reconnaissance) on 9 Oct 1943 and *activated* on 20 Oct. *Redesignated* 91st Reconnaissance Wing in Jun 1945. Moved to the Southwest Pacific, Feb–Mar 1944, and served with Fifth AF until the end of the war. *Inactivated* in Japan on 27 Jan 1946.

Allotted to the reserve. *Activated* in the US on 20 Dec 1946. *Redesignated* 91st Air Division (Reconnaissance) in Apr 1948. *Inactivated* on 27 Jun 1949.

GROUPS. *6th:* 1944–1945. *66th:* 1946–1949. *71st:* 1944–1945. *74th:* 1946–1949.

STATIONS. Will Rogers Field, Okla, 20 Oct 1943; Birmingham AAB, Ala, 9 Nov 1943–20 Feb 1944; Nadzab, New Guinea, 30 Mar 1944; Biak, 10 Aug 1944; Leyte, 12 Nov 1944; Mindoro, 28 Jan 1945; Clark Field, Luzon, 24 Mar 1945; Okinawa, 30 Jul 1945; Japan, Oct 1945–27 Jan 1946. Newark AAB, NJ, 20 Dec 1946–27 Jun 1949.

COMMANDERS. Lt Col James E Ilgenfritz, 13 Nov 1943; Col Elvin F Maughan, 18 Dec 1943; Col David W Hutchison, 12 Apr 1944; Col Ralph O Brownfield, 22 Apr 1944; Col John T Murtha, 23 Aug 1944; Col William C Sams, 16 Oct 1944–unkn.

CAMPAIGNS. Air Offensive, Japan; China Defensive; New Guinea; Bismarck Archipelago; Western Pacific; Leyte; Luzon; Southern Philippines; Ryukyus; China Offensive.

DECORATIONS. Philippine Presidential Unit Citation.

INSIGNE. None.

92d BOMBARDMENT WING

Constituted as 92d Combat Bombardment Wing (Heavy) on 25 Oct 1943. *Activated* in England on 1 Nov 1943. Assigned to Eighth AF. Entered combat on 11 Dec 1943 but its group were reassigned on 15 Dec. Re-entered combat with new groups in May 1944 and continued operations until the groups were taken away in Feb 1945. Moved to the US in Jul. *Disbanded* on 28 Aug 1945.

GROUPS. *351st:* 1943. *401st:* 1943. *486th:* 1944–1945. *487th:* 1944–1945.

STATIONS. Polebrook, England, 1 Nov 1943; Camp Blainey, England, c. 12 Dec 1943; Sudbury, England, c. 2 Mar 1944; Bury St Edmunds, England, c. 18 Nov 1944; Elveden Hall, England, 12 Feb–c. 13 Jul 1945; Sioux Falls AAFld, SD, 23 Jul–28 Aug 1945.

COMMANDERS. Col Julius K Lacey, 24 Nov–12 Dec 1943; Col Harold Q Huglin, c. 1 Apr–19 Nov 1944; Col Hunter Harris Jr, c. 12 Feb–11 May 1945.

CAMPAIGNS. Air Offensive, Europe; Normandy; Northern France; Rhineland; Ardennes-Alsace.

DECORATIONS. None.

INSIGNE. None.

93d BOMBARDMENT WING

Constituted as 93d Combat Bombardment Wing (Heavy) on 25 Oct 1943. *Activated* in England on 1 Nov 1943. Did not receive groups until the spring of 1944. Served in combat with Eighth AF in the European theater from May 1944 until Apr 1945. Moved to the US in Jul 1945. *Disbanded* on 28 Aug 1945.

GROUPS. *34th:* 1944–1945. *385th:* 1945. *490th:* 1944–1945. *493d:* 1944–1945.

STATIONS. Horsham St Faith, England, 1 Nov 1943; Elveden Hall, England, c. 10 Jan 1944; Mendlesham, England, c. 30

Mar 1944–11 Jul 1945; Sioux Falls AAFld, SD, c. 27 Jul–28 Aug 1945.

COMMANDERS. Brig Gen Walter R Peck, c. 27 Dec 1943–11 Jan 1944; Brig Gen John K Gerhart, Apr 1944–23 May 1945.

CAMPAIGNS. Air Offensive, Europe; Normandy; Northern France; Rhineland; Ardennes-Alsace; Central Europe.

DECORATIONS. None.

INSIGNE. None.

94th BOMBARDMENT WING

Constituted as 94th Combat Bombardment Wing (Heavy) on 2 Nov 1943. Activated in England on 12 Dec 1943. Assigned to Eighth AF. Served in combat in the European theater until Apr 1945. Received a DUC for an attack on German aircraft factories on 11 Jan 1944. Disbanded in England on 18 Jun 1945.

GROUPS. 351st: 1943–1945. 401st: 1943–1945. 457th: 1944–1945.

STATIONS. Polebrook, England, 12 Dec 1943; Alconbury, England, 12–18 Jun 1945.

COMMANDERS. Brig Gen Julius K Lacey, 12 Dec 1943; Col Eugene A Romig, 6–15 Jun 1945.

CAMPAIGNS. Air Offensive, Europe; Normandy; Northern France; Rhineland; Ardennes-Alsace; Central Europe.

DECORATIONS. Distinguished Unit Citation: Germany, 11 Jan 1944.

INSIGNE. None.

95th BOMBARDMENT WING

Constituted as 95th Combat Bombardment Wing (Heavy) on 2 Nov 1943. Ac-

tivated in England on 12 Dec 1943. Assigned to Eighth AF. Had no groups until Apr 1944. Flew in combat in the European theater from 2 Jun until 14 Aug 1944 when its groups were taken away. Moved to the US in Jul 1945. Disbanded on 28 Aug 1945.

GROUPS. 489th: 1944. 491st: 1944.

STATIONS. Attlebridge, England, 12 Dec 1943; Ketteringham, England, Feb 1944; Halesworth, England, c. 5 May 1944; Ketteringham, England, Aug 1944–c. 12 Jul 1945; Sioux Falls AAFld, SD, c. 23 Jul–28 Aug 1945.

COMMANDERS. Maj Albert W Osbourn, c. 6 Jan 1944; Lt Col Milton K Lockwood, c. 12 Jan 1944; Lt Col John H Diehl Jr, c. 26 Jan 1944; Col Frederick R Dent Jr, c. 1 Apr 1944; Col Irvine A Rendle, 30 Jun 1944; Col Frederick R Dent Jr, c. 15 Aug 1944; Col Troy W Crawford, c. 20 Aug 1944–unkn; Col Jack W Wood, c. 21 Oct 1944; Col Perry Norris, c. 18 Nov 1944–c. May 1945.

CAMPAIGNS. Air Offensive, Europe; Normandy; Northern France.

DECORATIONS. None.

INSIGNE. None.

96th BOMBARDMENT WING

Constituted as 96th Combat Bombardment Wing (Heavy) on 8 Nov 1943. Activated in England on 11 Jan 1944. Served in combat in the European theater with Eighth AF from Mar 1944 until Apr 1945. Redesignated 96th Bombardment Wing (Heavy) in Jun. Moved to the US in Aug. *Redesignated* 96th Bombardment Wing (Very Heavy) in Aug. *Inactivated* on 17 Oct 1945.

Allotted to the reserve. *Activated* on 12 Jun 1947. *Redesignated* 96th Air Division (Bombardment) in Apr 1948. *Inactivated* on 27 Jun 1949.

GROUPS. *44th:* 1945. *93d:* 1945. *351st:* 1948–1949. *381st:* 1947–1948. *392d:* 1945. *446th:* 1945. *448th:* 1945. *458th:* 1944–1945. *466th:* 1944–1945. *467th:* 1944–1945. *491st:* 1945.

STATIONS. Horsham St Faith, England, 11 Jan 1944; Ketteringham, England, c. 1 Jun–c. 5 Aug 1945; Sioux Falls AAFld, SD, c. 14 Aug 1945; Peterson Field, Colo, 16 Aug–17 Oct 1945. Scott Field, Ill, 12 Jun 1947–27 Jun 1949.

COMMANDERS. Brig Gen Walter R Peck, 11 Jan 1944; Col Irvine A Rendle, c. 10 May 1945; Brig Gen Walter R Peck, 1 Jun 1945–unkn; Col Fred Feasel, 31 Aug 1945–unkn.

CAMPAIGNS. Air Offensive, Europe; Normandy; Northern France; Rhineland; Ardennes-Alsace; Central Europe.

DECORATIONS. None.

INSIGNE. None.

97th BOMBARDMENT WING

Constituted as 97th Combat Bombardment Wing (Medium) on 2 Nov 1943 and *activated* in England on 12 Nov. Assigned to Ninth AF. *Redesignated* 97th Combat Bombardment Wing (Light) in Jul 1944. Participated in combat operations in the European theater, Apr 1944–

May 1945. *Redesignated* 97th Bombardment Wing (Medium) in Jun 1945. Moved to the US in Oct. *Inactivated* on 11 Oct 1945.

GROUPS. *409th:* 1944–1945. *410th:* 1944–1945. *416th:* 1944–1945.

STATIONS. Marks Hall, England, 12 Nov 1943; Little Walden, England, 13 Mar 1944; Voisenon, France, 13 Sep 1944; Marchais, France, 13 Feb 1945; Arrancy, France, 25 Apr 1945; Sandricourt, France, 24 May–1 Oct 1945; Camp Shanks, NY, 10–11 Oct 1945.

COMMANDERS. Capt Donald S Moloney, 26 Nov 1943; Lt Col Chris H W Rueter, 2 Mar 1944; Brig Gen Edward N Backus, 1 Apr 1944–1945.

CAMPAIGNS. Air Offensive, Europe; Normandy; Northern France; Rhineland; Ardennes-Alsace; Central Europe.

DECORATIONS. None.

INSIGNE. None.

98th BOMBARDMENT WING

Authorized on the inactive list as 3d Wing on 24 Mar 1923. *Redesignated* 3d Attack Wing in 1929. *Activated* on 15 Jun 1932. *Redesignated* 3d Wing in 1935. Became one of the original wings of GHQAF. *Redesignated* 3d Bombardment Wing in 1940. *Inactivated* on 5 Sep 1941.

Activated on 7 Jun 1942. Assigned to Eighth AF. Moved to the European theater, Aug–Sep 1942, and entered combat in May 1943. *Redesignated* 98th Combat Bombardment Wing (Medium) in Nov

1943. Assigned to Ninth AF and continued combat operations until Apr 1945. *Redesignated* 98th Bombardment Wing (Medium) in Jun 1945. *Inactivated* in Europe on 27 Nov 1945.

Redesignated 3d Bombardment Wing (Light) and allotted to the reserve. *Activated* in the US on 20 Dec 1946. *Redesignated* 3d Air Division (Bombardment) in Apr 1948. *Inactivated* on 27 Jun 1949.

GROUPS. *3d* Bombardment: 1932–1940. *13th* Bombardment: 1941. *20th* Pursuit: 1932–1939. *29th* Bombardment: 1940–1941. *44th* Bombardment: 1941. *305th* Bombardment: 1945. *306th* Bombardment: 1945. *310th* Bombardment: 1947–1949. *322d* Bombardment: 1942–1943. *323d* Bombardment: 1942–1945. *341st* Bombardment: 1947–1949. *344th* Bombardment: 1945. *386th* Bombardment: 1942–1943, 1945. *387th* Bombardment: 1942–1945. *391st* Bombardment: 1945. *394th* Bombardment: 1944–1945. *397th* Bombardment: 1944–1945.

STATIONS. Ft Crockett, Tex, 15 Jun 1932; Barksdale Field, La, 27 Feb 1935; MacDill Field, Fla, 2 Oct 1940–5 Sep 1941. Detrick Field, Md, 7 Jun–Aug 1942; Elveden Hall, England, c. 12 Sep 1942; Marks Hall, England, 12 Jun 1943; Earls Colne, England, Nov 1943; Beaulieu, England, 18 Jul–19 Aug 1944; Lessay, France, 23 Aug 1944; Chartres, France, 24 Sep 1944; Laon/Athies, France, 3 Oct 1944; Havrincourt, France, 1 Feb 1945; Venlo, Holland, c. 3 May 1945; Tirlemont, Belgium, c. Jul 1945; Kitzingen, Germany, Aug 1945; Namur, Belgium, c. Oct–Nov

1945. Bedford AAFld, Mass, 20 Dec 1946–27 Jun 1949.

COMMANDERS. Unkn, to 1 Mar 1935; Brig Gen Gerald C Brant, 1 Mar 1935; Brig Gen Frederick L Martin, 1 Apr 1937; Brig Gen Clarence L Tinker, c. Jan 1941; Brig Gen Follett Bradley, 1941–5 Sep 1941. Maj John P Carson, 7 Jun 1942; Maj William A Turner, 14 Jul 1942; Maj Thomas B Scott, 29 Jul 1942; Maj Jack E Caldwell, 29 Aug 1942; Col Charles T Phillips, 15 Sep 1942; Brig Gen Haywood S Hansell Jr, 6 Dec 1942; Brig Gen Frederick L Anderson, 27 Feb 1943; Brig Gen Francis M Brady, 27 Apr 1943; Col Samuel E Anderson, 12 Jul 1943; Col Carl R Storrie, Nov 1943; Col Millard Lewis, 21 Jan 1944; Brig Gen Harold L Mace, c. 2 Aug 1944–1945.

CAMPAIGNS. Air Offensive, Europe; Normandy; Northern France; Rhineland; Ardennes-Alsace; Central Europe.

DECORATIONS. None.

INSIGNE. None.

99th BOMBARDMENT WING

Constituted as 44th Bombardment Wing (Heavy) on 15 Feb 1943. *Activated* on 1 Mar 1943. Moved to England in Jul 1943 and assigned to Eighth AF. Combat elements apparently were not assigned and wing headquarters was not fully manned prior to Nov 1943. *Redesignated* 99th Combat Bombardment Wing (Medium). Served in combat with Ninth AF until May 1945. *Redesignated* 99th Bombardment Wing (Medium) in Jun 1945. Returned to the US, Sep–Oct 1945. *Inactivated* on 4 Oct 1945.

Redesignated 44th Bombardment Wing (Very Heavy) and allotted to the reserve. *Activated* on 26 Jun 1947. *Redesignated* 44th Air Division (Bombardment) in Apr 1948. *Inactivated* on 27 Jun 1949.

GROUPS. *312th:* 1947–1949. *322d:* 1943–1945. *344th:* 1943–1945. *386th:* 1944–1945. *391st:* 1944–1945. *394th:* 1945. *401st:* 1947–1949. *447th:* 1947–1949.

STATIONS. Salt Lake City AAB, Utah, 1 Mar 1943; Biggs Field, Tex, May–Jul 1943; Aldermaston, England, Jul 1943; Great Dunmow, England, 12 Nov 1943–Sep 1944; Beaumont, France, 25 Sep 1944; Tirlemont, Belgium, Apr 1945; Namur, Belgium, 1 Jul–Aug 1945; Camp Myles Standish, Mass, 3–4 Oct 1945. Brooks Field, Tex, 26 Jun 1947–27 Jun 1949.

COMMANDERS. Brig Gen Herbert B Thatcher, 12 Nov 1943; Col Reginald F C Vance, 7 Nov 1944; Maj Charles F Salter, 1 Jul 1945; Lt Col William W Brier, 13 Jul 1945; Brig Gen Richard C Sanders, 12 Aug–Oct 1945.

CAMPAIGNS. Air Offensive, Europe; Normandy; Northern France; Rhineland; Ardennes-Alsace; Central Europe.

DECORATIONS. None.

INSIGNE. None.

100th FIGHTER WING

Constituted as 100th Fighter Wing on 8 Nov 1943 and *activated* in England on 24 Nov. Assigned to Ninth AF. Engaged in combat in the European theater from Apr 1944 to May 1945. Moved to the US, Aug–Sep 1945. *Inactivated* on 7 Nov 1945.

GROUPS. *48th:* 1944. *354th:* 1943, 1944, 1945. *358th:* 1944. *361st:* 1944–1945. *362d:* 1944, 1945. *363d:* 1944. *365th:* 1944–1945. *367th:* 1944, 1945. *368th:* 1944–1945. *371st:* 1944, 1945. *405th:* 1945. *406th:* 1945. *474th:* 1944.

STATIONS. Boxted, England, 24 Nov 1943; Greenham Common, England, 6 Dec 1943; Ibsley, England, 13 Jan 1944; Lashenden, England, c. 15 Apr–Jun 1944; Criqueville, France, 1 Jul 1944; St-Pierre-Eglise, France, 10 Jul 1944; Rennes, France, 8 Aug 1944; Le Mans, France, 30 Aug 1944; St-Dizier, France, 19 Sep 1944; Metz, France, 29 Dec 1944; Konigstein, Germany, 14 Apr–Aug 1945; Seymour Johnson Field, NC, 6 Sep–7 Nov 1945.

COMMANDERS. Col David B Lancaster, Nov 1943; Brig Gen Homer L Sanders, c. 2 Jan 1944; Col Harry B Young, 23 May 1945–unkn.

CAMPAIGNS. Air Offensive, Europe; Normandy; Northern France; Rhineland; Ardennes-Alsace; Central Europe.

DECORATIONS. None.

INSIGNE. None.

301st FIGHTER WING

Constituted as 301st Fighter Wing on 5 Oct 1944 and *activated* on 15 Oct. Moved to Ie Shima, May–Jul 1945. Assigned to Twentieth AF. Engaged in combat during the last few days of the war. Assigned to Eighth AF in Aug 1945 and to Far East

Air Forces in 1946. *Inactivated* on Okinawa on 20 Jan 1949.

GROUPS. *51st:* 1946–1948. *408th:* 1944. *413th:* 1944–1946. *414th:* 1944–1945. *506th:* 1944–1945. *507th:* 1944–1945.

STATIONS. Seymour Johnson Field, NC, 15 Oct 1944; Mitchel Field, NY, 1 Nov 1944–30 May 1945; Ie Shima, 31 Jul 1945; Kadena, Okinawa, 29 Nov 1945; Naha, Okinawa, 14 Aug 1947–20 Jan 1949.

COMMANDERS. Lt Col George H Hollingsworth, 15 Oct 1944; Col Thayer S Olds, 19 Oct 1944; Brig Gen Francis H Griswold, 24 Aug 1945; Col Emmett F Yost, 11 Sep 1945; Col Hanlon H Van Auken, 1 Nov 1945; Col Mark E Bradley Jr, Apr 1946; Col Loring F Stetson Jr, 30 Oct 1946; Brig Gen Robert C Oliver, 1 Jan 1947; Col Loring F Stetson Jr, 24 Mar 1947; Brig Gen Hugo P Rush, 1 May 1947–31 Dec 1948.

CAMPAIGNS. Air Offensive, Japan.

DECORATIONS. None.

INSIGNE. None.

303d FIGHTER WING

Constituted as 303d Fighter Wing on 15 Nov 1943 and *activated* on 24 Nov. Moved to the European theater, Feb–Mar 1944. Assigned to Ninth AF. Served in combat from May 1944 until May 1945, operating with various groups that were assigned or attached for brief periods of time. *Disbanded* in Europe on 12 Aug 1945.

COMPONENTS. (See narrative.)

STATIONS. Norfolk AAFld, Va, 24 Nov 1943–12 Feb 1944; Ashford, England, 8

Mar 1944; La Combe, France, 31 Jul 1944; Houesville, France, 2 Aug 1944; Rennes, France, 24 Aug 1944; Vermand, France, 17 Sep 1944; Arlon, Belgium, c. 3 Oct 1944; Maastricht, Holland, 22 Oct 1944; Munchen-Gladbach, Germany, 8 Mar 1945; Haltern, Germany, 3 Apr 1945; Gutersloh, Germany, 14 Apr 1945; Brunswick, Germany, 22 Apr 1945–unkn.

COMMANDERS. Brig Gen Burton M Hovey Jr, 6 Jan 1944; Col John R Ulricson, c. May 1945–unkn.

CAMPAIGNS. Air Offensive, Europe; Normandy; Northern France; Rhineland; Ardennes-Alsace; Central Europe.

DECORATIONS. Cited in the Order of the Day, Belgian Army: 1 Oct 1944–; Dec 1944–Jan 1945. Belgian Fourragere.

INSIGNE. None.

304th BOMBARDMENT WING

Constituted as 304th Bombardment Wing (Heavy) on 7 Dec 1943 and *activated* in Italy on 29 Dec. Operated with Fifteenth AF in the Mediterranean and European theaters from Feb 1944 until May 1945. Moved to the US, Sep–Oct 1945. *Inactivated* on 13 Oct 1945. *Redesignated* 304th Bombardment Wing (Very Heavy) and allotted to the reserve. *Activated* on 19 Apr 1947. *Redesignated* 304th Air Division (Bombardment) in Apr 1948. *Inactivated* on 27 Jun 1949.

GROUPS. *448th:* 1947–1949. *452d:* 1947–1949. *454th:* 1944–1945. *455th:* 1944–1945. *456th:* 1944–1945. *459th:* 1944–1945; 1947–1949.

STATIONS. Cerignola, Italy, 29 Dec 1943–Sep 1945; Camp Kilmer, NJ, 12–13 Oct 1945. Long Beach, Calif, 19 Apr 1947–27 Jun 1949.

COMMANDERS. Col John K Brown Jr, c. 29 Dec 1943; Brig Gen Fay R Upthegrove, 27 Jan 1944; Lt Col William R Boutz, 5 Jul 1945–unkn.

CAMPAIGNS. Air Combat, EAME Theater; Air Offensive, Europe; Rome-Arno; Normandy; Northern France; Southern France; North Apennines; Rhineland; Central Europe; Po Valley.

DECORATIONS. None.

INSIGNE. None.

305th BOMBARDMENT WING

Constituted as 305th Bombardment Wing (Heavy) on 7 Dec 1943 and *activated* in Italy on 29 Dec. No combat components were assigned until 13 Jun 1945. *Inactivated* in Italy on 9 Sep 1945.

Redesignated 305th Bombardment Wing (Very Heavy) and allotted to the reserve. *Activated* in the US on 12 Jul 1947. *Redesignated* 305th Air Division (Bombardment) in Apr 1948. *Inactivated* on 27 Jun 1949.

GROUPS. *1st* Fighter: 1945. *14th* Fighter: 1945. *31st* Fighter: 1945. *52d* Fighter: 1945. *82d* Fighter: 1945. *325th* Fighter: 1945. *332d* Fighter: 1945. *445th* Bombardment: 1947–1949. *454th* Bombardment: 1947–1949. *456th* Bombardment: 1947–1949.

STATIONS. Foggia, Italy, 29 Dec 1943; Spinazzola, Italy, c. Feb 1944; Bari, Italy, c. Mar 1944; Torremaggiore, Italy, c. Dec 1944–9 Sep 1945. McChord Field, Wash, 12 Jul 1947–27 Jun 1949.

COMMANDERS. Lt Col [Julian M?] Bleyer, Mar–Apr 1944; Col William R Morgan, 13 Jun–9 Sep 1945.

CAMPAIGNS. European-African-Middle Eastern Theater.

DECORATIONS. None.

INSIGNE. None.

306th FIGHTER WING

Constituted as 306th Bombardment Wing (Heavy) on 7 Dec 1943. *Activated* in Italy on 15 Jan 1944. Assigned to Fifteenth AF. Entered combat in Mar as a fighter organization. *Redesignated* 306th Fighter Wing in May 1944. Operated in the Mediterranean and European theaters until the end of the war. Moved to the US, Jul–Aug 1945. *Inactivated* on 7 Nov 1945.

GROUPS. *1st:* 1944. *14th:* 1944. *31st:* 1944–1945. *52d:* 1944–1945. *82d:* 1944. *325th:* 1944–1945. *332d:* 1944–1945.

STATIONS. Bari, Italy, 15 Jan 1944; Foggia, Italy, 27 Jan 1944; Lucera, Italy, 23 Feb 1944; Torremaggiore, Italy, 8 Mar 1944; Lesina, Italy, 3 Sep 1944; Fano, Italy, 5 Mar–15 Jul 1945; Drew Field, Fla, Aug–7 Nov 1945.

COMMANDERS. Lt Col Sidney F Wogan, 15 Jan 1944; Lt Col Paul W Blanchard Jr, 23 Jan 1944; Brig Gen Dean C Strother, 26 Mar 1944; Brig Gen Yantis H Taylor, 3 Sep 1944–c. Aug 1945.

CAMPAIGNS. Air Combat, EAME Theater; Rome-Arno; Normandy; Northern France; Southern France; North Apennines; Rhineland; Central Europe; Po Valley.

DECORATIONS. None.

INSIGNE. None.

307th BOMBARDMENT WING

Constituted as 307th Bombardment Wing (Heavy) on 7 Dec 1943. *Activated* in Italy on 15 Jan 1944. No combat elements were assigned. *Disbanded* in Italy on 15 Jun 1944.

Reconstituted, redesignated 307th Bombardment Wing (Very Heavy), and allotted to the reserve, on 10 Feb 1947. *Activated* in the US on 31 Mar 1947. *Redesignated* 307th Air Division (Bombardment) in Apr 1948. *Inactivated* on 27 Jun 1949.

GROUPS. *482d*: 1947–1949.

STATIONS. Bari, Italy, 15 Jan–15 Jun 1944. New Orleans, La, 31 Mar 1947–27 Jun 1949.

COMMANDERS. Unkn.

CAMPAIGNS. European-African-Middle Eastern Theater.

DECORATIONS. None.

INSIGNE. None.

308th BOMBARDMENT WING

Constituted as 308th Bombardment Wing (Heavy) on 20 Jan 1944. *Activated* in New Guinea on 1 Feb 1944. Served in combat with Fifth AF from Feb 1944 to Aug 1945, operating with various groups

that were attached for brief periods. Moved to Korea late in 1945 and, as a component of Far East Air Forces, became part of the occupation force. *Redesignated* 308th Bombardment Wing (Light) in May 1946. Transferred, without personnel and equipment, to Japan in 1947 and was not remanned. *Inactivated* on 30 Jun 1948.

GROUPS. *475th* Fighter: 1945–1947.

STATIONS. Oro Bay, New Guinea, 1 Feb 1944; Owi, Schouten Islands, 2 Jul 1944; Hollandia, New Guinea, 10 Aug 1944; Leyte, 22 Oct 1944; Luzon, 11 Jan 1945; Okinawa, 16 Jun 1945; Seoul, Korea, 22 Sep 1945; Kimpo, Korea, 7 Jan 1946; Nagoya, Japan, Mar 1947–30 Jun 1948.

COMMANDERS. Col Dwight Divine II, 1 Feb 1944; Brig Gen David W Hutchison, 22 Apr 1944; Col Frank R Cook, 16 May 1946; Brig Gen David W Hutchison, 18 Jul 1946; Brig Gen Aubrey Hornsby, 22 Jul 1946; Col Leland S Stranathan, 1 Oct 1946–22 Mar 1947.

CAMPAIGNS. Air Offensive, Japan; China Defensive; New Guinea; Bismarck Archipelago; Western Pacific; Leyte; Luzon; Ryukyus; China Offensive.

DECORATIONS. Philippine Presidential Unit Citation.

INSIGNE. None.

309th BOMBARDMENT WING

Constituted as 309th Bombardment Wing (Heavy) on 20 Jan 1944. *Activated* in New Guinea on 1 Feb 1944. Assigned to Fifth AF. Served in combat until the end of the war, operating with various groups that were attached for short periods of time. *Inactivated* in Japan on 25 Mar 1946.

Redesignated 309th Bombardment Wing (Very Heavy). Allotted to the reserve. *Activated* in the US on 10 Jan 1947. *Redesignated* 309th Air Division (Bombardment) in Apr 1948. *Inactivated* on 27 Jun 1949.

GROUPS. *3d* Air Commando: 1946. *446th* Bombardment: 1947–1949. *455th* Bombardment: 1947–1949.

STATIONS. Lae, New Guinea, 1 Feb 1944; Saidor, New Guinea, c. Mar 1944; Noemfoor, 28 Jul 1944; Owi, Schouten Islands, 9 Nov 1944; San Marcelino, Luzon, 8 Feb 1945; Lingayen, Luzon, May 1945; Chitose, Japan, Oct 1945–25 Mar 1946. Hensley Field, Tex, 10 Jan 1947–27 Jun 1949.

COMMANDERS. Brig Gen Paul B Wurtsmith, 1 Feb 1944; Col Neel E Kearby, 26 Feb 1944; Maj Gen St Clair Streett, 3 Mar 1944; Lt Col Robert R Rowland, 5 Apr 1944; Col Jack W Saunders, 13 May 1944; Col Norman D Sillin, 16 Dec 1944; Col Herbert L Grills, 20 Oct 1945–unkn.

CAMPAIGNS. China Defensive; New Guinea; Western Pacific; Leyte; Luzon; China Offensive.

DECORATIONS. Philippine Presidential Unit Citation.

INSIGNE. None.

310th BOMBARDMENT WING

Constituted as 310th Bombardment Wing (Medium) on 20 Jan 1944. *Activated* in New Guinea on 1 Feb 1944. *Assigned* to Fifth AF. Engaged in combat from Feb 1944 until the end of the war, operating with various groups that were attached for short periods. *Inactivated* in Japan on 25 Mar 1946.

Redesignated 310th Bombardment Wing (Light). Allotted to the reserve. *Activated* in the US on 26 Jun 1947. *Redesignated* 310th Air Division (Bombardment) in Apr 1948. *Inactivated* on 27 Jun 1949.

GROUPS. *42d* Bombardment: 1946. *323d* Bombardment: 1947–1949. *340th* Bombardment: 1947–1949. *348th* Fighter: 1946.

STATIONS. Gusap, New Guinea, 1 Feb 1944; Hollandia, New Guinea, May 1944; Morotai, 18 Sep 1944; Leyte, 14 Nov 1944; San Jose, Mindoro, 15 Dec 1944; Clark Field, Luzon, 23 Aug 1945; Itami, Japan, 21 Oct 1945–25 Mar 1946. Tinker Field, Okla, 26 Jun 1947–27 Jun 1949.

COMMANDERS. Brig Gen Donald R Hutchinson, 1 Feb 1944; Col John T Murtha, 16 Oct 1944; Col Jack A Wilson, 15 Dec 1944; Col William M Morgan, 22 Mar 1945; Col Jack A Wilson, 17 Jul 1945; Col William M Morgan, 29 Aug 1945; Col Othel R Deering, 16 Dec 1945–unkn.

CAMPAIGNS. China Defensive; New Guinea; Western Pacific; Leyte; Luzon; Southern Philippines; China Offensive.

DECORATIONS. Philippine Presidential Unit Citation.

INSIGNE. None.

311th RECONNAISSANCE WING

Constituted as 311th Photographic Wing (Mapping and Charting) on 31 Jan 1944. *Activated* on 1 Feb 1944. Assigned directly to AAF. *Redesignated* 311th Reconnaissance Wing in Jul 1945. Operated in the US and sent detachments to various areas of the world to perform mapping and charting duties. Assigned to Continental Air Forces in Dec 1945. Became the major reconnaissance organization of Strategic Air Command in Mar 1946. *Redesignated* 311th Air Division (Reconnaissance) in Apr 1948, and 311th Air Division in Jan 1949. *Inactivated* on 1 Nov 1949.

COMPONENTS. *Groups. 1st:* 1944. *11th:* 1944. *55th:* 1947–1948. *91st:* 1947–1948. *Wings. 5th:* 1949. *9th:* 1949. *55th:* 1948–1949. *91st:* 1948–1949.

STATIONS. Bolling Field, DC, 1 Feb 1944; Buckley Field, Colo, c. 24 Nov 1944; MacDill Field, Fla, c. 17 Apr 1946; Andrews Field, Md, c. 1 Jun 1947; Topeka AFB, Kan, c. 20 Jul 1948; Barksdale AFB, La, c. 28 Oct–1 Nov 1949.

COMMANDERS. Col George G Northrup, 1 Feb 1944; Lt Col Roy W Gustafson, 16 Jan 1945; Col Karl L Polifka, 12 Feb 1945; Col James F Setchell, 16 Jul 1945; Col Karl L Polifka, 22 Oct 1945; Lt Col Albert M Welsh, c. 23 Feb 1946; Brig Gen Donald R Hutchinson, 23 May 1946; Brig Gen Paul T Cullen, c. 18 Jun 1947; Maj Gen Joseph H Atkinson, 17 Mar–1 Nov 1949.

CAMPAIGNS. American Theater.

DECORATIONS. None.

INSIGNE. None.

312th FIGHTER WING

Constituted as 312th Fighter Wing on 7 Mar 1944 and *activated* in China on 13 Mar. Assigned to Fourteenth AF. Served in combat in China from Jul 1944 until Aug 1945. Moved to the US, Oct–Nov 1945. *Inactivated* on 5 Nov 1945.

GROUPS. *33d:* 1944. *81st:* 1944–1945. *311th:* 1944–1945.

STATIONS. Kunming, China, 13 Mar 1944; Chengtu, China, c. 25 Mar 1944–c. 1 Oct 1945; Camp Kilmer, NJ, c. 3–5 Nov 1945.

COMMANDERS. Brig Gen Adlai H Gilkeson, c. 25 Mar 1944; Brig Gen Russell E Randall, c. 4 Sep 1944–c. Oct 1945.

CAMPAIGNS. China Defensive; China Offensive.

DECORATIONS. None.

INSIGNE. *Shield:* On an ultramarine blue rectangle, long axis vertical, corners engrailed, a golden orange dragon rampant, proper, tail entwined about bend checky blue and silver, edged golden orange, all within a neat line of the last. (Approved 28 Apr 1945.)

313th BOMBARDMENT WING

Constituted as 313th Bombardment Wing (Very Heavy) on 15 Apr 1944 and *activated* on 23 Apr. Moved to the Marianas late in 1944. Assigned to Twentieth AF. Engaged in very heavy bombardment operations from Jan to Aug 1945. Moved to the Philippine Islands and assigned to Far East Air Forces in Mar 1946. *Inactivated* in the Philippines on 15 Jun 1948.

Redesignated 313th Air Division. *Activated* on Okinawa on 1 Mar 1955. Assigned to Far East Air Forces.

COMPONENTS. *Groups.* *5th:* 1946–1948. *6th:* 1944–1948. *9th:* 1944–1948. *504th:* 1944–1946. *505th:* 1944–1946. *Wings.* *18th* Fighter: 1955–. *51st* Fighter: 1955–.

STATIONS. Peterson Field, Colo, 23 Apr–5 Nov 1944; North Field, Tinian, 24 Dec 1944; Clark Field, Luzon, 15 Mar 1946–15 Jun 1948. Kadena, Okinawa, 1 Mar 1955–.

COMMANDERS. Brig Gen John H Davies, 23 Apr 1944; Col George W Mundy, 26 Aug 1945–unkn. Maj Gen Fay R Upthegrove, 1 Mar 1955; Col Curtis D Sluman, 11 Jul 1955; Brig Gen William G Hipps, 3 Sep 1955–.

CAMPAIGNS. Air Offensive, Japan; Eastern Mandates; Western Pacific.

DECORATIONS. None.

INSIGNE. *Shield:* Azure, a silhouetted futuramic aircraft, volant in dexter chief, Air Force blue, fimbriated argent, with vapor trail forming an acute angular pattern from the aircraft to dexter base, the trail between three stars arched in bend sinister, one to chief, two to dexter of trail, all of the third; in sinister base an eagle volant of the second, fimbriated and detailed argent, grasping with his talons two bolts of lightning of the last. (Approved 15 Jul 1957.)

314th BOMBARDMENT WING

Constituted as 314th Bombardment Wing (Very Heavy) on 15 Apr 1944 and *activated* on 23 Apr. Moved to Guam, Dec 1944–Feb 1945. Assigned to Twentieth AF. Engaged in very heavy bom-

DESTRUCTIO AB ALTO

bardment operations from Feb to Aug 1945. *Redesignated* 314th Composite Wing in Jan 1946. Assigned to Far East Air Forces. Moved to Japan in Jun 1946. *Inactivated* on 20 Aug 1948.

Redesignated 314th Air Division. *Activated* in Japan on 1 Dec 1950. Assigned to Far East Air Forces. Provided air defense for Japan and logistic support for combat operations in Korea. *Inactivated* in Japan on 1 Mar 1952.

Activated in Korea on 15 Mar 1955. Assigned to Far East Air Forces.

COMPONENTS. *Groups. 3d* Bombardment: 1946–1948. *19th* Bombardment: 1944–1946. *29th* Bombardment: 1944–1946. *35th* Fighter: 1946–1948. *39th* Bombardment: 1944–1945. *49th* Fighter: 1946–1948. *330th* Bombardment: 1944–1945. *Wings. 35th* Fighter: 1951–1952. *58th* Fighter: 1955–. *374th* Troop Carrier: 1950–1951. *437th* Troop Carrier: 1950–1951.

STATIONS. Peterson Field, Colo, 23 Apr–9 Dec 1944; North Field, Guam, 16 Jan 1945; Johnson AB, Japan, 15 Jun 1946–20 Aug 1948. Nagoya, Japan, 1 Dec 1950–1 Mar 1952. Osan-Ni, Korea, 15 Mar 1955–.

COMMANDERS. Brig Gen Roger M Ramey, 1 Jun 1944; Lt Col Hewitt T Wheless, 15 Jun 1944; Col John G Fowler, 24 Jun 1944; Brig Gen Thomas S Power, 29 Aug 1944; Col Carl R Storrie, 23 Jul 1945–unkn; Brig Gen Jarred V Crabb, c. Jun 1946; Col Clarence D Wheeler, 30 Jul 1946; Brig Gen David W Hutchison, 23 Aug 1946; Brig Gen Herbert B Thatcher, 18 Feb 1947; Col Edward H Underhill, c. Apr 1947–1948. Brig Gen Delmar T Spivey, 1 Dec 1950–1 Mar 1952. Col William W Momyer, 15 Mar 1955; Col Thomas L Mosley, c. Sep 1955–.

CAMPAIGNS. Air Offensive, Japan; Western Pacific.

DECORATIONS. None.

INSIGNE. On an ultramarine blue disc, in sinister base, a globe, proper, with silver water areas and brown land areas, fimbriated gold, winged at dexter by a stylized wing of the last, charged with four aerial bombs gules palewise, points to base. *Motto:* DESTRUCTIO AB ALTO—Destruction from Above. (Approved 20 Jan 1945. This insigne was modified 9 May 1956.)

315th BOMBARDMENT WING

Constituted as 315th Bombardment Wing (Very Heavy) on 7 Jul 1944 and

activated on **17** Jul. Moved to Guam, Mar–Apr 1945. Assigned to Twentieth AF. Engaged in very heavy bombardment operations from Jun to Aug 1945. *Redesignated* 315th Composite Wing in Jan 1946. Assigned to Far East Air Forces. Moved to Japan in May 1946. *Inactivated* on 20 Aug 1948.

Redesignated 315th Air Division (Combat Cargo). *Activated* in Japan on 25 Jan 1951. Assigned to Far East Air Forces. Participated in aerial supply and evacuation operations for United Nations forces in Korea, 1951–1953. Assisted the French in Indochina, 1953–1954.

COMPONENTS. *Groups. 8th* Fighter: 1946–1947. *16th* Bombardment: 1944–1946. *38th* Bombardment: 1946–1948. *331st* Bombardment: 1944–1946. *501st* Bombardment: 1944–1946. *502d* Bombardment: 1944–1946. *Wings. 315th* Troop Carrier: 1952–1954. *374th* Troop Carrier: 1951–. *403d* Troop Carrier: 1952. *437th* Troop Carrier: 1951–1952. *483d* Troop Carrier: 1954–.

STATIONS. Peterson Field, Colo, 17 Jul 1944–7 Mar 1945; Northwest Field, Guam, 5 Apr 1945; Ashiya, Japan, 30 May 1946; Itazuke, Japan, 3 Sep 1946–20 Aug 1948. Ashiya, Japan, 25 Jan 1951; Fuchu, Japan, 4 Feb 1951; Tachikawa, Japan, 24 Apr 1954–.

COMMANDERS. Lt Col Robert A Koeper, 28 Jul 1944; Lt Col Stanley A Zidiales, 11 Aug 1944; Brig Gen Frank A Armstrong Jr, 18 Nov 1944; Col Leland S Stranathan, 25 Jan 1946; Col Vincent M Miles Jr, 15 Apr 1946; Col Hugh A Parker, c. Sep 1946; Col Travis M Hetherington, 7 Jun 1947; Col Joshua H Foster Jr, 19 Jun 1948; Col Marden M Munn, Jul–20 Aug 1948. Maj Gen William H Tunner, 25 Jan 1951; Brig Gen John P Henebry, 8 Feb 1951; Col Cecil H Childre, 26 Feb 1952; Maj Gen Chester E McCarty, 10 Apr 1952; Maj Gen Russell L Waldron, 3 Dec 1954–.

CAMPAIGNS. *World War II:* Air Offensive, Japan; Eastern Mandates; Western Pacific. *Korean War:* 1st UN Counteroffensive; CCF Spring Offensive; UN Summer-Fall Offensive; Second Korean Winter; Korea Summer-Fall, 1952; Third Korean Winter; Korea Summer-Fall, 1953.

DECORATIONS. Republic of Korea Presidential Unit Citation: 1 Jul 1951–27 Jul 1953.

INSIGNE. A white disc charged in base with a medium blue representation of Mt. Fujiyama, between a jagged lightning flash in dexter fesse and a like flash in sinister fesse of the last, each passing through a yellow, quarter moon, all within a border of the second, and surmounted by a large, dark red Torii pierced at center with a chevron couped inverted, above a sphere of the second outlined, marked, and charged with the Southern Cross constellation of the first, at the center of a stylized pair of golden orange wings in base. (Approved 25 Apr 1947. This insigne was modified 11 Oct 1954.)

316th BOMBARDMENT WING

Constituted as 316th Bombardment Wing (Very Heavy) on 4 Aug 1944 and *activated* on 14 Aug. Moved to Okinawa, Jul–Sep 1945. Assigned to Eighth AF and later (1946) to Far East Air Forces. *Redesignated* 316th Composite Wing in Jan 1946, and 316th Bombardment Wing (Very Heavy) in May 1946. *Inactivated* on Okinawa on 21 Jun 1948.

Redesignated 316th Air Division (Defense). *Organized* in French Morocco on 18 Sep 1953. Assigned to United States Air Forces in Europe.

COMPONENTS. *Groups. 22d:* 1946–1948. *333d:* 1944–1946. *346th:* 1944–1946. *382d:* 1944–1945. *383d:* 1944–1945. *Squadrons. 35th* Fighter: 1953–. *45th* Fighter: 1953–.

STATIONS. Peterson Field, Colo, 14 Aug 1944–7 Jul 1945; Kadena, Okinawa, 5 Sep 1945–21 Jun 1948. Rabat/Sale, French Morocco, 18 Sep 1953–.

COMMANDERS. Col Howard W Gray, 26 Aug 1944; Col Joseph J Nazzaro, 22 Nov 1944; Col Thomas J DuBose, 5 Dec 1944; Col Joseph J Nazzaro, 1 Dec 1945; Brig Gen Richard C Lindsay, 21 Jan 1946; Col Clarence A Neely, 3 Mar 1947; Col Francis L Rivard, 13 Sep 1947; Brig Gen Charles T Myers, 1 Oct 1947; Col John F Wadman, 11 Dec 1947; Col Walter E Arnold, 11 May–21 Jun 1948. Col John R Kane, 21 Sep 1953; Col Richard P Fulcher, 26 Dec 1953; Col Woodrow W Dunlop, 13 Nov 1954; Col Wallace S Ford, 23 Jun 1955–.

CAMPAIGNS. Asiatic-Pacific Theater.

DECORATIONS. None.

INSIGNE. On an ultramarine blue disc, marked with stylized latitude and longitude lines argent, a lion rampant, holding aloft in the dexter paw a sword, all of the last. (Approved 12 Feb 1945. This insigne was superseded by a new emblem on 15 Nov 1955.)

322d TROOP CARRIER WING

Constituted as 322d Troop Carrier Wing on 4 Dec 1944 and *activated* by Far East Air Forces on 30 Dec. Operated in the

southwestern and western Pacific areas until the end of the war. *Inactivated* in the Philippines on 15 Feb 1946.

Allotted to the reserve. *Activated* in the US on 12 Jun 1947. *Redesignated* 322d Air Division (Troop Carrier) in Apr 1948. *Inactivated* on 27 Jun 1949.

Redesignated 322d Air Division (Combat Cargo). *Activated* in Germany on 1 Mar 1954. Assigned to United States Air Forces in Europe.

COMPONENTS. *Groups. 374th:* 1945–1946. *440th:* 1947–1949. *Wings. 60th* Troop Carrier: 1955–. *317th* Troop Carrier: 1955–. *465th* Troop Carrier: 1955–.

STATIONS. Hollandia, New Guinea, 30 Dec 1944; Manila, Luzon, 22 Jul 1945–15 Feb 1946. Lowry Field, Colo, 12 Jun 1947–27 Jun 1949. Wiesbaden, Germany, 1 Mar 1954; Ramstein, Germany, c. 22 Mar 1954; Evreux/Fauville AB, France, 12 Aug 1955–.

COMMANDERS. Col Ray T Elsmore, 30 Dec 1944; Col Leo H Dawson, 17 Oct 1945–unkn. Col Lucion N Powell, 1 Mar 1954; Brig Gen Franklin Rose, 17 May 1954–.

CAMPAIGNS. Air Offensive, Japan; Western Pacific; Leyte; Luzon.

DECORATIONS. None.

INSIGNE. *Shield:* Argent between the points of a flying dart gules, a sphere of the field, with axis, latitude lines, longitude lines and outline sable; in dexter chief a cross couped of the second, winged of the first; in sinister base a parachute gules, lines and detail black; two points pointed bendwise, one in dexter base and one in sinister chief azure. (Approved 16 Aug 1956.)

323d COMBAT CREW TRAINING WING

Constituted as Boston Air Defense Wing on 6 Aug 1942 and *activated* on 11 Aug. *Redesignated* Boston Fighter Wing in Jul 1943. Defended the New England area; also trained fighter organizations and personnel. Apparently was not manned from Jul 1944 until Feb 1945. *Redesignated* 323d Combat Crew Training Wing. Trained very heavy bombardment personnel from Mar until Aug 1945. Apparently had no personnel assigned after Aug. *Inactivated* on 8 Apr 1946.

Redesignated 323d Troop Carrier Wing and allotted to the reserve. *Activated* on 1 Aug 1947. *Redesignated* 323d Air Division (Troop Carrier) in Apr 1948. *Inactivated* on 27 Jun 1949.

Redesignated 323d Air Division. *Activated* on 1 Jul 1958. Assigned to Military Air Transport Service.

GROUPS. *58th* Fighter: 1943. *79th* Fighter: 1942. *325th* Fighter: 1942–1943. *359th* Fighter: 1943. *434th* Troop Carrier: 1947–1949. *436th* Troop Carrier: 1947–1948. (Other groups assigned for short periods for operations or training, 1942–1944.)

STATIONS. Boston, Mass, 11 Aug 1942; MacDill Field, Fla, Feb 1945–8 Apr 1946. Stout Field, Ind, 1 Aug 1947–27 Jun 1949. Travis AFB, Calif, 1 Jul 1958–.

COMMANDERS. Col Minthorne W Reed, 11 Aug 1942; Col Glenn O Barcus, 25 Mar 1943; Col Laurence C Craigie, 6 Apr 1943; Lt Col Bingham T Kleine, 11 Jun 1943; Col Louis M Merrick, 22 Jul 1943; Lt Col J Marshall Booker, 29 Apr–c. 31 Jul 1944; Col Howard Moore, 22 Feb 1945; Col Frank Allen, 29 May 1945–unkn. Unkn, 1958–.

CAMPAIGNS. American Theater.
DECORATIONS. None.
INSIGNE. None.

325th RECONNAISSANCE WING

Constituted as 325th Photographic Wing (Reconnaissance) on 17 Jul 1944. *Activated* in England on 9 Aug 1944. Assigned to Eighth AF. Served in the European theater until after V–E Day. *Redesignated* 325th Reconnaissance Wing in Jun

1945. *Inactivated* in England on 20 Oct 1945.

Allotted to the reserve. *Activated* in the US on 9 Apr 1947. *Redesignated* 325th Air Division (Reconnaissance) in Apr 1948. *Inactivated* on 27 Jun 1949.

GROUPS. *7th* Reconnaissance: 1944–1945. *25th* Bombardment (Reconnaissance): 1944–1945. *68th* Reconnaissance: 1947–1949. *70th* Reconnaissance: 1947–1949. *72d* Reconnaissance: 1947–1949.

STATIONS. High Wycombe, England, 9 Aug 1944–20 Oct 1945. Hamilton Field, Calif, 9 Apr 1947–27 Jun 1949.

COMMANDERS. Col Elliott Roosevelt, 9 Aug 1944; Brig Gen Charles Y Banfill, 17 Jan 1945; Brig Gen Elliott Roosevelt, 22 Jan 1945; Col Leon W Gray, 13 Apr 1945; Col George W Humbrecht, 19 Jun–c. Oct 1945.

CAMPAIGNS. Northern France; Rhineland; Ardennes-Alsace; Central Europe.
DECORATIONS. None.
INSIGNE. None.

LOS ANGELES FIGHTER WING

Constituted as Los Angeles Air Defense Wing on 6 Aug 1942 and *activated* on 20 Aug. Assigned to Fourth AF. *Redesignated* Los Angeles Fighter Wing in Jul 1943. Provided air defense for the Los Angeles area. Also trained fighter groups and personnel. *Disbanded* on 7 Jun 1944.

GROUPS. *20th*: 1943. *329th*: 1943–1944. *360th*: 1943–1944. *364th*: 1943–1944. *412th*: 1943–1944. *473d*: 1943–1944. *474th*: 1943–1944. *479th*: 1943–1944.

STATIONS. Los Angeles, Calif, 20 Aug 1942–7 Jun 1944.

COMMANDERS. Col Robert S Israel Jr, Aug 1942; Maj Henry G Thorne Jr, c. 11 Dec 1942; Brig Gen Edward M Morris, c. 6 Jan 1943; Lt Col Henry G Thorne Jr, c. 21 Mar 1943; Col Ralph A Snavely, c. 25 Mar 1943; Lt Col Merrick Bayer, c. 4 Aug 1943; Col Romulus W Puryear, c. 16 Aug 1943; Col Ralph A Snavely, c. 8 Dec 1943; Lt Col Edward G Hillery, c. 26 Mar 1944; Lt Col John O Zahn, 5 Apr 1944; Maj Gomer Lewis, 1 May–c. 7 Jun 1944.

CAMPAIGNS. American Theater.

DECORATIONS. None.

INSIGNE. None.

NEW YORK FIGHTER WING

Constituted as New York Air Defense Wing on 6 Aug 1942 and *activated* on 11 Aug. Assigned to First AF. *Redesignated* New York Fighter Wing in Jul 1943. Served in defense of the New York area and also trained fighter groups and personnel. Evidently not manned after Jul 1944. *Inactivated* on 3 Apr 1946. *Disbanded* on 8 Oct 1948.

GROUPS. *56th:* 1942. *58th:* 1943. *80th:* 1942–1943. *326th:* 1942–1943. *348th:* 1942–1943. *352d:* 1942–1943. *356th:* 1943. *359th:* 1943. *362d:* 1943. *368th:* 1943. *370th:* 1943. *373d:* 1943. *402d:* 1943.

STATIONS. New York, NY, 11 Aug 1942–3 Apr 1946.

COMMANDERS. Col Davis D Graves, Aug 1942; Lt Col Othel R Deering, c. 19 Dec 1942; Col Morley F Slaght, c. 17 Jan 1943; Lt Col Othel R Deering, c. 19 Jan 1943; Brig Gen Earle E Partridge, c. 27 Jan 1943; Col Othel R Deering, c. 20 Apr 1943; Brig Gen Laurence C Craigie, Jun 1943; Maj Clayton J Larson, c. 22 Nov 1943; Col Stewart W Towle Jr, 2 Dec 1943–c. 29 Jul 1944.

CAMPAIGNS. American Theater.

DECORATIONS. None.

INSIGNE. None.

NORFOLK FIGHTER WING

Constituted as Norfolk Air Defense Wing on 6 Aug 1942 and *activated* on 11 Aug. Assigned to First AF. *Redesignated* Norfolk Fighter Wing in Jul 1943. Served in the defense of the Norfolk area. Not manned after Jul 1944. *Inactivated* on 3 Apr 1946. *Disbanded* on 8 Oct 1948.

COMPONENTS. (Operated with attached AAF organizations and cooperating naval aircraft.)

STATIONS. Norfolk, Va, 11 Aug 1942–3 Apr 1946.

COMMANDERS. Col Malcolm N Stewart, 11 Aug 1942; Col Murray C Woodbury, 24 Sep 1942; Maj Earl H Dunham, Apr 1943; Col Burton M Hovey Jr, c. 29 Jun 1943–unkn; Lt Col Earl H Dunham, 14 Aug 1943; Lt Col Otis F Tabler, c. 25 Nov 1943; Lt Col Charles A Gayle, c. 2 Apr–c. 26 Jul 1944.

CAMPAIGNS. American Theater.

DECORATIONS. None.

INSIGNE. None.

ORLANDO FIGHTER WING

Constituted as Air Defense Department, AAF School of Applied Tactics on 27 Nov 1942. *Activated* on 3 Dec 1942. Helped to develop air defense tactics and trained organizations and personnel in the techniques of air defense. Also served in defense of the Orlando area, using such tactical organizations as were assigned or attached. *Redesignated* Orlando Fighter Wing in Oct 1943. Continued to provide defense for the Orlando area but engaged primarily in training fighter and light bombardment organizations and personnel. *Disbanded* on 1 Apr 1944.

COMPONENTS. (See the narrative.)

STATIONS. Orlando, Fla, 3 Dec 1942–1 Apr 1944.

COMMANDERS. Col Earl W Barnes, Dec 1942; Col Orrin L Grover, c. 31 Jul 1943; Col Norman D Sillin, c. 1 Nov 1943; Lt Col Hervey H Whitfield, 8 Dec 1943; Col Orrin L Grover, 20 Feb 1944; Col Phineas K Morrill Jr, 1 Mar–1 Apr 1944.

CAMPAIGNS. American Theater

DECORATIONS. None.

INSIGNE. None.

PHILADELPHIA FIGHTER WING

Constituted as Philadelphia Air Defense Wing on 6 Aug 1942 and *activated* on 11 Aug. Assigned to First AF. *Redesignated* Philadelphia Fighter Wing in Jul 1943. Served in defense of the Philadelphia area

and also trained fighter groups and personnel. Not manned after 31 Jul 1944. *Inactivated* on 3 Apr 1946. *Disbanded* on 8 Oct 1948.

GROUPS. *33d:* 1942. *58th:* 1943. *83d:* 1943. *87th:* 1943. *324th:* 1942. *327th:* 1943. *353d:* 1942–1943. *355th:* 1943. *358th:* 1943. *361st:* 1943. *365th:* 1943. *366th:* 1943. *371st:* 1943.

STATIONS. Philadelphia, Pa, 11 Aug 1942–3 Apr 1946.

COMMANDERS. Col Elwood R Quesada, Aug 1942; Col Glenn O Barcus, Dec 1942; Col William R Morgan, c. 23 Mar 1943; Col Glenn O Barcus, c. 7 Apr 1943; Col William R Morgan, c. 13 Apr 1943; Brig Gen George F Schulgen, c. 21 May 1943; Col Burton M Hovey Jr, c. 5 Jul 1943; Brig Gen George F Schulgen, c. 12 Oct 1943; Brig Gen Richard E Nugent, c. 18 Oct 1943; Col Burton M Hovey Jr, c. 1 Nov 1943; Col Morris R Nelson, c. 2 Dec 1943; Maj Joseph S Littlepage, c. 27 Dec 1943– c. 31 Jul 1944.

CAMPAIGNS. American Theater.

DECORATIONS. None.

INSIGNE. None.

SAN DIEGO FIGHTER WING

Constituted as San Diego Air Defense Wing on 6 Aug 1942 and *activated* on 20 Aug. Assigned to Fourth AF. *Redesignated* San Diego Fighter Wing in Jul 1943. Served in defense of the San Diego area. *Disbanded* on 7 Jun 1944.

COMPONENTS. (Operated with an attached AAF squadron and cooperating naval aircraft.)

STATIONS. San Diego, Calif, 20 Aug 1942–7 Jun 1944.

COMMANDERS. Maj Kenneth R Martin, Aug 1942; Lt Col Paul W Blanchard Jr, c. 2 Nov 1942; Col Joseph A Bulger, c. 5 Feb 1943; Lt Col John O Zahn, 14 Oct 1943; Capt John W Etheredge, 27 Mar 1944; Lt Col Edward G Hillery, 7 Apr 1944; Lt Col Benjamin W Martin, 20 May–7 Jun 1944.

CAMPAIGNS. American Theater.

DECORATIONS. None.

INSIGNE. None.

SAN FRANCISCO FIGHTER WING

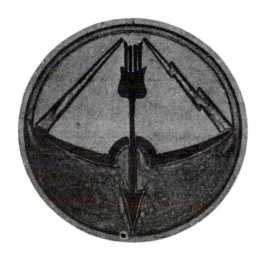

Constituted as San Francisco Air Defense Wing on 6 Aug 1942 and *activated* on 20 Aug. Assigned to Fourth AF. *Redesignated* San Francisco Fighter Wing in Jul 1943. Served in defense of the San Francisco area. Also trained fighter groups and personnel. *Disbanded* on 7 Jun 1944.

GROUPS. *328th:* 1943–1944. *354th:* 1943. *357th:* 1943. *363d:* 1943. *367th:* 1943–1944. *369th:* 1943–1944. *372d:* 1943. *478th:* 1943–1944.

STATIONS. San Francisco, Calif, 20 Aug 1942–7 Jun 1944.

COMMANDERS. Lt Col Ronald F Fallows, 20 Aug 1942; Col Jesse Auton, c. 16 Jan 1943; Lt Col John R Ulricson, c. 11 Apr 1943; Brig Gen Ned Schramm, c. 2 May 1943; Col John C Crosthwaite, 19 Nov 1943; Brig Gen Warren R Carter, 20 Dec 1943; Col John C Crosthwaite, 22 Jan 1944; Brig Gen Dean C Strother, 8 Feb 1944; Col Aaron W Tyer, 25 Feb 1944–unkn; Col Errol H Zistel, 1 Apr 1944; Maj Otis B Hocker, 16 May–7 Jun 1944.

CAMPAIGNS. American Theater.

DECORATIONS. None.

INSIGNE. *Shield:* On a bezant a hurt charged with a stylized red drawn-bow and arrow of four conventionalized feathers, points upwards, the bowstring consisting of a blue flash and a blue search light beam, within the lower arc of the ends of the bow, gold. (Approved 5 Feb 1943.)

SEATTLE FIGHTER WING

Constituted as Seattle Air Defense Wing on 6 Aug 1942 and *activated* on 20 Aug. Assigned to Fourth AF. *Redesignated* Seattle Fighter Wing in Jul 1943. Provided air defense for the northwest. Also trained fighter groups and personnel. *Disbanded* on 7 Jun 1944.

GROUPS. *55th:* 1943. *372d:* 1943–1944. *478th:* 1944.

STATIONS. Seattle, Wash, 20 Aug 1942–7 Jun 1944.

COMMANDERS. Col James W McCauley, 20 Aug 1942; Brig Gen Edward M Morris, c. 5 Dec 1942; Col James W McCauley, c. 18 Dec 1942; Lt Col Wilbur H Stratton, c. 22 Oct 1943; Col John C Crosthwaite, 22 Feb 1944; Lt Col John O Zahn, 1 Apr 1944; Col Clarence T Edwinson, 4 Apr 1944; Maj Norman S Archibald, 27 Apr 1944; Lt Col Richard E Carlgren, 1 May–c. 7 Jun 1944.

CAMPAIGNS. American Theater.

DECORATIONS. None.

INSIGNE. None.

TRINIDAD WING, ANTILLES AIR COMMAND

Constituted as VI Interceptor Command on 17 Oct 1941 and *activated* in Puerto Rico on 25 Oct. *Redesignated* VI Fighter Command in May 1942, and Trinidad Wing, Antilles Air Command in Oct 1943. *Disbanded* in Trinidad on 15 Mar 1944.

COMPONENTS. Unkn.

STATIONS. Borinquen Field, PR, 25 Oct 1941; Henry Barracks, PR, 20 Mar 1943; Waller Field, Trinidad, 15 May 1943–15 Mar 1944.

COMMANDERS. Brig Gen Edwin J House, Dec 1941—unkn; Brig Gen Charles F Born, Oct 1942–unkn.

CAMPAIGNS. American Theater.

DECORATIONS. None.

INSIGNE. None.

DIVISIONS

1st AIR DIVISION

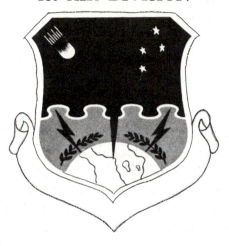

Constituted as 1st Bombardment Division on 30 Aug 1943. *Activated* in England on 13 Sep 1943. Assigned to Eighth AF. *Redesignated* 1st Air Division in Dec 1944. Served in combat in the European theater from Sep 1943 until Apr 1945, receiving a DUC for an attack on aircraft factories in central Germany on 11 Jan 1944. *Inactivated* in England on 31 Oct 1945.

Activated on Okinawa on 7 Jun 1946. Assigned to Far East Air Forces. Served as an air defense organization. *Inactivated* on 1 Dec 1948.

Activated in the US on 1 Jul 1954. Assigned to Strategic Air Command. Apparently had no combat components as-signed and was never adequately manned. *Inactivated* on 1 Apr 1955.

Activated on 15 Apr 1955. Assigned to Strategic Air Command. Had no combat elements assigned. Conducted high altitude meteorological research. *Inactivated* on 20 May 1956.

Redesignated 1st Missile Division. *Activated* on 15 Apr 1957. Assigned to Air Research and Development Command. No combat elements were assigned at the time of activation.

WINGS. *1st* Bombardment: 1943–1945. *2d* Bombardment: 1945. *32d* Composite: 1948. *40th* Bombardment: 1943–1945. *41st* Bombardment: 1943–1945. *51st* Fighter: 1948. *67th* Fighter: 1944–1945. *71st* Reconnaissance: 1948. *92d* Bombardment: 1943. *94th* Bombardment: 1943–1945. *301st* Fighter: 1946–1948. *316th* Bombardment: 1946–1948.

STATIONS. Brampton Grange, England, 13 Sep 1943; Alconbury, England, c. 20 Sep–31 Oct 1945. Kadena, Okinawa, 7 Jun 1946–1 Dec 1948. Westover AFB, Mass, 1 Jul 1954–1 Apr 1955. Offutt AFB, Neb, 15 Apr 1955–20 May 1956. Los Angeles, Calif, 15 Apr 1957–.

COMMANDERS. Maj Gen Robert B Williams, 16 Sep 1943; Maj Gen Howard M Turner, 22 Oct 1944; Brig Gen Bartlett

Beaman, 26 Sep 1945–unkn. Brig Gen Patrick W Timberlake, 7 Jun 1946; Maj Gen Albert F Hegenberger, Sep 1946; Maj Gen Charles T Myers, Dec 1947–1 Dec 1948. Lt Col Robert G Bradley, c. Jan 1955–unkn. Maj Gen William P Fisher, 15 Apr 1955–20 May 1956. Col William A Sheppard, 15 Apr 1957–.

CAMPAIGNS. Air Offensive, Europe; Normandy; Northern France; Rhineland; Ardennes-Alsace; Central Europe.

DECORATIONS. Distinguished Unit Citation: Germany, 11 Jan 1944.

INSIGNE. *Shield:* Per fess nebuly abased azure and or fimbriated argent, issuant from base a demi-sphere with grid lines and land masses of the third, the latter outlined of the first and water areas proper, heightened and encircled by two olive branches vert nerved of the second; surmounting the sphere in pale, a lightning flash gules terminating in chief accosted by two smaller flashes of the like in base radiant from the sphere; in dexter chief a descending nose cone in bend proper, with seven streaks of the third, in sinister chief four mullets of the like, all within a diminished border of the last. (Approved 17 Aug 1959.)

I TACTICAL AIR DIVISION

Constituted as IV Air Support Command on 21 Aug 1941. *Activated* on 3 Sep 1941. *Redesignated* IV Ground Air Support Command in Apr 1942, IV Air Support Command in Sep 1942, III Tactical Air Division in Aug 1943, and I Tac-

tical Air Division in Apr 1944. At various times, supervised heavy bomber flights to Hawaii, gave air support to ground units in training, participated in air-ground maneuvers, and put on air support demonstrations. *Inactivated* on 22 Dec 1945. *Disbanded* on 8 Oct 1948.

COMPONENTS. (Omitted because of large number and frequent changes.)

STATIONS. Fresno, Calif, 3 Sep 1941; Hamilton Field, Calif, 11 Sep 1941; Presidio of San Francisco, Calif, Feb 1942; Thermal AAFld, Calif, Jan 1943; Camp Young, Calif, c. Sep 1943; Thermal AAFld, Calif, c. 15 Dec 1943; Esler Field, La, Apr 1944; Alexandria AAFld, La, Sep 1945; Barksdale Field, La, c. 16 Nov 1945; Biggs Field, Tex, c. 23 Nov–22 Dec 1945.

COMMANDERS. Col Robert C Candee, Sep 1941; Lt Col Errol H Zistel, 27 Dec 1941; Brig Gen Jacob H Rudolph, 11 Apr 1942; Lt Col James R Gunn Jr, 23 Jan 1943; Col Clarence E Crumrine, 16 Feb 1943; Col Aubrey W Scholfield, 9 Nov 1943; Lt Col John T Shields, 18 Dec 1943; Brig Gen Ford L Fair, 24 Dec 1943; Col Charles G Chandler Jr, 1 May 1945; Col Joseph W Baylor, 15 Aug 1945–unkn.

CAMPAIGNS. American Theater.

DECORATIONS. None.

INSIGNE. None.

2d AIR DIVISION

Constituted as 2d Bombardment Division on 30 Aug 1943. *Activated* in England on 13 Sep 1943. Assigned to Eighth AF. *Redesignated* 2d Air Division in Dec

1944. Served in combat in the European theater from Sep 1943 until Apr 1945. Moved to the US in Jun 1945. *Disbanded* on 28 Aug 1945.

Organized in Germany on 1 Jun 1949. Assigned to United States Air Forces in Europe as a fighter-bomber organization. *Discontinued* in Germany on 7 May 1951.

Activated in Germany on 20 Apr 1953. Assigned to United States Air Forces in Europe. Was inadequately manned and had no combat components assigned. Transferred, without personnel and equipment, to Saudi Arabia in Mar 1954. Manned in the spring of 1954, but had no combat components assigned. Supervised USAF facilities in Saudi Arabia.

WINGS. *2d* Bombardment: 1943–1945. *14th* Bombardment: 1943–1945. *20th* Bombardment: 1943–1945. *36th* Fighter: 1949–1951. *65th* Fighter: 1944–1945. *86th* Fighter: 1949–1951. *93d* Bombardment: 1943–1944. *96th* Bombardment: 1944–1945.

STATIONS. Horsham St Faith, England, 13 Sep 1943; Ketteringham Hall, England, c. 10 Dec 1943–c. 22 Jun 1945; Sioux Falls AAFld, SD, c. 3 Jul–28 Aug 1945. Wiesbaden, Germany, 1 Jun 1949; Landsberg, Germany, 10 Jun 1949–7 May 1951. Ramstein, Germany, 20 Apr 1953–1 Mar 1954; Dhahran, Saudi Arabia, 1 Mar 1954–.

COMMANDERS. Brig Gen James P Hodges, 13 Sep 1943; Brig Gen Edward J Timberlake Jr, 16 Sep 1943; Maj Gen James P Hodges, 4 Oct 1943; Maj Gen William E Kepner, 1 Aug 1944; Brig Gen Walter R Peck, 10 May 1945; Col Harry McGee, c. 1 Jun 1945–unkn. Brig Gen Thomas C Darcy, 1 Jun 1949–May 1951. Brig Gen Orrin L Grover, 1 Mar 1954; Col George W Humbrecht, 13 Apr 1955; Brig Gen George F Schlatter, 27 Jun 1955–.

CAMPAIGNS. Air Offensive, Europe; Normandy; Northern France; Rhineland; Ardennes-Alsace; Central Europe.

DECORATIONS. None.

INSIGNE. *Shield:* Azure (dark blue) double bordered or and of the first (light blue) a stylized wing of the second, charged with two Doric columns, architrave and base all outlined of the first. (Approved 14 Oct 1954.)

II TACTICAL AIR DIVISION

Constituted as II Air Support Command on 21 Aug 1941. *Activated* on 1 Sep 1941. *Redesignated* II Ground Air Support Command in Apr 1942, II Air Support Command in Sep 1942, and II Tactical Air Division in Aug 1943. Partic-

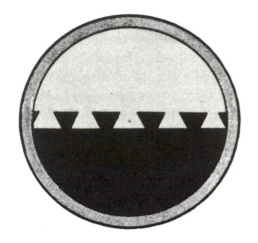

ton, 29 Sep 1943; Col Clarence D Wheeler, 5 May 1944; Col Yancey S Tarrant, 18 Jul 1945; Col Charles G Chandler Jr, 20 Aug 1945–unkn.

CAMPAIGNS. American Theater.

DECORATIONS. None.

INSIGNE. A disc per fess, dovetailed azure and vert, within a border argent. (Approved 15 Mar 1943.)

3d AIR DIVISION

ipated in various air-ground maneuvers, supported ground units in training, and put on air support demonstrations. *Inactivated* on 22 Dec 1945. *Disbanded* on 8 Oct 1948.

COMPONENTS. (Omitted because of large number and frequent changes.)

STATIONS. Ft Douglas, Utah, 1 Sep 1941; Will Rogers Field, Okla, c. Oct 1941; Birmingham, Ala, c. 1 Apr 1942; Geiger Field, Wash, 26 May 1942; Reno, Nev, 27 May 1942; Colorado Springs, Colo, Jul 1942; Barksdale Field, La, 15 Mar 1943; DeRidder AAB, La, c. 31 Mar 1944; Stuttgart AAFld, Ark, Feb 1945; Barksdale Field, La, c. 12 Nov 1945; Biggs Field, Tex, c. 23 Nov–22 Dec 1945.

COMMANDERS. Lt Col Bernard S Thompson, 4 Sep 1941; Col Hume Peabody, 11 Oct 1941; Brig Gen William E Lynd, 18 Mar 1942; Brig Gen John B Brooks, 15 Jun 1942; Col Arthur G Hamilton, 2 Dec 1942; Brig Gen Carlyle H Wash, 14 Dec 1942; Col Dache McC Reeves, 30 Jan 1943; Col Arthur G Hamil-

Constituted as 3d Bombardment Division on 30 Aug 1943. *Activated* in England on 13 Sep 1943. Assigned to Eighth AF. *Redesignated* 3d Air Division in Dec 1944. Served in combat in the European theater from Sep 1943 until Apr 1945. *Inactivated* in England on 21 Nov 1945.

Organized in England on 23 Aug 1948. Assigned first to United States Air Forces in Europe, later (Jan 1949) directly to USAF, and again (Jan 1951) to United States Air Forces in Europe. Had no combat elements assigned but directed the training of Strategic Air Command components on temporary duty in the United Kingdom. Also provided some logistic support for the Berlin airlift, 1948–1949. *Discontinued* in England on 1 May 1951.

Activated in Germany on 25 Oct 1953. Assigned to United States Air Forces in Europe. Apparently was inadequately manned and had no combat components assigned. *Inactivated* in Germany on 1 Mar 1954.

Activated on Guam on 18 Jun 1954. Assigned to Strategic Air Command. Given operational control over Strategic Air Command wings on temporary duty in the Far East.

WINGS. *4th* Bombardment: 1943–1945. *13th* Bombardment: 1943–1945. *14th* Bombardment: 1945. *20th* Bombardment: 1945. *45th* Bombardment: 1943–1945. *65th* Fighter: 1945. *66th* Fighter: 1944–1945. *67th* Fighter: 1945. *92d* Bombardment: 1943–1945. *93d* Bombardment: 1944–1945.

STATIONS. Camp Blainey, England, 13 Sep 1943; Honington, England, c. 27 Oct–21 Nov 1945. Marham, England, 23 Aug 1948; Bushy Park, England, 8 Sep 1948; Victoria Park Estate, England, 15 Apr 1949–1 May 1951. Wiesbaden, Germany, 25 Oct 1953–1 Mar 1954. Andersen AFB, Guam, 18 Jun 1954–.

COMMANDERS. Maj Gen Curtis E LeMay, 13 Sep 1943; Maj Gen Earle E Partridge, 21 Jun 1944; Brig Gen Norris B Harbold, 14 May 1945; Brig Gen Eugene L Eubank, 6 Jun 1945; Brig Gen Murray C Woodbury, c. 6 Sep 1945; Brig Gen Harold Q Huglin, 25 Sep 1945–unkn. Maj Gen Leon W Johnson, Aug 1948–1 May 1951. Maj Russel R Frederick, 26 Dec 1953–unkn. Brig Gen Joseph D C Caldara, 18 Jun 1954; Brig Gen Nils O Ohman, 10 Feb 1955–.

CAMPAIGNS. Air Offensive, Europe; Normandy; Northern France; Rhineland; Ardennes-Alsace; Central Europe.

DECORATIONS. None.

INSIGNE. *Shield:* Azure, three lightning bolts, points to base, radiating to chief or. (Approved 14 Mar 1955.)

9th AIR DIVISION

Constituted as 19th Composite Wing on 8 May 1929. *Activated* on 1 Apr 1931. Moved to the Panama Canal Zone in Jan 1933. *Redesignated* 19th Wing in 1937, and 19th Bombardment Wing in 1940. *Inactivated* in the Canal Zone on 25 Oct 1941.

Activated in the US on 24 Jul 1942. Moved to Egypt, Sep–Nov 1942. Assigned to Ninth AF. *Redesignated* IX Bomber Command in Nov 1942. Operated in the Mediterranean area until Oct 1943. Moved to the European theater, Oct–Nov 1943, and served as a tactical bombardment force in that area until V–E Day. *Redesignated* 9th Bombardment Division (Medium) in Aug 1944, and 9th Air Division in May 1945. *Inactivated* in Europe on 20 Nov 1945.

Redesignated 19th Bombardment Wing (Very Heavy). Allotted to the reserve. *Activated* in the US on 20 Dec 1946. *Redesignated* 19th Air Division (Bombardment) in Apr 1948. *Inactivated* on 27 Jun 1949.

Redesignated 19th Air Division. *Organized* on 16 Feb 1951. Assigned to Strategic Air Command.

COMPONENTS. *Groups.* *6th* Bombardment: 1931–1941. *9th* Bombardment: 1940–1941. *12th* Bombardment: 1942–1943. *16th* Pursuit: 1933–1940. *20th* Pursuit: 1931–1933. *37th* Pursuit: 1940. *94th* Bombardment: 1947–1949. *96th* Bombardment: 1947–1949. *98th* Bombardment: 1942–1943. *99th* Bombardment: 1947–1949. *321st* Bombardment: 1942–1943. *376th* Bombardment: 1942–1943. *Wings.* *7th* Bombardment: 1951–. *11th* Bombardment: 1951–. *97th* Bombardment: 1943–1945. *98th* Bombardment: 1943–1945. *99th* Bombardment: 1943–1945.

STATIONS. Mitchel Field, NY, 1 Apr 1931–Jan 1933; Albrook Field, CZ, 25 Jan 1933–25 Oct 1941. MacDill Field, Fla, 24 Jul–28 Sep 1942; Ismailia, Egypt, 12 Nov 1942; Bengasi, Libya, 15 Feb–1 Oct 1943; Marks Hall, England, 6 Nov 1943; Chartres, France, 18 Sep 1944; Reims, France, Oct 1944; Namur, Belgium, Apr–20 Nov 1945. Birmingham AAB, Ala, 20 Dec 1946–27 Jun 1949. Carswell AFB Tex, 16 Feb 1951–.

COMMANDERS. Lt Col William C McCord, 1933; Brig Gen George H Brett, c. Jun 1936; Brig Gen Herbert A Dargue, c. Sep 1938; Brig Gen Douglas B Netherwood, 30 Oct 1940; Brig Gen Edwin B Lyon, 4 Aug–25 Oct 1941. Brig Gen Patrick W Timberlake, 12 Nov 1942; Brig Gen Uzal G Ent, c. 18 Mar 1943; Maj Gen Samuel E Anderson, 16 Oct 1943; Brig Gen Richard C Sanders, 24 May 1945; Col Reginald F C Vance, 12 Aug–Nov 1945. Maj Gen Clarence S Irvine, 16 Feb 1951; Brig Gen J W Kelly, 10 Apr 1952; Brig Gen John D Ryan, 4 Aug 1953–.

CAMPAIGNS. Air Combat, EAME Theater; Egypt-Libya; Air Offensive, Europe; Tunisia; Sicily; Naples-Foggia; Normandy; Northern France; Rhineland; Ardennes-Alsace; Central Europe.

DECORATIONS. None.

INSIGNE. *Shield:* Azure, surmounting a lightning flash gules, a globe argent with latitude and longitude lines dark blue and encircled with a planetary ring of the last strewn with stars of the third and fimbriated of the like all bendwise, in chief an olive branch fesswise or, all within a diminished border of the third. (Approved 11 Mar 1959.)

COMMANDS

I BOMBER COMMAND

COMMANDERS. Brig Gen Westside T Larson, 15 Oct 1942; Col George A McHenry, c. 10 Sep 1943; Brig Gen Caleb V Haynes, c. 1 Oct 1943–unkn.

CAMPAIGNS. Antisubmarine, American Theater; Antisubmarine, EAME Theater.

DECORATIONS. None.

INSIGNE. On a disc azure, border or, a pile argent charged with a large, red aerial bomb palewise, all surmounted by a griffin or, facing toward dexter, fimbriated azure. (Approved 8 Jan 1946.)

I FIGHTER COMMAND

Constituted as Army Air Forces Antisubmarine Command on 13 Oct 1942 and *activated* in the US on 15 Oct. Assigned directly to AAF. *Redesignated* I Bomber Command in Aug 1943. Assigned to First AF. Conducted antisubmarine operations from bases in the US, the Caribbean, Newfoundland, Northwest Africa, and England from Oct 1942 until Oct 1943. Afterward, trained bombardment organizations and personnel. *Inactivated* on 21 Mar 1946. *Disbanded* on 8 Oct 1948.

WINGS. *25th* Antisubmarine: 1942–1943. *26th* Antisubmarine: 1942–1943.

STATIONS. New York, NY, 15 Oct 1942; Mitchel Field, NY, c. 1 Oct 1943–21 Mar 1946.

Constituted as I Interceptor Command on 26 May 1941. *Activated* on 5 Jun 1941. Assigned to First AF. *Redesignated* I Fighter Command in May 1942. Provided air defense for the east coast of the US (until Aug 1944); trained fighter personnel and organizations. *Inactivated* on 21 Mar 1946. *Disbanded* on 8 Oct 1948.

WINGS. Boston Fighter: 1942–1944. New York Fighter: 1942–1944. Norfolk Fighter: 1942–1944. Philadelphia Fighter: 1942–1944.

STATIONS. Mitchel Field, NY, 5 Jun 1941; New York, NY, 27 Dec 1941; Mitchel Field, NY, 9 Jun 1942–21 Mar 1946.

COMMANDERS. Brig Gen John C McDonnell, Jun 1941; Brig Gen John K Cannon, Mar–c. Sep 1942; Col Elwood R Quesada, c. 29 Sep 1942; Brig Gen Willis R Taylor, c. 25 Nov 1942; Brig Gen Glenn O Barcus, Apr 1943–c. 14 Apr 1944; Brig Gen John R Hawkins, c. 26 May 1944–unkn.

CAMPAIGNS. American Theater.

DECORATIONS. None.

INSIGNE. On a geometrical figure formed by an octagon with inverted sides azure, border gold, a pile argent debruised at base point by a mullet of the last and surmounted by a stylized falcon grasping two lightning bolts in claws, diving bendwise and emitting speed lines, all or. (Approved 11 Jun 1943.)

I TROOP CARRIER COMMAND

Established as Air Transport Command on 30 Apr 1942. Assigned directly to AAF. *Redesignated* I Troop Carrier Command in Jul 1942. Trained troop

carrier organizations and personnel. *Disbanded* on 4 Nov 1945.

WINGS. *50th:* 1942–1943, 1945. *51st:* 1942. *52d:* 1942–1943, 1945. *53d:* 1942–1944. *60th:* 1943–1945. *61st:* 1943–1945.

STATIONS. Washington, DC, 30 Apr 1942; Stout Field, Ind, c. 20 May 1942–4 Nov 1945.

COMMANDERS. Brig Gen Fred S Borum, 30 Apr 1942; Col Reed G Landis, 3 Aug 1943; Brig Gen Frederick W Evans, 4 Oct 1943; Brig Gen William D Old, 26 Aug 1944; Maj Gen Paul L Williams, c. Aug–c. 4 Nov 1945.

CAMPAIGNS. American Theater.

DECORATIONS. None.

INSIGNE. On a blue disc edged in gold, a stylized condor clutching in its dexter claw a Paratrooper carrying a "tommy" gun, ready for action. *Motto:* VINCIT QUI PRIMUM GERIT—He conquers who gets there first. (Approved 21 Oct 1942.)

II BOMBER COMMAND

Constituted as II Bomber Command on 4 Sep 1941 and *activated* on 5 Sep. Assigned to Second AF. Trained bombardment organizations. Also patrolled the west coast (until May 1943). *Disbanded* on 6 Oct 1943.

COMPONENTS. (Omitted because of large number and frequent changes.)

STATIONS. Ft George Wright, Wash, 5 Sep 1941–6 Oct 1943.

COMMANDERS. Brig Gen John B Brooks, 29 Sep 1941; Brig Gen Eugene L Eubank, c. 20 Jul 1942; Col Albert F Hegenberger, c. 4 Sep 1942; Brig Gen Robert B Williams, Oct 1942; Brig Gen Eugene L Eubank, c. 1 May 1943; Col Hugo P Rush, 28 Sep–6 Oct 1943.

CAMPAIGNS. American Theater.

DECORATIONS. None.

INSIGNE. None.

III AIR SUPPORT COMMAND

Constituted as III Air Support Command on 21 Aug 1941. *Activated* on 1 Sep 1941. Assigned to Third AF. Trained air force organizations for support operations and assisted in training ground forces. Also conducted antisubmarine patrols. *Disbanded* on 16 Mar 1942.

COMPONENTS. (Various observation and light bombardment organizations.)

STATIONS. Savannah AB, Ga, 1 Sep 1941; Drew Field, Fla, c. 1–16 Mar 1942.

COMMANDERS. Col Asa N Duncan, Sep 1941; Lt Col Herbert B Thatcher, c. 28 Jan–16 Mar 1942.

CAMPAIGNS. Antisubmarine, American Theater.

DECORATIONS. None.

INSIGNE. None.

III BOMBER COMMAND

Constituted as III Bomber Command on 4 Sep 1941 and *activated* on 5 Sep. Assigned to Third AF. Trained bombardment organizations and personnel. Also patrolled in search of enemy submarines, Dec 1941–Aug 1942. *Inactivated* on 8 Apr 1946. *Disbanded* on 8 Oct 1948.

COMPONENTS. (Omitted because of large number and frequent changes.)

STATIONS. Drew Field, Fla, 5 Sep 1941; MacDill Field, Fla, c. Sep 1941; Savannah AB, Ga, c. 10 Dec 1941; MacDill Field, Fla, c. 15 Dec 1941–8 Apr 1946.

COMMANDERS. Maj Gen Follett Bradley, Sep 1941; Col James P Hodges, 4 Mar 1942; Brig Gen Samuel M Connell, 20 Mar 1942; Brig Gen Robert Olds, 25 Apr 1942; Brig Gen James E Parker, 4 Nov 1942; Brig Gen Robert C Oliver, 5 Jul 1944; Brig Gen Joseph H Atkinson, 14 Aug 1944–unkn.

CAMPAIGNS. Antisubmarine, American Theater.

DECORATIONS. None.

INSIGNE. None.

III FIGHTER COMMAND

Constituted as III Interceptor Command on 26 May 1941. *Activated* on 17 Jun [or 14 Jul?] 1941. Assigned to Third AF. *Redesignated* III Fighter Command in May 1942. Trained fighter organizations and personnel. Also served in the defense of the southeastern US. *Inactivated* on 8 Apr 1946. *Disbanded* on 8 Oct 1948.

COMPONENTS. (Omitted because of large number and frequent changes.)

STATIONS. Drew Field, Fla, 1941; Mac-Dill Field, Fla, c. 1 Dec 1945–8 Apr 1946.

COMMANDERS. Maj Gen Walter H Frank, 1941; Brig Gen Clarence L Tinker, 6 Nov 1941; Col Willis H Hale, 16–30 Dec 1941; Brig Gen Ralph Royce, 28–29 Jan 1942; Brig Gen Carlyle H Wash, 2 Mar 1942; Col George P Tourtellot, 26 Jun 1942; Brig Gen Adlai H Gilkeson, 8 Oct 1942; Brig Gen Thomas W Blackburn, 14 Mar 1944–unkn.

CAMPAIGNS. American Theater.

DECORATIONS. None.

INSIGNE. None.

III RECONNAISSANCE COMMAND

Constituted as I Air Support Command on 21 Aug 1941. *Activated* on 1 Sep 1941. *Redesignated* I Ground Air Support Command in Apr 1942, I Air Support Command in Sep 1942, I Tactical Air Division in Aug 1943, III Tactical Air Division in Apr 1944, and III Reconnaissance Com-

mand in Jun 1945. Flew antisubmarine patrols off the east coast, 7 Dec 1941–15 Oct 1942. Trained light bombardment crews, participated in air-ground maneuvers, and demonstrated air support techniques, Sep 1941–May 1944. Trained reconnaissance personnel and organizations, May 1944–1946. *Inactivated* on 9 Apr 1946. *Disbanded* on 8 Oct 1948.

COMPONENTS. (Omitted because of large number and frequent changes.)

STATIONS. Mitchel Field, NY, 1 Sep 1941; Morris Field, NC, Nov 1942; Key Field, Miss, c. 3 Apr 1944; Rapid City AAB, SD, Nov 1945–9 Apr 1946.

COMMANDERS. Col William E Kepner, 1 Sep 1941; Col Dache McC Reeves, c. 22 Feb 1942; Col John P Doyle, 2 Sep 1942; Brig Gen Robert M Webster, 2 Oct 1942; Col John P Doyle, c. 23 Apr 1943; Brig Gen Ralph F Stearley, 2 May 1943; Col John E Bodle, 1 Apr 1944; Brig Gen Edmund C Lynch, 24 Jun 1944; Col Robin A Day, 28 Jan 1945–unkn.

CAMPAIGNS. Antisubmarine, American Theater.

DECORATIONS. None.

INSIGNE. On a blue octagon, edged in gold, a golden representation of the bust of the Egyptian mythological hawk god Horus. (Approved 23 Jul 1942.)

III TACTICAL AIR COMMAND

Constituted as III Ground Air Support Command on 15 May 1942 and *activated* on 19 May. Assigned to Third AF. *Redesignated* III Air Support Command in Sep 1942, III Reconnaissance Command in Aug 1943, and III Tactical Air Command in Mar 1944. At various times, trained dive bombardment, light bombardment, and reconnaissance organizations and personnel; also gave air support to ground units in training and participated in air-ground maneuvers and demonstrations. *Disbanded* on 24 Oct 1945.

DIVISIONS. *I* (formerly III) Tactical Air: 1944–1945. *II* Tactical Air: 1944–1945. *III* (formerly I) Tactical Air: 1944.

STATIONS. Birmingham, Ala, 19 May 1942; Barksdale Field, La, c. 1 Apr 1944–24 Oct 1945.

COMMANDERS. Brig Gen William E Lynd, 25 May 1942; Col Rosenham Beam, c. 21 Jun 1942; Brig Gen Arthur B McDaniel, 1 Oct 1942; Col John E Bodle, Dec 1943; Brig Gen Hume Peabody, 20 Mar 1944; Brig Gen John F McBlain, 17 Nov 1944; Brig Gen Gordon P Saville, 22 Mar 1945; Brig Gen Ford L Fair, 1 May 1945;

Brig Gen James W McCauley, 20 Jul–24 Oct 1945.

CAMPAIGNS. American Theater.

DECORATIONS. None.

INSIGNE. None.

IV BOMBER COMMAND

Constituted as IV Bomber Command on 4 Sep 1941 and *activated* on 19 Sep. Assigned to Fourth AF. Trained bombardment organizations and personnel. Also flew patrols along the west coast. *Disbanded* on 31 Mar 1944.

COMPONENTS. (Omitted because of large number and frequent changes.)

STATIONS. Tucson, Ariz, 19 Sep 1941; Hamilton Field, Calif, c. 8 Dec 1941; San Francisco, Calif, 5 Jan 1942–31 Mar 1944.

COMMANDERS. Brig Gen Frank D Lackland, Sep 1941; Col Ronald A Hicks, 9 Nov 1941; Brig Gen Barney McK Giles, 13 Mar 1942; Brig Gen Howard K Ramey, 12 Aug 1942; Col Thomas W Steed, 8 Nov 1942; Brig Gen Samuel M Connell, 11 Nov 1942;

Col Charles B Dougher, 19 Feb 1944; Col Elder Patteson, 18–31 Mar 1944.

CAMPAIGNS. American Theater.

DECORATIONS. None.

INSIGNE. On a blue disc with a yellow border, a winged aerial bomb, nose down, beneath an olive chaplet inclosing a bomb sight, all yellow. (Approved 4 Dec 1941.)

IV FIGHTER COMMAND

Constituted as IV Interceptor Command on 26 May 1941. *Activated* on 8 Jul 1941. Assigned to Fourth AF. *Redesignated* IV Fighter Command in May 1942. Provided air defense for the west coast; trained fighter organizations and personnel. *Disbanded* on 31 Mar 1944.

WINGS. Los Angeles Fighter: 1942–1944. Seattle Fighter: 1942–1944. San Diego Fighter: 1942–1944. San Francisco Fighter: 1942–1944.

STATIONS. March Field, Calif, 8 Jul 1941; Riverside, Calif, c. Jul 1941; Oakland, Calif, Jun 1942–31 Mar 1944.

COMMANDERS. Maj Gen Millard F Harmon, Jul 1941; Brig Gen William O Ryan, c. 3 Aug 1941; Brig Gen William E Kepner, c. 23 Feb 1942; Brig Gen Edward M Morris, 18 Mar 1943; Brig Gen Russell E Randall, 4 Dec 1943–31 Mar 1944.

CAMPAIGNS. American Theater.

DECORATIONS. None.

INSIGNE. On a bezant bordered blue a blue falcon with white talons volant holding in base in its beak two red flashes in saltire. (Approved 28 Nov 1942.)

V BOMBER COMMAND

Constituted as V Bomber Command on 28 Oct 1941. *Activated* in the Philippines on 14 Nov 1941. Participated in the defense of the Philippines in Dec 1941. Late in Dec the remaining bombers and some men were evacuated to Australia, and in Jan 1942 they were moved to Java to help delay the Japanese advance in the Netherlands Indies. The command ceased to function in Mar 1942 (the AAF bombardment organizations in the Southwest Pacific being under the control of American-British-Dutch-Australian Command and later Allied Air Forces). Headquarters was remanned in Sep 1942 and shortly afterward it assumed control of AAF bombardment groups in Australia and New Guinea. The command served in combat with Fifth AF until the end of the war. Brig Gen Kenneth N Walker, who was lost during a mission to Rabaul on 5 Jan 1943, was awarded the Medal of Honor; he had repeatedly taken part in combat missions and had developed an effective technique for bombing when opposed by enemy interceptors and antiaircraft fire. After the war the command became part of the occupation force for Japan. *Inactivated* on 31 May 1946. *Disbanded* on 8 Oct 1948.

GROUPS. *3d* Bombardment: 1942–1946. *6th* Reconnaissance: 1943. *7th* Bombardment: 1942. *8th* Fighter: 1942. *19th* Bombardment: 1941–1942. *22d* Bombardment: 1942–1945. *27th* Bombardment: 1941–1942. *35th* Fighter: 1945–1946. *38th* Bombardment: 1942–1945. *43d* Bombardment: 1942–1945. *49th* Fighter: 1945–1946. *71st* Reconnaissance: 1943. *90th* Bombardment: 1942–1945. *312th* Bombardment: 1944–1945. *345th* Bombardment: 1943–1945. *380th* Bombardment: 1943–1945. *417th* Bombardment: 1944–1945.

STATIONS. Clark Field, Luzon, 14 Nov 1941; Darwin, Australia, Dec 1941; Java, Jan–Mar 1942; Townsville, Australia, 5 Sep 1942; Port Moresby, New Guinea, Dec 1942; Nadzab, New Guinea, 21 Feb 1944; Owi, Schouten Islands, c. 15 Aug 1944; Leyte, Nov 1944; Mindoro, Jan 1945; Clark Field, Luzon, Mar 1945; Okinawa, Aug 1945; Murayama, Japan, Oct 1945; Irumagawa, Japan, c. 15 Jan–31 May 1946.

COMMANDERS. Col Eugene L Eubank, 14 Nov 1941–unkn; Brig Gen Kenneth N Walker, 5 Sep 1942; Brig Gen Howard K Ramey, Jan 1943; Brig Gen Roger M Ramey, 19 Apr 1943; Col John H Davies, Oct 1943; Brig Gen Jarred V Crabb, 27 Feb 1944–31 May 1946.

CAMPAIGNS. Philippine Islands; East Indies; Air Offensive, Japan; China Defensive; Papua; New Guinea; Northern Solomons; Bismarck Archipelago; Western Pacific; Leyte; Luzon; Southern Philippines; China Offensive.

DECORATIONS. Distinguished Unit Citations: Philippine Islands, 8–22 Dec 1941; Philippine Islands, 7 Dec 1941–10 May 1942; Papua, [Sep] 1942–23 Jan 1943. Philippine Presidential Unit Citation.

INSIGNE. None.

V FIGHTER COMMAND

Constituted as II Interceptor Command on 26 May 1941. *Activated* on 4 Jun 1941. *Redesignated* II Fighter Command in May 1942, and V Fighter Command in Aug 1942. Moved to the Southwest Pacific, Oct–Nov 1942, and operated with Fifth AF until the end of the war. Afterward, served with the occupation force in Japan. *Inactivated* on 31 May 1946. *Disbanded* on 8 Oct 1948.

(This V Fighter Command has no connection with a 5th Interceptor Command that was constituted on 14 Oct 1941, activated on 30 Oct, and redesignated Fighter Command School in Aug 1942. Nor is it related to a 5th Interceptor Command—probably a provisional organization—that was located in the Philippines in 1941–1942.)

GROUPS. *3d* Air Commando: 1944–1945. *8th* Fighter: 1942–1946. *35th* Fighter: 1942–1945. *38th* Bombardment: 1945–1946. *42d* Bombardment: 1946. *49th*

Fighter: 1942–1945. *54th* Fighter: 1941. *55th* Fighter: 1941. *58th* Fighter: 1943–1945. *312th* Bombardment: 1943–1944. *348th* Fighter: 1943–1945, 1946. *475th* Fighter: 1943–1945.

STATIONS. Ft George Wright, Wash, 4 Jun 1941; Ft Lawton, Wash, 19 Jun 1941–2 Oct 1942; Australia, Nov 1942; Port Moresby, New Guinea, Dec 1942; Nadzab, New Guinea, Jan 1944; Owi, Schouten Islands, Jul 1944; Leyte, Nov 1944; Mindoro, Jan 1945; Clark Field, Luzon, Mar 1945; Okinawa, Aug 1945; Fukuoka, Japan, Oct 1945–31 May 1946.

COMMANDERS. Brig Gen Carlyle H Wash, Jun 1941–unkn; Col Howard H Newman, 1942; Brig Gen Paul B Wurtsmith, 11 Nov 1942; Col Neel E Kearby, 24 Nov 1943; Brig Gen Paul B Wurtsmith, 13 Jan 1944; Brig Gen Frederic H Smith Jr, 10 Feb 1945; Col Hugh A Parker, 30 Sep 1945–31 Mar 1946.

CAMPAIGNS. American Theater; Air Offensive, Japan; China Defensive; Papua; New Guinea; Bismarck Archipelago; Western Pacific; Leyte; Luzon; Southern Philippines; China Offensive.

DECORATIONS. Distinguished Unit Citation: Papua, [Nov] 1942–23 Jan 1943. Philippine Presidential Unit Citation.

INSIGNE. None.

VI BOMBER COMMAND

Constituted as VI Bomber Command on 17 Oct 1941 and *activated* in the Panama Canal Zone on 25 Oct. Assigned to Caribbean (later Sixth) AF. Engaged in anti-

submarine operations; served as part of the defense force for the Panama Canal. *Inactivated* on 1 Nov 1946. *Disbanded* on 8 Oct 1948.

GROUPS. *6th:* 1941–1943. *9th:* 1941–1942. *25th:* 1941–1944. *40th:* 1941–1943.

STATIONS. Albrook Field, CZ, 25 Oct 1941–1 Nov 1946.

COMMANDERS. Brig Gen Edwin B Lyon, 25 Oct 1941; Col Forest G Allen, 13 May 1943; Col Edwin M Day, 18 Jun 1943; Col James E Roberts, 6 Oct 1944; Col Joseph P Bailey, 12 Apr 1945–unkn.

CAMPAIGNS. Antisubmarine, American Theater.

DECORATIONS. None.

INSIGNE. In front of a blue annulet bearing the motto "Alae Supra Canalem" in gold letters, a winged aerial bomb, the whole edged in gold. (Approved 18 Mar 1942.)

VII BOMBER COMMAND

Constituted as VII Bomber Command on 23 Jan 1942 and *activated* in Hawaii on

29 Jan. Assigned to Hawaiian (later Seventh) AF. Engaged in patrol operations from Hawaii until late in 1943. Afterward, served in combat in the Central and Western Pacific. *Inactivated* on Okinawa, [31?] Mar 1946. *Disbanded* on 8 Oct 1948.

GROUPS. *5th:* 1942. *11th:* 1942, 1943–1945. *30th:* 1943–1945. *41st:* 1943–1944, 1945. *307th:* 1942–1943. *312th:* 1945. *345th:* 1945. *380th:* 1945. *494th:* 1944–1945.

STATIONS. Hickam Field, TH, 29 Jan 1942; Funafuti, Nov 1943; Tarawa, Jan 1944; Kwajalein, Mar 1944; Saipan, Aug 1944; Okinawa, Jul 1945–Mar 1946.

COMMANDERS. Maj Gen Willis H Hale, Feb 1942; Col Albert F Hegenberger, 20 Jun 1942; Brig Gen William E Lynd, 25 Jun 1942; Brig Gen Truman H Landon, 20 Jan 1943; Brig Gen Lawrence J Carr, 11 Dec 1944; Col Roy D Butler, Oct 1945; Brig Gen Carl B McDaniel, 1 Dec 1945; Col John J Morrow, 7 Jan 1946–unkn.

CAMPAIGNS. Central Pacific; Air Offensive, Japan; Eastern Mandates; Western Pacific; Ryukyus; China Offensive.

DECORATIONS. None.

INSIGNE. None.

VII FIGHTER COMMAND

Constituted as VII Interceptor Command on 23 Jan 1942. *Activated* in Hawaii on 2 Feb 1942. *Redesignated* VII Fighter Command in May 1942. Assigned to Seventh AF. Engaged in patrol

activity from Hawaii. Later, served in combat in the Western Pacific. Remained in the theater as part of Far East Air Forces after the war. *Redesignated* 20th Fighter Wing in May 1946, and 46th Fighter Wing in Dec 1947. *Inactivated* in the Marianas on 24 Aug 1948.

GROUPS. *15th:* 1942–1945. *18th:* 1942–1943. *21st:* 1944–1946. *23d:* 1946–1948. *318th:* 1942–1945.

STATIONS. Ft Shafter, TH, 2 Feb 1942; Hickam Field, TH, 20 Oct 1944; Ft Kamehameha, TH, 18 Jan 1945; Iwo Jima, Mar 1945; Saipan, 1 Dec 1945; Guam, 15 Apr 1946–24 Aug 1948.

COMMANDERS. Brig Gen Howard C Davidson, Feb 1942; Brig Gen Robert W Douglass Jr, Oct 1942; Brig Gen Ernest Moore, May 1944; Col Thayer S Olds, 4 Sep 1945; Brig Gen Winslow C Morse, 26 Sep 1946; Col Romulus W Puryear, Jan–24 Aug 1948.

CAMPAIGNS. Air Offensive, Japan; Western Pacific; Ryukyus; China Offensive.

DECORATIONS. None.

INSIGNE. None.

VIII AIR SUPPORT COMMAND

Constituted as VIII Ground Air Support Command on 24 Apr 1942 and *activated* on 28 Apr. Assigned to Eighth AF. Moved to England, without tactical components, Jun–Aug 1942. *Redesignated* VIII Air Support Command in Sep 1942. Engaged in training, with one reconnaissance and one troop carrier group assigned, until Jul 1943. Afterward, carried out medium bombardment operations against the enemy on the Continent until Oct 1943 when all components and personnel were withdrawn from the command. *Disbanded* in England on 1 Dec 1943.

WINGS. *3d* Bombardment: 1943. *44th* Bombardment: 1943.

STATIONS. Bolling Field, DC, 28 Apr 1942; Savannah, Ga, 29 May–c. 20 Jul 1942; Bushy Park, England, Jul 1942; Membury, England, 21 Aug 1942; Sunninghill, England, 19 Oct 1942–1 Dec 1943.

COMMANDERS. Brig Gen Robert C Candee, May 1942–16 Oct 1943.

CAMPAIGNS. Air Offensive, Europe.

DECORATIONS. None.

INSIGNE. None.

VIII FIGHTER COMMAND

Constituted as VIII Interceptor Command on 19 Jan 1942. *Activated* on 1 Feb 1942. *Redesignated* VIII Fighter Command in May 1942. Moved to England, May–Jul 1942, and served with Eighth AF until after V–E Day. *Inactivated* in England on 20 Mar 1946. *Disbanded* on 8 Oct 1948.

WINGS. *6th:* 1942–1943. *65th* (formerly 4th Air Defense): 1943–1944, 1945. *66th* (formerly 5th Air Defense): 1943–1944, 1945. *67th:* 1943–1944, 1945.

STATIONS. Selfridge Field, Mich, 1 Feb 1942; Charleston, SC, c. 13 Feb–c. 1 May 1942; High Wycombe, England, c. 12 May 1942; Bushey Hall, England, c. 27 Jul 1942; Charleroi, Belgium, c. 15 Jan 1945; High Wycombe, England, 17 Jul 1945; Honington, England, 26 Oct 1945–c. 20 Mar 1946.

COMMANDERS. Col Lawrence P Hickey, c. 1 Feb 1942; Brig Gen Frank O'D Hunter, 14 May 1942; Maj Gen William E Kepner, 29 Aug 1943; Brig Gen Murray C Woodbury, 1 Aug 1944; Brig Gen Francis H Griswold, 3 Aug 1944; Col Benjamin J Webster, 17 Oct 1944; Col Robert W Humphreys, 19 Apr 1945; Maj Gen Westside T Larson, 17 Jul 1945; Maj Gen William E Kepner, 22 Jul 1945; Maj Gen Westside T Larson, 3 Aug 1945; Maj Gen Howard M Turner, 22 Sep 1945; Brig Gen Emil C Kiel, 13 Oct 1945–c. Mar 1946.

CAMPAIGNS. Air Offensive, Europe; Normandy; Northern France; Rhineland; Central Europe.

DECORATIONS. None.

INSIGNE. A figurehead consisting of a blue demi lion rampant outlined in gold. (Approved 23 May 1942.)

IX AIR DEFENSE COMMAND

Constituted as IX Air Defense Command on 19 Jun 1944. *Activated* in England on 1 Jul 1944. Assigned to Ninth AF. Provided air defense for areas behind the advancing ground forces in northern Europe. *Inactivated* in Europe on 25 Jun 1946. *Disbanded* on 8 Oct 1948.

WINGS. *71st* Fighter: 1944.

STATIONS. Hampstead Borough, England, 1 Jul 1944; Ecrammeville, France, Jul 1944; Rennes, France, 25 Aug 1944; Versailles, France, 8 Sep 1944; Paris, France, 16 Dec 1944; Neustadt, Germany, 24 May 1945–1946.

COMMANDERS. Brig Gen William L Richardson, 1 Jul 1944; Brig Gen Ned Schramm, 28 Jul 1944; Brig Gen William L Richardson, 27 Oct 1944; Col Matthew K Deichelmann, 5 Dec 1945–1946.

CAMPAIGNS. Normandy; Northern France; Rhineland; Ardennes-Alsace; Central Europe.

DECORATIONS. None.

INSIGNE. None.

IX FIGHTER COMMAND

Constituted as IX Interceptor Command on 19 Jan 1942. *Activated* on 1 Feb 1942. *Redesignated* IX Fighter Command in May 1942. Moved to Egypt, Nov 1942–Jan 1943. Assigned to Ninth AF. Operated in the Mediterranean area until Sep 1943. Moved to England, Oct–Nov 1943, for operations in the European theater. *Inactivated* in Europe on 16 Nov 1945. *Disbanded* on 8 Oct 1948.

WINGS. *8th:* 1942–1943. *9th:* 1942–1943. *70th:* 1943–1944. *71st:* 1943–1944. *84th:* 1944, 1944–1945. *100th:* 1943–1944. *303d:* 1944, 1944–1945.

STATIONS. New Orleans AAB, La, 1 Feb 1942; Drew Field, Fla, Jul–Oct 1942; El Kabrit, Egypt, 31 Jan 1943; Tripoli, Libya, 10 Apr–22 Sep 1943; Middle Wallop, England, 30 Nov 1943–Jul 1944; Les Obeaux, France, Jul 1944; Canisy, France, Aug 1944; Charleroi, Belgium, Sep 1944; Verviers, Belgium, Oct 1944; Bruhl, Germany, Mar 1945; Weimar, Germany, Apr 1945; Fritzlar, Germany, Jul 1945; Erlangen, Germany, Sep–Nov 1945.

COMMANDERS. Capt Phillip R Pattison, 1 Feb 1942; Col Thomas W Blackburn, 16 Feb 1942; Maj Phillip R Pattison, Jul 1942; Lt Col W C Warren, 6 Aug 1942; Maj Joseph A Kelly, 10 Aug 1942; Maj Arch G Campbell Jr, 15 Aug 1942; Maj Hugh E McConville, Aug 1942; Col John C Kilborn, Sep 1942; Brig Gen Auby C Strickland, Jan 1943; Col Charles D McAllister, 3 Jun 1943; Col Frederick M Byerly, 13 Sep 1943; Lt Col Ray J Stecker, 4 Oct 1943; Maj Gen Elwood R Quesada, 18 Oct 1943; Brig Gen Ralph F Stearley, 21 Apr 1945–unkn.

CAMPAIGNS. Air Combat, EAME Theater; Egypt-Libya; Air Offensive, Europe; Tunisia; Sicily; Naples-Foggia; Normandy; Northern France; Rhineland; Ardennes-Alsace; Central Europe.

DECORATIONS. Cited in the Order of the Day, Belgian Army: 6 Jun–30 Sep 1944. INSIGNE. None.

IX TACTICAL AIR COMMAND

Constituted as IX Air Support Command on 29 Nov 1943. *Activated* in England on 4 Dec 1943. Assigned to Ninth AF. *Redesignated* IX Tactical Air Command in Apr 1944. Operated in the European theater, primarily in support of US First Army, until V–E Day. Moved to the US in Oct 1945. *Inactivated* on 25 Oct 1945. *Disbanded* on 8 Oct 1948.

WINGS. *70th* Fighter: 1944–1945. *71st* Fighter: 1944. *84th* Fighter: 1944. *100th* Fighter: 1944.

STATIONS. Aldermaston Court, England, 4 Dec 1943; Middle Wallop, England, 1 Feb 1944; Uxbridge, England, 15 Feb–Jun 1944; Au Gay, France, 10 Jun 1944; Les Obeaux, France, 2 Jul 1944; Canisy, France, 2 Aug 1944; Coulouvray, France, 12 Aug 1944; Haleine, France, 22 Aug 1944; Versailles, France, 2 Sep 1944; Janoulx, Belgium, 11 Sep 1944; Verviers, Belgium, 2 Oct 1944; Bruhl, Germany, 26 Mar 1945; Marburg, Germany, 8 Apr 1945; Weimar, Germany, 26 Apr 1945; Fritzlar, Germany, 26 Jun–Sep 1945; Camp Shanks, NY, 24–25 Oct 1945.

COMMANDERS. Col Clarence E Crumrine, 4 Dec 1943; Maj Gen Elwood R Quesada, 1 Feb 1944; Brig Gen Ralph F Stearley, 21 Apr–Sep 1945.

CAMPAIGNS. Air Offensive, Europe; Normandy; Northern France; Rhineland; Ardennes-Alsace; Central Europe.

DECORATIONS. Cited in the Order of the Day, Belgian Army: 6 Jun–30 Sep 1944; 16 Dec 1944–25 Jan 1945. Belgian Fourragere.

INSIGNE. None.

IX TROOP CARRIER COMMAND

Constituted as IX Troop Carrier Command on 11 Oct 1943 and *activated* in England on 16 Oct. Assigned to Ninth AF. Served in the European theater, engaging in airborne and transport operations, until after V–E Day. Transferred, without personnel and equipment, in Sep 1945 to the US where the command was again manned and equipped. *Inactivated* on 31 Mar 1946. *Disbanded* on 8 Oct 1948.

WINGS. *50th*: 1943–1945, 1945–1946. *52d*: 1944–1945, 1945–1946. *53d*: 1944–1945.

STATIONS. Cottesmore, England, 16 Oct 1943; Grantham, England, 1 Dec 1943; Ascot, England, 20 Sep 1944–5 Sep 1945; Stout Field, Ind, 5 Sep 1945; Greenville AAB, SC, 1 Feb–31 Mar 1946.

COMMANDERS. Brig Gen Benjamin F Giles, 16 Oct 1943; Maj Gen Paul L Williams, 25 Feb 1944–c. 12 Jul 1945, and 5 Nov 1945–31 Mar 1946.

CAMPAIGNS. Normandy; Northern France; Rhineland; Ardennes-Alsace; Central Europe.

DECORATIONS. None.

INSIGNE. None.

XI BOMBER COMMAND

Constituted as XI Bomber Command on 4 Mar 1943 and *activated* in Alaska on 19 Mar. Operated in combat with Eleventh AF. *Disbanded* in Alaska on 31 Mar 1944.

GROUPS. *28th* Composite: 1943–1944.

STATIONS. Adak, 19 Mar 1943; Amchitka, 24 Jun 1943; Adak, 4 Sep 1943; Shemya, 3–31 Mar 1944.

COMMANDERS. Brig Gen Earl H De Ford, 19 Mar 1943; Col Robert H Herman, 2 Dec 1943–31 Mar 1944.

CAMPAIGNS. Air Offensive, Japan; Aleutian Islands.

DECORATIONS. None.

INSIGNE. None.

XI FIGHTER COMMAND

Constituted as XI Interceptor Command on 8 Mar 1942 and *activated* in Alaska on 15 Mar. Assigned to Eleventh AF. *Redesignated* XI Fighter Command in May 1942. Engaged in combat from Jun 1942 to Oct 1943. *Disbanded* in Alaska on 31 Mar 1944.

GROUPS. *343d:* 1942–1944.

STATIONS. Elmendorf Field, Alaska, 15 Mar 1942; Adak, 12 Sep 1943–31 Mar 1944.

COMMANDERS. Col Norman D Sillin, 15 Mar 1942; Col Phineas K Morrill Jr, 6 Sep

1942; Lt Col Donald E Meade, 15 Jul 1943; Col William E Elder, 25 Feb 1944; Lt Col Don L Wilhelm Jr, 20–31 Mar 1944.

CAMPAIGNS. Aleutian Islands.

DECORATIONS. None.

INSIGNE. None.

XII BOMBER COMMAND

Constituted as XII Bomber Command on 26 Feb 1942. *Activated* on 13 Mar 1942. Assigned to Twelfth AF in Aug 1942 and transferred, without personnel and equipment, to England where the command was re-formed. Moved to North Africa, with the first of its elements arriving during the invasion in Nov 1942. Served in combat in the Mediterranean theater until 1 Nov 1943 when most of the personnel were withdrawn. Received additional personnel in Jan 1944 and served in combat until 1 Mar 1944. *Disbanded* in Corsica on 10 Jun 1944.

WINGS. *5th:* 1943. *42d:* 1943, 1944. *47th* (formerly 7th Fighter): 1943. *57th:* 1944.

STATIONS. MacDill Field, Fla, 13 Mar 1942; High Wycombe, England, 31 Aug–10 Nov 1942; Tafaraoui, Algeria, 22 Nov 1942; Algiers, Algeria, 27 Nov 1942; Constantine, Algeria, 5 Dec 1942; Tunis, Tunisia, 23 Jul 1943; Bari, Italy, c. Dec 1943; Trocchia, Italy, 4 Jan 1944; Corsica, c. Apr–10 Jun 1944.

COMMANDERS. Brig Gen Samuel M Connell, 3–8 May 1942; Col Claude E Duncan, 2 Sep 1942; Col Charles T Phillips, 11 Dec 1942; Col Carlyle H Ridenour, 16 Dec 1942; Brig Gen John K Cannon, 1 Jan 1943; Maj Gen James H Doolittle, 26 Feb–1 Nov 1943; Brig Gen Robert D Knapp, c. Dec 1943–c. 29 Feb 1944.

CAMPAIGNS. Air Combat, EAME Theater; Algeria-French Morocco; Tunisia; Sicily; Naples-Foggia; Anzio; Rome-Arno.

DECORATIONS. None.

INSIGNE. None.

XII TACTICAL AIR COMMAND

Constituted as XII Ground Air Support Command on 10 Sep 1942 and *activated* on 17 Sep. Assigned to Twelfth AF. *Redesignated* XII Air Support Command in Sep 1942, and XII Tactical Air Command in Apr 1944. Moved to North Africa, Oct–Nov 1942. Col Demas T Craw was awarded the Medal of Honor for action during the invasion of Algeria-French Morocco: when the Allies landed on 8 Nov 1942, Col Craw volunteered to negotiate an armistice; while trying to pass through the lines near Port Lyautey, he was killed by machine-gun fire. The command served in combat in the Mediterranean and European theaters until May 1945. Afterward, remained in Europe as part of the occupation force. *Inactivated* in Germany on 10 Nov 1947. *Disbanded* on 8 Oct 1948.

WINGS. *5th* Bombardment: 1942. *7th* Fighter: 1942. *42d* Bombardment: 1945. *57th* Bombardment: 1943–1944. *63d* Fighter: 1945. *64th* Fighter (formerly 3d Air Defense): 1943–1944, 1945–1947. *70th* Fighter: 1945–1947. *71st* Fighter: 1945. *87th* Fighter: 1944.

STATIONS. Birmingham, Ala, 17 Sep 1942; Bolling Field, DC, 25 Sep–18 Oct 1942; French Morocco, 9 Nov 1942; Algeria, Jan 1943; Tunisia, 13 Mar 1943; Sicily, c. 12 Jul 1943; Italy, c. 9 Sep 1943; France, 18 Aug 1944; Germany, 27 Mar 1945; Erlangen, Germany, Jul 1945; Bad Kissingen, Germany, 1 Nov 1945–10 Nov 1947.

COMMANDERS. Col Rosenham Beam, 18 Sep 1942; Brig Gen John K Cannon, 22 Sep 1942; Col Rosenham Beam, c. 30 Dec 1942; Col Peter S Rask, 1 Jan 1943; Brig Gen Howard A Craig, 10 Jan 1943; Brig Gen Paul L Williams, 24 Jan 1943; Brig Gen John K Cannon, 12 May 1943; Col Lawrence P Hickey, 24 May 1943; Maj Gen Edwin J House, 13 Jun 1943; Brig Gen Gordon P Saville, 2 Feb 1944; Brig Gen Glenn O Barcus, 29 Jan 1945; Maj Gen William E Kepner, 3 Dec 1945; Brig Gen Glenn O Barcus, 9 Jan 1946; Brig Gen John F McBlain, 3 Aug 1946; Maj Gen Robert LeG Walsh, 27 Nov 1946; Brig Gen James M Fitzmaurice, 1 Apr–c. Oct 1947.

CAMPAIGNS. Air Combat, EAME Theater; Algeria-French Morocco; Tunisia; Sicily; Naples-Foggia; Anzio; Rome-Arno; Northern France; Southern France; North Apennines; Rhineland; Ardennes-Alsace; Central Europe.

DECORATIONS. None.

INSIGNE. None.

XIII BOMBER COMMAND

Constituted as XIII Bomber Command on 14 Dec 1942. *Activated* in the South Pacific on 13 Jan 1943. Served in combat with Thirteenth AF until the end of the war. *Inactivated* in the Philippines on 15 Mar 1946. *Disbanded* on 8 Oct 1948.

GROUPS. *5th:* 1943–1946. *11th:* 1943. *42d:* 1943–1945. *307th:* 1943–1945.

STATIONS. Espiritu Santo, 13 Jan 1943; Guadalcanal, 20 Aug 1943; Los Negros, 1 Jun 1944; Wakde, 3 Sep 1944; Morotai, 17 Oct 1944; Clark Field, Luzon, 27 Aug 1945–15 Mar 1946.

COMMANDERS. Col Harlan T McCormick, 13 Jan 1943; Col James M Fitzmaurice, 6 Apr 1943; Brig Gen Glen C Jamison, 16 Jun 1943; Brig Gen William A Matheny, 10 Aug 1943; Brig Gen Carl A Brandt, 2 Feb–c. Oct 1945.

CAMPAIGNS. Central Pacific; China Defensive; Guadalcanal; New Guinea; Northern Solomons; Eastern Mandates; Bismarck Archipelago; Western Pacific; Leyte; Luzon; Southern Philippines; China Offensive.

DECORATIONS. None.

INSIGNE. None.

XIII FIGHTER COMMAND

Constituted as XIII Fighter Command on 14 Dec 1942. *Activated* in the South Pacific on 13 Jan 1943. Served in combat with Thirteenth AF until the end of the war. *Inactivated* in the Philippines on 15 Mar 1946. *Disbanded* on 8 Oct 1948.

GROUPS. *18th:* 1943–1946. *347th:* 1943–1945. *414th:* 1946.

STATIONS. New Caledonia, 13 Jan 1943; Espiritu Santo, c. 22 Jan 1943; Guadalcanal, Dec 1943; Sansapor, New Guinea, 15 Aug 1944; Leyte, 10 Jan 1945; Puerto Princesa, Palawan, 1 Mar 1945; Manila, Luzon, c. Nov 1945–15 Mar 1946.

COMMANDERS. Brig Gen Dean C Strother, 13 Jan 1943; Brig Gen Earl W Barnes, Jan 1944; Col Willard R Wolfinbarger, 16 Nov 1944; Brig Gen Earl W Barnes, 31 Jan 1945–unkn.

CAMPAIGNS. China Defensive; Guadalcanal; New Guinea; Northern Solomons; Bismarck Archipelago; Western Pacific; Leyte; Luzon; Southern Philippines; China Offensive.

DECORATIONS. Philippine Presidential Unit Citation.

INSIGNE. None.

XIX TACTICAL AIR COMMAND

Constituted as XIX Air Support Command on 29 Nov 1943. *Activated* in England on 4 Jan 1944. Assigned to Ninth AF. *Redesignated* XIX Tactical Air Command in Apr 1944. Operated in the European theater, primarily in support of US Third Army, until V–E Day. Moved to the US in Aug 1945. *Inactivated* on 31 Mar 1946. *Disbanded* on 8 Oct 1948.

WINGS. *100th* Fighter: 1944–1945. *303d* Fighter: 1944.

STATIONS. Middle Wallop, England, 4 Jan 1944; Aldermaston Court, England, 1

Feb 1944; France, Jul 1944; Luxembourg, Jan 1945; Germany, Apr–Jul 1945; Drew Field, Fla, 21 Aug 1945; Barksdale Field, La, 17 Oct 1945; Biggs Field, Tex, 11 Dec 1945–31 Mar 1946.

COMMANDERS. Maj Gen Elwood R Quesada, 4 Jan 1944; Col Clarence E Crumrine, 1 Feb 1944; Maj Gen Otto P Weyland, 4 Feb 1944; Brig Gen Homer L Sanders, 23 May 1945; Col Roger J Browne, 5 Jul 1945; Brig Gen James W McCauley, 25 Oct 1945; Maj Gen Elwood R Quesada, 8 Feb 1946; Brig Gen Homer L Sanders, 25 Feb–Mar 1946.

CAMPAIGNS. Air Offensive, Europe; Normandy; Northern France; Rhineland; Ardennes-Alsace; Central Europe.

DECORATIONS. None.

INSIGNE. None.

XX BOMBER COMMAND
(formerly I Bomber Command)

Constituted as I Bomber Command on 4 Sep 1941 and *activated* on 5 Sep. Assigned to First AF. Engaged primarily in antisubmarine operations along the east coast. *Inactivated* on 15 Oct 1942.

Activated on 1 May 1943. Assigned to Second AF. *Redesignated* XX Bomber Command in Aug 1943. Trained bombardment organizations. *Disbanded* on 6 Oct 1943.

COMPONENTS. (Omitted because of large number and frequent changes.)

STATIONS. Langley Field, Va, 5 Sep 1941; New York, NY, c. 12 Dec 1941–15

Oct 1942. El Paso, Tex, 1 May–6 Oct 1943.

COMMANDERS. Brig Gen Arnold N Krogstad, 24 Sep 1941; Brig Gen Westside T Larson, c. 5 Mar–15 Oct 1942. Brig Gen Robert B Williams, 1 May 1943; Brig Gen Robert F Travis, 3 Jul 1943; Brig Gen Newton Longfellow, 18 Aug–6 Oct 1943.

CAMPAIGNS. Antisubmarine, American Theater.

DECORATIONS. None.

INSIGNE. On a blue disc, edged in gold, a gold aerial bomb. (Approved 24 Apr 1942.)

XX BOMBER COMMAND

Constituted as XX Bomber Command on 19 Nov 1943 and *activated* on 20 Nov. Assigned to Second AF. Moved to India early in 1944. Assigned to Twentieth AF. Engaged in very-long-range bombardment operations from Jun 1944 until all of its tactical components were relieved of assignment in Mar 1945. Moved to

Okinawa, Jun–Jul 1945. *Inactivated* on 16 Jul 1945. *Disbanded* on 8 Oct 1948.

WINGS. *58th:* 1943–1945. *73d:* 1943–1944.

STATIONS. Smoky Hill AAFld, Kan, 20 Nov 1943–12 Feb 1944; Kharagpur, India, 28 Mar 1944–17 Jun 1945; Sakugawa, Okinawa, 7–16 Jul 1945.

COMMANDERS. Brig Gen Kenneth B Wolfe, 27 Nov 1943; Brig Gen LaVern G Saunders, 6 Jul 1944; Maj Gen Curtis E LeMay, 29 Aug 1944; Brig Gen Roger M Ramey, 20 Jan 1945; Brig Gen Joseph Smith, 25 Apr–16 Jul 1945.

CAMPAIGNS. India-Burma; Air Offensive, Japan; China Defensive; Western Pacific; Central Burma.

DECORATIONS. None.

INSIGNE. On an ultramarine blue arc segment, couped at base, within border gold, two very large aerial bombs of the last, falling parallel to sides in perspective, toward and over a bezant in base, marked with latitude and longitude representations of the field. (Approved 20 Mar 1945.)

XXI BOMBER COMMAND

Constituted as XXI Bomber Command on 1 Mar 1944 and *activated* the same day. Assigned to Second AF. Moved to the Marianas late in 1944 and, assigned to Twentieth AF, engaged in very-long-range bombardment operations until mid-Jul 1945. The history of XXI Bomber Command terminated on 16 Jul 1945. (On that date Headquarters and Headquarters Squadron, XXI Bomber Command was redesignated Headquarters Squadron, Twentieth AF. This redesignation, which brought an end to XXI Bomber Command as an establishment, had no effect on the lineage of Twentieth AF.)

WINGS. *58th:* 1945. *73d:* 1944–1945. *313th:* 1944–1945. *314th:* 1944–1945. *315th:* 1945.

STATIONS. Smoky Hill AAFld, Kan, 1 Mar 1944; Peterson Field, Colo, 11 Jun–20 Oct 1944; Harmon Field, Guam, 4 Dec 1944–16 Jul 1945.

COMMANDERS. Col John B Montgomery, 7 Apr 1944; Brig Gen Roger M Ramey, 15 Jun 1944; Brig Gen Haywood S Hansell Jr, 28 Aug 1944; Maj Gen Curtis E LeMay, 20 Jan–16 Jul 1945.

CAMPAIGNS. Air Offensive, Japan; Eastern Mandates; Western Pacific.

DECORATIONS. None.

INSIGNE. None.

XXII BOMBER COMMAND

Constituted as XXII Bomber Command (Very Heavy) on 4 Aug 1944 and *activated* on 14 Aug. Assigned to Second AF. *Disbanded* on 13 Feb 1945.

WINGS. (Two attached.)

STATIONS. Peterson Field, Colo, 14 Aug 1944–13 Feb 1945.

COMMANDERS. Col William R Robertson Jr, 28 Aug 1944; Col Alan D Clark, 4 Sep 1944; Col Forrest G Allen, 6 Oct 1944; Col Robert F Worden, 11 Dec 1944; Col Merlin I Carter, 28 Dec 1944; Col Roscoe C Wriston, 5 Jan–13 Feb 1945.

CAMPAIGNS. None.

DECORATIONS. None.

INSIGNE. None.

XXII TACTICAL AIR COMMAND

Constituted as XII Interceptor Command on 26 Feb 1942. *Activated* on 5 Mar 1942. *Redesignated* XII Fighter Command in May 1942, and XXII Tactical Air Command in Nov 1944. Assigned to Twelfth AF in Aug 1942. Moved to England in Sep 1942 and to North Africa during Oct–Nov 1942. Served in combat in the Mediterranean theater until the end of the war. *Inactivated* in Italy on 4 Oct 1945. *Disbanded* on 8 Oct 1948.

WINGS. *3d* Air Defense: 1943. *62d* Fighter (formerly 1st Air Defense): 1943–1945. *63d* Fighter (formerly 2d Air Defense): 1943–1944. *87th* Fighter: 1944–1945.

STATIONS. Drew Field, Fla, 5 Mar–27 Aug 1942; Wattisham, England, 12 Sep 1942; Bushey Hall, England, 17 Sep–26 Oct 1942; Tafaraoui, Algeria, 8 Nov 1942; La Senia, Algeria, 12 Nov 1942; Tebessa, Algeria, Dec 1942; La Senia, Algeria, 12 Jan 1943; Algiers, Algeria, 20 Mar 1943; Caserta, Italy, 14 Jul 1944; Florence, Italy, 15 Sep 1944; Pomigliano, Italy, Aug–4 Oct 1945.

COMMANDERS. Maj Arch G Campbell Jr, 24 Aug–Sep 1942; Col Reuben C Moffat, 21 Sep 1942; Brig Gen Thomas W Blackburn, c. 27 Sep 1942; Col Lawrence P Hickey, c. 1 Mar 1943; Brig Gen Elwood R Quesada, c. Apr 1943; Brig Gen Gordon P Saville, 2 Oct 1943; Brig Gen Edward M Morris, 3 Jan 1944; Brig Gen Benjamin W Chidlaw, 12 Sep 1944; Brig Gen Thomas C Darcy, 6 Apr 1945; Brig Gen Robert S Israel Jr, 6 May 1945; Maj Gustav M Minton Jr, 7 Jun 1945–unkn.

CAMPAIGNS. Air Combat, EAME Theater; Algeria-French Morocco; Tunisia; Sicily; Naples-Foggia; Rome-Arno; North Apennines; Po Valley.

DECORATIONS. None.

INSIGNE. None.

XXVI FIGHTER COMMAND

Constituted as XXVI Interceptor Command on 28 Feb 1942. *Activated* in the Panama Canal Zone on 6 Mar 1942. Assigned to Sixth AF. *Redesignated* XXVI

Fighter Command in May 1942. Engaged in patrol operations in the defense of the Panama Canal. *Inactivated* on 25 Aug 1946. *Disbanded* on 8 Oct 1948.

GROUPS. *16th:* 1942–1943. *32d:* 1942–1943. *37th:* 1943. *53d:* 1942.

STATIONS. Albrook Field, CZ, 6 Mar 1942–25 Aug 1946.

COMMANDERS. Brig Gen Adlai H Gilkeson, 6 Mar 1942; Brig Gen Russell E Randall, 17 Aug 1942; Col Willis R Taylor, 16 Oct 1943; Col Robert T Cronau, 15 Jun 1945–unkn.

CAMPAIGNS. American Theater.

DECORATIONS. None.

INSIGNE. None.

XXXVI FIGHTER COMMAND

Constituted as XXXVI Fighter Command on 9 Aug 1942 and *activated* in Trinidad on 21 Aug. *Disbanded* on 30 Apr 1943.

COMPONENTS. Unkn.

STATIONS. Waller Field, Trinidad, 21 Aug 1942–30 Apr 1943.

COMMANDERS. Col Charles F Born, 21 Aug 1942–unkn.

CAMPAIGNS. American Theater.

DECORATIONS. None.

INSIGNE. None.

ANTILLES AIR COMMAND

Constituted as Antilles Air Task Force on 20 Feb 1943. *Activated* in Puerto Rico on 1 Mar 1943. *Redesignated* Antilles Air Command in Jun 1943. *Inactivated* in Puerto Rico on 25 Aug 1946. *Disbanded* on 8 Oct 1948.

COMPONENTS. Unkn.

STATIONS. San Juan, PR, 1 Mar 1943; Borinquen Field, PR, 1 Mar–25 Aug 1946.

COMMANDERS. Maj Gen Edwin J House, 1 Mar 1943; Brig Gen Edwin B Lyon, 14 May 1943; Col Bayard Johnson, 8 Jan 1944; Brig Gen Wolcott P Hayes, 22 Feb–Dec 1944; Brig Gen George G Lundberg, Feb 1945–unkn.

CAMPAIGNS. American Theater.

DECORATIONS. None.

INSIGNE. None.

AIR FORCES

FIRST AIR FORCE

Constituted as Northeast Air District on 19 Oct 1940. *Activated* on 18 Dec 1940. *Redesignated* First AF early in 1941. Trained new organizations and, later, replacements for combat units. Also provided air defense for the eastern US until 1943. Assigned to Air Defense Command in Mar 1946 and to Continental Air Command in Dec 1948, being concerned primarily with air defense until 1949 and with reserve and national guard activities thereafter.

COMMANDS. *I* Bomber (later assigned to Second AF and redesignated XX Bomber Command): 1941–1942. *I* Bomber (Antisubmarine Command prior to assignment to First AF): 1943–1946. *I* Fighter: 1941–1946. *I* Ground Air Support: 1941–1942.

STATIONS. Mitchel Field, NY, 18 Dec 1940; Ft Slocom, NY, 3 Jun 1946; Mitchel AFB, NY, 17 Oct 1949–.

COMMANDERS. Maj Gen James E Chaney, 18 Dec 1940; Maj Gen Herbert A Dargue, 24 Jun 1941; Brig Gen Arnold N Krogstad, 10 Dec 1941; Maj Gen Follett Bradley, 5 Mar 1942; Maj Gen James E Chaney, 23 Jul 1942; Maj Gen Ralph Royce, 18 Apr 1943; Maj Gen Frank O'D Hunter, 17 Sep 1943; Maj Gen Robert W Douglass Jr, 20 Oct 1945; Maj Gen Robert M Webster, 16 Jul 1947; Maj Gen Glenn O Barcus, 1 Sep 1949; Maj Gen Willis H Hale, 17 Jul 1950; Maj Gen James P Hodges, 27 Feb 1951; Col Joseph A Bulger, 1 Sep 1951; Maj Gen Howard M Turner, 9 Aug 1952; Maj Gen Roger J Browne, 10 May 1954–.

CAMPAIGNS. American Theater.

DECORATIONS. None.

INSIGNE. A white star charged with a red disc in the center and with golden orange stylized wings below the Arabic number "1" in white, all on a blue disc. (Approved 18 Jan 1944.)

SECOND AIR FORCE

Constituted as Northwest Air District on 19 Oct 1940. *Activated* on 18 Dec 1940. *Redesignated* Second AF early in 1941. Served as both an air defense and a training organization in 1941. Afterward, was engaged chiefly in training units and replacements for heavy and, later, very heavy bombardment operations. *Inactivated* on 30 Mar 1946.

Activated on 6 Jun 1946. Assigned to Air Defense Command. *Inactivated* on 1 Jul 1948.

Activated on 1 Nov 1949. Assigned to Strategic Air Command.

COMMANDS. *II* Air Support: 1941–1943. *II* Bomber: 1941–1943. *II* Fighter: 1941–1942. *IV* Air Support: 1942–1943. *XX* (formerly I) Bomber: 1943. *XX* Bomber (constituted Nov 1943): 1943–1944. *XXI* Bomber: 1944. *XXII* Bomber: 1944–1945.

STATIONS. McChord Field, Wash, 18 Dec 1940; Ft George Wright, Wash, 9 Jan 1941; Colorado Springs, Colo, Jun 1943–30 Mar 1946. Ft Crook, Neb, 6 Jun 1946–1 Jul 1948. Barksdale AFB, La, 1 Nov 1949–.

COMMANDERS. Maj Gen John F Curry, 18 Dec 1940; Maj Gen Millard F Harmon, 5 Aug 1941; Brig Gen John B Brooks, 19 Dec 1941; Maj Gen Frederick L Martin, 1 Feb 1942; Maj Gen Robert Olds, 14 May 1942; Maj Gen Davenport Johnson, 25 Feb 1943; Maj Gen St Clair Streett, 9 Sep 1943; Maj Gen Uzal G Ent, 15 Jan 1944; Maj Gen Robert B Williams, 28 Oct 1944; Brig Gen Julius K Lacey, 21 Nov 1945; Maj Gen Charles B Stone III, 21 Feb 1946; Brig Gen Charles F Born, 19–30 Mar 1946. Brig Gen Walter R Peck, 6 Jun 1946; Maj Gen Frederick W Evans, 15 Jul 1946; Brig Gen Walter R Peck, 23 Jun 1947; Maj Gen Paul L Williams, 15 Sep 1947–1 Jul 1948. Brig Gen Paul T Cullen, 1 Nov 1949; Maj Gen Joseph H Atkinson, 10 Nov 1949; Maj Gen Frank A Armstrong Jr, 16 Nov 1952–.

CAMPAIGNS. American Theater.

DECORATIONS. None.

INSIGNE. On a blue square, a golden orange falcon with jesses in striking attitude below a white star bearing a red disc. (Approved 16 Dec 1943. This insigne was superseded by another on 19 Oct 1954.)

THIRD AIR FORCE

Constituted as Southeast Air District on 19 Oct 1940. *Activated* on 18 Dec 1940. *Redesignated* Third AF early in 1941. Trained units, crews, and individuals for bombardment, fighter, and reconnaissance

operations. Also had some air defense responsibilities during 1940–1941 and engaged in antisubmarine activities from Dec 1941 to Oct 1942. Assigned in Mar 1946 to Tactical Air Command to serve as a troop carrier organization. *Inactivated* on 1 Nov 1946.

Organized in England on 1 May 1951. Assigned to United States Air Forces in Europe.

COMMANDS. *II* Air Support: 1943. *III* Air Support: 1941–1942. *III* Bomber: 1941–1946. *III* Fighter: 1941–1946. *III* Reconnaissance (formerly I Ground Air Support): 1942–1946. *III* Tactical Air: 1942–1945.

STATIONS. MacDill Field, Fla, 18 Dec 1940; Tampa, Fla, Jan 1941; Greenville AAB, SC, 21 Mar–1 Nov 1946. South Ruislip, England, 1 May 1951–.

COMMANDERS. Maj Gen Barton K Yount, 18 Dec 1940; Maj Gen Lewis H Brereton, 29 Jul 1941; Maj Gen Walter H Frank, 6 Oct 1941; Brig Gen Carlyle H

Wash, 25 Jun–26 Nov 1942; Maj Gen St Clair Streett, 12 Dec 1942; Maj Gen Westside T Larson, 11 Sep 1943; Brig Gen Edmund C Lynch, 14 May 1945; Brig Gen Thomas W Blackburn, 26 May 1945; Lt Gen Lewis H Brereton, 1 Jul 1945; Maj Gen Elwood R Quesada, 1–21 Mar 1946; Maj Gen Paul L Williams, 28 Mar–1 Nov 1946. Maj Gen Leon W Johnson, 3 May 1951; Maj Gen Francis H Griswold, 6 May 1952–20 Apr 1954; Maj Gen Roscoe C Wilson, 30 Apr 1954–.

CAMPAIGNS. Antisubmarine, American Theater.

DECORATIONS. None.

INSIGNE. On and over a blue disc within a yellow border an Arabic numeral "3" in white, in bend sinister, shaded in red perspective with a white star charged with a red disc in the lower loop. (Approved 1 Sep 1943.)

FOURTH AIR FORCE

Constituted as Southwest Air District on 19 Oct 1940. *Activated* on 18 Dec 1940. *Redesignated* Fourth AF early in 1941. Provided air defense for the western US until 1943, and at the same time trained new organizations. Later, was engaged primarily in training replacements for combat units. Assigned to Air Defense Command in Mar 1946 and to Continental Air Command in Dec 1948, being concerned chiefly with air defense until 1949 and with reserve and national guard activities thereafter.

CAMPAIGNS. American Theater.

DECORATIONS. None.

INSIGNE. *Shield:* Azure, a white star, charged with a red disc, all within a white winged annulet upheld by four golden yellow rays, radiating from base point, all within a border of the last. (Approved 1 Sep 1943. This insigne was superseded by another on 21 Mar 1957.)

FIFTH AIR FORCE

Constituted as Philippine Department AF on 16 Aug 1941. *Activated* in the Philippines on 20 Sep 1941. *Redesignated* Far East AF in Oct 1941, and Fifth AF in Feb 1942. This air force lost most of its men and equipment in the defense of the Philippines after 7 Dec 1941. Later in Dec 1941 headquarters and some crews and planes moved to Australia, and in Jan 1942 they were sent to Java to help delay Japanese advances in the Netherlands Indies. The Fifth did not function

COMMANDS. *IV* Bomber: 1941–1944. *IV* Fighter: 1941–1944. *IV* Ground Air Support: 1941–1942.

STATIONS. March Field, Calif, 18 Dec 1940; Riverside, Calif, 16 Jan 1941; Hamilton Field, Calif, 7 Dec 1941; San Francisco, Calif, 5 Jan 1942; Hamilton Field, Calif, 19 Jun 1946–.

COMMANDERS. Maj Gen Jacob E Fickel, 18 Dec 1940; Maj Gen George C Kenney, 2 Apr 1942; Maj Gen Barney McK Giles, 22 Jul 1942; Maj Gen William E Kepner, 18 Mar 1943; Maj Gen William E Lynd, 8 Jul 1943; Maj Gen James E Parker, 14 Jul 1944; Brig Gen Edward M Morris, 19 May 1945; Maj Gen Willis H Hale, 6 Jul 1945; Brig Gen Ned Schramm, 1 Nov 1947; Maj Gen John E Upston, 20 Jan 1948; Maj Gen Alvan C Kincaid, c. Sep 1950; Maj Gen William E Hall, 29 Jan 1951; Maj Gen Alfred A Kessler Jr, 8 Sep 1952; Maj Gen Robert B Landry, 4 Feb 1955–.

as an air force for some time after Feb 1942 (the AAF organizations in the Southwest Pacific being under the control of American-British-Dutch-Australian Command and later Allied Air Forces). Headquarters was remanned in Sep 1942 and assumed control of AAF organizations in Australia and New Guinea. The Fifth participated in operations that stopped the Japanese drive in Papua, recovered New Guinea, neutralized islands in the Bismarck Archipelago and the Netherlands East Indies, and liberated the Philippines. When the war ended in Aug 1945 elements of the Fifth were moving to the Ryukyus for the invasion of Japan. After the war the Fifth, a component of Far East Air Forces, remained in the theater, and from Jun 1950 to Jul 1953 it was engaged in the Korean War.

COMMANDS. *V* Bomber: 1941–1946. *V* Fighter: 1942–1946.

STATIONS. Nichols Field, Luzon, 20 Sep 1941; Darwin, Australia, Dec 1941; Java, Jan–Feb 1942; Brisbane, Australia, 3 Sep 1942; Nadzab, New Guinea, 15 Jun 1944; Owi, Schouten Islands, 10 Aug 1944; Leyte, c. 20 Nov 1944; Mindoro, Jan 1945; Clark Field, Luzon, Apr 1945; Okinawa, Jul 1945; Irumagawa, Japan, c. 25 Sep 1945; Tokyo, Japan, 13 Jan 1946; Nagoya, Japan, 20 May 1946; Seoul, Korea, 1 Dec 1950; Taegu, Korea, 22 Dec 1950; Seoul, Korea, 15 Jun 1951; Osan–Ni, Korea, 25 Jan 1954; Nagoya, Japan, 1 Sep 1954–.

COMMANDERS. Brig Gen Henry B Clagett, 20 Sep 1941; Maj Gen Lewis H Brereton, Oct 1941–Feb 1942; Lt Gen George C Kenney, 3 Sep 1942; Lt Gen Ennis C Whitehead, 15 Jun 1944; Maj Gen Kenneth B Wolfe, 4 Oct 1945; Maj Gen Thomas D White, 16 Jan 1948; Lt Gen Earle E Partridge, 6 Oct 1948; Maj Gen Edward J Timberlake, 21 May 1951; Maj Gen Frank F Everest, 1 Jun 1951; Lt Gen Glenn O Barcus, 30 May 1952; Lt Gen Samuel E Anderson, 31 May 1953; Lt Gen Roger M Ramey, 1 Jun 1954–.

CAMPAIGNS. *World War II:* Philippine Islands; East Indies; Air Offensive, Japan; China Defensive; Papua; New Guinea; Northern Solomons; Bismarck Archipelago; Western Pacific; Leyte; Luzon; Southern Philippines; China Offensive. *Korean War:* UN Defensive; UN Offensive; CCF Intervention; 1st UN Counteroffensive; CCF Spring Offensive; UN Summer-Fall Offensive; Second Korean Winter; Korea Summer-Fall, 1952; Third Korean Winter; Korea Summer-Fall, 1953.

DECORATIONS. Distinguished Unit Citations: Philippine Islands, 8–22 Dec 1941; Philippine Islands, 7 Dec 1941–10 May 1942; Papua, [Sep] 1942–23 Jan 1943. Philippine Presidential Unit Citation.

INSIGNE. On an ultramarine blue disc, the Southern Cross consisting of five stars in white between a flaming comet, the head consisting of a white five pointed star, charged with a red roundel, within a blue disc outlined in white, its tail consisting of three white streamers; all surmounted by an Arabic numeral "5," golden orange. (Approved 25 Mar 1943.)

SIXTH AIR FORCE

Constituted as Panama Canal AF on 19 Oct 1940. *Activated* in the Canal Zone on 20 Nov 1940. *Redesignated* Caribbean AF in Aug 1941, and Sixth AF in Feb 1942. Served primarily in defense of the Panama Canal; also engaged in antisubmarine operations. *Redesignated* Caribbean Air Command on 31 Jul 1946.

COMMANDS. *VI* Bomber: 1941–1946. *VI* Fighter: 1941–1942. *XXVI* Fighter: 1942–1946. *XXXVI* Fighter: 1942.

STATIONS. Albrook Field, CZ, 20 Nov 1940–.

COMMANDERS. Maj Gen Frank M Andrews, 6 Dec 1940; Maj Gen Davenport Johnson, 19 Sep 1941; Maj Gen Hubert R Harmon, 23 Nov 1942; Brig Gen Ralph H Wooten, 8 Nov 1943; Brig Gen Edgar P Sorensen, 16 May 1944; Maj Gen William O Butler, 21 Sep 1944; Brig Gen Earl H De Ford, 24 Jul 1945; Maj Gen Hubert R Har-

mon, 1 Feb 1946; Brig Gen Glen C Jamison, 4 Oct 1947; Maj Gen Willis H Hale, 13 Nov 1947; Brig Gen Rosenham Beam, 20 Oct 1949; Brig Gen Emil C Kiel, 15 Nov 1950; Maj Gen Reuben C Hood Jr, 11 Jun 1953–.

CAMPAIGNS. Antisubmarine, American Theater.

DECORATIONS. None.

INSIGNE. On a blue hexagon, a white star charged with a red disc partially over a pair of golden orange wings below a galleon in full sail, golden orange. (Approved 16 Jul 1943.)

SEVENTH AIR FORCE

Constituted as Hawaiian AF on 19 Oct 1940. *Activated* in Hawaii on 1 Nov 1940. *Redesignated* Seventh AF in Feb 1942. Provided air defense for the Hawaiian Islands and, after mid-1943, served in combat in the central and western Pacific areas. Transferred back to Hawaii in Jan 1946. *Redesignated* Pacific Air Command in Dec 1947. *Discontinued* on 1 Jun 1949.

Redesignated Seventh AF. *Activated* in Hawaii on 5 Jan 1955. Assigned to Far East Air Forces.

COMMANDS. *VII* Bomber: 1942–1946. *VII* Fighter: 1942–1945.

STATIONS. Ft Shafter, TH, 1 Nov 1940; Hickam Field, TH, c. 12 Jul 1941; Saipan, 13 Dec 1944; Okinawa, 14 Jul 1945; Hickam Field, TH, 1 Jan 1946–1 Jun 1949. Hickam AFB, TH, 5 Jan 1955; Wheeler AFB, TH, 24 Mar 1955–.

COMMANDERS. Maj Gen Frederick L Martin, 2 Nov 1940; Maj Gen Clarence L Tinker, 18 Dec 1941; Brig Gen Howard C Davidson, 9 Jun 1942; Maj Gen Willis H Hale, 20 Jun 1942; Maj Gen Robert W Douglass Jr, 15 Apr 1944; Maj Gen Thomas D White, 23 Jun 1945; Brig Gen Donald F Stace, 19 Oct 1946; Maj Gen Ralph H Wooten, 22 May 1947; Brig Gen Robert F Travis, 1 Sep 1948–1 Jun 1949. Maj Gen Sory Smith, 5 Jan 1955; Brig Gen Julian M Chappell, 25 Jul 1955–.

CAMPAIGNS. Central Pacific; Air Offensive, Japan; Eastern Mandates; Western Pacific; Ryukyus; China Offensive.

DECORATIONS. None.

INSIGNE. On a blue disc a golden orange Arabic numeral "7" enfiled in base by a white five-pointed star charged with a red disc, in perspective, all within a golden orange border. (Approved 21 May 1943.)

EIGHTH AIR FORCE
(originally VIII Bomber Command)

Constituted as VIII Bomber Command on 19 Jan 1942. *Activated* in the US on 1 Feb 1942. An advanced detachment was established in England on 23 Feb and units began arriving from the US during the spring of 1942. The command conducted the heavy bombardment operations of Eighth AF (see US Strategic Air Forces in Europe) from 17 Aug 1942 until early in 1944. *Redesignated* Eighth AF on 22 Feb 1944. Afterward, engaged primarily in bombardment of strategic targets in Europe. Transferred, without personnel, equipment, and combat elements, to Okinawa on 16 Jul 1945. Although some personnel and combat units were assigned before V–J Day, the Eighth did not participate in combat against Japan. Transferred, without personnel and equipment, to the US on 7 Jun 1946. Remanned and re-equipped as part of Strategic Air Command.

COMPONENTS. *1st* Bombardment Wing: 1942–1943. *2d* Bombardment Wing: 1942–1943. *3d* Bombardment Wing: 1942–1943. *4th* Bombardment Wing: 1942–1943. *12th* Bombardment Wing: 1942–1944. *301st* Fighter Wing: 1945–1946. *316th* Bombardment Wing: 1945–1946. *1st* Air Division: 1943–1945. *2d* Air Division: 1943–1945. *3d* Air Division: 1943–1945. *VIII* Fighter Command: 1944–1945.

STATIONS. Langley Field, Va, 1 Feb 1942; Savannah AB, Ga, c. 10 Feb 1942; Daws Hill, England, 23 Feb 1942; High Wycombe, England, 15 May 1942–16 Jul 1945; Okinawa, 16 Jul 1945–7 Jun 1946; MacDill Field, Fla, 7 Jun 1946; Ft Worth AAFld, Tex, 1 Nov 1946; Westover AFB, Mass, Jun 1955–.

COMMANDERS. Maj Gen Ira C Eaker, 23 Feb 1942; Brig Gen Newton Longfellow, 2 Dec 1942; Maj Gen Frederick L Anderson, 1 Jul 1943; Lt Gen James H Doolittle, 6 Jan 1944; Maj Gen William E Kepner, 10 May 1945; Maj Gen Westside T Larson, 21 Jun 1945; Lt Gen James H Doolittle, 19 Jul 1945; Maj Gen Earle E Partridge, 12 Sep 1945; Brig Gen Patrick W Timberlake, 30 Nov 1945–unkn; Col Neil B Harding, c. 16 Aug 1946; Brig Gen Roger M Ramey, 1 Nov 1946; Maj Gen Clements McMullen, 12 Nov 1946; Maj Gen Roger M Ramey, 16 Dec 1946; Maj Gen Archie J Old Jr, 15 Jun 1950; Lt Gen Samuel E Anderson, 14 Aug 1950; Maj Gen John B Montgomery, 8 May 1953;

Maj Gen James C Selser Jr, 13 Jun 1955; Maj Gen Walter C Sweeney Jr, 6 Aug 1955–.

CAMPAIGNS. Air Offensive, Europe; Normandy; Northern France; Rhineland; Ardennes-Alsace; Central Europe; Asiatic-Pacific Theater.

DECORATIONS. None.

INSIGNE. Azure, in the lower lobe of the winged Arabic numeral "8" or a mullet throughout argent charged with a torteaux. (Approved 20 May 1943.)

NINTH AIR FORCE

Constituted as V Air Support Command on 21 Aug 1941. *Activated* on 1 Sep 1941. *Redesignated* Ninth AF in Apr 1942. Moved to Egypt and began operations on 12 Nov 1942, participating in the Allied drive across Egypt and Libya, the campaign in Tunisia, and the invasions of Sicily and Italy. Moved to England in Oct 1943 to become the tactical air force for the invasion of the Continent. Helped prepare for the assault on Normandy, supported operations on the beach in Jun 1944, and took part in the drive that carried the Allies across France and culminated in victory over Germany in May 1945. *Inactivated* in Germany on 2 Dec 1945.

Activated in the US on 28 Mar 1946. Assigned to Tactical Air Command until Dec 1948 when the Ninth, reassigned to Continental Air Command, lost its role as a tactical air organization and became concerned chiefly with reserve and national guard activities. *Redesignated* Ninth AF (Tactical) in Aug 1950. Assigned to Tactical Air Command in Dec 1950 and again became concerned primarily with tactical air operations. *Redesignated* Ninth AF in Jun 1951.

COMPONENTS. *9th* Air Division (formerly IX Bomber Command): 1942–1945. *IX* Air Defense Command: 1944–1945. *IX* Fighter Command: 1942–1945. *IX* Tactical Air Command: 1943–1945. *IX* Troop Carrier Command: 1943–1944. *XIX* Tactical Air Command: 1944–1945. *XXIX* Tactical Air Command: 1945.

STATIONS. Bowman Field, Ky, 1 Sep 1941; New Orleans AAB, La, 24 Jan 1942; Bolling Field, DC, 22 Jul–Oct 1942; Egypt, 12 Nov 1942–Oct 1943; England, 16 Oct 1943–Sep 1944; France, 15 Sep 1944; Germany, 6 Jun–2 Dec 1945. Biggs Field, Tex, 28 Mar 1946; Greenville AAB, SC, 31 Oct 1946; Langley AFB, Va, 14 Feb 1949; Pope AFB, NC, 1 Aug 1950; Shaw AFB, SC, 20 Aug 1954–.

COMMANDERS. Brig Gen Junius W Jones, Sep 1941; Col Rosenham Beam,

1942; Lt Gen Lewis H Brereton, 12 Nov 1942; Lt Gen Hoyt S Vandenburg, 8 Aug 1944; Maj Gen Otto P Weyland, 23 May 1945; Maj Gen William E Kepner, 4 Aug–2 Dec 1945. Brig Gen Homer L Sanders, 28 Mar 1946; Maj Gen Paul L Williams, 1 Nov 1946; Maj Gen William D Old, 15 Sep 1947; Maj Gen Willis H Hale, 20 Oct 1949; Maj Gen Willard R Wolfinbarger, 1 Aug 1950; Maj Gen Edward J Timberlake, 7 Sep 1951–.

CAMPAIGNS. American Theater; Air Combat, EAME Theater; Egypt-Libya; Air Offensive, Europe; Tunisia; Sicily; Naples-Foggia; Normandy; Northern France; Rhineland; Ardennes-Alsace; Central Europe.

DECORATIONS. None.

INSIGNE. *Shield:* Azure, a bezant winged argent charged with the Arabic numeral "9" gules, in honor point a mullet of the second bearing a torteau. (Approved 16 Sep 1943.)

TENTH AIR FORCE

Constituted as Tenth AF on 4 Feb 1942 and *activated* on 12 Feb. Moved to India, Mar–May 1942. Served in India, Burma, and China until Mar 1943 when Fourteenth AF was activated in China. Then the Tenth operated in India and Burma until it moved to China late in Jul 1945. Returned to the US, Dec 1945–Jan 1946. *Inactivated* on 6 Jan 1946.

Activated on 24 May 1946. Assigned first to Air Defense Command and later (Dec 1948) to Continental Air Command.

Supervised reserve and national guard activities.

GROUPS. *3d* Combat Cargo: 1944–1945. *7th* Bombardment: 1942–1945. *12th* Bombardment: 1944–1945. *33d* Fighter: 1944–1945. *80th* Fighter: 1943–1945. *311th* Fighter: 1943–1944. *341st* Bombardment: 1942–1944. *443d* Troop Carrier: 1944–1945.

STATIONS. Patterson Field, Ohio, 12 Feb–8 Mar 1942; New Delhi, India, 16 May 1942; Myitkyina, Burma, 2 Nov 1944; Piardoba, India, 15 May 1945; Kunming, China, 1 Aug 1945; Liuchow, China, 9 Aug–15 Dec 1945; Ft Lawton, Wash, 5–6 Jan 1946. Brooks Field, Tex, 24 May 1946; Offutt AFB, Neb, 1 Jul 1948; Ft Benjamin Harrison, Ind, 25 Sep 1948; Selfridge AFB, Mich, 16 Jan 1950–.

COMMANDERS. Col Harry A Halverson, 17 Feb 1942; Maj Gen Lewis H Brereton, 5 Mar 1942; Brig Gen Earl L Naiden, 26 Jun 1942; Maj Gen Clayton L Bissell, 18 Aug 1942; Maj Gen Howard C Davidson, 19 Aug 1943; Maj Gen Albert F Hegen-

berger, 1 Aug 1945–unkn. Col Edward N Backus, 6 Jun 1946; Maj Gen Howard M Turner, 18 Jun 1946; Brig Gen Harry A Johnson, 6 Jan 1948; Maj Gen Paul L Williams, 1 Jul 1948; Maj Gen Harry A Johnson, 30 Apr 1950; Maj Gen Grandison Gardner, 20 Jan 1951; Maj Gen Harry A Johnson, 1 Apr 1951; Maj Gen Richard A Grussendorf, 2 Jul 1953; Maj Gen Robert E L Eaton, 15 Sep 1955–.

CAMPAIGNS. Burma, 1942; India-Burma; China Defensive; Central Burma; China Offensive.

DECORATIONS. None.

INSIGNE. On an ultramarine blue disc, a white shield in base, winged golden orange, the shield bearing the Arabic numeral "10" ultramarine blue, all below a white five pointed star charged with a red disc, encircled by a white annulet. (Approved 25 Jan 1944.)

ELEVENTH AIR FORCE

Constituted as Alaskan AF on 28 Dec 1941. *Activated* in Alaska on 15 Jan 1942. *Redesignated* Eleventh AF in Feb 1942. Participated in the offensive that drove the Japanese from the Aleutians, attacked the enemy in the Kuril Islands, and, both during and after the war, served as part of the defense force for Alaska. *Redesignated* Alaskan Air Command in Dec 1945.

(This Eleventh AF is not related to an organization of the same name that was constituted on 13 May 1946, assigned to Air Defense Command, activated on 13 Jun 1946, and inactivated on 1 Jul 1948.)

TWELFTH AIR FORCE

COMMANDS. *XI* Bomber: 1943–1944. *XI* Fighter: 1942–1944.

STATIONS. Elmendorf Field, Alaska, 15 Jan 1942; Adak, 10 Aug 1943; Elmendorf Field, Alaska, 1 Oct 1946–.

COMMANDERS. Lt Col Everett S Davis, 15 Jan 1942; Col Lionel H Dunlap, 17 Feb 1942; Maj Gen William O Butler, 8 Mar 1942; Maj Gen Davenport Johnson, 13 Sep 1943; Brig Gen Isaiah Davies, 4 May 1945; Maj Gen John B Brooks, 22 Jun 1945; Brig Gen Edmund C Lynch, 21 Dec 1945; Maj Gen Joseph H Atkinson, 1 Oct 1946; Maj Gen Frank A Armstrong Jr, 26 Feb 1949; Maj Gen William D Old, 27 Dec 1950; Brig Gen Walter R Agee, 27 Oct 1952; Maj Gen George R Acheson, 26 Feb 1953–.

CAMPAIGNS. Air Offensive, Japan; Aleutian Islands.

DECORATIONS. None.

INSIGNE. On an ultramarine blue shield, a red Arabic numeral "11" outlined in white, above a winged white star, bend sinisterwise, with a red disc in the center, wing golden yellow. (Approved 13 Aug 1943. This insigne was superseded by another on 23 May 1947.)

Constituted as Twelfth AF on 20 Aug 1942 and *activated* the same day. Moved to England, Aug–Sep 1942, and then on to North Africa for the invasion of Algeria and French Morocco in Nov 1942. Operated in the Mediterranean theater until the end of the war, serving with Northwest African Air Forces from Feb to Dec 1943, and afterward with Mediterranean Allied Air Forces. *Inactivated* in Italy on 31 Aug 1945.

Activated in the US on 17 May 1946. Assigned to Tactical Air Command until Dec 1948 when the Twelfth, reassigned to Continental Air Command, lost its functions associated with tactical airpower and became concerned primarily with reserve and national guard activities. *Discontinued* on 1 Jul 1950.

Organized in Germany on 21 Jan 1951. Assigned to United States Air Forces in Europe.

COMMANDS. *XII* Bomber: 1942–1944. *XII* Tactical Air: 1942–1944. *XXII*

Tactical Air (formerly XII Fighter): 1942–1945.

STATIONS. Bolling Field, DC, 20–28 Aug 1942; England, 12 Sep–22 Oct 1942; Algeria, 9 Nov 1942; Tunisia, 10 Aug 1943; Italy, 5 Dec 1943–31 Aug 1945. March Field, Calif, 17 May 1946; Brooks AFB, Tex, 1 Jan 1949–1 Jul 1950. Wiesbaden, Germany, 21 Jan 1951; Ramstein, Germany, 27 Apr 1953–.

COMMANDERS. Lt Col Roger J Browne, 26 Aug 1942; Lt Col Harold L Neely, 28 Aug 1942; Maj Gen James H Doolittle, 23 Sep 1942; Lt Gen Carl Spaatz, 1 Mar 1943; Lt Gen John K Cannon, 21 Dec 1943; Maj Gen Benjamin W Chidlaw, 2 Apr 1945; Brig Gen Charles T Myers, 26 May–31 Aug 1945. Brig Gen Yantis H Taylor, 17 May 1946; Brig Gen John P Doyle, 10 Jul 1946; Maj Gen William D Old, 24 Sep 1946; Brig Gen John P Doyle, 23 Jan 1947; Maj Gen Glenn O Barcus, 2 May 1947; Maj Gen Alden R Crawford, 1 Sep 1949; Col Ezekiel W Napier, 13 Jun–1 Jul 1950. Maj Gen Robert W Douglass Jr, 22 Jan 1951; Maj Gen Dean C Strother, 16 Mar 1951; Maj Gen Robert M Lee, 20 Nov 1953–.

CAMPAIGNS. Air Combat, EAME Theater; Algeria-French Morocco; Tunisia; Sicily; Naples-Foggia; Anzio; Rome-Arno; Southern France; North Apennines; Po Valley.

DECORATIONS. None.

INSIGNE. On an ultramarine blue equilateral triangle, one point down, a white star with a red disc in the center thereof bearing the numeral "12" in white, below a pair of stylized golden orange wings. (Approved 1 Dec 1943.)

THIRTEENTH AIR FORCE

Constituted as Thirteenth AF on 14 Dec 1942. *Activated* in New Caledonia on 13 Jan 1943. Served in the South Pacific and, later, Southwest Pacific, participating in the Allied drive north and west from the Solomons to the Philippines. Remained in the Philippines, as part of Far East Air Forces, after the war. Transferred, without personnel and equipment, to Okinawa in Dec 1948 and back to the Philippines in May 1949.

COMMANDS. *XIII* Bomber: 1943–1946. *XIII* Fighter: 1943–1946.

STATIONS. New Caledonia, 13 Jan 1943; Espiritu Santo, 21 Jan 1943; Guadalcanal, 13 Jan 1944; Los Negros, 15 Jun 1944; Hollandia, New Guinea, 13 Sep 1944; Noemfoor, 23 Sep 1944; Morotai, 29 Oct 1944; Leyte, 1 Mar 1945; Clark Field, Luzon, c. 1 Jan 1946; Ft William McKinley, Luzon, 20 May 1946; Clark Field, Luzon, 15 Aug

1947; Kadena, Okinawa, 1 Dec 1948; Clark AFB, Luzon, 16 May 1949–.

COMMANDERS. Maj Gen Nathan F Twining, 13 Jan 1943; Brig Gen Ray L Owens, 27 Jul 1943; Maj Gen Hubert R Harmon, 7 Jan 1944; Maj Gen St Clair Streett, 15 Jun 1944; Maj Gen Paul B Wurtsmith, 19 Feb 1945; Maj Gen Eugene L Eubank, 4 Jul 1946; Maj Gen Charles T Myers, 1 Dec 1948; Maj Gen Howard M Turner, Jun 1949; Maj Gen Ernest Moore, 16 Oct 1951; Maj Gen John W Sessums Jr, 10 Oct 1952; Brig Gen William L Lee, 27 Aug 1954–.

CAMPAIGNS. China Defensive; Guadalcanal; New Guinea; Northern Solomons; Eastern Mandates; Bismarck Archipelago; Western Pacific; Leyte; Luzon; Southern Philippines; China Offensive.

DECORATIONS. Philippine Presidential Unit Citation.

INSIGNE. On a blue disc, bordered golden orange, a pair of golden orange wings surmounted in base by a white star charged with a red disc; all below the Arabic numeral "13" in white. (Approved 18 Jan 1944.)

FOURTEENTH AIR FORCE

Constituted as Fourteenth AF on 5 Mar 1943 and *activated* in China on 10 Mar. Served in combat against the Japanese, operating primarily in China, until the end of the war. Moved to the US, Dec 1945–Jan 1946. *Inactivated* on 6 Jan 1946.

Activated on 24 May 1946. Assigned first to Air Defense Command and later

(1948) to Continental Air Command. Supervised reserve and national guard activities.

WINGS. *68th* Composite: 1943–1945. *69th* Composite: 1943–1945. *312th* Fighter: 1944–1945.

STATIONS. Kunming, China, 10 Mar 1943; Peishiyi, China, 7 Aug–15 Dec 1945; Ft Lawton, Wash, 5–6 Jan 1946. Orlando AB, Fla, 24 May 1946; Robins AFB, Ga, 29 Oct 1949–.

COMMANDERS. Maj Gen Claire L Chennault, 10 Mar 1943; Maj Gen Charles B Stone III, 10 Aug–31 Dec 1945. Maj Gen Leo A Walton, 24 May 1946; Maj Gen Ralph F Stearley, 27 Jul 1948; Maj Gen Charles E Thomas Jr, 17 Jul 1950; Maj Gen George G Finch, 1 Feb 1955–.

CAMPAIGNS. India-Burma; China Defensive; China Offensive.

DECORATIONS. None.

INSIGNE. On a blue disc, a winged Bengal tiger golden orange with black and white markings, below and partially covering a white star charged with a red disc. (Approved 6 Aug 1943.)

FIFTEENTH AIR FORCE

Constituted as Fifteenth AF on 30 Oct 1943. *Activated* in the Mediterranean theater on 1 Nov 1943. Began operations on 2 Nov and engaged primarily in strategic bombardment of targets in Italy, France, Germany, Poland, Czechoslovakia, Austria, Hungary, and the Balkans until the end of the war. *Inactivated* in Italy on 15 Sep 1945.

Activated in the US on 31 Mar 1946. Assigned to Strategic Air Command.

WINGS. *5th* Bombardment: 1943–1945. *42d* Bombardment: 1943. *47th* Bombardment: 1944–1945. *49th* Bombardment: 1944–1945. *55th* Bombardment: 1944–1945. *304th* Bombardment: 1943–1945. *305th* Bombardment: 1943–1945. *306th* Fighter: 1944–1945. *307th* Bombardment: 1944.

STATIONS. Tunis, Tunisia, 1 Nov 1943; Bari, Italy, 1 Dec 1943–15 Sep 1945. Colo-

rado Springs, Colo, 31 Mar 1946; March AFB, Calif, 7 Nov 1949–.

COMMANDERS. Maj Gen James H Doolittle, 1 Nov 1943; Maj Gen Nathan F Twining, 3 Jan 1944; Brig Gen James A Mollison, 26 May 1945; Brig Gen William L Lee, 3 Aug 1945; Col Elmer J Rogers Jr, 31 Aug–15 Sep 1945. Maj Gen Charles F Born, 31 Mar 1946; Brig Gen Leon W Johnson, 24 Apr 1947; Maj Gen Emmett O'Donnell Jr, 6 Oct 1948; Maj Gen Walter C Sweeney Jr, 20 Apr 1953; Maj Gen Archie J Old Jr, c. 20 Aug 1955–.

CAMPAIGNS. Air Combat, EAME Theater; Air Offensive, Europe; Naples-Foggia; Anzio; Rome-Arno; Normandy; Northern France; Southern France; North Apennines; Rhineland; Central Europe; Po Valley.

DECORATIONS. None.

INSIGNE. On a blue disc a white star charged with a red disc in the center and with golden orange stylized wings below a golden orange Arabic numeral "15", all within a golden orange annulet. (Approved 19 Feb 1944.)

TWENTIETH AIR FORCE

Constituted as Twentieth AF on 4 Apr 1944 and *activated* the same day. Some combat elements moved in the summer of 1944 from the US to India where they carried out very heavy bombardment operations against targets in Japan, Formosa, Thailand, and Burma. Other combat elements began moving late in 1944 from the US to the Marianas, being joined there

early in 1945 by the elements that had been in India. Headquarters, which had remained in the US, was transferred to Guam in Jul 1945. From the Marianas the Twentieth conducted a strategic air offensive that was climaxed by the dropping of two atomic bombs on Japan. After the war the Twentieth remained in the theater and eventually became part of Far East Air Forces. Served in combat for a short time at the beginning of the Korean War but later was concerned primarily with logistic support for the operations of other organizations and with air defense for the Ryukyus. *Inactivated* on Okinawa on 1 Mar 1955.

COMMANDS. *VII* Fighter: 1945. *XX* Bomber: 1944–1945. *XXI* Bomber: 1944–1945.

STATIONS. Washington, DC, 4 Apr 1944; Harmon Field, Guam, 16 Jul 1945; Kadena, Okinawa, 16 May 1949–1 Mar 1955.

COMMANDERS. General of the Army Henry H Arnold, 6 Apr 1944; Maj Gen Curtis E LeMay, 16 Jul 1945; Lt Gen Nathan F Twining, 2 Aug 1945; Maj Gen James E Parker, 15 Oct 1945; Brig Gen Frederick M Hopkins Jr, 19 Mar 1946; Maj Gen Francis H Griswold, 10 Sep 1946; Maj Gen Alvan C Kincaid, 8 Sep 1948; Maj Gen Ralph F Stearley, 31 Jul 1950; Maj Gen Fay R Upthegrove, 8 Feb 1953–1 Mar 1955.

CAMPAIGNS. *World War II:* American Theater; India-Burma; Air Offensive, Japan; China Defensive; Eastern Mandates; Western Pacific; Central Burma. *Korean War:* UN Defensive.

DECORATIONS. None.

INSIGNE. A disc of ultramarine blue marked with white parallels of latitude and meridians of longitude surmounted in base by a white star charged at center with a red disc and circumscribed by an annulet golden orange lined blue, tips enclosing the Arabic numeral "20". (Approved 26 May 1944.)

U.S. STRATEGIC AIR FORCES IN EUROPE
(originally Eighth Air Force)

Constituted as Eighth AF on 19 Jan 1942 and *activated* on 28 Jan. Moved to England, May–Jun 1942, and engaged primarily in bombardment of targets in Europe. *Redesignated* US Strategic Air Forces in Europe on 22 Feb 1944. Afterward, coordinated AAF activities in the EAME Theater, exercising some operational control over both Eighth AF (originally VIII Bomber Command) and

Fifteenth, and some administrative control over Eighth AF and Ninth. Served with the occupation forces in Europe after World War II. *Redesignated* United States Air Forces in Europe in Aug 1945. Directed USAF operations in the Berlin airlift, Jun 1948–Sep 1949.

COMMANDS. *VIII* Air Support: 1942–1943. *VIII* Bomber: 1942–1944. *VIII* Fighter: 1942–1944.

STATIONS. Savannah AB, Ga, 28 Jan–c. 20 May 1942; London, England, 18 Jun 1942; Bushy Park, England, 25 Jun 1942; St-Germain-en-Laye, France, 26 Sep 1944; Wiesbaden, Germany, c. 28 Sep 1945–.

COMMANDERS. Brig Gen Asa N Duncan, 28 Jan 1942; Maj Gen Carl Spaatz, 5 May 1942; Lt Gen Ira C Eaker, 1 Dec 1942; Gen Carl Spaatz, 6 Jan 1944; Lt Gen John K Cannon, 3 Jun 1945; Gen Carl Spaatz, 13 Jun 1945; Lt Gen John K Cannon, 4 Jul 1945; Maj Gen Idwal H Edwards, 2 Mar 1946; Brig Gen John F McBlain, 14 Aug 1947; Lt Gen Curtis E LeMay, 20 Oct 1947; Lt Gen John K Cannon, 16 Oct 1948; Gen Lauris Norstad, 22 Jan 1951; Lt Gen William H Tunner, 27 Jul 1953–.

CAMPAIGNS. Air Combat, EAME Theater; Air Offensive, Europe; Normandy; Northern France; Rhineland; Ardennes-Alsace; Central Europe.

DECORATIONS. None.

INSIGNE. Upon a shield argent charged with letters USSTAF gules, a chief azure charged with a pair of wings displayed or between three mullets one and two of the first in fess point a large mullet of the field that portion on shield fimbriated of the third charged with a torteau. (Approved 21 Dec 1944.)

APPENDIXES

APPENDIX I: ORGANIZATIONAL TERMS

Each unit of the Air Force has a unique lineage and history. The policy of first the War Department and later the Department of the Air Force has been to preserve the identity of each unit. There apparently has been only one deliberate violation of this basic policy—the bestowal of the histories of combat groups on similarly numbered combat wings, a practice that was started in 1954.

The lineage of each unit is determined by the language employed in orders relating to organizational actions. But before defining the various terms used in connection with such actions, some explanation concerning the structure of the Air Force may be in order.

During the period covered by this volume,* the Air Force was composed of a great number of primary components that were referred to as units. These units were divided into two categories. First, there were those units that served as headquarters for establishments and that may be identified by the use of the word "headquarters" in their designations. In the second category were squadrons and such miscellaneous organizations as bands and dispensaries.

These primary units were formed into larger "units" that were properly known as "establishments." An establishment (with some exceptions) came into being upon the constitution and activation, or designation and organization, of its headquarters; it ceased to exist when its headquarters was disbanded or discontinued. Headquarters was automatically part of the establishment, but other components could be—and usually were—assigned. Since the headquarters was the one constant element, an establishment traced its lineage, and thus its history, through the lineage of its headquarters. It will be noted that this volume on *Air Force Combat Units of World War II* is not concerned with the primary units (headquarters and squadrons) mentioned above; instead, it deals with the larger organizations (e.g., groups and wings) that commonly were referred to as "units" but in formal organizational terminology must be labeled "establishments."

Looking at the primary units of the Air Force from a different point of view, one finds that they fell into two classes: constituted and organized. The lineage—and history—of a constituted unit began when the unit was constituted. It continued through any number of activations, inactivations, and redesignations until the unit

---

*The organizational system described here was in effect until 2 October 1959, when important changes were made by the Air Force.

was disbanded. After disbandment, a unit could have its lineage continued by reconstitution. Further, the lineage of one unit could be merged with that of another (without violating the policy mentioned above) by formal action taken to consolidate the two units. Constitutions, disbandments, reconstitutions, and consolidations were accomplished by the Department of the Air Force, which also controlled all actions relating to activations, inactivations, and redesignations.

The lineage of an organized unit began when the unit was designated and organized. The unit could at any time be redesignated, but its lineage continued until the unit was discontinued. Designation, organization, redesignation, and discontinuance were usually controlled by the Department of the Air Force for organized units at higher echelons and by the major commands for units at lower echelons.

Sometimes a constituted headquarters was inactivated and replaced simultaneously by an organized headquarters that had essentially the same name and functions and often the same personnel. In other instances the reverse took place. When any such change was, in effect, merely a reorganization (usually associated with a shift from one system of manning to another), the Department of the Air Force disregarded the change in tracing the history of the establishment.

It may be noted in passing that provisional units were organized rather than constituted. They had no personnel assigned but were manned by persons who were attached. Likewise, provisional establishments had components attached but none assigned. Detachments were not units but segments of units.

The following glossary defines organizational terms, including those that relate to lineage:

Activate. To bring a constituted unit into physical existence by assigning personnel. (In some cases a token activation was accomplished by assigning a minimum number of personnel, generally one officer and one enlisted man; in other cases activation was recorded officially without assignment of personnel.)

Active list. The constituted units that were active and those that had been assigned to commands for activation.

Assign. To place a unit in a military organization, making it an element of that organization.

Attach. To place a unit with a military organization for administration, operational control, logistic support, or other purposes, without making the unit an integral part of the organization.

Authorize. To designate a unit and place it on the active or inactive list (used prior to World War II in the place of constitution of some units).

Consolidate. To combine two units, merging their lineage and histories into a single unit.

Constitute. To designate a unit and place it on the inactive list, thus making it available for activation.

Demobilize. To disband a unit (as used during the early period of Air Force history).

Designate. To give an official name, or name and number, to a unit.

Disband. To withdraw the designation of a constituted unit, thus making the unit unavailable for activation.

Discontinue. To withdraw all personnel from an organized unit and terminate the unit's existence.

Establishment. A military organization, at group or higher echelon, composed of a headquarters and any other elements that were assigned to the establishment.

Federal recognition. An action by which an Air Force unit, previously allotted by the Department of the Air Force (or War Department) to the National Guard Bureau and further allotted to a state, territory, or District of Columbia, was accepted by the Secretary of the Air Force (or Secretary of War) as an active component of the Air National Guard.

Inactivate. To withdraw all personnel and return a constituted unit to the inactive list. (In some cases all personnel were withdrawn without the unit being officially inactivated.)

Inactive list. Those constituted units that are inactive and have not been assigned to commands for activation.

Organize. To designate and activate a unit (as used in place of constitution and activation during the early period of Air Force history); to bring a previously designated, nonconstituted unit into physical existence by assignment of personnel.

Reconstitute. To return a disbanded unit to the inactive list and thus make it available for activation.

Redesignate. To change the name and/or number of a unit.

Unit. An air force squadron, a miscellaneous unit (such as a band), or the headquarters of a group or higher organization. (Also used, as it is in the title of this volume, in referring to groups, wings, and other establishments.)

APPENDIX II: THEATERS AND CAMPAIGNS

Units, as well as individual members of the Air Force, receive credit for wartime service. With proper authorization a unit may display on its flag or guidon a distinctive streamer denoting service in a specific theater. When embroidered with appropriate inscriptions or symbols, theater streamers represent campaign credits. The War Department or Department of the Air Force has prescribed limits in terms of time and area for each theater and campaign. All the campaigns in which Air Force units participated during World War I, World War II, and the Korean War are listed and described below. Some campaigns (e.g., Air Offensive, Japan) were exclusively aerial operations. Most of the campaigns, however, involved action on land or at sea as well as in the air; consequently, in the brief summaries that follow, the campaigns of the latter class are described in terms of general strategic or tactical situations rather than presented primarily from the standpoint of the aerial activities involved.

World War I

THEATER OF OPERATIONS: 6 April 1917 to 11 November 1918.

Somme Defensive: 21 March to 6 April 1918. After the German drive across France at the beginning of the First World War in 1914, the opposing armies had dug in. For three years a war of attrition had produced little change in the battle line. In the spring of 1918, however, the Germans launched a series of offensives in an effort to win the war. In the first of these offensives, which began on 21 March 1918, the British in the vicinity of Peronne were driven back more than 30 miles before the line was stabilized. It was during this campaign that units of the American Air Service entered combat in World War I.

Lys: 9 to 27 April 1918. The second German offensive in the spring of 1918 began with German forces breaking through the British line on the Lys River in Flanders on 9 April and culminated in the German capture of Mont-Kemmel on 25 April.

Champagne-Marne: 15 to 18 July 1918. As the attacks continued, the Germans drove a great salient into the line between Soissons and Reims before being stopped at Chateau-Thierry. Then, on 15 July, the enemy began a new offensive in the vicinity of Reims to open the front for a drive down the Marne to Paris. But the attack was repulsed, marking the turning point of the war.

Aisne-Marne: 18 July to 6 August 1918. Having stopped the enemy at Reims, the

Allies immediately took the offensive in the region between the Marne and the Aisne. The attack was a success, although the Germans were able to withdraw most of their forces. After reaching the Vesle on 6 August, the Allies temporarily abandoned their offensive on this part of the front.

Somme Offensive: 8 August to 11 November 1918. In August the Allies, under Foch, undertook a number of offensives to improve their position so that an attack could be made on the Hindenburg Line. One attack began on 8 August in the British sector before Amiens. Progress there was slow, but by early October the drive had smashed through the German's defensive line.

Oise-Aisne: 18 August to 11 November 1918. Another of the Allied offensives undertaken in August was in the French sector in the vicinity of Soissons and along the Vesle-Aisne line. The movement was bitterly contested as the attackers pushed in the direction of Laon. This offensive, like that in the Somme, merged later with the great Allied assault that was undertaken all along the front in September and that ended with the defeat of Germany in November.

St. Mihiel: 12 to 16 September 1918. On 12 September Pershing's forces attacked at St. Mihiel east of Verdun and within 36 hours had eliminated a salient that the enemy had held since 1914.

Meuse-Argonne: 26 September to 11 November 1918. Foch began his great assault on the Hindenburg Line on 26 September.

The Americans who attacked in the Meuse-Argonne sector west of Verdun made slow progress for three days. Then the offensive bogged down, but it was renewed on 4 October. By the end of the month the enemy's fixed positions had been taken, and by 7 November Pershing's troops had reached Sedan, thrown bridgeheads across the Meuse, and cut the Mezeires-Metz railroad that was so vital to the entire German front. Four days later the war ended.

NOTE: The War Department used the names of the Old Provinces (e.g., Lorraine) to award credit for combat outside the areas of the named campaigns.

World War II

AMERICAN THEATER: 7 December 1941 to 2 March 1946.

Antisubmarine, American Theater: 7 December 1941 to 2 September 1945. To protect Allied shipping from enemy submarines, AAF flew many antisubmarine patrols in the American Theater during World War II. Perhaps the most important of these operations were conducted from bases in Newfoundland and along the east coast of the United States. By the fall of 1942 these patrols, in conjunction with naval operations, had succeeded in driving off the German U-boat packs that had been taking such a heavy toll of shipping in the western Atlantic. In addition, AAF flew patrols in the Gulf of Mexico, in the Caribbean Sea, and along the west coast of the United States. In the latter part of 1943 the Navy assumed the antisubmarine responsibilities that had been assigned to AAF when the United States had entered the war in December 1941.

EUROPEAN-AFRICAN-MIDDLE EASTERN THEATER: 7 December 1941 to 8 November 1945.

Egypt-Libya: 11 June 1942 to 12 February 1943. Army Air Forces entered combat in the EAME Theater on 11 June 1942 when a small detachment equipped with B–24's and commanded by Col. Harry A. Halverson began operations in the Middle East. Shortly afterward the United States, answering a British appeal for assistance against Axis forces that were on the offensive in Libya, sent additional men and equipment into the area. In the Middle East, AAF units, which became part of Ninth Air Force in November 1942, helped to stop Rommel's drive toward the Suez Canal, took part in the Battle of El Alamein (25 October–5 November 1942), and worked with Montgomery's Eighth Army in driving Axis forces westward into Tunisia.

Algeria-French Morocco: 8 to 11 November 1942. Three days after their victory at El Alamein the Allies opened a new front with an assault on Algeria and French Morocco. Twelfth Air Force, with some units based on Gibraltar, some aboard the invasion fleet, and some bearing paratroops from England, entered combat at this time. The campaign was brief, for the French in Algeria and French

Morocco offered little resistance to the invaders.

Tunisia: 12 November 1942 to 13 May 1943. Having gained Algeria, the Allies quickly turned eastward, hoping to take Tunis and Bizerte before the Germans could send reinforcements into Tunisia. But the drive broke down short of the goal. In February 1943, after Rommel had been driven into Tunisia, the Axis took the offensive and pushed through Kasserine Pass before being stopped. With Ninth and Twelfth Air Forces in the battle, the Allies drove the enemy back into a pocket around Bizerte and Tunis, where Axis forces surrendered in May. Thus Tunisia became available for launching an attack on Sicily as a preliminary to an assault on Italy.

Sicily: 14 May to 17 August 1943. In preparation for the invasion of Sicily the Allies captured the islands in the Sicilian strait, with aerial bombardment forcing the capitulation of Pantelleria on 11 June 1943. By that time Allied air power had begun the attack on Sicily by bombing defenses and airfields. The invasion itself got under way on the night of 9/10 July with airborne landings that were followed the next day by an amphibious assault. The enemy offered strong resistance, but the Allies had superiority in the air and soon had planes operating from Sicilian bases to support Montgomery's Eighth Army and Patton's Seventh. Interdictory operations against communications in Italy and between Italy and Sicily convinced the enemy that it would be impossible to move strong reinforcements. By 17 August 1943 the Allies were in possession of the island, but they had not been able to prevent a German evacuation across the Strait of Messina.

Naples-Foggia: 18 August 1943 to 21 January 1944. After Allied bombardment of communications and airfields in Italy, Montgomery crossed the Strait of Messina on 3 September 1943 and started northward. Five days later Eisenhower announced that the Italian Government had surrendered. Fifth Army, under Clark, landed at Salerno on 9 September and managed to stay despite furious counter-attacks. By 18 September the Germans were withdrawing northward. On 27 September Eighth Army occupied the important airfields of Foggia, and on 1 October Fifth Army took Naples. As the Allies pushed up the peninsula, the enemy slowed the advance and brought it to a halt at the Gustav Line.

Anzio: 22 January to 24 May 1944. On 22 January 1944, in conjunction with a frontal assault, the Allies attempted to turn the Gustav Line by landing troops at Anzio. But the frontal attack failed, and the Allies were unable to break out of the beachhead at Anzio until the Gustav Line was breached in May 1944.

Rome-Arno: 22 January to 9 September 1944. The unsuccessful attempt to break the Gustav Line on 22 January was followed by another unsuccessful effort in March when the infantry failed to push through after bombers had endeavored to open the line at Monte Cassino. Allied air power then began a vigorous campaign against railroads, highways, and shipping that supported German forces in Italy. With supply lines strangled, the Germans could not repulse the new drive launched by the Allies in May. German resistance crumbled. By 4 June 1944 the Allies had taken Rome. But the advance ground to a halt against a new defensive line the enemy established along the Arno River.

Southern France: 15 August to 14 September 1944. While the Germans were retreating in Italy in the summer of 1944, the Allies diverted some of their strength in the theater to the invasion of Southern France. After preliminary bombardment, a combined seaborne-airborne force landed on the French Riviera on 15 August. Marseilles having been taken, Seventh Army advanced up the Rhone Valley and by mid-September was in touch with Allied forces that had entered France from the north.

North Apennines: 10 September 1944 to 4 April 1945. In Italy during the fall and winter of 1944–1945 the Allies used their air power against the enemy's communications as ground forces beat against the Gothic Line north of the Arno. Although little progress was made on the ground, the action in the Apennines tied down a large German army at a time when those troops could have been used in decisive campaigns being directed against Germany by the Allies in the west and the Russians on the east.

Po Valley: 5 April to 8 May 1945. The effectiveness of interdiction in northern

Italy was shown by the success of the final Allied drive in that area in April 1945. With communications shattered, the Germans were unable to move enough materiel to make a stand after being driven from their defensive positions south of the Po. Allied forces crossed the river on 25 April; and on 4 May, at the Italian end of the Brenner Pass, Fifth Army met the Seventh, which had driven into Germany and turned southward into Austria. With the joining of these forces the war in Italy was over.

Air Offensive, Europe: 4 July 1942 to 5 June 1944. At the time AAF entered combat in the Middle East in June 1942, Eighth Air Force was moving to England for operations against Germany. On 4 July six AAF crews, using Bostons (A–20's), joined six RAF crews for an attack on airdromes in Holland. Operations with heavy bombers began on 17 August with a raid on marshalling yards at Rouen, but in the fall of 1942 much of the Eighth's strength was diverted to North Africa. In 1943 the Eighth gradually increased the intensity of its operations, attacking factories, shipyards, transportation, airfields, and other targets on the Continent. Bomber formations frequently sustained heavy losses, as in the famous raids on Regensburg and Schweinfurt on 17 August 1943 and on Schweinfurt on 14 Oct 1943; but losses were reduced after long-range escort became available early in 1944, and after the Allies had waged a vigorous campaign, including the attacks of Big Week (20–25 February 1944), against the Ger-

man Air Force and aircraft industry. In the aerial offensive Eighth Air Force was joined by the Ninth, which was transferred from the Mediterranean to England in October 1943 to provide tactical air power for the invasion of France, and by the Fifteenth, which operated heavy bombers from Italy. As attacks on strategic objectives continued, AAF planes struck V-weapon sites in France and Belgium, and hit defensive positions, rail centers, bridges, and other targets in preparation for the invasion of Normandy.

Normandy: 6 June to 24 July 1944. Early on D–Day airborne troops landed in France to gain control of strategic areas. Aerial and naval bombardment followed. Then the invasion fleet, covered by an umbrella of aircraft, discharged Eisenhower's assault forces. Soon the beachhead was secure, but its expansion was a slow and difficult process in the face of strong opposition. It was not until late in July that the Allies were able to break out of Normandy.

Northern France: 25 July to 14 September 1944. Bombardment along a five-mile stretch of the German line enabled the Allies to break through on 25 July. While some armored forces drove southward into Brittany, others fanned out to the east and, overcoming a desperate counterattack, executed a pincers movement that trapped many Germans in a pocket at Falaise. The enemy fell back on the Siegfried Line, and by mid-September 1944 nearly all of France had been liberated. During these operations in France, while light and medium bombers and fighter-bomber aircraft of Ninth Air Force had been engaged in close support and interdictory operations, Eighth and Fifteenth Air Forces had continued their strategic bombing.

Rhineland: 15 September 1944 to 21 March 1945. Attempting to outflank the Siegfried Line, the Allies tried an airborne attack on Holland on 17 September 1944. But the operation failed, and the enemy was able to strengthen his defensive line from Holland to Switzerland. Little progress was made on the ground, but the aerial attacks on strategic targets continued. Then, having regained the initiative after defeating a German offensive in the Ardennes in December 1944, the Allies drove through to the Rhine, establishing a bridgehead across the river at Remagen.

Ardennes-Alsace: 16 December 1944 to 25 January 1945. During their offensive in the Ardennes the Germans drove into Belgium and Luxembourg, creating a great bulge in the line. For some time the weather was bad, but when it cleared the Allies could send their planes to assist their ground forces by bombing and strafing the enemy's columns, dropping paratroops and supplies, and interdicting the enemy's lines of communications. By the end of January 1945 the lost ground had been regained and the Battle of the Bulge, the last great German offensive, was over.

Central Europe: 22 March to 11 May 1945. Following the Battle of the Bulge the Allies had pushed through to the Rhine. On 22 March 1945 they began their assault across the river, and by 1 April

the Ruhr was encircled. Armored columns raced across Germany and into Austria and Czechoslovakia. On 25 April, the day American and Russian forces met on the Elbe, strategic bombing operations came to an end. Germany surrendered on 7 May 1945 and operations officially came to an end the following day, although sporadic actions continued on the European front until 11 May.

Air Combat, EAME Theater: 7 December 1941 to 11 May 1945. Some of the AAF's aerial operations in the EAME Theater—such as those in the Balkans (including the raids on Ploesti), over the Mediterranean Sea, and in Iceland—were outside the areas of the campaigns listed above. A special campaign, Air Combat, EAME Theater, was established to provide credits for these operations. (Provision was made for similar campaigns for the other theaters, but no aerial combat occurred in the American Theater, and no credits were awarded by the War Department for Air Combat, Asiatic-Pacific Theater.)

Antisubmarine, EAME Theater: 7 December 1941 to 2 September 1945. AAF antisubmarine operations began from England in November 1942 and from North Africa in March 1943. The most successful of these operations were carried out in the Bay of Biscay in the summer of 1943, and in the Mediterranean during the campaigns in Sicily and southern Italy. AAF units received credit for this campaign if they were engaged in antisubmarine warfare outside of the regularly designated campaign areas of the EAME Theater.

ASIATIC-PACIFIC THEATER: 7 December 1941 to 2 March 1946.

Philippine Islands: 7 December 1941 to 10 May 1942. A few hours after the raid on Pearl Harbor on 7 December 1941, Japanese aircraft attacked the Philippines. Three days later Japanese troops landed on Luzon. America's meager air power in the islands was soon destroyed. Unable to obtain reinforcements and supplies, Mac-Arthur could do nothing more than fight a delaying action. Between 16 and 18 December the few bombing planes that remained were evacuated, by their crews, to Australia, where US air power in the Far East was to be concentrated. Other members of the air units took up arms and fought as infantrymen in the battle that ended, at Bataan and Corregidor, with the loss of the Philippines in May 1942.

East Indies: 1 January to 22 July 1942. While engaged in the conquest of the Philippines, the Japanese thrust southward, landing troops in Sumatra, Borneo, Celebes, and elsewhere in the East Indies. Defeated in the Battle of the Java Sea at the end of February 1942, the Allies lost Java. Then the Japanese put forces into New Guinea and the Solomons, on the road to Australia. But a Japanese attempt to take Port Moresby early in May was thwarted when the Japanese were beaten in the Battle of the Coral Sea.

Papua: 23 July 1942 to 23 January 1943. In another effort to take Port Moresby the Japanese landed troops at Buna, Gona, and Sanananda in July 1942. At first the Allies could offer only feeble resistance to the enemy forces that pushed southward through Papua, but the Allies were building up their strength in Australia. By mid-September Fifth Air Force had superiority in the air over New Guinea, and the Japanese drive had been stopped. The Allies then began to push the enemy back, with Fifth Air Force ferrying supplies and reinforcements to the troops fighting in the jungle. Buna was taken on 2 January 1943, and enemy resistance at Sanananda ended three weeks later.

Guadalcanal: 7 August 1942 to 21 February 1943. The seizure of Guadalcanal in June 1942 marked the high tide of the Japanese advance in the Southwest Pacific. U.S. Marines landed on the island on 7 August and quickly took Henderson Field, which was needed in order to gain control of the air. The Japanese made several attempts to retake the field, and they repeatedly bombed the base to curtail Allied aerial activity. The contest, which became one of reinforcement and supply, was decided when Japanese troop transports that were heading for the island were destroyed by American ships and planes in November, but the Japanese held out on Guadalcanal until the following February.

Northern Solomons: 22 February 1943 to 21 November 1944. After the conquest of Guadalcanal, Halsey's forces, supported by Thirteenth Air Force, began a campaign to capture Japanese strongholds in the Northern Solomons. In February 1943

American forces landed in the Russell Islands to obtain an air strip. Air bases at Munda (New Georgia) and on Kolombangara Island were attacked as the Allies fought to gain superiority in the air. American troops landed on Rendova and on New Georgia at the end of June. The air base at Munda was taken in August, and the base on Kolombangara was neutralized. Landings were made in the Treasury Islands in October. Allied air power struck the great Japanese naval and air bases at Rabaul on New Britain to support the assault on Bougainville, which began on 1 November 1943. Enemy garrisons on Bougainville were contained, and other Japanese forces in the Northern Solomons were isolated. Although the enemy continued to resist, American air and naval power dominated the Solomons.

Bismarck Archipelago: 15 December 1943 to 27 November 1944. To isolate and neutralize Rabaul on New Britain and the Japanese base at Kavieng on New Ireland, American forces landed at Arawe and Cape Gloucester in December 1943, on Green and Los Negros Islands in February 1944, and at Talasea on New Britain and on Manus Island in March. Some other enemy forces in the Bismarck Archipelago were bypassed.

New Guinea: 24 January 1943 to 31 December 1944. After the loss of Buna and Gona in New Guinea, the Japanese fell back on their stronghold at Lae. Their attempt to reinforce Lae by sea in March 1943 met with disaster when American and Australian planes sank most of the convoy in the Battle of the Bismarck Sea. Salamaua and Lae then became the objectives for an Allied advance along the northern coast of New Guinea. Fifth Air Force bombers attacked airfields at Wewak, 300 miles west of Lae, to neutralize them. The Allies dropped paratroops at Nadzab, just beyond Lae. Enemy resistance at Salamaua broke on 14 September 1943; Lae fell two days later. In the months that followed, MacArthur's forces pushed westward, capturing some Japanese strongholds and bypassing others. After taking Hollandia in April 1944, the Allies attacked islands off the northern coast of New Guinea, taking Wakde and Biak in May, Owi in June, and Noemfoor in July. Sansapor on New Guinea also was gained in July. Aerial attacks on the Philippines began in August, and Morotai was seized in October to provide air bases for the invasion of the Philippines. Allied planes also bombed the oil center at Balikpapan and other targets in Borneo and Celebes.

Leyte: 17 October 1944 to 1 July 1945. On 17 October 1944, after preparatory bombardment, the invasion of the Philippines got under way with the seizure of islands guarding Leyte Gulf. The landing on Leyte itself on 20 October was strongly contested by Japanese forces on land and at sea. Organized resistance on the island did not end until after Christmas, and mopping up operations continued for a long time. Meanwhile, at the end of October, the neighboring island of Samar was occupied with little difficulty.

Luzon: 15 December 1944 to 4 July 1945. After Leyte came Mindoro, which was invaded on 15 December 1944, an air strip being obtained to provide a base for operations during the invasion on Luzon. American troops landed on the shores of Lingayen Gulf on 9 January 1945 and pushed to Manila, which the Japanese defended vigorously until 24 February. Rather than meet the Americans in a decisive battle, the Japanese decided to fight delaying actions in numerous places. Organized resistance ended in southern Luzon in April and in central and northern Luzon in June.

Southern Philippines: 27 February to 4 July 1945. After Luzon had been invaded and Manila taken, a series of landings were made in the southern Philippines, on Palawan, Mindanao, Panay, Cebu, Negros, and other islands. In some places the Japanese offered little resistance; in others they held out for considerable time. The liberation of the Philippines was announced by MacArthur on 5 July 1945.

Central Pacific: 7 December 1941 to 6 December 1943. The war in the Central Pacific began with the Japanese attack on Pearl Harbor on 7 December 1941. Six months later an AAF task force took part in the Battle of Midway, in which a great Japanese fleet was defeated. But another year and a half elapsed before American forces began an offensive against Japanese positions in the Central Pacific. It was then, on 20 November 1943, that landings were made in the Gilberts, on Makin and Tarawa, with the Marines at the latter place becoming engaged in one of the bloodiest battles of the war.

Eastern Mandates: 7 December 1943 to 16 April 1944. After the operations in the Gilberts, American air and naval forces bombed and shelled Japanese bases in the Marshall Islands. In February 1944 American troops went ashore on Kwajalein, Roi, Namur, and Eniwetok. Other islands, including Jaluit and Wotje in the Marshalls and Truk in the Carolines, were bombed and shelled but were bypassed.

Western Pacific: 17 April 1944 to 2 September 1945. Attacks on Truk, where the Japanese had a major base, continued as preparations were made for the invasion of the Marianas. The American troops that landed on Saipan on 15 June 1944 met bitter opposition; but, after a desperate Japanese counterattack on 7 July, organized resistance soon terminated. Tinian, invaded on 25 July, was won by 1 August. Guam, which had been seized by the Japanese on 10 December 1941, was invaded on 20 July and regained after 20 days of fighting. With the conquest of the Marianas, the United States gained valuable bases for an aerial offensive against Japan itself. To provide bases for operations against the Philippines, the Palaus were invaded in mid-September. Later, aerial attacks were made on Formosa to support the invasion of the Philippines and Okinawa.

Ryukyus: 26 March to 2 July 1945. Some small islands close to the southern tip of Okinawa were seized on 26–27 March 1945, and the invasion of Okinawa itself began on 1 April. Only light resistance was encountered in the northwestern part of the island, where the American troops landed. Japanese pilots, however, made suicidal (kamikaze) attacks on the invasion fleet. And savage opposition was met ashore as the troops moved southwest to clear the island. The campaign was costly, but it gave the United States a position from which it could use medium bombers and fighter aircraft of Seventh Air Force to attack the Japanese home islands.

Air Offensive, Japan: 17 April 1942 to 2 September 1945. The aerial offensive against the Japanese home islands began in April 1942 with the Doolittle raid, in which the B–25's of a special task force were launched from a carrier. The second AAF strike was made on 15 June 1944 by B–29's operating from China. Other missions were flown from Asia in the months that followed, but the strength of the offensive increased rapidly after B–29's of Twentieth Air Force began operating from the Marianas late in 1944. At first the raids from the Marianas were made at high altitude during daylight, with high-explosive bombs being used for precision bombardment of industrial targets. When such operations failed to produce good results, the tactics were changed, the B–29's being sent in at low altitude during the night to drop incendiary bombs on urban areas. To provide a base for fighter escort, as well as to gain emergency landing fields on the route from the Marianas to Japan, Marines landed on Iwo Jima on 25 February 1945 and took the island in a bloody battle that lasted a month. Support for the invasion of Okinawa was provided by B–29's that hit airfields the Japanese were using for their kamikaze attacks. To destroy Japanese shipping, the very heavy bombers sowed mines in the waters around Japan. And in the north Eleventh Air Force attacked targets in the Kurils. The offensive, increasing in intensity and effectiveness, reached its climax with the dropping of atomic bombs on Hiroshima (6 August 1945) and Nagasaki (9 August 1945).

Burma, 1942: 7 December 1941 to 26 May 1942. While some Japanese forces were conquering the Philippines, the East Indies, and islands of the South Pacific, others were penetrating Burma from Thailand. Moving rapidly, they controlled southern Burma by the end of January 1942, took Rangoon in March, and cut the Burma Road in April. Pushing on, the enemy forced the British westward into India and drove Stillwell's Chinese forces back into China. By the end of May the Japanese had taken all of Burma. Only the monsoon prevented an invasion of India.

India-Burma: 2 April 1942 to 28 January 1945. By 2 April 1942, Singapore, the Malay Peninsula, Sumatra, and Thailand, as well as most of Burma, were under Japanese domination. For a long time afterward the only counterblows were provided by the small air forces the Allies had in the area, and by Wingate's Raiders operating behind the enemy's lines. In the spring of 1944, while Anglo-Indian troops were resisting a Japanese invasion of the Imphal plain, Chinese troops and Merrill's Marauders in northern Burma started an offensive that captured the key town of Myitkyina in August and opened the Burma Road the following January.

Central Burma: 29 January to 15 July 1945. Having repulsed the Japanese invasion of India, Anglo-Indian troops took the offensive. They crossed the Irrawaddy River in February 1945, took Mandalay in March, and recaptured Rangoon on 4 May, by which time the Japanese were virtually beaten in Burma.

China Defensive: 4 July 1942 to 4 May 1945. The American Volunteer Group (Flying Tigers) under Chennault helped to defend China until 4 July 1942, when regular AAF units (formed into Fourteenth Air Force in March 1943) took over the task. The AAF support for Chiang Kai-shek's armies was limited, however, because of the small size of the force, and because of the lack of supplies, which had to be transported by air over the Hump route from India. A strong Japanese offensive along the Hankow railway in 1944 resulted in the loss of important air bases Fourteenth Air Force had been using in southeastern China. And by December 1944 the Japanese columns driving southward had met others that were moving up from Indochina.

China Offensive: 5 May to 2 September 1945. In the spring of 1945 the Chinese began an offensive in southern China. Some of the air bases lost the previous year being retaken, Fourteenth Air Force

was in a better position to support the Chinese as they recovered the territory lost to the Japanese during 1944.

Aleutian Islands: 3 June 1942 to 24 August 1943. On 3–4 June 1942, at the time of the Battle of Midway, a Japanese force attacked Dutch Harbor and inflicted considerable damage before it was driven off. The Japanese then occupied Attu and Kiska. For the rest of 1942 and into 1943, Eleventh Air Force struck enemy bases and installations whenever weather over the Aleutians permitted. The United States troops that landed on Attu on 11 May 1943 had possession of the island by the end of the month. The capture of Attu isolated Kiska, which was bombed repeatedly by American aircraft. The troops that invaded Kiska on 15 August 1943 discovered that the Japanese, under the cover of fog, had secretly evacuated their garrison.

NOTE: In the Asiatic-Pacific Theater the theater commander had authority to award campaign credits to units that were engaged in combat in the Northern Solomons, Bismarck Archipelago, New Guinea, Luzon, Southern Philippines, Eastern Mandates, Western Pacific, and Ryukyus after the closing dates shown above for those campaigns.

Korean War

KOREAN THEATER: 27 June 1950 to 27 July 1953.

UN Defensive: 27 June to 15 September 1950. Communist forces of North Korea attacked the Republic of Korea early on the morning of 25 June 1950. The following day, fighter planes of Far East Air Forces stood guard while American citizens were evacuated by ship from Inchon. On 27 June, when the Communists were at the gates of Seoul, FEAF transport planes began to evacuate Americans from the city. That same day USAF fighters covering the aerial evacuation encountered five North Korean fighter planes and destroyed three. Truman ordered MacArthur to use his air and naval forces to support ROK army. The United Nations Security Council recommended that UN members assist the Republic of Korea in repelling the invasion. Aerial attacks against military objectives in North Korea were authorized by the President on 30 June. And American army forces were thrown into the conflict. As the Communists drove southward, FEAF provided close support for UN ground forces, attacked the enemy's communications, and engaged in strategic operations against industrial targets in North Korea. UN forces were driven back to a defensive line around Pusan, where the North Korean offensive was stopped.

UN Offensive: 16 September to 2 November 1950. With the North Korean army virtually destroyed in the fighting around Pusan, the UN began an offensive in mid-September. UN troops landed at Inchon and soon had the important air base at Kimpo. Eighth Army attacked northward from Pusan. By 29 September the Communists had been driven from South Korea. As the offensive continued, UN forces moved beyond the 38th parallel, took the North Korean capital of Pyongyang, and pushed northward toward the Yalu River.

CCF Intervention: 3 November 1950 to 24 January 1951. The UN hoped to end the war by driving through to the Manchurian border, but the offensive was halted and turned by forces from Communist China. X Corps was evacuated, by air and sea, from the Hamhung-Hungnam area; Eighth Army withdrew over land. By the end of December 1950 the battle line was just below the 38th parallel, but the UN had to withdraw farther south, beyond Seoul, before the enemy's drive was stopped.

1st UN Counteroffensive: 25 January to 21 April 1951. Taking the offensive on 25 January 1951, the UN began operations that were directed more toward wearing down the enemy than toward capturing territory. Against strong resistance, UN forces advanced slowly, trying to maintain a solid line. Inchon and the airfield at Kimpo were taken on 10 February. Seoul was regained in mid-March. Having been pushed north of the 38th parallel, the Communists built up strength for a new offensive. Meantime, on 11 April, Truman had relieved MacArthur and made Ridgway commander in the Far East.

CCF Spring Offensive: 22 April to 8 July 1951. The enemy attacked on 22

April 1951, but the thrust was checked just short of Seoul. After a lull, in which the UN strengthened its positions along the new line, the Communists struck again, pushing back the eastern end of the line. Having again been driven south of the 38th parallel, the UN counterattacked and by 24 June not only had regained the territory lost during the enemy's spring offensive but had shoved the line deeper into North Korea. It was then that Malik suggested an armistice.

UN Summer–Fall Offensive: 9 July to 27 November 1951. Truce negotiations began on 10 July, but hostilities continued, although neither side was willing to begin a major offensive while the peace talks were being conducted. When negotiations were suspended in August, the UN began an offensive in the area known as the Punchbowl, and in the fierce fighting that followed was able to take some important positions, including Bloody and Heartbreak Ridges. After peace negotiations were resumed in October, Ridgway stopped offensive operations on the ground. In August FEAF had begun a strong campaign against the enemy's railroads. For three months the results of the latter campaign were good, but afterward the Communists provided stronger defenses and rushed repairs, thereby reducing the effectiveness of the interdictory operations.

Second Korean Winter: 28 November 1951 to 30 April 1952. Terminating its offensive, the UN waged a war of containment, but the aerial attacks on railroads in North Korea continued. The UN's interdictory operations, which destroyed some material and curtailed efforts to stockpile supplies, so damaged the Communists' railway system that it could not be used again to support a sustained offensive on the ground. But interdiction could not force the Communists to end the war. The enemy made some probing attacks, but there were no important changes in the battle line.

Korea Summer–Fall, 1952: 1 May to 30 November 1952. In May 1952 the Communists increased their probing and stepped up their artillery fire. As a result, in June the UN began a limited action to advance the patrol bases in front of the line, but the fighting was relatively of minor significance. Both sides made some small-scale attacks during the summer. After knocking out most of the electric plants in North Korea during June, FEAF began to apply continuous pressure on the Communists with the view of making the war as costly as possible in terms of enemy personnel, materiel, and facilities. The tempo of the action on the ground increased in October, but there were only minor changes in the line.

Third Korean Winter: 1 December 1952 to 30 April 1953. Activity along the front subsided during the winter, increased somewhat in March, but declined again in April. Negotiations for an armistice were approaching a decisive stage, but it was apparent from troop movements and other signs that the Communists were preparing for large-scale operations.

Korea Summer–Fall, 1953: 1 May to 27 July 1953. The Communists made a series of attacks on UN outposts during the last week in May, but the following week was relatively quiet. Then, on 10 June the Chinese struck, and in the fighting that followed, the heaviest since the spring of 1951, the UN lost some ground before agreement for an armistice was reached on 19 July. The war ended when the armistice papers were signed on 27 July 1953.

APPENDIX III: DECORATIONS

Air Force units, like individuals, receive citations and other awards for outstanding operations or for services of special significance.   The awards mentioned in this book, and the devices displayed by units as evidence of such awards, are described below:

Air Force Outstanding Unit Award.   A decoration for exceptionally meritorious achievement or service of great national or international significance not involving combat operations against an enemy.   Blue streamer, with a narrow red band center bordered by white lines, and red bands at each edge separated from the blue by white lines; embroidered in white with the name of the theater or area of operations and the inclusive dates, or whenever possible, with the service or achievement performed; separate streamer for each award.   Displayed on unit flag or guidon.

Belgian Fourragere.   A decoration that may be awarded, by separate decree of the Belgian Government, to units cited twice in the Order of the Day, Belgian Army.   Braided cord in red and green, looped, and ending in metal ferrule.   Displayed on unit flag or guidon.

Citation in the Order of the Day, Belgian Army.   A citation by decree of the Bel-

gian Government.   No emblem awarded to unit cited.

Distinguished Unit Citation.   A decoration for extraordinary heroism in action against an armed enemy of the United States.   Dark blue streamer, with the name of the action embroidered in white.   Separate streamer for each citation.   Displayed on unit flag or guidon.

French Croix de Guerre.   A citation by decree of the French Government.   Green and red streamer, embroidered with name of action or theater of operations.   Displayed on unit flag or guidon.

French Fourragere.   A decoration that may be awarded, by separate decree of the French Government, to units cited twice for the Croix de Guerre.   Braided cord, in colors of the Croix de Guerre.   Displayed on unit flag or guidon.

Philippine Presidential Unit Citation.   A citation for achievements while serving in the Philippines during periods 7 December 1941–10 May 1942 or 17 October 1944–4 July 1945.   No emblem awarded to unit.

Republic of Korea Presidential Unit Citation.   A citation for achievement during the Korean War.   No emblem awarded to unit.

APPENDIX IV: ABBREVIATIONS

The following glossary of abbreviations used in the volume does not include many standard abbreviations, such as those for months of the year, states and territories, and military grades and ranks.

AAB	Army Air Base	ETO	European Theater of Operations
AAF	Army Air Forces		
AAFld	Army Air Field	GHQ	General Headquarters
AB	Air Base	GHQAF	General Headquarters Air Force
ADC	Air Defense Command		
AEF	American Expeditionary Forces	Intl	International
		MTO	Mediterranean Theater of Operations
AF	Air Force		
AFB	Air Force Base	Mun	Municipal
AFOUA	Air Force Outstanding Unit Award	NAS	Naval Air Station
		OTU	Operational Training Unit
ANG	Air National Guard	PUC	Presidential Unit Citation
Aprt	Airport	RAF	Royal Air Force
c.	*circa* (about or approximately)	RTU	Replacement Training Unit
		SAC	Strategic Air Command
CBI	China-Burma-India	TAC	Tactical Air Command
CCF	Chinese Communist Forces	UN	United Nations
ConAC	Continental Air Command	unkn	unknown
DUC	Distinguished Unit Citation	US	United States
EAME	European-African-Middle Eastern	USAF	United States Air Force

INDEX OF UNITS

An asterisk (*) indicates that a history of the unit appears under the heading given in this index. Other entries refer to designations assigned at various times to units for which histories are provided in this volume.

WINGS

DIVISIONS

COMMANDS